T0229787

HANDBOOK OF
RESEARCH ON MACHINE LEARNING

Foundations and Applications

HANDBOOK OF
RESEARCH ON MACHINE LEARNING
Foundations and Applications

Edited by
Monika Mangla, PhD
Subhash K. Shinde, PhD
Vaishali Mehta, PhD
Nonita Sharma, PhD
Sachi Nandan Mohanty, PhD

First edition published 2023

Apple Academic Press Inc.
1265 Goldenrod Circle, NE,
Palm Bay, FL 32905 USA

4164 Lakeshore Road, Burlington,
ON, L7L 1A4 Canada

CRC Press
6000 Broken Sound Parkway NW,
Suite 300, Boca Raton, FL 33487-2742 USA

4 Park Square, Milton Park,
Abingdon, Oxon, OX14 4RN UK

© 2023 by Apple Academic Press, Inc.

Apple Academic Press exclusively co-publishes with CRC Press, an imprint of Taylor & Francis Group, LLC

Library and Archives Canada Cataloguing in Publication

Title: Handbook of research on machine learning : foundations and applications / edited by Monika Mangla, PhD, Subhash K. Shinde, PhD, Vaishali Mehta, PhD, Nonita Sharma, PhD, Sachi Nandan Mohanty, PhD.
Names: Mangla, Monika, editor. | Shinde, Subhash K., editor. | Mehta, Vaishali, editor. | Sharma, Nonita, editor. | Mohanty, Sachi Nandan, editor.
Description: First edition. | Includes bibliographical references and index.
Identifiers: Canadiana (print) 20220140839 | Canadiana (ebook) 2022014088X | ISBN 9781774638682 (hardcover) | ISBN 9781774638699 (softcover) | ISBN 9781003277330 (ebook)
Subjects: LCSH: Machine learning. | LCSH: Machine learning—Industrial applications.
Classification: LCC Q325.5 .H36 2022 | DDC 006.3/1—dc23

Library of Congress Cataloging-in-Publication Data

CIP data on file with US Library of Congress

ISBN: 978-1-77463-868-2 (hbk)
ISBN: 978-1-77463-869-9 (pbk)
ISBN: 978-1-00327-733-0 (ebk)

About the Editors

Monika Mangla, PhD
Associate Professor, Department of Information Technology,
Dwarkadas J. Sanghvi College of Engineering, Mumbai,
Maharashtra, India

Monika Mangla, PhD, is working as an Associate Professor in the Department of Information Technology at Dwarkadas J. Sanghvi College of Engineering, Mumbai, India. She has two patents to her credit as well as over 18 years of teaching experience at undergraduate and postgraduate levels, and she has guided many student projects. Her interest areas include IoT, cloud computing, network security, algorithms and optimization, location modeling, and machine learning. She has published several research papers and book chapters (SCI and Scopus-indexed) with reputed publishers. She has also been associated with several SCI-indexed journals, including the Turkish *Journal of Electrical Engineering & Computer Sciences* (TUBITAK), *Industrial Management & Data Systems,* etc., as a reviewer. She is a life member of the Computer Society of India and the Institution of Electronics and Telecommunication Engineers. Dr. Mangla received her PhD from Thapar Institute of Engineering & Technology, Patiala, Punjab, India.

Subhash K. Shinde, PhD
Professor and Vice Principal, Lokmanya Tilak College of Engineering
(LTCoE), Navi Mumbai, Maharashtra, India

Subhash K. Shinde, PhD, is a Professor and Vice Principal at Lokmanya Tilak College of Engineering (LTCoE), Navi Mumbai, India. He has over 20 years of rich teaching experience at both the undergraduate and graduate levels. His research areas include machine learning, computer networks, network security, data warehousing, and mining. He has also been guiding research scholars at the University of Mumbai. He has published numerous research papers in various reputed national and international conferences and journals (SCI and Scopus indexed) with reputed publishers, including

Elsevier and Inderscience, and has authored many books. He has also worked as Chairman of the Board of Studies in Computer Engineering under the Faculty of Technology at the University of Mumbai. Dr. Shinde earned his PhD in Computer Science and Engineering from Shri Guru Gobind Singhji Institute of Engineering and Technology, India.

Vaishali Mehta, PhD
Professor, Department of Information Technology,
Panipat Institute of Engineering and Technology, Panipat, Haryana, India

Vaishali Mehta, PhD, is working as a Professor in the Department Information Technology at Panipat Institute of Engineering and Technology, Panipat, Haryana, India. She has two patents published to her credit. She has over 17 years of teaching experience at undergraduate and postgraduate levels. Her research interests include approximation algorithms, location modeling, IoT, cloud computing, and machine learning. She has published research articles in quality journals (SCI and Scopus indexed), national and international conferences, and books of reputed publishers. She has also reviewed research papers of reputed journals and conferences. Dr. Mehta has a PhD in facility location problems from Thapar University, India.

Nonita Sharma, PhD
Assistant Professor, National Institute of Technology, Jalandhar,
Punjab, India

Nonita Sharma, PhD, is an Assistant Professor at the National Institute of Technology, Jalandhar, India. She has more than 10 years of teaching experience. Her major area of interest includes data mining, bioinformatics, time series forecasting, and wireless sensor networks. She has published several papers in the international and national journals and conferences and has written book chapters also. She received a best paper award for her research paper at the Mid-Term Symposium organized by CSIR, Chandigarh, India. She has authored a book titled *XGBoost: The Extreme Gradient Boosting for Mining Applications*. Dr. Sharma received her BTech degree in Computer Science Engineering, her MTech degree in Computer Science Engineering, and her PhD degree in Wireless Sensor Network from the National Institute of Technology, Jalandhar, India.

Sachi Nandan Mohanty, PhD

*Associate Professor, Department of Computer Science & Engineering,
Vardhaman College of Engineering (Autonomous), Hyderabad, India*

Sachi Nandan Mohanty, PhD, is an Associate Professor in the Department of Computer Science & Engineering at Vardhaman College of Engineering, Hyderabad, India. Professor Mohanty's research areas include data mining, big data analysis, cognitive science, fuzzy decision-making, brain-computer interface, and computational intelligence. He has received three best paper awards during his PhD studies and has since published 20 papers in SCI journals. As a Fellow of the Indian Society Technical Education, The Institute of Engineering and Technology, and the Computer Society of India, and as a Fellow of the Institute of Engineers and senior member of the IEEE Computer Society, he is actively involved in the activities of professional societies. He has received a Best Researcher Award from the Biju Pattnaik University of Technology in 2019, Best Thesis Award (first prize) from the Computer Society of India in 2015, and Outstanding Faculty in Engineering Award from Dept. of Higher Education, Govt. of Odisha in 2020. He has also received international travel funds from SERB, Dept. of Science and Technology, Govt. of India, for chairing a session at an international conference in the USA, 2020. Dr. Mohanty is currently acting as a reviewer of many journals, including *Robotics and Autonomous Systems, Computational and Structural Biotechnology, Artificial Intelligence Review,* and *Spatial Information Research*. He has also published four edited books and three authored books.

Contents

Contributors

Satheesh Abimannan
School of Computer Science and Engineering, Galgotias University, Uttar Pradesh, India,
E-mail: satheesha23@gmail.com

Rakhi Akhare
Faculty, Lokmanya Tilak College of Engineering, Navi Mumbai, Maharashtra, India

Dhruv Bansal
School of Automobile, Mechanical, and Mechatronics Engineering; Department of Mechatronics Engineering, Manipal University Jaipur, Rajasthan, India, E-mail: deebnsl65@gmail.com

Snehlata Beriwal
School of Computer Science and Engineering, Galgotias University, Uttar Pradesh, India

Priyanka Bhartiya
Gautam Buddha University, Greater Noida, Uttar Pradesh, India, E-mail: bhartiyapriyanka123@gmail.com

Gajanan K. Birajdar
Department of Electronics Engineering, Ramrao Adik Institute of Technology, Nerul,
Navi Mumbai – 400706, Maharashtra, India, E-mail: gajanan.birajdar@rait.ac.in

Yue-Shan Chang
Department of Computer Science and Information Engineering, National Taipei University, Taiwan

Santosh Chapaneri
Department of Electronics and Telecommunication Engineering, St. Francis Institute of Technology, University of Mumbai, Mumbai, Maharashtra, India, E-mail: santoshchapaneri@sfit.ac.in

Dipen Chawla
Computer Engineering Department, VESIT, Mumbai, Maharashtra, India,
E-mail: 2015dipen.chawla@ves.ac.in

Jijnasee Dash
Department of Computer Science and Engineering, College of Engineering and Technology, Bhubaneswar, Odisha, India

Sanjivani Deokar
Faculty, Lokmanya Tilak College of Engineering, Navi Mumbai, Maharashtra, Indian;
Research Scholar, Singhania University, Rajasthan, India, E-mail: sanjivanideokar@gmail.com

Hardik Deshmukh
Student, Lokmanya Tilak College of Engineering, Navi Mumbai, Maharashtra, India

Jaiditya Dev
University of Toronto, Toronto, Ontario, Canada, Email: jaiditya.dev@mail.utoronto.ca.

Pravin Ghatode
G H Raisoni College of Engineering, Nagpur, Maharashtra, India, E-mail: pravin.ghatode@raisoni.net

Nitin Goyal
Chitkara University Institute of Engineering and Technology, Chitkara University, Punjab, India

Lalit Gupta
School of Automobile, Mechanical, and Mechatronics Engineering; Department of Mechatronics
Engineering, Manipal University Jaipur, Rajasthan, India, E-mail: guptalalit1997@gmail.com

Arunima Hota
Department of Computer Science and Engineering, College of Engineering and Technology,
Bhubaneswar, Odisha, India

Samarth Jain
School of Automobile, Mechanical, and Mechatronics Engineering; Department of Mechatronics
Engineering, Manipal University Jaipur, Rajasthan, India, E-mail: samarthjain.119@gmail.com

Harsh Jalan
Department of Computer Engineering, St. Francis Institute of Technology, Mumbai, Maharashtra, India,
E-mail: harshjalan27@yahoo.com

Deepak Jayaswal
Department of Electronics and Telecommunication Engineering, St. Francis Institute of Technology,
University of Mumbai, Mumbai, Maharashtra, India

Shilpa Kapse
Assistant Professor, Lokmanya Tilak College of Engineering, Navi Mumbai, Maharashtra, India,
E-mail: shilpashrawane@gmail.com

Shahnawaz Khan
Department of Information Technology, University College of Bahrain, Bahrain

Sujata Khedkar
Computer Engineering Department, VESIT, Mumbai, Maharashtra, India,
E-mail: sujata.khedkar@ves.ac.in

Deepak Kochhar
School of Computer Science and Engineering, VIT, Vellore, Tamil Nādu, India

Vinay Kumar
Photogrammetry and Remote Sensing Department, Indian Institute of Remote Sensing, Indian Space
Research Organization, Dehradun, Uttarakhand, India

Monika Mangla
Associate Professor, Department of Information Technology, Dwarkadas J. Sanghvi College of
Engineering, Mumbai, India. E-mail: manglamona@gmail.com

Kavach Mishra
Geomatics Engineering Group, Civil Engineering Department, Indian Institute of Technology Roorkee,
Roorkee, Uttarakhand, India, E-mail: kmishra@ce.iitr.ac.in

Poonam Mittal
JC Bose University of Science and Technology YMCA, Faridabad, Haryana, India

Subhadarshini Mohanty
Department of Information Technology, College of Engineering and Technology, Bhubaneswar, Odisha,
India

Subasish Mohapatra
Department of Computer Science and Engineering, College of Engineering and Technology,
Bhubaneswar, Odisha, India, E-mail: smohapatra@cet.edu.in

Ayon Moitra
G H Raisoni College of Engineering, Nagpur, Maharashtra, India,
E-mail: moitra_ayon.ghrcecs@raisoni.net

Mamta Nain
Chitkara University Institute of Engineering and Technology, Chitkara University, Punjab, India

V. Lakshman Narayana
Department of IT, Vignan's Foundation for Science, Technology, and Research, Guntur,
Andhra Pradesh, India

Amanpratap Singh Pall
School of IT, APJIME, and Technical Campus, Punjab, India, E-mail: amanpall@hotmail.com

Dakshata Panchal
Department of Computer Engineering, St. Francis Institute of Technology, Mumbai, Maharashtra, India,
E-mail: dakshatapanchal@sfit.ac.in

R. S. M. Lakshmi Patibandla
Department of IT, Vignan's Foundation for Science, Technology, and Research, Guntur, Andhra
Pradesh, India, E-mail: patibandla.lakshmi@gmail.com

Mukesh D. Patil
Department of Electronics and Telecommunication Engineering, Ramrao Adik Institute of Technology,
Nerul, Navi Mumbai – 400706, Maharashtra, India

Rohini Patil
Research Scholar TCET, Assistant Professor, TEC, Navi Mumbai, Maharashtra, India,
E-mail: rohinipatil@ternaengg.ac.in

Princy Randhawa
School of Automobile, Mechanical, and Mechatronics Engineering; Department of Mechatronics
Engineering, Manipal University Jaipur, India, E-mail: princyrandhawa23@gmail.com

Sushant Rath
Research and Development Center for Iron and Steel, SAIL, Ranchi, Jharkhand, India,
E-mail: srath@sail.in

Reena
Department of Computer Science, Edge Hill University, United Kingdom,
Email: er_reenatechie@hotmail.com

Gopal Sakarkar
G H Raisoni College of Engineering, Nagpur, Maharashtra, India, E-mail: gopal.sakarkar@raisoni.net

Kamal Shah
Professor and Dean (R&D), TCET, Mumbai, Maharashtra, India

Manoj Shanti
G H Raisoni College of Engineering, Nagpur, Maharashtra, India

K. P. Sharma
Department of CSE, Dr. B. R. Ambedkar National Institute of Technology, Punjab, India,
E-mail: sharmakp@nitj.ac.in

Nonita Sharma
Department of CSE, Dr. B. R. Ambedkar National Institute of Technology, Punjab, India,
E-mail: nsnonita@gmail.com

P. S. Sheeba
Department of Computer Science & Engineering (IoT & Cyber Security including Blockchain Technology), Lokmanya Tilak College of Engineering, Navi Mumbai, Maharashtra, India, E-mail: sheebaps@gmail.com

Nilesh Shelke
Priyadarshini Indira Gandhi College of Engineering, Nagpur, Maharashtra, India, E-mail: nileshshelke08@gmail.com

Subhash K. Shinde
Department of Computer Engineering, Lokmanya Tilak College of Engineering, Navi Mumbai, Maharashtra, India

Asfa Siddiqui
Urban and Regional Studies Department, Indian Institute of Remote Sensing, Indian Space Research Organization, Dehradun, Uttarakhand, India

Jitendra P. Sonawane
Department of Electronics and Telecommunication Engineering, Ramrao Adik Institute of Technology, Nerul, Navi Mumbai – 400706, Maharashtra, India

K. Thirunavukkarasu
School of Computer Science and Engineering, Galgotias University, Uttar Pradesh, India, E-mail: thiruk.me@gmail.com

Sujay Varma
Computer Engineering Department, VESIT, Mumbai, Maharashtra, India, E-mail: 2015sujay.varma@ves.ac.in

Vaishali Wadhwa
Panipat Institute of Engineering and Technology, Panipat, Haryana, India, E-mail: wadhwavaishali@gmail.com

Sourabh Yadav
University of North Texas (UNT), Denton, Texas, USA, E-mail: sourabhy1797@gmail.com

Abbreviations

AdaIN	adaptive instance normalization
ADE	arbitrated dynamic ensemble
ADR	adverse drug reactions
AF	activation function
AI	artificial intelligence
AMC	Ahmedabad Municipal Corporation
ANFIS	adaptive neuro-fuzzy inference system
ANN	artificial neural network
AQI	air quality index
AR	autoregression
ARIMA	autoregressive integrated moving average
ARL	association rule learning
AUC	area under curve
AUV	autonomous underwater vehicle
AVIRIS-NG	airborne visible/near-infrared imaging spectrometer-next generation
BCRAT	breast cancer risk prediction tool
BDA	big data analytics
BE	binary encoding
BF	blast furnace
BP	blood pressure
BPA	backpropagation algorithm
BSE	Bombay stock exchange
CAD	coronary artery disease
CART	classification and regression tree
CASI	compact airborne spectrographic imager
CBC	complete blood count
CC	correlation coefficient
CGAN	conditional GAN
CHAID	chi-squared automatic interaction detection
CI	computational intelligence
CISDCP	China information system for disease control and prevention
CKD	chronic kidney disease

CLAHE	contrast limited adaptive histogram equalization
C-LSTME	convolutional long short-term memory neural network extended
CNEMC	China National Environmental Monitoring Center
CNN	convolution neural network
CNNA	convolutional neural network with attention
COD	chemical oxygen demand
CRF	conditional random field
CSS	cascading style sheet
CVDs	cardiovascular diseases
DBN	dynamic Bayesian network
DCNN	deep convolutional neural networks
DENFIS	dynamic evolving neuro-fuzzy inference system
DETS	dynamic ensemble for time series
DFD	data flow diagram
DIV	difference in variance
DL	deep learning
DLVM	deep latent variable models
DNN	deep neural networks
DoE	design of experiment
DRX	dynamic recrystallization
DT	decision tree
DTGP	direct TGP
E	entropy
EID	emerging infectious disease
ELM	extreme learning machine
EM	expectation maximization
ENVI	environment for visualization of images
ERF	effective receptive field
ERGAS	Erreur Relative Globale Adimensionnelle de Synthese
FBS	fasting blood sugar
FCC	false-color composite
FFHQ	Flickr faces HQ
FLAASH	fast line of sight atmospheric analysis of hypercubes
FN	false negatives
FOV	field of view
FP	false positives
FTP	file transfer protocol
FW	Frank-Wolfe

GA	genetic algorithm
GANs	generative adversarial networks
GBC	gradient boost classifier
GBM	gradient boosted model
GDP	gross domestic product
GFS	global forecasting system
GLM	generalized linear model
GNB	Gaussian Naïve Bayes
GP	Gaussian process
GPR	Gaussian process regression
GPS	global positioning systems
GRU	gated recurrent units
GUI	graphical user interface
HE	homomorphic encryption
HER	electronic health record
HF	heart failure
HMMs	hidden Markov models
HR	high resolution
HTD	hospital for tropical diseases
HYDICE	hyperspectral digital imagery collection experiment
ID3	iterative dichotomiser 3
IGM	input geometry
IHA	Indian Heart Association
IHDPS	intelligent heart disease prediction system
IIoT	industrial internet of things
IoT	internet of things
IWCV	importance weighted cross-validation
JM	Jeffries Matsushita
KL	Kullback-Leibler
KLIEP	Kullback-Leibler importance estimation procedure
KNN	k-nearest neighbor
KRR	kernel ridge regression
LDA	linear discriminant analysis
L-M	Levenberg-Marquardt
LPIPS	learned perceptual image patch similarity
LR	logistic regression
LS-SVM	least square support vector machine
LSTM	long short-term memory
MA	moving average

MAE	mean absolute error
MAPD	mean absolute percentage deviation
MAPE	mean absolute percentage error
MASE	mean absolute scaled error
MDRX	meta dynamic recrystallization
MERS	middle-east respiratory syndrome
MESMA	multiple endmember spectral mixture analysis
MFS	mean flow stress
ML	machine learning
MMH	maximum marginal hyperplane
MSE	mean square error
MTMF	mixture tuned matched filtering
MVN	multivariate normal
NAM	network animator
NCD	non-communicable disease
NDVI	normalized difference vegetation index
NF	neuro-fuzzy
NLP	natural language processing
NN	nearest neighbors
NN	neural network
NS	network simulator
NSE	national stock exchange
NTM	neural Turing machine
OTC	over-the-counter
PATE	private aggregation of teacher ensembles
PC	principal components
PCA	principal component analysis
PDF	packet delivery fraction
PERG	pattern electroretinography
PFWCS	pairwise Frank-Wolfe covariate shift
PG-GAN	progressive growing of GANs
PLC	programmable logic controller
PLS-DA	partial least square discriminant analysis
PM-KLIEP	PPCA-mixture KLIEP
PNN	probabilistic neural networks
PSNR	peak signal to noise ratio
PSO	particle swarm optimization
PV	photovoltaic
QoS	quality of service

RASE	relative average spectral error
RBF	radial basis function
RF	random forest
RFC	random forest classifier
RL	reinforcement learning
RMSE	root mean square error
RNN	recurrent neural network
ROC	receiver operating characteristic
ROI	regions of interest
ROV	remotely operated vehicles
SARIMA	seasonal ARIMA
SFF	spectral feature fitting
SGD	stochastic gradient descent
SIFT	scale-invariant feature transform
SIS	smart information systems
SLIC	straightforward straight iterative clustering
SM	Sharma-Mittal
SNR	signal to noise ratio
SNT	scalable network technologies
SOM	self-organizing maps
SRX	static recrystallization
SSIM	structure similarity measure
SSVM	structured support vector machine
SURF	speed up robust feature
SVM	support vector machine
SVR	support vector regression
SWIR	shortwave infrared
T2DM	type-2 diabetes mellitus
TB	tuberculosis
Tcl	tool command language
TD	transformed divergence
TDS	total dissolved solids
TF-IDF	term frequency-inverse document frequency
TGP	twin Gaussian process
USN	underwater sensor network
UTC	coordinated universal time
UTS	ultimate tensile strength
VAE	variational autoencoders
VNIR	visible near-infrared

WBCD	Wisconsin breast cancer dataset
W-ELM	weighted ELM
WGAN	Wasserstein GAN
WHO	World Health Organization
WSN	wireless sensor network
YS	yield stress

Acknowledgments

First of all, we express our gratitude to the Almighty, who blessed us with the zeal and enthusiasm to complete this book successfully.

We are extremely thankful to Prof. Lalit Kumar Awasthi, Director, Dr. B. R. Ambedkar National Institute of Technology Jalandhar; Prof. Ajay Kumar Sharma, Vice-Chancellor, Inder Kumar Gujral Punjab Technical University; Prof. Deepak Garg, Head of Department, Bennett University, Director-NVIDIA; Prof. Manju Sharma, Director, Khalsa College, Amritsar, for their continuous guidance and support throughout the life cycle of this book.

We would like to acknowledge the assistance and contribution of all the people engaged in this book project. We especially thank our authors for contributing their valuable work, without which it was impossible to complete this book.

We express our special and most sincere thanks to the reviewers involved in the review process who contributed their time and expertise to improve the eminence, consistency, and arrangement of the chapters in the book.

We also take the opportunity to express our thanks to personnel from the publishing house for giving it a final shape and presenting this book in this manner.

This book would not have been possible without the heartiest support of our families. Our deepest regards to our parents for their blessings and affection even during the tough period.

Last but not least, we thank GOD, for giving us the strength and wisdom to carry out this work successfully.

—*Editors*

Preface

Machine learning is one of the fastest growing domains that has dominated the software industry for the past few decades. The motive behind its success is it assists in discovering knowledge and trends in information that was quite cumbersome with conventional techniques. Additionally, machine learning also provides an approach to distinguish patterns and make actuality-based suggestions.

This book is an effort to present the diversified application areas of machine learning and its contribution to society/industry. In addition to discussing the multifarious applications of machine learning, the book also presents rudiments of the subject so as to maintain completeness.

The book is organized in a manner so as familiarize readers with the nuts and bolts of machine learning and the important ideas. Subsequently, they will also be able to figure out the integration of various machine learning methods with real-world problems. The first few chapters of the book deal with standard topics of machine learning, while the rest of the book covers the employment of machine learning in various industries. Emphasis has been given to the application of machine learning in healthcare, and the employment of machine learning in healthcare has completely transformed its facet. Apart from healthcare, several other domains have also been focused on with respect to the employment of machine learning.

The book aims to familiarize practitioners with a range of procedures and the other aspects of machine learning that can help them ace their skills. A book is also a great tool for aspiring data scientists who need to understand machine learning's real-world's application. The book helps both beginners and specialists by covering new contextual investigations and the most recent cutting-edge procedures.

The book is organized broadly into three diverse yet related sections focusing on rudiments, healthcare applications, and industrial applications, respectively. Part 1 covers the ethics, security, and privacy issues, future directions, and challenges in ML. Part 2 focuses on the applications of ML in healthcare, emphasizing current status, analytics, and future prospects. Part 3 adds a macro dimension to the book, highlighting the industrial applications, encompassing submissions in the steel industry, urban information retrieval, garbage detection, air pollution, stock market, fish detection in underwater video, fake news predictor, and many more. The book is coordinated into 21 chapters. A brief description of each of the chapters of this book is as follows:

Chapter 1 discusses ethical issues related to artificial intelligence for machine learning. Every sector not limited to health care, insurance, financial services, digital commerce industries, agriculture, privacy preservation, retail industry, automobile, logistics, manufacturing, aviation, transportation has endless opportunities due to the introduction of AI. While implementing above said applications, transparency, trust, cost-effectiveness, security, innovation, and privacy are the ethical backbones of the artificial intelligence system. The chapter deals with the challenges and strategies to deal with these issues.

Chapter 2 presents an overview of machine learning, machine learning security and privacy threat models, machine learning black-box attacks, and experimental methods related to these. In the chapter, a comparative study on secured frameworks that identify the attacks and provide security for the data is presented.

Chapter 3 explains the basic terms and some mandatory concepts related to deep learning techniques for image segmentation for a better understanding of the newcomer to the field. Then, the chapter focuses on different methods and network structures that are applicable for semantic image segmentation for deep analysis of images in different applications in contrast to conventional approaches. Also, the chapter outlines the strengths and weaknesses of the deep learning approach to present a better perspective to the individuals.

Chapter 4 makes an attempt to handle covariate shifts in ML occurring due to uneven probability distributions in training and testing data. In this chapter, the covariate shift is corrected by learning the importance of weights for re-weighting the train data such that the training samples get closer to the test data samples get more importance during modeling. To estimate the importance weights, a computationally efficient Frank-Wolfe optimization algorithm is used. A computationally efficient method of TGP is presented for covariate shift correction, and the performance is evaluated on the benchmark HumanEva dataset resulting in significantly reduced regression error.

Chapter 5 presents the brief history of generative models that existed before generative adversarial networks (GANs), such as the various types of autoencoders, Gaussian mixture models, and hidden Markov models. Following this, a deep dive into the architecture of GANs, the mathematics behind GANs, and how they are different from other generative models, specifically the vanilla GAN architecture, has been explored. A detailed analysis of vanilla GAN for the problems introduced in the training and the quality of generated data has been discussed.

Chapter 6 discusses the key applications of different types of supervised as well as unsupervised ML algorithms along with their utility in healthcare settings. The advantages and limitations of different algorithms and future prospects are also discussed.

Chapter 7 employs machine learning algorithms for predictive data analytics in healthcare. The authors in this chapter discuss the exuberance of machine learning and predictive data analytics in the healthcare domain. Employment of machine learning in various aspects of healthcare, viz. electronic record management, data integration, diagnoses, and disease predictions, have been focused on in the chapter. Finally, the chapter also presents the advantages of ML over traditional approaches, especially for predictive analytics.

Chapter 8 makes an attempt to predict heart disease using machine learning in an IoT scenario. In this chapter, different machine learning approaches have been applied for the early prediction of heart disease. It can be helpful for the necessary aid for chronic patients suffering from heart diseases. The authors discussed the methodologies and provided an insight into the framework for analysis. The chapter focused on the application of KNN and random forest classifier and concluded the predictive accuracy as 88.52%.

Chapter 9 presents ML-based data analytics for extracting meaningful information from the data that has been the major consideration for organizations. A number of research studies regarding the ML techniques used in the analysis of infectious diseases on the human body are reviewed. It has been found that techniques like KNN, SVM, Naive Bayes, random forest, k-means, and hierarchical Clustering are being majorly used. But random forest, GLM, GBM, K-Means are most suited in the field of infectious disease.

Chapter 10 establishes the need to develop a system for evaluating drug effectiveness by using a set of user comments which are annotated manually. A relation between the already available adverse reactions of a drug and those obtained by the developed system has been demonstrated in the chapter. A use case of seven drugs used for treating neurological disorders has been used for this study.

Chapter 11 provides an overview of the time series forecasting techniques for infectious disease prediction with a focus on enabling technologies, protocols, and implementation issues. The basic idea of this chapter is to have smart sensors working directly to achieve a new class of autonomous applications without human involvement. This chapter outlines a detailed survey of the time series forecasting techniques in the context of medical applications.

Chapter 12 presents a detailed overview and survey of ML application to the steel industry. This chapter also describes three case studies of the application of ML for the steel industry. A hybrid model, integrating mathematical model and ANN, was developed for level-2 mill set-up of an industrial hot strip mill. The second case study is about a mathematical-ANN hybrid model for the prediction of mechanical properties of hot rolled steel coils and. The third case study describes the methodology development of a cobble prediction system in a hot strip mill using statistical method and support vector machine (SVM), a classification algorithm.

Chapter 13 discuss in detail the geospatial big data produced by airborne or ground-based hyperspectral sensors have high spectral resolution and therefore account for the heterogeneity of urban areas. Machine learning approaches like support vector machines (SVM) successfully handle noise and variability in such datasets. SVM performs intermediate spectral angle mapper (SAM) and object-based image analysis (OBIA) in retrieving buildings and natural features from the 2 m airborne hyperspectral data over Reno. The chapter focuses on using iterative back projection (IBP) and bicubic interpolation over the Washington DC scene and concludes that IBP creates a higher spatial resolution image at the same scaling ratio without retaining spectral characteristics.

Chapter 14 works on garbage detection based on merchandise markers. The aim of this chapter is to detect different types of garbage based on a new algorithm which is a hybrid of the algorithms used in previous studies called the SURF algorithm. Three types of garbage images, namely paper, plastic, and a glass of garbage data (images), were collected, and by extracting feature points and descriptors from the data given, the identification of new upcoming images is made.

Chapter 15 provides a comprehensive discussion of various types of LSTMs being used to solve the problem of air pollution forecasting, along with discussing a general pipeline used for the same. Air pollution has become a topic of concern to all with the development of modern science, technology, transportation, and industrial pollution because of the exposure to high concentrations of PM (particulate matter) that contribute to several health hazards. Accurate air pollution forecasting thus becomes the need of the hour and has therefore evolved as an active field of research. Recent advancements in the field of deep learning and big data technologies have made LSTMs a state-of-the-art choice for predicting air quality. The chapter starts with a discussion of the LSTM architecture, its variants, and its applications across various domains.

Chapter 16 explores the application of ML in stock market prediction. Prediction of the stock market determines the future value of a stock traded in a stock exchange. With the accurate prediction of the future stock value of a company, an investor can maximize his gains. To increase efficiency and user-friendliness, stock market trading is getting adopted to new technologies. It has been estimated that 85% of the customer interaction in financial sectors will be without directly interacting with another human. This chapter gives an overview of various algorithms in the application of Machine Learning in stock market prediction.

Chapter 17 targets to perform univariate analysis on a historical dataset of Bombay stock exchange (BSE) SENSEX open value and compares the results of the ARIMA model, deep learning model, FBProhet model to predict the value of BSE SENSEX Open value, i.e., opening cost of stocks, with high exactness and accuracy.

Chapter 18 proposes a novel fish classification approach, where pre-processing is to be initiated by wavelet-based color correction techniques with different evaluation parameters followed by feature extraction to reduce the amount of redundant data for a given analysis. The proposed approach not only enhances the color content of the underwater video but also can maintain the structure of the original input videos.

Chapter 19 proposes a fake news detection model to efficiently check and predict the authenticity of the news with accuracy and precision. The latest machine learning algorithm with the perfect blend of natural language processing (NLP) techniques is employed for building this application. The model successfully gives considerable outcomes by filtering out the real news from fake news. Moreover, the model proposes the probability of truth, which makes this model different from others.

Chapter 20 gives an in-depth ML-based examination of numerous underwater simulation tools with key features and coding parameters. Due to complex network topology and tools, underwater sensor networks study is very inflated. But simulation environments and tools help to study the real underwater conditions. Numerous underwater network simulation tools are accessible nowadays, so the selection of a suitable tool is a significant task. The chapter helps researchers to identify the correct tool based on needs and availability.

Chapter 21 presents an analysis and prediction of heritage monuments images using machine learning techniques. Landmark acknowledgment could be a challenging issue within the space of picture classification due to gigantic varieties within the design of diverse landmarks. Diverse introductions of the structure play a vital role within the acknowledgment of the landmarks in their pictures. This chapter proposes an approach for the classification of various monuments based on the features of the monument images. Here, the demonstration is prepared on representations of distinctive Indian as well as outside landmarks, obtained from pictures, which show geographic and social differences. Further, tests have been carried out on the physically procured dataset that is composed of pictures of distinctive landmarks where each landmark has pictures from diverse precise sees with its ancient and modern pictures.

Thus, the aim of this book is to familiarize researchers with the latest trends in machine learning, starting from rudiments to its applications through healthcare and advanced applications like industries, underwater sensors, fish detection, monuments images, etc.

PART I

Rudiments of Machine Learning Approaches

CHAPTER 1

Ethics in AI in Machine Learning

SHILPA KAPSE

Assistant Professor, Lokmanya Tilak College of Engineering,
Navi Mumbai, Maharashtra, India, E-mail: shilpashrawane@gmail.com

ABSTRACT

A few years later, everything will be automated using a touch of artificial intelligence (AI) such as Siri, Google Assistant, Alexa, and Bixby. Every sector will enter into a service era where things will not be owned but accepted as a service. The way the service sector works will be totally changed. Every sector not limited to health care, insurance, financial services, digital commerce industries, agriculture, privacy preservation, retail industry, automobile, logistics, manufacturing, aviation, transportation; has endless opportunities due to introduction of AI. The massive volume of structured and unstructured data in most of the enterprises is so big to handle that it exceeds the current processing capacity. The information in the form of data is gathered from multiple sources. This data comprises of images, mobile devices, applications servers, and many more means. Various processes have been done on this gathered data. It includes capturing, formatting, manipulation, storing, and then analyzing. Once these processes have been done on the data, it becomes a trained one. This trained data is definitely helpful to an enterprise to acquire acumen, refine performance and make swift, more agile recommendations and ultimately improve operations. AI is more comprehensive and potentially more useful and holds tracked user data. AI offers analytic solutions while taking right decision. The focus of machine learning is to evolve AI pervaded with the human expertise set of troubleshoots, training, and recollection and provide a set of tools to handle massive user data.

While implementing above said applications using AI, customers must have faith on the service providers. This is possible only when transparency, trust, cost-effectiveness, security, innovation, and privacy are the ethical backbones of artificial intelligence system. The chapter aims at handling ethical issues related to Artificial Intelligence for machine learning.

1.1   INTRODUCTION

Since the last few years, machines are becoming more and smarter for the benefit of mankind. The world is getting closer with the help of cellular phones. People are becoming more tech-savvy. All the information is available at their palmtop. In these days of pandemic situation arrived on the world, it has also become need of the day. This information may be regarding healthcare, agriculture, retail industries, logistics, manufacturing, the weather, traffic conditions, education, office, home appliances, aviation industry, e-mails, online shopping and many more. Gadgets are getting smarter with the advent of technology. Machines and computer programs are able to solve problem and are learning like a human brain. In this era of computer technology, almost every field of science involves a vital role of artificial intelligence (AI). These fields may be biotechnology, bioinformatics, nanotechnology, etc. Recently, there is an enormous range of optimization problems in almost all engineering disciplines from size and complexity point of view. The use of conventional optimization techniques to get solution of such complex multimodal problems sometimes may prove uneconomical and strenuous. That is the reason why a special class of intelligence algorithms has become attentive. More often, they are cited to rational approaches and their basis lie on the interpretation motifs found in the human behavior. This computational technique has been implemented to numerous complications in the field of manufacturing and operative engineering, healthcare, agriculture, and many more.

Since the beginning of this decade, we find learning image analysis, machine learning (ML), deep learning (DL), Internet of things (IoT) image processing, reinforcement learning (RL), robotics, blockchain technology, sentiment analysis, drone are various applications evolved for the betterment of mankind and environment. Figure 1.1 shows all these applications.

Multinational companies such as Google, Microsoft, IBM, Amazon, Flip cart are the one who are working for the customer issues in every sector. These companies are infusing in the evolution of AI for healthcare, transportation, service industry. AI-enabled technology is widely used nowadays in the automobile industry. AI technology is widely used to resolve customer issues.

FIGURE 1.1   Various applications of AI technology.

1.2   DEFINITION OF AI

AI can be interpreted as the stream of science which deals with techniques aimed to make machines intelligent by using computer programs. In other words, using computers, machines can be made intelligent to understand human behavior. This intelligence is aimed at achieving desired objective. Human being is the only organism on the earth that has ability to think, plan for future and makemake smart decisions. Non-living things such as machines perform certain mechanism to complete certain desired tasks. An operator has to handle the machine to complete the task. The machines cannot think and can't make decisions on their own. Computer programs need very little time and too much memory. But it depends on how effectively the program has designed it to make the mechanism highly intellectual. When the machines complete certain task with highest efficiency, minimum time, accuracy, precisely, effectively then that machine is said to be intelligent.

In order to do so, a program designer has to program that machine to work accordingly. If after programming too machine takes more time than manual control, then the programming is to be revisited to give better results. So, by following a computational procedure, they can be made intelligent. This programming technique of making machines intelligent is called AI. Thus AI explored how to make computers carryout certain intelligent mechanisms. In order to carry out certain mechanism AI follows some algorithms that have capability similar to the human mind to carry out that task. These algorithms consist of sub-domains intended to execute different algorithmic steps.

AI represents a wide range of computational algorithm that fathoms solution of a system. Their peculiar characteristic is the human behavioral techniques that are at the roots of articulation and execution. Certainly, AI itself represents a particular category of new smart methodology pre-owned in almost all global control techniques. A typical AI system needs an environment, a set of sensors to sense various control parameters, computer algorithm to know-how is the world like you, a decision-maker to decide what actions have to be done, an effecter to represent the result of action taken and a continuous action rule.

The speculation of problems of widespread categories is called *computational complexity*. As yet, this hypothesis did not link with AI that would have been anticipated. Resources of difficulties and workout of these difficulties will decide the victory in problem solving by humans and by AI programs. Neither researchers nor AI section is able to find whether resources are complex or the workouts. The intricacy of algorithms is based on the reach of the shortest program which gives rise to discrete objects.

1.3   APPLICATIONS OF AI

There are many avenues are available for the modernization and implementation of AI. These applications are tremendous not limited to healthcare, agriculture, retail industries, logistics, manufacturing, the weather, traffic conditions, education, office, home appliances, aviation industry, e-mails, online shopping and many more. AI has its foundation based on human consciousness and computer science. As such it's an inherent blend of both cognitive methods and modern computation techniques. AI is capable of addressing many useful and important healthcare challenges. But the quality of this addressing is done on the basis of available healthcare data. AI cannot be as perfect as human being to determine the very cause of the disease.

1.3.1   HEALTHCARE

Moto of AI [1] is to mimic activities done by human consciously. Health care sector is touching new horizons. If we consider healthcare as one avenue for

AI application, then there are many sub-streams in healthcare. These include detection of disease, then decide whether it is chronic, then suggest the type of diagnosis to be provided, which medicines to be suggested and lastly the continuous research implementation to a patient. All these need the health-care data. The analytical data related to health issues is available to everyone and can protect our lives by proper diagnosis. This data may be in structured or non-structured form. Conventional support vector machine (SVM) and neural network (NN) are well accepted AI approaches that incorporate ML techniques for structured data. Whereas, modern DL and natural language processes methods are used for unstructured data [2]. Cancer, neurology, and cardiology are the major areas of healthcare issues where the application of AI finds better results of identification, therapeutics recommendations, along with consequences prognostications and prophecy assessment. In many of illustrations, AI performs healthcare activities better than human being due to whom it may put a stop to wide-ranging computerization, industrializa-tion, and mechanization of healthcare professional jobs for substantial time duration [1–3].

Figure 1.2 shows the statistical analysis of the data of number of cases of various types of diseases versus a number of patients in years 2013 to 2016 using AI [1]. The analysis of patients suffering from major diseases related to neoplasm, nervous, cardiovascular, urogenital, pregnancy, digestive system, respiratory system, skin diseases, endocrine, and nutritional.

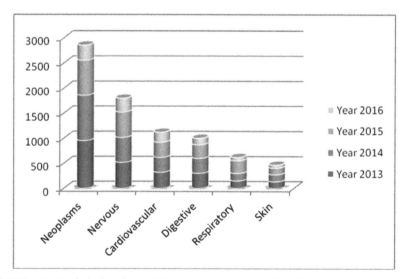

FIGURE 1.2   Statistical analysis of disease types considered in AI literature.

1.3.2 *AGRICULTURE*

In the developing country like India, most of the people being villagers depend upon agriculture as the only source of income. This agriculture sector faces many challenges in achieving maximum capitulate that together with inappropriate soil therapy, ailment, and epidemic invasion, very small amount of output, and an extensive comprehension breach connecting farmers and automation. The available agricultural machines have to be made more efficient and intelligent enough to carry out the agricultural works. Administrations of soil, crop, weed, and infection management are the different sectors where farmer has to apply his cognitive intelligence. Recently, it has been observed that the AI requisition [6] has been found noticeable in the wide spectrum of agriculture. Flexibility, revved up execution, precise full correctness; and. curmudgeonly of AI is its main concept in agriculture applications. An outstanding center of attention is imposed on the robustness and hindrances of the requisition and also the course of action in making use of expert systems for elevated productiveness.

The implementation of AI in agronomics assists the agronomists to understand the data insights such as temperature of the surrounding, precipitation in soil, speed of wind, and solar radiation; and many more. AI is being adopted in implementations such as computerized instrument acclimatization for weather forecasting and disease or pest recognition. [5] With the help of Chatterbot, farmers can be provided with exact updated information regarding soil moisture content, temperature, content of the soil, rainfall, etc. The State of Andhra Pradesh is an example in India where Microsoft Corporation has joined hands with around 175 farmers extending assistance and accommodating solutions for land tilling, scattering of seeds, addition of fungicides and pesticides, and other nutrient supplements for crop. It is observed that there was a increase in the production of crops by around 30% approximately as compared to the previous year's yield by simply making use of AI.

Smart information systems (SIS) [7] being used in agriculture has potential to retrieve different paradigms of data from the farmland, analyze the information, and mechanize the campaigns which would be done by all farmers, acknowledging for expenses reductions, rapid, and efficacious crop estimation, and improved administration and productivity of the landowners. Agricultural SIS also offers horticulture an supplementary returns, healthier clientele-relations, and diminished expenses from commissioning supplementary farmers and consultants. SIS is being confined as one hypothetical method to assist vegetation, seed, harvest, and manage farms better and more effectively. Many ethical apprehensions may arrive due to the implementation of agricultural SIS.

The plant's stress recognition system using ML and AI is shown in Figure 1.3. The measure and quantity of stress percentage and the information regarding weather database, stress forecasting are given as input parameters to the stress recognition system. This system then identifies and recognizes disease symptoms, spot on leaves and plants. It also categorizes stress into three categories absence of stress, mild stress and high stress. Using this framework, farmer can take effective steps to improve the crop yield.

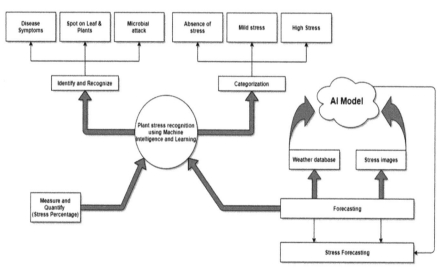

FIGURE 1.3   Plant's stress recognition using ML and AI.

As we already discussed, the use of SIS technology for many industries is motivated by its ability to shape agronomist's life straightforward, unchallenging, dynamic, effective, profitable, and cost worthy. The main motto of SIS is aim is to upgrade farm administration, not by increasing fertilizer use, but by more intelligent farming decisions and practices. The SIS project was drafted in such a way as to render farmers with the regional atmospheric prognostications, various diseases of plants and its early detection. Also, it works as a recommendation tool which helps in reducing the hazards, crop, and yield preliminary study and reviews, productivity of the farmland and measures for imperishable results. It also helps in timely detection to get rid of weeds, infections, and diseases.

At the national level, in the vegetables and fruits markets, AI-based computerized assessing and categorizing sorting have already been used. This technique is applied during export of things in order to create an international agriculture-commodity standard aiding reliable trading all over the world. In order to view images and pictures, the techniques used are DL and advanced image processing technique. Thus these techniques are found effective in digitizing the quality of food. There are enormous food products available in various geographical areas. And hence extending these applications may need millions and billions of images. We just can't imagine getting these many images to be collected, compiled together, analyzed, digitized, and interpreted across the globe. In fact government records carry massive agricultural data or information. Therefore, it is obligation solely to the government to elucidate and annotate in such a way that it can be effectively made at everyone's disposal. In consequence, quality as well as quantity has direct significance bearing on DL's potency. Furthermore, while applying DL in some applications such as solar or electricity power planning, information is needed over years to envisage the generation of power.

1.3.3 AVIATION

A typical framework of Blockchain in a particular aviation system is shown in Figure 1.4. It represents statistics collection, dissemination, and its use as mentioned in the framework. It includes information regarding data source, data providers, data disseminator and data users. The data sources include air travel demands, passengers, and freight. Here, the data providers are the stakeholders. They are airlines, airports, ANSPs, aircraft manufacturers, leasing companies, etc. States are the data collectors. Data disseminators include ISDB database which may be of temporary or permanent type [9]. This data can be used by the whole world.

Aviation industry works for the travel of passengers and goods to different locations. While doing so, functional, and reliable operations of operating systems and sub-systems are of utmost priority. This industry needs continued soundness and stability of operations, frequent flyer systems for customers as well as availability of flights, systems servers, planning objectives relating to support systems, related hardware, software, and other components' proper selection, development, and implementation are the various requirements for the proper functioning of aviation industry. Also there is surveillance systems often used to ascertain difficulties, issues or complications. Even though these systems advocate changes and solutions to be done, there are big challenges in aviation systems. These challenges may include estimating resource requirements and or implementation costs being very important jobs to be carried out [9]. AI finds major application for the effective completion of the abovementioned tasks. The toughest challenge in aviation may be to ensure that AI is developed and used must be transparent, reliable, and well suited with the public requirements and interest.

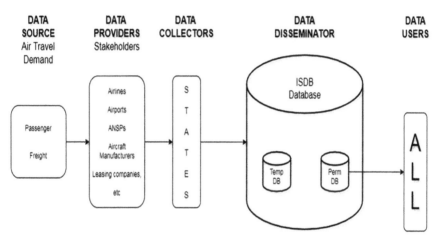

FIGURE 1.4 Framework of blockchain in aviation system.

1.3.4 RETAILING

The retailing is a very wide area. Its functioning can be made more effective with the use of AI and big data analysis. The apprehension structure authorizing big data and analytics in retailing is shown in Figure 1.5. It includes data from the customers, suppliers, and processes. This data is then collected, curetted, and analyzed. Next step involves data science models. These models may be descriptive, predictive or prescriptive [10].

These models work on these data are given as input to some algorithms and programs that work on and as a result provide learning and decisions. These decisions are worked upon by AI systems technology to provide automation [11].

In the retailing there is excessive share of human endeavor requirement although simultaneous profit margin is souring. The economy is dependent on work experience, order book, professional development; trade has the task of balancing spatial, temporal, qualitative, and quantitative distances between production and consumption.

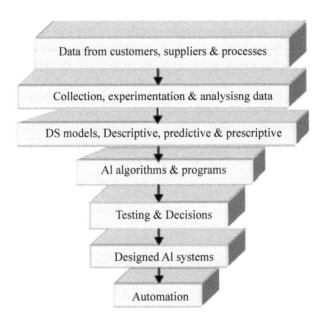

FIGURE 1.5   Apprehension structure authorizing big data and analytics in retailing.

Trading does purchasing of goods from manufacturers and pass on to suppliers, transporting, stocking, and combining goods to form assortment [10]. All these tasks are more or less are generic and can be mechanized smartly with the application of AI.

1.3.5   AUTOMOBILE

Worldwide, in the past decade, lots of people whose figure cannot be counted; have lost their lives or have become physically and mentally disabled due to road accidents. These accidents would have been caused due to vehicles or due to vehicle driver's state of mind at that moment for handling the tragic situation. Majority of these mishaps would have been due to human mistakes. Unfortunately, with the growing population, the occurrence of these accidents may double in near future. From the references obtained from the World Health Organization (WHO), it is observed that majority of the road traffic injuries caused, estimated 1.26 million deaths worldwide in the year 2000. Worldwide it was estimated in 2004 that 2.5 million people were killed in traffic accidents (4.7% of all deaths) [12]. Major automobile industries make use of their assets, measures, and technology to give the best solutions by making use of AI. From the records, it is observed that in 2015, the rate of installation of AI-based systems in brand new vehicles was just 8%. Definitely, this number may rise to 109% in 2025. As this is evident from the automobile research sector that the customers demand different kinds of AI systems to be installed in vehicles.

A typical framework of AIV shown in Figure 1.6 consists of various interfaces which work on automatic order creator, reporting module, robot device-mapper, bus routing and virtual dash buttons. Order management and monitoring, fleet monitoring, transfer handling, alarming, Web HMI, open interfacing are few of the works done by the AIV system. AI finds major applications areas such as vehicle accidents, thefts, maintenance, insurance, driver assistance, intelligent vehicles in automobiles [13].

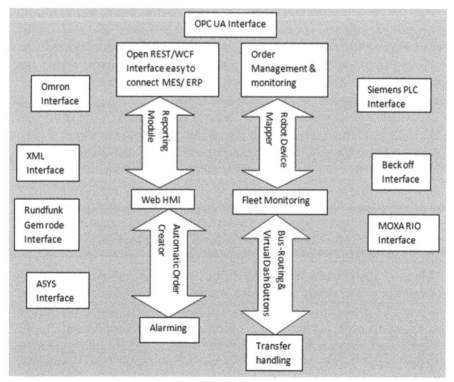

FIGURE 1.6   Typical AIV framework.

An immeasurable number of people lost their lives or became physically or mentally handicapped worldwide in the last 10 years because of on-road vehicle accidents. According to the statistical data available, a common reason for these accidents is nothing but the human mistake. These mistakes are due to driver distractions. Driver distractions occur due to talking to passengers, high volume music, drunk driving and many more. Hence safety of the passengers inside the vehicle as well as outside it is of major concern and priority. Every year thousands of vehicles get stolen and cannot be traced. If we try to estimate various asset losses due to the theft of motor vehicle, definitely their estimate is almost millions of rupee every year. Here we come to the term grand theft auto. Basically, this term deals with the stealing of the automobile. Routine maintenance is very necessary for the proper and smooth functioning of the vehicles. So maintenance scheduling plays a vital role to escalate the viability of the vehicles. This is a very important issue for vehicle owner. Proper maintenance of the motor vehicle elevates the performance as well as helps increasing the efficiency and productivity of the automobile [14].

Perhaps, these modern automobiles may not inscribe one or two additional miscellaneous issues. To mention one of them is a need of speed limiter predefined by the driver for properly controlling the speed of the vehicle. To be very frank yet none of the technique has been invented which can automatically recognize or discover the fault occurred in the vehicle, location of the fault, reason for the occurrence of the fault; in the particular part of the vehicle and suggestions about repair or replacement of the faulty part of the vehicle. Furthermore, there is a possibility that some concerns may be of miniature size but if ignored may lead to massive disasters during the run time of the vehicles on road. To illustrate this sentence let us take an example of a bad mechanical component in any of the system. This component may lead to destruction of the whole moving machine. In addition, unpleasant atmospheric conditions often can give rise to unforeseen disasters. We can definitely avoid such situations. Vehicle driver, though experienced one, may find critical situation due to bad weather conditions.

Many of the manufacturing industries have come forward to work on accomplishing completely auto controlled vehicles such as driverless cars, which will help the entire community for safe driving. By setting this idea or feature of driver less car in motion, a person who is not confident of driving can drive the vehicle without touching the steering wheel. This is possible only because of the use of features based on AI approach. Many companies are coming with the ideas of advanced safety features for betterment of the society. These safety features include automatic braking, collision avoidance systems, pedestrian, and also alerts given to cyclists, cross-traffic, and smart cruise controls. These features represent a few of supplemental attributes actually fueled by AI. State-of-art golden opportunities are revealed from the enthusiastic automobile manufacturers inclined to design and develop fully automated cars, 18-wheeler trailer trucks, good carriers and many more such vehicles.

With the advent of cloud computing, it has become convenient to make the computer system resources available for storing the data without directly carrying the data. This data can be deployed at any time and place without direct active management from the user's side. This cloud computing can easily deploy AI technology in the automotive field. Fast processing speed, big data access and analytics, and centralized connectivity are few of the important features of cloud computing. Many of such cloud-based platforms can evolve to walk hand in hand with the companies aspiring to evolve brand new ideas of fully controlled technology. The partnership between General Motors and IBM's Watson supercomputer stands for a best illustration of the platform where the power of clouds is being shared amongst.

Cognitive capabilities of AI have a great importance and usefulness to a wide range of vehicles ranging from small cars to heavy vehicles used in mines, civil constructions. These comprehensive systems are taken as granted to execute the tasks same as a person would interpret an actual-life circumstances, and to do that, a profound interpretation of unstructured data is essential [12]. AI needs an insight from abundant unstructured data to determine on how to acknowledge obviously in real-time. Furthermore, these systems would be capable of tackling dynamic operating conditions as well. Intelligent Risk Insurance Assessment is another major issue of insurance companies to partner with automotive and technology companies. They aim at helping to find out risky drivers. One such partnership involves Nauto, a technology developer, BMW I Ventures, and Toyota Research Institute, as well as the insurance company Allianz Group. Nauto has made agreements with the others to develop AI-based products that aid in fleet management, logistics, and driver safety.

Figure 1.7 indicates one illustration of the status of AI implementation of automotive organization from Capgemini research institute [12]. It gives the statistical analysis about the scaled implementation, selective implementation, pilots, and POCs and non-implemented any AI initiatives from mid-2017 till now. From this figure, we can conclude that the scaled implementation has found more applications than the rest.

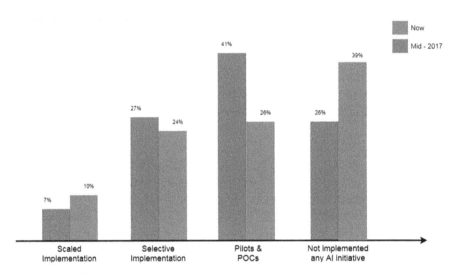

FIGURE 1.7   Illustration of status of AI implementation at automotive organization.

Table 1.1 indicates the statistical report of Road accidents occurred in India during the past four years. It tells us about an aggregate number of accidents happened, approx. number of persons lost lives and approx. number of persons got hurt yearly during 2014 to 2018. It is observed that the numbers are growing day by day. To avoid it, large steps have to be taken to automate the vehicles [15].

TABLE 1.1   Statistical Report of Road Accidents in India During 2014 to 2018

Year	Approx. No. of Road Accidents	Approx. No. of Persons Lost Their Lives	Approx. No. of Persons Got Hurt
2014	489,400	139,671	493,474
2015	501,423	146,133	500,279
2016	480,652	150,785	494,624
2017	464,910	147,913	470,975
2018	467,044	151,417	469,418

1.4   ETHICS IN AI

AI implementation makes use of technology and data. There are many ethical issues raised by the technology and the data usage while applying AI. We have come across the above said areas for the implementation of AI for making them more intelligent systems. While implementing these applications of AI, there are many risks, threats, ethics, and rights to be followed. If the system does not follow ethics, then the system will not last long. Also the commodity users will never have faith in the system and may lose interest. This aspect affects the whole market existence of the particular commodity. This may affect the future of the system. The transparency, trust, cost-effective, security, innovation, and privacy are the ethical backbones of AI system. This chapter aims at handling ethical issues related to big data for ML [8].

The ethics to be followed while applying AI areas in subsections.

1.4.1 INFORMATION SECURITY

AI has been implemented for the betterment of human being. The assurance of information security is very important. For instance, in banking sector, if the information of the account holder is not secure then it may lead to fraud. The security should be such that people should not be afraid of saving their money in the bank accounts.

Another example could be from the healthcare sector. If the analytical data of health information of a patient suffering from the certain disease is not secure, then the patient's life is at risk. Wrong medication can be given to the patient who may even lead death of the patient. AI technology defiantly helps to enhance the productivity of health care delivery and standard of patient care.

Further in retailing industry, if the trade information is not secure, then the whole business will be at risk. Millions of rupees have been invested in the business. Therefore, the business may get ruined if AI information security infringing happens.

1.4.2 TRANSPARENCY

There should be transparency while tackling with certain surgery where AI robot is used. All the staff, including doctors, nurses involved in surgery along with the patient must know the potential harms and hazards which come across while using AI technology. The AI industry aims at introducing numerous actions to ensure transparency in the AI industry [17]. A typical case denotes that the data sets and processes that are utilized in the establishment of the particular AI systems should be documented, accountable, and identifiable too. Of course, Also, AI systems should be derived such that everyone handling it is able to correlate and execute it as and when needed. Also, person handling it must be made aware of that he/she is interacting with an AI system. Furthermore, Accuracy, certainty, and articulateness are the fundamentals based on which the AI systems and related human decisions should be taken. Therefore, both AI system and the person handling it should be able to understand and trace out the peer objective. Transparency is the backbone of every system for its future endeavor.

1.4.3   CARE ABOUT THEIR PRIVACY AND DATA SECURITY

AI application in the healthcare sector is facing a lack of regulation and biases present in the encoded algorithms. Yet, patient data privacy is the most significant ethical challenge faced by the AI in healthcare. Privacy of every individual must be protected. If somebody knows more of your personal information, then that person may override you [4]. Whole control of yours will be with the person who may take important decisions of your life too. If stakeholder's personal information is in the wrong hands, then your whole life may be at risk. Consumers care about their privacy. For instance, in the banking sector if customer's privacy is not maintained online fraudulent may withdraw your money without your permission. Personal information should be confidential. Stakeholders should be able to supervise, manage, and must have full control over their data. AI developers should put in place surveillance and supervision techniques to control the quality of data sets. Also AI developers are ought to apply design techniques such as data encryption and data anonymity occurs.

Many times, patients are afraid of the fact that the details shared by them with the doctor may be put into one or the other algorithm and will be made reachable to anyone else to look at. This situation or to be very precise anxiety is obvious and seldom happens with everyone consulting doctor who makes use of AI technology-based systems. Patients also fear that hospital authority may share their information inappropriately without taking their approval. Nevertheless, numerous analysts fear bothers about data privacy may hinder lusty and robust experimentation plans.

1.4.4   CONSENT WILL NOT BE SUFFICIENT FOR AI

Consent is nothing but the ability to act according to an order or follow a set of rules or instructions. Compliance may include internal or external rules imposed upon a system. AI utilizes a set of instructions to perform certain task according to the program designer. It may not be often sufficient in every situation. Hence we can conclude that consent will not be sufficient for AI [19].

Employment is one more important ethical issue that has come across many projects quoted here which make use of AI systems. The SIS systems designed to automate various systems from enormous sections of healthcare, automobile, irrigation, agriculture; logistics are so efficient that they will replace human jobs. But the AI developer's teams state that the AI systems are designed to complement the human expert, rather than replacing them. Also, the team guarantees that with the use of strong security measures to avoid misuse and hacking, their customers' privacy is safeguarded. All the agronomists using AI have their data ownership. They have the flexibility to switchover to different farm management system supplier using the same data which they shared with earlier one. This means that there is no monopoly in the sector of SIS system. And all SIS system suppliers have a fair chance to survive and prosper.

With reference to the EU Data Protection Regulation, the certificate of consultation will be mandatory to all the service providers. This restriction of certification just contributes a solution with the help of which potential regulatory sanctions can be avoided. Perhaps, it is just insufficient to ensure that customers really trust a company.

1.4.5 MACHINES NEED TO ACT CONSCIENTIOUSLY ETHICALLY, NOT JUST INTELLIGENTLY

Physicians and surgeons will be defiantly benefited by the prediction of hazards or risks, recognizing the probable remedies, and also offering policy recommendations obtained from the decisions taken by AI systems in the healthcare sector. Further, these outcomes of AI technology benefit the patients who receive their care. Similarly, the laboratory operators in the hospitals who are handling the clinical machinery based on AI technology systems must be trained to handle the machinery in hospitals effectively as a clinical decision support tool, its benefits, limitations, and precautions in using such a tool. Therefore, stakeholder may have realistic sense and will realize what AI can do and can't. Hence computer programming of these machines should be designed in such a way that machines have to operate ethically and their operation should not be completely dependent on the basis of algorithmic rules [4]. Algorithm users cannot furnish a valid explanation of how they have got the outcome of the algorithm they are using on a particular situation. In such cases, there are fair chances that the use of "black-box" algorithm may lead to dereliction of medical duties and accountability of the product. Therefore, these end-users must be must be educated about the operation of the unknown algorithm. It concludes that full control should not be given to the machines equipped with AI technology. Hence, supervisory control should be with the operator. Humans should always posses' right or power to revoke the system's auto-generated decisions ultimately. The machines are automated to take the decisions. But there should always be the control of the console user to control the outcome of the decisions. At the same time the person handling the console should also be worthy of it. Otherwise, because of human interventions, some decisions may go wrong who may lead to destructive work.

1.4.6   TECHNICAL ROBUSTNESS, SAFETY, AND SECURITY

Safety is the first priority requirement of any system whose control is done with the help of AI. If this system belongs to healthcare, then it may lead to death of a patient whose diagnosis is done. There is a probability that the decisions taken by AI may contain errors. In such scenario it is very difficult to trace the part of AI system from where the error has developed. Also there will be a series of unexpected results that may be very hazardous for the whole system. For instance, if a patient is treated for brain tumor and diagnosis is done with devices which are controlled using AI, there are many chances that the medication given on the basis of decisions taken by AI-controlled equipments may lead to damage the brain of the patient forever. The AI implemented system essentially requires possessing secure and reliable systems and software. Reliability is another ethical issue of AI implementation. AI implemented equipment's may suggest you unnecessary tests and treatments. An ethical and reliable AI system requires algorithms it makes use of must-have security, reliability, and robustness sufficient to patronage errors or inconsistencies during all life-cycle phases of an AI system [17]. This requirement is about ensuring cyber security. While designing AI system, its vulnerability to cyber-attacks and hacking must be taken into consideration with great care. Also, system should be able to understand and mitigate these risks significantly. If the AI system fails to mitigate the risks, then the human control must be there to override the system control.

Automated vehicles have framed safety claims. The claims are based on the decisions taken by the AI technology based on some standard problematic situations handled by the human drivers. Many times due to fatigue, distraction, intoxications, human driver may make wrong decisions while driving vehicle that may lead to massive road accidents. These poor decisions can be defiantly overridden with the help of AV. Yet, the arguments may be troublesome because it depends on the capability of the AI technique to make decisions based on the wide spectrum of human driving decisions [13]. Regardless of the self-driving car prioritizes life of occupants or of pedestrians or neither is a trolley problem. Or safety of one person at the cost of safety of others is a very big issue. As a matter of fact that it is an assumption that AI can be used in real sense. Explicitly we can presume that AV will bring new accident metrics to the safety figures. There will undoubtedly be RTAs uniquely tied to AV decision making capacity in the global context, such as sensor error, programming bugs, unanticipated objects, classification error, and hardware faults [14].

Application of Big Data in agronomics is also unsafe from customer privacy and security threats. Wicked and abominable people functioning as corrupt governments, competitors, or even market traders may misuse it [5, 6, 8]. There are many chances of causing harm, distress, and damage to animal welfare and the environment due to the use of various sensors, robots, and devices required for operation of AI systems. Many researchers, experienced people from the fields and the manufacturing company personnel can come together to resolve these ethical issues complying SIS projects. There is also a tension between ensuring an agribusinesses' intellectual property and the protection of the farmer's data ownership. SIS systems are very costly because of which there are possibilities of originating digital divide. The company's agricultural apprehension to supervise their farm productively and information obtained from farmers are combined together for better results using AI project.

EU addresses key ethical prerequisites, specifications, and recommendations to all AI stakeholders involved in the design, development, deployment, implementation of various AI system techniques [18].

According to European Union guidelines, three measures must be reflected in practice. They are:

- To ensure that an AI systems doesn't disobey EU fundamental rights. While implementing AI fundamentals rights should not be violated or infringements of fundamental rights should not happen. This is ensured by the feedback taken from outside agency.

- Full control should not be with the AI system and definitely human control must be there to understand and interact with AI systems to a satisfactory degree. Human intervention should always be there at the end such that decisions are not solely dependent on automated processing.
- Human influence on the machine decisions must be taken care of so as to avoid misuse of the gadget.

1.5   CONCLUSION

There is a wide spectrum of applications of AI aimed at improving the efficiency, performance effectiveness, ease, consuming less time, robust, and behaving ethically. Healthcare, farming, aviation, automobiles, banking, logistics are a few examples to quote where AI proves to be best. With the help of AI technologies, farmers can analyze present scenario of soil conditioning and crop health. Nowadays, AI is helping farmers, enable them to take right decisions to take right crop with increased yield in particular season. Farmers are saving money and lots of labor and earning with profit too. AI has made agriculture industry to leverage emerging technology for the goodwill of farmers. Chatbot helps farmers to resolve their issues related to crops, soil, and the environment provides answers to all their queries and recommend relevant advices for better yield. This will defiantly propel the growth of the AI market in agriculture ethically.

AI systems are made smarter with the development of more advanced ML models. This task is carried out by the tech giants such as AgriData, CropX, etc. Recently we find the wide applications of AI in various consumer tools covering home automation to industrial automation. Most probably by the end of few years one third jobs in retail industry will be replaced by AI systems following proper ethical norms and regulations.

With the evolution of AI technology, the vehicles are getting smarter day by day. Aviation industry found a boon in the form of AI to have smart remote sensing and control of communication signals. AI has a big challenging role in developing logistics sector referring all the ethics. All aspects of researches need to be ethics-free so that AI can be used for human welfare whether it is biomedical sciences. It is an amalgamation of computer ethics and bioethics.

Regulations won't be implemented overnight. Optimized AI implementation without biased datasets will help the community to live better life.

All ethical aspects will be implemented properly for the smooth functioning of the advanced technology. It won't be an exaggeration to say that AI will always be used in a responsible and ethical manner.

With the help of AI technology, man can reach to such heights of betterment and advancement of life that human beings can never expect. All the consumers will be satisfied with the service they get from the providers. A great day lies in near future when AI will be present in every aspect of life leveraging AI to its best possible extent.

KEYWORDS

- artificial intelligence
- internet of things
- machine learning
- neural network
- smart information systems
- World Health Organization

REFERENCES

1. Fei, J., Yong, Z., Hui, Z., Yi, D., Jiang, F., Jiang, Y., Zhi, H., et al., (2017). Artificial intelligence in healthcare: Past, present, and future. *Stroke and Vascular Neurology, 2*(4), 230–243. PMCID: PMC5829945.
2. Thomas, D., & Ravi, K., (2019). The potential for artificial intelligence in healthcare. *Future Healthcare Journal, 6*(2), 94–98.
3. Anubha, D., (2019). Artificial intelligence: Ethics in healthcare. *Journal of Pharmaceutics and Drug Research, 2*(4), 140, 141.
4. Ramesh, A. N., Kambhampati, C., Monson, J. R. T., & Drew, P. J., (2004). Artificial intelligence in medicine. *Ann. R Coll. Surg. Engl., 86*(5), 334–338.
5. Paras, K., & Himanshu, C., (2019). artificial intelligence in agriculture: An emerging era of research. *TY Journal.*
6. Eli-Chukwu, N. C., (2019). Applications of artificial intelligence in agriculture: A review. *Engineering, Technology & Applied Science Research, 9*(4), 4377–4383.
7. Dharmaraj, V., & Vijayanand, C., (2018). Artificial intelligence (AI) in agriculture. *International Journal Curr. Microbiol. App. Sci., 7*(12), 2122–2128.
8. Mark, R., (2019). Ethics of using AI and big data in agriculture: The case of a large agriculture multinational. *Medicine, Orbit.* 10.29297/orbit. V2i2.109.
9. Assem, M., (2019). Artificial intelligent in aviation/AI in aviation. *Artificial Intelligence and Soft Computing.* Paris.

10. Felix, D. W., & Reinhard, S., (2019). State of the art and adoption of artificial intelligence in retailing. *Digital Policy Regulation and Governance, 21*(3).
11. Venky, S., (2019). Big data and analytics in retailing. Sciendo. doi. 10.2478, Nimmir 2019–0006, Big data in retailing. *NIM, Marketing Intelligence Review, 11*(1).
12. Shubham, S., (2018). Artificial intelligence in automobiles: An overview. *IJIRSET, 7*(5).
13. Andrea, R., (2018). *Ethics, Algorithms, and Self-Driving Cars: A CSI of the 'Trolley Problem.* Policy Insights, Thinking Ahead of Europe, No 2018/02.
14. Martin, C., Martin, M., & Finbarr, M., (2019). Autonomous vehicles and embedded artificial intelligence: The challenges of framing machine driving decisions. *Applied Artificial Intelligence, 33*(8).
15. *Report on Road Accidents in India,* (2018). Ministry of Road Transport & Highways, Government of India.
16. Muller, V. C., (2020). *Ethics of Artificial Intelligence and Robotics. First published Standard Encyclopedia of Philosophy.* URL= https://plato.stanford.edu/archives/sum2020/entries/ethics-ai/ (accessed on 11 November 2021).
17. Michael, J. R., (2019). Ethical dimensions of using artificial. *AMA Journal of Ethics, Illuminating the Art of Medicines, 21*(2), E121–124.
18. Tambiama, M., (2019). *EU Guidelines on Ethics in Artificial Intelligence: Context and Implementation, European Guidelines.* EPRS: European Parliamentary Research Service Author: Members' Research Service PE 640.163.
19. Vargas, F. G., Rio De, J., Brasil, R. J., & Doutor, E. D., (2018). Governance of internet of things and ethics of artificial intelligence. *Revista Direitos Culturais, Santo Angelo, 13*(31), 153–190. http://dx.doi.org/10.20912/rdc.v13i31.2816.

CHAPTER 2

Advances in Artificial Intelligence Models for Providing Security and Privacy Using Machine Learning Technique

R. S. M. LAKSHMI PATIBANDLA and V. LAKSHMAN NARAYANA

Department of IT, Vignan's Foundation for Science, Technology, and Research, Guntur, Andhra Pradesh, India,
E-mail: patibandla.lakshmi@gmail.com (R. S. M. L. Patibandla)

ABSTRACT

Advances in ML (AI) starting late have enabled a puzzling bunch of uses, for instance, data assessment, self-administering structures, and security diagnostics. ML is at present inescapable new structures and models are being sent in every territory reasonable, inciting no matter how you look at its course of action of programming-based acceptance and dynamic. Specifically, deep neural systems have indicated extraordinary execution brings about numerous fields. Numerous applications are deeply associated with our day-by-day life, for example, settling on noteworthy choices in application territories dependent on forecasts or characterizations, in which a DL model could be significant. Thus, if a DL model causes mispredictions or misclassifications because of pernicious outer impacts, at that point, it can cause extremely huge troubles, all things considered. Also, preparing DL models to include a huge measure of information, and the preparation information regularly incorporates delicate data. In this manner, DL models would not uncover the privacy of such information. In this chapter, we describe an overview of machine learning, machine learning security and privacy threat models, machine learning black-box attacks and experimental methods that are used in this work. In the proposed work, a comparative study on secured frameworks that identify the attacks and provide security for the data.

2.1   OVERVIEW OF MACHINE LEARNING

ML is a multidisciplinary exploration area that traverses different controls comprising software engineering, likelihood, and measurements, brain research, and cerebrum science. The goal of ML is how to viably mimic human learning exercises by PCs with the end goal that the information can be consequently found and procured. As per the distinctions of criticisms, ML-related works can be ordered into three gatherings, specifically directed, solo, and fortification learning. In the administered learning, the preparation tests with class names ought to be nourished into classification or relapse replicas in their preparation stage. The commonly administered erudition methods incorporate an optimal tree, support vector machine (SVM), Neural Systems, and so forth. The solo learning, in contrast, incites prototypes utilizing the preparation tests by no information on relating class marks. Bunching and auto-encoder are two ordinary instances of unaided learning strategies.

The support learning streamlines conduct methodologies through attempt and mistake, which is unique to the learning strategy of the over two kinds of strategies. The security examination of ML with the thought of hostile information was proposed. At that point, analysts suggested mutually reflecting the objective and the ability of antagonists into the model. As of late, Biggio et al. contended that a well-defined antagonistic exemplary ought to be developed by four measurements, objective, information, ability, and attacking technique.

Specifically, the antagonistic objective can be portrayed utilizing both the normal effects and the attack specificity of security dangers. For instance, the objective of an aggressor is to dispatch an unpredictable respectability attack that initiates high spurious optimistic, and genuine destructive paces of classifiers or to dispatch a focused on secrecy infringement attack that wrongfully acquires delicate information of the focused on the client. For hostile information, it tends to be partitioned into two gatherings named obliged information and complete information by inspecting whether an aggressor knows preparing information, highlights, learning calculations, choice capacities, classifier boundaries, and input data [1] The antagonistic capacity of an aggressor alludes to their ability to control preparing and testing information. Moreover, the ability can be subjectively deciphered as of three viewpoints:

- Remains the effect of security dangers causal or empirical?
- Whatever is the level of preparing and challenging information that remains constrained by the aggressor? and

- Whatever is the degree of highlights and boundaries that are identified by the assailant?

Finally, the attacking technique is the identified practices of controlling preparing then testing information to adequately accomplish his/her objectives. For instance, an assailant settles on choice in regards to control of information, modification of class names, and messing with highlights. ML is as a rule progressively used for an assortment of utilizations from interruption identification to suggesting new films. Some ML applications require private people's information. Such private information is transferred to concentrated areas in clear content for ML calculations to extricate examples, and assemble models from them [2] The issue isn't constrained to the dangers related with having this private information presented to insider danger at these organizations, or outcast danger if the organizations holding these informational collections were hacked. Likewise, it is conceivable to gather additional data about the private informational indexes regardless of whether the information was anonymized 1, or the information itself and the ML models were out of reach and just the testing results were uncovered [2].

2.1.1 MACHINE LEARNING SECURITY AND PRIVACY THREAT MODELS

The scientific categorization of security dangers for ML models is particularly supported by three alternate points of view. They're the impact on classifiers, the wellbeing infringement, and along these lines, the attack specificity. From the disposition of those three impacts, security dangers towards ML models are regularly additionally isolated into seven classes they're referenced below:

1. **Causative Attack:** This attack incorporates the adjustment inside the dispersion of instructing information like a difference in the boundaries of the preparation models. This change inside the effectively-prepared classifiers prompts diminishing the exhibition of classifiers inside the grouping errands [3].
2. **Exploratory Attack:** This attack makes misclassification with reference antagonistic examples that winds up in uncovering the touchy data from preparing information likewise as learning models.

3. **Respectability Attack:** The honesty attack accomplishes an ascent of the false negatives (FN) inside the exhibition proportion of existing classifiers while grouping unsafe examples.
4. **Accessibility Attack:** This attack is inverse to the respectability attack. Not at all like trustworthiness attack, has this attack accomplished an ascent of the false positives (FP) inside the exhibition proportion of classifiers for the positive examples [4].
5. **Security Violation Attack:** With the privacy infringement attack, enemies are prepared to get delicate additionally as a tip from preparing information and learning models.
6. **Directed Attack:** This attack is particularly wont to lessen the presence of the classifiers on a chosen test or on a chosen gathering of tests.
7. **Drifting Attack:** This kind of attack makes the classifiers bomb in an undiscriminating manner on a more extensive scope of tests.

Deep learning (DL) has risen along with the significant spaces in ML. Specialists have discovered a few vulnerabilities during this space. Inside the instance of deep neural systems, there are a few hostile attacks as referenced underneath:

1. **Security Threats against the Training Phase:** Poisoning attack might be a run-of-the-mill kind of security danger that disturbs the flexibly and, in this manner, the trustworthiness of ML models using infusing hostile examples to the preparation dataset. It's a sort of causative attack which is uncommonly assigned to have practically comparative highlights with vindictive examples and wrong names [5]. The security and privacy threat models are depicted in Figure 2.1.

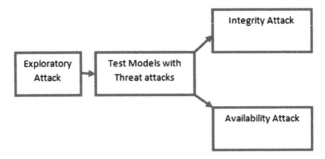

FIGURE 2.1   Security and privacy threat models.

2. **Security Threats Counter to the Testing/Inferring Phase:** Satirizing like avoidance and mimic dangers and reversal attacks are frequently said because the commonest sorts of security dangers against the testing/deriving stage, differential privacy gives a numerical structure that will be wont to comprehend the degree to which an ML calculation 'recollects' data about people that it shouldn't, in this manner offering the ability to measure ML calculations for security ensures they will give [5]. This is frequently significant because we might need replicas to discover broad ideas as of a dataset yet not explicit traits that will uncover the personality or delicate information of entities through dataset, e.g., John's pay is X. Also, during take-off from the attack exemplary accepted thru 'k-secrecy' and its companion's gap privacy makes no presumptions about the degree or degree of foundation accessible to the assailant.

Despite the way that the term 'differential security' [6] has become to some degree notable enunciation, it is principal as in fundamental exertion is fact contributed thru scientists entirely different ML spaces to guarantee that calculations and edifice squares of ML be able to prepare' differentially private.' Distinction security accomplishes its target by the expansion of a controlled measure of 'commotion' during handling to produce enough uncertainty downstream that privacy affecting inductions can't be made dependent on expectations from the framework [7]. Also, this is done while as yet guaranteeing that the forecasts are sufficiently precise to be handy. It takes a shot at the thought of a fixed 'security spending plan' and gives a premise to assessing privacy misfortune from a different procedure on the information, at last determining how that misfortune might be limited while achieving satisfactory tradeoffs with misfortune in the utility of the information. The differential privacy model is depicted in Figure 2.2 and definition of differential privacy levels are depicted in Figure 2.3.

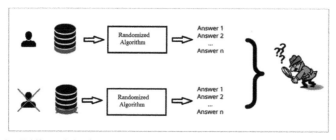

FIGURE 2.2   Differential privacy.

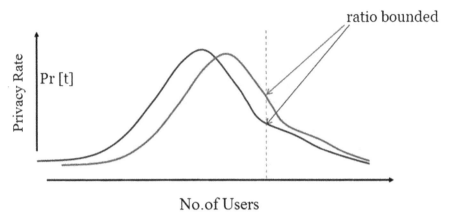

FIGURE 2.3   Definition of differential privacy.

2.2   MACHINE LEARNING BLACK-BOX ATTACKS

The attacking needs to make responses misclassified by the ML exemplary by the solitary uttermost compasses of getting to the name O˜(~x) dispatched by the classifier for any picked input ~x. The structure is to get settled with an auxiliary for the target model with an arranged dataset made by the antagonist and named by study prophet yield. By that point, incapably planned models are made using this auxiliary [21]. We expect the goal of deep neural networks (DNN) to misclassify them considering transferability among plans [7]s. To raise the exertion of driving the snare beneath this peril exemplary, survey reinforcing the seriously engineered target of outcome irrelevant trouble that controls the concentrated on the prophet to misclassify. A shut structure system can't be initiated after the goal is a non-raised ML exemplary. The explanation behind most undermining attacks is to evaluate its answer consuming edge set up smoothing out concerning limits portrayed thru a DNN. Since estimating these cut-off focuses and their edges require data on the DNN arranging and cut-off focuses, such an attack is awesome under our disclosure condition. It was indicated that adversaries with access to a self-sufficiently assembled named planning set from a close to individuals distributing than the prophet could set up a model with trade building and use it as a substitute: undermining models expected to control the substitute is as normal as possible misclassified by the concentrated on the model [21].

In any case, the unique forefront ML structures require beast and unreasonable getting ready groups for organizing. For example, we deliberate facsimiles planned over a couple of countless named models. This makes ambushes reliant on this perspective unfeasible for foes without huge named datasets. In this study, the producers show revelation outbreaks can be exhausted at a much minor cost, without demonstrating a free orchestrating set. In our methodology, to interface with the antagonist to set up an auxiliary model starved of a genuinely named dataset, we use the goal DNN as a prophet to build up an arranged dataset. The wellsprings of information are untrustworthily passed on and the yields are marks seen from the prophet. Using this made dataset, the aggressor aggregates a measure F of the model O learned by the prophet. This substitute structure F is then used to make undermining models misclassified by F Indeed, with its full data on the substitute DNN F limits, the foe can use one of them beginning late delineated ambushes to make truly planned models misclassified by F [21]. For whatever time allotment that the transferability property holds among F and O, adversarial models made for F will in like manner be misclassified by O. This primes us to advise the standard with the framework:

1. **Substitute Model Training:** the assailant requests the prophet with collected information sources picked by a Jacobian-based heuristic to develop a model F resembling the prophet model O's decision cut-off focuses.

2. **Amazing Sample Creating:** The assailant occupations substitute framework F to make repudiating models, which are then misclassified by prophet O considering the transferability of strong models. We portray the perspective used to play out the disclosure not a lot of organized ML attacks on Tor traffic delineation models [8]. The insufficiently sorted out attack is acted in two phases; explicitly, substitute model masterminding, and negating model creation. Figure 2.1 gives a made outline out of the way of thinking used to play out a disclosure subverting trap on the Tor traffic diagram.

3. **Training on Substitute Model:** Rendering to the suppositions gave in III-A, the enemy can simply demand the sent ML/DL praiseworthy F through made information Q to get a name as reaction Y. These requesting reaction sets are then reused for setting up a helper model structure S. The goal is preparing S is to mimic the choice farthest reaches of the passed on classifier F. This method is isolated into two segments; to be unequivocal, substitute model sorting out

strategy and made dataset blend and substitute DNN preparing on a fabricated dataset [8]. The substitute model structure plan and made dataset game-arrangement are attempting assignments. As the challenger has no data about F's structure and sorting out movement, the validation of the fitting structure for S and arranging frameworks are performed heuristically. In our assessments, we picked DNN as our substitute arranging. The truly sifted through trap proposed in this chapter is what's more sensible to other ML/DL models with express acclimations to the availability framework. The foe can likewise prepare explicit ML/DL models to locate the best-prepared substitute model Approx [9]. Substitute model S is set up to utilize passed on information tests Q filtered through by watching out for F for names Y. We utilized a moderate number of deals to make passed on information for planning S. From the most punctual beginning stage, the enemy sends requesting to F from a set "Q" of made traffic tests got by utilizing Tor and a standard program to get marks Y. 86 Each mentioning near its reaction mark is overseen as a passed on information pair in sorted out dataset word reference D. Right when we get a moderate level of sorted out information—for our condition, 2644 requesting reaction orchestrates—the substitute DNN is set up on this made dataset. Twofold cross-entropy and straight out cross-entropy occasion limits are utilized in an indistinguishable and multi-class gathering. We used the stochastic grade drop figuring for setting up the substitute model S. The enduring arranging procedure is portrayed in Algorithm 1.

Calculation 1 DNN Training for Substitution
Info: F, S, and Q
Yield: Sapprox and D
Instate: Y = {} for all x ∈ Q do y ← F(x) Y ← y
end for
D = {Q, Y} Sapprox = min S L (D; S)
return Sapprox, D

Undermining sample crafting once the substitute classifier S is prepared, it is utilized to make the antagonistic trap. Since the adversary has a deep comprehension of the prepared substitute model Sapprox, it is certainly not difficult to make a hostile disturbing for Sapprox. To inconvenience Sapprox, an enemy needs to locate the most discriminant consolidate and to indistinctly trouble it. Definitively, an unfriendly aggravation for sifting through traffic is information that, when added to the veritable information doesn't lose it's utilitarian direct yet gets arranged in a substitute class. In our twofold class demand case, a little difficulty in the Tor test will drive the classifier to arrange the Tor test in the non-Tor portrayal. We use MI (intelligent documentation: $I(X; Y)$) for most discriminative part conspicuous confirmation for threatening model creation. The MI $I(X; Y)$ is depicted as the degree of quantifiable reliance between two abstract segments. The MI between two eccentric factors X and Y are given as $I(X; Y) = X, Y\ p(x, y)\ log(p(x, y)/p(x)p(y))$ (1) To pick the most discriminative segment from fabricated information "D," we process MI between each part and name pair. The top "n" ("n" can change between 1 to any quick number of highlights while keeping up the important lead) highlights having the most basic estimations of MI are picked as the most discriminant highlights [11]. MI estimation of any part besides portrays its impact on the mentioning theory. Right when the most discriminative highlights are picked, they are aggravated pitifully utilizing L1 standard minimization.

The antagonistic model creation calculation is given in Algorithm 2. At the point when the restricting models caused utilizing the Algorithm 2 to have effectively sidestepped Approx, as per the undermining ML transferability property, the threatening models evading the respectability of Approx are essentially certain to bargain the uprightness of F. In our assessments, we assessed the compromising models on F and the relating results are given, where for both equivalent and multi-class demand, the made revelation opposing models have sufficiently avoided the sent ML-based structure (Tor) traffic strategy framework. For a compromising attack to be useful in mental systems association, it is colossal that the essential pack's handiness is saved, paying little heed to how the attacker is irritating the group to bewilder the classifier. We expect that the bothers can be turned around through a middlebox utilized by the rival or that the enemy utilizes the bits of bundles for the unsettling influence that is in any case unessential to the gathering's handiness.

Information: F, S, and Q
Output: Sapprox and D
Introduce: Y = {}
for all x ∈ Q
do y ← F(x)
Y ← y

end for

D = {Q, Y} Sapprox = min S L (D; S)

return Sapprox, D

2.2.1 DEFENSIVE ADVERSARIAL TRAINING AND DEFENSIVE DISTILLATION IN ML

Monotonous schemes for making ML models progressively vigorous, for example, weight rot and dropout, for the most part, don't give a down-to-earth resistance against antagonistic models. Up until this point, just three techniques have given a huge barrier:

1. **Hostile Planning:** This is a monster power course of action where we essentially produce a huge amount of antagonistic models and explicitly train the excellent not to be deceived by all of them. An open-source execution of opposing planning is available in the clever hand's library, and its usage spoke to in the going with instructional exercise.

2. **Monitored Refining:** This is the place we train the model to yield probabilities of different classes, rather than hard decisions about which class to yield. The probabilities are given by a past model, arranged on a comparable task using hard class marks. This makes a model whose surface is smoothed in the manners an enemy will conventionally endeavor to mishandle, making it difficult for them to discover badly arranged data changes that lead to an incorrect course of action. (Refining was at first introduced in distilling the knowledge in a neural network (NN) as a strategy for model weight, where somewhat model is set up to reflect a colossal one, to get computational speculation reserves.) Anyway, even these specific counts can without a very remarkable stretch be broken by giving the progressively computational ability to the assailant.

3. **A Bombed Resistance:** "Angle concealing" to give a case of how straightforward privacy can fizzle, how about we look at why as a method called "angle concealing" doesn't work. "Slope concealing" is a term presented in practical black-box attacks against DL systems utilizing adversarial examples. To portray a whole class of bombed resistance strategies that work by attempting to deny the aggressor access to a valuable angle. Most hostile

model development methods utilize the inclination of the model to make an attack. As such, they take a gander at an image of a plane, they test which bearing in picture space makes the likelihood of the "feline" class increment, and afterward, they give a little push (as it were, they annoy the contribution to) that course. The new, adjusted picture is misperceived as a feline. In any case, imagine a scenario where there was no slope — consider the possibility that a minuscule alteration to the picture caused no adjustment in the yield of the model. This appears to give some safeguard because the assailant doesn't know what direction to "push" the picture. We can without much of a stretch envision some extremely minor approaches to dispose of the slope. For instance, most picture grouping models can be run in two modes: one mode where they yield only the personality of the most probable class, and one mode where they yield probabilities. If the model's yield is "99.9% plane, 0.1% feline," at that point a negligible change to the info gives a minuscule change to the yield, and the slope reveals to us which changes will expand the likelihood of the "feline" class.

On the off chance that we run the model in a mode where the yield is simply "plane," at that point a minuscule change to the info won't change the yield by any stretch of the imagination, and the inclination doesn't reveal to us anything. We should run a psychological study to perceive how well we could protect our model against antagonistic models by running it "in all likelihood class" mode rather than "likelihood mode." The aggressor no longer realizes where to go to discover inputs that will be named felines, so we may have some barrier. Sadly, every picture that was delegated a feline before is despite everything named a feline at this point. If the aggressor can figure which focuses are antagonistic models, those focuses will in any case be misclassified. We haven't made the model progressively strong; we have quite recently given the aggressor fewer signs to make sense of where the openings in the model's privacy are. Significantly more shockingly, for reasons unknown, the assailant has an excellent procedure for think about where the gaps in the resistance are. The aggressor can prepare their model, a smooth model that has a slope, make antagonistic models for their model, and afterward send those hostile models against our non-smooth model. All the time, our model will misclassify these models as well. At long last, our psychological test uncovers that concealing the angle didn't go anyplace.

The barrier techniques that perform inclination veiling regularly bring about a model that is smooth in explicit ways and neighborhoods of preparing focuses, which makes it harder for the enemy to discover slopes demonstrating great up-and-comer headings to annoy the contribution to a harming path for the model. Nonetheless, the enemy can prepare a substitute model: a duplicate that mirrors the shielded model by watching the names that the safeguarded model doles out to inputs picked cautiously by the antagonist. A strategy for performing such a model extraction attack was presented operating at a profit box attack paper. The antagonist would then be able to utilize the substitute model's slopes to discover hostile models that are misclassified by the protected model also. In the figure above, repli-cated from the conversation of inclination concealing found in towards the science of security and privacy in ML, we show this attack technique with a one-dimensional ML issue. The inclination concealing wonder would be exacerbated for higher dimensionality issues, however harder to portray. The ML defensive techniques are depicted in Figure 2.4.

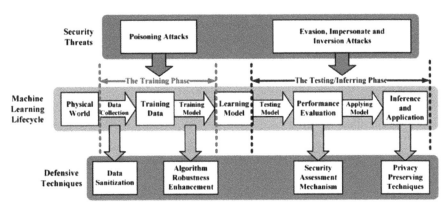

FIGURE 2.4   ML defensive techniques.

We locate that both antagonistic preparing and protective refining inad-vertently play out a sort of inclination covering. Neither one of the algorithms was expressly intended to perform angle concealing, however, inclination covering is a resistance that ML calculations can imagine generally effec-tively when they are prepared to safeguard themselves and not given explicit directions about how to do as such. On the off chance that we move antago-nistic models from one model to a second model that was prepared with either hostile preparing or guarded refining, the attack frequently succeeds, in any event, when an immediate attack on the subsequent model would come up short.

This recommends both preparing methods accomplish more to level out the model and expel the inclination than to ensure it characterizes more focuses effectively. For what reason is it difficult to safeguard against antagonistic models? Hostile models are difficult to safeguard against because it is hard to develop a hypothetical model of the antagonistic model-making process. Antagonistic models are answers for a streamlining issue that is non-straight and non-curved for some, ML models, including neural systems. Since we don't have great hypothetical instruments for portraying the answers for these convoluted enhancement issues, it is difficult to make any sort of hypothetical contention that a guard will preclude a lot of antagonistic models. Hostile models are additionally difficult to shield against because they require ML models to deliver great yields for each conceivable info. More often than not, ML models work very well however just work on a modest quantity of all the numerous potential sources of info they may experience. Each methodology we have tried so far comes up short since it isn't versatile: it might square one sort of attack, however, it leaves another weakness open to an assailant who thinks about the guard being utilized. Planning guards that can secure against an amazing, versatile aggressor is a significant examination region.

2.2.2 OPEN PROBLEMS IN DEFENSES

ML has made a genuine impact in the assurance region, particularly in the military. This is in regions, for instance, military intelligence modern battling is getting overwhelmingly subject to ML and ML. As opposed to normal structures, ML programming can process a huge amount of data. This improves the dynamic and precision of fight structures. Governments that get ML in their military divisions will have an edge in battling circumstances. China and the US are the most observable of ML and ML for military use. In 2017, the US Department of defense consumed $7.4 billion on ML and big data. China has in like manner made huge hypotheses and is foreseen to be the primary ML nation by 2030. Weaponry new battling systems and weapons right now come introduced with ML, making them progressively compelling and less subject to human movement. This has moreover achieved a more coordinated effort of exercises and systems similarly as diminishing the help required for apparatus and weapons. Cybersecurity A computerized ambush on military workplaces can achieve the loss of outstandingly delicate data and cause mischief to military bodies. The usage of ML in military workplaces helps with preventing these sorts of attacks, by protecting frameworks from unapproved interference.

By relying upon setting up structures, security systems can pre-empt attacks and make countermeasures. Transportation A gainful transportation structure is huge for achievement in the military. Ammunition, food, weapons, troops, and various items need to get to their objective on time and in incredible condition. Consolidating ML into the military's key system will lessen human effort, limit slip-ups, and prohibitions, inciting shorter lead times, and separate variations from the norm speedier. Target recognition combat circumstances are baffling. Regions, atmosphere conditions, and enemy direct can make target affirmation inconvenient. ML systems can help such conditions by separating land data, news channels, and information data, to give an unrivaled cognizance of the target. For instance, DARPA'S TRACE program relies upon ML to perceive targets using radar.

Combat area Healthcare In 2018, the University of North Carolina got a $1.6 million honor from the US Department of Defense, for example, financing for an endeavor expected to make ML and ML answers for dealing with wounds in fight conditions. The system will dismember data and predict the capacities and patient thought strategies that apply in a particular circumstance. Having such a mechanical assembly to oversee dynamic will ensure each outcome is the best one. Fight training the military uses PC delivered circumstances to set up their work power. For these test frameworks to be feasible, they have to make useful conditions and be flexible. This suggests they have to modify their lead to suit a combination of conditions. This is cultivated through fortress acknowledging, where virtual or human experts learn by getting prize or control hails in the wake of playing out explicit exercises. This system helps with improving fight getting ready for virtual authorities and human troopers. Peril monitoring intelligence and reconnaissance missions are noteworthy for risk care. For mystery purposes, watch bodies have taken to using unmanned systems, for instance, drones. These are fitted with programming that licenses them to recognize borders, see expected threats, and report or mount an attack. Machines are especially useful in remote districts.

2.2.3   DIFFERENTIAL PRIVACY AND PRIVACY-PRESERVING MACHINE LEARNING WITH THE PATE FRAMEWORK

Differential security gives a general methodology that can be applied in different propensities in ML settings. The private aggregation of teacher ensembles (PATE) Framework applies differential assurance to give a general security certification on the model being set up from client information. The key instinct in the PATE system is that "on the off chance that two models masterminded on self-ruling information respect some result, by then it is more sketchy than sharing that result to the customer will release any delicate information about a particular client." The system distributes private information into subsets and wholeheartedly prepares various models (called 'instructors') on the entirety of the subsets. The general check is made by blending the individual wants for this 'gathering' of teacher models. This in itself prohibits any security fixing in with the general miss-arrange [20]. That is created by two enormous advances. In the first place, the unsettling influence is fused while consolidating the delayed consequences of individual educators, so the joined outcome is a 'loud storing up' of individual teacher wants. Second, these uproarious wants from the teacher troupe are utilized as 'named arranging information' to set up a downstream 'understudy' model. It is this understudy model that is acquainted with end-clients for utilization. This chapter by the writers of the PATE system completely clarifies. Bound together learning grasps a striking method to guarantee security in unreservedly maintained learning conditions. The key anyway is that 'why in any case, join all information accepting, rather, we can devise propensities by which we can get from subsets (islands) of information and a brief timeframe later adequately complete our learnings?.' This makes learning conceivable in a few hypnotizing conditions. For example, a get-together of clinical offices might be amped up for applying ML methodologies to improve the human organizations of patients, in any case:

- Specific emergency communities likely won't have adequate information to do as such with no other individual
- They won't have any desire to chance to discharge their information for focal variety and assessment. This is perfect for applying united learning. Another conventional situation is the capacity to utilize ML to improve client experience over a contraption stage without moving client advancement information from lone gadgets to focal help. In the last case, every contraption downloads a (dependably improving) model from a focal zone and applies ML locally to make 'humbler extension moves ups to the model to be submitted back to the focal server. This method is getting balance in a like way considering the broadening extravagance of information open locally on every gadget (so changing locally is astoundingly valuable with fewer security

objectives) and the extensively logically ground-breaking contraption side processors stood apart from pasts making register concentrated ML calculations possible to run. The PATE framework is depicted in Figure 2.5.

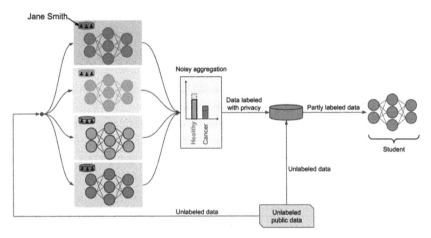

FIGURE 2.5   PATE framework.

With everything taken into account, endeavors have additionally been in progress for utilizing cryptography to give security ensures in ML by utilizing an encryption method called homomorphic encryption (HE). Right when information is encoded utilizing standard procedures, it gets hard to do any basic calculation on it in the blended structure. With regardless of what you look like at it the decision of scattered preparing, one once in a while experiences conditions where a social gathering having touchy information needs to redistribute some depend on that information to an unapproachable which it doesn't trust with the plaintext information. HE fundamentally empowers us to play out the assorted basic techniques on blended information without having direct access to the encryption keys or the plain substance information itself. Utilizing HE, the association can play out the referenced calculation on the blended information and return the (encoded) result to a customer.

The customer would then have the alternative to utilize the encryption key (which was never conceded to the association) to interpret the returned information and get an authentic outcome. HE is with no other individual an impelling field. Execution is a noteworthy concern and certain hindrances, for example, the constraint to process polynomial cutoff points (different request confines in ML are non-polynomial) and just increases and additions of numbers modulo-n, deduce that there are so far different difficulties to persevere. Regardless, with the rising reputation of ML as help (MLaaS), there is a ton of vitality for improving methods that sway HE to perform 'blended' ML. The two assortments are being analyzed the capacity to perform learning/want over encoded information and the capacity to utilize a blended model for learning in with plaintext information [19].

2.2.4   CODEDPRIVATEML FRAME WORK

CodedPrivateML system comprises of four fundamental stages that are first portrayed at an elevated level:

1. **Quantization:** In request to ensure data hypothetical protection, one needs to veil the dataset and the weight vector in a limited field F utilizing consistently random networks, with the goal that the additional arbitrariness can make every information point show up similarly likely

2. **Encoding and Secret Sharing:** In the subsequent stage, the ace parcels the quantized dataset X into K submatrices and encodes them utilizing the as of late proposed Lagrange coding strategy.

3. **Polynomial Approximation and Local Computations:** In the third stage, every laborer plays out the calculations utilizing its neighborhood stockpiling and sends the outcome back to the ace.

4. **Deciphering and Model Update:** The ace gathers the outcomes from a subset of the quickest laborers and translates the angle over the limited field.

5. **PrivacyML Frame Work:** This methodology is to build up a general structure that upholds security inside empowering various types of AI to be built up that are naturally protection saving. This decoupling of security conservation and AI-based investigation is significant because it diminishes the extra weight of security assurance. We will probably shield the information from experts who need to investigate it for different purposes while as yet empowering its utility.

2.3   EXPERIMENTAL METHODS

We proposed a comparative study on various machine learning (ML) models on secured frameworks that identify the attacks and provide security for the data. In this study, we have got the following results while comparing the different frameworks on various ML models.

2.3.1 DECISION TREE (DT)

A tree has various analogies, taking everything into account and it turns out that it has affected a wide region of AI, covering both gathering and backslide. In the decision assessment, a DT can be used to apparently and unequivocally address decisions and elements. As the name goes, it uses a tree-like model of decisions. Regardless of the way that a normally used gadget in data burrowing for inducing a framework to show up at a particular target, it's similarly comprehensively used in AI, which will be the essential point of convergence of this chapter [11]. An ideal tree is drawn upside down with its root at the top. In the image on the left, the exceptional substance in dim addresses a condition/internal center, taking into account which the tree parts into branches/edges.

The completion of the branch that doesn't part any more drawn out is the decision/leaf, for this circumstance, whether or not the explorer passed on or suffer, addressed as red and green substance independently. Albeit, a genuine dataset will have significantly more highlights and this will simply be a branch in a lot greater tree, yet you can't overlook the effortlessness of this calculation. The component significance is clear and relations can be seen without any problem. This system is all the more normally known as taking in the choice tree from the information or more tree is called clas- sification tree as the objective is to arrange a traveler as enduring or passed on. Relapse trees are spoken to similarly; just they foresee constant qualities like the cost of a house. By and large, DT calculations are alluded to as CART or classification and regression trees. All in all, what is going on out of sight? Growing a tree includes settling on which highlights to pick and what conditions to use for parting, alongside realizing when to stop. Like a tree, for the most part, develops subjectively, you should trim it down for it to look lovely. We should begin with a typical strategy utilized for parting.

2.3.2 LINEAR DISCRIMINANT ANALYSIS (LDA)

Determined lapse is a gathering estimation generally limited to only two-class request issues. If you have different classes, by then, LDA is the supported straight gathering technique [11]. In this post, you will locate the

LDA estimation for gathering judicious exhibiting issues. In the wake of examining this post you will know.

The depiction of LDA is straight forward [11]. These quantifiable properties are assessed from your data and fitting into the LDA condition to make desires. These are the model characteristics that you would extra to appeal to for your model. The model uses Bayes Theorem to check the probabilities [13]. Rapidly Bayes 'Theory can be used to measure the probability of the yield class (k) given the data (x) using the probability of each class and the probability of the data having a spot with each class:

$$P(Y=x|X=x) = (PIk \times fk(x))/sum(PIl \times fl(x)) \qquad (1)$$

where; PIk implies the base probability of each class (k) found in your planning data (for instance, 0.5 for a 50–50 split in a two-class issue). In Bayes' Theorem, this is known as the prior probability.

$$PIk = nk/n \qquad (2)$$

The f(x) above is the surveyed probability of x having a spot with the class. A Gaussian allotment work is used for f(x) [13]. Associating the Gaussian to the above condition and smoothing out we end up with the condition underneath. This is known as a different limit and the class is resolved as having the greatest worth will be the yield request (y):

$$Dk(x) = x \times (muk/siga^2) - (muk^2/(2 \times sigma^2)) + ln(PIk) \qquad (3)$$

Dk(x) is the isolated work for class k given data x, the muk, sigma^2, and PIk are evaluated from your data.

2.3.3   RANDOM FOREST CLASSIFIER (RFC)

Random forest (RF) calculations are utilized for arrangement and relapse. The RF is a troupe learning technique, made out of different choice trees. By averaging out the effect of a few choice trees, Random timberlands will in general upgrade expectations. There are numerous different models accessible to frame expectations on grouping information. Strategic relapse is one of the premier normal for binomial information. Different procedures incorporate help vector machines (SVMs), guileless Bayes, and k-closest neighbors [15]. Arbitrary woods will in the general sparkle in situations where a model highlights a sizable measure of highlights that separately have frail prescient force however a lot more grounded power collectively.

2.3.4   GRADIENT BOOST CLASSIFIER (GBC)

Gradient boosting classifiers are the Ada boosting technique joined with weighted minimization, after which the classifiers and weighted data sources are recalculated. The objective of gradient boosting classifiers is to constrict the misfortune or the distinction between the specific class estimation of the preparation model and in this way, the anticipated class esteem. It isn't required to know the strategy for decreasing the classifier's misfortune, however, it works also to angle plunge during a neural system [14]. Refinements to the current procedure were made and gradient boosting machines were made. Inside the instance of Gradient Boosting Machines, at whatever point a substitution feeble student is added to the model, loads of the past students are solidified or established in situ, left unaltered because the new layers are presented. This is regularly particular from the methodologies used in AdaBoosting, where the qualities are balanced when new students are included. The office of inclination boosting machines originates from the very certainty that they will be utilized on very paired order issues; they will be utilized on multi-class arrangement issues and even relapse problems [16].

2.3.5   K-NEAREST NEIGHBOR (KNN)

KNN's fundamental inconvenience of turning out to be essentially slower because the volume of information builds settles on it an unreasonable decision in situations where expectations got the chance to be made quickly. Besides, there are quicker calculations that will create progressively exact order and relapse results. Notwithstanding, gave you have adequate figuring assets to rapidly deal with the data you're utilizing to shape forecasts, KNN can even now help take care of issues that have arrangements that rely on distinguishing comparable items [17]. A case of this is frequently utilizing the KNN calculation in recommender frameworks, an utilization of KNN-search. Any place we got our information, there could likewise be something-things amiss with it that we'd prefer to address to sort out it for the KNN calculation. For example, the data probably won't be inside the arrangement that the calculation expects, or there could likewise be missing qualities that we ought to consistently fill or expel from the information before channeling it into the calculation [18]. Our KNN usage above depends on organized information. It must be during a table organization. Moreover, the user expects that every one segments contain numerical information which the last section of our information has names that we will play out some capacity on. In this way, any place we got our information from, we'd prefer to frame it adjust to those limitations.

2.3.6   GAUSSIAN NAÏVE BAYES (GNB)

Gaussian naive Bayes might be a variation of naive Bayes that follows Gaussian dissemination and supports persistent information. We've investigated the idea behind Gaussian naive Bayes nearby a model. Before going into it, we will experience a fast outline of naive Bayes. Gullible Bayes might be a gathering of directed AI arrangement calculations that supported the Bayes hypothesis. It's a simple characterization procedure yet has high usefulness. They discover use when the dimensionality of the information sources is high. Complex arrangement issues additionally can be actualized by utilizing the Naive Bayes classifier.

2.3.7   SUPPORT VECTOR MACHINE (SVM)

Support vectors are information focuses that are nearer to the hyperplane and impact the position and direction of the hyperplane. Utilizing these help vectors, we boost the sting of the classifier. Erasing the assistance vectors will change things of the hyperplane. These are the focuses that assist us in building our SVM. Inside the SVM calculation, we hope to expand the sting between the info focuses and, during this manner, the hyperplane. The misfortune work that expands the sting is pivot misfortune. Pivot misfortune works the price is 0 if the foreseen esteem and during this way the real worth is of a proportionate sign. On the off chance that they are not, we at that time ascertain the misfortune esteem. We likewise add a regularization boundary to the price capacity. The target of the regularization boundary is to regulate the sting expansion and misfortune. After including the regularization boundary, the price capacities look as underneath.

Since we have the misfortune work, we take fractional subsidiaries as for the hundreds to get the angles. Utilizing the slopes, we will refresh our loads. When there's no misclassification, i.e., our model accurately predicts the category of our information point, we just got to refresh the inclination from the regularization boundary. When there's a misclassification, i.e., our model commits a mistake on the expectation of the category of our information point, we incorporate the misfortune alongside the regularization boundary to perform slope update. The comparative study on Various ML models on different secured frameworks are noted in Table 2.1.

$$w = w + \alpha.(y_i.x_i - 2\lambda w)$$

TABLE 2.1   Comparative Study on Various ML Models on Different Secured Frameworks

Model	Mean Accuracy of PATE Framework	Mean Accuracy of CodedPrivateML	Mean Accuracy of PrivacyML
Decision tree (DT)	99.47%	100%	100%
Linear discriminant analysis (LDA)	99.82%	99.67%	99.76%
Gaussian naïve bayes (GNB)	92.35%	98.78%	99.09%
Gradient boost classifier (GBC)	99.42%	99.93%	99.97%
K-nearest neighbor (KNN)	65.85%	71.31%	70.65%
Random forest classifier (RFC)	90.36%	92.60%	93.75%
Support vector machine (SVM)	52.78%	89.10%	90.61%

2.4   CONCLUSION

Early work in security and defense in ML has taken an activity security tack concentrated on making sure about a current ML framework and keeping up its information trustworthiness. Security standards to give an operational point of view on ML security. In this chapter, we have described all the security and privacy frameworks and compared them on various ML models and according to that results which is better.

KEYWORDS

- **artificial intelligence**
- **deep learning**
- **linear discriminant analysis**
- **machine learning**
- **support vector machine**

REFERENCES

1. Huang, L., Joseph, A. D., Nelson, B., Rubinstein, B. I. P., & Tygar, J. D., (2011). Adversarial machine learning. In: *Proceedings of the 4th ACM Workshop on Security and Artificial Intelligence* (pp. 43–58). New York, NY, USA.
2. Patibandla, R. S. M. L., Kurra, S. S., & Mundukur, N. B., (2012). A study on scalability of services and privacy issues in cloud computing. In: Ramanujam, R., & Ramaswamy, S., (eds.), *Distributed Computing and Internet Technology, 7154*, 212–230 ICDCIT 2012: Lecture Notes in Computer Science.
3. Lakshmi, P. R S M., Santhi, S. K., & Kim, H. J., (2014). Electronic resource management using cloud computing for libraries. *International Journal of Applied Engineering Research, 9*(23), 18141–18147.
4. Akhtar, N., & Mian, A., (2018). The threat of adversarial attacks on deep learning in computer vision: A survey. *IEEE Access, 6*, 14410–14430.
5. Biggio, B., & Roli, F., (2018). Wild patterns: 10 years after the rise of adversarial machine learning. *Pattern Recognition, 84*, 317–331.
6. Chakraborty, A., Alam, M., Dey, V., Chattopadhyay, A., & Mukhopadhyay, D., (2018). *Adversarial Attacks and Defenses: A Survey, 1*, 1–31.
7. Liu, Q., Li, P., Zhao, W., Cai, W., Yu, S., & Leung, V. C. M., (2018). A survey on security threats and defensive techniques of machine learning: A data-driven view. *IEEE Access, 6*, 12103–12117.
8. Patibandla, R. S. M. L., & Veeranjaneyulu, N., (2018). Survey on clustering algorithms for unstructured data. In: Bhateja, V., Coello, C. C., Satapathy, S., & Pattnaik, P., (eds.), *Intelligent Engineering Informatics: Advances in Intelligent Systems and Computing, 695*, 421–429.
9. Patibandla, R. S. M. L., & Veeranjaneyulu, N., (2018). Performance analysis of partition and evolutionary clustering methods on various cluster validation criteria. *Arab J. Sci. Eng., 43*(8), 4379–4390.
10. Lakshmi, P. R S M., & Veeranjaneyulu, N., (2020). A SimRank based ensemble method for resolving challenges of partition clustering methods. *Journal of Scientific & Industrial Research, 79*(4), 323–327.
11. Tarakeswara, R. B., Patibandla, R. S. M. L., & Murty, M. R., (2020). A comparative study on effective approaches for unsupervised statistical machine translation. In: Bhateja, V., Satapathy, S., & Satori, H., (eds.), *Embedded Systems and Artificial Intelligence: Advances in Intelligent Systems and Computing, 1076*, 895–905.
12. Lakshmi, P. R. S. M., Tarakeswara R. B., Sandhya K. P., & Venkata, R. M., (2020). Medical data clustering using particle swarm optimization method. *Journal of Critical Reviews, 7*(6), 363–367.
13. Sandhya, K. P., Ummadi, J. R., Lakshmi, P. R. S. M., & Reshmi, K. S., (2020). Identification of lung cancer stages using efficient machine learning framework. *Journal of Critical Reviews, 7*(6), 385–390.
14. Banavathu, M., Reshmi, K. S., Venkata, R. M., & Lakshmi, P. R. S. M., (2020). Data distribution method with text extraction from big data. *Journal of Critical Reviews, 7*(6), 376–380.
15. Dumala, A., Divakara, R. D. V., Lakshmi, P. R. S. M., & Reshmi, K. S., (2020). Digital certificate validation for improving security in ad hoc networks. *Test Engineering and Management, 83*(3), 11026–11034.

16. Naresh, A., Lakshmi, P. R S M., Vidya, L., G., & Meghana, C. M., (2020). Unsupervised text classification for heart disease using machine learning methods. *Test Engineering and Management, 83*(3), 11005–11016.

17. Narayana, V., Lakshman, B., Naga, S., Venkata, R. M., & Anusha, P., (2020). Fuzzy based artificial neural network model for text extraction from images. *Journal of Critical Reviews, 7*(6), 350–354.

18. Saxe, J., Harang, R., Wild, C., & Sanders, H., (2018). A deep learning approach to fast, format-agnostic detection of malicious web content. In: *Proceedings of the 2018 IEEE Security and Privacy Workshops (SPW)* (pp. 8–14). San Francisco, CA, USA.

19. Carlini, N., & Wagner, D., (2017). Adversarial examples are not easily detected. In: *Proceedings of the 10th ACM Workshop on Artificial Intelligence and Security—AISec'17* (pp. 3–14). New York, NY, USA.

20. Meng, D., & Chen, H., (2017). MagNet: A two-pronged defense against adversarial examples. In: *Proceedings of the 2017 ACM SIGSAC Conference on Computer and Communications Security—CCS'17* (pp. 135–147). New York, NY, USA.

21. Tariq, M. I., Tayyaba, S., Rasheed, H., & Ashraf, M. W., (2017). Factors influencing the cloud computing adoption in higher education institutions of Punjab, Pakistan. In: *Proceedings of the 2017 International Conference on Communication, Computing, and Digital Systems (C-CODE)* (pp. 179–184). Islamabad, Pakistan.

CHAPTER 3

A Systematic Review of Deep Learning Techniques for Semantic Image Segmentation: Methods, Future Directions, and Challenges

REENA,[1] AMANPRATAP SINGH PALL,[2] NONITA SHARMA,[3] K. P. SHARMA,[3] and VAISHALI WADHWA[4]

[1]*Department of Computer Science, Edge Hill University, United Kingdom, Email : er_reenatechie@hotmail.com*

[2]*School of IT, APJIME, and Technical Campus, Punjab, India, E-mail: amanpall@hotmail.com*

[3]*Department of CSE, Dr. B. R. Ambedkar National Institute of Technology, Punjab, India, Email : nsnonita@gmail.com (N. Sharma), sharmakp@nitj.ac.in (K. P. Sharma)*

[4]*Panipat Institute of Engineering and Technology, Panipat, Haryana, India, E-mail: wadhwavaishali@gmail.com*

ABSTRACT

The advancements in the methods and techniques in the field of computer vision have enabled numerous applications based on understanding and analysis of image data. Moreover, deep learning has brought a massive shift in image analysis, thereby attracting the attention of researchers worldwide. Many real-life application areas used the image segmentation techniques for the identification of different regions in an image and classify them into clusters depending upon the similarity. Many conventional techniques, namely thresholding, k-means clustering histogram-based segmentation, and edge detection algorithms were applied for the segmentation; these pre-existing methods were found to be less efficient because of human intervention. But with the turn-up of deep learning, it is considered as a predominant method in image processing.

In today's era where computer vision is contemplating image segmentation for various applications, it is of utmost importance to have a detailed review of it. In the past decade, image segmentation has evolved a lot and is defined on two levels of granularity, namely semantic segmentation and instance segmentation. Furthermore, semantic segmentation segments unknown objects or new objects and classify pixels which are semantically together. This approach can lay down the foundations for new models to improve prior existing computer vision methods. It is entrenched as a vigorous implement for the critical analysis of the different areas in given images. Firstly, we elucidate the basic terms and some mandatory concepts related to this particular field for a better understanding of the naive. Then, the chapter focuses on different methods and network structures which are applied in semantic image segmentation for deep analysis of images in different applications in contrast to conventional approaches. Also, we outline the strengths and weaknesses of this approach to present a superior perspective to the individuals. At last, we strive to disclose challenges of semantic image segmentation processes concurrence with deep learning and point out a set of promising future works.

3.1 INTRODUCTION

In the past decade, artificial intelligence and deep learning (DL) emerged adequately in the computer vision sector. Image segmentation is viewed as a fundamental technique in the processing of an image and critical process in computer vision. The images or videos are divided into different segments based on similarity in their neighboring pixels for efficient analysis of the image [1]. Before the advent of DL, there were numerous methods mentioned in the literature such as thresholding, histogram-based bundling, conditional, and Markov fields, edge detection, graph cuts for the image segmentation. From the past years, DL networks have introduced a substantial improvement in the image segmentation methods and achieved a higher efficiency than pre-defined techniques, and this is also a reason why semantic segmentation is becoming a more focused research area these days. In computer vision, it is the most critical task which lays the basis for a complete understanding of the scene. Putting together the number of pixels based on some properties leads to two granularity levels of image segmentation, i.e., semantic segmentation and instance segmentation. The former approach assigns a semantic class label to every pixel which is related to real-world categories whereas, in later technique, each object of the same class is considered as a single instance [2, 3]. Semantic segmentation is different from image classification and object detection where the entire image is categorized into one class and individual objects are recognized from the classification (Figure 3.1).

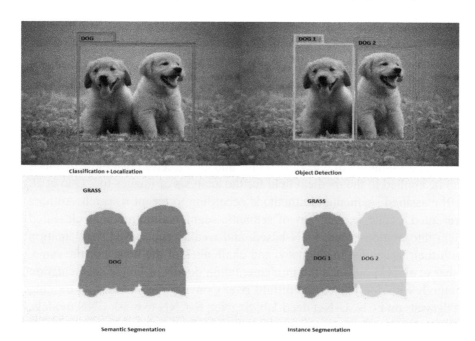

FIGURE 3.1   Object detection and segmentation.

Numerous applications derive information from images, e.g., autonomous driving, video surveillance, robot navigation, industrial inspection and augmented reality to name a few [5]. For example, in medical image analysis, it is mandatory to detect unhealthy tissue for the diagnosis, monitoring, and treatment of that particular organ and it is only feasible when each pixel is labeled based on their segments. Despite a variety of computer vision techniques, semantic image segmentation is tackled by deep architectures, mainly by convolution neural networks (CNNs) because it provides faster and precise outputs as compared to traditional methods [6].

DL is a subset of the machine learning (ML) field, is mushrooming day by day, making it strenuous to keep track of all the improvements, new developments, and their application in new domains. Various authors have produced a huge literature on the advancements and innovations of semantic segmentation with DL. Zue et al. [7] summarized discrete and continuous bottom-up image segmentation methods with a new concept of superpixel to produce much faster image segmentation. His studies included interactive methods, object region proposals, semantic parsing, and image co segmentation with its advantages and limitations. Boundary matching, Region covering, Variation of information and probabilistic random index are few proposed parameters to measure performance of the above-mentioned segmentation methods. Thoma [8] illustrated the categorization of semantic segmentation, summarize completely automatic, passive semantic segmentation algorithms succinctly. Author shed a light on accuracy, speed, stability, usage of memory factors for the evaluation of segmentation methods. The primary aim of segmentation is to present a real-time application that is described by Niemeijer et al. [9] with the help of neural networks (NN). Authors applied segmentation techniques on an autonomous driving car for a better understanding of the entire scene, and they inferred that these methods can be applied to the medical field for the analysis of images too. Guo et al. [10] classified segmentation methods according to recent research. Authors presented a concise overview of semantic segmentation methods classified them into, region-based, FCN-based, and weakly supervised segmentation with their strengths, inadequacy, and challenges of the area. For the same, Vihar et al. [11] outlined the implementation details of image segmentation methods with dominance and pitfalls over Convolutional NN. After training of datasets on FCN, U-Net deep-lab, SegNet, R-CNN to mask CNN models, they mentioned R-CNN, the most productive approach for locating objects in an image, and to perform the segmentation part, the U-Net framework generates fine results. The paramount objective of the study [12] is to give a detailed overview of traditional semantic image segmentation methods, i.e., K-means clustering, Support vector machines (SVMs), thresholding, edge detection, Markov random network, and concisely list all the recent progress made in this field. Gen et al. [13] discussed the progression of the image segmentation in context with CNNS. In CNNs, resolution of feature maps kept on decreasing with higher semantic levels which inhibits accuracy of segmentation methods. Probabilistic graphic models, CRFs, and MRFs are proposed to tackle accuracy issues and RNN, LSTM, survey latest outcomes on PASCAL VOC 2012 dataset. They also concluded that the association of features with different layers can ameliorate segmentation results. Regardless of having various techniques in this research field, semantic segmentation is a stimulating task even now. Hongshan Yu et al. [68] mentioned three categories of methods, i.e., hand-engineered features (MRF, CRF to secure spatial consistency), learned features (CNN for dense predictions) and weakly supervised learning (for annotated datasets) to epitomize advantages, disadvantages owing to comparisons among them.

3.2 BACKGROUND CONCEPTS

Image processing, computer vision, ML, and artificial intelligence (AI) subject areas complement each other. In computer vision and image processing, the feature is an elementary concept to perform all the computational chores while processing. However, the cardinal purpose of both approaches is different, image processing works to intensify different properties of an image for later use, but the objective of computer vision is a thorough understanding of the scene with all its image or video content and environment. Computer vision is a subset of AI that makes computers capable of processing, extract visual information, and comprehend what they are representing in a scene [14]. ML enlarged the scope of computer vision because it has methods for effective acquisition, object focus for better recognition, and tracking. With a rise in DL, there is a tremendous improvement in the processing of data as compared to older ML approaches. Another reason for the upsurging of DL is massive, high-quality complex data accompanied by GPU computing which accelerated the processing time as compared to CPUs [15]. For a complete understanding of the linkage between modern DL methods and image segmentation, it is imperative to perceive the amalgamation of different areas with DL. Historically, image segmentation was only classified in two categories: the one is a background and another is foreground, but as the complexity of images kept on increasing, researchers were more focused to identify every single element of the image and this is how semantic segmentation of images or video has started and taken a pace with the discovery of modern architectures. Now, the question arises that how semantic image segmentation works with recognition and labeling of image or video content. Image is always comprised of a large number of pixels which have information about different objects reflected in that image. To deduce a logical outcome, the processing of digital content involves several stages.

The foremost step is to do prognostication of given input and generate classification labels that are followed up by localization and object detection to reveal multiple objects where they are placed in an image. This is implemented by the computation of some numerical parameters concerning image boundary. Finally, each pixel is tagged with the class of its enfolded object so that a high resolution image is constructed at the output. To have in-depth knowledge of this technique, readers must have some background knowledge. The following subsections will recapitulate traditional methods of semantic image segmentation and DL basic architectures.

3.2.1 TRADITIONAL METHODS

Nowadays, image segmentation is an acutely diverse and complex field, as a result of the application of various segmentation techniques on different dimensions of data, i.e., 2D image or 3D video. The following methods will shed light on methods before the emergence of DL.

3.2.1.1 THRESHOLDING

It is a very fundamental algorithm which partitions image into separate regions. The gray levels of pixels belonging to one object are entirely different from background pixel levels, or we can even say that gray levels distinguish between foreground and background. Threshold segmentation is categorized into local and global threshold techniques. Later one distinguishes between foreground and background on account of the intensity distribution. But the former approach decides for each pixel going by certain parameters. The upper hand of the threshold method is its uncomplicated computation, momentum of performing operations [66]. Precisely, the segmentation effect can be derived when the target and the background have a high contrast. Less distinction or high overlapping among images acts as an obstacle in achieving accurate results in this method.

It is often composite with different procedures because it only gauges gray information without contemplating spatial information of that image. Moreover, its sensitivity to noise and grayscale jaggedness is also one reason to have them amalgamated with different methods.

3.2.1.2 EDGE DETECTION SEGMENTATION

The procedure of grouping and setting out sharp discontinuities in an image is called edge detection. Pixel concentration is altered by including discontinuities which can discern boundaries of objects in a scene [67]. Derivative operations can help in the recognition of discontinuity [66]. Objects, their boundaries among different objects and background are identified and delineated by this process. Edge detection is the closest method for detecting significant discontinuities by targeting intensity values.

3.2.1.3 SEGMENTATION BASED ON CLUSTERING

Clustering is a method to generate groups of objects which are sharing some similarities among them. While dealing with segmentation and clustering simultaneously, a feature space clustering approach segments the pixels with relative feature space points. For an outcome, feature space is sectioned primarily and aligned back to initial space afterward. One of the most commonly used methods in clustering is K-means, to congregate different clusters according to distance. The positive aspect of this method is its rapid action and effortless processing. It is immensely productive and extensible for large data sets and its linear time complexity makes it suitable for mining also. While making clusters, K, i.e., clustering figure has no specific election benchmark so that it is hard to extrapolate [22]. This framework traverse all samples in every iteration which makes it expensive too. K-means distance portioning method is only applicable to the convex data sets and not convenient for generating non-convex clusters [23].

3.2.2 OVERVIEW OF DEEP NEURAL NETWORKS

3.2.2.1 CONVOLUTIONAL NEURAL NETWORKS

CNNs are examined as the highest productive, commonly used frameworks in DL for computer vision tasks. CNN networks are inspired by the brain [18] when Hubel and Wiesel were scrutinizing the brain of mammals, and they proposed a model on visual perceiving power of mammals.

CNN mainly comprises of two components:

1. **Hidden Layers/Feature Extraction:** Many convolutions and pooling operations are performed for the extraction of features. To exemplify the same, consider an image of a cat then hidden layer will identify its ears, legs, tail. Each convolution layer acts as a filter or linear operation.
2. **Classification Part:** A fully connected layer which acts as a classifier aligns extracted features into the final output. Kernels are trained by using optimization algorithm, i.e., backpropagation, and gradient descent to lessen the difference between outputs and ground truth labels.

The main advantage of CNN is it automatically finds features without human intervention. It has efficiency in terms of memory and complexity because it has weight sharing. An assortment of well-known CNN architectures include: AlexNet [19], VGGNet [61], ResNet [63], GoogleNet [62], MobileNet [64], and DenseNet [65] (Figure 3.2).

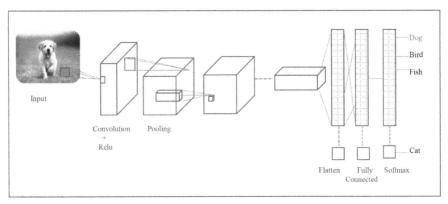

FIGURE 3.2   The framework of CNN [18].

3.2.2.2   RECURRENT NEURAL NETWORKS (RNNS) AND THE LSTM

Traditional NNs we make an assumption that all inputs are independent but for prediction based on the previous inputs, a new model was required. Recurrent networks, are models to solve above mentioned problem. In RNNs, same task is carried out for each of the inputs and the outcome of the current input is dependent on the previous calculation. The inputs are processed sequentially through the use of internal memory. RNNs are used across a wide range of applications like language modeling and text generation, machine translation, generating image descriptions and speech recognition, etc. [22].

Figure 3.3 illustrates a view of deeper network in context of MLP [69]. Input is fed to the network where activation functions (AFs) are applied to hidden layers successively. Hidden layers have similar weights, bias so that they can combine on later stages to produce an accurate output. After rolling all hidden layers into a single recurrent layer, we have another network, i.e., Recurrent network. A recurrence formula which is shown in Figure 3.4 is applied to input vector and its previous state to generate output. To accurately classify input, the network relies on backpropagation through time which generates a sequence of calculations from one time step to next. To write down a simple recurrence formula at time step t, we have following parameters:

x_t is current input, h_{t-1} is previous input state h_t is new state, tanh is AF, Wh weight of recurrence neuron, Wx weight of input neuron, y_t output state and Wy weight at output state.

$$h_t = \tanh(Whh_{t-1} + WxXT) \tag{1}$$

$$y_t = Wy\, h_t \tag{2}$$

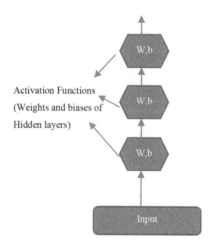

FIGURE 3.3   Deeper network [68].

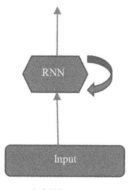

FIGURE 3.4   Folded recurrent network [68].

RNNs remember information for small durations, i.e., If an element is required within limited duration, it is able to reproduce it, but once a lot of information is fed into the network, it becomes difficult to regenerate it. This difficulty is solved in long short term memory networks which are capable of recalling their past data. LSTM is more capable to categorize, progress, and anticipate time series, and backpropagation is used for learning. An LSTM network has three gates (Figure 3.5).

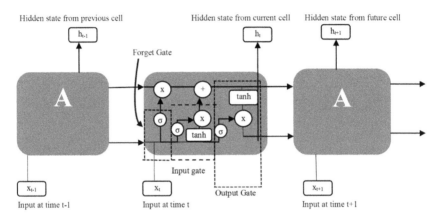

FIGURE 3.5   Description of three gates of LSTM [56].

h_{t-1} is hidden state at time step t–1 and xt is input at time t [60]:

1. **Input Gate**: Elects input value which will be utilized to amend the contents of memory.
2. **Forget Gate:** Its basic aim is to find details that need to be omitted from the block.
3. **Output Gate:** Memory and input consecutively decides output.

3.2.2.3   GENERATIVE ADVERSARIAL NETWORKS (GANS)

GAN is related to unsupervised learning, to generate or produce new patterns or examples that are possibly generated from original datasets. It is a conjunction of two models: one is a generator that is trained to produce new examples, and another one is a discriminator to classify fake or real examples. It is similar to a zero-sum game, where the discriminator either rewarded or mention no change in model parameters after recognition of real or fake examples, but a generator is penalized with either updating of model parameters or adjusting weights of the generator. In the given figure generator will try to produce some data a € dfake which is similar to the real data Ddata. Generator tries to transfigure v vector from dv, i.e., a=G(v). All the real word samples and synthetic data is available to discriminator to predict the fake or real ones. GAN's are prepared by solving the given optimization problem. V (D,G) is the objective function [24] (Figure 3.6).

$$\min G \max D \ V(D,G) = E\ [\log D(a)] + E\ [\log\ (1 - D(G(v)))] \qquad (3)$$

$$a{\sim}Ddata\ v{\sim}pv$$

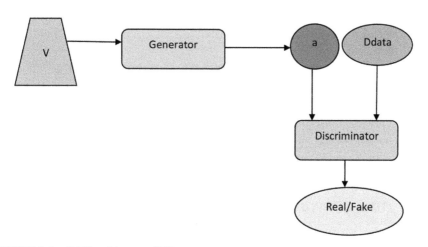

FIGURE 3.6   GAN architecture [24].

Different applications of GAN's are action planning using predicted future states, generating missing data and labels, high-quality speech recognition, and quality improvement for images.

3.2.2.4   AUTOENCODERS

The objective of autoencoders is to comprehend the inherent data that works better for a predefined task than raw data. These are feed-forward networks which compress the input by reducing their dimensionality and reconstruct output [25]. These are considered unsupervised models, but it is not fallacious even if we tag them self-supervised because they generate labels from training data on their own. An autoencoder consists of three components: encoder, code, and decoder. Before training of data in an auto-encoder, few parameters are needed to be set, i.e., size of code, a number of layers, nodes per layer, and loss function. The basic architecture of auto-encoder is to refrain some of the nodes in the hidden layers so that model itself can learn important attributes of input. In sparse autoencoders, a loss function is constructed by regularizing the activations. A more generalized model referred to as denoising autoencoder, in which input is reformed by adding noise but the output phase still maintains to get uncorrupted data. A contractive autoencoder is an unsupervised DL technique for the encoding of unmarked training data. Different applications of autoencoders are Abnor-mality detection, Denoising of data, e.g., images, audio, Image inpainting, Information retrieval.

3.3 IMAGE SEGMENTATION METHODS AND APPROACHES

This section will brief image segmentation methods, approaches, and models. An overview of numerous well-known DL architectures for computer vision tasks. The following subsections include different frameworks with their numerous techniques and modules in detail.

3.3.1 FULLY CONVOLUTION NETWORKS

Long et al. [26] main objective was to build a FCN which takes any input and produces similar size output with logical inferences and learning. ILSVRC classifiers are supplemented for the dense prediction whereas skip architec-ture is embodied for the rectification of semantics and spatial precision of the output. To design a dense FCN from classifiers, PASCAL VOC 2011 was considered, and three architectures were taken into account Alexnet, VGG Nets, and GoogLeNet where VGG's 16 layer and GoogLeNet's final loss layer is used to upgrade performance. Further, fully connected layers were converted to convolutions and coarse inputs were upsampled to pixel-dense outputs but unable to get better implementation results. Finally, a fully convolution net was developed which blends feature hierarchy layers to fine-tune apatial fidelity of output.

Testing was done on PASCAL VOC, NYUDv2 and SIFT flow which leads to a conclusion that FCN-8s is the best in Pascal VOC 2011 but FCN-16s is the best in NYUDv2 and SIFT Flow. Improvements in the architecture with multi resolution layers improve performance, speed up learning, and deductions. For the same, a network is designed by [27] that follows up global features and normalization in layers to get better results. The network achieves 20% relative improvement on PASCALVOC 2011 and 2012 test sets and reduces inference time. Although, it is examined as efficient for the segmentation of variable-sized images but its acceleration is not good for conclusion in real-time cases. Moreover, global information is not taken into account and not workable for 3D images (Figure 3.7).

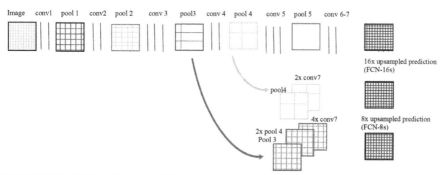

FIGURE 3.7   FCN architecture [27].

Liu et al. [28] proposed a new network model, i.e., ParseNet that uses a global context in an end-to-end fully convolution layers as opposed to patch-based approach with minimal computation overhead. A network makes a collaborative prediction for all pixels. Firstly, Global pooing is used to get context features from higher layers and add up global feature to local features map by using early or late fusion. Secondly, normalization is applied to every feature to understand scale factor before classification stage for an efficient training. Finally, by unpooling global features are replicated spatially with a similar size as of local feature map, concatenated further with feature map to produce a combined feature (Figure 3.8).

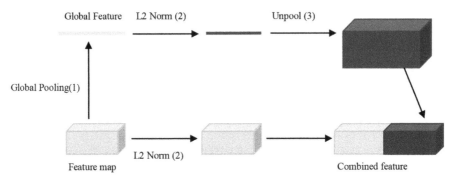

FIGURE 3.8   ParseNet architecture [28].

3.3.2 DCNN

FCNN was observed as a standard tool for image segmentation which generates class labels for an image at once. But DCNNs are more powerful than fully convolutional networks because they capture a lot of information from nearby pixels by their convolution layers. Additionally, pooling layers expands the impression of consecutive layers in an input image. Marmanisa et al. [31] presented a segmentation method that includes class boundaries (with different semantic class) in the form of pixel wise contours. Primarily, SEGNET encoder-decoder architecture is augmented with boundary detection to make it memory efficient module and later on FCN are also employed with boundary detection to build up high end classifiers. The model achieves approximately 90% accuracy on the ISPRS Vaihingen benchmark.

Chai et al. [32] mentioned that DCNN's are failed to learn spatial context because repetitive convolutions are applied to the same pixels, leading to inconsistent labeling of nearby pixels. They proposed a method for semantic segmentation of aerial images (high resolution) in which primarily a signed distance map is acquired from the ground truth label map for every semantic class. The obtained distance map holds spatial context with a score map of different semantic classes because it makes it feasible to compute the distance between target and object boundary nearby pixels. Segmentation results are smoother than existing techniques, better than fully connected CRF used for post-processing (Figure 3.9).

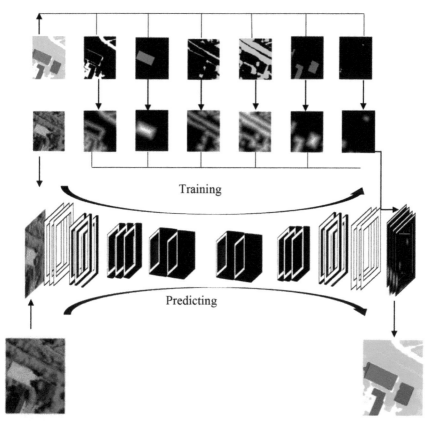

FIGURE 3.9 The stages of the segmentation process. The input image is at the left-hand side, which extracts numerous features while passing through convolution layers and finally deconvoluted at the right end with the output image, which has the equivalent resolution as of input image. Training images are shown with ground truth maps and distance maps related to different channels.[32].

3.3.3 CNNS WITH CRF

DCNN has proved better segmentation results than previous methods. Chen et al. [33] discussed that while performing object segmentation, localization results are poor because of invariance properties. To resolute this problem, they represented a model which is a combination of DCNN and fully connected conditional random field (CRF). For definite segmentation results, responses recorded at the concluding layer of DCNNs are not adequately restrained. The prevalence of DCNNs for high level tasks is due to the invariance properties. The authors repressed this unproductive localization property of deep networks by integrating the feedback at the concluding layer with a fully connected CRF. Their aforementioned method works with higher accuracy as compared to existing approaches as per the authors claim. CRF is considered a highly favorable graphical model in DL. It has been found that FCN generated rough segmentation results, this is a reason CRFs are chosen for post-processing steps in segmentation Figure (3.10).

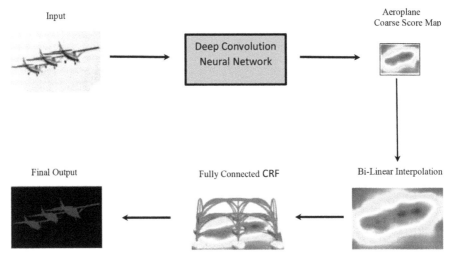

FIGURE 3.10   Deep convolution generates a coarse score map, is upsampled by bi-linear interpolation. Segmentation results are produced by fully connected CRF [33].

Zheng et al. [34] combined CNN with CRF for a better description of visual objects. They devised mean-field approximate inference for the CRFs with Gaussian pairwise potentials as recurrent NNs, including backpropagation for the better training of the model. To learn from patch to patch and to capture semantic correlations between neighboring pixels

Lin et al. [35] presented a combination of CRF with CNN, implemented a traditional multiscale input image with pyramid pooling for effective performance. Initially, local patches are made from images, and later on, a patch wise network is constructed. Training data is processed in different ways with the characteristics of images and scale variation problem is solved by the author's above-mentioned strategy. Besides, precision is ameliorated by studying the impact of conditional random field (CRF).

Zhou et al. [36] also mentioned an analogous combination of FCN and CRF in which FCN will assimilate features from an input image, create local predictions and global structure. CRF utility is to calculate the sensitivity of neurons and transfer it to FCN for further processing. Experiments conducted reveal improved accuracy with numerous other methods on Pascal VOC 2012 dataset (Figure 3.11).

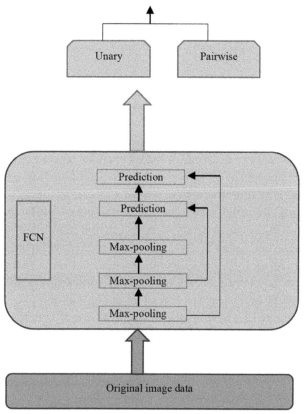

FIGURE 3.11 Different steps involved in the processing of image data with FCN and CRF [36].

Zhao et al. [37] improved segmentation by employing FCN to acquire semantic features on pixel level and clustering method to gather super-pixel level region data. Accuracy is improved by incorporating CRFs for the anticipation of the semantic information of every pixel to get better information on local features, global, and get smoothness (Figure 3.12).

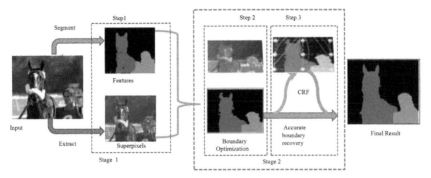

FIGURE 3.12   Proposed architecture (FCN+CRF) [37].

3.3.4   ENCODER-DECODER BASED MODELS

Badrinarayanan et al. [38] proposed an architecture, SegNet name refers to semantic pixel-wise segmentation. It has an encoder where convolutions and poolings are performed with VGG-16 layers. The decoding side performs upsampling and convolutions with a SoftMax classifier for each pixel at the end. SegNet provides good functioning with competitive inference time and most productive inference memory-wise as compared to other architectures with two datasets, i.e., CamVid dataset for road scene segmentation and SUN RGB-D dataset for Indoor scene segmentation. Later on, Kendall et al. [39] discussed a similar method Bayesian SegNet (probabilistic framework for semantic segmentation), an extension of deep convolution encoder-decoder network architecture. They followed up the concept of uncertainty, a larger performance is recorded for CamVid dataset and 2–3% improvement is also recorded with SegNet, FCN, Dilated networks, and DenseNet (Figure 3.13).

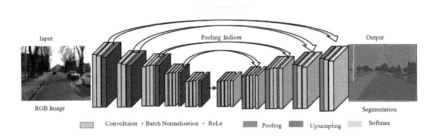

FIGURE 3.13   A schematic of the Bayesian SegNet architecture. The figure gives a view of a channel which describes all the transformations included in the process. The encoder has VGG-16 network convolution layers and decoder has all in reverse [38].

Existing techniques for pix are accurate enough but for real-time applications but they need to be more concerned about the various factors for efficient use of an approach. Chaurasia et al. [40] tried to get a more accurate prediction without sacrificing processing time. The information lost in convolutions at the encoder end is recovered by pooling indices. LinkNet proposed architecture pass spatial information from the encoder to the corresponding decoder for better accuracy and consumption of less processing. Cityscapes and CamVid datasets were trained on this network, whose results prove that these architectures can work better for high resolution images (Figure 3.14).

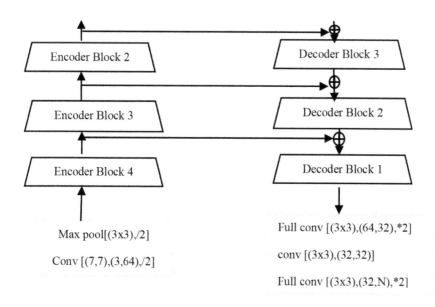

FIGURE 3.14 LinkNet architecture [40].

With a large number of vision-based systems, scene understanding is becoming a more focused research area. Robail [41] designed an architecture for pixel wise predictions, encoder can work for any size and resolution of images, whereas decoder upsamples lower resolution features passed by the encoder. High performance is computed with less overhead with a simplified CNN model. The model was tested on CamVid Dataaset which has better results than FCN and VGG16 (Figure 3.15).

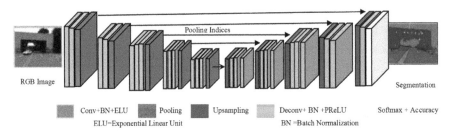

FIGURE 3.15   EURU architecture [41].

There are so many areas in daily life where object detection, localization, and segmentation plays a critical role, e.g., vehicle tracking for traffic monitoring. Y.G et al. [42] discussed encoder-decoder based deconvolution network for semantic segmentation in autonomous driving scenarios. Inclusion of residual learning decrease the size of feature maps between convolutional layers, resolution is also preserved. A good performance is recorded while comparing their presented model performance with pre-existing models. Image segmentation is also equally favorable in medical image analysis. For diagnosis and clinical application of diseases, it has great significance especially in MR (magnetic resonance) because tissue boundary has low contrast values from which inference making is hard. So, in order to resolve this, Geng et al. [43] presented an encoder-decoder structure with dense dilated spatial pyramid pooling. Encoder task is to capture spatial data for lowering feature maps where decoder will retrieve space details progressively. Experimental results prove that this method has good accuracy and robustness (Figure 3.16).

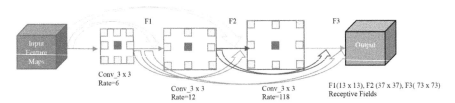

FIGURE 3.16   Dense dilated spatial pyramid pooling [43].

Following above-said technique, Bindu [44] mentioned that for diagnosis, a high-resolution medical image segmentation is required. The author also presented an encoder/decoder model where feature maps are kept at a lower resolution to make a distinction between classes and later on upsample

sample to have a high-resolution segmentation map for analysis. This method helps in reducing the testing time.

3.3.5 DILATED CONVOLUTIONS

The word dilation emerges from wavelet decomposition, also called Altrous convolution. It has worked well in real life images, e.g., some small or objects placed in crowded areas were unable to be taken into account in remote sensing imagery. Hamaguchi et al. [46] proposed a module local feature extraction to identify small objects in remote sensing images. The arrangement of module consists of a number of convolution layers with a drop in dilation factors. Feature extractor is sealed at the dilated front end section for accumulation of local features. The collection of features depends upon weights of kernels which turn more close as they pass through the module. Another model for high resolution images was discussed by Mehta et al. [47], and efficient spatial pyramid with better computation, memory, and power. An evaluation was done on datasets cityscapes, PASCAL VOC, and breast biopsy images. Under certain constraints, ESPNet performs better than existing models (Figure 3.17).

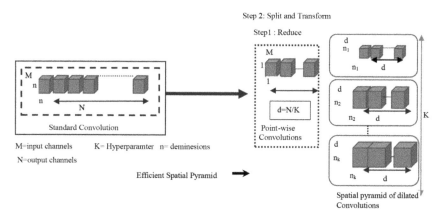

FIGURE 3.17 Efficient spatial pyramid (ESP) module follows the reduce strategy in first stage and split, transform in second stage.[47].

Dense predictions are highly required for high resolution images; it is the reason why dilated convolutions are taken into account while developing semantic segmentation models. Yu et al. [45] mentioned that dilated convolutions work for multiscale feature selection without loss. The presented model ameliorates the accuracy of semantic segmentation methods. Image segmentation methods are widely used in different application areas, e.g., pavement extraction, structures investigation, vegetable, and analysis, agriculture groundwork, urban planning, and navigation systems, etc. Satellites provide images of such areas for further analysis of pixel level segmentation. A parallel dilated convolution module is applied with U-net (Dilated Deep UNet) architecture [48]. The design of the network includes Relu with convolution layers at one end, a receptive field that is based on module and decoding end which has deconvolutions (Figure 3.18).

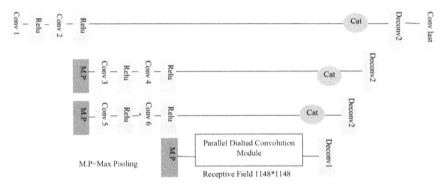

FIGURE 3.18   Dilated deep UNet architecture [48].

The point of difference between deep dilated UNet and original UNet is a parallel hole convolution module which is appended to the terminating layer of UNet. A parallel dilated convolution module acts as an interface between the encoder part and the decoder part of the framework. Results generated by the model are more accurate and clear.

For the same, one more model attention dilation-LinkNet [49] were developed for context information in satellite images. This structure adopts encoder-decoder, dilated convolutions in serial-parallel combination. Even data processing, transfer learning is also used to limit semantic label requirements. The concept of parallel expansion is added with a short circuit connection to get connected with receptive fields and also arrange multi-scale features parallelly. The channel-wise attention technique is developed for surroundings details in the satellite image. Segmentation accuracy was improved effectively while doing testing on different satellite spheres, e.g., road extraction.

When dilated convolutions have achieved success in DL tasks with DCNNs, there is one thing which was focused, i.e., "gridding artifacts." Connecting elements of outputs are evaluated from different collections of members in the input if dilation figures are greater than one. It results in a discrepancy of local data and inhibits the execution of DCNNs with dilated convolutions [50]. resolved this effect by smoothing dilated convolutions itself without a decreasing number of parameters. Experimental responses show that augmentation of DCNNs with dilated convolutions improved functioning by only including other parameters. The effective receptive field (ERF) analysis is employed to envision a smoothing effect for DCNNs with our dilated convolutions (Figure 3.19).

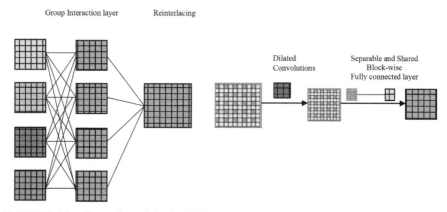

FIGURE 3.19 Illustration of the degridding method on left-hand side which shows group interaction layer before reinter lacing and gray box shows local information. Right-hand side shows a proposed method for achieving smoothing by adding an SS block after dilation [50].

3.3.6 GAN

Luc et al. [51] presented a method that discriminates segmentation maps whether it is surfacing from ground truth or the segmentation network. A hybrid loss function which is a combination of two terms, one is multi-class entropy which predicts appropriate class label for each pixel and other is for above mentioned discrimination. Standford Background dataset has better accuracy than PASCAL VOC 2012. Semi segmentation is another challenging task for computer vision due to assigning labels to every pixel which leads to a lack of annotations.

This issue is resolved by presenting a semi-supervised framework [52]. In this GAN, a generator provides extra training samples to a multi-class classifier, and after assigning label, some can be marked as fake tuples. With this procedure, factual specimens will be very near in feature space for the classification task (Figure 3.20).

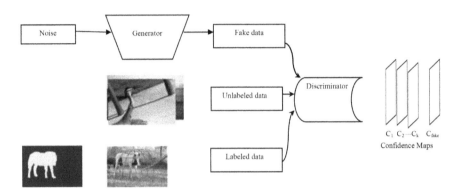

FIGURE 3.20   GAN architecture with semi-supervised convolution. Fake data is generated by a generator that is fed up to discriminator. The discriminator makes use of fake data, unlabeled data, and labeled data to learn class confidences and produces confidence maps for each class as well as a label for fake data [52].

Another framework SegGAN [53] is presented, in which a prior trained deep semantic segmentation network is fitted into a generative adversarial framework for the fine calculation of masks in segmentation. To get improved segmentation results, combined networks are blended fine-tuned. There is a loss between generator images with ground truth masks as input and original images, which need to be reduced in the pre-training of GAN. Anticipated masks should have a similar relationship with original images as GAN has with ground truth masks and original images (Figure 3.21).

In medical images analysis, segmentation plays a pivotal role for diagnosis. For the detection of abnormalities to discover possible pathological factors, a laborious task is required to assess multiple spinal structures in MRIs. The basic aim of this initiative is to conduct classification and automated segmentation at once to assist spinal clinicals for diagnosis.

However, semantic segmentation of intervertebral discs, vertebrae, and neural foramen has not been attained concurrently due to these mentioned challenges: (1) It is difficult to segment multiple structures at one time; (2) High variety and variability is another issue; (3) complexity is increased by fragile spatial associations and minute dissimilarities between normal and abnormal structures. The authors proposed a Spine-GAN to sort out above mentioned issues. Initially, altrous convolution helps solve high variation complex spine structures. Preservation of fine structural information and semantic task aware representation is performed by autoencoder. Secondly, the proposed model's long short-term memory (LSTM) module assists in developing spatial pathological interrelationships among normal and abnormal structures. Thirdly, Spine-GAN obtains steady productivity and organized induction by attaching a discriminative network to correct forestall errors and contiguity at the global level (Figure 3.22).

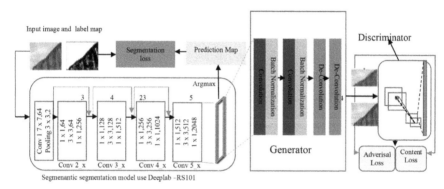

FIGURE 3.21 The proposed framework for SegGAN [53].

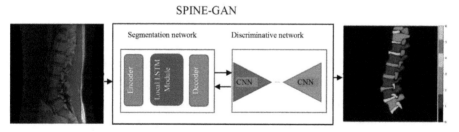

FIGURE 3.22 Spine GAN architecture [54].

3.3.7 OTHER MODELS

Image resolution tends to decrease by recurring pooling or convolution actions in deep CNNs [55]. RefineNet, a generic multi-path refinement network makes use of obtainable information of the downsampling process for projecting high resolution. This is how the hidden layers that perceive high-level semantic features can be rectified using fine-grained features from prior convolutions. Every component of the model follows up connections for an effective end to end training. To acquire rich background context information a chained residual pooling is implemented.

Scene parsing is challenging for diverse scenes [56]. The proposed model used feature maps for final predictions with a pyramid pooling module. Good quality results can be produced by global prior representation, at the same time PSPNet provides a superior framework for pixel-level prediction (Figure 3.23).

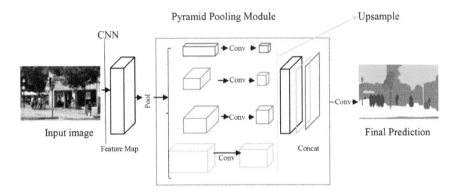

FIGURE 3.23   Overview of our proposed PSPNet. Feature map is constructed by a convolutional neural network which is pooled in input and upsampled concatenated at the output of the pyramid pooling module. The final output of per-pixel prediction is obtained by the convolution layer [56].

CNNs are used for segmentation tasks effectively, but the key difficulty with DCNN is successive pooling operations that leads to reduction in feature resolution. To overcome this problem, altrous convolution was again taken into account [57] with ImageNet to control the resolution of feature responses so that and it may not obscure dense predictions. Another issue is related to different objects of multiple scales. Authors considered Image Pyramid, Encoder-Decoder, Deeper altrous convolution and Spatial Pyramid pooling methods to segment objects for context knowledge. Then, Atrous Spatial pyramid pooling module is presented that is able to capture multi-scale information effectively with different rates (Figure 3.24).

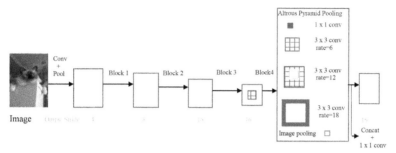

FIGURE 3.24 Illustration of the process with ASPP and image pooing [57].

It is discerned that in previous methods [69, 70], integration of CNN directly with MRF is not registered as an effective method due to a problem in optimization and its rate of deduction [58]. Additionally, CNN, and Markov Random Fields have a huge range of variables which makes it quite inadequate for optimum performance.

To resolve above mentioned issues, a Deep parsing network is propounded for modeling of two dimensional segmentation for images and 3D for video segmentation. The MRF is depicted as an undirected graph where each node is depicted as a voxel, connected with edges through a method of Dynamic node linking to get accurate information of surroundings in a spatio-temporal space. DPN is an extension of CNN for modeling of classifications (which are related to per voxel) and to approximate mean algorithm for smoothness constraints. The first property of this approach is its no recurrent inference in backpropagation. Moreover, pairwise terms can cipher huge information related to background conditions. Additionally, its base is totally designed upon convolutions which ensure its pace and parallel processing (Figure 3.25 and Table 3.1).

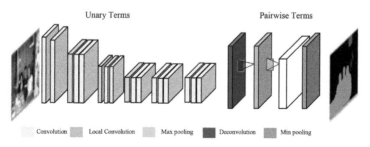

FIGURE 3.25 (a) Overall design of DPN shows basic processing stages in a network. (b) Representing extension of original CNN structure for modeling of unary and pairwise terms. (c) DPN is facilitating the dynamic linking of nodes [58].

TABLE 3.1 Summary of all Reviewed Semantic Image Segmentation Methods

Author	Architecture/ Model	Dataset	Method / Technique	Results
Long et al. [26]	FCN with AlexNet, VGG Net, GoogleNet	PASCAL VOC 2011	Fine-tuning from classification to segmentation along with multiple resolution layers	FCN VGG16 performed better than other datasets computed by mean intersection over union (IU) and inference time. Dataset PASCAL VOC 11 with FCN 8s shows 20% improvement
Shelhamer et al. [27]	FCN with AlexNet, VGG Net, GoogleNet	PASCAL VOC 2011	Layer fusion, Skip architecture for segmentation	This model has 30% improvement on PASCAL VOC 2011 with FCN 8s as compared to above mentioned model
Liu et al. [28]	ParseNet	PASCAL VOC 2011, PASCAL-context, SiftFlow	Add global feature and normalization	Segmentation results are similar to post-screening FCN with graphical model.
Marmanisa et al. [31]	DCNN with SegNet encoder-decoder architecture	ISPRS Vaihingen benchmark	Boundary detection, High end classifier ensemble	Segmentation is improved with boundary detection and model achieves > 90% accuracy on mentioned dataset.
Chaia et al. [32]	DCNN (with modification in SegNet)	ISPRS semantic labeling dataset	Distance maps	Smooth segmentation results for high resolution images
Chen et al. [33]	DCNN +CRF	PASCAL VOC 2012	Feature extraction with hole algorithm	71.6% IOU accuracy is recorded with given dataset

TABLE 3.1 *(Continued)*

Author	Architecture/ Model	Dataset	Method / Technique	Results
Zheng et al. [34]	CRF-RNN	PASCAL VOC 2012	Mean-field approximate inference + Gaussian pairwise potentials	74.7% accuracy is recorded with given dataset
Lin et al. [35]	CRF, Altrous convolution, DCNN (deep lab)	ISPRS WG II/4 and dataset was compiled from a capital city in West China	Patch wise segmentation	Better results than U-net, CNN-FPL, and SVL_1
Zhou et al. [36]	FCN-CRF	PASCAL VOC 2012	Backpropagation algorithm with calculating sensitivity of neurons	Better mean IU accuracy than FCN 8s and CNN as RNN
Zhao et al. [37]	CRF	PASCAL VOC 2012 dataset, cityscapes dataset	Superpixels application, Feature extraction, Boundary optimization	mIOU scores improved as compared to FCN 8s
Badrinarayan et al. [38]	SegNet (encoder-decoder)	CamVid, SUNRGB-D	Max pooling indices	SegNet more memory efficient during inference model as compared to DeepLab-LargeFOV, FCN, and DeconvNet
Kendall et al. [39]	Bayesian SegNet	CamVid, SUNRGB-D	Posterior distribution was produced from Monte Carlo sampling with dropout at test time	Smaller datasets showed better performance
Chaurasia et al. [40]	LinkNet	CamVid, cityscapes	Pooling indices	Highly efficient on high end GPUs for high resolutions image processing

TABLE 3.1   *(Continued)*

Author	Architecture/ Model	Dataset	Method / Technique	Results
Robail [41]	ECRU	CamVid	Images are processed with batch normalization and exponential linear unit activation functions.	Good as driving assistant system. Better performance than DeepLab, FCN, DeconvNet
Y.G et al. [42]	Residual encoder-decoder	CamVid, Cityscapes	Feature map size decreased and resolution is preserved	Better than SegNet, Enet for some classes of CamVid. Good mean IOU with cityscapes
Geng et al. [43]	Encoder-decoder with dense dilated spatial pyramid pooling	MR Images	Multi-scale features are extracted and upsampled for prediction	High accuracy and robustness
Bindhu [44]	Encoder-decoder	Biomedical images Kaggle lung CT dataset and the UCSB	V-net architecture to analyze images with AlexNet	Good performance with rational amount of training
Hamaguchi et al. [46]	Dilated convolutions (local feature extraction)	Toyota city dataset, Massachusetts buildings dataset and Vaihingen dataset	Local features were agglomerated by lessen up dilation factor	Small object cases showed extraordinary productivity with Unet and Deeplab architecture
Metha et al. [47]	ESPNet	Cityscapes, PASCAL VOC, and a breast biopsy	Pointwise convolutions and spatial pyramid dilated convolutions	Outperforms than MobielNet, ShuffNet, ENet
Piao et al. [48]	Dilated deep Unet with convolution	DeepGlobe road extraction	Paralleled dilated convolution	67.32 mIOU score as compared to Unet and deep dilated Unet

TABLE 3.1 *(Continued)*

Author	Architecture/ Model	Dataset	Method / Technique	Results
Wu et al. [49]	AD-LinkNet	DeepGlobe road extraction inner Mongolia	Serial paralled dilated convolution with global pooling	More accurate and precise for deep globe for edge processing, segments
Wang et al. [50]	DeepLabv2 with ResNet-101	PASCAL VOC 2012, cityscapes	Degridding method	Smooth effects, better performance
Luc et al. [51]	GAN	Stanford background dataset, PASCAL VOC 2012	Adversarial training, detecting, and correcting high order inconsistencies	Recorder higher accuracy in Sandford dataset.
Souly et al. [52]	GAN	PASCAL, SiftFLow, Stanford, and CamVid	Semi-supervised learning	Achieved better performance as compared to previous methods
Zhang et al. [53]	SegGAN	Stanford background dataset, PASCAL VOC 2012	Finding a correlation between masks and input images	Best performance is recorded with Stanford BG.
Han et al. ([54]	Spine-GAN	MRI images	LSTM for modeling	Pixel accuracy 96.2%
Lin et al. [55]	Refine net	PASCAL VOC 2012, PASCAL-Context, NYUDv2, SUNRGBD, Cityscapes, ADE20K, and the object parsing person-parts dataset	High-resolution segmentation maps are generated by fusing high-level semantics and low-level features	83.4 IOU score for PASCAL VOC 2012, best reported result.
Zhao et al. [56]	PSPnet	PASCAVL VOC 2012, cityscapes	Pyramid pooling	mIoU accuracy 85.4% on PASCAL VOC 2012 and accuracy 80.2% on cityscapes.

TABLE 3.1   *(Continued)*

Author	Architecture/ Model	Dataset	Method / Technique	Results
Chen et al. [57]	DeepLabv3	PASCAL VOC 2012	Altrous convolution	DeepLabv3 has better performance than DeepLab
Liu et al. [58]	Markov random field	PASCAL VOC 2012, cityscapes dataset and CamVid dataset.	Mean-field algorithm	Up to date performance achieved on VOC12, Cityscapes, and CamVid datasets

3.4   FUTURE DIRECTIONS AND CHALLENGES IN SEMANTIC SEGMENTATION WITH DEEP LEARNING

3.4.1   NEED FOR LARGE AND HIGH-QUALITY DATASETS

Semantic segmentation requires a massive amount of labeled data for better results. This means that if labeled data sets are unavailable, some algorithms will not work efficiently. Furthermore, real-time data (images, video) has high resolutions which also involves a large number of objects and overlapped data. So, to train a model with utmost performance a large dataset is required for deep processing. With the rising popularity of DL in biomedical image analysis, large 3D datasets are in need of effective evaluation and processing of images. The size of datasets and DL is positively linked to each other. For better results, current methods need a colossal dataset which is a diligent task to produce it. This is also a reason for the demand of semi-supervised and weakly supervised methods among researchers because they do not need labeled data and they show significant results in performance by using additional annotations. Though there are already some promising works, there is still room for better data which will lead to better outputs of models or networks.

3.4.2   SEQUENCE DATASETS

Though, there is a great rise in the development of image segmentation methods in past few years but video series are still processed frame by frame.

The major drawback in this approach is that temporal information is not taken into account which is beneficial to enhance the performance of the method. So, there is also a need for video segmentation methods to take advantage of temporal information for better results. Generating more 3D images and video datasets will unlock new research areas.

3.4.3 OVERFITTING

This is one fundamental issue in DL because models have to learn a large number of parameters. Even noise patterns present in the training data are also learned by a model that generates a large gap between training and test error. Different methods, e.g., regularization, LI regularization, L2 regularization, drop out are applied to solve this issue. Data augmentation was used to reduce overfitting. There is a need for some more methods to be developed for improving the performance of the network.

3.4.4 HIGH MEMORY REQUIREMENTS

It is another important factor for DL models and methods. High-end graphical processing units that stimulate DL networks demand high memory. DNN are not available for mobile devices due to high memory requirements and a problem arises with the inference stage of a model. In order to fit them into mobile devices, networks must be simplified, compression techniques can be used to make it available for small, memory efficient network. Also, a point of investigation is how to increase efficiency with less memory but better accuracy. A dense outlook is needed on how potential issues with DNN can be resolved with basic operations.

3.4.5 SEGMENTATION IN REAL-TIME

Without sacrificing accuracy, it is very difficult to perform real-time segmentation. This is beneficial in certain applications where execution duration is very crucial for the performance of the model, e.g., autonomous driving. This research area is not covered by most of the researchers, but currently, numerous efforts are in action for the designing of productive architectures which may make it possible through convolutions. This is a challenging task to have a model with high accuracy with low running time.

3.5 CONCLUSION

In this chapter, we have presented an exhaustive review of semantic segmentation methods based on the perspective of DNN with an emphasis on CNN, RNN, GAN, and Autocencoders. We have tried to review some of the latest models based on or which are a combination of the above-mentioned technology/techniques. Each model has been reviewed and conclusive summary pertaining to the three perspective viz. Underlying Framework, datasets, and the performance results has been duly discussed. The primary goal was to extract the effectiveness and efficiency associated with each of these methods, as based on these techniques, we would try to construct new models that can deliver better results and can subdue the disadvantages attached with the present methods. Certain issues which need to be demystified for a productive outcome has also been discussed in the chapter.

KEYWORDS

- **artificial intelligence**
- **conditional random field**
- **effective receptive field**
- **generative adversarial networks**
- **recurrent neural networks**

REFERENCES

1. Minaee, S., Boykov, Y., Porikli, F., Plaza, A., Kehtarnavaz, N., & Terzopoulosences, D., (2020). *Image Segmentation Using Deep Learning: A Survey*. Retrieved from: https://arxiv.org/abs/2001.05566 (accessed on 11 November 2021).
2. Sharma, N., Mangla, M., Mohanty, S. N., Gupta, D., Tiwari, P., Shorfuzzaman, M., & Rawashdeh, M., (2021). A smart ontology-based IoT framework for remote patient monitoring. *Biomedical Signal Processing and Control, 68*, 102717.
3. Huang, Z., Wang, C., Wang, X., Liu, W., & Wang, J., (2019). Semantic image segmentation by scale-adaptive networks. *IEEE Transactions on Image Processing, 29*, 2066–2077.
4. Singh, S., Kaushik, S., Vats, R., Jain, A., & Thakur, N., (2019). Semantic segmentation using deep learning. *International Research Journal of Engineering and Technology, 6*(4).
5. Garcia-Garcia, A., Orts-Escolano, S., Oprea, S. O., Villena-Martinez, V., & Garcia-Rodriguez, J., (2017). *A Review on Deep Learning Techniques Applied to Semantic Segmentation*. Retrieved from: https://arxiv.org/abs/1704.06857 (accessed on 11 November 2021).

6. Lateef, F., & Ruichek, Y., (2019). Survey on semantic segmentation using deep learning techniques. *J. Neurocomputing, 338,* 321–348.

7. Zhu, H., Meng, F., Cai, J., & Lu, S., (2016). Beyond pixels: A comprehensive survey from bottom-up to semantic image segmentation and co-segmentation. *Journal of Visual Communication and Image Represent, 34,* 12–27.

8. Thoma, M., (2016). *A Survey of Semantic Segmentation.* Retrieved from arxiv.org/abs/1602.06541.

9. Niemeijer, J., Fouopi, P. P., Knake-Langhorst, S., & Barth, E., (2017). A review of neural network-based semantic segmentation for scene understanding in context of the self-driving car. *Proceedings of the BioMedTech Studierenden Tagung.*

10. Guo, Y., Liu, Y., Georgiou, T., & Lew, M. S., (2018). A review of semantic segmentation using deep neural networks. *Int. J. Multimedia Information Retrieval, 7*(2), 87–93.

11. Kurama, V., Alla, S., & Vishnu, K. R., (2018). Image semantic segmentation using deep learning. *I. J. Image, Graphics, and Signal Processing, 12,* 1–10.

12. Liu, X., Deng, Z., & Yang, Y., (2018). Recent progress in semantic image segmentation. *Artificial Intelligence Review.* https://doi.org/10.1007/s10462-018-9641-3.

13. Geng, Q., Zhou, Z., & Cao, X., (2018). Survey of recent progress in semantic image seg-mentation with CNNS. *Science China Information Sciences, 61*(5), 051–101. Springer.

14. Voulodimos, A., Doulamis, N., Doulamis, A., & Protopapadaki, E., (2018). Deep learning for computer vision: A brief review. *Computational Intelligence and Neuroscience.* https://doi.org/10.1155/2018/7068349.

15. Shaikh, F., (2017). *Deep Learning vs. Machine Learning the Essential Differences you Need to Know*! Retrieved From https://www.analyticsvidhya.com/blog/2017/04/comparison-between-deep-learning-machine-learning/ (accessed on 11 November 2021).

16. Liu, Y., Liu, J., Li, Z., et al., (2013). Weakly-supervised dual clustering for image semantic segmentation *IEEE Conference on Computer Vision and Pattern Recognition (CVPR), 2075–2082.*

17. Zhang, C. F., (2012). Image semantic segmentation based on conditional random filed. *Journal Computer CD Software and Applications, 9,* 21–23.

18. Cornelisse, D., (2018). *An Intuitive Guide to Convolutional Neural Networks.* Retrieved from https://www.freecodecamp.org/news/an-intuitive-guide-to-convolutional-neural-networks-260c2de0a050/ (accessed on 11 November 2021).

19. Krizhevsky, A., Sutskever, I., & Hinton, G. E., (2012). ImageNet classification with deep convolutional neural networks. *Advances in Neural Information Processing Systems,* 1097–1105.

20. LeCun, Y., Bottou, L., Bengio, Y., Haffner, P., et al., (1998). Gradient-based learning applied to document recognition. *Proceedings of the IEEE, 86*(11), 2278–2324.

21. Yamashita, R., Nishio, M., Kinh, G. R. D., & Togashi, K., (2018). Convolutional neural networks: An overview and application in radiology. *Insights into Imaging, 9,* 611–629.

22. Nisbet, R., Gary, M., & Yale, K., (2018). Deep learning. *Handbook of Statistical Analysis and Data Mining Applications* (2nd edn., pp. 741–751).

23. Browniee, J., (2017). *A Gentle Introduction to Long Short-Term Memory Networks by the Experts.* Retrieved from: https://machinelearningmastery.com/gentle-introduction-long-short-term-memory-networks-experts/ (accessed on 11 November 2021).

24. Wolterinka, J. M., Kamnitsasb, K., Ledigc, C., & Išguma, I., (2020). Deep learning: Generative adversarial networks and adversarial methods. In: Kevin, Z. S., Daniel, R., & Gabor, F., (eds.), *Handbook of Medical Image Computing and Computer-Assisted Intervention* (1ˢᵗ edn., pp. 547–574).

25. Baldi, P., (2012). Autoencoders, unsupervised learning, and deep architectures. *JMLR: Workshop and Conference Proceedings, 27,* 37–50.

26. Long, J., Shelhamer, E., & Darrell, T., (2015). Fully convolutional networks for semantic segmentation. In: *Proceedings of the IEEE Conference on Computer Vision and Pattern Recognition* (pp. 3431–3440).

27. Shelhamer, E., Long, J., & Darrell, T., (2017). Fully convolutional networks for semantic segmentation. *IEEE Transactions on Pattern Analysis and Machine Intelligence, 39*(4).

28. Liu, W., Rabinovich, A., & Berg, A. C., (2015). *Parsenet: Looking Wider to See Better.* arXiv preprint arXiv:1506.04579.

29. Wang, G., Li, W., Ourselin, S., & Vercauteren, T., (2017). Automatic brain tumor segmentation using cascaded anisotropic convolutional neural networks. *International MICCAI Brain Lesion Workshop,* 178–190. Springer.

30. Li, Y., Qi, H., Dai, J., Ji, X., & Wei, Y., (2017). Fully convolutional instance aware semantic segmentation. In: *Proceedings of the IEEE Conference on Computer Vision and Pattern Recognition* (pp. 2359–2367).

31. Marmanisa, D., Schindlerb, K., Wegnerb, J. D., Gallianib, S., Datcua, M., & Stillac, U., (2018). Classification with an edge: Improving semantic image segmentation with boundary detection. *ISPRS Journal of Photogrammetry and Remote Sensing, 135,* 158–172.

32. Chaia, D., Newsamb, S., & Huang, J., (2020). Aerial image semantic segmentation using DCNN predicted distance maps. *ISPRS Journal of Photogrammetry and Remote Sensing, 160,* 309–322.

33. Chen, L. C., Papandreou, G., Kokkinos, I., Murphy, K., & Yuille, A. L., (2014). *Semantic Image Segmentation with Deep Convolutional Nets and Fully Connected CRFs.* arXiv preprint arXiv:1412.7062.

34. Zheng, S., Jayasumana, S., Romera-Paredes, B., Vineet, V., Su, Z., Du, D., Huang, C., & Torr, P. H., (2015). Conditional random fields as recurrent neural networks. In: *Proceedings of the IEEE International Conference on Computer Vision* (pp. 1529–1537).

35. Lin, G., Shen, C., Van, D. H. A., & Reid, I., (2016). Efficient piecewise training of deep structured models for semantic segmentation. In: *Proceedings of the IEEE Conference on Computer Vision and Pattern Recognition* (pp. 3194–3203).

36. Zhou, H., Zhang, J., Lei, J., Li, S., & Tu, D., (2016). Image semantic segmentation based on FCN-CRF model. *International Conference on Image, Vision, and Computing.* doi: 10.1109/ICIVC.2016.7571265.

37. Zhao, W., Fu, Y., Wei, X., & Wang, H., (2018). An improved image semantic segmentation method based on superpixels and conditional random fields. *Applied Sciences, 8*(5), 837. https://doi.org/10.3390/app8050837

38. Badrinarayanan, V., Kendall, A., & Cipolla, R., (2017). Segnet: A deep convolutional encoder-decoder architecture for image segmentation. *IEEE Transactions on Pattern Analysis and Machine Intelligence, 39*(12), 2481–2495.

39. Kendall, A., Badrinarayanan, V., & Cipolla, R., (2015). *Bayesian Segnet: Model Uncertainty in Deep Convolutional Encoder-Decoder Architectures for Scene Understanding.* arXiv preprint arXiv:1511.02680.

40. Chaurasia, A., & Culurciello, E., (2017). Linknet: Exploiting encoder representations for efficient semantic segmentation. *IEEE Visual Communications and Image Processing (VCIP)*, 1–4.

41. Yasrab, R., (2018). ECRU: An Encoder-Decoder Based Convolution Neural Network (CNN) for Road-Scene Understanding. *Journal of Imaging, 4*(10), 116. doi: 10.3390/jimaging4100116.

42. Naresh, Y. G., Little, S., & O'Connor, N. E., (2018). A residual encoder-decoder network for semantic segmentation in autonomous driving scenarios. In: *26*[th] *European Signal Processing Conference (EUSIPCO).* doi: 10.23919/EUSIPCO.2018.8553161

43. Geng, L., Wang, J., Xiao, Z., Tong, J., Zhang, F., & Wu, J., (2019). Encoder-decoder with dense dilated spatial pyramid pooling for prostate MR images segmentation. Research article. Online access. *Journal Computer Assisted Surgery, 24,* 13–19. Taylor and Francis. https://doi.org/10.1080/24699322.2019.1649069.

44. Bindhu, V., (2019). Biomedical image analysis using semantic segmentation. *Journal of Innovative Image Processing, 1*(2), 91–101.

45. Yu, F., & Vladlen, K., (2016). Multi-scale context aggregation by dilated convolutions. *International Conference on Learning Representations (ICLR).*

46. Hamaguchi, R., Fujita, A., Nemoto, K., Imaizumi, T., & Hikosaka, S., (2017). *Effective Use of Dilated Convolutions for Segmenting Small-Object Instances in Remote Sensing Imagery.* https://arxiv.org/abs/1709.00179.

47. Mehta, S., Rastegari, M., Caspi, A., Shapiro, L., & Hannaneh, H., (2018). *ESPNet: Efficient Spatial Pyramid of Dilated Convolutions for Semantic Segmentation.* arXiv:1803.06815.

48. Piao, S., & Liu, J., (2019). Accuracy improvement of UNet based on dilated convolution. *Journal of Physics: Conference Series 1345052066.* doi: 10.1088/1742-6596/1345/5/052066.

49. Wu, M., Zhang, C., Liu, J., Zhou, L., & Li, X., (2019). Towards accurate high resolution satellite image semantic segmentation. *IEEE Access: Special Section on AI-Driven Big Data Processing: Theory, Methodology, and Applications.* Digital object identifier. 10.1109/ACCESS.2019.2913442.

50. Wang, Z., & Ji, S., (2018). *Smoothed Dilated Convolutions for Improved Dense Prediction.* Research track paper KDD 2018. London, United Kingdom.

51. Luc, P., Couprie, C., Chintala, S., & Verbeek J., (2016). *Semantic Segmentation using Adversarial Networks.* arXiv:1611.08408.

52. Souly, N., Spampinato, C., & Shah, M., (2017). Semi-supervised semantic segmentation using generative adversarial network. *IEEE International Conference on Computer Vision (ICCV).*

53. Zhang, X., Zhu, X., Xiao-Yu, Z., Zhang, N., Li, P., & Wang, L., (2018). SegGAN: Semantic segmentation with generative adversarial network. *IEEE Fourth International Conference on Multimedia Big Data (BigMM).*

54. Han, Z., Wei, B., Mercado, A., Leung, S., & Li, S., (2018). Spine-GAN: Semantic segmentation of multiple spinal structures. *Medical Image Analysis, 50,* 23–35. Accepted manuscript.

55. Lin, G., Milan, A., Shen, C., & Reid, I., (2016). *RefineNet: Multi-Path Refinement Networks for High-Resolution Semantic Segmentation.* arXiv:1611.06612.

56. Zhao, H., Shi, J., Qi, X., Wang, X., & Jia, J., (2017). Pyramid scene parsing network. *IEEE Conference on Computer Vision and Pattern Recognition (CVPR).*

57. Liang-Chieh, C., Papandreou, G., Schroff, F., & Adam, H., (2017). *Rethinking Atrous Convolution for Semantic Image Segmentation.* arXiv:1706.05587.

58. Liu, Z., Li, X., Luo, P., Loy, C. C., & Tang, X., (2018). Deep learning Markov random field for semantic segmentation. *IEEE Transactions on Pattern Analysis and Machine Intelligence.*

59. Parmar, R., (2018). *Detection and Segmentation through ConvNets.* Retrieved from https://towardsdatascience.com/detection-and-segmentation-through-convnets-47aa42de27ea (accessed on 11 November 2021).

60. Colah's Blog, (2015). *Understanding LSTM Networks.* Retrieved from: https://colah.github.io/posts/2015-08-Understanding-LSTMs/ (accessed on 11 November 2021).

61. Simonyan, K., & Zisserman, A., (2014). *Very Deep Convolutional Networks for Large-Scale Image Recognition.* arXiv:1409.1556.

62. He, K., Zhang, X., Ren, S., & Sun, J., (2016). Deep residual learning for image recognition. *Proceedings of the IEEE Conference on Computer Vision and Pattern Recognition,* 770–778.

63. Szegedy, C., Liu, W., Jia, Y., Sermanet, P., Reed, S., Anguelov, D., Erhan, D., et al., (2015). Going deeper with convolutions. *Proceedings of the IEEE Conference on Computer Vision and Pattern Recognition,* 1–9.

64. Howard, A. G., Zhu, M., Chen B., Kalenichenko, D., Wang, W., Weyand, T., Andreetto, M., & Adam, H., (2017). *MobileNets: Efficient Convolutional Neural Networks for Mobile Vision Applications.* arXiv:1704.04861.

65. Iandola, F., Moskewicz, M., Karayev, S., Girshick, R., Darrell, T., & Keutzer, K., (2014). *DenseNet: Implementing Efficient ConvNet Descriptor Pyramids.* https://arxiv.org/pdf/1404.1869.pdf (accessed on 11 November 2021).

66. Yuheng, S., & Hao, Y., (2017). *Image Segmentation Algorithms Overview.* arXiv:1707.02051.

67. Muthukrishnan, R., & Radha, M., (2011). Edge detection techniques for image segmentation. *International Journal of Computer Science & Information Technology, 3*(6).

68. Gupta, D., (2017). *Fundamentals of Deep Learning-Introduction to Neural Networks.* Retrieved from: https://www.analyticsvidhya.com/blog/2017/12/introduction-to-recurrent-neural-networks/ (accessed on 11 November 2021).

69. Kr¨ahenb¨uhl, P., & Koltun, V., (2011). *Efficient Inference in Fully Connected CRFs with Gaussian Edge Potentials.* NIPS.

70. Vineet, V., Warrell, J., & Torr, P. H., (2012). *Filter-Based Mean-field Inference for Random fields with Higher-Order Terms and Product Label-Spaces.* ECCV.

CHAPTER 4

Covariate Shift in Machine Learning

SANTOSH CHAPANERI and DEEPAK JAYASWAL

Department of Electronics and Telecommunication Engineering,
St. Francis Institute of Technology, University of Mumbai, Mumbai,
Maharashtra, India, E-mail: santoshchapaneri@sfit.ac.in (S. Chapaneri)

ABSTRACT

Covariate shift occurs in machine learning when the input train and test probability distributions are different even though the conditional distribution of output given the train and test inputs remain unchanged. Most existing supervised machine learning techniques make an assumption that the train and test data samples follow the same probability distribution, but this is violated in practice for many real-world applications. In this work, the covariate shift is corrected by learning the importance weights for re-weighting the train data such that the training samples closer to the test data samples get more importance during modeling. To estimate the importance weights, a computationally efficient Frank-Wolfe optimization algorithm is used. Structured prediction is required to model the dependency that can exist in the multi-dimensional target variables, for example, in the application of human pose estimation. Twin Gaussian process (TGP) structured regression is used to model this dependency for improving the prediction performance relative to learning the multiple target dimensions separately. A computationally efficient method of TGP is presented for covariate shift correction and the performance is evaluated on the benchmark HumanEva dataset resulting in significantly reduced regression error.

4.1 INTRODUCTION

A fundamental assumption in most supervised machine learning (ML) methods is that the train and test data points are sampled from the *same* underlying probability distribution. Given the joint training distribution $p_{tr}(\mathbf{x}, \mathbf{y})$ and the joint test distribution $p_{te}(\mathbf{x}, \mathbf{y})$ where $\mathbf{x} \in \chi$ is the feature vector and $\mathbf{y} \in \gamma$ is the target, the assumption is that the joint distributions remain the same, that is $p_{tr}(\mathbf{x}, \mathbf{y}) = p_{te}(\mathbf{x}, \mathbf{y})$. However, this assumption is generally not valid for real-life test data. For example, consider the problem of price prediction of an insurance policy based on age, income, employment type, etc. With the typical ML pipeline of preprocessing, data cleaning, feature selection, and model training, the model performance can be evaluated on the test data. The test performance can degrade if the test distribution of age is different from the train distribution of age, i.e., if the model was learned on the age group of 15 to 45, but the test data also includes customers belonging to the age group of 50 and above. Due to this potential mismatch between the distributions, the test performance is always lower than the training performance.

Broadly, there are three types of dataset shift studied in the literature:

1. **Covariate Shift:** which occurs due to a shift in the distribution of independent variables for $\chi \rightarrow \gamma$ problems. In this case, the conditional distributions remain the same but the marginal distributions of inputs differ, i.e., $p_{tr}(x,y) = p_{tr}(y|x)p_{tr}(x)$ and $p_{te}(x,y) = p_{te}(y|x)p_{te}(x)$, so $p_{tr}(y|x) = p_{te}(y|x)$ and $p_{tr}(x) \neq p_{te}(x)$.
2. **Prior Probability Shift:** which occurs due to a shift in the distribution of dependent variables. This dataset shift scenario is applicable to $\gamma \rightarrow \chi$ problems where the target variable determines the covariate values. An example is the field of medical diagnosis where the disease label determines the symptoms. In this case, we have $p_{tr}(x|y) = p_{te}(x|y)$ and $p_{tr}(y) \neq p_{te}(y)$.
3. **Concept Shift:** Also referred to as concept drift, can occur in both $\chi \rightarrow \gamma$ and $\gamma \rightarrow \chi$ problems due to a changing relationship between the independent and dependent variables. In this case, we have $p_{tr}(y|x) \neq p_{te}(y|x)$ and $p_{tr}(x) = p_{te}(x)$ for $\chi \rightarrow \gamma$ problems and $p_{tr}(x|y) \neq p_{te}(x|y)$ and $p_{tr}(y) \neq p_{te}(y)$ for $\gamma \rightarrow \chi$ problems.

A detailed overview of dataset shift is presented in [1, 2], illustrating its various types, causes, and several applications. We focus on covariate shift since it is widely applicable to many existing supervised ML methods. The covariate shift can be corrected by estimating the importance weight $w(x) = \frac{p_{te}(x)}{p_{tr}(x)}$ from the probability distributions of train and test data. But this is non-trivial to solve due to the problem of curse of dimensionality and can also be not reliable for input data in high dimensions [3]. A feasible solution is to thus learn the importance weight directly from the given data without the need to estimate the train and test probability densities.

For correcting the covariate shift, various techniques are proposed in the literature, e.g., Kullback-Leibler importance estimation procedure (KLIEP) [3], least-squares importance fitting (LSIF) [4], relative unconstrained least-squares importance fitting (RuLSIF) [5], log-linear KLIEP (LL-KLIEP) [6], KLIEP based on Gaussian mixture models (GM-KLIEP) [7], KLIEP based on mixture of probabilistic principal component analyzers (PM-KLIEP) [8], etc. These important weight estimation techniques are unsupervised since only the features are required for estimating the importance weight without requiring the target variable. The LSIF and RuLSIF have a closed-form analytical solution for the importance weights; however, their resulting estimates can be biased [5]. KLIEP is used in this work for estimating the importance weights since a) it has a convex optimization problem with a unique global solution, b) its weight estimate is unbiased and c) the Frank-Wolfe (FW) algorithm can be used to solve its optimization problem efficiently.

In this work, the correction of covariate shift is done following the unsupervised principle (i.e., without the target variables) using the *projection-free* FW optimization algorithm [9]. The FW optimization algorithm can iteratively solve constrained convex optimization problems efficiently using the linearization principle and can obtain sparser solutions [9, 10]. In Ref. [11], a covariate shift based on the standard FW method was proposed to compute the importance weights of KLIEP. Instead of using the standard FW algorithm, a more efficient FW covariate shift algorithm using the pairwise steps is used in this work resulting in a more sparser solution with significantly better computational efficiency.

Structured regression is an increasingly studied concept in ML when the multi-dimensional target variables are dependent on each other across dimensions. The task is to learn the functional mapping $f : \mathbb{R}^{d_x} \to \mathbb{R}^{d_y}$ from input $\mathbf{x} \in \mathbb{R}^{d_x}$ to target $\mathbf{y} \in \mathbb{R}^{d_y}$ (both multivariate) by exploiting any correlation that may exist between multivariate data dimensions. Twin Gaussian process (TGP) regression [12] is used in this work for modeling the dependency to reduce the regression error. The TGP regression model is updated to correct the covariate shift during the training phase. Experimental results on the benchmark HumanEva dataset show that the PFWCS algorithm used with the importance weighted TGP method outperforms the non-weighted TGP method, thus reducing the effect of covariate shift.

4.2   ESTIMATION OF THE IMPORTANCE WEIGHTS

4.2.1   KULLBACK LEIBLER IMPORTANCE ESTIMATION PROCEDURE

KLIEP was proposed in [3] to compute the importance weight $w(\mathbf{x}) = \hat{p}_{te}(\mathbf{x}) / p_{tr}(\mathbf{x})$. This is achieved by reducing the Kullback-Leibler (KL) divergence from the actual test probability density $p_{te}(\mathbf{x})$ to its estimate $\hat{p}_{te}(\mathbf{x})$ without the need to compute the train and test probability densities explicitly. Based on mixtures of Gaussians, the importance weights are modeled as Eqn. (1), where $\alpha = \left[\alpha_1,\ldots,\alpha_{n_{te}}\right]^{\mathrm{T}}$ denote the mixing coefficients, $\kappa(\cdot)$ is a kernel function satisfying Mercer's conditions, n_{tr} is the number of train samples and n_{te} is the number of test samples. The importance weights can be intuitively understood as follows: if the training sample is closer to the test distribution, then this sample should be given more importance; likewise, if the training sample is far from the test distribution, then such a sample should be assigned a less weight. This implies that the training samples should be re-weighted by $w(\mathbf{x}^{tr})$.

$$w\left(\mathbf{x}^{tr}\right) = \sum_{l=1}^{n_{te}}\alpha_l \kappa_l\left(\mathbf{x}^{tr}\right) = \sum_{l=1}^{n_{te}}\alpha_l \exp\left(\frac{-\mathbf{x}^{tr} - \mathbf{x}_l^{te\,2}}{2\sigma^2}\right) \qquad (1)$$

Using the importance weights, the test probability density can be estimated as $\hat{p}_{te}(\mathbf{x}) = w(\mathbf{x}^{tr})p_{tr}(\mathbf{x})$. Accordingly, the KL divergence measure from the true test probability density to its estimated version is given by Eqn. (2).

$$KL\left[p_{te}(\mathbf{x})\,\hat{p}_{te}(\mathbf{x})\right] = \int p_{te}(\mathbf{x})\log\frac{p_{te}(\mathbf{x})}{\hat{p}_{te}(\mathbf{x})}d\mathbf{x}^{te} = \int p_{te}(\mathbf{x})\log\frac{p_{te}(\mathbf{x})}{w(\mathbf{x})p_{tr}(\mathbf{x})}d\mathbf{x}^{te}$$

$$= \int p_{te}(\mathbf{x})\log\frac{p_{te}(\mathbf{x})}{p_{tr}(\mathbf{x})}d\mathbf{x}^{te} - \int p_{te}(\mathbf{x})\log w(\mathbf{x})d\mathbf{x}^{te} \qquad (2)$$

Since the first term of the KL divergence does not involve the parameter α, it can be ignored for the optimization process. The objective function can be empirically approximated by Eqn. (3), which is to be maximized, since maximizing J_{KLIP} is equivalent to minimizing the KL divergence. Further, the integral of $\hat{p}_{te}(\mathbf{x})$ should be one, since it is a probability density, resulting in the constraint given by Eqn. (4).

$$J_{\mathrm{KLIEP}} = \int p_{te}(\mathbf{x})\log w(\mathbf{x})d\mathbf{x}^{te} \approx \frac{1}{n_{te}}\sum_{j=1}^{n_{te}}\log w\left(\mathbf{x}_j^{te}\right) = \frac{1}{n_{te}}\sum_{j=1}^{n_{te}}\log\left(\sum_{l=1}^{n_{te}}\alpha_l \kappa_l\left(\mathbf{x}_j^{te}\right)\right) \qquad (3)$$

$$\int \hat{p}_{te}(\mathbf{x})\,d\mathbf{x}^{te} = 1 = \int w(\mathbf{x})\,p_{tr}(\mathbf{x})\,d\mathbf{x}^{tr} \approx \frac{1}{n_{tr}}\sum_{i=1}^{n_{tr}} w\left(\mathbf{x}_i^{tr}\right) = \frac{1}{n_{tr}}\sum_{i=1}^{n_{tr}}\sum_{j=1}^{n_{te}} \alpha_j \kappa_j\left(\mathbf{x}_j^{tr}\right) \quad (4)$$

The constrained convex optimization problem of KLIEP given by Eqn. (5) can be solved using the *projected gradient method* [3] as shown in Figure 4.1.

$$\max_{\acute{a}} F(\acute{a}) = \sum_{j=1}^{n_{te}} \log\left(\sum_{l=1}^{n_{te}} \alpha_l \kappa_l\left(\mathbf{x}_j^{te}\right)\right)$$

$$s.t. \sum_{i=1}^{n_{tr}}\sum_{j=1}^{n_{te}} \alpha_j \kappa_j\left(\mathbf{x}_i^{tr}\right) = n_{tr}; \alpha_1, \alpha_2, \ldots, \alpha_{n_{te}} \geq 0 \quad (5)$$

Algorithm KLIEP

Input: $\{\mathbf{x}_i^{tr}\}_{i=1}^{n_{tr}}, \{\mathbf{x}_j^{te}\}_{j=1}^{n_{te}}$, **Output:** $\mathbf{w} = \{w(\mathbf{x}_i^{tr})\}_{i=1}^{n_{tr}}$

1: $(\mathbf{A})_{j,l} = \kappa_l(\mathbf{x}_j^{te}) = \exp\left(-\frac{1}{2\sigma^2}\|\mathbf{x}_j^{te} - \mathbf{x}_l^{te}\|^2\right)$ for $j, l = \{1, \ldots, n_{te}\}$

2: $b_l = \frac{1}{n_{tr}}\sum_{i=1}^{n_{tr}} \kappa_l(\mathbf{x}_i^{tr}) = \frac{1}{n_{tr}}\sum_{i=1}^{n_{tr}} \exp\left(-\frac{1}{2\sigma^2}\|\mathbf{x}_i^{tr} - \mathbf{x}_l^{te}\|^2\right)$

3: Initialize $\alpha\,(>0)$ and $\epsilon\,(0 < \epsilon \ll 1)$

4: **repeat**   ▷ projected gradient ascent

5: $\quad \alpha \leftarrow \alpha + \epsilon \mathbf{A}^\top(1./\mathbf{A}\alpha)$ ▷ element-wise division

6: $\quad \alpha \leftarrow \alpha + \dfrac{(1 - \mathbf{b}^\top\alpha)\mathbf{b}}{(\mathbf{b}^\top\mathbf{b})}$

7: $\quad \alpha \leftarrow \max(\alpha, \mathbf{0})$ ▷ element-wise maximum

8: $\quad \alpha \leftarrow \dfrac{\alpha}{(\mathbf{b}^\top\alpha)}$ ▷ constraint satisfaction

9: **until** convergence

10: Estimate the importance weights $w(\mathbf{x}_i^{tr}) = \sum_{l=1}^{n_{te}} \alpha_l \kappa_l(\mathbf{x}_i^{tr}) \quad \forall i = 1, \ldots, n_{tr}$

FIGURE 4.1 Algorithm for Kullback-Leibler importance estimation procedure.

The tuning parameter σ needs to be obtained with the likelihood cross-validation method of model selection; however, the resulting value can be biased due to the covariate shift [3]. Thus, the unbiased importance weighted cross-validation (IWCV) [13] procedure is utilized for determining the optimum σ of the KLIEP kernel function as shown in Figure 4.2. In IWCV, the test data set is split into T disjoint subsets $\{\mathcal{X}_t^{te}\}_{t=1}^{T}$ in line 1. In lines 2 to 8, the importance weights are obtained for each possible σ_m candidate $(m \in \mathcal{M})$

for each split t and the score is computed as $J(m)$. The optimum σ is obtained as the one that maximizes the score in line 9. The importance weight is then obtained in line 10 using the optimum σ value.

Algorithm Frank-Wolfe
___
Input: $g_0 \in \mathcal{G}$, **Output:** Optimal point g

1: **for** iteration $t = 0, 1, 2, \ldots$ **do**

2:     **if** $\nabla F(g_t) = 0$, **return** g_t ▷ convergence

3:     Find $s_t \leftarrow \underset{s \in \mathcal{G}}{\mathrm{argmin}} \, \langle s, \nabla F(g_t) \rangle$ ▷ linear minimization principle

4:     Update: $g_{t+1} = (1 - \rho_t)g_t + \rho_t s_t,$ for $\rho_t \in [0, 1]$ ▷ ρ_t obtained with line-search

        $= g_t + \rho_t(s_t - g_t)$

5: **end for**

FIGURE 4.2   Algorithm for importance weighted cross-validation.

4.2.2   VARIANTS OF KLIEP

Some variants of KLIEP model are proposed in the literature with respect to the parameterization of the importance weights. The log-linear KLIEP method [6] uses a non-linear parameterization given by Eqn. (6) with the denominator representing the normalization constant. The non-linear model with the log function can take only non-negative values and thus the *unconstrained* optimization problem of LL-KLIEP is given by Eqn. (7).

$$w\left(x^{tr}\right) = \frac{\exp\left(\sum_{l=1}^{n_{te}} \alpha_l \kappa_l\left(x^{tr}\right)\right)}{\frac{1}{n_{tr}} \sum_{i=1}^{n_{tr}} \exp\left(\sum_{l=1}^{n_{te}} \alpha_l \kappa_l\left(x_i^{tr}\right)\right)} \tag{6}$$

$$J_{\mathrm{LL-KLIEP}} = \frac{1}{n_{te}} \sum_{l=1}^{n_{te}} \alpha_l \kappa_l\left(x^{tr}\right) - \log \frac{1}{n_{tr}} \sum_{i=1}^{n_{tr}} \exp\left(\sum_{l=1}^{n_{te}} \alpha_l \kappa_l\left(x_i^{tr}\right)\right) \tag{7}$$

Since the implementation of KLIEP uses a spherical Gaussian kernel $\kappa(\cdot)$, it cannot capture any correlation existing in the data. To solve this problem, KLIEP based on Gaussian mixture model (GM-KLIEP) method was proposed in [7] to learn the covariance matrix directly from the data by using a mixture of Gaussians given by Eqn. (8).

$$w\left(x^{tr}\right) = \sum_{l=1}^{K} \pi_l N\left(x^{tr} \mid \mu_l, \Sigma_l\right) \tag{8}$$

Here, K is the number of Gaussian mixtures, π_l are the mixing coefficients and $N\left(x^{tr}|\mu_l,\Sigma_l\right) \propto \exp\left(-\frac{1}{2}\left(x^{tr}-\mu_l\right)^T \Sigma_l^{-1}\left(x^{tr}-\mu_l\right)\right)$ is the multivariate Gaussian probability density having mean vector μ_l and covariance matrix Σ_l of the lth Gaussian. The constrained optimization problem of GM-KLIEP given by Eqn. (9) can be solved using the expectation-maximization (EM) algorithm [14].

$$\max_{\{\pi_l,\mu_l,\Sigma_l\}_{l=1}^{K}} \left[\sum_{j=1}^{n_{te}} \log\left(\sum_{l=1}^{K} \pi_l N(x_j^{te}\mid\mu_l,\Sigma_l) \right) \right]$$

$$s.t. \sum_{i=1}^{n_{tr}}\sum_{l=1}^{K} \pi_l N(x_i^{tr}\mid\mu_l,\Sigma_l) = n_{tr}; \pi_1,\pi_2,\ldots,\pi_K \geq 0 \tag{9}$$

The GM-KLIEP method can handle the correlation in the data, but its training involves computing the inverse of covariance matrices, which can be unstable numerically when the data has a rank-deficient covariance matrix. This problem of coping with rank deficient data is solved in [8] using the dimensionality reduction method of principal component analysis (PCA). The importance weight is thus modeled by Eqn. (10) using the mixture of probabilistic principal component analyzers (PPCA) [15] resulting in the PPCA-mixture KLIEP (PM-KLIEP) method, where K refers to the number of PPCA mixtures, π_l are the mixing coefficients, and $\{p_l(x^{tr})\}_{l=1}^{K}$ are the probabilistic principal component analyzers.

$$w\left(x^{tr}\right) = \sum_{l=1}^{K}\pi_l p_l\left(x^{tr}\right) = \sum_{l=1}^{K}\pi_l \frac{1}{\left(2\pi\sigma_l^2\right)^{d/2}|C_l|^{1/2}}\exp\left(-\frac{1}{2}\left(x^{tr}-\mu_l\right)^T C_l^{-1}\left(x^{tr}-\mu_l\right)\right) \tag{10}$$

Here, $C_l = W_l W_l^T + \sigma_l^2 I_d$, d is the data dimensionality, I_d is the d-dimensional identity matrix, μ_l is the mean vector of the lth Gaussian and $W \in \mathbb{R}^{d\times m}$ is the projection matrix onto a m-dimensional ($m \leq d$) reduced space. The constrained optimization problem of PM-KLIEP given by Eqn. (11) can also be solved using the expectation-maximization (EM) algorithm similar to that of GM-KLIEP.

$$\max_{\{\pi_l,\mu_l,W_l,\sigma_l\}_{l=1}^{K}} \left[\sum_{j=1}^{n_{te}} \log\left(\sum_{l=1}^{K} \pi_l p_l\left(x_j^{te}\right) \right) \right]$$

$$s.t. \sum_{i=1}^{n_{tr}}\sum_{l=1}^{K} \pi_l p_l\left(x_i^{tr}\right) = n_{tr}; \pi_1,\pi_2,\ldots,\pi_K \geq 0 \tag{11}$$

When the reduced feature space dimensionality is the same as that of the data dimensionality, i.e., $m = d$, the PM-KLIEP method becomes equivalent to the GM-KLIEP method. Both GM-KLIEP and PM-KLIEP are non-convex optimization problems and thus the optimal solution found is only local but not global.

4.3 FRANK-WOLFE COVARIATE SHIFT

4.3.1 FRANK-WOLFE OPTIMIZATION CONCEPT

The FW optimization algorithm is used to solve problems of the form $\min_{g \in \mathcal{G}} F(g)$ for any function $F : \mathcal{G} \to \mathbb{R}$ that is continuously differentiable and convex with $\mathcal{G}$ as the convex set having the inner product $\mathbf{u}, \mathbf{v} = \sum_j u_j v_j$. The working of the standard FW algorithm for minimization problems is shown in Figure 4.3, where for the initial point $g_0 \in \mathcal{G}$, the goal is to determine the optimal point g. Iteratively, the algorithm determines the point $s_t \in \mathcal{G}$ such that the inner product of gradient of F at the current point g_t and the current candidate s is minimized, thus utilizing the linearization principle instead of the costly projected gradient. The next iterate g_t+1 is updated by moving toward the direction of s_t using a convex combination of g_t and s_t with ρ_t as the step-size, which can be obtained using line-search. The standard FW algorithm converges at the rate $\mathcal{O}(1/T)$ with T iterations required to achieve convergence [16].

Algorithm IWCV for KLIEP

Input: $\{\mathbf{x}_i^{tr}\}_{i=1}^{n_{tr}}, \{\mathbf{x}_j^{te}\}_{j=1}^{n_{te}}$, **Output:** $\mathbf{w} = \{w(\mathbf{x}_i^{tr})\}_{i=1}^{n_{tr}}$

1: Split the test data $\{\mathbf{x}_j^{te}\}_{j=1}^{n_{te}}$ into T disjoint subsets $\{\mathcal{X}_t^{te}\}_{t=1}^{T}$

2: **for** each candidate σ_m **do**

3:     **for** each test split $t = 1, \ldots, T$ **do**

4:         $w_t(\mathbf{x}) \leftarrow KLIEP\left(\{\mathbf{x}_i^{tr}\}_{i=1}^{n_{tr}}, \{\mathcal{X}_j^{te}\}_{j \neq t}\right)$ using σ_m

5:         $J_t(m) \leftarrow \dfrac{1}{|\mathcal{X}_t^{te}|} \sum_{\mathbf{x} \in \mathcal{X}_t^{te}} \log w_t(\mathbf{x})$

6:     **end for**

7:     $J(m) \leftarrow \dfrac{1}{T} \sum_{t=1}^{T} J_t(m)$

8: **end for**

9: Optimum $m' \leftarrow \underset{m}{\operatorname{argmax}} J(m), \sigma_{opt} \leftarrow \sigma_{m'}$

10: Estimate the importance weights $\mathbf{w} \leftarrow KLIEP\left(\{\mathbf{x}_i^{tr}\}_{i=1}^{n_{tr}}, \{\mathbf{x}_j^{te}\}_{j=1}^{n_{te}}\right)$ using σ_{opt}

FIGURE 4.3 Algorithm for standard Frank-Wolfe optimization.

The FW optimization concept has been applied in the literature for various applications: (i) matrix factorization where the convergence was shown using the approximation quality obtained with the FW duality gap [9], (ii) image and video co-localization formulated using FW leading to an improved computational efficiency [10], (iii) structured support vector machine (SSVM) with the SVM duality gap equivalent to the FW duality gap [11], etc. To remove the influence of "bad" visited vertices, the away-steps FW algorithm [18] was shown to converge at a linear convergence rate in [19].

The iterates g_t obtained by the FW algorithm converges to an optimal value at a linear convergence rate only when this optimal solution belongs to the interior of a polytope. If this is not the case, then the convergence rate can be sublinear because of the zig-zagging effects as demonstrated in [20]. To obtain a linear convergence rate, the FW modifications, namely Away-steps FW and Pairwise FW are suggested in the literature [18, 20–22]. These variants of FW algorithms were studied in detail in [20] and a global linear convergence rate was derived for these modifications.

Figure 4.4 shows the directions of the standard FW algorithm as well as the away-steps and pairwise FW from the current solution α_t with α^* as the optimal solution for maximization problems. The toward direction d_t^{FW} is chosen during each iteration by determining the location l_t^{FW} in the standard FW algorithm since this is the direction that maximizes the gradient. But, if the optimal solution lies closer to the boundary of the polytope, the iterates of the standard FW algorithm would zig-zag and thus the algorithm need more iterations to converge [20]. Thus, the away-step direction d_t^{AFW} is preferred by moving away from the location l_t^{AFW} that minimizes the gradient. In the pairwise FW variant, the iterates move pairwise from the away direction to the toward direction to obtain the pairwise direction $d_t^{PFW} = d_t^{FW} + d_t^{AFW}$. Since the pairwise FW variant is efficient in arriving at the optimum solution quickly [20], we present the pairwise FW covariate shift algorithm for computing the importance weights [23].

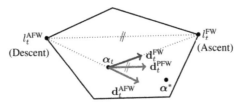

FIGURE 4.4   Toward, away, and pairwise Frank-Wolfe directions for maximization problems [23].

4.3.2   PAIRWISE FRANK-WOLFE COVARIATE SHIFT ALGORITHM

To use the pairwise FW variant for computing the importance weights of KLIEP, the gradient $g = \left[g_1, ..., g_{n_{te}}\right]^{\mathrm{T}}$ of the objective function and the upper bound $\beta = \left[\beta_1, ..., \beta_{n_{te}}\right]^{\mathrm{T}}$ for the constraint on α is given by Eqn. (12) with $0 \leq \alpha_l \leq \beta_l$, for $l = 1, ..., n_{te}$.

$$g_l = \frac{\partial F(\alpha)}{\partial \alpha_l} = \sum_{j=1}^{n_{te}} \frac{\kappa_l\left(\mathbf{x}_j^{te}\right)}{\sum_{l'=1}^{n_{te}} \alpha_{l'} \kappa_{l'}\left(\mathbf{x}_j^{te}\right)}; \beta_l = \frac{n_{tr}}{\sum_{i=1}^{n_{tr}} \kappa_l\left(\mathbf{x}_i^{tr}\right)} \tag{12}$$

Figure 4.5 shows the working of pairwise FW covariate shift (PFWCS) method with the inputs as the train and test data and the output as the importance weight for each input data sample. The iterate α_t can be written as an atomic decomposition given by Eqn. (13) with $\beta^{(l)} = \beta \odot e^{(l)}$ where the basis vector $e^{(l)}$ has 0 everywhere except 1 at the l index, and $\odot$ refers to the Hadamard product. $S_t = \{l : \mu_t(l) \neq 0\}$ (the active set) maintains the locations visited by the algorithm up to the tth iteration such that μ_t is non-zero at those locations. In line 1, the upper bound β is computed and t (iteration counter) is set to 0. In line 2, the following quantities are initialized: α (the mixing coefficients), μ (the atoms) and S (the active set).

$$\alpha_t = \sum_{l=1}^{n_{te}} \mu_t(l) \beta^{(l)}; \text{constraints} : \sum_{l=1}^{n_{te}} \mu_t(l) = 1, \mu_t(l) \geq 0 \tag{13}$$

Lines 3–15 are repeated till the convergence of F to obtain the optimum α. The gradient g_t of F is calculated with Eqn. (12) using which the toward location l_t^{FW} is determined as the index of the largest element-wise product of g_t and β. Using the FW linear maximization principle, the toward (ascent) direction is obtained as $d_t^{FW} = \beta^{(l_t^{FW})} - \alpha_t$. The away direction is also found in line 6 using the location l_t^{AFW}, which corresponds to the index of the smallest element-wise product of g_t and β. A smaller active set S_t is used to find the location l_t^{AFW} making it fundamentally easier to find relative to l_t^{FW}. The away direction is given by $d_t^{AFW} = \alpha_t - \beta^{(l_t^{AFW})}$ since we move away from the location of descent. The algorithm proceeds in the pairwise direction given by Eqn. (14) at each iteration t in line 7 instead of either the toward or away direction, i.e., the solution gets closer to the location l_t^{FW} and also moves away from the location l_t^{AFW} in the *same* iteration.

Algorithm Pairwise Frank-Wolfe Covariate Shift (PFWCS)

Input: $\{\mathbf{x}_i^{tr}\}_{i=1}^{n_{tr}}, \{\mathbf{x}_j^{te}\}_{j=1}^{n_{te}}$, **Output:** $\mathbf{w} = \{w(\mathbf{x}_i^{tr})\}_{i=1}^{n_{tr}}$

1: Compute upper bound β using Eq. (12) and set $t \leftarrow 0$

2: Initialize: $\alpha_0 \leftarrow \mathbf{0}$, $i_\beta \leftarrow \text{argmin}_i(\beta)_i$, $\alpha_0(i_\beta) \leftarrow \beta(i_\beta)$, $\mu_0 \leftarrow \mathbf{0}$, $\mu_0(i_\beta) \leftarrow 1$, $S_0 \leftarrow \{i_\beta\}$

3: **repeat**

4:     Compute gradient $\mathbf{g}_t$ using Eq. (12)   ▷ using previous α_t

5:     Find $l_t^{FW} \leftarrow \text{argmax}_l (\mathbf{g}_t \odot \beta)_l$;

    Compute $\mathbf{d}_t^{FW} \leftarrow \beta^{(l_t^{FW})} - \alpha_t$ ▷ toward direction

6:     Find $l_t^{AFW} \leftarrow \text{argmin}_{l \in S_t} (\mathbf{g}_t \odot \beta)_l$;

    Compute $\mathbf{d}_t^{AFW} \leftarrow \alpha_t - \beta^{(l_t^{AFW})}$ ▷ away direction

7:     Compute $\mathbf{d}_t^{PFW} \leftarrow \mathbf{d}_t^{FW} + \mathbf{d}_t^{AFW}$ ▷ pairwise direction

8:     Compute $\rho_{max} \leftarrow \mu_t(l_t^{AFW})$ ▷ maximum step of pairwise direction

9:     Find $\rho_t \leftarrow \text{argmax}_{\rho \in [0, \rho_{max}]} F(\alpha_t + \rho \mathbf{d}_t^{PFW})$ ▷ found using line search

10:    Update: $\alpha_{t+1} \leftarrow \alpha_t + \rho_t \mathbf{d}_t^{PFW}$

11:    Update: $\mu_{t+1} \leftarrow \mu_t$;

       $\mu_{t+1}(l_t^{FW}) \leftarrow \mu_t(l_t^{FW}) + \rho_t$;

       $\mu_{t+1}(l_t^{AFW}) \leftarrow \mu_t(l_t^{AFW}) - \rho_t$

12:    Update: $S_{t+1} \leftarrow S_t \cup \{l : \mu_{t+1}(l) \neq 0\}$

13:    **if** $(\rho_t == \rho_{max})$ **do**   ▷ modify the active set

      if $(l_t^{FW} \in S_t)$ **do**

         $S_{t+1} \leftarrow S_{t+1} \setminus \{l_t^{AFW}\}$,   ▷ drop step

         $\mu_{t+1}(l_t^{AFW}) \leftarrow 0$

      else

         $S_{t+1} \leftarrow S_{t+1} \cup \{l_t^{FW}\} \setminus \{l_t^{AFW}\}$ ▷ swap step

14:    $t \leftarrow t + 1$

15: **until** the convergence of objective function F in Eq. (5)

16: Compute weights $\mathbf{w}$ with α_t using Eq. (1)

FIGURE 4.5   Algorithm for pairwise Frank-Wolfe covariate shift.

$$\mathbf{d}_t^{PFW} = \underbrace{\beta^{(l_t^{FW})} - \alpha_t}_{} + \underbrace{\alpha_t - \beta^{(l_t^{AFW})}}_{} = \beta^{(l_t^{FW})} - \beta^{(l_t^{AFW})} = \mathbf{d}_t^{FW} + \mathbf{d}_t^{AFW}$$

(14)

In lines 8 and 9, the maximum step-size ρ_{max} guarantees the current solution feasibility with a line search method shown in Figure 4.6, which iterates till the Armijo condition [24] given by Eqn. (15) is satisfied to guarantee an increase in the value of F, where C is the Lipschitz constant.

$$F\left(\alpha_t + \rho d_t\right) \geq F\left(\alpha_t\right) + \tau\rho g_t, d_t \; \forall \rho \in \left[0,\rho^*\right], \text{where } \rho^* = \frac{2\left(\tau-1\right)g_t,d_t}{Cd_{t2}^2} \qquad (15)$$

Algorithm Armijo Line Search

Input: $\alpha_t, \mathbf{d}_t, F, \mathbf{g}_t, \rho_{\max}, \tau \in (0, 1), \xi \in (0, 1),$ **Output:** ρ_t

1: Set $\rho \leftarrow \rho_{\max}$

2: **while** $F(\alpha_t + \rho\mathbf{d}_t) < F(\alpha_t) + \tau\rho\langle \mathbf{g}_t, \mathbf{d}_t \rangle$ **do**

3:     $\rho \leftarrow \xi\rho$

4: **end while**

5: $\rho_t \leftarrow \rho$

FIGURE 4.6   Algorithm for Armijo line search.

For any ρ_t of the PFWCS algorithm, we have:

$$\alpha_t + \rho_t d_t^{\text{PFW}} = \alpha_t + \rho_t\left(\beta^{\left(l_t^{\text{FW}}\right)} - \beta^{\left(l_t^{\text{AFW}}\right)}\right) = \sum_{l=1}^{n_{te}}\mu_t(l)\beta^{(l)} + \rho_t\left(\beta^{\left(l_t^{\text{FW}}\right)} - \beta^{\left(l_t^{\text{AFW}}\right)}\right)$$

$$= \sum_{l \neq l_t^{\text{FW}},\, l_t^{\text{AFW}}}\mu_t(l)\beta^{(l)} + \mu_t\left(l_t^{\text{FW}}\right)\beta^{\left(l_t^{\text{FW}}\right)} + \mu_t\left(l_t^{\text{AFW}}\right)\beta^{\left(l_t^{\text{AFW}}\right)} + \rho_t\left(\beta^{\left(l_t^{\text{FW}}\right)} - \beta^{\left(l_t^{\text{AFW}}\right)}\right)$$

$$= \sum_{l \neq l_t^{\text{FW}},\, l_t^{\text{AFW}}}\mu_t(l)\beta^{(l)} + \left\{\mu_t\left(l_t^{\text{FW}}\right) + \rho_t\right\}\beta^{\left(l_t^{\text{FW}}\right)} + \left\{\mu_t\left(l_t^{\text{AFW}}\right) - \rho_t\right\}\beta^{\left(l_t^{\text{AFW}}\right)}$$

$$= \sum_{l=1}^{n_{te}}\hat{\mu}_t^{\text{PFW}}(l)\beta^{(l)} \qquad (16)$$

To guarantee a feasible solution, it is required that $\sum_{l=1}^{n_{te}}\hat{\mu}_t^{\text{PFW}}(l)=1$ and $\hat{\mu}_t^{\text{PFW}}(l) \geq 0$. From Eqn. (16), it follows that:

$$\sum_{l=1}^{n_{te}}\hat{\mu}_t^{\text{PFW}}(l) = \sum_{l \neq l_t^{\text{FW}},\, l_t^{\text{AFW}}}\mu_t(l) + \left\{\mu_t\left(l_t^{\text{FW}}\right) + \rho_t\right\} + \left\{\mu_t\left(l_t^{\text{AFW}}\right) - \rho_t\right\}$$

$$= \sum_{l \neq l_t^{\text{FW}},\, l_t^{\text{AFW}}}\mu_t(l) + \rho_t - \rho_t = 1, since \sum_{l=1}^{n_{te}}\mu_t(l) = 1$$

Since $\hat{\mu}_t^{\text{PFW}}(l) \geq 0 \forall l$, the maximum value of the step-size $\rho_{\max}$ is given by Eqn. (17).

$$\mu_t\left(l_t^{\text{AFW}}\right) - \rho_{\max} = 0 \therefore \rho_{\max} = \mu_t\left(l_t^{\text{AFW}}\right) \tag{17}$$

After obtaining the optimum step size using the line search algorithm, α, μ and S are updated using Eqns. (18)–(20). Due to the use of the pairwise direction instead of the toward or away directions, only the atoms related to l_t^{FW} and l_t^{AFW} are updated in line 11 without changing the other atoms, resulting in higher computational efficiency. In contrast, the standard FW and its away-steps variant would require to update *all* atoms in each iteration.

$$\alpha_{t+1} = \alpha_t + \rho_t \mathbf{d}_t^{\text{PFW}} \tag{18}$$

$$\mu_{t+1}(l) = \begin{cases} \mu_t(l) \, if \, l \neq l_t^{\text{FW}} \, and \, l \neq l_t^{\text{AFW}}, \\ \mu_t(l) + \rho_t \, if \, l = l_t^{\text{FW}}, \\ \mu_t(l) - \rho_t \, if \, l = l_t^{\text{AFW}} \end{cases} \tag{19}$$

$$S_{t+1} = \begin{cases} S_t \setminus \{l_t^{\text{AFW}}\} \, if \, \rho_t = \rho_{\max} \, and \, l_t^{\text{FW}} \in S_t \, (\text{drop step}), \\ S_t \cup \{l_t^{\text{FW}}\} \setminus \{l_t^{\text{AFW}}\} \, if \, \rho_t = \rho_{\max} \, and \, l_t^{\text{FW}} \notin S_t \, (\text{swap step}), \\ S_t \, if \, \rho_t < \rho_{\max} \, and \, l_t^{\text{FW}} \in S_t, \\ S_t \cup \{l_t^{\text{FW}}\} \, if \, \rho_t < \rho_{\max} \, and \, l_t^{\text{FW}} \notin S_t \end{cases} \tag{20}$$

The PFWCS algorithm can take several steps as follows:

- *Good step,* if rmax = 1, or rmax < 1 and rt < rmax;
- *Drop step,* if rt = rmax < 1 and $l_t^{\text{FW}} \in S_t$; in this case, $\mu_t\left(l_t^{\text{AFW}}\right) = 0$ as well as the location l_t^{AFW} is removed from the active set St;
- *Swap step,* if rt = rmax < 1 and $l_t^F W \notin S_t$; in this case, the locations l_t^{AFW} and l_t^{FW} are swapped in St.

For the PFWCS algorithm, with the set $\mathcal{A} \subseteq \mathbb{R}^d$ consisting of a finite number of atoms, the number of good steps, drop steps and swap steps till the tth iteration are bounded by $t/(3|\mathcal{A}|!+1)$, $t/2$ and $3|\mathcal{A}|!$, respectively [20]. The computational complexity of the PFWCS algorithm is $\mathcal{O}(1/t)$ since the error function $h_t = F(\alpha_t) - F(\alpha^*)$ for an optimal solution α^* follows a linear convergence rate $h_t < h_0 \exp(-vs(t))$ where v depends on the curvature constant of the objective function F.

To determine the importance weights $\mathrm{w} = \left\{ w\left(\mathrm{x}_i^{\mathrm{tr}}\right)\right\}_{i=1}^{n_{\mathrm{tr}}}$, we can use the PFWCS algorithm instead of the original KLIEP algorithm as illustrated in the next subsection and the optimum tuning σ parameter can be obtained using the importance-weighted cross-validation as before using PFWCS algorithm in the place of KLIEP. The KLIEP algorithm uses only a random subset of the test data for the Gaussian centers to reduce the computational overhead; however, this may not be an optimal approach due to the randomness involved. An advantage of the PFWCS algorithm is that the entire test data set can be used for determining the optimum mixing coefficients, since during each iteration, only one Gaussian center is activated due to the FW linear maximization and minimization principle.

4.3.3   ILLUSTRATIVE RESULTS OF KLIEP AND PFWCS

To evaluate the performance of PFWCS algorithm relative to the original KLIEP algorithm, synthetic data is generated using $y = 1 - 2x^3 + 3$ sinc $(x) + \epsilon$ with the noise $\epsilon \sim \mathcal{N}(0, 0.1^2)$. For simulating the covariate shift, 500 training data points are sampled from $\mathcal{N}(0.5, 0.5^2)$ and 300 testing data points are sampled from $\mathcal{N}(0, 0.3^2)$. Figures 4.7(a) and 4.7(b) shows the importance weights of KLIEP as well as PFWCS algorithms on this synthetic data, where it is observed that both algorithms obtain identical importance weights; however, as shown in Figure 4.7(c), the PFWCS algorithm results in significantly sparser mixing coefficients α. Figure 4.7(d) illustrates the log-scale run-time with changing sample size of the synthetic data ($n_{\mathrm{tr}} = n_{\mathrm{te}}$). It is observed that the PFWCS algorithm is consistently faster relative to the KLIEP algorithm for estimating the importance weights. Thus, the PFWCS algorithm is computationally efficient and obtains sparse solutions.

4.4   IMPORTANCE WEIGHTED STRUCTURED REGRESSION

The regression theory aims at predicting a real value from the observed variables. Specifically, structured regression is applicable when the output target variable is multi-dimensional and these target dimensions may be dependent on each other. Some examples are i) human pose estimation is a structured regression problem in computer vision since the target pose is multi-dimensional and ii) music mood estimation is a structured regression problem in music information retrieval since the music mood represented as a numerical vector value on the two-dimensional valence arousal space is correlated to a certain degree between valence and arousal [25]. Instead of estimating inaccurately each target dimension separately, structured regression aims to consider the dependency between the target dimensions to improve the prediction performance. We discuss TGP structured regression concept proposed in [12] to address this aspect and apply the PFWCS importance weights to correct the covariate shift during the learning of structured regression.

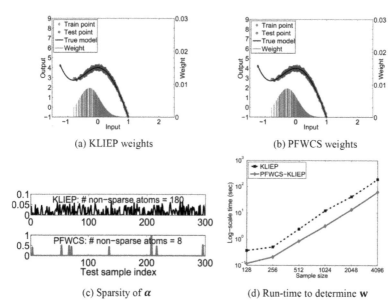

(a) KLIEP weights   (b) PFWCS weights

(c) Sparsity of α (d) Run-time to determine $\mathbf{w}$

FIGURE 4.7   Comparison of KLIEP and PFWCS algorithms.

4.4.1   GAUSSIAN PROCESS REGRESSION

Gaussian process regression (GPR) is used to describe distributions over functions and can be interpreted as a nonparametric Bayesian version of support vector regression (SVR) [26]. Formally, the gaussian process (GP) is defined as "a collection of random variables any finite number of which has a joint Gaussian distribution" [26]. Consider the feature matrix $X \in \mathbb{R}^{N \times D}$ of N input instances with D dimensions. Any finite number of function values $f(x)$ has a joint multivariate normal (MVN) distribution defined by the mean function $\mu:\mathbb{R}^D \to \mathbb{R}$ and the covariance function $\Sigma:\mathbb{R}^D \times \mathbb{R}^D \to \mathbb{R}$ with the elements $\Sigma_{ij} = \kappa(\mathrm{x}_i,\mathrm{x}_j)$ where κ is any kernel function satisfying Mercer's conditions. The GP defines a prior over functions given by Eqn. (21) using which the posterior predictive density can be obtained using the observed training data.

$$f(\mathrm{x}) \sim GP(m(\mathrm{x}),\kappa(\mathrm{x},\mathrm{x}'))$$
$$m(\mathrm{x}) = E\left[f(\mathrm{x})\right]; \kappa(\mathrm{x}_i,\mathrm{x}_j) = E\left[(f(\mathrm{x}_i) - m(\mathrm{x}))(f(\mathrm{x}_j) - m(\mathrm{x}))^{\mathrm{T}}\right] \qquad (21)$$

Consider the noisy observations with training data $\mathcal{D} = \{(\mathrm{x}_i, y_i = f(\mathrm{x}_i) + \epsilon)\}_{i=1}^{N}$ where $\epsilon \sim \mathcal{N}(0, \sigma_y^2)$. For the test data $\mathrm{X}_* \in \mathbb{R}^{N_* \times D}$, the task is to predict the corresponding outputs y_*. Using the GP definition, the joint distribution is given by Eqn. (22) assuming zero-mean, where $\mathrm{K} = \kappa(\mathrm{X},\mathrm{X}) \in \mathbb{R}^{N \times N}$ is the Gram matrix, $\mathrm{K}_* = \kappa(\mathrm{X},\mathrm{X}_*) \in \mathbb{R}^{N \times N_*}$, $\mathrm{K}_{**} = \kappa(\mathrm{X}_*,\mathrm{X}_*) \in \mathbb{R}^{N_* \times N_*}$ and I_N is the identity matrix.

$$\begin{pmatrix} \mathrm{y} \\ \mathrm{y}_* \end{pmatrix} \sim \mathcal{N}\left(0, \begin{bmatrix} \mathrm{K} + \sigma_y^2 \mathrm{I}_N & \mathrm{K}_* \\ \mathrm{K}_*^{\mathrm{T}} & \mathrm{K}_{**} \end{bmatrix}\right) \qquad (22)$$

Using the Bayes' rule, the posterior predictive density is given by Eqn. (23) and for a single test sample, the posterior is given by Eqn. (24) where $\mathrm{k}_* = \left[\kappa(\mathrm{x}_*,\mathrm{x}_1),\dots,\kappa(\mathrm{x}_*,\mathrm{x}_N)\right] \in \mathbb{R}^N$ and $k_{**} = \kappa(\mathrm{x}_*,\mathrm{x}_*) \in \mathbb{R}$. The log marginal likelihood of GP is given by Eqn. (25), where the first term is the only term that involves the output data and controls the quality of model fit, the second (regularization) term penalizes the complexity of the GP model and the third term is a constant.

$$p(\mathrm{y}_* \mid \mathrm{X}_*,\mathrm{X},\mathrm{y}) = N(\mathrm{y}_* \mid \mu_*,\Sigma_*),$$
$$\mu_* = \mathrm{K}_*^{\mathrm{T}}\left(\mathrm{K} + \sigma_y^2 \mathrm{I}_N\right)^{-1}\mathrm{y}, \Sigma_* = \mathrm{K}_{**} - \mathrm{K}_*^{\mathrm{T}}\left(\mathrm{K} + \sigma_y^2 \mathrm{I}_N\right)^{-1}\mathrm{K}_* \qquad (23)$$

$$p(y_* \mid \mathrm{x}_*,\mathrm{X},\mathrm{y}) = \mathcal{N}\left(y_* \mid \mathrm{k}_*^{\mathrm{T}}\left(\mathrm{K} + \sigma_y^2 \mathrm{I}_N\right)^{-1}\mathrm{y}, k_{**} - \mathrm{k}_*^{\mathrm{T}}\left(\mathrm{K} + \sigma_y^2 \mathrm{I}_N\right)^{-1}\mathrm{k}_*\right) \qquad (24)$$

$$\log p(\mathrm{y} \mid \mathrm{X}) = -\frac{1}{2}\mathrm{y}^{\mathrm{T}}\left(\mathrm{K} + \sigma_y^2 \mathrm{I}_N\right)^{-1}\mathrm{y} - \frac{1}{2}\log\left|\mathrm{K} + \sigma_y^2 \mathrm{I}_N\right| - \frac{N}{2}\log 2\pi \qquad (25)$$

The performance of GPR depend on the kernel choice as well as its hyper-parameters. For the squared exponential kernel $\kappa\left(x_i, x_j\right) = \sigma_f^2 \exp\left(-\dfrac{1}{2l^2}\left\|x_i - x_j\right\|^2\right)$, l represents the function's horizontal scale, σ_f^2 and σ_y^2 refers to the function's vertical scale and the noise variance, respectively. Overfitting is a less significant problem in GP since a relatively small number of parameters needs to be estimated. An illustration of the GP prediction with various hyper-parameter settings is shown in Figure 4.8, where the result varies from a smooth fit to a wiggly fit.

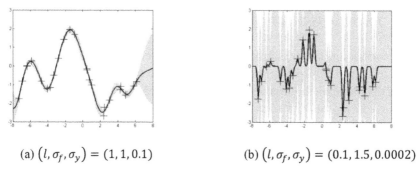

(a) $\left(l, \sigma_f, \sigma_y\right) = (1, 1, 0.1)$ (b) $\left(l, \sigma_f, \sigma_y\right) = (0.1, 1.5, 0.0002)$

FIGURE 4.8   1D GPs fitted to 25 noisy observations using a squared exponential 1 kernel.

An algorithm to compute the mean, variance, and the log marginal likelihood of GPR is shown in Figure 4.9, where Cholesky decomposition is used for $K_y = K + \sigma_y^2 I = LL^T$ to determine the inverse of K_y instead of directly finding the inverse to avoid numerical instability. The computational complexity is $\mathcal{O}(N^3)$ for the Cholesky decomposition and $\mathcal{O}(N^2)$ for $\zeta = K_y^{-1}y$.

Algorithm Gaussian Process Regression

    Input: $\mathbf{X}$ (features), $\mathbf{y}$ (target), κ (kernel), σ_y^2 (noise variance), $\mathbf{x}_*$ (test data)

    Output: Mean, variance and log marginal likelihood

1: $\mathbf{L} = \mathrm{chol}(\mathbf{K} + \sigma_y^2 \mathbf{I})$ ▷ Cholesky decomposition

2: $\zeta = \mathbf{L}^{-\top}\mathbf{L}^{-1}\mathbf{y} = \mathbf{L}^\top \setminus (\mathbf{L} \setminus \mathbf{y})$

3: Predictive mean: $\mathbb{E}[\mathbf{x}_*] = \mathbf{k}_*^\top \zeta$

4: Predictive variance: $\mathbb{V}[\mathbf{x}_*] = k_{**} - \mathbf{k}_*^\top \mathbf{L}^{-\top}\mathbf{L}^{-1}\mathbf{k}_*$

5: Log marginal likelihood: $\log p(\mathbf{y} \mid \mathbf{X}) = -\dfrac{1}{2}\mathbf{y}^\top \zeta - \displaystyle\sum_i \log L_{ii} - \dfrac{N}{2}\log(2\pi)$

FIGURE 4.9   Algorithm for gaussian process regression.

To maximize the log marginal likelihood, the gradient with respect to the hyper-parameters of the kernel denoted by θ is computed by Eqn. (26). The value for $\frac{\partial \mathbf{K}_y}{\partial \theta}$ depends on the kernel used in GP and any standard gradient-based optimizer can be used to estimate the hyper-parameters of GP.

$$\frac{\partial}{\partial \theta_j} \log p(\mathbf{y} \mid \mathbf{X}) = \frac{1}{2}\mathbf{y}^\mathsf{T}\mathbf{K}_y^{-1}\frac{\partial \mathbf{K}_y}{\partial \theta_j}\mathbf{K}_y^{-1}\mathbf{y} - \frac{1}{2}tr\left(\mathbf{K}_y^{-1}\frac{\partial \mathbf{K}_y}{\partial \theta_j}\right)$$
$$= \frac{1}{2}tr\left(\left(\zeta\alpha^\mathsf{T} - \mathbf{K}_y^{-1}\right)\frac{\partial \mathbf{K}_y}{\partial \theta_j}\right) \tag{26}$$

4.4.2 TWIN GAUSSIAN PROCESS REGRESSION

The conventional GPR technique does not model any dependency existing in the structured (multi-dimensional) output, and thus TGP can be used that models this dependency between the target dimensions. The TGP structured regression based on Kullback-Leibler divergence [12] uses the input joint probability distribution given by $p(X,x) = \mathcal{N}_X\left(0,K_{X\cup x}\right)$ and the output joint probability distribution given by $p(Y,y) = \mathcal{N}_Y\left(0,K_{Y\cup y}\right)$. The joint kernels are defined by Eqn. (27) where x is the test data corresponding to the unknown structured output y. The input and output Gaussian similarity kernels are given by Eqn. (28), where λ_x and λ_Y are the regularization parameters, ρ_x and ρ_Y correspond to the kernel bandwidths, and δ is the Kronecker delta function. Here, K_X is a $N \times N$ kernel matrix, k_X^x is a vector with elements given by $\left(k_X^x\right)_i = K_X\left(x_i,x\right)$, $k_X(x,x)$ is a scalar, and thus $K_{X\cup x} \in \mathbb{R}^{(N+1)\times(N+1)}$. The output kernels $K_{Y\cup y}$, K_Y, k_Y^y and $k_Y(y,y)$ can be similarly defined.

$$K_{X\cup x} = \begin{bmatrix} K_X & k_X^x \\ k_X^{xT} & k_X\left(x,x\right) \end{bmatrix}, K_{Y\cup y} = \begin{bmatrix} K_Y & k_Y^y \\ k_Y^{yT} & k_Y\left(y,y\right) \end{bmatrix} \tag{27}$$

$$\left(K_X\right)_{ij} = \exp\left(-\frac{\left\|x_i - x_j\right\|^2}{2\rho_X^2}\right) + \lambda_X\delta_{ij}; \left(K_Y\right)_{ij} = \exp\left(-\frac{\left\|y_i - y_j\right\|^2}{2\rho_Y^2}\right) + \lambda_Y\delta_{ij} \tag{28}$$

The goal of KLTGP is to ensure that (i) the training data samples distant from the test data should be given less importance towards prediction, (ii) the training data samples close to the test data but with corresponding training outputs distant from the test output should also be given less importance towards prediction, and (iii) the similar training and test inputs and outputs should contribute significantly for the prediction [12]. KLTGP minimizes the KL divergence between the marginal input and output GPes and the predicted multivariate output is obtained using the optimization problem given by Eqn. (29), where $u_x = K_X^{-1} k_X^x$ and $\eta_x = k_X(x,x) - k_X^{xT} u_x$. The gradient with respect to the rth multivariate output dimension is given by Eqn. (30). For Gaussian kernels, $\dfrac{\partial k_Y(y,y)}{\partial y^{(r)}} = 0$ and the remaining partial derivatives are given by Eqn. (31).

$$\hat{y} = \operatorname{argmin}_y \left[L_{KL}(x,y) = k_Y(y,y) - 2k_Y^{yT} u_x - \eta_x \log\left(k_Y(y,y) - k_Y^{yT} K_Y^{-1} k_Y^y \right) \right] \tag{29}$$

$$\frac{\partial L_{KL}(x,y)}{\partial y^{(r)}} = \frac{\partial k_Y(y,y)}{\partial y^{(r)}} - 2u_x^T \frac{\partial k_Y^y}{\partial y^{(r)}} - \eta_x \frac{\log\left[\dfrac{\partial k_Y(y,y)}{\partial y^{(r)}} - 2k_Y^{yT} K_Y^{-1} \dfrac{\partial k_Y^y}{\partial y^{(r)}} \right]}{\left(k_Y(y,y) - k_Y^{yT} K_Y^{-1} k_Y^y \right)} \tag{30}$$

$$\frac{\partial k_Y^y}{\partial y^{(r)}} = \begin{bmatrix} -\dfrac{1}{\rho_Y^2}\left(y_1^{(r)} - y^r\right) k_Y(y_1, y) \\[2mm] -\dfrac{1}{\rho_Y^2}\left(y_2^{(r)} - y^r\right) k_Y(y_2, y) \\[2mm] \cdots \\[2mm] -\dfrac{1}{\rho_Y^2}\left(y_N^{(r)} - y^r\right) k_Y(y_N, y) \end{bmatrix} \tag{31}$$

Another TGP model based on the generalized Sharma-Mittal divergence (SMTGP) was proposed in [27] with two parameters (τ, ψ) and was found to perform better than KLTGP on several datasets. The Sharma-Mittal (SM) divergence between two Gaussian distributions $\mathcal{N}_p = \mathcal{N}(\mu_p, \Sigma_p)$ and $\mathcal{N}_q = \mathcal{N}(\mu_q, \Sigma_q)$ is given by Eqn. (32) where $\Delta\mu = \mu_p - \mu_q$, $|\cdot|$ denotes the matrix determinant and $\tau\Sigma_p^{-1} + (1-\tau)\Sigma_q^{-1}$ is a positive definite matrix.

$$L_{\tau,\psi}(\mathcal{N}_p, \mathcal{N}_q) \& = \frac{1}{\psi - 1} \left[\left(\frac{|\Sigma_p|^\tau |\Sigma_q|^{1-\tau}}{\left| \left(\tau\Sigma_p^{-1} + (1-\tau)\Sigma_q^{-1} \right)^{-1} \right|} \right)^{-\frac{1-\psi}{2(1-\tau)}} \times \exp\left(-\frac{\tau(1-\psi)}{2} \Delta\mu^T \left(\tau\Sigma_p^{-1} + (1-\tau)\Sigma_q^{-1} \right)^{-1} \Delta\mu \right) - 1 \right] \tag{32}$$

Applying the closed-form expression of SM divergence given in Eqn. (32) between the input and output joint probability distributions with $\Delta\mu = 0$ results in

$$L_{\tau,\psi}\left(p(X,x),p(Y,y)\right)=\frac{1}{\psi-1}\left[\left(\frac{\left|K_{X\cup x}\right|^{\tau}\left|K_{Y\cup y}\right|^{1-\tau}}{\left|\left(\tau K_{X\cup x}^{-1}+(1-\tau)K_{Y\cup y}^{-1}\right)^{-1}\right|}\right)^{-\frac{1-\psi}{2(1-\tau)}}-1\right] \tag{33}$$

Using the concept from matrix algebra that $\left|A^{-1}\right|=1/\left|A\right|=\left|A\right|^{-1}$ and $\left|AB\right|=\left|A\right|\left|B\right|$, the SM divergence under the TGP setting is simplified as Eqn. (34) and applying this to Eqn. (33) results in Eqn. (35).

$$L_{\tau,\psi}\left(\mathcal{N}_p,\mathcal{N}_q\right)=\frac{1}{\psi-1}\left[\left(\frac{\left|\Sigma_p\right|^{1-\tau}\left|\Sigma_q\right|^{\tau}}{\left|\tau\Sigma_q+(1-\tau)\Sigma_p\right|}\right)^{\frac{1-\psi}{2(1-\tau)}}-1\right] \tag{34}$$

$$L_{\tau,\psi}\left(p(X,x),p(Y,y)\right)=\frac{1}{\psi-1}\left[\left(\frac{\left|K_{X\cup x}\right|^{1-\tau}\left|K_{Y\cup y}\right|^{\tau}}{\left|(1-\tau)K_{X\cup x}+\tau K_{Y\cup y}\right|}\right)^{\frac{1-\psi}{2(1-\tau)}}-1\right] \tag{35}$$

Since the joint kernel matrix $K_{X\cup x}$ is square and non-singular, it can be decomposed as Eqn. (36) using the Aitken block-diagonalization formula [28]. Here, $\eta_x=k_x\left(x,x\right)-k_x^{xT}K_x^{-1}k_x^x$ refers to the Schur complement of $K_{X\cup x}$ whose determinant is $\left|K_{X\cup x}\right|=\left|K_X\right|\times\eta_x$. Similarly, $\eta_y=k_y\left(y,y\right)-k_y^{yT}K_y^{-1}k_y^y$ refers to the Schur complement of $K_{Y\cup y}$ whose determinant is $\left|K_{Y\cup y}\right|=\left|K_Y\right|\times\eta_y$.

$$K_{X\cup x}=\begin{bmatrix}I & 0\\ k_x^{xT}K_x^{-1} & I\end{bmatrix}\begin{bmatrix}K_X & 0\\ 0 & \eta_x\end{bmatrix}\begin{bmatrix}I & K_x^{-1}k_x^x\\ 0 & I\end{bmatrix} \tag{36}$$

The Schur complements η_x and η_y can be interpreted as the change in the variance of GP relative to the test data x. Both η_x and η_y have an upper bound of $k_X(x,x)$ and $k_Y(y,y)$ and they decrease when the test data x becomes close to X. The terms of Eqn. (35) can be written as:

$$\left|K_{Y\cup y}\right|^{\frac{\tau(1-\psi)}{2(1-\tau)}}=\left|K_Y\right|^{\frac{\tau(1-\psi)}{2(1-\tau)}}\left(k_Y\left(y,y\right)-k_Y^{yT}K_Y^{-1}k_Y^y\right)^{\frac{\tau(1-\psi)}{2(1-\tau)}}$$

and

$$\left|(1-\tau)K_{X\cup x}+\tau K_{Y\cup y}\right|^{-\frac{(1-\psi)}{2(1-\tau)}}=\left|(1-\tau)K_X+\tau K_Y\right|^{-\frac{(1-\psi)}{2(1-\tau)}}$$
$$\times\left(k_{XY}^{\tau}-k_{XY}^{xyT}\left((1-\tau)K_X+\tau K_Y\right)^{-1}k_{XY}^{xy}\right)^{-\frac{(1-\psi)}{2(1-\tau)}}$$

where $k_{XY}^{\tau} = (1-\tau)k_X(x,x) + \tau k_Y(y,y) \in \mathbb{R}$, $k_{XY}^{xy} = (1-\tau)k_X^x + \tau k_Y^y \in \mathbb{R}^N$ and

$K_{XY} = (1-\tau)K_X + \tau K_Y \in \mathbb{R}^{N \times N}$. Ignoring the constants $\left| K_{X \cup x} \right|^{\frac{1-\psi}{2}}$, $\left| K_Y \right|^{\frac{\tau(1-\psi)}{2(1-\tau)}}$,

$\left| (1-\tau)K_X + \tau K_Y \right|^{-\frac{(1-\psi)}{2(1-\tau)}}$ and (-1) that do not depend on the unknown y, the
SMTGP optimization function to determine the predicted output is given by
Eqn. (37).

$$\hat{y} = \mathrm{argmin}_y \frac{1}{\psi-1}\left[\left(k_Y(y,y) - k_Y^{yT}K_Y^{-1}k_Y^y \right)^{\frac{\tau(1-\psi)}{2(1-\tau)}} \times \left(k_{XY}^{\tau} - k_{XY}^{xyT}K_{XY}^{-1}k_{XY}^{xy} \right)^{-\frac{(1-\psi)}{2(1-\tau)}} \right] \qquad (37)$$

The gradient of the SMTGP optimization function with respect to the rth
structured output dimension is given by Eqn. (38) obtained using chain-rule
and rearrangement.

$$\frac{\partial L_{\tau,\psi}}{\partial y^{(r)}} = \frac{-\tau}{2(1-\tau)} \& \left[\left(k_Y(y,y) - k_Y^{yT}K_Y^{-1}k_Y^y \right)^{\frac{\tau(1-\psi)}{2(1-\tau)}-1} \right.$$
$$\times \left(-2k_Y^{yT}K_Y^{-1}\frac{\partial k_Y^y}{\partial y^{(r)}} \right) \times \left(k_{XY}^{\tau} - k_{XY}^{xyT}K_{XY}^{-1}k_{XY}^{xy} \right)^{-\frac{(1-\psi)}{2(1-\tau)}} \right]$$
$$+ \frac{1}{2(1-\tau)}\left[\left(k_Y(y,y) - k_Y^{yT}K_Y^{-1}k_Y^y \right)^{\frac{\tau(1-\psi)}{2(1-\tau)}} \right.$$
$$\times \left(k_{XY}^{\tau} - k_{XY}^{xyT}K_{XY}^{-1}k_{XY}^{xy} \right)^{-\frac{(1-\psi)}{2(1-\tau)}-1} \times \left(-2k_{XY}^{xyT}K_{XY}^{-1}\tau \frac{\partial k_Y^y}{\partial y^{(r)}} \right) \right] \qquad (38)$$

4.4.3 DIRECT TGP

An efficient version of KLTGP known as direct TGP (DTGP) was proposed
in [29] using simple algebraic manipulations of the KLTGP optimization
problem. Instead of directly optimizing for y, DTGP optimizes the output
kernel function $t_y = k_Y^y$ having elements $\left(k_Y^y \right)_i = K_Y(y_i, y)$. After estimating
t_y, the top P nearest outputs are obtained by ranking based on t_y and then the
prediction is obtained as the weighted sum over these P nearest neighbors
(NN). The optimization function of DTGP is given by Eqn. (39) where
$k_Y(y,y) = 1 + \lambda_Y$ due to Gaussian kernels.

$$\min_{t_y} \left[1 + \lambda_Y - 2t_Y^T u_x - \eta_x \log\left(1 + \lambda_Y - t_Y^T K_Y^{-1} t_y\right) \right]$$
$$s.t. \, 0 \le t_{y,i} \le 1 + \lambda_Y, i = 1,2,\dots,N \tag{39}$$

Differentiating Eqn. (39) with respect to t_y without considering the constraints and equating to zero results in Eqn. (40), where μ is a scalar given by Eqn. (41).

$$t_y = \mu K_Y u_x \tag{40}$$

$$\mu = \frac{1 + \lambda_Y - t_Y^T K_Y^{-1} t_y}{\eta_x} \tag{41}$$

Plugging Eqn. (40) into Eqn. (39), the optimization problem can now be re-written as:

$$\min_{\mu} \left[1 + \lambda_Y - 2\mu a - \eta_x \log\left(1 + \lambda_Y - \mu^2 a\right) \right] \tag{42}$$

where; $a = u_x^T K_Y u_x$ is a constant. This is a much easier problem to solve since only a scalar μ has to be optimized instead of optimizing for t_y or y. Differentiating Eqn. (42) with respect to μ and equating to zero, the closed-form solution is given by:

$$\hat{\mu} = \frac{-\eta_x + \sqrt{\eta_x^2 + 4a\left(1 + \lambda_Y\right)}}{2a} \tag{43}$$

The final optimal solution is given by Eqn. (44) with the computational complexity of $O(N)$. Here, the min and max operations for vectors are applied element-wise.

$$\hat{t}_y = \min\left(\left(1 + \lambda_Y\right)1, \, \max\left(0, \hat{\mu} K_Y u_x\right)\right) \tag{44}$$

To simplify the computations of DTGP, P nearest neighbors (NN) $\left\{ y_p, \hat{t}_{y,p} \right\}_{p=1}^P$ are found from $\{y_i\}_{i=1}^N$ for each test sample x depending on the weights γ_p. The structured output $\hat{y}$ is predicted using the weighted sum of P nearest training data samples given by Eqn. (45). Since $\hat{t}_{y,p}$ is a Gaussian kernel, i.e., $\hat{t}_{y,p} = \exp\left(-\frac{1}{2\rho_Y^2} \|y - y_p\|^2\right)$, it can also be re-written as $\log\left(\hat{t}_{y,p}\right) \propto -\|y - y_p\|^2$. The weight γ_p captures the input-output and between-output dependency for structured regression [29].

$$\hat{y} = \sum_{p=1}^{P} \gamma_p \mathbf{y}_p ; \gamma_p = \frac{\hat{t}_{y,p}}{\sum_{p=1}^{P} \hat{t}_{y,p}} \tag{45}$$

The DTGP method is easy to implement and can estimate the predicted output $\hat{y}$ without the need for computationally expensive non-linear optimizers that are required for KLTGP and SMTGP structured regression methods.

4.4.4 IMPORTANCE WEIGHTED TGPS

The likelihood of the GP regression model for the rth dimension under the covariate shift is given by Eqn. (46) [30, 31], where $\hat{y}$ is the predicted regression value.

$$\prod_{i=1}^{n_{tr}} p\left(y_i^{(r)tr} \mid x_i^{tr}\right)^{w\left(x_i^{tr}\right)} \propto \prod_{i=1}^{n_{tr}} \frac{1}{\sqrt{2\pi\sigma^2}} \exp\left[-\frac{1}{2\sigma^2} w^{\frac{1}{2}}\left(x_i^{tr}\right) y_i^{(r)tr} - w^{\frac{1}{2}}\left(x_i^{tr}\right) \hat{y}_i^{(r)tr2}\right] \tag{46}$$

Thus, the GPR model can therefore be updated by re-weighting each data point by $w^{\frac{1}{2}}\left(x_i^{tr}\right)$. Accordingly, the KLTGP, SMTGP, and DTGP structured regression methods can be modified with the importance weights to correct the covariate shift. The importance weighted joint and marginal kernels of IW-KLTGP, IW-SMTGP, and IW-DTGP are defined in Eqn. (47), where $W = \text{diag}\left\{w(x_1),\ldots,w(x_{n_{tr}})\right\}$ is a diagonal matrix consisting of the importance weights w.

$$\left(K_{X_W}\right)_{ij} = w^{\frac{1}{2}}(x_i) w^{\frac{1}{2}}(x_j) \exp\left(-\frac{x_i - x_j}{2\rho_X^2}^2\right) + \lambda_X \delta_{ij} \Rightarrow K_{X_W} = W^{\frac{1}{2}} K_X W^{\frac{1}{2}},$$

$$\left(K_{Y_W}\right)_{ij} = w^{\frac{1}{2}}(x_i) w^{\frac{1}{2}}(x_j) \exp\left(-\frac{y_i - y_j}{2\rho_Y^2}^2\right) + \lambda_Y \delta_{ij} \Rightarrow K_{Y_W} = W^{\frac{1}{2}} K_Y W^{\frac{1}{2}},$$

$$\left(k_{X_W}^x\right)_i = K_{X_W}(x_i, x) = w^{\frac{1}{2}}(x_i) \exp\left(-\frac{x_i - x^2}{2\rho_X^2}\right) \Rightarrow k_{X_W}^x = W^{\frac{1}{2}} k_X^x,$$

$$\left(k_{Y_W}^y\right)_i = K_{Y_W}(y_i, y) = w^{\frac{1}{2}}(x_i) \exp\left(-\frac{y_i - y^2}{2\rho_Y^2}\right) \Rightarrow k_{Y_W}^y = W^{\frac{1}{2}} k_Y^y,$$

$$k_{XY_W}^{xy} = (1-\tau)k_{X_W}^x + \tau k_{Y_W}^y = W^{\frac{1}{2}} k_{XY}^{xy}, K_{XY_W} = (1-\tau)K_{X_W} + \tau K_{Y_W} = W^{\frac{1}{2}} K_{XY} W^{\frac{1}{2}} \tag{47}$$

The optimization problems of IW-KLTGP, IW-SMTGP, and IW-DTGP are thus given by Eqns. (48), (49) and (50), respectively, using the weighted kernels, where $u_{x_w} = K_{X_w}^{-1} k_{X_w}^{x}$ and $\eta_{x_w} = k_x(x,x) - k_{X_w}^{xT} u_{x_w}$. Note that $k_Y(y,y) = 1 + \lambda_Y$ when using Gaussian kernels and thus is not affected by the importance weights. The corresponding gradients can be accordingly updated with the importance weighted kernels.

$$\hat{y} = \arg\min_y \left[k_Y(y,y) - 2k_{Y_w}^{yT} u_{x_w} - \eta_{x_w} \log\left(k_Y(y,y) - k_{Y_w}^{yT} K_{Y_w}^{-1} k_{Y_w}^{y} \right) \right] \qquad (48)$$

$$\hat{y} = \arg\min_y \frac{1}{\psi - 1} \left[\left(k_Y(y,y) - k_{Y_w}^{yT} K_{Y_w}^{-1} k_{Y_w}^{y} \right)^{\frac{\tau(1-\psi)}{2(1-\tau)}} \times \left(k_{XY}^{\tau} - k_{XY_w}^{xyT} K_{XY_w}^{-1} k_{XY_w}^{xy} \right)^{-\frac{(1-\psi)}{2(1-\tau)}} \right] \qquad (49)$$

$$\min_{t_y} \left[1 + \lambda_Y - 2t_Y^T u_{x_w} - \eta_{x_w} \log\left(1 + \lambda_Y - t_Y^T K_{Y_w}^{-1} t_y \right) \right]$$
$$s.t.\, 0 \le t_{y,i} \le 1 + \lambda_Y, i = 1,2,\dots,N \qquad (50)$$

Using the procedure outlined for DTGP, the analytical solution of IW-DTGP is given by Eqn. (51), where the scalars are obtained using Eqn. (52). The predicted value of IW-DTGP can be obtained using Eqn. (45) by substituting Eqn. (51).

$$\hat{t}_y = \min\left((1+\lambda_Y)1, \ \max\left(0, \hat{\mu}_w K_{Y_w} u_{x_w} \right) \right) \qquad (51)$$

$$\hat{\mu}_w = \frac{-\eta_{x_w} + \sqrt{\eta_{x_w}^2 + 4a_w(1+\lambda_Y)}}{2a_w}; a_w = u_{x_w}^T K_{Y_w} u_{x_w} \qquad (52)$$

4.5   APPLICATION: HUMAN POSE ESTIMATION

Human pose estimation is a challenging research topic in the computer vision domain with several applications such as sports performance analysis, gaming, human-robot interaction, video surveillance, etc. The estimation of structured pose from a single image frame is an ill-posed problem, since multiple joints of body limbs can obtain the same pose projection. Also, the prediction model should be robust to several aspects such as skin color, background scenes, clothing texture and shape, lighting, etc. Covariate shift can be observed in these applications due to changing conditions of pose changes, background, location, etc. The standard benchmark HumanEva dataset [32] is used in this work to evaluate the performance of KLIEP and PFWCS for computing the importance weights as well as the importance weighted TGP structured regression methods.

The HumanEva dataset [32] comprises of multiple view video and motion data with the extracted histogram of oriented Gradients features $\left(\mathbf{x} \in \mathbb{R}^{270}\right)$ of 3 subjects (S_1, S_2, S_3) performing the following motions: gesturing, jogging, boxing, walking, and throwing/catching. Both motion and video captures were synchronized by the software. The associated ground truth given by the output structured pose $\left(\mathbf{y} \in \mathbb{R}^{60}\right)$ is represented using 20 joint markers via torsoDistal, captured with three cameras (C_1, C_2, C_3) resulting in 9,630 image-poses for each camera. Figure 4.10 illustrates sample examples of the HumanEva dataset. Five possible covariate shift scenarios can be observed in the HumanEva dataset for the pose estimation:

1. **Selection Bias (C_1):** All subjects (S_1, S_2, S_3) are considered in the training phase and one subject, either S_1 or S_2 or S_3, is considered in the testing phase. Only the camera C_1 data is used in this scenario.
2. **Selection Bias (C_{1-3}):** The subjects are selected as above but all three camera data C_1, C_2, C_3 is used.
3. **Subject Transfer (C_1):** The subjects in the training and testing phases are different, for example, the subjects S_1 and S_2 are included in the training phase and the subject S_3 is included in the testing phase.
4. **Motion Transfer (C_{1-3}):** Different motions are used in the training and testing phase. The motions used in the training phase are gesturing, jogging, and boxing, and the motions used in the testing phase are walking and throwing/catching.
5. **Camera Transfer:** The camera data used in the training and testing phases is different. C_1 data is used in the training phase and C_2 data is used in the testing phase.

4.5   APPLICATION: HUMAN POSE ESTIMATION

Human pose estimation is a challenging research topic in the computer vision domain with several applications such as sports performance analysis, gaming, human-robot interaction, video surveillance, etc. The estimation of structured pose from a single image frame is an ill-posed problem, since multiple joints of body limbs can obtain the same pose projection. Also, the prediction model should be robust to several aspects such as skin color, background scenes, clothing texture and shape, lighting, etc. Covariate shift can be observed in these applications due to changing conditions of pose changes, background, location, etc. The standard benchmark HumanEva dataset [32] is used in this work to evaluate the performance of KLIEP and PFWCS for computing the importance weights as well as the importance weighted TGP structured regression methods.

The HumanEva dataset [32] comprises of multiple view video and motion data with the extracted histogram of oriented Gradients features $\left(\mathbf{x} \in \mathbb{R}^{270}\right)$ of 3 subjects (S_1, S_2, S_3) performing the following motions: gesturing, jogging, boxing, walking, and throwing/catching. Both motion and video captures were synchronized by the software. The associated ground truth given by the output structured pose $\left(\mathbf{y} \in \mathbb{R}^{60}\right)$ is represented using 20 joint markers via torsoDistal, captured with three cameras (C_1, C_2, C_3) resulting in 9,630 image-poses for each camera. Figure 4.10 illustrates sample examples of the HumanEva dataset. Five possible covariate shift scenarios can be observed in the HumanEva dataset for the pose estimation:

1. **Selection Bias (C_1):** All subjects (S_1, S_2, S_3) are considered in the training phase and one subject, either S_1 or S_2 or S_3, is considered in the testing phase. Only the camera C_1 data is used in this scenario.
2. **Selection Bias (C_{1-3}):** The subjects are selected as above but all three camera data (C_1, C_2, C_3) is used.
3. **Subject Transfer (C_1):** The subjects in the training and testing phases are different, for example, the subjects S_1 and S_2 are included in the training phase and the subject S_3 is included in the testing phase.
4. **Motion Transfer (C_{1-3}):** Different motions are used in the training and testing phase. The motions used in the training phase are gesturing, jogging, and boxing, and the motions used in the testing phase are walking and throwing/catching.
5. **Camera Transfer:** The camera data used in the training and testing phases is different. C_1 data is used in the training phase and C_2 data is used in the testing phase.

All of the above scenarios obey the definition of covariate shift due to different train and test data distributions.

The comparison of PFWCS and KLIEP algorithms for computing the importance weights $\mathbf{w}$ of the HumanEva dataset is shown in Table 4.1 for four sample covariate shift scenarios. To determine the optimal σ parameter of Eqn. (1) for both KLIEP and PFWCS algorithms, the IWCV algorithm is used. The PFWCS algorithm obtains a lower number of non-sparse atoms of α relative to the number of test samples in all covariate shift scenarios. Each experiment is run for 50 trials and the average training run time (seconds) along with the standard deviation is shown. The PFWCS algorithm outperforms the KLIEP algorithm due to its capability of providing sparser solutions with higher computational efficiency. The PFWCS algorithm is thus used for further experiments to determine the importance weights in all covariate shift scenarios.

 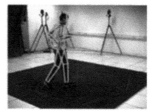 

FIGURE 4.10   Samples of the HumanEva dataset.

TABLE 4.1   Comparison of KLIEP and PFWCS for the HumanEva Dataset

Covariate Shift	Method	# Non-Sparse Atoms of a	Time (s) to Find w
Subject transfer (C_1)	KLIEP	2019 (64%)	27.1 ± 0.24
Train: S_2, S_3; Test: S_1 (# samples: 3135)	PFWCS	471 (15%)	5.4 ± 0.21
Motion transfer (C_{1-3})	KLIEP	2608 (72%)	29.3 ± 0.19
Train: S_1, S_2, S_3; Test: S_2 (# samples: 3622)	PFWCS	689 (19%)	6.2 ± 0.27
Selection bias (C_1)	KLIEP	1792 (62%)	26.7 ± 0.23
Train: S_1, S_2, S_3; Test: S_3 (# samples: 2873)	PFWCS	364 (12%)	4.8 ± 0.41
Camera transfer (C_1)	KLIEP	2341 (74%)	28.5 ± 0.47
Train: S_1, S_2, S_3; S_1, C_2 Test: (# samples: 3135)			

The computational complexity of the various TGP structured regression methods is shown in Table 4.2. The inverse W^{-1} can be trivially computed as $W^{-1} = \mathrm{diag}\left\{ w\left(x_1\right)^{-1}, \dots, w\left(x_{n_{tr}}\right)^{-1} \right\}$ since W is a diagonal matrix. Thus, the complexity of IW-{KL/SM/D}TGP methods is the same as that of the respective {KL/SM/D}TGP methods.

TABLE 4.2   Computational Complexity of TGP Structured Regression Methods

Method	Complexity
KLTGP & IW-KLTGP	$O(N^3)$
SMTGP & IW-SMTGP	$O(N^3)$
DTGP & IW-DTGP	$O(N)$

Both IW-KLTGP and IW-SMTGP has $O(N^3)$ complexity, where N is the number of training data samples, due to the matrix inversion required for solving the optimization function. However, the complexity of IW-DTGP is only $O(N)$ due to the use of simple algebra solution given by Eqn. (51) instead of solving the optimization problem of Eqn. (50), thus avoiding the matrix inversion. Thus, for subsequent experiments, the DTGP and IW-DTGP methods are used for the performance evaluation of covariate shift correction. Even though IW-SMTGP performs relatively better than IW-KLTGP [23], the IW-DTGP method is preferred due to its significantly lower computational complexity.

The evaluation metric for human pose estimation is the joint pose prediction error measured using the Euclidean distance given by Eqn. (53). Here, the true pose is $\mathbf{y}^*$, the estimated pose is $\hat{y}$ and i ranges from 1 to 20 due to the use of 20 3D joint markers.

$$Error_{pose}\left(\mathbf{y}^*,\hat{y}\right) = \frac{1}{20}\sum_{i=1}^{20}\mathbf{y}^{*(i)} - \hat{y}^{(i)} \tag{53}$$

For DTGP, the parameter setting of [12] is used: $\lambda_x = 10^{-3}, \lambda_y = 10^{-3}, 2\rho_x^2 = 5$ and $2\rho_y^2 = 5\times10^5$. To predict the pose $\hat{y}$, the number (P) of the nearest training instances for (IW-)DTGP is empirically set to 30. The performance of (IW-)DTGP is relatively insensitive to the changes in the value of P since the distance between the samples of both input and output are taken into account using Gaussian kernels [29].

The performance of the joint prediction error for DTGP and IW-DTGP structured regression methods is shown in Table 4.3 for five covariate shift scenarios with different train and test data distributions, averaged across all 5 motions. 50% non-overlapping training and testing sets are chosen randomly for the performance evaluation. This procedure is repeated for 10 trials to avoid the bias due to random sampling, and the resulting average joint errors are reported. The parameter settings are shared by both DTGP and IW-DTGP, but the importance weights $\mathbf{w}$ from the PFWCS algorithm leads to an improved pose estimation thus reducing the regression error of IW-DTGP for all scenarios of covariate shift correction.

TABLE 4.3 Performance Evaluation of Covariate Shift Correction for the HumanEva Dataset

Covariate Shift	Train	Test	DTGP	IW-DTGP
Selection	–	S_1	53.18	52.24
Bias	S_1,S_2,S_3	S_2	52.43	51.65
(C_1)	–	S_3	57.93	56.08
Selection	–	S_1	84.78	82.31
Bias	S_1,S_2,S_3	S_2	85.61	82.76
(C_{1-3})	–	S_3	87.28	85.39
Subject	S_2,S_3	S_1	122.77	120.41
Transfer	S_1,S_3	S_2	106.82	105.18
(C_1)	S_1,S_2	S_3	149.21	135.69
Motion	–	S_1	146.92	143.14
Transfer	S_1,S_2,S_3	S_2	155.28	152.76
(C_{1-3})	–	S_3	149.31	147.83
Camera	–	S_1,C_2	148.66	146.38
Transfer	S_1,S_2,S_3	S_2,C_2	149.29	147.12
(C_1)	–	S_3,C_2	146.71	144.19

Figure 4.11 illustrates the performance of the baseline GPR as well as the DTGP and IW-DTGP structured regression methods for 15 possible covariate shift combinations. For each case, the average joint pose error is shown with respect to the number of training data samples averaged over 10 trials and all 5 motions. If the number of training samples is less, the samples n_{tr} are randomly sampled with replacement from the full training set. These graphs show that the IW-DTGP structured regression method improves the performance significantly relative to the baseline GPR and DTGP for all scenarios. Also, the results of IW-DTGP are significantly better than GPR and DTGP statistically based on a 5% significance level paired t-test.

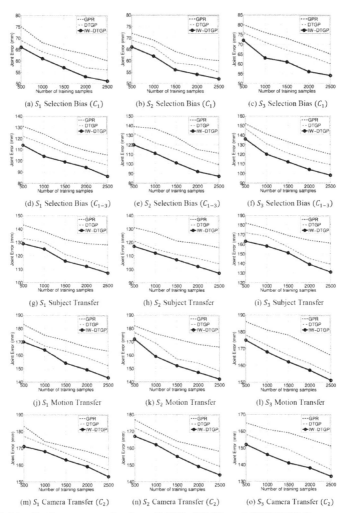

FIGURE 4.11 Performance evaluation of GPR, DTGP, and IW-DTGP for covariate shift correction of the HumanEva dataset.

4.6 CONCLUSION

In many real-world supervised ML applications (such as language processing, intrusion detection systems, etc.), the phenomenon of covariate shift is evident due to the mismatch between the train and test data probability distributions. This problem is solved by computing the importance weights directly from the data without performing the hard task of density estimation in high dimensions.

The training data samples are re-weighted using the importance weights to give more significance to the training data samples closer to the test data. For computing the importance weights, the KLIEP method is used since it has a constrained convex optimization problem which can be efficiently solved. The pairwise FW covariate shift optimization algorithm is presented as an alternative to the KLIEP method resulting in a sparser solution. The PFWCS algorithm is based on the linear maximization/minimization principle of the FW optimization concept, and thus the number of updates required to reach the optimal solution is less leading to higher computational efficiency.

For structured regression problems such as human pose estimation, it is necessary to model the dependency between the multiple target dimensions. Twin GPR methods based on Kullback-Leibler or Sharma-Mittal divergence measures can be used for these problems; however, they require a non-linear optimizer during the training procedure. The direct TGP method has an analytical solution obtained with simple algebra and is thus preferred over KLTGP and SMTGP methods since DTGP can be trained with $O(N)$ cost. These TGP methods are modified for covariate shift correction during the learning process by incorporating the importance weights. The performance is evaluated on the HumanEva dataset for estimating human poses and the covariate shift correction in the learning process results in a reduced regression error. The importance weighted DTGP outperforms DTGP due to the PFWCS importance weights. Following this line of research, correcting the covariate shift for supervised, structured classification problems can be a promising direction to pursue.

KEYWORDS

- **multivariate normal**
- **principal component analysis**
- **structured support vector machine**
- **Twin Gaussian process**
- **Pairwise Frank-Wolfe covariate shift**

REFERENCES

1. Moreno-Torres, J., Raeder, T., Alaiz-Rodriguez, R., Chawla, N., & Herrera, F., (2012). A unifying view on dataset shift in classification. *Pattern Recognition, 45*(1), 521–530.

2. Quionero-Candela, J., Sugiyama, M., Schwaighofer, A., & Lawrence, N., (2009). *Dataset Shift in Machine Learning*. The MIT Press.

3. Sugiyama, M., Suzuki, T., Nakajima, S., Kashima, H., Von, B. P., & Kawanabe, M., (2008). Direct importance estimation for covariate shift adaptation. *Annals of the Institute of Statistical Mathematics, 60*(4), 699–746.

4. Kanamori, T., Hido, S., & Sugiyama, M., (2009). A least-squares approach to direct importance estimation. *Journal of Machine Learning Research, 10*, 1391–1445.

5. Yamada, M., Suzuki, T., Kanamori, T., Hachiya, H., & Sugiyama, M., (2013). Relative density-ratio estimation for robust distribution comparison. *Neural Computation, 25*(5), 1324–1370.

6. Tsuboi, Y., Kashima, H., Bickel, S., & Sugiyama, M., (2009). Direct density ratio estimation for large-scale covariate shift adaptation. *Journal of Information Processing, 17*, 138–155.

7. Yamada, M., & Sugiyama, M., (2009). Direct importance estimation with Gaussian mixture models. *IEICE Transactions on Information and Systems, 92*(10), 2159–2162.

8. Yamada, M., Sugiyama, M., Wichern, G., & Simm, J., (2010). Direct importance estimation with a mixture of probabilistic principal component analyzers. *IEICE Transactions on Information and Systems, 93*(10), 2846–2849.

9. Jaggi, M., (2013). Revisiting Frank-Wolfe: Projection-free sparse convex optimization. *Proc. of the 30th Intl. Conf. on Machine Learning (PMLR), 28*(1), 427–435.

10. Joulin, A., Tang, K., & Fei-Fei, L., (2014). Efficient image and video co-localization with Frank-Wolfe algorithm. *Proc. European Conf. on Computer Vision, 8694*, 253–268.

11. Wen, J., Greiner, R., & Schuurmans, D., (2015). Correcting covariate shift with the Frank-Wolfe algorithm. *Proc. of the 24th Intl. Joint Conf. on Artificial Intelligence*, 1010–1016.

12. Bo, L., & Sminchisescu, C., (2010). Twin Gaussian processes for structured prediction. *Intl. Journal of Computer Vision, 87*(28), 1–25.

13. Sugiyama, M., Krauledat, M., & Muller, K., (2007). Covariate shift adaptation by importance weighted cross-validation. *Journal of Machine Learning Research, 8*, 985–1005.

14. Bishop, C., (2006). *Pattern Recognition and Machine Learning*; Springer-Verlag.

15. Tipping, M., & Bishop, C., (1999). Mixtures of probabilistic principal component analyzers. *Neural Computation, 11*(2), 443–482.

16. Garber, D., & Hazan, E., (2015). Faster rates for the Frank-Wolfe method over strongly-convex sets. *Proc. of the 32nd Intl. Conf. on Machine Learning*, 541–549.

17. Osokin, A., Alayrac, J., Lukasewitz, I., Dokania, P., & Lacoste-Julien, S., (2016). Minding the gaps for block Frank-Wolfe optimization of structured SVMs. *Proc. of the 33rd Intl. Conf. on Machine Learning, 48*, 593–602.

18. GueLat, J., & Marcotte, P., (1986). Some comments on Wolfe's away step. *Mathematical Programming, 35*(1), 110–119.

19. Beck, A., & Shtern, S., (2017). Linearly convergent away-step conditional gradient for non-strongly convex functions. *Mathematical Programming, 164*(1, 2), 1–27.

20. Lacoste-Julien, S., & Jaggi, M., (2015). On the global linear convergence of Frank-Wolfe optimization variants. *Proc. Conf. Advances in Neural Information Processing Systems*.

21. Allende, H., Frandi, E., Nanculef, R., & Sartori, C., (2013). Pairwise away steps for the Frank-Wolfe algorithm. *Proc. Conf. Advances in Neural Information Processing Systems.*

22. Nanculef, R., Frandi, E., Sartori, C., & Allende, H., (2014). A novel Frank-Wolfe algorithm: Analysis and applications to large-scale SVM training. *Information Sciences, 285,* 66–99.

23. Chapaneri, S., & Jayaswal, D., (2019). Covariate shift adaptation for structured regression with Frank-Wolfe algorithms. *IEEE Access, 7,* 73804–73818.

24. Sun, W., & Ya-Xiang, Y., (2006). *Optimization Theory and Methods: Non-linear Programming.* Springer-Verlag.

25. Chapaneri, S., & Jayaswal, D., (2017). Structured prediction of music mood with twin gaussian processes. *Proc. Pattern Recognition and Machine Intelligence (PReMI), 10597,* 647–654.

26. Rasmussen, C., & Williams, C., (2006). *Gaussian Processes for Machine Learning.* The MIT Press.

27. Elhoseiny, M., & Elgammal, A., (2015). Generalized twin Gaussian processes using Sharma-Mittal divergence. *Journal of Machine Learning, 100*(2), 399–424.

28. Tian, Y., & Takane, Y., (2009). More on generalized inverses of partitioned matrices with Banachiewicz-Schur forms. *Linear Algebra and its Applications, 430*(5, 6), 1641–1655.

29. Yamada, M., Sigal, L., & Chang, Y., (2014). Domain adaptation for structured regression. *Intl. Journal of Computer Vision, 109*(2), 126–145.

30. Yamada, M., Sigal, L., & Raptis, M., (2014). Covariate shift adaptation for discriminative 3D pose estimation. *IEEE Tran. Pattern Analysis and Machine Intelligence, 36*(2), 235–247.

31. Shimodaira, H., (2000). Improving predictive inference under covariate shift by weighting the log-likelihood function. *Journal of Statistical Planning and Inference, 90*(2), 227–244.

32. Sigal, L., Balan, A., & Black, M., (2010). HumanEva: Synchronized video and motion capture dataset and baseline algorithm for evaluation of articulated human motion. *Intl. Journal of Computer Vision, 87*(1, 2), 4–27.

CHAPTER 5

Understanding and Building Generative Adversarial Networks

HARSH JALAN and DAKSHATA PANCHAL

Student, Department of Computer Engineering, St. Francis Institute of Technology, Mumbai, Maharashtra, India,
E-mails: harshjalan27@yahoo.com; dakshatapanchal@sfit.ac.in

ABSTRACT

In this chapter, the evolution of generative models such as the various types of autoencoders, gaussian mixture models and Hidden Markov models (HMMs), and generative adversarial networks (GANs) has been discussed in the beginning. Following this, a deep dive into the architecture of GANs, the mathematics behind GANs, and how they are different from other generative models, specifically the vanilla GAN architecture have been explored. A detailed analysis of vanilla GAN for the problems introduced in the training and the quality of generated data, and the limitations of Vanilla GAN that resulted in the growth of the host of GAN architectures that propelled the research forward has been explored. Some of these new versions of GAN architectures such as conditional GAN (CGAN), Wasserstein GAN, StackGAN (v1 and v2), PG-GAN, and StyleGAN (v1 and v2) along with their pros and cons have been addressed. Moreover, various methods for latent-space disentanglement in GANs which helps in controlling the GAN output have been discussed. Although all the above-mentioned architectures were initially developed to generate images, some recent GAN architectures used to generate other types of data such as text and audio have been presented. Finally, various scientific as well as day-to-day life applications of GANs such as data augmentation, Face generation, music generation, and art generation have been presented. New research directions and open-ended questions in GAN have been presented.

5.1   A BRIEF HISTORY OF GENERATIVE MODELS

5.1.1   INTRODUCTION

In machine learning (ML), classification problems can be solved by two main approaches, namely, generative approach and discriminative approach. These approaches mainly differ from each other in the degree of statistical modeling required by each approach:

- In generative approach, given a set of features X and label(s) Y, a generative model can be described as the statistical model of the joint probability distribution on $X \times Y$, $P(X,Y)$. In case there are no labels, the generative model can be described as a statistical model of $P(X)$ [1] (Figure 5.1).

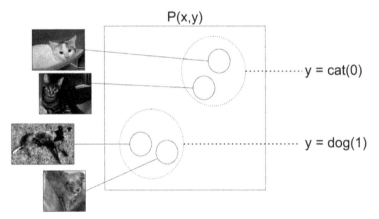

FIGURE 5.1   Generative model.

- A discriminative model, in contrast, tries to model the conditional probability of label(s) Y given a set of features X, i.e., $P(Y|X)$ (Figure 5.2).

In simpler terms, we can say that given a set of features X and label(s) Y, the generative approach asks the question for any given example, "Which label (Y) has the most probability to generate the features X" for example, let's take a problem of captioning bird images, if a caption is given as "A red bird with a yellow beak sitting on a tree branch," A suitable generative model would be capable of understanding what the content of such an image will be, while a discriminative model, on the other hand, cannot derive any meaning from the given label as it can only predict the label (Y) of a given image (X).

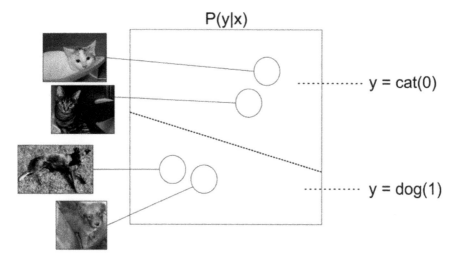

FIGURE 5.2   Discriminative model.

5.1.2   *TYPES OF GENERATIVE MODELS*

A number of popular generative models have been studied in the literature. They are as follows:

- Gaussian mixture models;
- Hidden Markov model;
- Variational autoencoders;
- Boltzmann machines;
- Bayesian networks; and
- Generative adversarial networks, etc.

5.1.3   *GAUSSIAN MIXTURE MODELS*

A mixture model is a probabilistic model which is used for finding the existence of subpopulations within an overall population, without the need of observable labels (identity) for each data point. In some implementations of mixture models, labels or ranks may be given to the individual observations after determining the subpopulation to which the observations belong; this step is very similar to clustering, which is a category of Unsupervised ML, although it is not necessary to label/rank the observations. Therefore, it can be said that mixture models are used to determine properties of different subpopulations from a pooled population without giving the model the identities of the subpopulations (Figure 5.3).

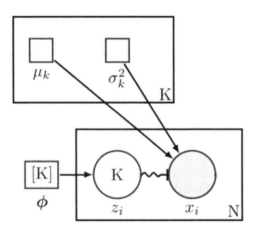

FIGURE 5.3   Non-Bayesian Gaussian mixture models using plate notation.

The mathematical description of a parametric mixture model is as follows:
- K = number of mixture components.
- N = Number of observations.
- $\theta_{i=1\ldots K}$ = Parameter of distribution of observation with component i.
- $\phi_{i=1\ldots K}$ = Mixture weight of a given component i.
- $Z_{i=1\ldots N}$ = Components of an observation i.
- $x_{i=1\ldots N}$ = Observation i.
- $F(x|\theta)$ = Probability distribution of an observation, parameterized on θ.
- $z_{i=1\ldots N} \sim$ Categorical (ϕ).
- $xi = 1\ldots N \sim F(\theta_z)$.

Gaussian mixture models can be derived from parametric mixture models by simply substituting the function F with a normal (if data is continuous) or categorical (if data is discrete) Distribution, collectively known as a Gaussian. Therefore, the Gaussian mixture model can be described as:

- K, N = Same as above;

- $\phi_{i=1...K}$ = Same as above;
- $z_{i=1...N}, x_{i=1...N}$ = Same as above;
- $\theta_{i=1...K} = \{\sigma^2_{i=1...K}\}$;
- $\mu_{i=1...K}$ = Mean of component i;
- $\sigma^2_{i=1...K}$ = Variance of component I;
- $z_{i=1...N} \sim$ Categorical (ϕ);
- $xi = 1 ...N \sim N(\mu_{zi}, \sigma^2_{zi})$.

The expectation-maximization or EM is one of the most popular algorithms which is used for determining the parameters for a gaussian mixture model. Some applications of Gaussian mixture models include image segmentation, point set registration, building financial models, etc. (Figure 5.4).

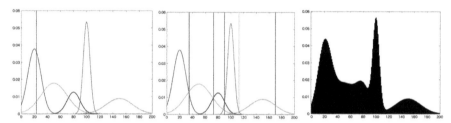

FIGURE 5.4 Image segmentation using GMMs [2]. (Reprinted from [2]. © 2006 Jianhong (Jackie) Shen. https://creativecommons.org/licenses/by/3.0/)

5.1.4 HIDDEN MARKOV MODELS

Hidden Markov models (HMMs) are stochastic statistical models which are used mainly to model randomly changing systems. The system being modeled is assumed to be a Markov Process, say X, which has multiple hidden (or unobservable) states. HMM makes the assumption that another process Y is dependent on X such that at any instance in time n_0, the conditional probability of Y_{n0} given the history $\{X_n = x_n\}_{n \leq n0}$ should only depend on the latest observation that is, x_{n0}.

The mathematical definition of a HMM is given as follows:

$$P(Y_n \in A | X_1 = x_1,..., X_n = x_n) = P(Y_n \in A | X_n = x_n) \tag{1}$$

where; X_n and Y_n are discrete-time stochastic processes; n is the time ($n \geq 1$) and A is a measurable arbitrary set. The states of the process X_n are called unobservable (or hidden) states and $P(Y_n \in A \mid X_n = x_n)$ is called emission (or output) probability.

The goal of the HMM is to calculate the hidden state x for the next time step given the emission output y for the next time step, the transition probabilities linking the hidden states x and the emission probabilities from a hidden state x to an emission output y. The transition and emission probabilities are either calculated on a dataset which contains historic records of the occurrence of hidden states and emission outputs as a time sequence or determined by expert knowledge.

HMMs, when used for inference, generate a time sequence of emission outputs, i.e., one emission output at each time step. This makes HMMs generative in nature. HMMs are widely known for their use in reinforcement learning (RL), speech recognition, gesture recognition (3) and part-of-speech tagging.

In Figure 5.5, the HMM parameters are described as follows:

- **Hidden States:** {Rainy, Sunny}
- **Emission Outputs:** {Happy, Sad}
- **Starting Probabilities $P(x_0)$:** {Rainy: 0.4, Sunny: 0.6}
- **Transition Probabilities $P(x_{n+1} \mid x_n)$:** {Rainy: {Rainy: 0.6, Sunny: 0.4};
  Sunny: {Rainy: 0.3, Sunny: 0.7}}
- **Emission Probabilities $P(y_n \mid x_n)$:** {Rainy: {Sad: 0.8, Happy: 0.2};
  Sunny: {Sad: 0.25, Happy: 0.75}}

Now, given a sequence such as START $\rightarrow$ SAD $\rightarrow$ SAD $\rightarrow$ HAPPY $\rightarrow$ SAD $\rightarrow$ HAPPY $\rightarrow$ END, and the given probabilities, HMMs can predict the weather for each day of the sequence.

5.1.5   VARIATIONAL AUTOENCODERS

Autoencoders are a form of artificial neural networks (ANN), which perform unsupervised learning to learn and compress the underlying features of a dataset into a smaller vector space which is not observed during the training. This smaller space is known as latent space, which is usually represented by Z.

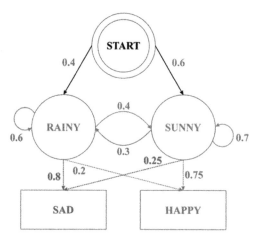

FIGURE 5.5 Hidden Markov model representation.

Figure 5.6 shows a simple autoencoder architecture; this architecture can be divided into two main components from left to right, the first three layers from the left are called the encoder component, while the last two layers are called the decoder component. The input given to the Encoder is a set of features $\{x_1, x_2, ..., x_n\}$ which are then converted into a k-dimensional latent vector $\{z_1, z_2, ..., z_k\}$, this latent vector is then passed through the decoder component, whose task is to predict the original features where the predicted features are denoted by $\{\hat{x}_1, \hat{x}_2, ..., \hat{x}_n\}$. The entire architecture is trained end-to-end using backpropagation and the choice of the loss function depends on the type of features we are trying to predict (usually sigmoid is used if feature values are between 0 and 1 for each feature, and mean squared/absolute error otherwise).

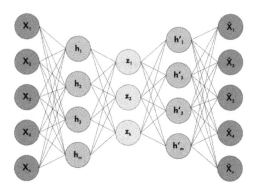

FIGURE 5.6 A simple autoencoder architecture.

These types of autoencoders have various applications such as dimensionality reduction, image denoising, information retrieval and even machine translation. Autoencoders are also known as deep latent variable models (DLVM) [4].

Variational autoencoders (VAEs) differ from regular autoencoders or DLVMs in their choice of a latent-space distribution and their choice of optimization objective (or loss function). VAEs consist of an encoder component, also known as an Inference model and a decoder component, also known as the generative model [4].

For the inference model, q_ϕ, Φ denotes the parameters of the model and it is optimized as follows:

$$q_\phi(z \mid x) \approx p_\theta(z \mid x) \tag{2}$$

where; $p_\theta(z|x)$ is the true posterior probability of the generative model. $p_\theta(z|x)$ is very difficult to control (i.e., intractable) and therefore the inference model is used to approximate it.

The generative model learns a joint distribution $p_\theta(x|z)$ which is often calculated as:

$$p_\theta(x, z) = p_\theta(z) p_\theta(x \mid z) \tag{3}$$

where; $p_\theta(z)$ is a prior distribution over the latent-space Z; and $p_\theta(x|z)$ is the output of the generative model.

Overall, a VAE learns stochastic mapping between the input space X, whose distribution is typically complicated and the latent space Z, whose distribution is comparatively simpler (such as a spherical distribution).

The steps to calculate $q_\phi(z|x)$ are as follows:

$$(\mu, log(\sigma)) = EncoderNeuralNet_\phi(x) \tag{4}$$

$$q_\phi(z \mid x) = N(z; \mu, diag(\sigma)) \tag{5}$$

The optimization objective is the Evidence Lower Bound [4] or ELBO which is written as:

$$L_{\theta, \Phi(x)} = \mathbb{E}_{q\Phi(z|x)} [log[p_\theta(x, z)] - log[q_\phi(z \mid x)]] \tag{6}$$

where; $\mathbb{E}_{q\Phi(z|x)}$ represents the expected value of $q_\Phi(z|x)$. The maximization of $L_{\theta,\Phi(x)}$ w.r.t θ and Φ will concurrently optimize two things:

- It will approximately maximize the marginal likelihood term $p_\theta(x)$, which means that the generative model will become better.
- The Kullback-Leibler (KL) Divergence of $q_\Phi(z|x)$ from $P_\Phi(z|x)$ will be minimized, so the inference model or $q_\Phi(z|x)$ becomes better. This is because:

$$log\left(p_\theta\left(x\right)\right) = L_{\theta,\Phi(x)} + D_{KL}\left(q_\Phi\left(z|x\right) \| p_\theta\left(z|x\right)\right) \qquad (7)$$

where; $D_{KL}(.)$ is the KL-divergence term and $D_{KL}(.)$ is always non-negative.

Alternatively, the KL-Divergence of $q_\Phi(z|x)$ from $P_\Phi(z)$ can be minimized to train the inference and generative models.

VAEs are used for solving a wide variety of problems such as drug discovery [5], population data synthesis [6], image synthesis, language model generation, text generation and text interpolation among many others.

5.2 GENERATIVE ADVERSARIAL NETWORKS

5.2.1 VANILLA GAN

Generative adversarial networks is a framework for generative model estimation via an adversarial (combative or oppositional) process, introduced in 2014 by Goodfellow et al. The framework, which is comparable to a two-player minimax game, pits two neural network (NN) models (a Generator and a Discriminator) against each other [7].

The generator is tasked with generating data $\hat{x}$ given an input vector z, i.e., $\hat{x}=G(z)$ where G is the generator function. The discriminator, on the other hand, is tasked with recognizing whether the given input data *(X)* is coming from the actual training data or from the generator, i.e., $\hat{y}=D(X)$, where $\hat{y}\in[0,1]$, here, 0 means the image is fake and 1 means the image is real. The generator wins if the discriminator is unable to classify the fake image from the real image and vice versa [7].

The idea of GANs can be best understood by comparing it with the idea of a Currency Forger and the Police, where the Currency Forger tries to produce fake currency to fool the Police, which is tasked with differentiating the Fake Currency with Real Currency. Here the generator is analogous with the currency forger and the discriminator is analogous to the police [7]. Figure 5.7 gives an overview of how the training in GANs progresses with time.

Initially, the Generator will not be able to output anything meaningful which makes it very easy for the Discriminator to recognize the fake images from the real ones.

However, after a few epochs (iterations) of training, the Generator starts figuring out some of the basic structures in the dataset, which are reflected in its output.

Then, after a sufficient number of epochs have passed, the Generator, in theory, should be able to generate data which is good enough to fool the Discriminator, at this point the training is stopped as the Discriminator cannot provide any meaningful outputs to train the Generator.

FIGURE 5.7   Training progress of GANs.

5.2.2   *VANILLA GAN ARCHITECTURE*

The generator and the discriminator network architectures make up the entire vanilla GAN architecture. Although, there are no hard-set rules to define the generator and discriminator except that the output layer of the generator should have the same shape as the input layer of the discriminator. In Figure 5.8, the vanilla GAN architecture for generating CIFAR-10 images (CIFAR-10 is a dataset containing RGB images of size 32 x 32) which was introduced in Goodfellow et al.'s GAN paper [7].

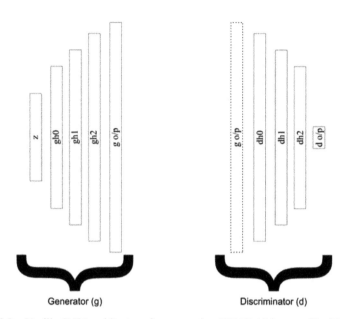

Generator (g)   Discriminator (d)

FIGURE 5.8 Vanilla GAN architecture for generating CIFAR-10 images. Vanilla GAN has two variations, this is the deep convolutional GAN, the other one is a more simplistic fully-connected GAN.

The layer-wise information for the above architecture is as follows:

- **Generator (g):**
  - **z:** The input latent-vector (100-dimensional vector in original paper)
  - **gh0:** Fully-Connected Layer – 8000 Neurons & ReLU Activation
  - **gh1:** Fully-Connected Layer – 8000 Neurons & Sigmoid Activation
  - **gh2:** Space Converter – dim(8000,) → dim(10,10,80) where height = 10, width = 10 & num. channels = 80
  - **g o/p:** Transpose Convolution Layer – kernel_shape = (5,5), strides = (3,3), num_channels = 3, therefore, dim(10,10,80) → dim(32,32,3)

- **Discriminator (d):**
  - **g o/p:** The output of generator is given as input to the Discriminator
  - **dh0:** Convolution Layer followed by Max Pooling – kernel_shape = (8,8), strides = (1,1), num_channels = 32, pooling_shape

= (4,4), pooling_stride = (2,2), padding = 4, maxout_pieces = 2, therefore, dim(32,32,3) → dim(15,15,32)

o **dh1:** Convolution Layer followed by Max Pooling – kernel_ shape = (8,8), strides = (1,1), num_channels = 32, pooling_shape = (4,4), pooling_stride = (2,2), padding = 3, maxout_pieces = 2, therefore, dim(15,15,32) → dim(6,6,32)

o **dh2:** Convolution Layer followed by Max Pooling – kernel_shape = (5,5), strides = (1,1), num_channels = 192, pooling_shape = (2,2), pooling_stride = (2,2), padding = 3, maxout_pieces = 2, therefore, dim(6,6,32) → dim(3,3,192)

o **dh3:** Maxout Layer – 500 Neurons & maxout_pieces = 5, therefore, dim(4,4,192) → dim(500,)

o **d o/p:** Fully-connected Layer – 1 Neuron & sigmoid activation

Maxout is a regularization function which applies Maximum Pooling to a linearly ordered set of inputs (taken k at a time) in case of Dense Layers and a Maximum Pooling through k feature maps in addition to spatial locations in case of Convolution Layers, where k is the number of maxout pieces [8].

5.2.3   LOSS FUNCTION AND TRAINING ALGORITHM

The generator and discriminator are playing a minimax game with each other with the following value function [7]:

$$min_G max_D V(D,G) = \mathbb{E}_{x \sim p_{data}} \left[log(D(x)) \right] + \mathbb{E}_{z \sim p_z(z)} \left[log(D(G(z))) \right] \qquad (8)$$

where; p_{data} is the dataset distribution; and $p_z(z)$ is the latent-space distribution of the generator.

The loss functions used for training the Generator and Discriminator components are based on the above Value Function. The Discriminator loss has two parts, one for the real image from the dataset and the other for the generated image and it is defined as [7]:

$$J_D^{(i)} = \left(log(D(x^{(i)})) + log(1 - D(G(z^{(i)}))) \right) \qquad (9)$$

where; D(.) is the discriminator, G(.) is the generator, $x^{(i)}$ is the ith sample from the dataset and $z^{(i)}$ is the ith latent-vector.

Whereas since the generator never gets to observe the actual dataset, the Generator loss is defined as [7]:

$$J_G^{(i)} = log\left(1 - D\left(G\left(z^{(i)}\right)\right)\right)$$

(10)

For the above equations, since $0 \leq D(.) \leq 1$ due to the sigmoid activation in the output layer, $J_D \geq 0$ and $J_G \leq 0$.

In training a GAN architecture, the generator and discriminator are trained simultaneously but asynchronously. Minibatch gradient descent is used for training the networks and the training algorithm is defined as follows [7]:

for number of training iterations do

for k steps do

- Sample minibatch of m noise samples $\left\{z^{(1)}, z^{(2)}, ..., z^{(m)}\right\}$ from noise prior $p_g(z)$
- Sample minibatch of m examples $\left\{z^{(1)}, x^{(2)}, ..., x^{(m)}\right\}$ from data generating distribution $p_{data}(x)$
- Update the discriminator by ascending its stochastic gradient.

$$\Delta_{\theta_d} \cdot \frac{1}{m} \sum_{i=1}^{m} \left(log\left(D\left(x^{(i)}\right)\right) + log\left(1 - D\left(G\left(z^{(i)}\right)\right)\right)\right)$$

(11)

end for

- Sample minibatch of m noise samples $\{z^{(1)}, z^{(2)}, ..., z^{(m)}\}$ from noise prior $p_g(z)$
- Update the generator by descending its stochastic gradient.

$$\Delta_{\theta_g} \cdot \frac{1}{m} \sum_{i=1}^{m} \left(log\left(1 - D\left(G\left(z^{(i)}\right)\right)\right)\right)$$

(12)

end for

In the above algorithm, k is the number of steps for which to train the discriminator, for one training step of the generator, k is a hyperparameter that needs to be tuned to get the best results and faster training.

Generative adversarial networks opened up a plethora of new application ideas and brought about a great paradigm shift in the area of generative models, but the vanilla GAN architecture's loss function and training algorithm introduced their own set of problems that needed to be solved.

5.2.3.1   QUALITY OF GENERATOR OUTPUT

Although Vanilla GANs are able to generate a satisfactory output with smaller image sizes, the generator is not able to scale up successfully to higher resolution of data. For images, it means high resolution images, and for other data, it simply means data with a higher number of features.

The fully-connected model is a GAN architecture consisting of only fully-connected layers and no convolutional layers. The Generator produces good outputs for the MNIST dataset containing 28x28 grayscale images but as the number of channels, resolution and variation in the datasets are increased, the GAN architecture doesn't scale up well. For a more detailed look at the results, please refer to figure 2 in Ref. [7].

5.2.3.2   NON-CONVERGENCE

The GAN Architecture is trained by simultaneously training a generator and a discriminator network which are working against each other playing a minimax game. This, in turn, leads to both the networks' losses to oscillate or even destabilize, thus causing the training to go haywire and the models never reaching the state of convergence. In GANs, convergence is the state where the Value Function of the GAN achieves Nash equilibrium, which is a state where the generator and discriminator essentially stop learning anything new. The imbalance between generator and discriminator training is also a cause for overfitting.

5.2.3.3   MODE COLLAPSE

In the GAN training algorithm, the generator model is trained for too long without updating the discriminator model, it can reach a state where too many values of z collapse (point towards) a single value in the dataset. For example, a Generator generates only 2 to 3 types of data in a dataset containing 10 classes (or modes) in total, such as the MNIST dataset (Figure 5.9).

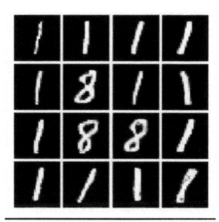

FIGURE 5.9   Example of mode collapse in GANs trained on MNIST dataset where the generator is only generating output for classes 1 and 8.

Mode collapse destroys the diversity of the generator, and it occurs because the Generator essentially learns to fool the discriminator by outputting similar data since the discriminator is trained less often than the generator. Avoiding mode collapse is also the reason that in the training algorithm of GANs we train discriminator for k steps where $k \geq 1$ for each training step of the generator.

5.2.3.4   VANISHING GRADIENTS PROBLEM

The Vanishing Gradient Problem occurs when the gradient updates of a NN model get too small to pass any information in the backpropagation step and the model essentially stops learning at a premature stage of training. In the case of GANs, vanishing gradients may occur in different parts of the architecture due to different reasons. The discriminator may suffer from vanishing gradient problem due to the choice of activation functions (AFs) used in its hidden layers, where using logistic AFs makes the model more prone to vanishing gradients problem than using AFs like ReLU, eLU, and Leaky ReLU. The generator, on the other hand, suffers from vanishing gradients when the discriminator gets too good at differentiating real data from fake data, thus reducing the gradients of the generator, which are backpropagated through the discriminator (see Generator Loss Function), to a negligible magnitude causing them to vanish.

5.2.3.5   CONTROL OVER GENERATOR OUTPUT

The Vanilla GAN architecture describes the Generator and Discriminator networks for the estimation of $P(x)$ and not $P(x,y)$. This means that the learning is completely Unsupervised and there is no way to control the Generator Output. However, Goodfellow et al. in their GAN paper [7], have talked about a way to model $P(x,y)$ by providing the one-hot encoded labels to the Generator and Discriminator models. The next section describes an architecture which can model the probability $P(x,y)$.

5.2.3.6   MODEL COMPARISON DURING TRAINING OF GANS

In Discriminative Models, the model loss can be seen as a representation of the accuracy of the model in predicting $P(y|x)$, but in the case of GANs, the generator and discriminator model loss represents how well a network is performing against its adversary network. This makes the model losses of generator and discriminator unsuitable metrics for describing the quality of the generated output. The quality of generated outputs have to be checked manually at periodic intervals by making inferences from the generator as it is completely possible that the Generator loss is high, but the output quality is better than a point in training where the Generator loss was low. The next section will discuss some of the other metrics which are used for measuring output quality of GANs.

5.3   IMPROVEMENTS IN GENERATIVE ADVERSARIAL NETWORKS

5.3.1   CONDITIONAL GAN (CGAN)

5.3.1.1   CGAN ARCHITECTURE

Conditional GAN architecture introduces the label(s) y as input to the generator and discriminator components of vanilla GAN [9] (Figure 5.10).

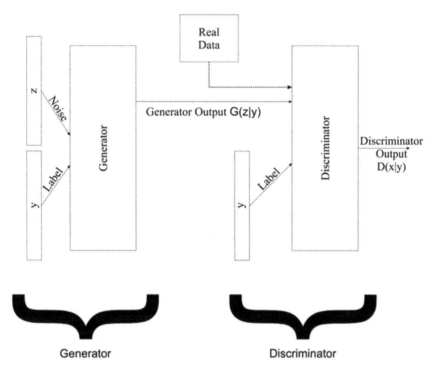

FIGURE 5.10 CGAN architecture.

The only significant difference between Vanilla GAN and Conditional GAN is that CGAN is able to model $P(x,y)$ while Vanilla GAN can only model $P(x)$.

5.3.1.2 CHANGES IN THE VALUE FUNCTION

The value function for CGAN has the same structure as Vanilla GAN, but the only change is that the label y is now incorporated in the Value Function to account for the class labels [9].

$$\min_G \max_D V(D,G) = \mathbb{E}_{x \sim p_{data}}\left[log(D(x \mid y))\right] + \mathbb{E}_{z \sim p_z(z)}\left[log(D(G(z \mid y)))\right] \tag{13}$$

5.3.1.3   SINGLE LABEL (UNIMODAL) VS. MULTI-LABEL (MULTIMODAL)

Conditional GANs work well with both single label and multi-label data. An example of a single label dataset is the MNIST Dataset where each number is given only one class label. The CGAN generator is trained by providing it a random noise z but this time along with z, a class label y is also provided. Thus, instead of just depending on d, the generator now depends on both z and y for generating an output. Similarly, the discriminator now checks reality of data for each class, as it is provided the class label as input along with a real/fake image. The class labels in case of MNIST data are one-hot encoded (Figure 5.11).

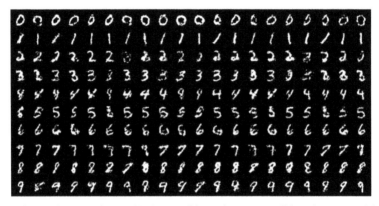

FIGURE 5.11   Generated MNIST Data with each row conditioned on one label [9]. (Reprinted from [9]. https://creativecommons.org/licenses/by/4.0/)

An example of multi-class data is image annotations where each image is given multiple tags. A CGAN can be built such that given any image, the CGAN will tag the image with multiple tags which define the image. This is done by feeding the generator with noise vector z along with the feature vector calculated for the image by passing it through a pre-trained convolutional network (in this case, AlexNet trained on ImageNet 21k) where the output layer of the CNN is removed, and thus the output is fetched from the second last layer. This calculated feature vector for an image acts as a label which is then passed to the CGAN Generator, which generates multiple tags based on the noise and the image feature vector. The generated/real tags are then passed through a pre-trained Language Model before being given as input to the discriminator along with the image feature vector. In this way, the generator learns to assign multiple tags to an image [9] (Figure 5.12).

User tags + annotations	Generated tags
 montanha, trem, inverno, frio, people, male, plant life, tree, structures, transport, car	taxi, passenger, line, transportation, railway station, passengers, railways, signals, rail, rails
 food, raspberry, delicious, homemade	chicken, fattening, cooked, peanut, cream, cookie, house made, bread, biscuit, bakes

FIGURE 5.12   Multimodal output tags generated for images [9]. (Reprinted from *[9]*. *https://creativecommons.org/licenses/by/4.0/)*

5.3.2   *WASSERSTEIN GAN (WGAN)*

5.3.2.1   *WASSERSTEIN DISTANCE*

If $\pi(P_r, P_g)$ is the set of all joint distributions $\gamma(x,y)$ whose marginals are respectively P_r and P_g figuratively, $\gamma(x,y)$ indicates the amount of "mass" that must be transported from x to y in order to transform the distribution P_r into P_g then the Wasserstein (or Earth Mover) Distance is defined as "cost" of the optimal transport plan and is given by:

$$W\left(P_r, P_g\right) = \inf_{\gamma \in \pi\left(P_r, P_g\right)} \mathbb{E}_{(x,y)\sim\gamma}\left[\left\|x - y\right\|\right] \tag{14}$$

5.3.2.2   *WGAN LOSS FUNCTION AND TRAINING*

There are no major changes in the architectural specifications of WGAN from standard vanilla GAN, but the loss function of WGAN has a lot of advantages over Vanilla GAN. WGAN uses the Wasserstein distance as the loss metric for evaluating the generator and discriminator. Wasserstein distance calculates the distance between the generated and the real distributions and provides the generator and discriminator with much better stability and metric during training and evaluating, respectively. The loss function of the discriminator is given by [10]:

$$J_D = \frac{1}{m}\sum_{i=1}^{m} D\left(x^{(i)}\right) - \frac{1}{m}\sum_{i=1}^{m} D\left(G(z^{(i)})\right) \tag{15}$$

The loss function of the Generator is given by:

$$J_G = -\frac{1}{m}\sum_{i=1}^{m} D\left(G(z^{(i)})\right)$$

(16)

The above loss functions have several advantages over the loss function used for Vanilla GANs:

- They are easier to compute than the Vanilla GAN losses as seen in the above equations.
- Using Wasserstein Distance Loss avoids the Vanishing Gradient Problem because of the removal of the log from the loss function which was responsible for diminishing gradients in the network.
- The WGAN loss also provides improved stability as the need for balancing the generator and discriminator training goes away, and the discriminator can now be trained to optimality. This is possible because of the linear nature of WGAN Loss. Due to this linear nature, the better the discriminator is at classifying real/fake images, the better the gradients passed to the generator during the training process.
- Unlike vanilla GAN Loss, WGAN Loss is a meaningful metric to evaluate GAN training since it reports the distances between the real and generated data distributions, and a lower distance can be seen as a more optimal result.
- Since the Discriminator can be trained to complete optimality, it also makes mode collapse in the generator impossible in such a scenario, since the generator can never fool an optimal discriminator by collapsing its noise vectors to generate data of the same class.

The training algorithm for the WGAN remains the same as a Vanilla GAN, but the gradients are now calculated on the WGAN Loss instead of the Vanilla GAN Loss and RMSProp Optimizer is used instead of stochastic gradient descent (SGD) [10] (Figure 5.13).

FIGURE 5.13   WGAN results (top) vs. traditional GAN (bottom) [10]. (Reprinted from [10]. https://creativecommons.org/licenses/by/4.0/)

5.3.3 STACKGAN

5.3.3.1 STACKGAN ARCHITECTURE

Although the vanilla GAN and WGAN architectures work well with low resolution data, they were unable to give satisfactory results for images with higher resolution like 256×256 images. This disadvantage of GANs was the driving force behind the idea of StackGANs which are meant to tackle the problem of generating higher resolution data in a satisfactory manner. StackGANs were built on the principle that the high-resolution images when scaled down to lower resolutions are still related to their higher resolution counterparts, therefore, the team behind StackGAN hypothesized that by breaking the generative task into smaller sub-problems having progressive goals will help stabilize GAN training for higher resolution. StackGANs are effective at modeling lower-to-higher resolution data. The architecture of StackGAN is as follows [11]:

The architecture in Figure 5.14 has three major components working together as explained below:

1. **Conditional Augmentation:** The text description t is converted into embedding vector φ_t by using any embedding algorithms like Word2Vec, GloVe, Elmo, etc. However, the vector φ_t is a high dimensional vector (>100) and it cannot be directly downsampled to a lower-dimensional vector using non-linear transformations because that will cause discontinuities in the latent data created by such transformations which is undesirable for training GANs where one of the requirements is smooth interpolation between images. Thus, the authors suggest a new technique called Conditional Augmentation to produce conditional variables $\hat{c}$, which are randomly sampled from the normal distribution $N\left(\mu(\varphi_t), \Sigma(\varphi_t)\right)$ where the mean $\mu(\varphi_t)$ and diagonal covariance matrix $\Sigma(\varphi_t)$ are functions of the embedding vector φ_t. In order to avoid overfitting and enforcing smoothness over the conditional manifold, the following regularization term is added to the Generator Loss Function [11].

$$D_{KL}\left(N\left(\mu(\varphi_t), \Sigma(\varphi_t)\right) \| N(0,1)\right) \qquad (17)$$

This is the Kullback-Leibler Divergence between a standard Gaussian Distribution and the Conditional Distribution. Conditional Augmentation helps in modeling text to image translations in GANs due to its randomness, since a piece of text can correspond to various images. For example, in Figure 5.15, try imagining the possible images for the text t, the described bird can be in various positions and can have slightly differing appearances as well.

2. **Stage-1 GAN:** The Generator G_0 obtains text conditioning variable $\hat{c}_0$ from previous layer, where $\hat{c}_0 = \mu_0 + \sigma_0 \odot \in$ where $\in \sim N(0,1)$ and $\odot$ is element-wise multiplication. μ_0, σ_0 are obtained by connecting fully-connected layers to the embedding vector φ_t. $\hat{c}_0$, with dimensions N_g, is then concatenated with z vector with dimension N_z. The resulting vector is then passed through a series of upsampling blocks to generate an image of size $W_0 \times H_0$.

   In the Discriminator D_0, the embedding vector φ_t is passed through a dense layer to compress it to N_d dimensions and then replicated spatially to form a $M_d \times M_d \times N_d$ tensor. The input (real/fake) image is fed through a series of down-sampling blocks to reduce its spatial dimensions to $M_d \times M_d$. The image filter map is then concatenated with the tensor obtained from the embedding vector φ_t and then 1×1 convolutions are applied to learn features across the image and text together. Finally, a fully-connected layer with one neuron is used to produce the final decision score [11].

3. **Stage-2 GAN:** The Stage-2 Generator G is designed as an Encoder-Decoder network with residual blocks. The embedding vector φ_t is again passed through the Conditional Augmentation block to obtain $\hat{c}_0$, which is then spatially replicated to a $M_g \times M_g \times N_g$ tensor. The output image of G_0 is passed through several downsampling blocks until it reaches a spatial dimension of $M_g \times M_g$. The tensor, which represents text features and the image features obtained are concatenated along the channel dimension. These coupled features are then passed through several residual blocks, which learn the multi-modal representation across the text and image features. Finally, upsampling layers are employed to transform these representations into a high-resolution image of dimensions $W \times H$.

The architecture of Discriminator D remains the same as D_0; the only change is that two more downsampling blocks are added since the input image dimensions of D are bigger than the input image dimensions of D_0 [11].

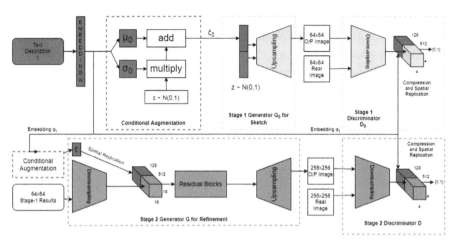

FIGURE 5.14   StackGAN-v1 architecture [11].

5.3.3.2   STACKGAN LOSS FUNCTION AND TRAINING

The Stage-1 GAN is trained by the loss functions J_{D0} and J_{G0} where [11]:

$$J_{D_0} = \mathbb{E}_{(I_0,t) \sim pdata}\left[log\left(D_0\left(I_0,\varphi_t\right)\right)\right] + \mathbb{E}_{z \sim pz(z), t \sim pdata}\left[log\left(1 - D_0\left(G_0\left(z,\hat{c}_0\right),\varphi_t\right)\right)\right] \quad (18)$$

$$J_{G_0} = \mathbb{E}_{z \sim pz(z), t \sim pdata}\left[-log\left(1 - D_0\left(G_0\left(z,\hat{c}_0\right),\varphi_t\right)\right)\right] + \lambda D_{KL}\left(N\left(\mu\left(\varphi_t\right),\Sigma\left(\varphi_t\right)\right) \| N\left(0,1\right)\right) \quad (19)$$

The Stage-2 GAN is trained by the loss functions J_D and J_G where [11]:

$$J_D = \mathbb{E}_{(I, t) \sim P_{data}}\left[log\left(D\left(I,\varphi_t\right)\right)\right] + \mathbb{E}_{s_0 \sim P_{G_0}, t \sim P_{data}}\left[log\left(1 - D\left(G\left(s_0,\hat{c}_0\right),\varphi_t\right)\right)\right] \quad (20)$$

$$J_G = \mathbb{E}_{s_0 \sim P_{G_0}, t \sim P_{data}}\left[-log\left(1 - D\left(G\left(s_0,\hat{c}_0\right),\varphi_t\right)\right)\right] + \lambda D_{KL}\left(N\left(\mu\left(\varphi_t\right),\Sigma\left(\varphi_t\right)\right) \| N\left(0,1\right)\right) \quad (21)$$

The upsampling blocks consist of nearest neighbor upsampling and a 3×3 Convolution with stride 1. Batch Normalization and ReLU are applied after every convolution except the last one. The residual blocks also consist of 3×3 Convolutions with stride 1, with Batch Normalization and ReLU. Depending on the size of the model, there may be two Residual Blocks for (128×128) images and four residual blocks for (256×256) images. The downsampling blocks consist of 4×4 Convolutions with stride 2, Batch Normalization, and LeakyReLU Activation.

The first downsampling convolution does not have Batch Normalization. The default configuration for all the hyperparameters described in the StackGAN-v1 architecture is

$$N_g = 128, N_z = 100, M_g = 16, M_d = 4, N_d = 128, W_0 = H_0 = 64, W = H = 128$$

First, the Stage-1 GAN is trained for 600 epochs while keeping Stage-2 GAN fixed, then the Stage-2 GAN is trained for 600 epochs by fixing the Stage-1 GAN. The optimizer used is ADAM with beta 1 = 0.5, batch size is taken as 64, the learning rate is taken as 0.0002 and then decayed to 0.5 of its previous value every 100 epochs [11].

5.3.3.3   INCEPTION SCORE AND FRÉCHET INCEPTION DISTANCE

Inception score and fréchet inception distance are some of the popular metrics which are used currently to judge the quality of GANs. These metrics are observed when training GANs and they provide a good measure of the quality of the generated images.

The inception score (IS) is a metric which was created to replace subjective human evaluations of generated images, since then it has been used in almost every paper introducing a new GAN architecture or training algorithm. It is calculated by first passing the generated images through a pre-trained Inception-v3 model and predicting the class probabilities. These are conditional probabilities and a strong probability for one class over all the other classes indicate high image quality. The conditional probability distribution for each image should have a low entropy. The other goal is to have varying images, this is checked by taking the marginal probability, that is, the probability distribution of all generated images. The integral of this marginal probability should have a high entropy to ensure high image variety. Here entropy is given by [12]:

$$H = -\Sigma p_i * log(p_i) \tag{22}$$

The final inception score is taken as the exponent of the KL-divergence between the conditional and marginal probability distributions given as [12]:

$$IS = exp(D_{KL}(C \| M)) \tag{23}$$

where; C is the conditional distribution; and M is the marginal distribution. This score is calculated over a distribution of a large number of generated images (usually 50,000). The higher the Inception Score, the better, the upper bound for IS is the number of classes present in the training dataset. The Inception Score has its limitations when it comes to training dataset whose labels are not present in the ImageNet Dataset (on which Inception-v3) is trained, then inception score is always low, if the generator generates the same image multiple times for a class, but different images for different classes, then IS is still high since IS does not check for intra-class diversity.

Another metric which is used is the Fréchet inception distance or FID Score. The FID score, instead of calculating the class probabilities, calculates the distance between the feature vectors calculated for real and generated images, this feature vector is calculated by using the pre-trained Inception-v3 model, removing its output layer and taking outputs from the final pooling layer with 2048 neurons, hence each feature vector has 2048 neurons [13].

The inception score measures the goodness of the generated images amongst themselves while the FID is responsible for comparing some statistics of the generated images with that of the real images. Therefore, FID along with IS gives a complete view of the quality of GAN Outputs. The FID is calculated as [13]:

$$FID = ||\mu_r - \mu_g||^2 + Tr\left(\sigma_g + \sigma_g - 2 * \sqrt{\sigma_r . \sigma_g}\right) \tag{24}$$

where; μ_r and μ_g are the mean of the calculated feature vectors for real and generated image, respectively, σ_r and σ_g are the covariance matrices for the real and generated images' feature vectors respectively and Tr(.) is the trace operation, i.e., the sum of the main diagonal of a square matrix. The lower the FID for a set of images, the better is the quality of the generator. The FID, like IS, is calculated for a large set of images, usually 50,000 and this is also sometimes dubbed as FID50k.

5.3.3.4 STACKGANV2 ARCHITECTURE

StackGAN-v2 takes the idea of StackGAN-v1 to the next level by making various updates to the architecture as well as the loss function of the GAN. StackGAN-v2 has a tree-like architecture which is used to generate images at multiple scales (ex. 64×64, 128×128, 256×256), all from a single architecture. This is made possible by branching out the output heads (G_i) of the Generators at different intervals in the overall architecture, with the first head generating the minimum-scale images and the last head generating the maximum-scale images. All the generator output heads are paired with a JCU Discriminator (D_i).

The JCU discriminator is a novel discriminator introduced with Stack-GANv2 which uses both the conditional (with labels) and unconditional (without labels) discriminator loss for training. The specialty of this architecture is that after training is completed, the generator is able to generate both random images without any label provisions as well as specific images for a provided label [11].

5.3.3.5   STACKGANV2 LOSS FUNCTION AND TRAINING

The loss function used for training StackGAN-v2 are J_G and J_{Di} where [11]:

$$J_G = \sum_{i=1}^{m} J_{G_i} \text{ and } J_{G_i} = \mathbb{E}_{s_i \sim pG_i}\left[-log\left(D\left(s_i\right)\right)\right] + \mathbb{E}_{s_i \sim pG_i}\left[-log\left(D\left(s_i,c\right)\right)\right] \qquad (25)$$

$$\left(J_{D_i} = -\mathbb{E}_{x_i \sim pdata_i}\left[log\left(D_i\left(x_i\right)\right)\right] - \mathbb{E}_{s_i \sim P_{G_i}}\left[log\left(1-D_i\left(s_i\right)\right)\right] + \left(-\mathbb{E}_{x_i \sim P_{data_i}}\left[log\left(D_i\left(x_i,c\right)\right)\right] - \mathbb{E}_{s_i \sim P_{G_i}}\left[log\left(1-D_i\left(s_i,c\right)\right)\right]\right)\right) \qquad (26)$$

where; m is the number of generator output heads; c is the conditional variables calculated from the embedding vector; s_i is the image generated by G_i, x_i is a real image sampled from p_{data}, the first term in J_{Gi} and the first two terms in J_{Gi} represent the unconditional loss, and the rest of the terms in both loss functions represent the conditional loss [11].

For a StackGAN-v2 with 256×256 output, the input vector (z for unconditional StackGAN-v2 or concept (z,c) for conditional StackGAN-v2) is first converted into a $4 \times 4 \times 64N_g$ tensor, this tensor is then gradually converted to $64 \times 64 \times 4N_g$ (here, 2 branches are created, see Figure 5.15), then $128 \times 128 \times 2Ng$ and finally $256 \times 256 \times 1N_g$ by a total of 6 upsampling blocks. Here N_g is the number of channels in the tensor. The conditional variables c or unconditional variables z are also fed into the intermediate layers so that their information is not omitted. All Discriminators D_i use downsampling blocks with 3×3 Convolutions to downsample the input image to $4 \times 4 \times 8N_d$ tensor, finally sigmoid is used for outputting probabilities. By default, N_g = 32, Nd = 64, 2 residual blocks are used between two generators, ADAM optimizer with beta 1 = 0.5 and learning rate of 0.0002 is used [11].

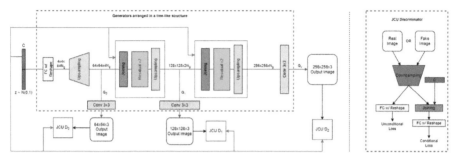

FIGURE 5.15   The StackGAN-v2 architecture [11].

5.3.3.6   *STACKGANV1 VS. STACKGANV2*

StackGAN-v2 was created to be an improvement upon StackGAN-v1. The generated image quality of StackGAN-v2 is much higher than its predecessors. A detailed look at output comparisons for StackGAN-v2 and its predecessors can be found in figure 3 in Ref. [11]. Some of the output metrics of both the models are shown below for comparison [11]:

In Table 5.1, HR: average human ranks; ↓: lower the better; and ↑: higher the better, IS, and FID are explained in Section 5.3.3.

TABLE 5.1   Comparison of Metrics for StackGAN-v1 and StackGAN-v2 for 3 Datasets [11]

Dataset		CUB	Oxford-102	COCO
FID ↓	StackGAN-v1	51.89	55.28	74.05
	StackGAN-v2	15.30	48.68	81.59
IS ↑	StackGAN-v1	3.07 ± 0.04	3.20 ± 0.01	8.45 ± 0.03
	StackGAN-v2	4.04 ± 0.05	3.26 ± 0.01	8.30 ± 0.01
HR ↓	StackGAN-v1	1.81 ± 0.02	1.70 ± 0.03	1.45 ± 0.04
	StackGAN-v2	1.19 ± 0.02	1.30 ± 0.03	1.55 ± 0.05

5.3.4   PROGRESSIVE GROWING OF GANS (PG-GAN)

5.3.4.1   INTRODUCTION

The progressive growing of GANs or PG-GAN is a research paper published by Nvidia which mainly focuses on a GAN training algorithm where the layers of the Generator and Discriminator are slowly grown, that is, added to the architecture, while training.

In many ways, this algorithm resembles a learning process where the NN starts off with a very small task, and progressively learns to perform bigger and bigger tasks. This algorithm has been shown to stabilize as well as speed up GAN training. However, the greatest advantage of this algorithm is seen in its ability to create hyper-realistic images with resolutions of 1024×1024 and higher. Some other ideas which deal with increasing the variation in generated images were also introduced in this chapter [14].

5.3.4.2   THE PROGRESSIVE GROWING OF GANS ALGORITHM

All the GAN Architectures and Training Algorithms that were released before PG-GAN dealt with images of size up to 256×256, which is an extremely low resolution by current standards. This low quality was mainly a result of trying to train a complete GAN Architecture at once on a high-resolution dataset. The PG-GAN Algorithm was created for improving the quality of the generated images, as well as stabilizing GAN training [14].

This algorithm resolves the problem of training GANs on high resolution data by making the training process progressive in nature. What this means is that the training starts with a small Generator and Discriminator architecture which trains on downscaled, low resolution data (say 4×4 images), as the training progresses, the Generator and Discriminator architecture is now grown, and the model is now trained on higher resolution data (say 8×8 images), this process continues till the target resolution (say 1024×1024 images) is reached. In this way, in the initial phases of training, the GAN model learns about the coarse features of the dataset and as the training progresses and the architecture as well as image resolution is grown, the model starts learning finer and finer features of the dataset.

During training, the GAN does not transition from a lower resolution to a higher resolution instantly, instead, as the training progresses, the lower resolution training examples are smoothly faded out while fading in the higher resolution example, this step is necessary for stabilizing GAN training, since transitioning the resolution directly in one step can destabilize training due to the sudden change in training data. This kind of fade in fade out effect is implemented by making some additions to the architecture [14].

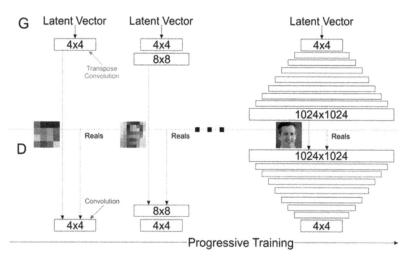

FIGURE 5.16   Progressive training in GANs.

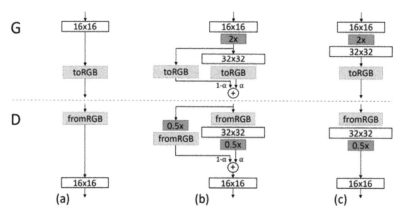

FIGURE 5.17   Illustrates the transition from 16×16 (a) images to 32×32 (c) images, the transitioning as shown in (b) is done by adding the upsampling and downsampling blocks for 32×32 in G and D respectively, while also retaining the original toRGB and fromRGB layers shown in (a) as a residual block. The parameter $1-\alpha$ is the weight of the residual layer, and α increases linearly from 0 to 1. It can be observed that in (a) $\alpha = 0$ and in (c) $\alpha = 1$. 2x and 0.5x operations are performed by using nearest neighbor filtering and average pooling [14]. (Reprinted from [14]. https://creativecommons.org/licenses/by/4.0/)

The variation of generated images is increased by using a minibatch standard deviation layer, which is appended towards the end of the Discriminator. This layer takes the minibatch and computes the standard deviation over each spatial location in the minibatch, these estimates are then averaged over each feature and spatial location to get a single value, which is then replicated into a constant feature map and concatenated to the feature maps coming from the previous layer. This gives the Discriminator access to these statistics of the minibatch, thus increasing overall variation of the generated images while training, this happens because the Discriminator cannot be fooled as easily by invariant data as before due to access to the standard deviation of a minibatch.

The generator is trained by WGAN Loss and the Discriminator architecture is trained using WGAN Loss Function with added Gradient Penalty as a substitute for gradient clipping, it is given by ($\gamma = 750$ for PG-GAN) [14]:

$$J_D = \mathbb{E}_{s_0 \sim P_G}\left[D\left(s_0\right)\right] - \mathbb{E}_{x \sim P_{data}}\left[D\left(x\right)\right] + \lambda \; \mathbb{E}_{\hat{x} \sim P_{\hat{x}}}\left[\left(\left\|\nabla_{\hat{x}}D\left(\hat{x}\right)\right\|_2 - \gamma\right)^2 / \gamma^2\right] \quad (27)$$

$$\hat{x} = ts_0 + \left(1 - t\right)x \, where \, 0 \leq t \leq 1 \quad (28)$$

5.3.4.3   RESULTS

The PG-GAN Algorithm was able to produce hyper-realistic face images when trained on the CELEB-A HQ Dataset which contains 30,000 images with 1024×1024 resolution, made from the images sampled from CELEB-A dataset (Figure 5.18).

FIGURE 5.18   Fake celebrity images generated by PG-GAN [14]. (Reprinted from [14]. https://creativecommons.org/licenses/by/4.0/)

5.3.5   STYLEGAN

5.3.5.1   INTRODUCTION

The PG-GAN algorithm introduced a new training algorithm for training GANs and StyleGAN, which is another paper by Nvidia, introduces a new style-based generator architecture for GANs which makes use of the concept of style transfer to produce more diverse results closer to the original data.

The style-based generator provides more controllability over the generated images, along with a smoother, unwarped latent space. These advantages improve the overall quality of the generated images and also increases the explainability of the generator layers in a way.

5.3.5.2   THE STYLE-BASED GENERATOR ARCHITECTURE

The style-based generator consists of two-component networks, these are the mapping network and the synthesis network [15] (Figure 5.19).

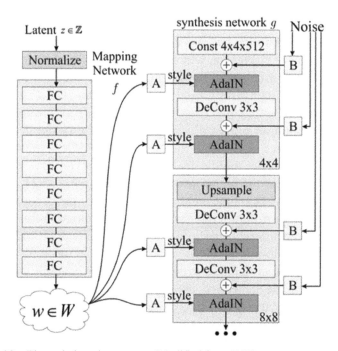

FIGURE 5.19   The style-based generator. (Modified from [15].)

The mapping network (f) converts the random latent vector z into a learned latent vector w by passing it through 8 fully-connected layers, this is done in order to undo the warping caused by mapping z to the image features directly like the traditional GAN architecture [15] (Figure 5.20).

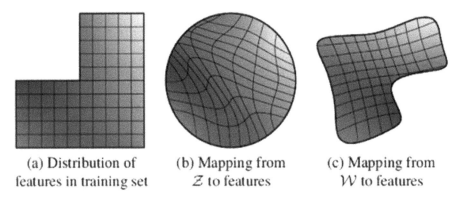

| (a) Distribution of features in training set | (b) Mapping from $\mathcal{Z}$ to features | (c) Mapping from $\mathcal{W}$ to features |

FIGURE 5.20   An informative diagram showing the unwarping of latent space by the mapping network [15]. (Reprinted from [15]. https://creativecommons.org/licenses/by/4.0/)

This new latent vector w is replicated to match the number of the learned affine transform layers (A). The synthesis network (g) consists of a learnt constant 4×4×512 tensor, which is used as the first layer of the architecture of g, using a constant Tensor and injecting features later proved more effective than converting random latents to tensors directly. The A layers are responsible for converting w to a style $y = (y_s, y_b)$. where the style in the lower resolution blocks $4^2 - 8^2$ represents the coarse features like pose, eyeglasses, face shape, etc., the one in the middle resolution blocks $16^2 - 32^2$ represents the middle features like hairstyle, eyes open/close, etc., lastly, the one in the higher resolution blocks $64^2 - 1024^2$ represents the finer features like skin tone and hair color, etc., of the generated image. These latent w from different images can be sent to these different resolution blocks during inference of g to control the generated image output, this is known as style-mixing [15].

An additional noise input is provided to g have random variations in some features of the generated image in order to model some random features like hair placement, freckles, and skin pores. The layer B is a learnt per-channel noise scaling layer which scales the noise input to g according to each channel of the other input tensor to the addition layer.

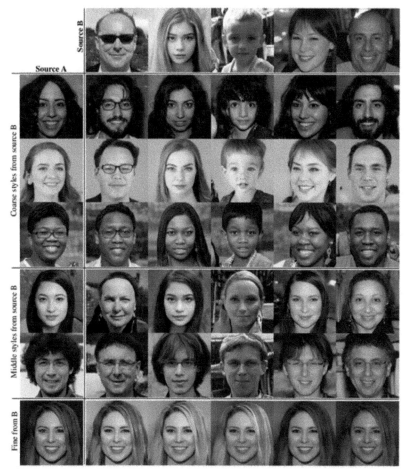

FIGURE 5.21 Style mixing in StyleGANs [15]. (Reprinted from [15]. https://creativecommons.org/licenses/by/4.0/)

The adaptive instance normalization (AdaIN) layers adds the style to the input tensor by first normalizing each feature map x_i of the input tensor separately and then multiplying it with the corresponding style weight $y_{s,i}$, and style bias $y_{b,i}$ [15].

$$AdaIN\left(x_i, y\right) = y_{s,i} \cdot \frac{x_i - \mu\left(x_i\right)}{\sigma\left(x_i\right)} + y_{b,i} \qquad (29)$$

Currently, there are six different configurations of the style-based generator from A to F and Figure 5.19 is config-A. Each of the configurations make little changes to the base configuration (A). For example, instead of using the PG-GAN Algorithm for training, config-E adds residual layers to the Generator Architecture and it is observed that the effect is the same as performing progressive training. These changes in configuration were also successful in removing a few artifacts (anomalies) like eyes facing in the same direction for images with different poses, occurring in the generated images of config-A. Config-F is also known as StyleGAN2 [16].

5.3.5.3   RESULTS AND DISCUSSIONS

StyleGAN is the state-of-the-art for image generation using GANs. The images in Figure 5.24 are from a StyleGAN trained on the Flickr faces HQ (FFHQ) Dataset containing 70000 images (1024×1024) of people from various ethnicities having a diverse set of features.

FIGURE 5.22   StyleGAN (Config-F) results showing the quality and diversity of generated images [16].

There was a considerable boost in performance with each new iteration of the styleGAN Architecture. The papers [15] [16] show FID50k results for different GANs trained on the FFHQ dataset (Table 5.2).

TABLE 5.2   FID50k of GAN Configurations Trained on FFHQ Dataset

GAN Method/Architecture	FID50k ↓
Progressive GAN	8.04
StyleGAN Config-A	4.40
StyleGAN Config-B	4.39
StyleGAN Config-C	4.38
StyleGAN Config-D	4.34
StyleGAN Config-E	3.31
StyleGAN Config-F	2.84

In [16] some discussion on some additional functionalities such as projection of images to latent space for recreating these images in the StyleGAN and the linear separability of image features for image manipulation is mentioned. Some of these features are discussed in the later sections.

5.4   VARIOUS METHODS FOR GAN LATENT-SPACE DISENTANGLEMENT

The previous section dealt with constructing and training different GAN Architectures by using a variety of loss functions and training algorithms. This section deals with controlling the output generated by a GAN. Generative Models as a whole are only considered useful when the output generated by these models can be controlled and manipulated by a user.

One way of implementing control over the GAN Outputs is by using conditional inputs as seen in CGAN in the previous section. The major downside to this method is that for adding a new label or new information to an existing label, the entire GAN Architecture would need to be retrained.

The answer to this problem of retraining GANs in order to add new input conditions lies in the Disentanglement of the Latent-Space of the GAN. The word latent means hidden, and latent-space is named so because the vectors in the latent-space contain information about the output they are generating, for example, the latent space W of styleGAN contains information about the styles in each image. Disentangling the latent-space of a GAN means learning to predict these latent vectors using the required features that are wanted in a generated image, since there is clearly a relation between the features of an image and the latent space.

One example of latent-space disentanglement is the projection algorithm used in styleGAN, which takes a real image as input and then optimizes the input vector w of the synthesis network in order to generate the same image from the styleGAN, the optimization objective used to optimize w is the learned perceptual image patch similarity (LPIPS) of the real and generated images [16] (Figure 5.25).

FIGURE 5.23   (Left) Real image from CELEB-A HQ dataset (right) generated image from styleGAN2 trained on FFHQ dataset using projection.

Another method of disentanglement of latent space could be on the basis of multiple labels describing the generated image such as gender, age, hair color, etc., in case of face images. This would require the use of 2 ML models other than the GAN and the flow of learning the mapping from these labels to the latent space Z (or W) would be as follows [17]:

1. **Generation:** Generating an ample amount of images using a Generator of your choice. The latent-vector z should be stored along with the image as it will be required later.
2. **Feature Extraction**: Using a trained ML model (usually CNNs) to extract the probability of each feature being present for each image.
3. **Correlation:** Finding the correlation between the labels and Z, this can also be done by using simple ML models like a generalized linear model (GLM) or ANNs. In this case, the labels become your input X, and the latent vector becomes your output Y.
4. **Exploration:** Finally, the model in the above step can be used to explore the latent space for different label probabilities.

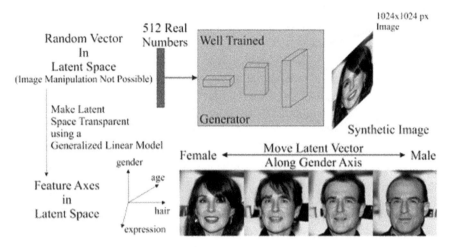

FIGURE 5.24 Latent space disentanglement using feature labels.

5.5 GAN ARCHITECTURES FOR TEXT SEQUENCES AND AUDIO

In almost all the above examples, GANs are being used for generating images. However, GANs can also be used for generating other kinds of data such as text and audio.

There have been some research efforts in Text and Audio generation using GANs although most of the research papers stick to image data due to the fact that image data does not require as much cleaning and preprocessing as texts and audios. Some efforts to generate text data using GANs are LeakGAN [18] and SeqGAN [19]. Audio (Music) data generation using GANs has been explored in GANSynth [20] meanwhile GAN-TTS [21] by deep mind explores Text-to-Speech using GANs.

5.6 APPLICATIONS OF GANS AND FURTHER RESEARCH DIRECTIONS

Generative Adversarial Networks are still more of a research subject, and there are a lot of opportunities right now to make software solutions for industries using GANs. Some applications of GAN are:

1. **Data Augmentation:** GANs can be used to increase the size of datasets used for training classifiers where there is a shortage of data.

2. **Content Generation:** GANs can be used for generating new content like images of products, logos, etc., or even music (like DeepComposer on AWS) and text.
3. **Smart Editing:** Using latent-space disentanglement, the generated output of the GAN can be edited as per the user's requirements; this can be a powerful tool since the machine is aware of the features that constitute the data and can generate data directly from such features.

Currently, most of the research related to GANs is focused on Image Data, and thus, there is a whole almost unexplored field of using GANs with other types of data such as texts and audios. There are also various opportunities for research in disentanglement studies in GANs. In the above section, disentanglement with respect to generated images using real images or features of generated images is explained. Some other ideas may be generating data using text description or direct audio input to predict latent vector and, for example, using a person's voice samples in order to reconstruct their face by predicting the latent vector.

KEYWORDS

- **conditional GAN**
- **deep latent variable models**
- **generative adversarial networks**
- **hidden Markov models**
- **Wasserstein GAN**

REFERENCES

1. Ng, A., & Jordan, M., (1987). On discriminative vs. generative classifiers: A comparison of logistic regression and naive Bayes. *Advances in Neural Information Processing Systems.*
2. Shen, J., (2006). A stochastic-variational model for soft Mumford-shah segmentation. *International Journal of Biomedical Imaging.*
3. Starner, T., & Pentland, A., (1995). *Real-Time American Sign Language Visual Recognition from Video Using Hidden Markov Models.* Master's Thesis, Massachusetts Institute of Technology, Cambridge, MA.
4. Kingma, D., & Welling, M., (2019). *An Introduction to Variational Autoencoders: Foundations and Trends® in Machine Learning, 12*(4), 1–18.

5. Zhavoronkov, A., Ivanenkov, Y., Aliper, A., Veselov, M., Aladinskiy, V., Aladinskaya, A., Terentiev, V., et al., (2019). Deep learning enables rapid identification of potent DDR1 kinase inhibitors. *Nature Biotechnology, 37*(9), 1038–1040.

6. Borysov, S., Rich, J., & Pereira, F., (2019). How to generate micro-agents? A deep generative modeling approach to population synthesis. *Transportation Research Part C: Emerging Technologies, 106,* 73–97.

7. Goodfellow, I., Pouget-Abadie, J., Mirza, M., Xu, B., Warde-Farley, D., Ozair, S., Courville, A., & Bengio, Y., (2014). Generative adversarial nets. In: *Proceedings of the 27th International Conference on Neural Information Processing Systems*. Cambridge, MA.

8. Goodfellow, I., Warde-Farley, D., Mirza, M., Courville, A., & Bengio, Y., (2013). Maxout networks. In: *Proceedings of the 30th International Conference on International Conference on Machine Learning.*

9. Mirza, M., & Osindero, S., (2014). *Conditional Generative Adversarial Nets.* CoRR, abs/1411.1784.

10. Arjovsky, M., Chintala, S., & Bottou, L., (2017). *Wasserstein GAN.* CoRR, abs/1701.07875.

11. Zhang, H., Xu, T., Li, H., Zhang, S., Wang, X., Huang, X., & Metaxas, D., (2019). StackGAN++: Realistic image synthesis with stacked generative adversarial networks. *IEEE Transactions on Pattern Analysis and Machine Intelligence, 41*(8), 1947–1962.

12. Salimans, T., Goodfellow, I., Zaremba, W., Cheung, V., Radford, A., & Chen, X., (2016). Improved techniques for training GANs. In: *Proceedings of the 30th International Conference on Neural Information Processing Systems*. Curran Associates Inc.: Red Hook, NY.

13. Heusel, M., Ramsauer, H., Unterthiner, T., Nessler, B., & Hochreiter, S., (2017). GANs trained by a two time-scale update rule converge to a local Nash equilibrium. In: Guyon, I., Von, L. U., Bengio, S., Wallach, H. M., Fergus, R., Vishwanathan, S. V. N., & Garnett, R., (eds.), *NIPS* (pp. 6626–6637).

14. Karras, T., Aila, T., Laine, S., & Lehtinen, J., (2018). Progressive Growing of GANs for improved quality, stability, and variation. In: *ICLR*. OpenReview.net.

15. Karras, T., Laine, S., & Aila, T., (2019). A Style-based generator architecture for generative adversarial networks. In: *CVPR* (pp. 4401–4410). Computer Vision Foundation / IEEE.

16. Karras, T., Laine, S., Aittala, M., Hellsten, J., Lehtinen, J., & Aila, T., (2019). *Analyzing and Improving the Image Quality of StyleGAN.* CoRR, abs/1912.04958.

17. Guan, S., (2021). *Generating Custom Photo-Realistic Faces Using AI.* https://blog.insightdatascience.com/generating-custom-photo-realistic-faces-using-ai-d170b1b59255 (accessed on 11 November 2021).

18. Guo, J., Lu, S., Cai, H., Zhang, W., Yu, Y., & Wang, J., (2018). Long text generation via adversarial training with leaked information. In: McIlraith, S. A., & Weinberger, K. Q., (eds.), *AAAI* (pp. 5141–5148). AAAI Press.

19. Yu, L., Zhang, W., Wang, J., & Yu, Y., (2017). SeqGAN: Sequence generative adversarial nets with policy gradient. In: Singh, S. P., & Markovitch, S., (eds.), *AAAI* (pp. 2852–2858). AAAI Press.

20. Engel, J. H., Agrawal, K. K., Chen, S., Gulrajani, I., Donahue, C., & Roberts, A., (2019). *GANSynth: Adversarial Neural Audio Synthesis.* CoRR, abs/1902.08710.

21. Binkowski, M., Donahue, J., Dieleman, S., Clark, A., Elsen, E., Casagrande, N., Cobo, L. C., & Simonyan, K., (2020). High fidelity speech synthesis with adversarial networks. In: *ICLR*. OpenReview.net.

PART II

Application of Machine Learning in Healthcare

CHAPTER 6

Machine Learning in Healthcare: Applications, Current Status, and Future Prospects

ROHINI PATIL[1] and KAMAL SHAH[2]

[1]Research Scholar TCET, Assistant Professor, TEC, Navi Mumbai, Maharashtra, India, E-mail: rohinipatil@ternaengg.ac.in (R. Patil)

[2]Professor and Dean (R&D), TCET, Mumbai, Maharashtra, India

ABSTRACT

Significant progress in science related to an understanding of disease and treatment has contributed to an increase in the life span of people. With increasing urbanization and changing lifestyles, the burden of disease patterns has transitioned from communicable diseases to non-communicable diseases. In resource-limited countries, increasing rates of illness and economic challenges both are significant concerns related to healthcare. Long-term diseases such as diabetes mellitus, heart diseases, kidney diseases, and different types of malignancies are associated with significant morbidities. Reduction in mortality rates and improving quality of life are the key goals.

Early diagnosis and better care with reasonable cost are key aspects for improving patient satisfaction. Enormous data and increased complexities have led to rising interest in the use of machine learning (ML) in healthcare. Disease prediction using ML is gaining significant attention in data science. ML is used to learn from a set of examples and evaluate the criteria by using training examples. Different classification algorithms include supervised learning, unsupervised learning, semi-supervised, and reinforcement learning.

In this chapter, we discuss the key applications of different types of ML algorithms along with their utility in healthcare settings. The advantages and limitations of different algorithms and future prospectus are also discussed.

6.1 INTRODUCTION

Artificial intelligence (AI) is a buzzword today in health sciences and engineering. AI techniques and tools are not new concepts. They have been used in healthcare applications or diagnoses of medical problems for more than 40 years. ML is a subdivision of AI. The intention of using AI and ML in healthcare is to increase the diagnostic accuracy, effectiveness of therapy, and help clinicians in their practice of patient management with improved outcomes. With improvements in the rates of accuracy and availability of a large amount of data, the choice of using AI in the diagnostic field is rapidly gaining pace.

With an increase in awareness and understanding of diseases, increase in earning of people, improved access to healthcare, access to technology such as internet and mobile phones, there has been significant growth in the disease-associated information in the medicinal field. The collection of data from the patient, physician, hospital records, and insurance agencies has become easier today than before because of the advances in technology. The growth of healthcare coupled with technology has fueled the expanded need for ML in healthcare. As expected, ML helps in removing significant information from enormous available data. ML is helping healthcare by providing innovative and relevant information which is practically difficult to analyze manually given the constraints of time, manpower, and other resources.

Accuracy of diagnostic rates and quick results are the well-known benefits of AI and ML. Today, increasing costs is one of the important challenges in healthcare. Government and others involved in healthcare always seek cost-effective options. The solutions provided for healthcare should be cost-effective without compromising patient access, delivery of healthcare care resulting in better health outcomes. In this regard, AI and ML have all the required potential to fulfill such demand. The wide and diverse utility of AI in the medical field underlines its long presence over four decades and applications and research is expected to further increase over a while. Considering accuracy and cost efficiency, AI offers the advantage of replication.

Here, we have discussed key trends among supervised and unsupervised ML algorithms. AI, the development of intelligent systems, their evaluation in the healthcare system are discussed with examples. Overall, how ML is assisting in improved patient health, community health with improved efficiency and cost savings. Different ML algorithms with their current and potential applications are also discussed.

6.1.1 EVOLUTION AND THE CURRENT ERA OF ML IN GLOBAL HEALTHCARE

The era of AI began several years before and it has evolved into ML and currently into deep learning (DL) (Figure 6.1).

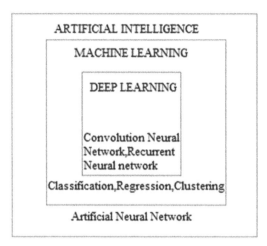

FIGURE 6.1   Subdivision of artificial intelligence.

"AI" term was invented by John McCarthy, an American scientist, in 1956 at the Dartmouth Conference. AI works for a large data sets by applying an intelligence. Overall, AI software automatically learns from patterns. It is a simulation of human intelligence processes using a computer. The process includes the ability to learn, rule-based reasoning, planning, problem-solving approach, representation of knowledge, perception, manipulation, and creativity [9].

Different factors contributing to the progression of AI are listed in Table 6.1.

TABLE 6.1   Factors Contributing to the Progression of AI

- The rapid and fast growth of data;
- Complexity in the datasets;
- The capacity of rapid analysis of trends and patterns;
- Technological advances;
- Better storage capacities;
- Increase of computing power;
- Accessible cost.

ML, a division of AI allows the machine to study from prior cases and identify patterns from multifaceted datasets [27]. Through ML, computers learn to act without specific programming *(Stanford University)* more advanced techniques and models help computers to sort out required analysis from the large data. Algorithms are used to discover specific patterns to get the required insights from the data.

DL helps the machines to think and work like a human. It uses multi-layered neural networks (NNs) that provide high accuracy in different applications like language translation, speech recognition and detection of object [9].

6.1.2   AI: APPLICATION DOMAIN

AI plays an important role in data analysis in several fields. AI remains in existence in computer science due to its advanced intelligent skills in learning, predicting patterns, decision-making capability, and ability to do language processing.

Out of several essential components on which AI systems works, some are:

1. **Knowledge Depiction:** Knowledge needs to be represented in a systematic form. There are many ways for the representation of knowledge including if-then rules, semantic network, frame-based system, or in the form of connection weights of NN.
2. **Learning Ability:** Knowledge can be built from the environment by gaining rules for an expert system. Apply this learning to train the network.
3. **Rule Generation:** Rules can be specifically incorporated into an expert system, or learned by a NN.
4. **Searching:** For instance, searching is a sequence of states which can lead to a quick solution for a given problem. By applying minimal fitness function we can easily identify connection weights in a NN.

Different application domains of AI are shown in Figure 6.2.

1. **Evolutionary Computing:** These techniques can produce optimized solutions in a wide range of problem settings such as genetic algorithms (GAs) or genetic programming.

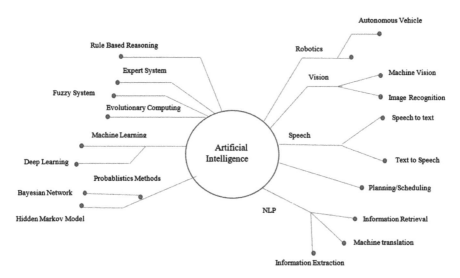

FIGURE 6.2 Different domains of AI.

2. **Vision:** Image or video sources are processed to extract meaningful information and take action based on it. Examples of related to vision in AI include object recognition or machine vision.

3. **Robotics:** The application of robots is commonly recognized and used. Interacting robots with the surrounding reality in a dynamic situation is being explored. Some examples related to this include intelligent control and autonomous exploration.

4. **Expert Systems:** This program is designed to solve the problems with human expertise or experience. The system can perform analysis, design, or monitoring by mimicking the thinking of human experts. The system can even take decisions and perform even more functions. Examples of the expert system include decision support systems and teaching systems.

5. **Speech Processing:** In this program, system identifies the specific arguments and transforms them into machine-understandable format. This can have applications in speech recognition and production.

6. **Natural Language Processing (NPL):** In this program systems is proficient in interacting with people through discussion are developed. This system can have applications in machine translation, information retrieval, and information extraction.

7. **Planning:** This is a process of selecting the right sequence of stages to resolve a given problem. Planning can have applications in scheduling and playing a game.

8. **ML:** This is used for improving the capability of algorithms to work on a database consisting of enormous data. The applications of ML include DTs learning and version space learning.

9. **DL:** It has can be used in computer vision for identification of object or labeling of video [9].

6.2   MACHINE LEARNING (ML)

ML originated from pattern recognition and the concept of ability to learn without programming to perform specific tasks. "ML" was invented by Samuel during the early 1950s [27] in one of his papers. In his paper, he solved the checker game problem by training the computer for 8–10 hours to perform better than its human creator. At the same time, the work of Alan Turing caught attention with the proposal of an analogy "Can machine thinks?"

ML uses several approaches to automatically learn and improvise the prediction without explicit programming. It develops on existing statistical methods and finds patterns in the data. These patterns help in generating hypotheses [21]. The flow of the ML process is depicted in Figure 6.3.

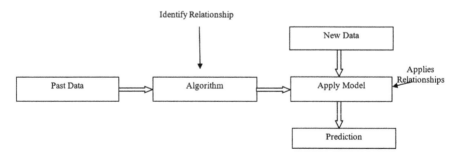

FIGURE 6.3   Flow of ML process.

6.2.1   *CLASSIFICATIONS OF MACHINE LEARNING ALGORITHMS*

ML is used to optimize system parameters and get the expected outcome with the use of training examples. Statistical techniques are often used for making computers able to "learn." Once computer learning is done, the resulting system is used for different applications including automatic prediction of the type of data, feature extraction, or generating artificial examples. Various types of ML algorithms work with certain hypotheses and mathematical models for data. Types of ML and their several algorithms are shown in Figure 6.4.

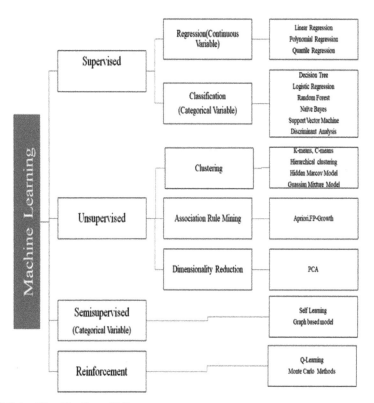

FIGURE 6.4   Classification of ML

6.2.1.1   SUPERVISED LEARNING

In this learning, the training consists of input vectors and target vectors. For each instance target vector is represented as, $y(n)$. The model is in the form $[(x(n), y(n)) \, n = 1,\ldots, N]$. The multiple feature vector as $x_1, x_2, \ldots, x_k$ where x is input. The model is represented as $f(x) = cx + d$, where $f(x)$ is the predictor variable, c, and d are constant variables, and the noise in the data.

For each input vector, loss functions are the difference between output and target vector. This procedure is repeated until the system reaches to optimized value for c and d. In this way, the machine learns through experience and becomes ready for use [11, 22, 32] Primary categories under supervised learning consist of classification and regression.

6.2.1.1.1 Classification

If the dependent variable is categorical, the problems are called classification. Classification algorithms use features based on some predefined criteria to determine how to classify data in classes, such as "diabetes" or "no diabetes."
Example: Independent variable consists of many features. At instance, if the input feature is "fasting blood glucose (FBS)" which may read as:

$$\{x\_training, output\} \rightarrow \{\text{"FBS, 140," "Diabetes"}\}$$

From classification algorithms, the machine learns to classify data items. Classification problems require labeled data for identification of patterns, through the correctly classified instances model's accuracy is validated.

6.2.1.1.2 Regression

If the dependent variable is continuous, the problems are known as regression. In the regression problem based on the pattern in the information, the machine predicts continuous variables. For example, if the continuous value is HbA1c = 7.1%. Three groups can be defined based on the level of HbA1c:

- Diabetes (Group 1) → HbA1c ≥ 6.5%
- Pre-diabetes (Group 2) → HbA1c = 5.7% to 6.4%
- Normal (Group 3) → HbA1c < 5.7%.

Important algorithms of supervised learning are explained below:

1. **Logistic Regression (LR):** It is a classification problem which classifies the data in the form of binary variable means if the person has diabetes or not. The objective includes-To identify independent variables that have an impact on the dependent variable. To develop a logit model-based classification system for determining group membership.

For analyzing a dataset where >1 independent variables which find an outcome using logit function where logit (z) = log (Event Probability/No event probability) =log(z/1-z)=log(odds). LR is based on the maximum likelihood estimation technique. The importance of input features is determined by the coefficients of the model. LR requires large sample sizes. For prediction and classifications of medical problems, such as diagnosis of disease LR algorithm is used. The advantages of these are, it is a probabilistic model, and this model can be updated easily. Limitations include does not show a linear relationship, a complex relationship between variables does not give good accuracy of the model and due to sampling bias may overstate prediction accuracy [22, 32]. Figure 6.5 demonstrates the data into two classes.

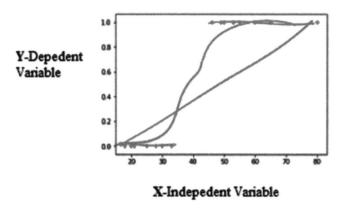

FIGURE 6.5 Graphical representation of logistic regression.

2. **Decision Trees (DTs):** These are prepared using an algorithm that identifies a mechanism to divide features based on conditions. A DTs make a hierarchical decision about the sequential, outcomes variable based on the predictor data. Figure 6.6 shows DTs.

In DTs, each node, transition path, and leaf represents a feature, decision, and outcome respectively and decisions are provided in the form of if-then-else statements. Through entropy and Gini index information gain is calculated which is used for the splitting of a node. It can work with small data, both continuous and categorical, can easily handle outliers it is also used for feature selection. The size of the DTs is reduced by the pruning method. DTs can generate strong classifier validated through statistical tests. Limitations include if non-leaf node variable value is missing it cannot branch and will work on the order of variables [22, 31, 32].

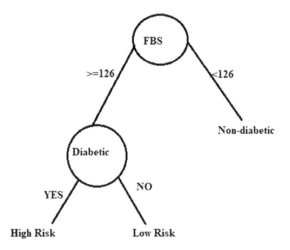

FIGURE 6.6   Decision tree with n = 2 nodes.

3. **Random Forest (RF):** It is an ensemble classifier formed by training multiple DTs simultaneously and hence called "forest." DTs cause overfitting of the training data, RFs prevent this. Accuracy is proportional to the number of DTs. For decision, each RF takes a dataset sample and a subset of features. Each tree performs classification the forest then selects the classification having the more 'votes' or the average votes [22]. It reduces the variance resulted from a single DTs. It also works for the large dataset and can provide the estimation of important variables in classification. However, it is computationlly complex,expensive and favors only higher values of variables.

4. **Artificial Neural Networks (ANN):** This was developed based on the idea of the function of nervous systems in the brain. Like brain neuron, ANN algorithms is an interconnected group of nodes, allows the system to learn and streamline itself by analyzing new data. The components of ANN are the Input, hidden, and an output layer (Figure 6.7). The total number of neurons in the network is equal to the total number of variables. Input layer has input = n, output =

(n/2). The hidden layer has variables equal to the sum of the input and output variables= (n+1) where n= number of features. Activation function (AF) plays an important role in NN, e.g., sigmoidal function given by, $f(x) = 1/1+e^x$. A cost function is used for optimization. A backpropagation NN is used to learn the parameter and optimal parameters can be identified using the gradient descent algorithm. The advantage of this algorithm is that it is suitable for both categorical and numeric variables. It needs lesser statistical training. Moreover, it can identify nonlinear relationships between outcome and independent variables. The limitation include for complex classification problems it is computationally expensive to and predictor variables require pre-processing step [11, 22, 32].

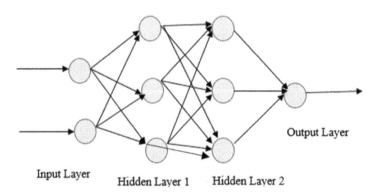

FIGURE 6.7   Basic neural network with two hidden layers.

5.   **Naïve-Bayes:** This classification algorithm is based on probability theory with consideration of all variables are independent of each other. Ability to handle continuous and discrete data and make probabilistic predictions. The algorithm works on the simple Naïve-Bayes formula, i.e., posterior probability α likelihood probability x prior probability of predictor/ prior probability of a class, which is represented as:

$$P(C|B)=((P(B|C) \times P(C))/P(B)$$

where; P(C|B) is the posterior probability of target class; P(B|C) is the likelihood probability of given class; P(C) is the prior probability of predictor; P(B) is the prior probability of class [22].

From the training data, the prior distribution and likelihood probability can be calculated. This classifier is used for high dimensional
data. Due to dependency between variable affects classification
performance. By default, this algorithm assumes the normal distribution for the numerical data [22].

6. **Support Vector Machine (SVM):** It is one of the standard model
applicable to classification and regression problems of non-linear and
linear data. The aim is to find the highest-margin separating hyperplane and minimizing the classification errors. For better generalization, hyperplane should be far from the data points. Support vectors
are the points that lie nearest to the hyperplane [22, 32]. Figure 6.8
shows the working of SVM.

Original training data is transferred into higher dimensional space
that can be done using a Kernel based approach. In linear SVM
minimum number of features are used and for more features, Kernel
trick applied. SVMs work well on small datasets. Less risk of over
fitting, it can work for semi-structured or unstructured data. Limitations are, less capable of noisy data, computationally expensive for
complex data, and generic SVM extension is required cannot classify
more than two classes.

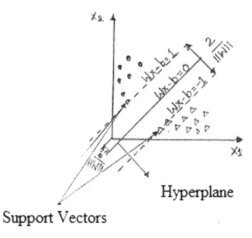

FIGURE 6.8   Working of support vector machine.

7. **K-Nearest Neighborhood (kNN):** This algorithm determines the
unclassified points by measuring the majority class vote from its

k-nearest neighbor. Applicable to regression and classification, kNN is a nonparametric technique. kNN is considered lazy learners as there is no learning of the model. The algorithm first measures the distance between any two points then finds distance based nearest neighbors (NN) and the majority vote to give to a class based on the NLP [22].

If a variable is a categorical variable, then uses hamming distance, and if it is continuous variables, the distance measure is Minkowski distance, Euclidean distance performs well for categorical and numerical datasets. Advantages include can classify instances quickly and used for both classification and regression. Limitations include, The distances between vectors cannot be calculated on missing data hence kNN is not well missing data. Expensive to increasing attributes, weightage is given to all attributes which may lead to poor classification performance.

8. **Linear Regression:** This supervised learning algorithm is used for predictive modeling (Figure 6.9). It applies to a continuous variable Model predict outcome variable value 'y' based on independent variable values x_1, x_2, x_3..., x_n. With multiple independent variables analysis, a linear regression model is represented by $y = b_0 + b_1 x_1 + b_2 x_2 + ... + b_n x_n + \varepsilon$ where 'y' is the outcome variable, b_0 is intercept, ε is an error term and b_1, b_2, b_3, ..., b_n are coefficients of x_1, x_2, x_3, ..., x_n. There must be a linear relationship, either positive, negative or no relationship. It is very sensitive to outliers. As variance increases which may lead to instability in coefficient estimations [8].

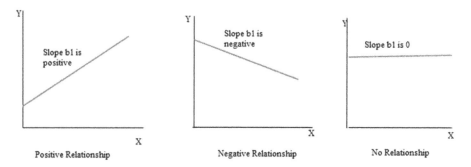

FIGURE 6.9 Linear regression.

6.2.1.2 UNSUPERVISED ML ALGORITHMS

A learning model is trained on unlabeled data, to predict outcomes. It is pattern based learning. This algorithm is used for instances where experts are unable to analyze data. This technique is used in descriptive modeling and pattern detection. Unsupervised learning algorithms are clustering, dimensionality reduction algorithm, and association rule learning (ARL):

1. **K-Means Clustering:** It is unsupervised learning algorithms for cluster analysis. It is basically distance-based, i.e., Minkowski distance, Euclidean distance, Manhattan distance used as a measure of similarity. The algorithm operates on a given data through the number of clusters, k. The number of the cluster varies between the range of 2 and 10. Elbow method to find the number of clusters the elbow technique is used. The algorithm works as:
   - Consider k = 2 as an initial point of the cluster;
   - Calculate centroid for each cluster;
   - For each point, find the nearby cluster centroid and then recalculate centroid for the new cluster until centroid remains unchanged [22].
2. **Principal Component Analysis (PCA):** It is a technique to convert an orthogonal transformation of correlated variables into uncorrelated variables. Principle components (PC), the new variables are either less or equal to the initial variables. The first component explains the maximum percentage and the second component with the next maximum percentage and so on in dimensional dataset, therefore, it reduces the number of original variables. Through covariance, variance PCA minimizes the redundancy and maximizes the information [26].
3. **Association Rule Learning (ARL):** It is used to extract rules which explain best relationships among variables, which can be used to drive and optimize. The association probability can be predicted by analyzing transactional datasets. Different ARL algorithms are the FP-Growth algorithm and the Apriori algorithm.

6.2.1.3 SEMI-SUPERVISED ML ALGORITHMS

Semi-supervised learning originates from supervised and unsupervised learning. The higher cost of labeling is due to the need for an expert's knowledge. To overcome this limitation, some models have been developed with labels for fewer observations and unlabeled data for others. For limited dataset, this method is used.

6.2.1.4 REINFORCEMENT ML ALGORITHMS

Reinforcement learning (RL) is a type of learning of behavior in a certain condition for a certain reward/ penalty signal. In this type of learning, a current state and environment is defined. Through a set of policies, a basis function, assess the current state to produce a proper honor or penalty action. It is self-sustainable and with each task completed and upgrades on its own. By simulating positive and negative rewards, learning is done. If the actions are as per expectations considered to be positive otherwise its negative reward. Popular RL algorithms are the Monte Carlo method and Q-learning.

6.2.2 EVALUATION METRICS

- Confusion matrix (Table 6.2) shows the correct and incorrect classifications prepared by the model.

TABLE 6.2   Confusion Matrix

	Actual Class	Predicted Class
True positive (TP)	+	+
False-positive (FP)	−	+
True negative (TN)	−	−
False-negative (FN)	+	−

Note: + = yes, − = no.

- **Accuracy:** Determines the accuracy of a classifier = correctly classified instances/Total no of instances = (TP + TN)/(TP + TN + FP + FN).
- **Precision:** Positive predicted value =correctly predicted Positive instances/total predicted Positive instances= True Positive/ (True Positive+ False Positive).
- **Sensitivity:** True positive/ (True Positive+ False Negative).
- **Specificity:** True negative/ (True Negative + False Positive).

- **F-Measure:** 2 (Precision × Recall) / (Precision + Recall).
- **Area Under Curve (AUC):** AUC gives true positives rate to the FP rate. The graph is termed as Receiver Operating Characteristics (ROC)
- Root mean square error (RMSE)= $\sqrt{\sum i\left(Yi - Yi'\right)^2} / 2$

6.3   SCOPE AND UTILITY OF ML IN HEALTHCARE

With transitioning of epidemiology from communicable diseases to non-communicable diseases (NCD), the growth of lifestyle diseases is driven by several factors including rapid urbanization, unhealthy lifestyles and population aging [11, 12]. Lifestyle diseases has relations with the environment in which people live. Such diseases are avoidable, and their frequency can be minimized with modifications in dietary patterns, lifestyle, and environmental conditions. Examples include type 2 diabetes, heart disease, stroke, depression, and obesity. The onset of such lifestyle diseases is slow; they take years to develop, and once established, pose difficulties in their management and impair the quality of life of patients. These diseases also add to a financial burden to the families and at large to the healthcare utilization of the country.

The occurrence of chronic diseases controlled by healthy lifestyles such as avoidance of smoking, maintaining ideal body weight, regular physical activity/exercise, consumption of healthy diet including plenty of fruits and vegetables and limiting the intake of excessive calories or sugar, etc.

Considering the large burden of diseases and economic stress on the patients, the healthcare sector has become an obvious and one of the most popular targets for AI, ML, and DL used to analyze huge data and develops predictive models. ML, by virtue of its ability of computational techniques can handle complex and large datasets to provide meaningful results. With increasing advances in technologies such as ML and a better understanding of the disease process today it is possible to diagnose the disease at an early stage and reduce the burden of diseases and their complications.

Data collection, a critical step in the overall process, is associated with several challenges, including continuous growth in the amount of data, costs related to data storage cost, different types of data, complex data, heterogeneity of data, and diverse sources for data collection. Even though massive tasks have been performed by the ML domain, manpower cannot be entirely replaced by machines.

6.3.1   USE OF ML IN DISEASE DIAGNOSIS

Diseases are diagnosed by healthcare professionals based on the history of a patient, clinical examination, and related laboratory, imaging, or other related investigations. Medical diagnostics comprises of different types of tests/investigations for the diagnosis of a certain disease. Correct and timely identification of a disease with effective treatment is important for better patient outcomes. Diagnostic errors can account for patient morbidity, hospital admissions, and mortality. ML has significant potential for assisting clinicians in the diagnostic process. Some of the uses of ML in disease prediction are given in subsections.

6.3.1.1   DIABETES MELLITUS

Due to different complications, long term diabetes mellitus can increase the risk of premature mortality. Diabetes can be associated with complications related to heart, kidney, eyes, nerve, extremities, and brain, increased risk of infections, and depression. Therefore, early diagnosis and interventions are required for living well with diabetes [7].

Dagliati et al. [5] developed a model which predicts for retinopathy, neuropathy, and nephropathy at 3, 5, and 7-year time span using LR with an accuracy of 83.8%. Perveen et al. [24] showed a correlation between metabolic syndrome risk factors and diabetes mellitus. LR is used for validation of predictive power of risk along with data sampling techniques. A female-centric study [10] showed how stress is a robust risk factor for type 2 diabetes mellitus. They showed a direct and indirect effect of stress on diabetes through factors such as hypertension, body mass index, and exercise. In 2018, Zou et al. [35] published a paper on the prediction of diabetes with ML techniques. The authors used algorithm-RF, DT, ANN with PCA, and minimum redundancy maximum prevalence (mRMR) and compared with Luzhou (China-82694 healthy and DB data) and Pima dataset (768 to 392). By using all features, they found good results with mRMR (RF with acc-0.8084). According to them, blood glucose does not give good results. Olivera et al. [20] showed a predictive model for detecting undiagnosed diabetes. They identified results with an ML algorithm with discretization and without discretization. In their study, RF resulted in less accuracy while ANN, LR showed the best result. In another female-centric study (Pima dataset), Sisodia et al. [29] designed a system using NB and showed an accuracy of 76.30%. Zarkogianni et al. [34] assessed the risk of developing cardiovascular disease using advanced ML techniques in type 2 diabetes population. Martinez et al. [15] also reported the effect of stress on diabetes. The result showed increased risk for type 2 diabetes in with stressful work culture or traumatic events, personality type or psychiatric conditions. Patil et al. [23] developed a stress based model showed SVM gives best accuracy in comparison with other classifier.

6.3.1.2   HEART DISEASE

Coronary artery disease (CAD), it is one of the leading cause of mortality, which reduces blood supply to the heart. It was estimated that in 2017, 365,914 people died due to CAD (CDC, 2019).

Singh et al. [28] developed a model for prediction of heart disease using 15 variables with 303 records. The proposed system has been developed using ANN, multilayer NN along with backpropagation algorithm and the result shows that ANN gives approximately 100% accuracy [1]. Electrocardiogram classification based on heartbeat signals using ML was proposed by Alarsan and Younes [1]. Models based on DTs, RFs, and Gradient-Boosted Trees algorithm can classify different ECG heartbeat types and perform a quick and reliable diagnosis with an accuracy of RF is 98.03% for multi-class classification. Beunza et al., [3] compared different supervised algorithms on Framingham database for the prediction of coronary heart disease. The database containing 4240 records. This comparative study suggested the best results with vector machines (AUC=0.75). Swain et al. (2019) developed a prediction system for assisting no specialized healthcare workers using several algorithms and found that LR produces the highest accuracy of 88.29%. Awan, Bennamoun, Sohel, Sanfilippo, and Dwivedi [2] proposed a system for predicting events of 30-day heart failure (HF) readmission and death using MLP based approach and other regression models and showed the MLP approach gives the best result.

6.3.1.3   BREAST CANCER

Breast cancer is the leading type of cancer in Indian women, which accounts for 14% of all cancers in women new cancer cases diagnosed in 2018. The peak incidence of breast cancer is reported in the age of 50–64 years (CDC, 2019).

According to the results of a meta-analysis, the SVM algorithm can calculate breast cancer risk with better accuracy, which is more than 90% than other ML algorithms [19, 30]. Based on the use of personal health data for prediction of five-year breast cancer risk, breast cancer risk prediction tool (BCRAT) provided a better result in comparison with other models [14]. Prediction system using LR, KNN, SVM algorithm and showed that KNN gives better accuracy of 99.28% for predicting the incidence of breast cancer at an early stage by analyzing the clinical dataset of Wisconsin breast cancer dataset (WBCD) [8]. A system for the prediction of the type of breast cancer recurrence reported better performance of NNs than others [16]. Mohebian and colleagues designed a hybrid system for predicting the recurrence of breast cancer. In this study, the authors used optimized ensemble learning on 579 breast cancer patients.

6.3.1.4   CHRONIC KIDNEY DISEASE

Among the NCDs, chronic kidney disease (CKD) [4] is an important contributor to morbidity and mortality. Worldwide, in 2017, about 1.2 million people died due to CKD. Kidney disease as a contributor to cardiovascular disease.

With the help of ML [13] designed a system for prediction of mortality among patients receiving continuous renal replacement therapy. In this study, for the mortality in the intensive care unit, the RF model showed the highest AUC. Rady and Anwar [25] developed a system for prediction of the stage of kidney disease. In this study, probabilistic neural networks (PNN) provided better performance in classification and prediction than MLP, SVM, and radial basis function (RBF) algorithms. Xiao et al. [33] have developed a predictive model for quick prediction of CKD severity using demographic and biochemical features. They used statistical, ML, and NN approaches for building an online tool for prediction of proteinuria progress during follow-up.

Other possible uses of ML in healthcare are:

1.   Pathology: It is the branch of medical science that is involved in the diagnosis of diseases by analyzing tissue samples and body fluids like urine and blood.
2.   Genetic Diseases: Rare genetic diseases can be diagnosed by a combination of algorithms with facial recognition software.

3. Cancer: Algorithms in ML can be useful to identify or predict the occurrence of cancer.

6.3.2 MACHINE LEARNING CHALLENGES

Although ML has been used widely it has some challenges as discussed below:

- There is no uniformity in the data collection process, data collection tools used by healthcare professionals this results in difficulty in streamlining in data and infrastructures;
- Availability of sufficient resources including knowledgeable and trained manpower, technology, and financial resource;
- Data standardization and optimization for effective utilization in the improvement of existing knowledge;
- Regular update of the datasets;
- Issues related to data privacy and data integrity;
- Differences in results of prediction by different algorithms resulting in biased diagnosis;
- Although it can significantly help in automation it cannot completely replace all tasks.

6.3.3 FUTURE PROSPECTUS OF MACHINE LEARNING IN HEALTHCARE

With a better understanding of diseases, their pathophysiology, challenges in the diagnosis of newer and rare diseases, an increasing amount of data, and ethical issues in data collection, applications of ML in healthcare are expected to evolve over some time.

Chronic neurological diseases such as disorders of movement and speech because of spinal cord injury or brain-related problems are associated with significant morbidity. The use of brain-computer interfaces can be used for such patients. The decoding of neural activities using a brain-computer interface may be useful in them. Similarly, it will be of immense use in the diagnosis and prediction of other chronic diseases.

In future healthcare professionals having knowledge and using applications of AI and ML will have an advantage over those who are not knowledgeable in this domain. AI will not be the replacement for healthcare workers but instead, it may help in assisting clinicians in early diagnosis and allow them more time for patient care. It may also help to reduce the stress and burnout and cognitive burden on healthcare workers. As healthcare practitioners adapt and utilize AI into their practice, it will help to enhance patient care resulting in better patient outcomes.

6.4 CONCLUSION

With the increasing burden of diseases and complexity in health-related data, several data sources, and other challenges in the diagnosis of diseases, applications of ML are evolving. ML cannot replace manpower, but it has significant potential for assisting clinicians in the accurate and timely diagnosis of diseases. Supervised, unsupervised, and RL algorithms can be used in healthcare-related applications for improvement of disease prediction. The performance measures used in ML are useful parameters for disease prediction. With an increase in the use of technology, mobile phones, and access to healthcare, the opportunity for the use of AI and ML is unlimited. It should be noted that AI has implications related to privacy, data protection, and the rights of individuals.

KEYWORDS

- **artificial intelligence**
- **artificial neural networks**
- **coronary artery disease**
- **principal component analysis**
- **support vector machine**

REFERENCES

1. Alarsan, F. I., & Younes, M., (2019). Analysis and classification of heart diseases using heartbeat features and machine learning algorithms. *Journal of Big Data, 6*(1). https://doi.org/10.1186/s40537-019-0244-x.
2. Awan, S. E., Bennamoun, M., Sohel, F., Sanfilippo, F. M., & Dwivedi, G., (2019). Machine learning-based prediction of heart failure readmission or death: Implications of choosing the right model and the right metrics. In: *ESC Heart Failure* (Vol. 6). https://doi.org/10.1002/ehf2.12419.

3. Beunza, J. J., Puertas, E., García-Ovejero, E., Villalba, G., Condes, E., Koleva, G., & Landecho, M. F., (2019). Comparison of machine learning algorithms for clinical event prediction (risk of coronary heart disease). *Journal of Biomedical Informatics, 97*, 103257. doi.org/10.1016/j.jbi.2019.103257.

4. Bikbov, B., Purcell, C. A., Levey, A. S., Smith, M., Abdoli, A., Abebe, M., & Murray, C. J. L., (2020). Global, regional, and national burden of chronic kidney disease, 1990–2017: A systematic analysis for the global burden of disease study 2017. *The Lancet, 395*(10225), 709–733. https://doi.org/10.1016/S0140-6736(20)30045-3.

5. Dagliati, A., Marini, S., Sacchi, L., Cogni, G., Teliti, M., Tibollo, V., & Bellazzi, R., (2018). Machine learning methods to predict diabetes complications. *Journal of Diabetes Science and Technology, 12*(2), 295–302. https://doi.org/10.1177/1932296817706375.

6. Debabrata, S., Preeti, B., Vishal, D., Dash, B., & Santhappan, J., (2019). An Efficient heart disease prediction system using machine learning. In: *Machine Learning and Information Processing* (pp. 39–50).

7. Federation, I. D., (2017). Diabetes atlas 2017. In: *IDF Diabetes Atlas*. https://doi.org/ http://dx.doi.org/10.1016/S0140-6736(16)31679-8.

8. Goyal, K., Aggarwal, P., & Kumar, M., (2018). Prediction of breast cancer recurrence: A machine learning approach. In: *Computational Intelligence in Data Mining* (Vol. 990, pp. 101–114). Springer Nature Singapore.

9. Harkut, D. G., Kasat, K., & Harkut, V. D., (2019). Artificial intelligence-scope and limitations. *Artificial Intelligence-Scope and Limitations*, 1–5. https://doi.org/10.5772/ intechopen.77611.

10. Harris, M. L., Oldmeadow, C., Hure, A., Luu, J., Loxton, D., & Attia, J., (2017). Stress increases the risk of type 2 diabetes onset in women: A 12-year longitudinal study using causal modeling. *PLoS One, 12*(2), 1–13. https://doi.org/10.1371/journal.pone.0172126.

11. Jain, V., & Chatterjee J., (2020). *Machine Learning with Healthcare Perspective* (Vol. 13). Springer Science and Business Media LLC.

12. Kamdar, J. H., Jeba P. J., & John, J. G., (2020). Artificial intelligence in medical diagnosis: Methods, algorithms, and applications. In: *Machine Learning with Health Care Perspective* (pp. 27–38).

13. Kang, M. W., Kim, J., Kim, D. K., Oh, K. H., Joo, K. W., Kim, Y. S., & Han, S. S., (2020). Machine learning algorithm to predict mortality in patients undergoing continuous renal replacement therapy. *Critical Care, 24*(1), 1–9. https://doi.org/10.1186/ s13054-020-2752-7.

14. Kumari, M., & Singh, V., (2018). Breast cancer prediction system. *Procedia Computer Science, 132*, 371–376. https://doi.org/10.1016/j.procs.2018.05.197.

15. Martinez, A., Sánchez, W., Benitez, R., González, Y., Mejia, M., & Ortiz, J., (2018). A job stress predictive model evaluation through classifiers algorithms. *IEEE Latin America Transactions*, 16(1), 178–185. https://doi.org/10.1109/TLA.2018.8291471.

16. Mohebian, M. R., Marateb, H. R., Mansourian, M., Mañanas, M. A., & Mokarian, F., (2017). A hybrid computer-aided-diagnosis system for prediction of breast cancer recurrence (HPBCR) using optimized ensemble learning. *Computational and Structural Biotechnology Journal, 15*, 75–85. https://doi.org/10.1016/j.csbj.2016.11.004.

17. National Center for Chronic Disease Prevention and Health Promotion, (2021). *Division for Heart Disease and Stroke prevention.* https://www.cdc.gov/heartdisease/facts.htm (accessed on 11 November 2021).

18. National Cancer Registry Program, (2021). *Breast Cancer*. http://cancerindia.org.in/cancer-statistics/ (accessed on 11 November 2021).

19. Nindrea, R. D., Aryandono, T., Lazuardi, L., & Dwiprahasto, I., (2018). Diagnostic accuracy of different machine learning algorithms for breast cancer risk calculation: A meta-analysis. *Asian Pacific Journal of Cancer Prevention, 19*(7), 1747–1752. https://doi.org/10.22034/APJCP.2018.19.7.1747.

20. Olivera, A. R., Roesler, V., Iochpe, C., Schmidt, M. I., Vigo, A., Barreto, S. M., & Duncan, B. B., (2017). Comparison of machine learning algorithms to build a predictive model for detecting undiagnosed diabetes-ELSA-Brazil: Accuracy study. *Sao Paulo Med. J., 135*, 234–246.

21. Panch, T., Szolovits, P., & Atun, R., (2018). Artificial intelligence, machine learning, and health systems. In: The *Journal of Global Health* (Vol. 8). https://doi.org/10.7189/jogh.08.020303.

22. Panesar, A., (2019). Machine learning and AI for healthcare. In: *Machine Learning and AI for Healthcare*. https://doi.org/10.1007/978-1-4842-3799-1.

23. Patil, R., & Shah, K., (2019). Assessment of Risk of type 2 diabetes mellitus with stress as a risk factor using classification algorithms. *International Journal of Recent Technology and Engineering, 8*(4), 11273–11277. https://doi.org/10.35940/ijrte.d9509.118419.

24. Perveen, S., Shahbaz, M., Keshavjee, K., & Guergachi, A., (2019). Metabolic syndrome and development of diabetes mellitus: Predictive modeling based on machine learning techniques. *IEEE Access, 7*, 1365–1375. https://doi.org/10.1109/ACCESS.2018.2884249.

25. Rady, E. H. A., & Anwar, A. S., (2019). Prediction of kidney disease stages using data mining algorithms. *Informatics in Medicine Unlocked, 15*, 100178. https://doi.org/10.1016/j.imu.2019.100178.

26. Roopa, H., & Asha, T., (2019). A linear model based on principal component analysis for disease prediction. *IEEE Access, 7*, 105314–105318. https://doi.org/10.1109/access.2019.2931956.

27. Samuel, A. L., (1959). Eight-move opening utilizing generalization learning. (See Appendix B, game G-43.1 some studies in machine learning using the game of checkers. *IBM Journal*, 210–229.

28. Singh, P., Singh, S., & Pandi-Jain, G. S., (2018). Effective heart disease prediction system using data mining techniques. *International Journal of Nanomedicine, 13*, 121–124. https://doi.org/10.2147/IJN.S124998.

29. Sisodia, D., & Sisodia, D. S., (2018). Prediction of diabetes using classification algorithms. *Procedia Computer Science, 132*(Iccids), 1578–1585. https://doi.org/10.1016/j.procs.2018.05.122.

30. Stark, G. F., Hart, G. R., Nartowt, B. J., & Deng, J., (2019). Predicting breast cancer risk using personal health data and machine learning models. *PLoS One, 14*(12), 1–17. https://doi.org/10.1371/journal.pone.0226765.

31. Mitchell, T. M., (1997). *Machine Learning* (Vol. 45, No. 37, pp. 870–877). McGraw Hill, Burr Ridge, IL.

32. Uddin, S., Khan, A., Hossain, M. E., & Moni, M. A., (2019). Comparing different supervised machine learning algorithms for disease prediction. *BMC Medical Informatics and Decision Making, 19*(1), 1–16. https://doi.org/10.1186/s12911-019-1004-8.

33. Xiao, J., Ding, R., Xu, X., Guan, H., Feng, X., Sun, T., & Ye, Z., (2019). Comparison and development of machine learning tools in the prediction of chronic kidney disease

progression. *Journal of Translational Medicine, 17*(1), 1–13. https://doi.org/10.1186/s12967-019-1860-0.

34. Zarkogianni, K., Athanasiou, M., Thanopoulou, A. C., & Nikita, K. S., (2018). Comparison of machine learning approaches toward assessing the risk of developing cardiovascular disease as a long-term diabetes complication. *IEEE Journal of Biomedical and Health Informatics, 22*, 1637–1647.

35. Zou, Q., Qu, K., Luo, Y., Yin, D., Ju, Y., & Tang, H., (2018). Predicting diabetes mellitus with machine learning techniques. *Frontiers in Genetics, 9*, 1–10. https://doi.org/10.3389/fgene.2018.00515.

CHAPTER 7

Employing Machine Learning for Predictive Data Analytics in Healthcare

RAKHI AKHARE,[1] MONIKA MANGLA,[2] SANJIVANI DEOKAR,[1,3] and HARDIK DESHMUKH[1]

[1]*Lokmanya Tilak College of Engineering, Navi Mumbai, Maharashtra, India*

[2]*Department of Information Technology, Dwarkadas J. Sanghvi College of Engineering, Mumbai, India*

[3]*Research Scholar, Singhania University, Rajasthan, India, E-mail: sanjivanideokar@gmail.com*

ABSTRACT

Technological advancements have transformed and revolutionized several fields, including transportation, agriculture, finance, weather monitoring, etc. Apart from these, healthcare has also been completely transformed and revamped owing to the technological revolution. The major aspects of the technological revolution that has transformed the facet of healthcare are the emergence of IoT, machine learning, and data analytics. This has brought a systematic change in health systems in order to significantly improve the efficiency and quality of patient care. This improvement in efficiency is gained due to the competence of machine learning in handling massive and unstructured data. As a result, the system is capable of extracting relevant information and thus taking recommended action at the right time, much needed in healthcare systems. It enables real-time medical monitoring of patients.

The authors in this chapter aim to discuss the exuberance of machine learning and predictive data analytics in the healthcare domain. Employment of machine learning in various aspects of healthcare viz. electronic record management, data integration, diagnoses, and disease predictions have been focused in this chapter. Finally, the chapter also presents the advantages of ML over traditional approaches, especially for predictive analytics.

7.1 INTRODUCTION

The technological revolution has revamped the facet of each industry. This transformation in the industry has been termed as Industry 4.0 by the experts. There have been significant advancements and transformations in the fields like education, transportation, finance, etc. Apart from these fields, healthcare has also witnessed a tremendous transformation. The witnessed revolutionary transformation in healthcare is further necessitated owing to frequent emergence of novel diseases and associated treatments methodologies. In such complex scenarios, traditional healthcare systems fail to provide the required quality of service (QoS) which opens avenues for some sophisticated and intelligent method to handle massive data produced by the modern healthcare systems.

In the modern healthcare era, the patient is continuously monitored in terms of various parameters like blood pressure (BP), fever, pulse rate, oxygen level with help of various sensors attached to the body of the concerned. These monitored values are analyzed in order to assess the condition of the patient which enables the health profession to take corrective actions. Competence of handling huge data enables processing of patient health history during the past few years and thus achieves effective patient care. However, this automated healthcare system has some associated challenges. Among various challenges, the first and foremost challenge is to extract useful data from a huge pool of databases. Another challenge is the ability to analyze the extracted data in order to infer meaningful information that could assist a patient's treatment. In order to address these challenges, the area needs to have substantial improvement so as to incorporate data mining and machine learning (ML) concepts [1].

The prime motive behind implementing ML in healthcare is the integration of unstructured data coming from various sources. Owing to such nature of health data, manual handling gets cumbersome. Hence, it necessitates a ML based system that can aid in automated monitoring and decision making in real-time. Owing to the competence of ML, it has been widely accepted as a promising approach in healthcare, primarily for data analytics. Additionally, the popularity of ML is further supported by its ability to address various challenges like data integration and electronic record management. Also, ML has proved its efficiency in disease diagnosis and prediction. Resultantly, it won't be incorrect to say that the future of healthcare lies in ML.

In the current situation, hospitals are in the possession of prolonged historical data which is the most vital and helpful asset to garner maximum benefit from ML. This data can be easily utilized effectively in association with appropriate technologies to assess a patient's health. Furthermore, it can also suggest short-term and long-term strategies to improve a patient's health. Thus, it becomes quite helpful for the medical field with respect to treatment cost and time [2].

Health care industries have been rigorously exploiting BDA to perform analysis on the health data. As a result, the facet of healthcare systems has significantly transformed [2]. The health data consists of the patient's data related to electronic health reports (EHR), diagnostic reports, doctor's prescription, medical images, pharmacy records. On the other side, it also refers to the research data from medicinal journals. In order to handle such a variety of data, digitization of data is absolutely mandatory to optimize the time and cost of disease diagnosis. Additionally, systematic handling of such health data aids to handle all associated challenges during the initial stage. Also, it helps to improve information management in health organizations like hospitals. Considering this, it becomes vital to analyze big data in order to assist automated healthcare systems.

Big data is an emerging technology for efficiently handling complex, unstructured, varying, and voluminous data. It is characterized by four Vs viz. Velocity, volume, variety, and veracity. Big data and data mining algorithms go hand in hand for efficient analysis of such complex data to predict some useful outcomes like hidden patterns and association, etc. In order to cope up with the unmatched demand of big data analytics (BDA) in healthcare, healthcare industries are evolving to frame future policies so as to accommodate it for enhanced efficiency. BDA enables hospitals to collect and process the data in order to discover insights for fact-based and informed decision making. Thus, BDA has established its potential and competency in diverse domains among which healthcare is the most drastically revolution-ized. The reason behind this unmatched popularity of BDA in healthcare is its improved QoSs owing to proper maintenance of multidimensional data. This data consists of information related to historical data, patient's appointments, user experience and diseases diagnosis. The analytics in healthcare using BDA can be broadly classified into four categories as shown in following Figure 7.1:

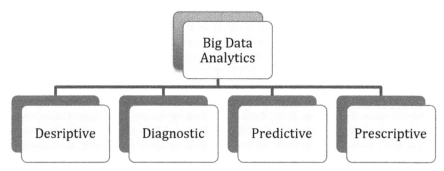

FIGURE 7.1   Classification of BDA in healthcare.

1. **Descriptive Analytics:** It indicates about what is happening and provides statistical data regarding date of occurrence, volume, patient details, etc., in healthcare.
2. **Diagnostic Analytics:** It takes the descriptive data a step ahead and provides a deeper analysis. Often, diagnostic analysis is also referred to as root cause analysis. Diagnostic analytics generally explores the data and tries to infer correlations.
3. **Predictive Analytics:** It is used to make predictions in healthcare regarding patient's conditions, disease outbreak, etc. Predictive analytics helps the help professionals to anticipate the condition beforehand so that it can be handled efficiently.
4. **Prescriptive Analytics:** It reads the predictive data and then processes it. Prescriptive analysis uses the inference of predictive analytics and plans the future infrastructure requirement in terms of manpower and medical equipment.

Among these classifications, descriptive analytics and diagnostic analytics uses past data to understand what happened and its cause, whereas predictive analytics and prescriptive analytics use historical data to forecast future conditions and corresponding actions so as to handle it in the best possible manner.

This chapter is organized into various sections. The first section of the chapter briefly introduces the concept of predictive data analytics and its application in the healthcare industry. Various approaches of predictive data analytics have also been discussed. Background and related work has been elaborated in Section 7.2. Section 7.3 focuses on predictive data analytics in healthcare. The various models for predictive data analytics have been presented in Section 7.4. This section also discusses the various challenges and limitations involved. The authors attempt to propose a framework for predictive data analytics in Section 7.5. Finally, the conclusion and future direction for research has been presented in Section 7.6.

7.2 RELATED WORK

As discussed in the previous section, the capability and competence of ML to handle massive data has widely deployed in healthcare as it handles a lot of unstructured data coming from various sources. As a result, numerous researchers and health professionals have been attracted to undertake this domain as a research area. This section briefly presents the related work presented by various researchers in the context of healthcare and disease prediction.

Authors in Ref. [3] utilize neural networks (NNs), decision tree (DT) and genetic algorithms (GAs) to assess and evaluate various risk factors like age, family history, diabetes, hypertension, cholesterol, smoking, alcohol intake, obesity or physical inactivity [3] in order to predict the heart disease. Implementation of various ML algorithms such as RF, LR, gradient boosting machines and NNs on samples of 378,256 patients for the prediction of cardiovascular risk has been undertaken by authors in Ref. [4]. Continuing the same research line, authors in Ref. [5] developed a prototype for an intelligent heart disease prediction system (IHDPS) using DTs, naive Bayes and NN. During result evaluation of the proposed prototype, it is noticed that each technique has its unique strength in realizing the goals.

Authors in Ref. [6] proposed a framework to identify Type-2 diabetes mellitus (T2DM) patients using electronic health record (EHR) data. In this study, samples of a total of 300 patients were collected, and 114 features were extracted on which different ML algorithms were applied. These ML algorithms mainly included k-nearest neighbor (kNN), random forest (RF), DT, Naïve Bayes, support vector machine (SVM) and LR. From the results, it is observed that SVM produces the best result with an accuracy of 96%. The competence of SVM is also established by research in Ref. [7] where the performance of Naïve Bayes classifier, RBF network and SVM Classifier for heart, cancer, and diabetes datasets is compared. The comparative analysis demonstrates that the SVM classifier produces better accuracy in classification. Thus, it is well established that SVM is the most robust and effective classifier for medical data sets.

Further, authors in Ref. [8] hybridize SVMs with various ML methods to conduct diagnosis of hepatitis disease. It used DTs C4.5 algorithm, ID3 algorithm and CART algorithm in addition to SVM to categorize the diseases. During this research, the prime focus was on the aspect of Medical diagnosis by learning patterns through the collected data of hepatitis and to develop intelligent medical decision support systems to help the physicians.

Authors in Ref. [9] employed predictive data analytics using HER, natural language processing (NLP) for expert decision. Similar methodology can be implemented in various industries. In healthcare, competence to accurately and quickly diagnose patient condition boosts the patient confidence and also fosters the association among patient and health professionals. Similarly, authors in Ref. [10] attempted to diagnose kidney stones. For the same, authors integrated two NN approaches viz. Backpropagation algorithm (BPA) and radial basis function (RBF) and SVM and validated the performance of each. From the experiment, it is demonstrated that the BPA significantly outperforms the diagnosis process in comparison to other techniques.

Similarly, SVM and RF is also used by authors in Ref. [11] to perform classification of cancer and other ailments related to heart and liver with varying kernels and kernel parameters. During result verification, it is observed that different kernels lead to variations in the obtained results. ANN is also implemented for diagnosis of pattern electroretinography (PERG) of optic nerve [12]. During results evaluation, it is observed that the proposed method can be quite helpful for making an accurate interpretation. Various algorithms like Naive Bayes, ANN, and DTs have also been incorporated in the healthcare domain to classify diseases related to liver disorder [13]. Such an efficient system is definitely a boon for the medical domain as early diagnosis of liver related diseases a key to its treatment. The importance of applying AI for health data analytics is also presented by [14] as an automated system will be competent to efficiently monitor the health data and thus will support decision making.

The usage of ML based techniques for detecting breast cancer is also advocated in Ref. [15]. Conventional methods rely on X-ray and eliminate the lump which is tested for hormone receptor status. Integration of ML hugely enhances the diagnosis accuracy and also reduces the recurrence possibility. Authors in Ref. [16] implemented predictive data analytics in heart diseases so as to improve the detection of such diseases. University of California developed a predictive model to analyze such data and identified 13 risk factors. The developed model achieves an accuracy of 93.02%. The patient inflow may also be predicted with the help of work of [14] which will enhance the patient service and care. Such a system also enables hospital management to plan for resources in an effective manner. Hence, it is evident from this section that ML has significantly revamped and revolutionized the facet of healthcare.

7.3 PREDICTIVE ANALYTICS IN HEALTHCARE

From the past few years, the healthcare field has generated massive data about clinical evaluation and report in regards to patients, treatment, subsequent follow-ups, medicine, and so on. All this data should be efficiently handled in order to produce superior outcomes. Hence, some attractive and efficient strategic decisions need to be devised so as to garner maximum advantage of technological development. However, usage of historical data in healthcare fails to perform optimally due to technological constraints. Moreover, data quality is also affected by improper handling of the data. So there is an urge for an efficient method to give promising results. Considering this growing demand, predictive data analytics is emerging as a promising approach to grasp large information and predict the activity, behavior, and future trends for any domain [17]. In healthcare, it may help to predict the progression of disease, recurrence of disease, patient's visit, number of staff and services in emergency conditions, etc. Hence, it is gaining unmatched popularity among researchers and academicians. Predictive data analytics acts up to obtain the desired results while using straightforward methods. This employs predictive data analytics methods with some ML approach ML improves the capability of predictive data analytics.

Following are existing models for predictive data analytics [18]:

- Classification model;
- Clustering model;
- Outliers model; and
- Time series model.

Here, authors restrain from having a detailed discussion of these models. However, readers may refer [18] for a detailed explanation of these models. There are some common predictive algorithms used by these models.

The predictive algorithm is mainly classified into two groups viz. ML and deep learning (DL). ML works for mainly linear as well as nonlinear data. DL is a specialized ML technique that is basically used for audio, text, and images with better optimization results. There are several algorithms for ML based predictive analytics. Some of these algorithms are briefly discussed below:

1. **Support Vector Machine (SVM):** It is basically a classification algorithm. In this algorithm, each data item can be plotted as a point in n-dimensional space (where n is a number of features) with the value of a particular coordinate for each feature.

2. **Logistic Regression:** Unlike classification algorithms, it is used to estimate discrete values, e.g., binary values like 0/1, yes/no, true/false based on a given set of independent variable(s). In simple words, it predicts the probability of occurrence of an event, e.g., for predicting weather, there can be only two possibilities, it may occur or it does not.

3. **CART:** Classification and regression trees are a specific flavor of DTs. The root and internal nodes of CART are the non-terminal nodes while terminal nodes are the leaf nodes. This model predicts the value present at the leaf node after traversing the path with reference to some predefined condition.

4. **Random Forest:** It can also be used for classification as well as regression. Also, it is capable of handling huge volumes of data. RF implements bagging where a subset of training data is used to train the network. The training process may be repeated with another subset in parallel thus achieving a strong learning.

5. **Generalized Linear Model (GLM):** It narrows down the list of variables and thus achieves enhanced performance. Also, it gets trained quickly. The only limitation of this model is that it requires relatively huge training data sets.

6. **Gradient Boosted Model (GBM):** it generates a model that uses DT for classification. In this approach, each tree rectifies errors present in previously trained trees. As it builds one tree at a time, it takes longer but gives better performance. Hence, it is used in ML based ranking in Yahoo, among others.

7. **K-Means:** It is a simple and most popular algorithm to classify input data into different clusters. It calculates the minimum distance from centroid to different variables and assigns it to the nearest center. It is a fast method to classify input data based on similarity index.

On account of these algorithms, ML has gained unprecedented popularity in handling huge volumes of data generated in healthcare industries. Further, it implements a variety of algorithms to enhance the capabilities of healthcare systems and also provides promising results in less time and cost. The subsequent subsection discusses the employment of ML for predictive data analytics in the Healthcare industry.

7.4   ML FOR PREDICTIVE DATA ANALYTICS IN HEALTHCARE

As a result of increasing population and environmental changes, it is observed that incidence of diseases are exponentially rising and hence healthcare necessitates the incorporation of innovative technologies to cope up with these increasing instances.

Conventional drug discovery is a very time-consuming and costly process. Using traditional methods, it takes around 10 years to discover a drug for a disease. It has been witnessed recently during drug discovery for COVID-19. Each leading country is spending a huge share of its national economy to discover drugs for fighting COVID-19. Most rigorous research is taking place at the topmost priority in all leading countries [19]. It is estimated that for this drug discovery, nations are putting up around 100 million dollars. This huge time and cost can be optimized by using existing clinical data with ML algorithms which can boost such research in the following ways:

- Monitoring live data from patients and feeding it directly into the system helps the model to adapt to the ever-changing patient's medical history.
- Helps in spotting complex patterns from massive data for detection of disease and diagnosis to produce better decisions about treatment plans.
- Using predictive modeling helps to eliminate the overall cost and time required for trial and monitor processes in drug discovery [2].
- For healthcare, supervised learning is used for predicting patient mortality, hospitalization duration, and drug response. The supervised learning algorithm tries to learn how to build a classifier for predicting the outcome variable y for given input x, which is a mapping function f where $y = f(x)$. The classifier is built by an algorithm along with a set of data $\{x_1, x_2, \ldots x_n\}$ with the corresponding outcome label$\{y_1, y_2, \ldots y_n\}$ [20].

On the contrary, unsupervised learning only finds associations or clusters within the data. For example, it may discover hidden subtypes within a disease. For example, the agent (for example, Reinforcement learning (RL) algorithm) tries to improve the model parameters through iteratively simulating the state (patient condition) and action (giving fluid or vasopressor for hypotension) to obtain the feedback reward (mortality or not) that eventually converge to a model that yields optimal decisions [21].

In recent times diagnosis and prediction on various diseases like cardiovascular diseases (CVDs), cancers, Diabetes, Hepatitis Asthma, Tuberculosis (TB) blood pressure (BP) monitoring and infectious diseases have been carried out using various ML predictions techniques. Here are some instances for the same as follows:

1. **Image Analysis:** ML helps radiologists to find the changes in medical images (X-Ray, Scans, etc.), to detect and diagnose the malignancy during early stages.
2. **Drug Discovery:** Bio-medical data is highly complex as it contains genetic and imaging data. ML algorithms help researchers to design new drugs and their chemical structures. Also, it helps to evaluate the benefits and side-effects of drugs.
3. **Identify Diseases and Diagnosis:** ML helps doctors to diagnose diseases which were beyond diagnosis until ML evolved such as tumors/cancers.
4. **Personalized Treatment:** By leveraging on patient medical history, ML can help to develop customized treatment and medicines that can target specific diseases in individual patients.
5. **Prediction in Epidemic Outbreaks:** ML algorithms help to monitor and predict the possible epidemic outbreaks that can take various parts of the world by collecting data from satellites, real time updates on social media, and vital information from the web. ML algorithms like SVM have helped to predict the outbreaks of malaria by considering factors such as temperature, average monthly rainfall, etc.
6. **Maintaining Healthcare Records:** Document classification methods using vector machines like ML based OCR recognition is used to sort and classify healthcare data.

7.5   USE CASE: ML FOR HEART DISEASE

This section basically considers the application of predictive data analytics for various diseases. For the sake of better understanding, authors consider the example of heart disease so as to enhance the readers' understanding.

Here, it is worth mentioning that such an automated system can be basically demonstrated with the help of a block diagram as shown in Figure 7.2.

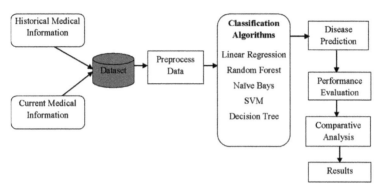

FIGURE 7.2   Illustration of ML application in healthcare.

Here, as demonstrated in Figure 7.2, the first and foremost step in such a system is data collection related to health. This multi-perspective data is in various forms (text, image, quantitative value) and may be collected form of prescriptions, discharge slips, patient's history. Thereafter, data is cleaned so as to remove any unnecessary data. Following this, important features are extracted to find important features. Then, a model is developed which is trained on the huge dataset so as to enhance its prediction accuracy. After sufficient training of the model, it is deployed and leveraged for further improvement [1].

Here, in this section, the authors discuss the employment of ML algorithms with reference to heart diseases. For the same, the dataset is taken from 2 different data sources viz. [22] and [23] created by Hungarian Institute of Cardiology, University Hospital (Zurich), and University Hospital (Basel, Switzerland). This is multivariate type of dataset thus involves a variety of mathematical and statistical variables.

	A	B	C	D	E	F	G	H	I	J	K	L	M	N
1	age	sex	cp	trestbps	chol	fbs	restecg	thalach	exang	oldpeak	slope	ca	thal	target
2	63	1	3	145	233	1	0	150	0	2.3	0	0	1	1
3	37	1	2	130	250	0	1	187	0	3.5	0	0	2	1
4	41	0	1	130	204	0	0	172	0	1.4	2	0	2	1
5	56	1	1	120	236	0	1	178	0	0.8	2	0	2	1
6	57	0	0	120	354	0	1	163	1	0.6	2	0	2	1
7	57	1	0	140	192	0	1	148	0	0.4	1	0	1	1
8	56	0	1	140	294	0	0	153	0	1.3	1	0	2	1
9	44	1	1	120	263	0	1	173	0	0	2	0	3	1
10	52	1	2	172	199	1	1	162	0	0.5	2	0	3	1

FIGURE 7.3   Illustration of health data considered for heart disease.

This database includes 76 attributes, but all published studies relate to the use of a subset of 14 of them. These 14 attributes viz. age, sex, chest pain type, resting blood pressure (BP), serum cholesterol, fasting blood sugar (FBS), resting ECG, maximum heart rate achieved, exercise-induced angina, old peak-ST depression induced by exercise relative to rest, the slope of the peak exercise ST segment, number of major vessels and Thalassemia as shown in Figure 7.3. Researchers have primarily worked on the Cleveland database till date. The prime task here is to predict whether a particular person has a heart disease or not based on various attributes. Another task of this study is to diagnose various insights that could be helpful for an enhanced understanding. The association of all these 14 variables with heart disease or heart attack can be understood and visualized using a Heatmap as shown in Figure 7.4. From the heatmap, it becomes evident that chest pain is most highly correlated with the target variable (heart attack in this case). Thus, it implies that compared to other attributes, chest pain contributes the most in prediction of presences of a heart disease.

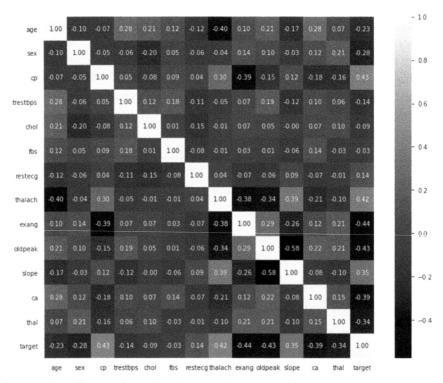

FIGURE 7.4   Heatmap for various factors with target variable.

Apart from finding the association, the dataset can also be used to infer the susceptibility among individuals. Here this susceptibility is analyzed along sex of the patient and the result is demonstrated in Figure 7.5. It is evident from Figure 7.5 that males are more susceptible to get heart disease than females.

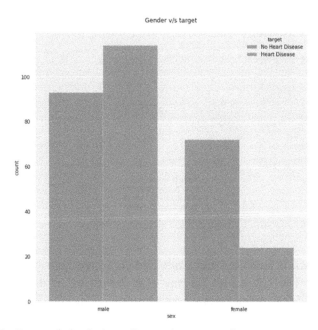

FIGURE 7.5   Data analytics for heart disease along sex attribute.

Additionally, men experience sudden heart attacks, i.e., between 70–89%. On the contrary, women may experience a heart attack with no chest pressure; they usually experience nausea or vomiting which is often confused with acid reflux or the flu. The data is also analyzed along chest pain attributes and the result is shown in Figure 7.6.

The chest pain is broadly classified into four classes as asymptomatic, atypical angina, non-anginal pain and typical angina. Most of the heart disease patients are found to have asymptomatic chest pain. These groups of people might show a typical symptom like indigestion, flu or a strained chest muscle. An asymptomatic attack, like any heart attack, involves, blockage of blood flow to your heart and possible damage to the heart muscle. Asymptomatic Heart attack puts you at a greater risk of having another heart attack which could turn to be fatal. Unfortunately, there is no test to determine the potential for asymptomatic heart attack. The only way to determine it is through an electrocardiogram test. These tests can reveal changes that signal a heart attack.

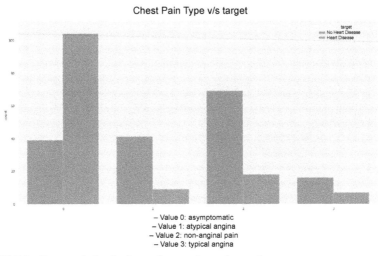

FIGURE 7.6   Data analytics for heart disease along chest pain.

Heart disease is analyzed along age and cholesterol attributes with help of count plot. The count plot for age and cholesterol is demonstrated in Figures 7.7 and 7.8, respectively. From Figure 7.7, it is evident that Heart Disease is common among people in the age group 60 and above followed by age group 41 to 60. Similarly, the association of cholesterol is represented in Figure 7.8.

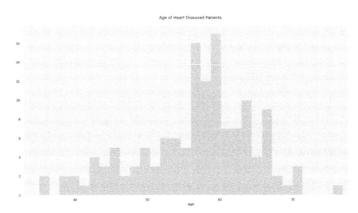

FIGURE 7.7   Count plot along age attribute.

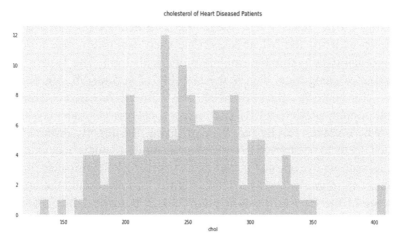

FIGURE 7.8   Count plot along cholesterol attribute.

Further, authors analyze heart disease with respect to two different attributes at the same time. For the same, authors select age and cholesterol level. The impact of two attributes on heart disease can be represented by the joint plot in seaborn as shown in Figure 7.9. From this trend among two features, it is evident that patients in the age group 50–60 tend to have Cholesterol between 200 mg/dl to 300 mg/dl.

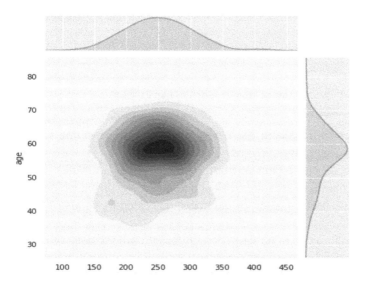

FIGURE 7.9   Joint plot for age and cholesterol level.

In order to analyze the data, the authors performed some further processing on the dataset. For the same, data needs to be prepared in a manner so as it fits the ML models. One such example is the conversion of categorical data to suitable (mainly numerical) form. The motive behind conversion of categorical data is the inability of several ML algorithms to work on non-numeric values and needs only numeric values, a constraint for efficient implementation of ML. For instance, categorical data may be color names where values can be red, blue or green. Resultantly, some efficient approach needs to be devised to convert such values to numerical values. For the same, authors use one-hot encoding to transform categorical attributes of the dataset to numerical values. Here, Figure 7.10 represents the attributes categories of the dataset. From Figure 7.10, it is evident that there are a total of six numerical attributes, four categorical attributes and four Boolean attributes in the dataset containing 303 observations.

Overview	Reproduction	Warnings 3			
Dataset statistics			**Variable types**		
Number of variables		14	NUM		6
Number of observations		303	CAT		4
Missing cells		0	BOOL		4
Missing cells (%)		0.0%			
Duplicate rows		1			
Duplicate rows (%)		0.3%			
Total size in memory		33.3 KiB			
Average record size in memory		112.4 B			

FIGURE 7.10   Description of various attributes in the dataset.

In order to transform the categorical attribute to numerical value, the attribute is minutely analyzed. For instance, Figure 7.11 demonstrates the description of chest pain attribute (a categorical attribute). This analysis describes that there are total distinct categories for this attribute as discussed previously. The frequency of each distinct category is also represented in Figure 7.11.

Further, in order to implement a regression model, data values are generally normalized. Here, authors use the min-max normalization method for the same so as to scale the data ranges into [0,1]. Further, the same is used to perform classification. The implemented classification model shows that 91% prediction of absence of heart disease was predicted correctly while the accuracy regarding presence of heart disease is found to be 83%. The same is also represented by the confusion matrix for the system in Figure 7.12.

FIGURE 7.11   Detailed analysis of chest pain attribute (a categorical attribute).

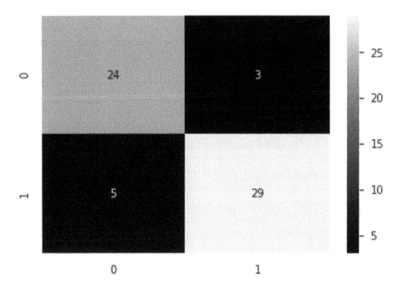

FIGURE 7.12   Confusion matrix for the developed system.

From the confusion matrix, it is evident that the proposed system performs efficiently for detecting heart diseases as both true-false and true-negative show exciting results as true positive value is 24 and true negative 29. In order to further validate the model, the authors also demonstrate the ROC curve for heart disease classifier in Figure 7.13. This ROC curve demonstrates the competency of the classifier algorithm to distinguish among positive and negative classes. A most sophisticated classifier algorithm achieves this value to be 1. Here it is observed in the ROC curve that true positive rate reaches near to 1 which is quite exciting.

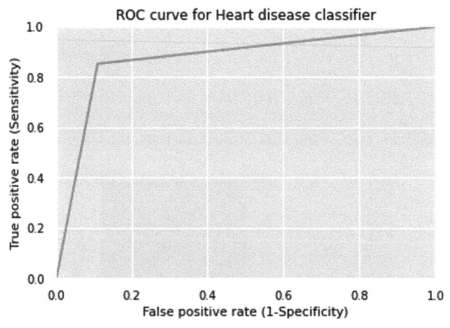

FIGURE 7.13   ROC curve for heart disease classifier.

The accuracy of the model is obtained to be 87.09%.

7.6   LIMITATIONS AND CHALLENGES

ML has observed its intense deployment in healthcare since its inception. However, it still bears some limitations and challenges. The major challenge is handling enormous data coming from various sources in semi-structured and unstructured form. In order to use the data, it necessitates proper handling so as it could infer meaningful information. Another concerning challenge is security and privacy of health data. Moreover, it also necessitates skilled health professionals so as to develop a coherent model. Also, as the health data is voluminous in terms of timeliness also, it further adds to the associated challenges [2]. Moreover, in order to completely implement the ML in healthcare, EHR needs to be digitized, which is a huge challenge as it requires a lot of effort in terms of people, technology, and process. Construction of efficient classifiers for biological application is another challenge in ML [24].

7.7 CONCLUSION

The advancements in ML has revamped the facet of healthcare in an unmatched and unprecedented manner. Integration of ML in healthcare significantly improves the diagnosis result which is a great achievement. However, it still has some limitations which still needs research in order to garner maximum advantage of the technology. Here, in this chapter, the authors present the employment of ML in the context of heart disease considering the authentic data set comprising 14 attributes. The classification, regression, join plot of the data is illustrated. The effectiveness of the implemented system is also demonstrated using a confusion matrix and ROC curve which shows exciting achievement. The work can be further extended in order to address the limitations of ML so as to achieve the maximum advantage of the technological revolution.

KEYWORDS

- **backpropagation algorithm**
- **generalized linear model**
- **machine learning**
- **radial basis function**
- **support vector machine**

REFERENCES

1. Science, C., (2018). *Disease Prediction Using Machine.* 8(1), 1–8. doi: 10.5121/cseij.2018.8101.
2. Kaur, P., Sharma, M., & Mittal, M., (2018). Big data and machine learning based secure healthcare framework. *Procedia Comput. Sci., 132,* 1049–1059. doi: 10.1016/j.procs.2018.05.020.
3. Ayatollahi, H., Gholamhosseini, L., & Salehi, M., (2019). Predicting coronary artery disease: A comparison between two data mining algorithms. *BMC Public Health, 19*(1), 1–9. doi: 10.1186/s12889-019-6721-5.

4. Weng, S. F., Reps, J., Kai, J., Garibaldi, J. M., & Qureshi, N., (2017). Can machine-learning improve cardiovascular risk prediction using routine clinical data? *PloS One, 12*(4), e0174944.

5. Siegel, E., (1991). German standards for ventilation devices. *Anasthesiol. und Intensivmed., 32*(2), 52–54.

6. Zheng, T., et al., (2017). A machine learning-based framework to identify type 2 diabetes through electronic health records. *Int. J. Med. Inform., 97*, 120–127. doi: 10.1016/j.ijmedinf.2016.09.014.

7. Huang, S., Nianguang, C. A. I., Penzuti, P. P., Narandes, S., Wang, Y., & Wayne, X., (2018). Applications of support vector machine (SVM) learning in cancer genomics. *Cancer Genomics and Proteomics, 15*(1), 41–51. doi: 10.21873/cgp.20063.

8. Jain, D., & Singh, V., (2018). Feature selection and classification systems for chronic disease prediction: A review. *Egypt. Informatics J., 19*(3), 179–189. doi: 10.1016/j.eij.2018.03.002.

9. Boukenze, B., Mousannif, H., & Haqiq, A., (2016). Predictive analytics in healthcare system using data mining techniques. *Comput. Sci. Inf. Technol., 1*, 1–9.

10. Verma, J., Nath, M., Tripathi, P., & Saini, K. K., (2017). Analysis and identification of kidney stone using Kth nearest neighbor (KNN) and support vector machine (SVM) classification techniques. *Pattern Recognit. Image Anal., 27*(3), 574–580.

11. AhmedK, A., Aljahdali, S., & Naimatullah, H. S., (2013). Comparative prediction performance with support vector machine and random forest classification techniques. *Int. J. Comput. Appl., 69*(11), 12–16. doi: 10.5120/11885-7922.

12. Vijayarani, S., & Dhayanand, S., (2015). Kidney disease prediction using SVM and ANN algorithms. *Int. J. Comput. Bus. Res., 6*(2), 2229–6166. ISSN Online.

13. Baitharu, T. R., & Pani, S. K., (2016). Analysis of data mining techniques for healthcare decision support system using liver disorder dataset. *Procedia Comput. Sci., 85*(Cms), 862–870. doi: 10.1016/j.procs.2016.05.276.

14. Kaur, J., & Mann, K. S., (2018). AI based healthcare platform for real time, predictive, and prescriptive analytics. *Commun. Comput. Inf. Sci., 805*, 138–149. doi: 10.1007/978-981-13-0755-3_11.

15. Shukla, R., Yadav, V., Pal, P, R., & Pathak, P., (2019). Machine learning techniques for detecting and predicting breast cancer. *Int. J. Innov. Technol. Explor. Eng., 8*(7), 2658–2662.

16. Alharthi, H., (2018). Healthcare predictive analytics: An overview with a focus on Saudi Arabia. *J. Infect. Public Health, 11*(6), 749–756. doi: 10.1016/j.jiph.2018.02.005.

17. Lepenioti, K., Bousdekis, A., Apostolou, D., & Mentzas, G., (2020). Prescriptive analytics: Literature review and research challenges. *Int. J. Inf. Manage., 50*, 57–70. doi: 10.1016/j.ijinfomgt.2019.04.003.

18. Van, C. B., Wynants, L., Timmerman, D., Steyerberg, E, W., & Collins, & G, S., (2019). Predictive analytics in healthcare: How can we know it works?. *J. Am. Med. Informatics Assoc., 26*(12), 1651–1654. doi: 10.1093/jamia/ocz130.

19. Mangla, M., & Sharma, N. *Fuzzy Modeling of Clinical and Epidemiological Factors for COVID-19.*

20. Haq, A, U., Li, J, P., Memon, M, H., Nazir, S., Sun, R., & Garciá-Magarinð, I., (2018). A hybrid intelligent system framework for the prediction of heart disease using machine learning algorithms. *Mob. Inf. Syst., 2018.* doi: 10.1155/2018/3860146.

21. Basurto, N., Arroyo, Á., Vega, R., Quintián, H., Calvo-Rolle, J, L., & Herrero, Á., (2019). A Hybrid Intelligent System to forecast solar energy production. *Comput. Electr. Eng., 78,* 373–387.
22. https://archive.ics.uci.edu/ml/datasets/Heart+Disease (accessed on 11 November 2021).
23. https://www.kaggle.com/ronitf/heart-disease-uci (accessed on 11 November 2021).
24. Meena, S. D., & Revathi, M., (2013). Predictive analytics on healthcare: A survey. *Int. J. Sci. Res., 4,* 2319–7064. [Online]. Available: www.ijsr.net (accessed on 11 November 2021).

CHAPTER 8

Prediction of Heart Disease Using Machine Learning

SUBASISH MOHAPATRA,[1] JIJNASEE DASH,[1]
SUBHADARSHINI MOHANTY,[2] and ARUNIMA HOTA[1]

[1]Department of Computer Science and Engineering,
College of Engineering and Technology, Bhubaneswar, Odisha, India,
E-mail: smohapatra@cet.edu.in (S. Mohapatra)

[2]Department of Information Technology, College of Engineering and
Technology, Bhubaneswar, Odisha, India

ABSTRACT

The heart is the organ that controls the progression of blood in the body or the focal point of human feeling. It is the most vital organ found in the chest pit of people. Due to the lack of proper diagnosis and early-stage prediction of heart disease, many people die every year. In today's era, the modern lifestyle and the polluted atmosphere is the main cause of the growth in mortality rate. As per the Indian heart association (IHA), every minute around four-person dies in India whose age group belongs to 30–50. It does not mean that children and other age groups are not affected. As per WHO data, cardiovascular diseases (CVDs) are the number one reason for death all around, taking an expected 17.9 million lives every year that is approximately 31% of deaths around the globe. CVDs are a gathering of clutters of the heart and veins and incorporate coronary illness, cerebrovascular ailment, rheumatic coronary illness, and different conditions. Four out of five CVD passing are because of cardiovascular failures and strokes, and 33% of these passing happen rashly in individuals under 70 years old. Irrespective of gender and age group cardiovascular illness is a major issue in India. Hence, it is necessary that early prediction with accuracy can save a million lives. In this chapter, different machine learning approaches have been applied for the early prediction of heart disease. Finally, after all, the model evaluation conclusion drawn is that KNN and random forest classifier (RFC) produces a more accurate prediction than others. It can be helpful for the necessary aid for chronic patients suffering from heart diseases.

8.1   INTRODUCTION

The heart is the most important organ present in the left-center of the human body, though it is small in size that is the same as the size of our fist, it has a vital role to make a human life. Any disorder that affects the normal functionality of the heart is known as heart disease. Under the term heart illness, it consists of blood vessel diseases, such as coronary artery problems, heart rhythm problems (arrhythmias) and heart faults you're born with (congenital heart problem), and many more [1]. Insufficient or less blood flow can affect a healthy heart by not getting proper oxygen it requires and affects other body parts with insufficient oxygen. Types of heart diseases are there with various symptoms that can be different for men and women [2]. In blood vessel (atherosclerotic) heart disease, men are likely to get chest pain, pain in the upper abdomen or back during heavy work or exercise, whereas women can get chest discomfort, nausea, fatigue, and shortness of breath, weakness, etc.

It can be detected with early diagnosis of symptoms. Abnormal heartbeats (heart arrhythmias) disease causes the heart to beat very fastly or very slowly. Symptoms are like shortness of breath, dizziness, bradycardia, tachycardia, syncope, etc. Heart disease generated by heart defects causes symptoms like cyanosis, swelling around the eyes, leg, poor weight gain in the case of a child. Weak heart muscle (dilated cardiomyopathy) disease symptoms are not visible earlier. At worst condition symptoms like fatigue, breathlessness at rest, a fluttering of the heart can be seen. Heart infections can cause skin rashes, swelling of body parts, dry cough, etc. [2]. Our heart consists of four valves, namely aortic, mitral, pulmonary, tricuspid valves. They generally open and closes to coordinate blood course through our heart. Stenosis, insufficiency, prolapse are the conditions that may damage our valves to cause valvular heart disease. The visible symptoms are swollen legs, irregular heartbeat, and syncope. Individuals with high blood pressure (BP), hypertension, overweight, high lipid, diabetics are at risk of cardiovascular disease [1, 20]. If at the primary stage they get a proper diagnosis and primary health care facilities, the premature death rate can be prevented.

With proper treatment and right counseling at an earlier stage can cure their disease [3, 21].

Therefore many researchers have tried to give a solution for the prediction of heart disease. But accuracy has always been a major issue. In this chapter, machine learning (ML) techniques have been used, and the result is compared with different algorithms to get more accuracy in predicting whether a person is having heart disease or not. Various attributes of the dataset and the performance of the model are evaluated using a confusion matrix.

The organization of the chapter is as follows: Next section contains the Literature review. Then the subsequent sections contain the proposed model, Model analysis, result discussion, conclusion, and future works respectively.

8.2   LITERATURE SURVEY

Rovina Dbritto et al. proposed a model and discussed the major techniques of data mining for early detection of heart illness and they concluded that SVM is more accurate that is up to 80% for large datasets [3]. Dwivedi discussed various algorithms of ML and those were assessed on the receiver operative characteristic curve. With LR, approximately 85% accuracy recorded [4]. De Menezes et al. proposed a methodology for data classification with the binary response through the Boosting algorithm and LR. Binomial boosting with LR was effective for noisy data and described more accurate information about the problem of binary response [5]. Beyene et al. proposed a methodology to compare different data mining techniques using the WEKA tool to do a prior diagnosis of heart disease. They failed to predict the accurate performance of each algorithm as feature selection was a major concern. So accuracy was not so good [6]. Haq et al. proposed a system that was helpful to doctors to diagnose heart patients easily. They have discussed all classifiers and feature selection algorithms and validated their model with ROC and AUC. But the reduction in feature and optimization resulting accuracy was not up to the mark [7]. Gunasekaran Manogaran et al. Proposed a system where a wearable body sensor technique used to measure BF, glucose level, and heartbeat rate of patients to predict the illness of heart using a linear regression model with 81% accuracy [8]. SD Desai et al. proposed a methodology where LR and BPNN classification models were used with 10 fold cross-validation to predict heart illness by considering attributes of the Cleveland dataset. But visible accuracy was not achieved by them [9]. R

Kannan et al. proposed a methodology where they compared the accuracy of four different ML algorithms with receiver operating characteristic (ROC) curve for predicting heart illness by the 14 attributes from UCI Cardiac Datasets [10]. Muhammad Affan Alim et al. proposed a model to predict heart disease using ML algorithms. They focused on finding features by using correlation on UCI vascular heart disease dataset for robust prediction of results. They achieved an accuracy of 86.94% [17].

From the above reviews, it is clear that the prediction accuracy rate of classifiers and other algorithms is still a major concern for heart disease prediction [11, 12]. So different ML techniques such as LR, KNN classification, SVM algorithm, Naïve Bayes algorithm, decision tree (DT) algorithm, random forest (RF) classification have been discussed [13–15]. Data exploration and model validation has been evaluated to get a more accurate prediction of the occurrence of heart disease in a person irrespective of age group and gender.

8.3   PROPOSED MODEL

A new methodology has been proposed in Figure 8.1 given that collects data from the dataset, data exploration is done then pre-processes the data as the dataset may contain null values, dummy variables are created for categorical data. Then the whole dataset is divided into two sets that is training set and testing set.

Different supervised ML techniques applied for examining the accuracy rate for the prediction of heart disease. Plots of each algorithm's prediction accuracy rate in one place to compare the best accuracy achieved. Finally, the confusion matrix for each technique has been demonstrated for model validation.

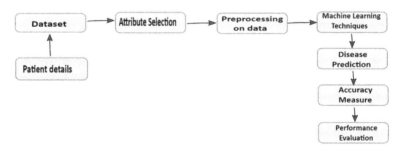

FIGURE 8.1   Block diagram of the proposed model.

8.4   WORKING OF MODEL

Dataset is collected from UCI repository that is the Cleveland dataset. Some rows with all 14 attributes we are using are given below. Purpose of all attributes described later. Basic attributes taken into consideration and description of each attribute were presented in Tables 8.1 and 8.2, respectively.

TABLE 8.1   Basic Attributes of Dataset

	age	sex	cp	trestbps	chol	fbs	restecg	thalach	exang	oldpeak	slope	ca	thal	traget
0	63	1	3	145	233	1	0	150	0	2.3	0	0	1	1
1	37	1	2	130	250	0	1	187	0	3.5	0	0	2	1
2	41	0	1	130	204	0	0	172	0	1.4	2	0	2	1
3	56	1	1	120	236	0	1	178	0	0.8	2	0	2	1
4	57	0	0	120	354	0	1	163	1	0.6	2	0	2	1

TABLE 8.2   Description of Each Attribute of Dataset

SL. No.	Attributes	Description
1.	age	Age in years
2.	sex	(1 = male; 0 = female)
3.	cp	Chest pain type
4.	trestbps	Resting blood pressure (in mm Hg on admission to the hospital)
5.	chol	Serum cholesterol in mg/dl
6.	fbs	(fasting blood sugar > 120 mg/dl) (1 = true; 0 = false)
7.	restecg	Resting electrocardiographic results
8.	thalach	Maximum heart rate achieved
9.	exang	Exercise-induced angina (1 = yes; 0 = no)
10.	oldpeak	ST depression induced by exercised relative to rest
11.	slope	Slope of the peak exercise ST segment
12.	ca	Number of major vessels (0–3) colored by fluoroscopy
13.	thal	3 = normal; 6 = fixed defect; 7 = reversible defect
14.	target	Have disease or not (1 = yes, 0 = no)

Datasets ideally is a consummately curated gathering of perceptions with no missing qualities or abnormalities. Be that as it may, this isn't correct. True information can be of any size. It tends to be chaotic, that implies it should be spotless and hassles. Data cleaning is a very vital process. ML algorithms gain from the information. It is critical, in any case, that the information you provide them is explicitly prearranged and refined for the troublesome you have to understand. It incorporates information cleaning, preprocessing, highlight building, etc.

Data pre-processing is very important because the dataset is not cent percent correct and error-free. So various operations should be carried out before using the actual algorithm. The NaN values present in the dataset are a major problem, so first of all, we have to remove those fields not containing values. NAN can't be processed so that it has been converted to numerical values. We have to replace it with column mean value. So that those NAN values can be removed. In a few ML algorithms range of values for raw data varies widely, so without feature scaling objective functions work is not proper. For example, the majority of classifiers figure the separation between two focuses by the Euclidean separation. If one of the highlights has a wide scope of qualities, the separation will be represented by this specific component.

In this way, the scope of all highlights ought to be scaled so each element contributes around proportionately to the last separation. So we will scale the different fields to get them closer as far as qualities. Age has simply two qualities for example 0,1 and cholesterol have high qualities like 100. In this way, to get them closer to one another we should scale them. Factorization is another important step where we relegated importance to the qualities with the goal that the calculation doesn't befuddle between them. For instance, allotting importance to 0 what's more, 1 in the age area with the goal that the calculation doesn't think about 1 as more prominent than 0 in that area.

8.4.1   SPLITTING

The entire dataset has been divided into two categories that are training and testing set. For training purposes, 80% of data is used and the rest 20% for testing purposes.

8.4.2   CLASSIFIERS

The training data is trained by using six different ML algorithms, i.e., LR, KNN, SVM, Naive Bayes, DT, and RF. Each algorithm detail explanation is given in subsections.

8.4.2.1   LOGISTIC REGRESSION

LR is a ML technique that comes under supervised learning which can work with labeled data specially used to predict the probability of occurrence of a target variable[16]. The target or dependent variable has binary values that are 0 (No) or 1(Yes). The output is a sigmoid curve always. P-value lies between 0 to 1. Below is the equation of LR.

$$\log\left[\frac{y}{1-y}\right] = b_0 + b_1 x_1 + b_2 x_2 + \ldots + b_n x_n \tag{1}$$

where; y is the independent variable; x is the dependent variable; b0 is Y-intercept, b_1, b_2, ..., b_n are slopes.

8.4.2.2   KNN (K-NEAREST NEIGHBORS) CLASSIFICATION

KNN is a ML technique that comes under supervised learning which can solve both classification and regression problems. It assumes that similar things existence is very close to each other. Selecting the right K value is the most important task here. For the given data that is unknown to the machine, we can test with different K values to get reduced error for better prediction. First of all number K of neighbors is selected then Euclidean distance is evaluated and as per the calculation selection of K nearest neighbors [26, 27] done. No. of data points in each category is counted. For the category having max neighbor, new data points are assigned. Then the model is ready. We have used Sklearn to direct import this classifier.

$$Euclidean\ Distance\ D(P,Q) = \sqrt{(x_2 - x_1)^2 + (y_2 - y_1)^2} \tag{2}$$

8.4.2.3   SVM (SUPPORT VECTOR MACHINE) ALGORITHM

SVM is very popular as a supervised ML technique [22]. Mainly, to solve classification as well as regression problems, it is used. A set of training data is given, set apart as having a place with both of two classifications, an SVM preparing calculation at that point fabricates a model that allocates new guides to one classification or the other, making it a no probabilistic double direct classifier. An SVM model is a portrayal of the models as focuses in space, mapped so the instances of the different classifications are isolated by a reasonable hole that is as wide as could be expected under the circumstances [23] marked as belonging to either one of two categories, an SVM [31] training algorithm then builds a model that assigns new examples to one category or the other, making it a no probabilistic binary linear classifier [24]. An SVM model is a representation of the examples as points in space, mapped so that the examples of the separate categories are divided by a clear gap that is as wide as possible [25]. New examples are then mapped into that same space. The focuses are isolated based on the hyperplane that different them. SVM algorithm's Objective is to make the best line or choice limit that can isolate n-dimensional space into classes with the goal that we can without much of a stretch, put the new information point in the right classification later on. This best choice limit is known as a hyperplane. We are using the Sklearn library to import the SVM classifier directly.

8.4.2.4　NAÏVE BAYES CLASSIFIER ALGORITHM

It comes under Supervised learning and based on Bayes theorem to solve classification problems with a large dataset and very effective for quick prediction. Based on the object's probability prediction is done here. The first given dataset is converted to frequency tables. Then the likelihood table is generated by finding the probabilities of given features. Finally, Bayes theorem used to calculate the posterior probability [28, 29]. Bayes theorem formula is given as:

$$P(A|B) = \frac{P(B|A)P(A)}{P(B)} \tag{3}$$

where; P (A|B) represents the posterior probability; P(B) represents predictor prior probability; P (B|A) represents likelihood; P(A) represents class prior probability.

8.4.2.5　DECISION TREE ALGORITHM

It is a simple supervised learning technique for solving classification problems. In the tree structure, features of the dataset are represented in internal nodes, and decision rule represented by branches and outcome is represented by each leaf node [20]. There are two hubs, namely Decision Node and

Leaf Node [33, 34]. Choice hubs are utilized to settle on any choice having various branches, though Leaf hubs are the yield of those chosen choices and does not contain any extra branches. The tree begins with root node S with a complete dataset [25]. Attribute Selection Measure is used to find the best attribute. Node S is divided into subsets containing best attribute possible values [19]. The node which contains the best attribute is generated, then new DTs made recursively using a subset of the dataset. This process continues until the stage it is not possible to classify the nodes known as a final leaf node [6]. ASM contains two techniques.

Below given equations are used for decision making.

$$\text{Information Gain} = \text{Entropy}(S) - \left[(\text{Weighted Avg})*\text{Entropy}(\text{each feature}) \right] \quad (4)$$

$$\text{Gini Index} = 1 - \sum_j (Pj)^2 \quad (5)$$

$$\text{Entropy}(s) = -P(\text{yes}) \log_2 P(yes) - P(\text{no}) \log_2 P(no) \quad (6)$$

where; S is the total number of samples; P (yes) is the probability of yes; P (no) is the probability of no.

Where information gain represents the estimation of changes in entropy after the division of a dataset dependent on an attribute [25]. Gini index is a proportion of polluting influence or immaculateness utilized at the time of making a choice tree in the CART calculation. Entropy measures the randomness of data.

8.4.2.6   RANDOM FOREST ALGORITHM

It depends on the idea of the group realizing, which is a procedure of joining different classifiers to take care of a perplexing issue and to improve the presentation of the model. As the name recommends, RF [18] is a classifier that contains various choice trees on different subsets of the given dataset and takes the normal to improve the prescient exactness of that dataset. Instead of depending on one choice tree, the irregular backwoods take the expectation from each tree and dependent on the lion's share votes of forecasts, and it predicts the last yield. By combining the N DT, the RF is created in the first phase. In the second phase, the prediction is made for each tree created in the first phase. Random K data points are chosen from dataset then decision tree made and number N chosen for trees that are required to build. Repetition of the above two steps done for the old one. For new data, point calculates prediction of each tree and new data point assignment done to the majority vote winner category.

8.5 SIMULATION AND RESULT DISCUSSION

Jupyter notebook for programming is used for the implementation of the proposed model in Python language. Different libraries like NumPy that is to deal with arrays, pandas for CSV file and different data frames, train_ test_split that means for splitting the dataset into two different sets that is training and testing data, StandardScaler for scaling features, so as for better adaption of datasets by ML algorithms, matplotlib to plot charts using pyplot and cm.rainbow used to color them, seaborn to plot charts and warnings for ignoring all warnings of notebook caused, due to past/future depreciation of a feature, etc., are imported and different functions that have been used for model validation and visualization. Initially, the dataset is read from the repository, and then data exploration is done.

The plots have been constructed for the heart disease frequency with attributes age, sex, FBS, slope, chest pain type to get a clear visualization of disease frequency. We got a clear idea about how many patients have the disease and which gender group they belong to. The obtained dataset is the Cleveland dataset. The first step is to do data cleaning and preparation. Then in the second step visual exploratory data analysis is done. This is a great opportunity to envision the information with the assistance of the seaborn bundle. Recurrence plot of coronary illness underneath shows the two classes namely having heart disease and no heart disease are roughly adjusted, with nearly 45.54% of perceptions having coronary illness and the rest of the populace not having coronary illness.

In any case, how about we see the relationship grid of highlights and attempt to break down it. The figure size is characterized to 12 × 8 by utilizing rcParams. At that point, we utilized a pyplot to show the connection lattice. Utilizing xticks and yticks, we have added names to the relationship framework. Colorbar () shows the color bar for the grid. It's anything but difficult to see that there is no single element that has a high connection with our objective worth. Additionally, a portion of the highlights have a negative relationship with the objective esteem and some have positive. Figure 8.2 is the correlation matrix that clearly shows us a better understanding of data of dataset.

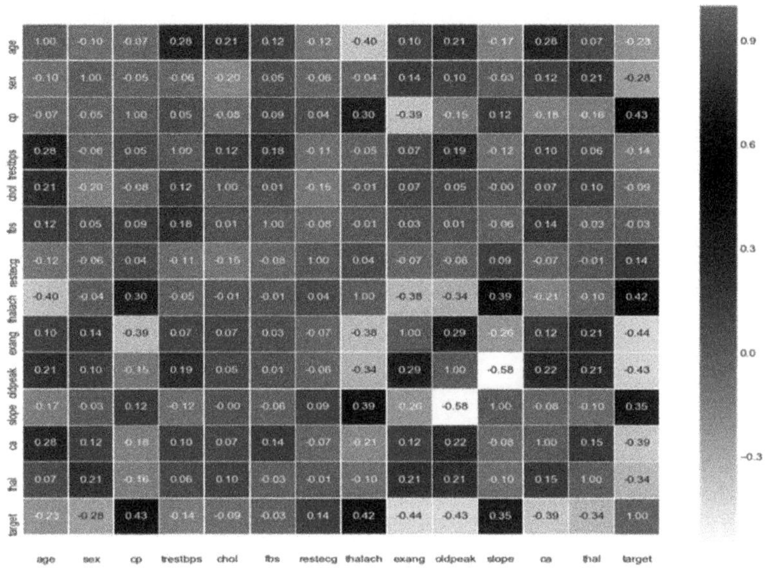

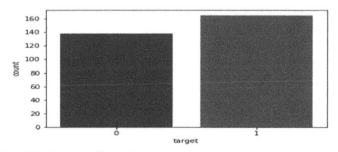

FIGURE 8.2 Visualization of the correlation matrix.

It's extremely fundamental that the dataset we are taking a shot at ought to be roughly adjusted. An amazingly imbalanced dataset can render the entire model preparing pointless and along these lines, will be of no utilization. How about we comprehend it with a model.

Suppose we take the dataset consists of 100 individuals with 99 non-patients and one patient. The model can generally forecast, the new individual would be not a sufferer with an exactness of 99%. For the scenario, where we progressively keen on distinguishing the one individual who is a sufferer, we require adjusted datasets with the goal that is learned by the model.

Figure 8.3 depicts that as a result of data exploration, 45.54% of patients have no heart disease and 54.46% of patients have heart disease.

FIGURE 8.3 Visualization of heart disease percentage.

Figure 8.4 gives us a clear visualization of heart disease frequency based on Sex. 31.68% are female patients and 68.32% are male patients.

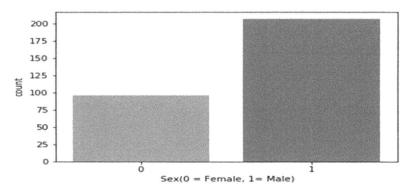

FIGURE 8.4   Visualization of heart disease percentage based on sex.

As we see data are well-balanced no need to equalize classes. In Figure 8.5 pair plot is shown to get a detailed idea of relationship among factors.

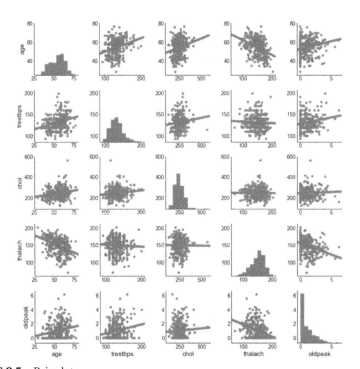

FIGURE 8.5   Pair plot.

The pair plot above permits us to see the dissemination and relationship of numerical factors. The inclining shows portion thickness plots demonstrating the unpleasant conveyances of the two populaces. The dissipate plots show the connection between plots. We can mention a couple of objective facts from the pair plot:

- Resting circulatory strain will in general increment with age paying little mind to coronary illness.
- We can see that maximum pulses are altogether lower for individuals without coronary illness.

From Figure 8.6, we get a clear visualization of heart disease frequency for ages. The age groups belong to 29 to 77. Frequency is very high for age groups between 41 to 54.

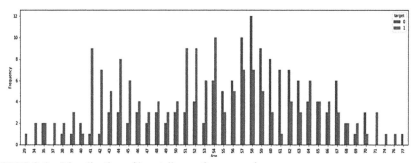

FIGURE 8.6   Visualization of heart disease frequency for ages.

We need a scatter plot to show the correlation between variables. Figure 8.7 represents the relationship between age and heart rate.

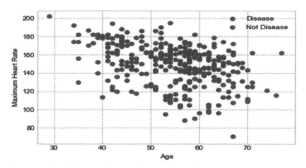

FIGURE 8.7   Scatter plot of heart disease frequency for ages.

In Figure 8.8, the relationship between frequency and the slope of the peak Exercise ST segment is shown. In Figure 8.9, the relationship between frequency and Fasting blood sugar (FBS) is shown.

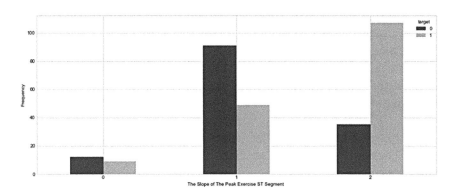

FIGURE 8.8   Visualization of heart disease frequency for slope.

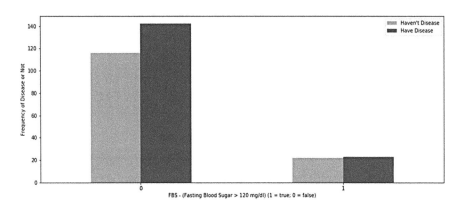

FIGURE 8.9   Visualization of heart disease frequency for FBS.

In Figure 8.10, relationship between chest pain type and frequency of disease is shown.

Dummy variables are created to deal with categorical values. In steps three and four we do training and testing of models. Model selection is the way toward joining information and earlier data to choose among a gathering of factual models. we have analyzed our data with different combinations. In step five, we look forward to improvement. One approach to improve our model is to decrease the number of highlights in your information grid by picking those with the most noteworthy prescient worth is fitting. The quantity of critical highlights is not exactly the all outnumber of highlights, so the irrelevant highlights are dispensed with.

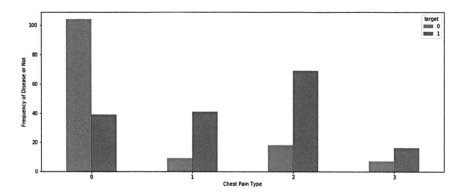

FIGURE 8.10 Visualization of heart disease frequency for chest pain type.

Table 8.3 clearly shows the accuracy rate in percentage for each classifier that we have discussed earlier to predict heart disease.

TABLE 8.3 Accuracy Rate of Each Model

	Model Name	Accuracy (%)
0	Logic regression	86.89
1	K-nearest neighbors	88.52
2	Support vector machine	86.89
3	Naïve Bayes	86.89
4	Decision tree	78.69
5	Random forest	88.52

A Sklearn library is used to import classifiers directly to predict the score. Then each model's accuracy is compared through visualization plot. All model works correctly but the best accuracy rate predicted by KNN and RF with 88.52%. The confusion matrix table helps to evaluate the performance of classification models for a set of test data for known truth values. We can see the performance evaluation of all our models with a confusion matrix visualization plot. Comparison results were shown in Figure 8.11.

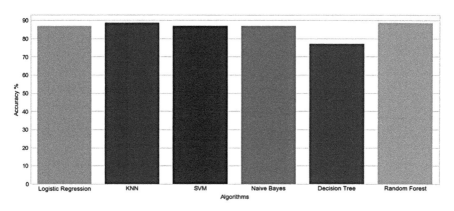

FIGURE 8.11   Comparison of accuracy rate of each classifier.

Confusion matrix for each model performance evaluation shown in Figure 8.12.

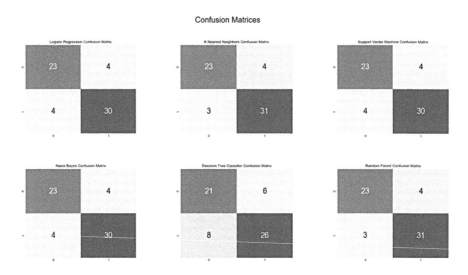

FIGURE 8.12   Confusion matrix for each model performance evaluation.

From the confusion matrix in Figure 8.12, we see that the most 'precise' model will in general exacerbate the sort of slip-up. Like above, the right expectations show up on the primary corner to corner, while all off-inclining esteems compare to wrong characterizations. Precision is estimated on how well all cases were ordered [35, 36]. The two kinds of misclassifications:

naming a sound individual is undesirable and naming an ill individual as solid. Both are not similarly awful. It's unquestionably more terrible to mislabel a patient as solid if they have coronary illness, as their coronary illness would go untreated, and they may proceed with an unfortunate eating routine or seek after perilous movement levels.

As far as grouping measurements, that sort of forecast botch is a false negative. The elective misstep (a False Positive) is to mark somebody as ill when they are sound, which would prompt somebody pointlessly changing their eating routine and way of life, which would be undesirable, yet not possibly deadly, as in the other case. For all the models it is observed that TP and TN values are maximum, especially for KNN and RF less FP and FN values, we are getting. Where TP is a true positive, TN is a true negative, FP is false positive and FN is a false negative. After performance evaluation, we are clear that the KNN and RF algorithm [37, 38] outperforms over all other algorithms in predicting heart disease [39] with more accuracy.

8.6   CONCLUSION

In the present chapter, various ML methodologies have been discussed for heart disease prediction [40, 41]. Early diagnosis can save millions of life so an effective methodology can become a helping hand for doctors for predicting whether a patient is having heart illness or not. Based upon our dataset training and testing of data are performed and various classifiers are involved in the prediction process individually. Finally, after all, the model evaluation conclusion drawn is that KNN and RF classifier [32] produces a more accurate prediction that is 88.52%. With the confusion matrix plot, it can be visualized that our model performance is good. In the future, aiming to work with real clinical data and with more advanced classifiers, feature selection algorithms, and boosting algorithms so that accuracy rate can be enhanced. Further, this comparison can be done with unsupervised learning algorithms where labeled data is not present to predict heart disease.

KEYWORDS

- **cardiovascular diseases**
- **fasting blood sugar**
- **Indian Heart Association**
- **receiver operating characteristic**
- **support vector machine**

REFERENCES

1. https://www.who.int/health-topics/cardiovascular-diseases/#tab=tab_1 (accessed on 11 November 2021).
2. https://www.mayoclinic.org/diseases-conditions/heart-disease/symptoms-causes/syc-20353118 (accessed on 11 November 2021).
3. Dbritto, R., Srinivasaraghavan, A., & Joseph, V., (2016). Comparative analysis of accuracy on heart disease prediction using classification methods. *International Journal of Applied Information Systems, 11*(2), 22–25.
4. De Menezes, F. S., Liska, G. R., Cirillo, M. A., & Vivanco, M. J., (2017). Data classification with binary response through the Boosting algorithm and logistic regression. *Expert Systems with Applications, 69*, 62–73.
5. Dwivedi, A. K., (2018). Performance evaluation of different machine learning techniques for prediction of heart disease. *Neural Computing and Applications, 29*(10), 685–693.
6. Beyene, C., & Kamat, P., (2018). Survey on prediction and analysis of the occurrence of heart disease using data mining techniques. *International Journal of Pure and Applied Mathematics, 118*(8), 165–174.
7. Haq, A. U., Li, J. P., Memon, M. H., Nazir, S., & Sun, R., (2018). A hybrid intelligent system framework for the prediction of heart disease using machine learning algorithms. *Mobile Information Systems, 2018*, p. 21, Article ID: 3860146. https://doi.org/10.1155/2018/3860146.
8. Manogaran, G., & Lopez, D., (2018). Health data analytics using scalable logistic regression with stochastic gradient descent. *International Journal of Advanced Intelligence Paradigms, 10*(1, 2), 118–132.
9. Desai, S. D., Giraddi, S., Narayankar, P., Pudakalakatti, N. R., & Sulegaon, S., (2019). Back-propagation neural network versus logistic regression in heart disease classification. In: *Advanced Computing and Communication Technologies* (pp. 133–144). Springer, Singapore.
10. Kannan, R., & Vasanthi, V., (2019). Machine learning algorithms with ROC curve for predicting and diagnosing the heart disease. In: *Soft Computing and Medical Bioinformatics* (pp. 63–72). Springer, Singapore.
11. Wright, V., (2019). *Machine Learning: Using the Logistic Regression Model to Predict Coronary Heart Disease*.
12. Wu, C. S. M., Badshah, M., & Bhagwat, V., (2019). Heart disease prediction using data mining techniques. In: *Proceedings of the 2019 2nd International Conference on Data Science and Information Technology* (pp. 7–11).
13. Baggen, V. J., Venema, E., Živná, R., Van, D. B. A. E., Eindhoven, J. A., Witsenburg, M., & Roos-Hesselink, J. W., (2019). Development and validation of a risk prediction model in patients with adult congenital heart disease. *International journal of cardiology, 276*, 87–92.
14. Beunza, J. J., Puertas, E., García-Ovejero, E., Villalba, G., Condes, E., Koleva, G., & Landecho, M. F., (2019). Comparison of machine learning algorithms for clinical event prediction (risk of coronary heart disease). *Journal of Biomedical Informatics, 97*, 103257.
15. Panda, D., & Dash, S. R., (2020). Predictive system: Comparison of classification techniques for effective prediction of heart disease. In: *Smart Intelligent Computing and Applications* (pp. 203–213). Springer, Singapore.

16. Vaidya, N., Kandu, M., Yadav, R. K., & Bharadwaj, N., (2020). The working of various prediction techniques for heart diseases: A case study. *IJRAR-International Journal of Research and Analytical Reviews (IJRAR), 7*(1), 447–453.

17. Alim, M. A., Habib, S., Farooq, Y., & Rafay, A., (2020). Robust heart disease prediction: A novel approach based on significant feature and ensemble learning model. In: *2020 3rd International Conference on Computing, Mathematics, and Engineering Technologies (iCoMET)* (pp. 1–5). IEEE.

18. Mohan, S., Thirumalai, C., & Srivastava, G., (2019). Effective heart disease prediction using hybrid machine learning techniques. *IEEE Access, 7*, 81542–81554.

19. Guo, Y., Hao, Z., Zhao, S., Gong, J., & Yang, F., (2020). Artificial intelligence in health care: Bibliometric analysis. *Journal of Medical Internet Research, 22*(7), e18228.

20. Noah, C. A., (2014). *Kids Playing for Keeps: A Feasibility Study of Coronary Heart Disease Intervention in a Rural African American Community*.

21. Sharma, H., & Rizvi, M. A., (2017). Prediction of heart disease using machine learning algorithms: A survey. *International Journal on Recent and Innovation Trends in Computing and Communication, 5*(8), 99–104.

22. Gavhane, A., Kokkula, G., Pandya, I., & Devadkar, K., (2018). Prediction of heart disease using machine learning. In: *2018 Second International Conference on Electronics, Communication, and Aerospace Technology (ICECA)* (pp. 1275–1278). IEEE.

23. Gonsalves, A. H., Thabtah, F., Mohammad, R. M. A., & Singh, G., (2019). Prediction of coronary heart disease using machine learning: An experimental analysis. In: *Proceedings of the 2019 3rd International Conference on Deep Learning Technologies* (pp. 51–56).

24. Yekkala, I., Dixit, S., & Jabbar, M. A., (2017). Prediction of heart disease using ensemble learning and particle swarm optimization. In: *2017 International Conference on Smart Technologies for Smart Nation (SmartTechCon)* (pp. 691–698). IEEE.

25. Nikhar, S., & Karandikar, A. M., (2016). Prediction of heart disease using machine learning algorithms. *International Journal of Advanced Engineering, Management, and Science, 2*(6).

26. Bhardwaj, A., Kundra, A., Gandhi, B., Kumar, S., Rehalia, A., & Gupta, M., (2019). Prediction of heart attack using machine learning. *IITM Journal of Management and IT, 10*(1), 20–24.

27. Malav, A., Kadam, K., & Kamat, P., (2017). Prediction of heart disease using k-means and artificial neural network as hybrid approach to improve accuracy. *International Journal of Engineering and Technology, 9*(4), 3081–3085.

28. Pahwa, K., & Kumar, R., (2017). Prediction of heart disease using hybrid technique for selecting features. In: *2017 4th IEEE Uttar Pradesh Section International Conference on Electrical, Computer, and Electronics (UPCON)* (pp. 500–504). IEEE.

29. Pouriyeh, S., Vahid, S., Sannino, G., De Pietro, G., Arabnia, H., & Gutierrez, J., (2017). A comprehensive investigation and comparison of machine learning techniques in the domain of heart disease. In: *2017 IEEE Symposium on Computers and Communications (ISCC)* (pp. 204–207). IEEE.

30. Jabbar, M. A., (2017). Prediction of heart disease using k-nearest neighbor and particle swarm optimization. *Biomedical Research (0970-938X), 28*(9).

31. Raihan, M., Mandal, P. K., Islam, M. M., Hossain, T., Ghosh, P., Shaj, S. A., & More, A., (2019). Risk prediction of ischemic heart disease using artificial neural network.

In: *2019 International Conference on Electrical, Computer, and Communication Engineering (ECCE)* (pp. 1–5). IEEE.

32. Magesh, G., & Swarnalatha, P., (2020). Optimal feature selection through a cluster-based DT learning (CDTL) in heart disease prediction. *Evolutionary Intelligence*, 1–11.

33. Dinesh, K. G., Arumugaraj, K., Santhosh, K. D., & Mareeswari, V., (2018). Prediction of cardiovascular disease using machine learning algorithms. In: *2018 International Conference on Current Trends Towards Converging Technologies (ICCTCT)* (pp. 1–7). IEEE.

34. Maji, S., & Arora, S., (2019). Decision tree algorithms for prediction of heart disease. In: *Information and Communication Technology for Competitive Strategies* (pp. 447–454). Springer, Singapore.

35. Dhar, S., Roy, K., Dey, T., Datta, P., & Biswas, A., (2018). A hybrid machine learning approach for prediction of heart diseases. In: *2018 4th International Conference on Computing Communication and Automation (ICCCA)* (pp. 1–6). IEEE.

36. Dileep, P., & Rao, K. N., (2019). A review on machine learning techniques for data-driven heart disease prediction. *Journal of the Gujarat Research Society, 21*(3), 304–316.

37. Sinha, A., & Mathew, R., (2019). Machine learning algorithms for early prediction of heart disease. In: *International Conference on Computer Networks, Big data and IoT* (pp. 162–168). Springer, Cham.

38. Chadha, R., & Mayank, S., (2016). Prediction of heart disease using data mining techniques. *CSI Transactions on ICT, 4*(2–4), 193–198.

39. Sajeev, S., Maeder, A., Champion, S., Beleigoli, A., Ton, C., Kong, X., & Shu, M., (2019). Deep learning to improve heart disease risk prediction. In: *Machine Learning and Medical Engineering for Cardiovascular Health and Intravascular Imaging and Computer-Assisted Stenting* (pp. 96–103). Springer, Cham.

40. Ramotra, A. K., Mahajan, A., Kumar, R., & Mansotra, V., (2020). Comparative analysis of data mining classification techniques for prediction of heart disease using the weka and SPSS modeler tools. In: *Smart Trends in Computing and Communications* (pp. 89–97). Springer, Singapore.

41. Singh, D., & Samagh, J. S., (2020). A comprehensive review of heart disease prediction using machine learning. *Journal of Critical Reviews, 7*(12).

CHAPTER 9

Detection of Infectious Diseases in Human Bodies by Using Machine Learning Algorithms

SNEHLATA BERIWAL,[1] K. THIRUNAVUKKARASU,[1]
SHAHNAWAZ KHAN,[2] and SATHEESH ABIMANNAN[1]

[1]School of Computer Science and Engineering, Galgotias University, Uttar Pradesh, India, E-mail: thiruk.me@gmail.com (K. Thirunavukkarasu)

[2]Department of Information Technology, University College of Bahrain, Bahrain

ABSTRACT

Today extracting and analyzing meaningful information from the data has been the major consideration for organizations. In fact, every sector relies upon data analysis for future directions for efficient working and time saving. Machine learning in data analytics helps to do such analysis efficiently. Machine learning is being used in various fields like stock exchange, weather forecasting, ecommerce, prediction of disease, etc. Therefore, a number of research studies regarding the techniques of Machine Learning used in analysis of infectious disease on human body are reviewed. It has been found that techniques like KNN, SVM, naive Bayes, random forest, K-means, and hierarchical clustering are being majorly used. But random forest, GLM, GBM, K-means are mostly suited in the field of infectious disease.

9.1 INTRODUCTION

This introductory section covers the main concepts related to diseases and serves as the starting point for the chapter. This section gives a detail about the diseases which exist in the human body and their effects also. The next section describes how different infectious diseases are predicted by ML algorithms and also a comparison is given among the techniques used. Later part describes the dataset used for the research work and also the implementation techniques.

9.1.1   DISEASES IN HUMAN BODY

A disease is a specific pathological disorder that adversely affects the whole or part of an organism's structure or function and is not caused by any immediate external injury [1]. In general, a disease is a disorder of progressive onset, having formed over a relatively long period of time [2]. For example, a back injury caused by repetitive lifting, carrying or bending at work that induces degenerative changes in the spine of an individual can be considered a disease. Equally a condition of the shoulder that has gradually developed over a period of time due to repetitive activity or repetitive use of the upper limb of a person, where symptoms have gradually developed or deteriorated.

A disease in humans is a medical condition that can lead to discomfort, pain, disorders, abnormal behavior and also can because of death of a person. Similar problem can also be shown in people who are in contact with the infected person. Every disease is associated with some specific symptoms which help in its diagnosis. Jackie Leach Scully [3], in his work, stated that with time the notion of disease also changes due to the technological advancement in the medical field and also due to social and economic reasons. One example is osteoporosis; previously it was considered normal with increasing age but in 1994 WHO officially recognized it as a disease. Diseases can be classified as communicable (infectious) and non-communicable (non-infectious) diseases [4]. A disease affects people physically and also mentally, since contracting and living with a disease can change the life perspective of the person concerned.

9.1.2   INFECTIOUS DISEASE

Pathogenic microorganisms such as parasites, viruses, fungi, or bacteria are the cause of infectious disease as stated by WHO [5]. The spread of infectious disease can be direct or indirect and specific symptoms may vary among individuals. Infectious disease such as zoonotic of animals can cause disease to humans when transmitted. Depending on the infection causing microorganism, signs, and symptoms vary, but fever and fatigue are often common. Sometimes mild infections may lead to rest and home remedies, while hospitalization may be needed for some life-threatening infections [6]. Infectious diseases pose a significant threat to human and animal health. In modern times, the pace at which diseases can spread globally and the path to deadly pandemics means that surveillance must be able to track diseases that can cause outbreaks and catch unknown threats that can occur from a wide range of sources [7].

Major epidemics have already marked the 21st century. Old diseases have returned-cholera, plague, and yellow fever-and new ones have emerged-SARS, MERS, pandemic influenza, Ebola, and Zika [8]. These emerging infectious disease (EID) area significant threat to world economy as well public health also.

According to WHO some of the infectious diseases are [9]: Ebola virus disease, yellow fever, Lassa fever, Zika, chikungunya, Crimean-Congo hemorrhagic fever, avian, and other zoonotic influenza, pandemic influenza, seasonal influenza, Middle-East respiratory syndrome (MERS), plague, leptospirosis, cholera, meningococcal meningitis, monkeypox, and the latest being COVID-19.

9.1.3 NON INFECTIOUS DISEASE

Non-communicable diseases (NCD) are those diseases that cannot be transmitted directly from one person to another [10]. NCD contain diseases like Parkinson's disease, most heart diseases, osteoarthritis, osteoporosis, autoimmune diseases, strokes, diabetes, most cancers, Alzheimer's disease, chronic kidney problems, cataracts, and others. NCDs, which are also known as chronic diseases, tend to exist for long duration and a combination of genetic, physiological, behavioral, and environmental factors are responsible for their cause. These NCDs kills 41 million people every year alone as compared to 71% of all deaths globally. The major cause of death in high income countries are NCDs. However, in low- and middle-income countries, NCDs cause 78% of the global deaths due to NCDs [11].

On an average, every year, almost 15 million people die between the ages of 30 and 69 years due to NCDs. A majority of these premature deaths (almost 85%) happen in the countries having low- and middle-income. More than half of the world's 56.9 million deaths in 2016 (54%) were attributed to the top 10 causes. Ischemic heart disease and stroke are the biggest killers in the world, accounting for 15.2 million deaths overall in 2016. For the past 15 years, these diseases are the leading cause of death worldwide.

9.2   CASE STUDY: INFECTIOUS DISEASES DETECTION USING MACHINE LEARNING ALGORITHMS

9.2.1   BAYESIAN NETWORKS

A Bayesian network, Bayes network, [12] belief network, decision network or probabilistic directed acyclic graphic model is a probabilistic graphic model (a type of statistical model) which represents a set of variables (nodes) and a conditional probability distribution in each of the node through a Directed Acyclic Graph. Bayesian networks are best suited to find the probability of an event given the conditional probability of an event. For example, the probabilistic relationship between diseases and symptoms may be represented by a Bayesian network. The network can be used to measure the probability of the occurrence of different diseases, provided the symptoms.

Bayesian networks can be applied in a wide range of fields in health services research (economic assessment of health, measurement of health quality, monitoring of health outcomes, analysis of cost-effectiveness), but also in epidemiology, clinical research, medical decision making or public health. Some case studies are being given below that used Bayesian Networks as their main tool for research [13].

Tao Zhang et al. [14] Suggested that dynamic Bayesian network (DBN) can be used for improving the quality of infectious diseases surveillance. In this study, the evaluation of the performance of DBN was done through two simulations.

The performance of deep belief network was evaluated based on the techniques granger causality hypothesis test and least absolute shrinkage and selection operator in the first simulation.

Forecasting ability of infectious diseases could be improved for Deep Belief Network in the second simulation. Also, the simulation environments were adapted from real-world studies so that situations are close to the real world.

The simulation scenarios were adapted from previous studies which includes HFMD and meteorological factors by Wei Y and Chinese J (2013). Simulation is close to real-world surveillance.

HFMD cases reported in Sichuan province from 2010 to 2013 were obtained from the China information system for disease control and prevention (CISDCP) in a daily basis.

Retno A. Vinarti and Lucy M. Hederman [15], presented a model for predicting a person's risk of getting infected based on their personal characteristics and surroundings like region, climatic conditions. In this model, it enables the system to help epidemiologists and represent their knowledge in an easy way.

In this model, the IDR knowledge-base is converted to an infectious disease risk BN using the BN builder in this model.

9.2.2 SUPPORT VECTOR MACHINE

Mostly used for classification problems, SVM is a supervised ML algorithm. In this also, every data item is plotted as a point in space. The space used is n-dimensional, and the coordinate values indicated as the value of each feature. Then classification is performed by finding the hyperplane which divides the two classes.

In 2019, Rajeev et al. present a model for early detection of dengue. An analytical study was conducted by collecting symptoms and tests were conducted. The SVM classification ML technique was used for doing the analyzes. It was found that four factors are very crucial for prediction of dengue [16].

In 2017, Amani Yahiaoui et al. [17] developed a recognition system using SVM technique for the early diagnosis of tuberculosis (TB) infection for the first time. The data was taken from the 'chest diseases department of a hospital in Diyarbakir' located in the south of Turkey. The designed system included a sample of 150 patients, 50 patients diagnosed with TB and 100 individuals having no disease. The diagnostic results showed that the proposed model was far better than other systems used for the disease.

In 2018, Yaecob Girmay Gezahegn et al. proposed malaria detection model and also for classification of species using ML approach. Techniques like Scale Invariant Feature Transform (SIFT) and support vector machine (SVM) were used. The dataset was taken from CDC. If a large database of images of species is available, then malaria is easily detected, this model can further be enhanced by using deep learning (DL) approach [18].

9.2.3   K-NEAREST NEIGHBOR

It is most simple supervised ML algorithm which is majorly used for classification problems. KNN training phase is very negligible so it is often called lazy algorithm. Also, no assumption is made on the distribution of the data, so it is also known as non-parametric algorithm. It adopts the similarity approach for predicting the data points of new values. A value is assigned to the data points if it is similar to the points in the training set.

9.2.4   RANDOM FOREST

Random forest (RF) classifier is a ML technique that belongs to the supervised learning algorithms family. RF is a commonly used technique for regression and classification. However, the most common use of this techniques can be seen in classification. It is an ensemble technique that ensembles decision trees (DTs) [37]. Ensemble methods/techniques produce results by combining multiple algorithms. Combining results from multiple methods to obtain the final results usually overcome or at least reduce the problem of over-fitting. Therefore, RFs being an ensemble method reduces the over-fitting and improve accuracy. Technique's name 'RF' is based on the analogy to real world forests. The forests are made of trees. Similarly, RF is implemented using multiple DTs. It is one of the most powerful classification algorithms of ML [35, 44]. It works by creating a forest of large number of DTs. Each individual tree gives a prediction and the decision of one tree is not affected by others. The final result comes on the basis of committee (group of trees) and not on the basis of individual tress. The trees are uncorrelated, and as the number of uncorrelated trees increases in the forest, the accuracy of prediction also increases.

DTs are high speed classifier. However, as the complexity of the trees increase, there is a possible loss of accuracy especially for the unseen data [36, 45]. This limitation usually leads to suboptimal accuracy. RF classifiers (see Figure 9.1) are constructed from multiple DTs. These DTs are built-in subspaces that are randomly selected from the feature space. By doing so, the combined capacity of the decision trees can be expanded, and the accuracy also improves for training and unseen data as well. Different trees generalized their classifications from different subspaces in a complimentary way. The combined classification results obtained from multiple DTs built on different subspaces can be monotonically improved [37].

The algorithm for RF can be outlined into the following steps:

- Create multiple random samples of the dataset;
- Build a DT from each sample and obtain the results from each tree;
- Combine the prediction results by voting or summing; and
- Produce the final prediction results based on the results of Step 3.

There are several studies by various researchers in the direction of developing computing models to assist in detecting the infectious disease using ML and big data, etc. [23–27]. While building a ML model for predicting the disease, selection of the optimal parameter is the primary criteria for developing a high accuracy performing model. Though, there are several ML algorithms as discussed among various sections of this chapter. However, RF is a commonly used technique for infectious disease prediction. A research study was conducted by [28] on ML algorithms for disease prediction including RFs, SVM, Naive Bayes algorithm, etc. The study concludes that the RF performs better than any other technique.

In a study, researchers [22] have developed a model for recognizing a virus protein for predicting the host tropism. Classifying medical data is a complex task and there are several research studies and models are available for medical data classification. There are several other research studies that have used RF technique for developing the infectious diseases such as screening between COVID-19 and Pneumonia [33], avian influenza H5N1 outbreaks prediction [32], Epidemic Curve prediction [31], etc.

A research study for developing the predictor for classifying medical data RF techniques is applied for feature ranking and classifier is built. The study concludes that RF-based classifier outperforms its counterpart such as evolutionary extreme learning machine, SVM, multilayer perceptron, and Bayes network, etc. [29]. Another research study for comparing ML techniques such as conventional and penalized logistic regression (LR), boosted regression trees and RFs for H1N1pdm influenza infections detection has concluded that RFs results are highly accurate in comparison to other techniques [30]. Building a classifier for imbalanced data set is one of the major challenges while developing ML models. A model on predicting the disease risks using RFs technique has been developed that use a highly imbalanced data for prediction. The model has shown a better accuracy than the previously developed model for the same tasks [34]. Based on the above discussion, it can be concluded that RFs algorithms usually outperforms other classification techniques and should be considered as one of the most valuable classification techniques for infectious disease predictions.

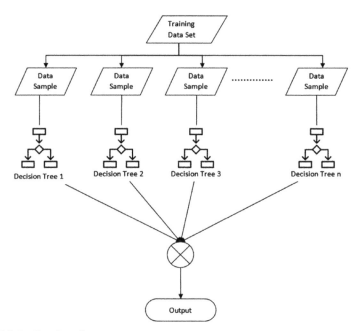

FIGURE 9.1   Random forest.

9.2.5   *NAIVE BAYES*

Although ML has made tremendous advancement in the last decade or so but Naïve Bayesian still remain a simple and accurate technique for the construction of the classifiers. It belongs to probabilistic algorithm family and works on the principle of Bayes theorem. It works very well with large data sets. Naïve Bayesian classifiers works on the assumption that values of features are not related to each other or they are independent of each other for a given text. The probability of each feature is calculated based on the previous conditions.

In 2018, Manish Jaiswal and co-authors [19], compared different ML techniques for the prediction of Anemia disease. Naive Bayes, RF, and DT algorithm were compared for anemia using complete blood count (CBC). The data was collected from local pathology centers. The dataset consists of 200 test samples and contained 18 attributes but only those were selected which are required for anemia disease prediction. It was observed that the Naive-Bayes technique outperforms in terms of accuracy as compared to C4.5 and RF.

9.2.6 *UNSUPERVISED ML ALGORITHM*

In unsupervised ML, no labeled data is provided to the machine; only the inputs are given, the model has to train itself on the basis of the input and tries to find complex hidden patterns from it. Since there is no supervision, it is known as unsupervised learning.

An simple example in real life can be like sorting different colors of balls into separate piles. This is specifically not taught but by just looking at the features of ball like color, one can group them into different clusters.

Unsupervised learning is more complicated than supervised learning, because by removing the supervision the problem cannot be defined properly. To look for what pattern The model has to do more work.

Let's take an example If a person tries to learn to play cricket under the supervision of a teacher, he would learn quickly by the techniques taught to him by the teacher. But if he tries to learn by himself, then it is quite tough to know where to start from.

In unsupervised learning, the start is from scratch and without any biasness, so it may be possible that a much better model can be developed, hence it is also known as knowledge discovery. Unsupervised learning is very useful when conducting exploratory data analysis.

Manivannan and Isakki Devi [20], presented a research work to predict people affected by dengue based on age group categorization using the K-means clustering algorithm. This chapter focused on four stages, namely the preprocessing, selection of attributes, clustering, and prediction of dengue fever. R-programing language (Version 3.3.2) was used to pre-process dengue dataset household. Method D wins has been applied to generate filled data set by replacing all missing values with mode and mean value for nominal and numeric attributes. Different mining techniques can be used to detect dengue disease. Data on the dengue patient was collected from dengue household clustering, which was collected in Ho Chi Minh City in Vietnam between October 2010 and January 2013. The hospital for tropical diseases (HTD) is the infectious disease guideline hospital in southern Vietnam, situated in central HCMC. The dataset included 1910 records and 171 attributes initially It was concluded that K-Means clustering adds to an increase of the proficiency of the output. This is the most effective technique to For predicting the dengue patients with serotypes and with clustered dengue dataset KNN was found to be most effective.

9.2.7 SUPERVISED ML ALGORITHMS

In supervised learning, the machine is trained to identify or learn the association or rules between a set of inputs and outputs. A simple approach is used in this, like a teacher guides a student in learning a particular subject and the student is then tested whether he has learned properly or not. If he passes the test, then the student is properly trained; otherwise, he is made to learn what mistakes he has made. So the teacher here is the supervisor and student is the model which is being trained.

For example, the inputs could be the different pictures of fruits which are labeled like apple, grapes, banana, pear, etc. The aim in supervised learning would be to learn the mapping which can describe the relationship between images and the name of fruits: Here, the model learns by differentiation made on the basis of features like color, size, shape, weight of the fruits. So when a new picture of any of these fruit is fed in to algorithm should be able to classify it.

The key generalization aspect of ML is being able to adapt to new inputs and make prediction. In order to make supervised model capable of defining the real underlying general relationship or mapping, maximum generalization should be the key aspect in training.

It is very much known that supervision always adds to biasness in learning and so it is very important to provide unbiased examples when the model is being trained. To make the model more effective, it should be fed with a large amount of reliable labeled: data which can normally be hard to find.

If the output of a supervised model is in the form of such a category (Orange, Watermelon, Pomegranate). The input is classifying that some categorical distribution is made between the data, and then it is known as a classification problem (Figure 9.2).

FIGURE 9.2   Input, model, category classification.

When the output from the supervised learning is an numerical value the it is known as regression (Figure 9.3).

FIGURE 9.3 Classification problem.

In 2019, K Shasvat and co-authors, proposed a model which was an ensemble of three ML techniques: Support vector regression (SVR), NN, linear regression. The data of dengue and Typhoid for the year 2014 to 2017 was taken from integrated disease Surveillance program, Government of India [21].

In 2019, Mehrbakhsh Nilashi and co-authors, proposed a model which used ensemble learning for accurate prediction of hepatitis. DT was used in the selection of the features. It was found that the model proposed was superior to SVM, KNN, and NN [22].

In 2019, Saiprasath G and co-authors, proposed a malaria detection system using shallow ML algorithms like DT, RF, KNN. The accuracy of the model can help the laboratory technicians for decision making. The dataset obtained after feature extraction can further be used for diagnostic testing of diseases like TB, worm infestations and hemoparasites [23].

In 2019, Peiffer-Smadja and co-authors, conducted a thorough study of ML-CDSS in infectious diseases. It was observed that the machine learning tools provides prediction and diagnosis of various diseases, but they could not gather any evidence regarding their impact in actual life clinical settings [24].

In 2018, Tulika Bhardwaj and Pallavi Somvanshi, reviewed different ML techniques for diagnosis of infectious diseases. The techniques considered were SVM, Fuzzy logic, artificial neural network (ANN). It was observed that analysis and interpretation of huge dataset is possible through ML techniques. It was further concluded that a combination of these techniques can be also used to enhance the diagnosis [25].

In 2016, Mustafa Aydın and co-authors, proposed a model for detecting jaundice in infants. The dataset was taken from Fırat University Faculty of Medicine Neonatal Department(turkey). KNN and SVR ML Regressions are used on the dataset after feature extraction. The success rate achieved was about 85%. Also this study can further be used for other diseases as well [26].

9.2.8 DATASET

Author Names	Title	Abstract	Technique	Dataset Source	Advantages	Future Work
Mehrbakhsh, Nilash Hossein Ahmadi Leila Shahmorad Othman Ibrahim Elna Zakbarief, (2019)	A predictive method for hepatitis disease diagnosis using ensembles of neuro-fuzzy technique	To develop ensemble model for hepatitis	Neural network, ANFIS, K-nearest neighbors and support vector machine.	Data mining repository UCI	The performance of the ensemble model is greater than other models under consideration.	This method can be developed so that the trained models can be incrementally updated when the new information arrives thus making memory efficient.
• Rajeev Kapoor Virender Kadyan Sachin Ahuja (2020) •	Identification of influential parameter for early detection of dengue using machine learning approach	Analytical study and use of ml techniques for finding symptoms	SVM	Tuli medico Lab, Amritsar, Punjab)	Fever, headache, skin rash, and abdominal pain are the crucial symptoms in dengue prediction. Proposes a dataset for dengue.	This research can further be used by researchers for developing a predictive model for early dengue detection.
• Shashvat, K, Basu, R, Bhondekar, P Kaur, A	An ensemble model for forecasting infectious diseases in India	Develop a model based on the models of SVR, NN, LR.	SVR, NN, and LR.	From 2014 to 2017 data was taken from integrated diseases surveillance program, Government of India	The models outperform the already applied model on the basis of accuracy.	The efficiency of the proposed model can further be enhanced.

Author Names	Title	Abstract	Technique	Dataset Source	Advantages	Future Work
• Yaccob Girmay Gezahegn • Yirga Hagos G. Medhin • Eneyew Adugna Etsub (2018) • Gereziher Nigus G. Tekele	Malaria detection and classification using machine learning algorithms	Image segmentation techniques are compared for extracting malaria	Scale-invariant feature transform (SIFT) Support vector machine (SVM)	CDC (center for disease and control)	With large databases of images of different species and stages of malaria parasite then it is easily predicted.	Deep learning approach can be used to detect malaria and also identify various stages.
Mustafa Aydin& Firat Hardalaç & Berkan Ural& Serhat Karap (2016)	Neonatal jaundice detection system	Creation of non-invasive system to detect jaundice	kNN and SVR	Firat university faculty of medicine neonatal department (turkey)	Jaundice was detected in the infants successfully and within a span of short time and success rate of 85% was achieved by the system.	The study can be used further for the diagnosis of other diseases as well.
IN. Peiffer-Smadja T. M. Rawson R. Ahmad A. Buchard P. Georgiou F.-. Lescure G. Birgand A. H. Holmes (2019)	Machine learning for clinical decision support in infectious diseases: a narrative review of current applications	Informing the clinicians that ML can be used for diagnosis, classification, prediction of infectious diseases.	Supervised, unsupervised, deep learning	Data from ML-DSS (88% from HIC and 12% from LIC)	–	ML-CDSS in ID can also be developed in varying health settings and should be integrated with clinical settings.

Author Names	Title	Abstract	Technique	Dataset Source	Advantages	Future Work
• Tulika Bhardwaj • Pallavi Somvanshi (2018)	Machine learning toward infectious disease treatment	The mining of diagnostic techniques has to be done so that correct disease diagnosis can be done.	Support vector machine fuzzy logic, artificial neural network	—	Analysis and interpretation of huge dataset is possible through ML	A combination of machine learning platforms can be used for the identification of disease
Saiprasath G, Naren Babu R, Arun Priyan J, Vinayakumar R, Sowmya V, Soman K P (2019)	Performance comparison of machine learning algorithms for malaria detection using microscopic images.	To detect malaria by using the captured patient images without expert	Decision trees, naive Bayes, random forest tree, Adaboost, logistic regression	Captured using oil immersion objective lens from 133 individuals using with 1000x magnification	It can be used in countries where there is lack of resources and experts.	More accuracy can be achieved by using deep learning methods.
Ayon Dey (2016)	Machine learning algorithms: A review	To study various ML techniques	Decision trees, naive Bayes, random forest tree, SVMt, logistic regression, KNN, K-means clustering	—	ML is used in every field now	—
P. Manivannan and P. Isakki Devi [27]	Dengue fever prediction using K-means clustering algorithm	—	K-means clustering	Ho Chi Minh City in Vietnam between October 2010 and January 2013, the hospital for tropical diseases (HTD)	K-means is effective in predicting dengue	—

9.3 REINFORCEMENT LEARNING

Reinforcement learning (RL) is a form of ML technique that enables an agent to learn through trial and error, using input from their own actions and experiences, in an interactive environment (Figure 9.4). Like in Supervised learning where the agent learns through labeled data but in RL the agent leans through the feedback automatically without any labeled data. The agent gets a reward for the good action and a penalty for any bad actions.

Imagine of like training a cat, good behaviors of the cat are rewarded and become frequent. Bad behaviors are punished and become less frequent. This reward-motivated behavior is the principal of RL. RL is more effective for problems which require sequential decision making and target for a long-term goal, like game-playing, robotics, etc.

RL problems are best suited for the game's problem and can be well explained through them. Let's take the game of snake. Here the agent is Snake and the environment is the field where it is moving. In this game user control a snake that wants to eat apples, and if it does, then the snake gains a reward and also grows in size. The snake is free to move around the field, but if the snake hits the walls, then the game is over.

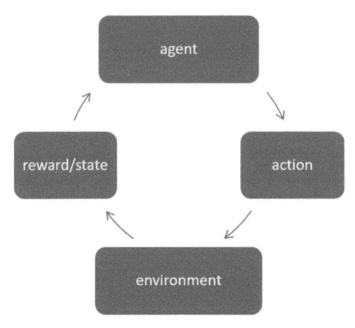

FIGURE 9.4 Reinforcement learning.

9.4 SUMMARY

It is quite evident from the facts provided that ML has spanned its roots into the healthcare industry and that too strongly. In developing countries like India, the burden of infectious disease is quite high. ML techniques can help in early detection and outbreak of these diseases. People are struggling now with COVID 19 during pandemic situation, it is also an example of an infectious disease. Early detection can help the government to take rapid response and plan of action that could control the spread of infection. ML can thus avert infectious diseases and can help in enhancement of quality of life.

KEYWORDS

- **dynamic Bayesian network**
- **emerging infectious disease**
- **middle-east respiratory syndrome**
- **non-communicable disease**
- **scale-invariant feature transform**

REFERENCES

1. Scully J. L. (2004). What is a disease? *EMBO Reports, 5*(7), 650–653. https://doi.org/10.1038/sj.embor.7400195.
2. https://www.who.int/topics/infectious_diseases/en/ (accessed on 11 November 2021).
3. Mayo Clinic Staff, (2020). *Infectious Diseases-Symptoms and Causes*. https://www.mayoclinic.org/diseases-conditions/infectious-diseases/symptoms-causes/syc-20351173 (accessed on 11 November 2021).
4. Dixon, M. A., Dar, O. A., & Heymann, D. L., (2014). Emerging infectious diseases: Opportunities at the human-animal-environment interface. *Veterinary Record, 174*, 546–551.
5. Jones, K., Patel, N., Levy, M., et al., (2008). Global trends in emerging infectious diseases. *Nature, 451*, 990–993. https://doi.org/10.1038/nature06536.
6. https://www.who.int/topics/infectious_diseases/factsheets/en/ (accessed on 11 November 2021).
7. https://www.who.int/news-room/fact-sheets/detail/noncommunicable-diseases (accessed on 11 November 2021).
8. Zhang, T., Ma, Y., Xiao, X., et al., (2019). Dynamic Bayesian network in infectious diseases surveillance: A simulation study. *Sci Rep., 9*, 10376. https://doi.org/10.1038/s41598-019-46737-0.

9. Retno, A. V., & Lucy, M. H., (2019). A personalized infectious disease risk prediction system. *Expert Systems with Applications, 131*, 266–274. ISSN 0957-4174.

10. Kapoor, R., Kadyan, V., & Ahuja, S., (2019). *Identification of Influential Parameter for Early Detection of Dengue Using Machine Learning Approach.* Available at SSRN 3511419.

11. Yahiaoui, A., Er, O., & Yumusak, N., (2017). A new method of automatic recognition for tuberculosis disease diagnosis using support vector machines. *Biomedical Research, 28*(9). Google Scholar.

12. Gezahegn, Y. G., Medhin, Y. H. G., Etsub, E. A., & Tekele, G. N. G., (2018). Malaria detection and classification using machine learning algorithms. In: Mekuria, F., Nigussie, E., Dargie, W., Edward, M., & Tegegne, T., (eds.), *Information,* and *Communication Technology for Development for Africa* (Vol. 244). ICT4DA 2017. Lecture Notes of the Institute for Computer Sciences, Social Informatics and Telecommunications Engineering, Springer, Cham.

13. Jaiswal, M., Srivastava, A., & Siddiqui, T. J., (2019). *Machine Learning Algorithms for Anemia Disease Prediction: Select Proceedings of IC3E 2018.* 10.1007/978-981-13-2685-1_44.

14. Manivannan, P., & Devi, P. I., (2017). Dengue fever prediction using K-means clustering algorithm. In: *2017 IEEE International Conference on Intelligent Techniques in Control, Optimization, and Signal Processing (INCOS)* (pp. 1–5). Srivilliputhur. doi: 10.1109/ITCOSP.2017.8303126.

15. Shashvat, K., Basu, R., Bhondekar, P. A., & Kaur, A., (2019). An ensemble model for forecasting infectious diseases in India. *Tropical Biomedicine, 36*(4), 822–832.

16. Mehrbakhsh, N., Hossein, A., Leila, S., Othman, I., & Elnaz, A., (2019). A predictive method for hepatitis disease diagnosis using ensembles of neuro-fuzzy technique. *Journal of Infection and Public Health, 12*(1), 13–20. ISSN 1876-0341.

17. Saiprasath, G. B., (2019). Performance comparison of machine learning algorithms for malaria detection using microscopic images. *IJRAR, 6*(1).

18. Peiffer-Smadja, N., Rawson, T. M., Ahmad, R., Buchard, A., Georgiou, P., Lescure, F. X., Birgand, G., & Holmes, A. H., (2020). Machine learning for clinical decision support in infectious diseases: A narrative review of current applications. *Clinical Microbiology and Infection, 26*(5).

19. Bhardwaj, T., & Somvanshi, P., (2019). Machine learning toward infectious disease treatment. In: Tanveer, M., & Pachori, R., (eds.), *Machine Intelligence and Signal Analysis: Advances in Intelligent Systems and Computing* (p. 748). Springer, Singapore.

20. Aydin, M., Hardalaç, F., Ural, B., & Karap, S., (2016). Neonatal jaundice detection system. *Journal of Medical Systems, 40.* 10.1007/s10916-016-0523-4.

21. Dey, A., (2016). Machine learning algorithms: A review. *International Journal of Computer Science and Information Technologies, 7*(3), 1174–1179.

22. Eng, C. L., Tong, J. C., & Tan, T. W., (2014). Predicting host tropism of influenza A virus proteins using random forest. *BMC Med. Genomics, 7*, S1. https://doi.org/10.1186/1755-8794-7-S3-S1

23. Lampos, V., Miller, A. C., Crossan, S., & Stefansen, C., (2015). Advances in nowcasting influenza-like illness rates using search query logs. *Sci. Rep., 5*, 12760. doi: 10.1038/srep12760.

24. Khan, S., & Kannapiran, T., (2019). *Indexing Issues in Spatial Big Data Management.* Available at SSRN 3387792.

25. Rohart, F., Milinovich, G. J., Avril, S. M., Lê Cao, K. A., Tong, S., & Hu, W., (2016). Disease surveillance based on Internet-based linear models: An Australian case study of previously unmodeled infection diseases. *Scientific Reports, 6*, 38522.

26. Balcan, D., Hu, H., Goncalves, B., Bajardi, P., Poletto, C., Ramasco, J. J., & Colizza, V., (2009). Seasonal transmission potential and activity peaks of the new influenza A (H1N1): A Monte Carlo likelihood analysis based on human mobility. *BMC Medicine, 7*(1), 45.

27. Colizza, V., Barrat, A., Barthelemy, M., Valleron, A. J., & Vespignani, A., (2007). Modeling the worldwide spread of pandemic influenza: baseline case and containment interventions. *PLoS Medicine, 4*(1).

28. Uddin, S., Khan, A., Hossain, M., et al., (2019). Comparing different supervised machine learning algorithms for disease prediction. *BMC Med. Inform. Decis. Mak., 19*, 281. https://doi.org/10.1186/s12911-019-1004-8.

29. Alam, M. Z., Rahman, M. S., & Rahman, M. S., (2019). A Random Forest based predictor for medical data classification using feature ranking. *Informatics in Medicine Unlocked, 15*, 100180.

30. Mansiaux, Y., & Carrat, F., (2014). Detection of independent associations in a large epidemiologic dataset: A comparison of random forests, boosted regression trees, conventional, and penalized logistic regression for identifying independent factors associated with H1N1pdm influenza infections. *BMC Med. Res. Methodol., 14*, 99. https://doi.org/10.1186/1471.2288-14-99.

31. Nsoesie, E. O., Beckman, R., Marathe, M., & Lewis, B., (2011). Prediction of an epidemic curve: A supervised classification approach. *Statistical Communications in Infectious Diseases, 3*(1).

32. Kane, M. J., Price, N., Scotch, M., et al., (2014). Comparison of ARIMA and random forest time series models for prediction of avian influenza H5N1 outbreaks. *BMC Bioinformatics, 15*, 276. https://doi.org/10.1186/1471-2105-15-276.

33. Shi, F., Xia, L., Shan, F., Wu, D., Wei, Y., Yuan, H., & Shen, D., (2020). *Large-Scale Screening of Covid-19 from Community-Acquired Pneumonia Using Infection Size-Aware Classification.* arXiv preprint arXiv:2003.09860.

34. Khalilia, M., Chakraborty, S., & Popescu, M., (2011). Predicting disease risks from highly imbalanced data using random forest. *BMC Med. Inform. Decis. Mak., 11*, 51. https://doi.org/10.1186/1472-6947-11-51.

35. Shahnawaz, M. R., (2011). ANN and rule based model for English to Urdu-Hindi machine translation system. In: *Proceedings of National Conference on Artificial Intelligence and Agents: Theory& Application (AIAIATA 2011)* (pp. 115–121).

36. Shahnawaz, & Mishra, R. B., (2015). An English to Urdu translation model based on CBR, ANN, and translation rules. *International Journal of Advanced Intelligence Paradigms, 7*(1), 1–23.

37. Ho, T. K., (1995). Random decision forests. In: *Proceedings of 3rd International Conference on Document Analysis and Recognition* (Vol. 1, pp. 278–282). IEEE.

38. Horný, M., (2014). *Bayesian Networks.* In Technical report No. 5. 2014, Department of Health Policy & Management: Boston University School of Public Health.

39. White, T., (2014). *What is the Difference Between an 'Injury' and 'Disease' for Commonwealth Injury Claims?* Tindall Gask Bentley.

40. https://web.archive.org/web/20140111192614/http://dorlands.com/ (accessed on 11 November 2021).

41. WHO, (2020). *Noncommunicable Diseases*. World Health Organization. https://www. who.int/news-room/fact-sheets/detail/noncommunicable-diseases (accessed on 11 November 2021).

42. Ben, G. I., (2007). Bayesian networks, In: Ruggeri, F., Kennett, R. S., & Faltin, F. W., (eds.), *Support-Page. Encyclopedia of Statistics in Quality and Reliability*. John Wiley & Sons; ISBN 978-0-470-01861-3.

43. McWhinney, I. R., (1987). Health and disease: Problems of definition. *CMAJ., 136*(8), 815.

44. Shahnawaz, & Mishra, R. B., (2013). Statistical machine translation system for English to Urdu. *International Journal of Advanced Intelligence Paradigms, 5*(3), 182–203.

45. Khan, S. N., & Usman, I., (2019). A model for English to Urdu and Hindi machine translation system using translation rules and artificial neural network. *Int. Arab J. Inf. Technol., 16*(1), 125–131.

CHAPTER 10

Medical Review Analytics Using Social Media

DIPEN CHAWLA, SUJAY VARMA, and SUJATA KHEDKAR

Computer Engineering Department, VESIT, Mumbai, Maharashtra, India,
E-mails: 2015dipen.chawla@ves.ac.in (D. Chawla),
2015sujay.varma@ves.ac.in (S. Varma),
sujata.khedkar@ves.ac.in (S. Khedkar)

ABSTRACT

Drug adverse reactions have always been a threat to human life. It has been observed that, at times even expensive laboratory testing is also not sufficient to detect all the adverse reactions caused by a drug. Detecting all adverse reactions caused by a drug-using patient reviews is the need of the hour. This would be help detect even minor side effects caused by a drug which would otherwise be difficult. Social media networks are connecting patients and health seekers in online communities to improve the patients' healthcare, and also facilitate communication between medical professionals and health seekers to ask health related queries, share information, opinions, observations, etc. Here, we develop a system for evaluating drug effectiveness by using a set of user comments which are annotated manually. A relation between the already available adverse reactions of a drug and those obtained by the developed system has been also obtained by us. For this purpose, the system uses user reviews of those drugs. User comments generally contain a vast variety of complex sentences and phrases which pose as an interesting natural language challenge. These user reviews provide immense scope for further exploration as well. A use case of seven drugs used for treating neurological disorders has been used for this study.

10.1   INTRODUCTION

Most of us tend to look up the internet for obtaining reviews of a medicine administered to us. At times the list of side effects is horrific. The next thought in this order is only if there would have been some system which could provide the extent to which these side effects were observed among the people. Patient reviews about a drug are readily available over the World Wide Web.

Data mining combined with sentiment analysis is an ongoing field of research in the area of natural language processing (NLP) using machine learning (ML). It uses computational linguistics to systematically identify, extract, and study of complex data. Here we have discussed an approach to develop a framework to analyze reviews from various medical blogs for drugs prescribed for neurological disorders. This would give an in-depth idea about the effectiveness of the drugs from the user's point of view. User reviews even provide the pros and cons of the drug and would also be helpful in generating an overall summary of a drug. The development framework takes data in the form of reviews from three medical websites. The framework as a whole would be quite useful for both medical professionals as well as common users in general to obtain the effects of the drug as well as the comparison between them to suggest alternatives for drugs.

Extracting adverse drug reactions (ADR) from user comments is a very important feature of the healthcare industry, adding up to loads of data analysis, the majority of which is due to the progress of social media as a tool for analyzing healthcare data. Here we have described a novel approach that can be used for the analysis of patient reviews from social media platforms to generate concise visualization and summaries from tons of reviews. Drug reviews can be broadly classified into four categories viz:

1. **Effective:** Reviews indicating a positive effect of a drug on the patient.
2. **Ineffective:** Reviews indicating that the drug did not work as expected and had no effect, either positive or negative on the patient.
3. **Adverse:** Patient has experienced side effects on consumption of a drug.
4. **Other:** Reviews which do not fall in any of the above categories.

Medical reviews have been analyzed to a certain extent previously using lexicon-based approaches. These use a dictionary-based approach for categorizing user reviews. Whereas the system described below makes use of ML as well as deep learning (DL) approaches rather than the traditional lexicon-based models. This is because lexicon-based models are not capable of covering the huge subjective and descriptive complexities present in user reviews.

It has been commonly observed that users post reviews which do not contain general medical terms, which are the heart of lexicon-based approaches. In fact, these reviews contain common everyday terms which are not covered by traditional dictionary-based approaches. Below examples show some of the inefficiencies of lexicon-based approaches:

- "My eyes never adjust to the changes in light and everything becomes a huge swirling mass of shadows." -incorrectly classified as 'EFFECTIVE;'
- "It keeps me from crashing after mania because the mania never peeks." -incorrectly classified as 'OTHER;'
- "It helps with the intense mood swings; negative emotions are less severe." -incorrectly classified as 'ADVERSE.'

The above examples show that review number 1 contains phrases indicating severe reactions to the patient's eyes after consuming the drug, but these terms do not match with those present in a typical medical dictionary. On the other hand, review numbers 2 and 3 indicate the effectiveness of the drug for the patient but since they either contain terms used to express adverse effects of the drug and do not contain terms indicating a positive effect on the user. Because of this, they were wrongly classified. We can overcome these inefficiencies by using a non-lexicon-based approach.

The rest of the chapter is organized as follows: Section 10.2 reviews related work. Section 10.3 describes the Proposed Methodology. Section 10.4 describes the experiments, evaluation. Conclusion and future work are described in Section 10.5.

10.2 RELATED WORK

Extracting information about post-marketing drug safety, including BioMed literature and electronic health records (EHRs) is an important field, and multiple organizations are working to manually curate the data for those tasks. However, automatic extraction of drug reactions from online reviews is a complicated task, and very little work has been carried out in said domain. A short review of the related work in the said domain is described below.

Kuhn et al. [1] introduce a public, computer-readable drug side effect resource (SIDER) that is a complete matrix connecting 888 drugs to 1450 side effect terms, as a method for studying Adverse Drug Reactions (ADR's), for academic and commercial research. The resource is available at the website http://sideeffects.embl.de. The resource is potentially an important source of data for model testing and comparative analysis using lexicon approach.

After mining relationships between drugs and ADR's of drugs from patient's opinion reviews mined from daily strength website, comparing terms from lexicon to user comments using a sliding window method is used by Leaman et al. [2]. The novel approach to pharmacovigilance by comparing comments to a lexicon is appreciated. The combined dataset is also immensely useful for the preparation of a corpus.

Nikfarjam et al. [3] propose a ML-based CRF tagger for automatically extracting ADR from user reviews. Using a combination of comments from Twitter and dailystrength.com, the model uses a highly efficient approach to obtain drug adverse reactions from comments using a combination of CRF classification technique and learning using word embeddings.

A novel approach to classify medication data from social media is to train a deep convolutional neural network (NN) to obtain sentiment word distribution for medical conditions and medication is used by Yadav et al. [4]. The five-layered CNN model trained using a dataset is highly accurate in extracting emotions from medication reviews. The baseline models used for training are strong and provide necessary direction to the actual training of models.

Huynh et al. [5] have established the classification models for drug reactions using two separate models, CRNN (a combination of CNN'S and RNN's) and convolutional neural network with attention (CNNA). The classification is done on a Twitter dataset containing informal language and ADR data from MEDLINE reports. The neural networks constructed by this chapter are extremely insightful and would go a long way in helping us to build our own models. The results are accurate as well for both of the DL models.

Yang et al. [6] use association mining to mine relations between drugs and adverse reactions of drugs from users of med help, an online medical community. The novel idea of using association mining algorithms and lexicon for the classification of diseases and drug names is appreciated.

A semi-supervised approach for detecting the ADR'S in tweets collected is provided by Lee et al. [7]. The use of a semi-supervised CNN-based framework for classification of adverse drug events in tweets is considerably unique but is highly efficient as it performs better than other SOTA models trained on Twitter datasets.

Xia et al. [8] have introduced the use of DL and NLP for high-performance extraction of ADR's of drugs from comments, from PubMed dataset as well as automatic crawlers for mining user comments. The chapter establishes the need for crawling newer comments rather than importing a dataset for review classification. Various adverse reactions are expected as results.

Previous studies used various types of data sources such as disease-related forums [10, 11], general medicine related discussion forums [12–14], social media platforms like Twitter [15], Medical terms specific lexicon dictionaries are also used for further analysis in some studies [16]. Supervised ML approaches are used for finding Adverse drug effect's as discussed in Refs. [17–20]. Convolution neural network (CNN) is also effective in the classification of medical reviews for addressing adverse drug effect's [21].

After researching the extensive work in the automated pharmacovigilance domain, we felt the need for building an accurate system that would be accessible and understandable to the end-user for him/her to make an informed decision before consuming the aforementioned drugs.

10.3   PROPOSED METHODOLOGY

The proposed methodology is summarized in Figure 10.1.

10.3.1   MODULE 1: DATA SCRAPER/WEB CRAWLER

This module uses a python based web crawler for parsing web pages of three healthcare websites and scraping them. The obtained comments are then stored in the database. We have scraped around 5000 user reviews from WebMD, drugs.com and Everyday health. The web crawler parses only the most helpful comments on these websites, ensuring the reliability of our dataset.

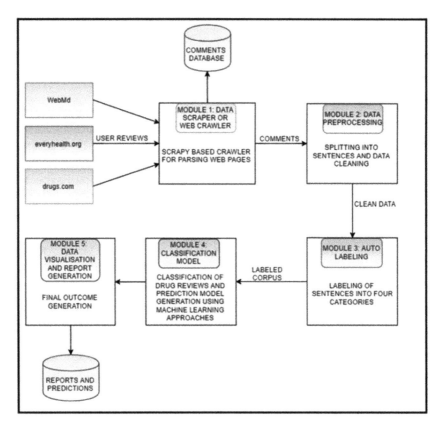

FIGURE 10.1   Proposed methodology.

10.3.2   MODULE 2: DATA PREPROCESSING

The preprocessing module includes splitting the reviews into sentences. These sentences are then steamed and corrected for any errors. These steps ensure that the data is clean for training the model.

10.3.3   MODULE 3: LABELING OF DATA

This phase includes labeling the clean data. The reviews are labeled based on four categories, i.e., Effective, ineffective, adverse, and other as shown in Table 10.1. This module provides data which is ready for training.

TABLE 10.1   Sample Categorization of Sentences

Data	Category
It has been working a lot better than the medicines II was taking before.	Effective
When I was on the dosage, my levels were not as stable.	Ineffective
Was experiencing Stevens-Johnson Syndrome when I first started taking this drug.	Adverse
I hold a full-time job and I drive, so my number 1 priority every night is to take the medicines.	Other

10.3.4   MODULE 4: CLASSIFICATION MODEL

The data is trained using a classification model comparing and contrasting various ML approaches. The algorithms to be used include SVM, decision tree (DTs) forests, logistic regressor, etc. The efficiency of these algorithms is compared to obtain the most efficient approach.

10.3.5   MODULE 5: VISUALIZATION OF DATA AND REPORT GENERATION

The top reviews for each category for all drugs under consideration are generated. A report including the pros and cons is also generated. A comparison between drugs for the same disorder can be obtained, however this does warrant further look and does not serve as a medicine recommender under any circumstance. This should be used only as a suggestion of alternative drugs for a drug having severe adverse effects for medical professionals. Graphical analysis of various drugs with respect to a particular disease is generated via our system.

10.4   ALGORITHMS USED

1. **OneVsRestClassifier:** This strategy, also known as one vs all classification, consists of fitting one classifier per class in the problem. For each classifier, the class is then fitted against all other classes. Apart from the efficiency of computation (only n_classes classifiers are needed), the advantage of this approach is the interpretability.

Since each class is represented by one classifier only, it is possible to know more about the class by inspecting its corresponding classifier. This is a commonly used strategy for multiclass classification and therefore is a fair choice for our problem.

2. **Logistic Classifier:** LR is another oft used strategy for classification problems, binary, and multiclass. LR is named for the famous function used at the core, the logistic function. The logistic function, also called the sigmoid curve, which is an S-shaped curve that can take any real-valued number and map it into a value between 0 and 1, but never exactly those limits.

   A linear classifier provides the outcome (dependent variable) in a continuous behavior. It can have any one of infinite possible values. On the other hand, in logistic classifiers, the outcome (dependent variable) has only a limited number of possible values. Such classifiers are quite useful when the response variable is categorical in nature.

3. **Random Forest Classifier:** Random forest (RF) is a supervised learning algorithm. It creates a forest and makes it somehow random. RF builds multiple DTs and merges them together to get a sufficiently accurate prediction of the class for a prediction. Instead of searching for the most important feature while splitting a node, it searches for the best feature among a random subset of features. This results in a wide diversity leading to a better model. It is very easy to measure the relative importance of each feature on the prediction.

   It randomly selects "k" features from total "m" features, where k << m. Then among those "k" features, it starts calculating the node "d" using the best split point. Further, the node is divided into daughter nodes using the same strategy. The entire procedure is looped until the number of nodes has been achieved. There is no overfitting problem in classification using the RF Algorithm.

4. **F1 and Weighted F1 scores:** Accuracy of the predictions is defined as:

$$\text{Accuracy} = (TP + TN) / (TP + TN + FP + FN)$$

Other model prediction metrics like F1-score, precision, and recall are defined as:

$$\text{Precision} = (TP) / (TP + FP)$$
$$\text{Recall} = (TP) / (TP + FN)$$

F1 Score = 2 × (Recall × Precision) / (Recall + Precision)

We considered the weighted F1 score from sklearn for model evaluation to account for the class imbalance in the dataset, which takes into account the support (number of true instances) for each class and then finds their mean score.

Weighted F1 score = $(1+ \beta^2)$ × precision × recall / $(\beta^2$ × precision) + recall

10.5 EXPERIMENTS AND EVALUATION

The final dataset consisted of an average of 200 reviews for each of the seven neurological drugs, which was then split into training and test datasets in the ratio of 80:20. Python 3 libraries such as NumPy, pandas, scrapy, nltk, spacy, matplotlib, textblob, etc., which are standard libraries for text and numerical analysis, Scikit Learn for Model creation and result prediction., Anaconda Navigator and Jupyter Notebook as an Integrated environment for running python and notebook files, TensorFlow, and Keras for neural network, Google Colab as shared environment with enhanced processing capabilities, VADER for sentiment score calculation and Bokeh for creating dynamic visualization of drug effectiveness are used for carrying out experiments.

The entire development process has been divided into three stages. The first stage describes the steps involved in data collection and preprocessing. The data prepared here is ready to be fed into the model. The second stage describes the process of model development. Multiple combinations of models have been used to obtain the best-fitting model for the dataset. Several reports generated by the system and their significance is described in the third stage of development.

A detailed description of the development process along with essential code snippets can be found in our blog on medium mentioned in the references [20].

10.5.1   STAGE 1: COLLECTING AND PREPROCESSING THE DATA

1. **Scraping the Reviews:** For developing a decisive system, a subset of the extensive review data available on the Internet is taken. The reviews for neurological drugs for the treatment of epilepsy, seizures,

and bipolar disorders were scraped using scrapy, a library for developing custom web crawlers as shown in Figure 10.2.

(taken for 1 to 6 months)

"I started tegretol about 4 days ago and I've had the most crazy side effects ever. I've been on this medication several years ago I never had all these side effects before. It feels like I'm high all the time. My face is a little numb I'm very wobbly when I walk and have vertigo. I'm considering stopping it and consulting my doctor. I'm very nauseous when I take it in the morning in combination with my iron pill, (ferrious Sulfate)."

(taken for less than 1 month)

"This medicine helped tremendously with neurological pain from multi-level spinal cord compression. This was the only nerve pain medication which helped me to some degree by lowering the severity of the nerve pain from 10 ER level to about a 6 level I-Can-Get-Through-This pain. Unfortunately, I could only stay on it for a couple of months because it had very bad interactions with amlodipine BP med, causing increased severe side effects and loss of vision."

FIGURE 10.2   Example of a scraped review.

The final dataset consisted of an average of 200 reviews for each of the seven drugs, which was then split into training and test dataset in the ratio of 80:20.

2. **Cleaning the Reviews:** We tokenized the reviews into sentences using sent_tokenize from Natural Language Toolkit(nltk).

   The standardization of text which involved lowercase conversion, splitting of conjugate words, and correcting misspelled words was done. The words were lemmatized to get the root word form of the words using nltk.

   The stop words, negation, and punctuation are retained in this step to preserve the information contained in the reviews as best as possible. At the end of this step, the cleaned sentences are ready to be labeled into appropriate categories.

3. **Labeling the Training Dataset:** The sentence can be classified into one of the three categories:

4. **Effective:** The reviews in which the improvement of a patient's health is implied after use of the drug.

5. **Ineffective:** The reviews which imply no change in or worsening of the condition of the patient but contain no mentions of any adverse reactions after use of the drug.

6. Adverse: The reviews which contain explicit mentions of adverse reactions to the patient after use of the drug.

An auto-labeler evaluated the sentence on three parameters.

- A dictionary consisting of a collection of 'problem' words which tend to occur in the case of adverse category sentences.
  problems= 'hallucinations weakness hair loss tired hair loss nausea shakiness tremor tremors stones weight pounds flu flus lbs drowsiness dizziness appetite manic maniac cold vomiting seizures nauseous vision inflammation tingling numb numbness swollen swelling depression attacks blisters skin rash diarrhea headache headaches head severe fever sleep pain stress numb'

- The POS (parts-of-speech) tags of individual words of the sentence, generated using the nltk library.
  review = 'laying down is excruciating and I'm in the process of running test'
  [('laying,' 'VBG'), ('down,' 'RP'), ('is,' 'VBZ'), ('excruciating,' 'VBG'), ('and,' 'CC'), ('im,' 'NN'), ('in,' 'IN'), ('the,' 'DT'), ('process,' 'NN'), ('of,' 'IN'), ('running,' 'VBG'), ('test,' 'NN')]

- The compound VADER sentiment score of each sentence. VADER is a python module which is used for scoring the sentiment of a review in terms of polarity (positive or negative) and intensity(score). The compound score is an integer value ranging between −1 and 1 to evaluate the sentiment conveyed in the text. A value of 0 is the center point of the scale signifying neutral sentiment as shown in Figure 10.3.

	Review	Category	Drug	category_id	neg	pos	neu	compound
0	But since I started alternating I haven't had ...	Effective	Phenytoin	0	0.000	0.0	1.000	0.0000
1	About the Half Life of Phenytoin, about Sudden...	Adverse	Phenytoin	1	0.245	0.0	0.755	-0.5994
2	I think it's time to switch back to what works	Ineffective	Phenytoin	2	0.000	0.0	1.000	0.0000
3	SICK	Adverse	Phenytoin	1	1.000	0.0	0.000	-0.5106
4	It does work!"	Effective	Phenytoin	0	0.000	0.0	1.000	0.0000

FIGURE 10.3 Sentiment scores for few examples.

Thus, a preliminary labeling scheme for reviews was developed which was further refined by manual labeling of sentences.

The reviews misclassified by the auto-labeler were manually labeled by two independent annotators, and the conflicts were resolved by an unbiased third annotator. The dataset was then verified by a medical health professional. The training set is now ready for input to the classification algorithm.

10.5.2   STAGE 2: CHOOSING THE RIGHT APPROACH

1. **Vectorizing:** The vectorizer is used to convert every word into a vector of size equal to the unique count of words in the entire collection of documents(reviews). This approach is known as the 'bag-of-words' model. This model converts the text into numerical features form required by the ML algorithm.

    For example, a review of a certain drug reads 'This drug has made me worse' while another review says 'This drug has made me better.' The count of unique words in the reviews is found to be 7 ('this,' 'drug,' 'has,' 'made,' 'me,' 'worse,' 'better').

    Thus, the vectors for the reviews are
    - 'This drug has made me worse' = [1,1,1,1,1,1,0].
    - 'This drug has made me better' = [1,1,1,1,1,0,1].

    We can use either the CountVectorizer approach (creation of a sparse matrix of the size of words * reviews) or the term frequency-inverse document frequency (TF-IDF) approach (measures the frequency of a word along with the rareness of the word in the collection).

2. **Creation of Bi-Grams and Tri-Grams:** In NLP, each word in the text document is referred to as a 'gram.' Thus, a combination of co-occurring words is known as an n-gram, where n is the length of the combination considered.

    For example, 'bipolar disorder' would be an often occurring combination in our corpus of words. Thus, it can be represented with a bi-gram instead of the unigrams for individual words 'bipolar' and 'disorder,' as both of these words may not appear as separate words as frequently.

    bigram = gensim.models.Phrases(words, min_count=5, threshold=100)
    trigram = gensim.models.Phrases(bigram[words], threshold=100)
    bigram_mod = gensim.models.phrases.Phraser(bigram)
    trigram_mod = gensim.models.phrases.Phraser(trigram)
    def make_bigrams(texts):

return [bigram_mod[doc] for doc in texts]
def make_trigrams(texts):
return [trigram_mod[bigram_mod[doc]] for doc in texts]

The bi-grams or tri-grams may be obtained as features independently using Gensim (as above) or by using scikit-learn's feature extraction module to automatically generate them during vectorization.

3. **Choosing the Algorithms:** The reviews need to be classified into three categories, that is, effective, ineffective, and adverse, therefore we need to use a multi-class classifier instead of a binary classifier. For comparative analysis, four multi-class algorithms are used for prediction of categories:

   i.   OneVsRest SVM classifier: It involves the fitting of a single SVM classifier per class while considering all other classes as one class, effectively turning the problem into a binary classification problem;

   ii.   Logistic regression multi-class classifier;

   iii. Random forest classifier;

   iv.   Bagging meta-estimator with logistic regressor base: This ensemble technique uses random subsets of data to fit individual classifiers of the base type and then aggregates their predictions to obtain a single prediction.

4. **Creation of Feature Selections:** The performance of the algorithms was tested against a variety of feature selections as shown in Figure 10.4. Thus, various combinations of features were generated by combining vectorization techniques, the number of words considered as features and sentiment scores of the reviews. An example is shown in Figure 10.4.

	0	1	2	3	4	5	6	7	8	9	...	14994	14995	14996	14997	14998	14999	neg	pos	neu	compound
0	0.000000	0.0	0.000000	0.0	0.0	0.0	0.0	0.0	0.0	0.0	...	0.0	0.0	0.0	0.0	0.0	0.0	0.000	0.0	1.000	0.0000
1	0.000000	0.0	0.000000	0.0	0.0	0.0	0.0	0.0	0.0	0.0	...	0.0	0.0	0.0	0.0	0.0	0.0	0.245	0.0	0.755	-0.5994
2	0.000000	0.0	0.000000	0.0	0.0	0.0	0.0	0.0	0.0	0.0	...	0.0	0.0	0.0	0.0	0.0	0.0	0.000	0.0	1.000	0.0000
3	0.000000	0.0	0.000000	0.0	0.0	0.0	0.0	0.0	0.0	0.0	...	0.0	0.0	0.0	0.0	0.0	0.0	1.000	0.0	0.000	-0.5106
4	0.249827	0.0	0.321899	0.0	0.0	0.0	0.0	0.0	0.0	0.0	...	0.0	0.0	0.0	0.0	0.0	0.0	0.000	0.0	1.000	0.0000

FIGURE 10.4   Example of features.

Here, we convert the top 15,000 occurring words and their bi-grams (as ngram_range is set between 1–2) to feature vectors using TF-IDF. The vectors of each review are combined with the VADER sentiment scores to obtain the features, which are to be fed to the classification algorithm to decide the class of that review.

Similarly, 7 other such feature sets are created as below:

- **FS-1:** CountVectorizer
- **FS-2:** CountVectorizer + VADER Sentiment Scores
- **FS-3:** CountVectorizer top 10000 features + VADER Sentiment Scores + n-gram range 1–3
- **FS-4:** CountVectorizer all features + VADER Sentiment Scores + n-gram range 1–3
- **FS-5:** TfidfVectorizer
- **FS-6:** TfidfVectorizer + VADER Sentiment Scores
- **FS-7:** Tfidf Vectorizer top 10000 features + VADER Sentiment Scores + n-gram range 1–3
- **FS-8:** Tfidf Vectorizer top 15000 features + word tokenize analyzer + VADER Sentiment Scores + n-gram range 1–3

10.5.3   STAGE 3: OBSERVATIONS AND RESULTS

The highest accuracy of the model is obtained by feeding a combination of top 15,000 TF-IDF features from the review texts and VADER sentiment scores to a OnevsRestClassifier with a Linear SVM core and cross-validated across 10 folds. This results in an accuracy of ~75% across three categories-adverse, effective, ineffective. The detailed output is shown in the table below.

Comparison over feature sets-Eight feature sets from TF-IDF features and VADER sentiment scores were used to evaluate four models as below:

- **FS-1:** CountVectorizer
- **FS-2:** CountVectorizer + VADER Sentiment Scores
- **FS-3:** CountVectorizer top 10000 features + VADER Sentiment Scores + n-gram range 1–3
- **FS-4:** CountVectorizer all features + VADER Sentiment Scores + n-gram range 1–3
- **FS-5:** TfidfVectorizer
- **FS-6:** TfidfVectorizer + VADER Sentiment Scores
- **FS-7:** Tfidf Vectorizer top 10000 features + VADER Sentiment Scores + n-gram range 1–3

- **FS-8:** Tfidf Vectorizer top 15000 features + word tokenize analyzer + VADER Sentiment Scores + n-gram range 1–3
- **M1:** OneVsRest Classifier with linear SVM core
- **M2:** Logistic Regression
- **M3:** Random Forest Classifier
- **M4:** Bagging meta-estimator with linear regressor core.

The results obtained using these feature sets are shown in Table 10.2.

TABLE 10.2   Various Approaches, Feature Selections and Their Respective Weighted F1-Scores

	FS-1	FS-2	FS-3	FS-4	FS-5	FS-6	FS-7	FS-8
OneVsRest classifier with linear SVM core	67.21	69.21	70.42	72.07	69.83	71.11	72.61	73.37
Logistic regression	67.11	68.48	70.80	72.25	68.43	70.32	72.71	73.56
Random forest	66.30	67.93	67.58	66.35	64.54	66.70	65.84	68.10
Bagging meta-estimator with linear regressor core	67.21	69.12	71.96	–	69.38	71.37	71.82	72.77

All scores printed are weighted F1 scores averaged for each of the three categories-effective, adverse, ineffective-, and cross validated over 10 folds. The comparison of results is shown in Figure 10.5.

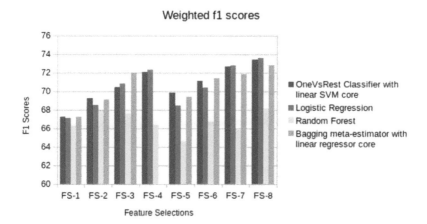

FIGURE 10.5   Various approaches, feature selections and their respective weighted F1-scores.

Various DL algorithms like LSTM, CNN + LSTM, LSTM with recurrent dropout were implemented as well. This gave results of around ~75% with high bias towards the dominant class, i.e., effective category. Thus, we conclude that the ML approach is more effective as it gives a prediction model which equally favors all classes.

10.5.4   VISUALIZATIONS

The final user interface is generated using flask and aids the user to get an concise overview of the drugs he/she intends to use. The application allows the user to upload his/her own reactions to the selected drugs, read the reviews in a summarized format or at length, and visualize the drug reactions in an interactive format using graphs and charts as shown in Figures 10.6 and 10.7. The informative reports with statistical graphs are generated by the system.

The adverseness comparison of seven drugs is shown in Figure 10.8. Phenobarbital drug for treating neurological diseases is having minimum adverse effects as compared to other drugs:

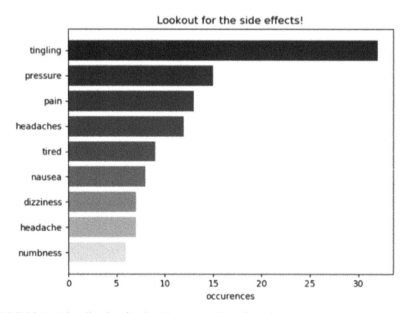

FIGURE 10.6   Visualization for the adverse reactions for a drug

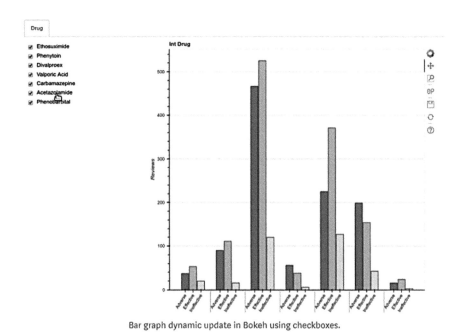

Bar graph dynamic update in Bokeh using checkboxes.

FIGURE 10.7   Visualization for comparison between drugs for the neurological disorder.

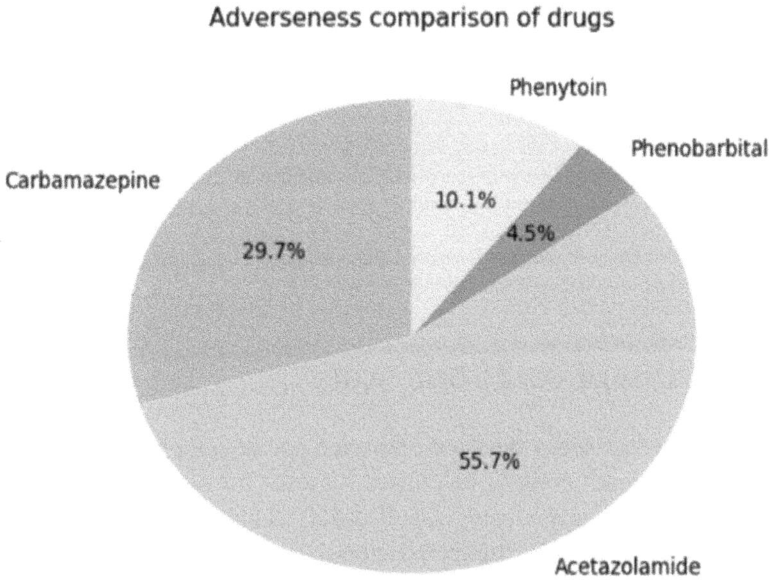

Adverseness comparison of drugs

Phenytoin

Phenobarbital

Carbamazepine

10.1%

29.7%

4.5%

55.7%

Acetazolamide

FIGURE 10.8   Visualization for % adverse reviews in each category.

➢ **Ranking Reviews with Text Rank:** The TextRank algorithm uses the similarity graph of TF-IDF vectors to calculate the importance of each node. The node or review which is most similar to most other reviews is considered 'central' to the class it belongs to.

Here, the reviews for the effective category are ranked for a particular drug. The phrases 'best drug,' 'helped me lots,' 'would not be able to live without it' best reflect the theme of the effective class, and therefore the reviews containing them are ranked at the top using TextRank as shown in Figure 10.9.

Top Effective Sentences for carbamazepine

Rank	Effective Sentences	Score
1	But it is the best drug I have been on to control seizures.	0.0098746145 7807941
2	I was scared about the side effects but I had to weigh up the pros and cons and took it has helped me lots.	0.0096904245 5776571
3	Do not know why my review did not show up, but here I go again I have been taking this for depression for several years and it has brought me out of the funk.	0.0096780234 82178248
4	This medicine has helped me SO much, and I would not have been able to live without it!".	0.0094046688 0911016
5	It did make me a bit sleepy and unsteady in the beginning, but that has waned and now I really do not have any side effects.	0.0093380682 42233726

FIGURE 10.9   Top effective sentences for drug carbamazepine.

10.6   CONCLUSION AND FUTURE SCOPE

Here we have proposed a detailed approach for development of a system for classification and analysis of patient reviews for seven drugs given as medication for treating neurological disorders. This system is designed in such a way that it provides better efficiency and usability as compared to existing systems.

In the future, the system can be improved in many ways by providing support for authentication of reviews, considering reviews of other domains, and improving the efficiency by employing neural networks.

KEYWORDS

- **adverse drug reactions**
- **convolutional neural network with attention**
- **deep learning**
- **pharmacovigilance**
- **term frequency-inverse document frequency**

REFERENCES

1. Kuhn, M., Monica, C., Ivica, L., Lars, J. J., & Peer, B., (2010). A side effect resource to capture phenotypic effects of drugs. *Molecular Systems Biology, 6*(1), 343.
2. Leaman, R., Laura, W., Ryan, S., Annie, S., Jian, Y., & Graciela, G., (2010). Towards internet-age pharmacovigilance: Extracting adverse drug reactions from user posts to health-related social networks. In: *Proceedings of the 2010 Workshop on Biomedical Natural Language Processing* (pp. 117–125). Association for Computational Linguistics.
3. Nikfarjam, A., Abeed, S., Karen, O., Rachel, G., & Graciela, G., (2015). Pharmacovigilance from social media: mining adverse drug reaction mentions using sequence labeling with word embedding cluster features. *Journal of the American Medical Informatics Association, 22*(3), 671–681.
4. Yadav, S., Asif, E., Sriparna, S., & Pushpak, B., (2018). *Medical Sentiment Analysis Using Social Media: Towards Building a Patient Assisted System.* In: LREC.
5. Huynh, T., Yulan, H., Alistair, W., & Stefan, R., (2016). *Adverse Drug Reaction Classification with Deep Neural Networks.* Cooling.
6. Yang, C. C., Haodong, Y., Ling, J., & Mi, Z., (2012). Social media mining for drug safety signal detection. In: *Proceedings of the 2012 International Workshop on Smart Health and Wellbeing* (pp. 33–40). ACM.
7. Lee, K., Ashequl, Q., Sadid, A. H., Vivek, D., Aaditya, P., Joey, L., & Oladimeji, F., (2017). Adverse drug event detection in tweets with semi-supervised convolutional neural networks. In: *Proceedings of the 26th International Conference on World Wide Web* (pp. 705–714). International World Wide Web Conferences Steering Committee.
8. Xia, L., Alan, W. G., & Weiguo, F., (2017). A deep learning based named entity recognition approach for adverse drug events identification and extraction in health social media. In: *International Conference on Smart Health* (pp. 237–248). Springer, Cham,
9. Krittika, K., (2018). *Using Data Science to Help Women Make Contraceptive Choices.* Insight data science via medium.

10. Liu, X., & Chen, H., (2015). A research framework for pharmacovigilance in health social media: Identification and evaluation of patient adverse drug event reports. *J. Biomed. Inform. 58*, 268–279.

11. Benton, A., Ungar, L., Hill, S., Hennessy, S., Mao, J., Chung, A., Leonard, C. E., & Holmes, J. H., (2011). Identifying potential adverse effects using the web: A new approach to medical hypothesis generation. *J. Biomed. Inform., 44*, 989–996.

12. Leaman, R., Wojtulewicz, L., Sullivan, R., Skariah, A., Yang, J., & Gonzalez, G., (2010). Towards internet-age pharmacovigilance: Extracting adverse drug reactions from user posts to health-related social networks., In: *Proceedings of the 2010 Workshop on Biomedical Natural Language Processing.* Association for Computational Linguistics.

13. Nikfarjam, A., & Gonzalez, G. H., (2011). Pattern mining for extraction of mentions of adverse drug reactions from user comments. *AMIA Annual Symposium Proceedings.*

14. Wu, H., Fang, H., & Stanhope, S. J., (2013). Exploiting online discussions to discover unrecognized drug side effects. *Methods Inf. Med., 52*, 152–159.

15. Bian, J., Topaloglu, U., & Yu, F., (2012). Towards large-scale twitter mining for drug-related adverse events. In: *Proceedings of the 2012 International Workshop on Smart Health and Wellbeing.* ACM.

16. Basch, E., (2010). The missing voice of patients in drug-safety reporting. *N. Engl. J. Med., 362*, 865–869.

17. Aagaard, L., Nielsen, L. H., & Hansen, E. H., (2009). Consumer reporting of adverse drug reactions: A retrospective analysis of the Danish adverse drug reaction database from 2004 to 2006. *British Journal of Clinical Pharmacology.*

18. Vinodhini, G., & Chandrasekaran, R., (2017). Patient opinion mining to analyze drugs satisfaction using supervised learning. *Journal of Applied Research and Technology, 15.*

19. Dipen, C., Disha, M., Varsha, S., Sujay, V., & Sujata, K., (2019). Drug review analytics of neurological disorders. In: *2019 International Conference on Nascent Technologies in Engineering (ICNTE 2019).*

20. Dipen, C., (2021). *How Machine Learning Can Help Identify Effectiveness and Adverseness of a Drug.* by towardsdatascience.com (accessed on 11 November 2021).

21. Mark, H., Irene, L., Spyros, K., & Toyotaro, S., (2016). Medical text classification using convolutional neural networks. *International Journal of Computational Linguistics and Applications.*

CHAPTER 11

Time Series Forecasting Techniques for Infectious Disease Prediction

JAIDITYA DEV,[1] MONIKA MANGLA,[2] NONITA SHARMA,[3] and
K. P. SHARMA[3]

[1]*University of Toronto, Toronto, Ontario, Canada*
E-mail: jaiditya.dev@mail.utoronto.ca

[2]*Department of Information Technology, Dwarkadas J. Sanghvi College of*
Engineering, Mumbai, India, E-mail: manglamona@gmail.com

[3]*Dr. B. R. Ambedkar National Institute of Technology, Jalandhar, Punjab,*
India, E-mails: nonita@nitj.ac.in (N. Sharma),
sharmakp@nitj.ac.in (K. P. Sharma)

ABSTRACT

This chapter provides an overview of the Time Series Forecasting techniques for infectious disease prediction with a focus on enabling technologies, protocols, and implementation issues. Recent developments in RFID, smart sensors, communications technologies, and Internet protocols enable the latest technological advances in the field of epidemiology. The basic idea of this chapter is to have smart sensors working directly to achieve a new class of autonomous applications without human involvement. One of the significant challenges in the medical domain is the effective handling of large volumes of time series data and the associated algorithms. Apart from the sheer volume of data, the diversity of data sources gives rise to considerable complexity: without comprehensive semantic meaning data on signals, objects, and their location, users cannot comprehend the raw time-series data. This further augments the complexity by considering predictive models for capturing regularities and time series statistical patterns, often as a function of other time series influenced through co-location and physical processes.

This chapter outlines a detailed survey of the time series forecasting techniques in the context of medical applications.

11.1   INTRODUCTION

The rising prevalence of IoT and sensor networks leads to the collection of a vast amount of time-series data that enables forecasting for many IoT applications [1]. The multitude of use cases for time series applications in IoT exists from optimization problems to anomaly detection, prediction, and many more. The prime focus of these applications is to automate a conventional manual system. This automation enables the evaluation of numerous data points ranging from tens to millions along a data series [2]. In particular, time series forecasting applies a statistical model to predict future values based on past results. In such applications, data is collected over time, and the time series model uses that data to forecast future values [3]. The objective of data learning is to analyze the observed environment and/or extract useful information that supports decision-making [4]. The ability to predict the next value in a time series helps to estimate how a specific factor will evolve over time. A higher level of confidence in the prediction model helps to take appropriate action or business decisions accordingly [5].

The research community is increasingly relying on clinical databases for potential study and accurate forecasting, which allows people to take appropriate precautions to prevent future diseases [6]. Time-series forecasting models are frequently used to design forecasting systems for disease prediction through a collection of clinical datasets. These models discover patterns and trends in the time series data and use that in conjunction with the current year patterns to estimate the future occurrences [7]. Time series can be defined as a series of measurements over a period of time which could be weekly, monthly, quarterly, annually, etc. In addition to finding meaningful patterns in the data, time series forecasting models offer several advantages like reliability, seasonal patterns identification, and trend estimations [8]. However, these models suffer from the drawback of the high generalization error of prediction. To overcome this problem, innovative combinations of different forecasting models or the ensemble model could be used for significantly reducing the generalization error and enhancing accuracy [9].

Ensemble models are meta-algorithms that combine several ML techniques into one predictive model to decrease variance and improve prediction accuracy. Ensemble converts multiple weak learners into a single strong learner [8]. An ensemble model is mostly used due to good performance in several tasks like classification or regression problems. Ensembling of different models can be done in two ways, namely: sequential ensembling and parallel ensembling. In sequential ensembling, the base learners are produced consecutively. The results of the previous model are used in the next model (e.g., AdaBoost), so the upcoming model handles error in the last model. In parallel ensembling model, the base learners are produced in parallel, i.e., side by side (e.g., Random Forest), and training data are provided to each model parallelly and further combining the results of all models [10].

This chapter outlines the different time series forecasting techniques applicable to the medical domain. Section 11.1 introduces the process of time series forecasting in detail. Section 11.2 gives a brief explanation of the time series forecasting process. Section 11.3 describes how technology is implemented in the forecast. Integration of methods in order to further optimize results has been discussed in Section 11.4. Section 11.5 is dedicated to the implementation and results are discussed in Section 6. Finally, the last Section 11.7 presents the conclusion and future scope.

11.2   TIME SERIES FORECASTING PROCESS

Time-series Forecasting is carried out in almost every organization that uses quantifiable data [11]. The purpose of time series forecasting is:

- To understand or to find out the probability of an event that gives rise to an observed series;
- To predict or forecast the future possibilities of that observation by looking at historical data.

The various factors that affect the values of an observation in a time series are the components of a time series. The most vital component is trend, which is a general tendency of the data to rise or diminish in the given data. Generally, the trend is smooth over the long-term. The second component is seasonality, which is a cyclic change in an observed set of data over a fixed period of time. Many times, the recorded data shows a seasonal variation annually; it may be an uptrend or a downtrend.

Apart from these components, the process of time-series follows can be best described as shown in Figure 11.1. Here follows the brief introduction of each block in Figure 11.1 for enhanced understanding.

11.2.1 GOAL DEFINITION

Generally, the data analysis starts with Goal Definition during which data is collected, refined, and is analyzed using various visualization tools. It is followed by choosing an appropriate forecasting method based on the nature of data. For finalizing the forecasting method, the accuracy of various forecasting models is compared. After finalizing the forecasting method, it is used to generate the forecast. The method of finalizing the forecasting goal is a vital process for achieving targets. Primarily, there are two types of goals in time series forecasting (Figure 11.1):

1. **Descriptive Goal:** In this case, the time series is structured in a manner that it helps to define its components in terms of seasonal patterns, trends, and relations to external factors, etc. This can further be used for decision making and strategy planning by using time series data to predict the future values of the series.
2. **Predictive Goal:** In this case, time-series data is used to predict the future values for a time variable. It is a useful model that is assessed by its predictive precision.

The predictive goal is a better method to obtain accurate forecasting along the time series. However, in order to understand how rigorously a person can forecast and whether to forecast all the data in one instance or at a constant rate, forecast horizon, forecast updating, forecast use and level of automation should be considered.

The forecast horizon, "k" is the number of periods in the future that can be forecasted, and F_{t+k} is k steps ahead forecast value. For instance, if a company wants to predict its revenue after three months, it will use the model F_{t+3} (three months ahead forecast) [12].

It is important to have realistic anticipations with respect to forecast accuracy. The longer duration we consider for forecasting, the higher becomes the possibility of uncertainty as there becomes a possibility that situation may change in an unforeseen manner. Hence, the model should be updated regularly so as to handle these uncertainties over time. This is referred to as forecast updating; and constant refreshing of the old data with the new data is called Roll-Forward Forecasting. To find out how these forecasts will be useful to different stakeholders, it is indeed important to accurately forecast the correct type of data. This helps to understand the correct use of this data referred to as forecast use.

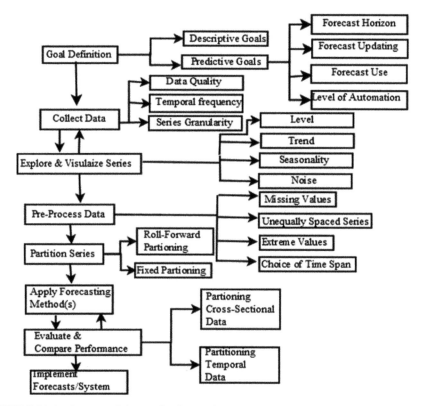

FIGURE 11.1 Process of time series forecasting.

The required level of automation in time series forecasting basically depends on two things viz. The nature of the task and the manner in which it will be used by stakeholders. Hence, some basic questions that are quite necessary to be asked during the start of every goal definition stage are:

- How many series are to be forecasted?
- Is forecasting an ongoing process or a one-time event?
- Which kind of data and software will be available during the time series forecasting period?

11.2.2 DATA COLLECTION

The second process after the Goal Definition is Data Collection. After carefully examining the data received, it is proceeded towards the Time Series

Forecasting process. However, Prior to this, the collected data is carefully investigated as it has a huge impact on forecasting accuracy. Some of the investing factors are as follows:

1. **Data Quality:** The data quality is determined in terms of its measurement accuracy, missing values, corrupted data and data entry errors. An optimal data quality is strongly required in a time series if the number of the data points is very small otherwise it may lead to suboptimal performance. When there are multiple data sources, it is recommended to evaluate data quality so as to finalize the best data source. Moreover, data collection is not a single time task; additional data is to be collected again for future reference from the same source.

2. **Temporal Frequency:** With today's technological advancements, the data is recorded in a frequent time scale. Though this data is recorded at a frequent time scale, it is not always required to consider this frequency scale. Rather, it is suggested to choose a temporal frequency by considering the forecasting requirement and data noise.

3. **Series Granularity:** Granularity refers to the level of detail of the data. This is generally referred to in terms of geographical area, population, time of operation, etc., of this data. With temporal frequency, the level of granularity of the data should also be taken care of for the forecasting goal. The level of granularity will ultimately affect the range of pre-processing, forecasting methods and the evaluation methods.

11.2.3 COMPONENTS OF TIME SERIES

It is suggested to divide the time series data into systematic part and a non-systematic part so as to select the appropriate components of time series forecasting [13]. The systematic components are divided into three parts: level, seasonality, and trend:

- Level provides the average value of the series;
- Trend is the net change in the initial value and the final value of the data; and
- Seasonality describes a short-termed recurring behavior of data that is observed multiple times in a series.

While some of the series don't compulsorily have Trend and Seasonality, it is always observed to have a Level. Moreover, time series are also observed to possess a noise (non-systematic part of the Time Series), which is caused by measurement errors or some different reasons that aren't accounted for. Noise is always assumed to be there in a time series; however sometimes it may be minor enough that it is not directly noticed.

The forecasting methods aim to segregate the systematic part and compute the level of noise. The systematic part of the time series helps in prediction whereas the magnitude of noise helps to ascertain the uncertainty associated with forecasted values. These components of the time series trends are generally estimated by linear, exponential, and other types of mathematical functions. Figure 11.2 underneath shows the decomposition of a time series into its components.

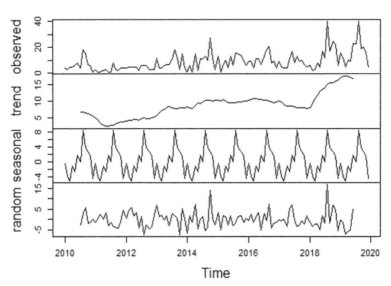

FIGURE 11.2   Decomposition of a time series into components.

11.2.4   *EXPLORING AND VISUALIZING THE TIME SERIES*

To illustrate the nature of time series, data visualization is the most commonly used. Data visualization helps to find initial patterns, identify components and look out for some potential problems (such as extreme values, unequal spacing, and missing values). One of the elementary graphs that helps to visualize a time series is the time plot. In the most basic form, the time plot is a line chart of our time series model values $(y_1, y_2, \ldots\ldots)$ over time $(t = 1, 2, 3, \ldots.)$ with temporal labels (e.g., calendar dates) on the horizontal axis [14]. An example of time series plot is given in Figure 11.3. It is advisable to carry out data visualization in steps in order to obtain the maximum benefit. These steps are as follows:

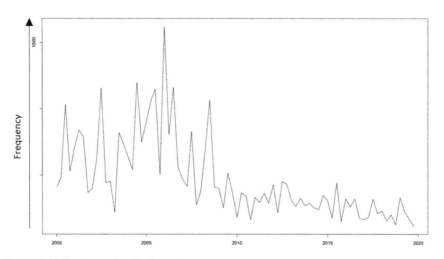

FIGURE 11.3   Example of a time plot.

1. **Zooming In:** To discover a few hidden patterns in a time series, shorter periods in the time series can be zoomed in. This gives satisfactory performance when the time series is particularly long.
2. **Changing the Scale:** It is usually recommended to change the scale of the time series so as to be able to recognize the shape of the trend. One such solution is to change the vertical axis(y-axis) to a logarithmic scale. If the trend in the new scale shows a linear trend, it demonstrated that the original scale has an exponential trend.
3. **Adding Trend Lines:** While fitting different trend lines (e.g., linear, exponential, cubic, etc.), it can be evaluated that what type of trend best approximates the data points.
4. **Suppressing Seasonality:** If the data in a time series is expanded, the trends get more evident and easier to interpret. Plotting the series at a sketchier time scale (e.g., accumulating monthly data into yearly data) also helps in suppressing seasonal patterns.

Time plots are beneficial for identifying the global and local trends in the data. The global pattern is one which remains constant throughout the series. Whereas, local pattern persists for a shorter duration of time and then it changes.

11.2.5   PRE-PROCESSING OF DATA

Data exploration and pre-processing helps to handle issues like missing values, unequal spacing and irrelevant periods in the Time Series model [15]. Hence, it basically prepares the data so as to enable further actions. Some of the actions performed during pre-processing are as follows:

1. **Missing Values:** The missing values in a particular time series create "holes" or "voids" in the given series. This may hinder the forecasting process hence it becomes imperative to fill this "hole/void" in the time series.
2. **Unequally Spaced Series:** Equally spaced data means that the data has uniform spaced time intervals. However, some data may have unequal spaced intervals. In order to convert unequally spaced data to equally spaced data, the interpolation of data is required.
3. **Extreme Values:** The values of data throughout the series of the time series are somewhat similar, but there may be some values that are remarkably large or small. These extreme values influence the forecasting to a different extent. Hence, it needs to be decided whether to keep these extreme values or discard them. Therefore, it is suggested to make two different forecasts for the same data one including extreme values and another without extreme values.
4. **Choice of Time Span:** Another vital parameter is to determine the time span that should be considered for data so as to give an accurate prediction. A very short time series may fail to give optimal performance while a prolonged historical data may also be harmful from performance perspective. Thus, the time span should be decided so as it performs optimally.

11.2.6   PERFORMANCE EVALUATION

At times, we might think that it is appropriate to choose a forecasting model that generates the best forecasts [16]. However, there may be some instances that when selected model is used on some other data, it generates *bias*. Hence, the following steps must be performed:

1. **Data Partitioning:** Sometimes the data for evaluation is overfitted and unorganized. Therefore, it is a necessary step to apply *data partitioning* in the forecasting method. During data partitioning, given time series is split into two periods. Among these partitions, the first partition is used to develop the forecasting model. Thereafter, second partition is used to analyze performance of the model by measuring the errors (difference in the predicted values and the actual values).
    i. **Partitioning Cross-Sectional Data:** When built models uses cross-sectional data, it generates partitions viz. *training set, validation set* and occasionally an extra *test set*. Among these partitions, the *training set* is the largest partition which includes the data used for analysis. The *validation set* is used to evaluate the performance of each model and finally selecting the best one. Finally, the *test partition* is used to judge the performance of the selected model with new data.
    ii. **Temporal Partitioning:** Unlike earlier partitioning methods, partitioning of data into *training* and *validation sets* is done differently in temporal partitioning. The series is clipped into two periods, in which the earlier period ($t = 1,2,3,...n$) is labeled as the *training period* and the later one ($t = n+1, n+2... ...$) as the *validation period.* A graphed example of this process is given in Figure 11.4.

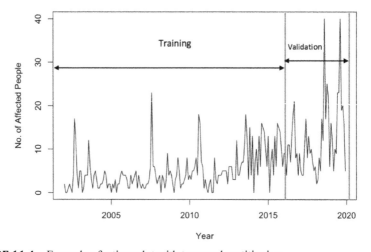

FIGURE 11.4   Example of a time plot with temporal partitioning.

2. **Joining Partitions for Forecasting:** During forecasting, the training period and the validation period must be integrated into a single series. Thereafter, the chosen method is re-applied on the whole data. This final model is used to predict future values.

3. **Choosing the Validation Period:** The idea of selecting the time duration *for the validation period* depends on the forecasting goal. Its main objective is to simulate the forecast horizon, so as to allow the evaluation of actual predictive performance. This period should neither be too short nor too long. As in both such cases, the model won't be able to function accurately and appropriately.

4. **Fixed and Roll-Forward Partitioning:** The process of dividing the data into fixed training period and validation periods makes the process of predictive evaluation somewhat limited. Hence, instead of applying this approach, a different method known as the roll-forward validation period can be applied. Unlike Fixed partitioning, training-validation periods continuously move one period at a time in roll-forward validation. Resultantly, it helps to gain more information about the short-term forecasts leading to a decrease in the amount of data.

5. **Measuring Predictive Accuracy:** In order to measure the effectiveness of a forecasting model, various standard performance metrics are in existence. The limitation of these standard measures is that they are unable to evaluate the ability of the given model to forecast new values. Hence, several measures are generally integrated to judge the predictive accuracy of a forecasting method. Few performance metrics are discussed as follows:

6. **Common Prediction Accuracy Measures:** The *forecast error* for time period t, is denoted by e_t. This is the difference between the actual value y_t and the forecasted value at the time t.

$$e_t = y_t - F_t$$

To understand better, let us consider a validation period of v periods. Thus, time will be: $t = n + 1, n + 2 \ldots \ldots \ldots \ldots n + v$

The popular methods of predictive accuracy are:

MAE or MAD (mean absolute error/deviation) $= \dfrac{1}{v} \sum_{t=1}^{v} |e_t|$.

It is also useful to get the magnitude of the average absolute error as follows:

$$\textbf{Average Error} = \frac{1}{v}\sum_{t=1}^{v} e_t .$$

This measure of average error is similar to MAD, but it doesn't include a modulus function due to which it can have either positive or negative magnitude:

$$\textbf{MAPE (mean absolute percentage error)} = \frac{1}{v}\sum_{t=1}^{v} \left|\frac{e_t}{y_t}\right| \times 100$$

This measure gives a percentage value that tells how the forecast is going to deviate from the average or the original value.

$$\textbf{RMSE (root mean-squared error)} = \sqrt{\frac{1}{v}\sum_{t=1}^{v} e_t^2}$$

All of the above measures using the above methods using the training period do not tell us about the predictive accuracy of the model; rather it tells us about how good the model fits in the training period.

Zero Counts: If the series contains a zero, then the calculation leads to infinity due to division by y_t. One way to omit this issue to remove zeros and compute the data with MAPE. Though it solves the problem of getting infinity, but leads to the omission of some important value from the series. Therefore, another solution is to use measures like MAE and RMSE if applicable [17].

Although MAPE appeals to be a scale-independent measure, there is another scale-independent measure which can handle zero count, i.e., mean absolute scaled error (MASE) defined as follows:

$$MASE = \frac{validation\,MAE}{training\,MAE\,of\,naive\,forecasts} = \frac{\frac{1}{v}\sum_{t=n+1}^{n+v}|e_t|}{\frac{1}{n-1}\sum_{t=1}^{n}|y_{t-1} - y|}$$

As MASE evaluates the forecasting functioning (MAE) to the naive forecast, hence following conditions hold:

- Values less than 1 represent that the model has a lower average error than the naive forecast.

- Values more than 1 signify the poor performance in comparison to the naive forecast.

11.3 IMPLEMENTATION OF FORECASTS

The various methods that are used to generate the forecast are:

1. **Model-Based Method:** It uses a mathematical or any other scientific model to estimate a data series. Here training data is used to approximate the parameters of the model. These models are therefore advantageous when the series is very short. Model based methods are used for forecasting series with global patterns that usually spreads throughout the whole data period.
2. **Data-Driven Method:** This method is used when the model assumptions are violated or when the time series changes its structure with the passage of time. For instance, naïve forecast is a data driven method that simply uses the last data point in the series for prediction. The prime advantage of such method is that it requires less input from the user.
3. **Extrapolation Method:** It is the method that is based on the history of its forecast, e.g., *naive forecasts*. When multiple related time series are provided assuming that the value of one series is in correlation to the other; the most common method for such forecasting is *extrapolation method*. It is very simple to use with the only problem that it does not take into account the probable connections among series.
4. **Econometric Model:** These models are based on the theories of casualty that originated from theoretical models.
5. **Using External Information:** A substitute method where the casual, econometric, and multivariate time series models are used for the sake of forecasting.

11.4 COMBINING METHODS AND ENSEMBLES

It is often observed that when various forecasting methods are used together in a model, it leads to improved performance. These methods can be combined in different manners. For instance, different types of forecasting methods are applied to the series which give different results. Then the subsequent forecast is averaged to produce the final forecast. The most beneficial part of averaging out data of the forecasts is that it tends to make the forecast values more tough and precise. Such a model is called ensemble model. A simple example of ensemble modeling can be built using a data analysis software like R, Python, etc. It takes place in the following steps:

- The data for previous years is uploaded and subsequently filtered out;
- The data is uploaded into the programming software and segregated on the basis of its frequency as desired. It could be monthly, quarterly or as desired;
- A time series is created and a graph plot is generated to validate the data;
- Basic autoregressive integrated moving average (ARIMA) model is applied in order to find the best forecasting model that can be applied to data;
- The data is then forecasted and the final graph is plotted;
- The data is checked for its error metrics (as discussed previously) and then it is applied to various other models like NNAR, ETS, Holt Winter, etc.;
- On the basis of the various forecasting models, an appropriate ensemble is created.

11.5 IMPLEMENTATION

Here, R Studio has been used as the programming software to forecast the occurrence of diseases like Tuberculosis (TB), Dengue, Chickenpox, and, Food Poisoning. The data is taken from www.chp.gov.hk and cleaned on the basis of time. This data tells us about the number of people affected by Dengue in Hong Kong (From 2002–2019), chickenpox (From 1999–2019), food poisoning (From 2000–2019) and the number of deaths that were caused due to TB (From 1995–2019) in the same area:

1. **Dengue:** It is observed that the data has a monthly frequency, throughout the given time span. *ARIMA* function is applied to find the best forecasting model for the data [18]. The forecasted values till the year 2025 are demonstrated through a graph in Figure 11.5.
    In Figure 11.5, the black graph line shows the number of people who were affected by Dengue from 2002 till 2019. The blue line shows the projection of the number of people who might get affected by the

disease in the upcoming five years, starting from 2019. From this, we can infer that the number of dengue affected people will be less than the year 2018 and 2019 and this will continue to decrease in the coming years.

Forecasts from ARIMA(2,1,1)(2,0,0)[12]

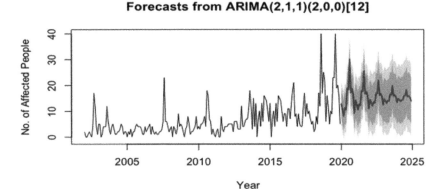

FIGURE 11.5   Forecast graph of dengue using ARIMA.

2. **Tuberculosis:** The data for TB is also taken from the same source. It has a frequency of 18 in a given year, starting from 1995 till 2019. The data provides a number of deaths due to TB. ARIMA is applied to this data to find the best prediction model [19]. The obtained data is then plotted to study the future trend of the disease. Figure 11.6 shows the graph for the number of total deaths caused by TB.

Forecasts from ARIMA(0,0,1)(1,1,1)[18]

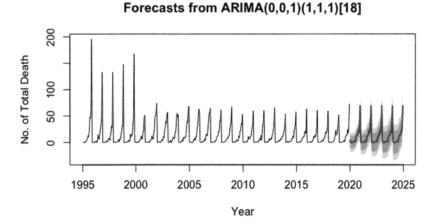

FIGURE 11.6   Forecast graph of tuberculosis using ARIMA.

In Figure 11.6, the black line demonstrates the number of people who died because of TB and the blue line shows the predicted number of people who might die in the coming five years. Broadly, the figure shows the general death rate pattern since 2000, therefore model tells that somewhat similar pattern may be observed in the forthcoming years also.

3. Food Poisoning: The data of food poisoning contains the number of people who suffered from Food Poisoning from the year. Here also, the black line shows the number of people affected by Food Poisoning from 2000 till 2019 and the blue line shows the forecast for coming years by ARIMA model (Figure 11.7).

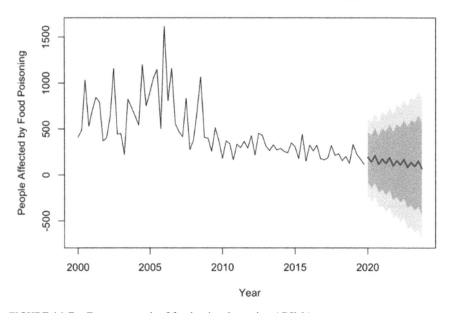

FIGURE 11.7   Forecast graph of food poisoning using ARIMA.

4. **Chickenpox:** The data of chickenpox deaths from 1999 to 2019 is used to predict the same for coming years using the ARIMA model and the obtained values are demonstrated in Figure 11.8.

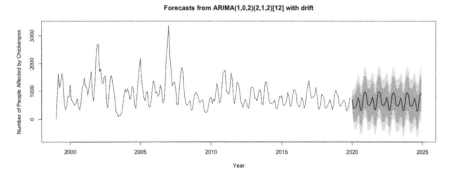

FIGURE 11.8   Forecast graph of chickenpox using ARIMA.

In Figure 11.8, the black graph line shows the number the people who were affected by Chickenpox from 1999 till 2019. The blue line shows the projection of the number of people who might get affected by the disease in the upcoming five years, starting from 2019. From this, we can infer that the number of people who will be affected by Chickenpox will be similar to that of the year 2018 and 2019, and the count will continue to be the same in the coming years.

11.6   RESULTS AND DISCUSSION

Table 11.1 comprises of average errors of predictions as different error metrics for base models and the ensemble model. The results show that the ensemble model outperforms all the independent base models, justifying the applicability of the ensemble model where the error metrics are minimum for all the disease datasets. Also, the datasets of Chickenpox and Food poisoning which uncovers higher values of error metrics for base models have also shown a significant decline in the values of error metrics [19]. MAE, i.e., the mean average error of the ensemble model for the Tuberculosis (TB), Dengue, Food Poisoning, and Chickenpox are 1.58, 1.89, 11.45, and 15.68 respectively. Amongst the base models, NNAR has shown the best performance with the MAE error metrics being: 2.97, 2.75, 14.59, and 24.12 for diseases in the same order as given above, respectively. The detailed comparison of all the models reflecting the values of all error metrics is given in Table 11.1 as appendix. The ensemble model enhances the predictive accuracy for the TB, Dengue, Food poisoning, and Chickenpox by 46.80%, 31.27%, 21.52%, 34.99% as compared to the independent NNAR model, respectively.

TABLE 11.1   Average Errors of Prediction as Different Error Metrics for Base Model and the Ensemble Model[#]

Time Series Forecasting Models	MAE (Mean Absolute Error)			
	TB*	DG*	FP*	CP*
Theta forecasting	13.4	2.48	49.65	54.12
Moving average	14.63	4.58	56.01	46.86
Spline	13.64	4.19	37.06	33.71
Naïve	9.56	3.84	21.58	30.41
Random walk with drift	9.55	3.84	42.25	44.25
Croston's method	16.58	3.31	49.96	47.97
Holt winter	12.57	3.36	47.58	44.41
Simple exponential smoothing	12.55	3.34	65.38	43.44
Seasonal naïve	3.59	3.43	18.57	39.24
NNAR	2.97	2.75	14.59	24.12
ETS	4.26	2.88	88.31	56.46
ARIMA	3.5	2.92	31.78	37.78
DETS (Time-series ensemble model)	2.17	1.95	12.95	18.12
ADE (Time-series ensemble model)	2.56	2.31	13.34	20.12
Random forest	3.04	3.56	21.87	24.53

[#]Mean absolute error (MAE) metrics obtained by trend modeling of disease datasets using base models. (TB* = Tuberculosis, DG* = Dengue, FP* = Food poisoning, CP* = Chickenpox).

Further, the base models selected to model the trends of the dataset shows the minimum value of the error metrics which further justifies the selection of base models. NNAR, ARIMA, SNAIVE, SPLINE demonstrates the lowest value of error metrics with NNAR outperforming all the base models with values being 2.97, 2.75, 14.59, and 24.12 for TB, Dengue, Food Poisoning, and Chickenpox respectively.

Further, state of art ensemble models namely dynamic ensemble for time series (DETS), arbitrated dynamic ensemble (ADE), and RF are implemented, and a comparison is made with the proposed ensemble model [20, 21]. DETS follows a conventional approach by training heterogeneous base models, and the final forecast is the weighted average based on the performance of the base models [22]. ADE is based on combining base models using a meta learner and a strategy called arbitrating [23]. RF is the ensemble of DTs [24]. The proposed model shows the reduced value of

MAE by 27.18%, 3.07%, 11.58%, 13.46% for TB, Dengue, Food Poisoning, and Chickenpox, respectively.

11.7   CONCLUSION

In summary, the research work exhibits the application of ensemble approach to blend forecasts from multiple models of disease incidence prediction. The work presented here focuses on three main properties, specifically concept drift, overfitting, and handling outliers. The proposed model shows promising results in terms of error metrics when compared with state-of-art ensemble models. As more data related to communicable disease outbreaks are operationalized and merged into public health data repositories, it becomes more significant to combine dissimilar forecasts and merge information so as to obtain the most accurate prediction of a disease outbreak. The work can be further extended to incorporate geographical and temporal dependencies so as to obtain a robust model with respect to regional outbreaks.

KEYWORDS

- **arbitrated dynamic ensemble**
- **autoregressive integrated moving average**
- **dynamic ensemble for time series**
- **mean absolute error**
- **mean absolute scaled error**

REFERENCES

1. Brockwell, P. J., & Davis, R. A., (2016). *Introduction to Time Series and Forecasting.* Springer.
2. Singh, B., Kumar, P., Sharma, N., & Sharma, K. P., (2020). Sales forecast for amazon sales with time series modeling. In *2020 First International Conference on Power, Control, and Computing Technologies (ICPC2T)* (pp. 38–43).
3. Verma, S., & Sharma, N., (2019). Time-series forecasting models for predicting conjunctivitis disease cases. *IUP J. Inf. Technol., 15*(4).
4. Wang, K. W., Deng, C., Li, J. P., Zhang, Y. Y., Li, X. Y., & Wu, M. C., (2017). Hybrid methodology for tuberculosis incidence time-series forecasting based on ARIMA and a NAR neural network. *Epidemiol. Infect., 145*(6), 1118–1129.
5. Zhai, B., & Chen, J., (2018). Development of a stacked ensemble model for forecasting and analyzing daily average PM2. 5 concentrations in Beijing, China. *Sci. Total Environ., 635*, 644–658.

6. Azari, A. A., & Barney, N. P., (2013). Conjunctivitis: A systematic review of diagnosis and treatment. *JAMA, 310*(16), 1721–1730.

7. Verma, S., & Sharma, N., (2018). Statistical models for predicting chikungunya incidences in India. In: *2018 First International Conference on Secure Cyber Computing and Communication (ICSCCC)* (pp. 139–142).

8. Drucker, H., Cortes, C., Jackel, L. D., LeCun, Y., & Vapnik, V., (1994). Boosting and other ensemble methods. *Neural Comput., 6*(6), 1289–1301.

9. Sharma, N., & Juneja, A., (2017). Combining of random forest estimates using LSboost for stock market index prediction. In *2017 2ⁿᵈ International Conference for Convergence in Technology (I2CT)* (pp. 1199–1202).

10. Sharma, N., (2018). *XGBoost. The Extreme Gradient Boosting for Mining Applications.* GRIN Verlag.

11. Kalekar, P. S., (2004). Time series forecasting using holt-winters exponential smoothing. *Kanwal Rekhi Sch. Inf. Technol., 4329008*(13).

12. Lai, D., (2005). Monitoring the SARS epidemic in China: A time series analysis. *J. Data Sci., 3*(3), 279–293.

13. Mendes-Moreira, J., Soares, C., Jorge, A. M., & De Sousa, J. F., (2012). Ensemble approaches for regression: A survey. *Acm Comput. Surv., 45*(1), 1–40.

14. Sultana, N., Sharma, N., & Sharma, K. P., (2020). *Ensemble Model Based on NNAR and SVR for Predicting Influenza Incidences.* Available SSRN 3574620.

15. Verma, S., Sharma, N., & Sharma, K. P., (2020). *Comparative Analysis of Time Series Models for the Prediction of Conjunctivitis Disease.* Available SSRN 3572573.

16. Shashvat, K., Basu, R., Bhondekar, A. P., & Kaur, A., (2019). A weighted ensemble model for prediction of infectious diseases. *Curr. Pharm. Biotechnol., 20*(8), 674–678.

17. Shashvat, K., Basu, R., Bhondekar, A. P., Lamba, S., Verma, K., & Kaur, A., (2019). Comparison of time series models predicting trends in typhoid cases in northern India. *Southeast Asian J. Trop. Med. Public Health, 50*(2), 347–356.

18. Ko, C., Sohn, G., Remmel, T. K., & Miller, J., (2014). Hybrid ensemble classification of tree genera using airborne LiDAR data. *Remote Sens., 6*(11), 11225–11243.

19. Opitz, D., & Maclin, R., (1999). Popular ensemble methods: An empirical study. *J. Artif. Intell. Res., 11*, 169–198.

20. Ren, Y., Zhang, L., & Suganthan, P. N., (2016). Ensemble classification and regression-recent developments, applications, and future directions. *IEEE Comput. Intell. Mag., 11*(1), 41–53.

21. Sultana, N., & Sharma, N., (2018). Statistical models for predicting swine flu incidences in India. In: *2018 First International Conference on Secure Cyber Computing and Communication (ICSCCC)* (pp. 134–138).

22. Tamuli, J., Jain, A., Dhan, A. V., Bhan, A., & Dutta, M. K., (2015). An image processing based method to identify and grade conjunctivitis infected eye according to its types and intensity. In: *2015 Eighth International Conference on Contemporary Computing (IC3)* (pp. 88–92).

23. Teoh, D. L., & Reynolds, S., (2003). Diagnosis and management of pediatric conjunctivitis. *Pediatr. Emerg. Care, 19*(1), 48–55.

24. Wolpert, D. H., (1992). Stacked generalization. *Neural Networks, 5*(2), 241–259.

PART III

Towards Industrial Automation Through Machine Learning

CHAPTER 12

Machine Learning in the Steel Industry

SUSHANT RATH

Research and Development Center for Iron and Steel, SAIL, Ranchi, Jharkhand, India, E-mail: srath@sail.in

ABSTRACT

Machine learning is the core of Industry 4.0, the fourth industrial revolution, which is in progress in manufacturing industries. Machine learning tools like linear regression, logistic regression, artificial neural network, support vector machine, and random forest regression are being used in industry 4.0 for making automated informed decisions. In this chapter, different applications of machine learning tools in different areas of the steel Industry are discussed. Application of machine learning in coke oven, blast furnace, sinter plant, rolling mills, and product development areas are described in the chapter. Three case studies of the application of artificial neural networks and support vector machines in the steel industry are also discussed in the chapter. A mill set-up model in a rolling mill of steel plants automatically generates draft and speed schedules. Traditionally, mathematical models were used in mill set-up models. The methodology for the development of the mill-setup model by integrating a mathematical model with an artificial neural network is discussed in the first case study. The hybrid model is found to be more accurate and fast converging compared to standalone models. The second case study is about the prediction of mechanical properties like yield stress, ultimate tensile strength, and percentage elongation of steel products using a combination of empirical equations and an artificial neural network. The third case study is about the prediction of cobble generation in a hot strip mill of an industrial steel plant using statistical and support vector machine techniques.

12.1 INTRODUCTION

The manufacturing industries throughout the world are passing through a phase of transformation: from the third industrial revolution to the fourth industrial revolution. The fourth industrial revolution is also known as Industry 4.0 or industrial internet of things (IIoT). Cyber-physical systems have a prominent role in Industry 4.0. The cyber systems are data storage, communication, and computation. The physical systems are sensors, actuators, and control systems. These cyber-physical systems can communicate with each other without human interference. These systems will also communicate with different units of the industry, engineers, managers, and operators in real-time for making informed, calculated, and optimized decisions. Machine learning (ML) is the core of this automatic decision-making process of Industry 4.0.

The steel industry, one of the largest manufacturing industries, has lots of applications of ML. ML is not new to the steel industry. ML tools such as artificial neural network (ANN), linear regression, logistic regression (LR), random forest (RF) regression, convolution neural network (CNN), fuzzy logic, genetic algorithm (GA) and support vector machine (SVM) are being extensively used in the steel industry since last three decades. In a review paper published in 1993, Carayannis [1] described various ML-based systems used in the steel industry at that time. An automation system, consisting of 700 sensors, an artificial intelligent (AI) processor and a programmable logic controller (PLC), was used to determine the condition of a blast furnace (BF). ML tools were also used for blowing control systems in steelmaking, tundish level control in continuous casting and mill setup in rolling mills.

An integrated steel plant consists of different units. Major production units of the steel plant are coke oven, sinter plant, BF, steel melting shop and rolling mills. New product development is also an important activity in the steel industry. The prediction of the mechanical properties of the material is the most important aspect of product development. The application of ML in these areas is discussed in the chapter.

This chapter also discusses three case studies of the application of ML in the steel industry. In the first case study, a mathematical-ANN model was used for calculation of optimized draft schedule in a hot strip mill. This on-line model trains itself after rolling of each coil and predicts roll force and temperatures for the next coil. In the second case study, a mathematical-ANN hybrid model has been developed to predict the material properties of hot rolled coils. The third case study describes the methodology of the development of a cobble prediction system in a hot strip mill using combined statistical and SVM-based ML algorithms.

12.1.1 MACHINE LEARNING APPLICATION IN COKE OVEN

In coke ovens, ML tools are being used for prediction of coke strength, gas flow, gas holder level, wastewater quality, etc. A Gaussian process (GP) based echo states network-based model was developed by Zhao et al. [2] to predict the real-time gas flow and the gasholder level in a coke oven gas system. North et al. [3] predicted coke strength using self-organizing maps (SOM). They have developed a method of classifying vitrinite reflectance distributions using the SOM algorithm. Khandelwal et al. [4] predicted coke plant wastewater quality using ML algorithms. The model predicts the effluent stream of by-product plant, in terms of chemical oxygen demand (COD) and total dissolved solids (TDS) with coal constituents and coke making process parameters as inputs.

12.1.2 MACHINE LEARNING APPLICATION IN SINTER PLANT

A coke powder ratio prediction model was developed by Beskardeş and Cevik [5] using multiple linear regression and SVMs by correlating it to coke analysis information, raw material quality parameters and process data of an industrial sinter plant.

12.1.3 MACHINE LEARNING APPLICATION IN BLAST FURNACE

Condition monitoring is a challenging task in BFs. As discussed earlier, Carayannis [1] had described an automation system, consisting of 700 sensors, an AI processor and a PLC, which was used to determine the condition of a BF. The silicon content of the molten metal is an important index reflecting the product quality and thermal status of the BF iron making process. An improved extreme learning machine (ELM) model was developed by Zhou et al. [6] to correlate Si content with hot blast pressure, hot blast temperature, oxygen enrichment percentage, volume of coal injection, blast humidity and gas volume of bosh. A weighted ELM (W-ELM) algorithm was employed by Zhang et al. [7] to predict the changing trend of silicon content. Kim et al. [8] used a multivariate time series forecasting algorithm using convolutional neural networks (CNNs) and long short-term memory (LSTM) models to predict the opening and closing time for an industrial BF.

12.1.4   MACHINE LEARNING APPLICATION IN STEEL MAKING

ML has a lot of applications in the steel making process. Carayannis [1] had also described applications of ML in blowing control system in steelmaking, tundish level control in continuous casting. Laha et al. [9] predicted the yield of steel in steel making process using different ML tools like RFs, ANN, dynamic evolving neuro-fuzzy (NF) inference system (DENFIS) and support vector regression (SVR). Laha [10] also used a multi-layer feed-forward neural network with Levenberg-Marquardt (L-M) backpropagation algorithm (BPA) to predict the output yield of steel during the steel making process. Das et al. [11] used ANN with Bayesian regularization and adaptive NF inference system (ANFIS) to predict the amount of oxygen to be lanced at different sampling instants based on the values of the individual chemical constituents of the collected molten samples. Based on the prediction, two control strategies were devised: one with full sampling and the other with limited or reduced sampling. Rajesh et al. [12] developed a feed-forward neural network using BPA for prediction of end blow oxygen in the LD converter steel making using 6 input parameters: weight of hot metal, weight of scrap, end blow oxygen, intermediate stoppage temperature, intermediate stoppage carbon level and end blow temperature.

12.1.5   MACHINE LEARNING APPLICATION IN ROLLING MILLS

Steel plants throughout the world are using ML extensively for rolling mill applications. In 1996, an ANN based model was developed by Pican et al. [13] to calculate the draft set-up of a temper rolling mill. The ANN model was using 12 process parameters as input to predict roll force during temper rolling. They found that the mean model error of prediction of roll force by ANN model was 13.2% against 24.7% error of prediction by theoretical mathematical models. An ANN model was developed by Cho et al. [14] to predict the roll force of a tandem cold rolling mill. They had used BPA for training and validation of 4944 process data collected from an industrial mill. In comparison to mathematical models, the model error was lower by 33.88% with the ML model. Schlang et al. [15] described mathematical model-ANN hybrid systems for edger gap control, temperature prediction and laminar cooling control in the hot rolling process. An ANN model was also developed by Kusiak et al. [16] for calculating the rolling schedules of a 4-hi reversing cold rolling mill.

ML is being used in different automation systems of rolling mills of steel plants. An ANN model was also developed by Kim et al. [17] to calculate the rolling load of a hot strip mill. Lee and Lee [18] had also developed an ANN model to predict the roll force of an industrial rolling mill. Yang et al. [19] had also developed an ANN model to predict rolling parameters. They used the design of experiment (DoE) technique for generating training data from an orthogonal array (OA). A back-propagation algorithm was used for training the ANN model. An on-line adaptable ANN model was developed by Lee and Choi [20] for an industrial plate mill. An on-line ANN model was also developed by Son et al. [21] to predict the rolling load. An adaptable ANN model was developed by Yang et al. [22] to predict the rolling load of a cold rolling mill. The predicted roll force was used as a component of the draft schedule optimization model. Rath et al. [23, 24] have described ANN models to predict the rolling load of an industrial plate mill. The model uses a variable learning rate. The model has been validated with measured data of the mill. An ANN model is described by Ding et al. [25] which correlates measured parameters of threaded stands with thickness and flow stress errors. These errors are used for modification of draft schedules of the unthreaded stands. Cao et al. [26] used ANN to predict roll force during strip casting. An auto-adaptive ANN model has been developed by Chen [27] for mill set-up of an industrial hot strip mill.

ML techniques have been used in a lot of applications in rolling mills in the last few years. A mathematical-ANN hybrid model was developed by Rath et al. [28] to predict rolling load during the hot rolling of steel. Vannucci et al. [29] have described the methodology of applying ANN for calculation of mean flow stress (MFS) of material during rolling of steel in a hot rolling mill. An ANN based hybrid intelligent system was developed by Jose et al. [30]. This system is used for tunning of controllers of rolling mills. Lechwar [31] describes a ML based system for the classification of mill scale defects. Krajewski et al. [32] have described ML based methods for the prediction of mechanical properties of AHSS grades of steel. The application of ANN for calculating the flow stress of steel is described by Rath et al. [33]. Flow stress is the most important material property required for mill setup models. Tian [34] describes the method of identification of surface defects using GA and ELM techniques.

12.1.6   ML APPLICATION IN PRODUCT DEVELOPMENT

ML tools are also used to predict the material properties of steel products. Bhadeshia [35], in a review paper, discusses the use of ANN to predict mechanical properties of hot-rolled coils. The properties like yield stress (YS), ultimate tensile strength (UTS), percentage elongation and chapry impact toughness are correlated with chemical composition and rolling mill process parameters. Dumortier and Lehert [36] described an ANN model for the prediction of UTS of steel products. Initially, they had carried out multivariate data analysis of process data obtained from an industrial rolling mill. Datta et al. [37] developed a Petri neural network model, a multilayered feed-forward network model, for predicting material properties of steel. An ANN model was developed by Warde and Kimowles [38] to predict the yield strength of polycrystalline superalloys. They used the ANN within a Bayesian framework. Femminella [39] developed a NF model to predict material property from microstructure. They have shown that data pre-processing and model initialization factors are very important in developing such a model. Wang et al. [40] described an ANN model to study the effects of the carbon in steel composition and cooling rate on phase transformation. Lenard et al. [41] have compiled literature on grain evolution during hot rolling, correlation of grain size with mechanical properties and application of ANN to predict grain size and roll force during the hot rolling process. Doll et al. [42] of Siemens AG developed a hybrid empirical-ANN model to predict the mechanical properties of steel.

12.2   CASE STUDY-I: MACHINE LEARNING IN MILL SET-UP MODEL

A mill set-up model in a rolling mill calculates draft and speed schedule in different passes based on the primary data input and target thickness and temperature. Accurate prediction of roll force is important for a mill setup model. The methodology of developing a mathematical-ANN hybrid roll force model developed for the mill set-up model for an industrial rolling mill is discussed in the section. The optimized drafting and speed schedule calculated by the hybrid model was successfully communicated to the mill automation system. Industrial trials were conducted successfully using the system.

12.2.1   METHODOLOGY OF DEVELOPMENT OF HYBRID MILL SET-UP MODEL

Mathematical theories for calculation of roll force have been developed by different researchers using the mechanical theory of plastic deformation. In this work, the two most popular theories, Sims' theory and Tselikov's theory, were selected for prediction of roll force. Pressure distribution in roll bite, according to Sims' theory, is given by:

$$\frac{s^+}{k} = \frac{\pi}{4}(1 + \ln\frac{h}{h_x}) + \sqrt{\frac{R}{h_x}}\tan^{-1}\left(\sqrt{\frac{R}{h_x}}\varphi\right) \tag{1}$$

$$\frac{s^-}{k} = \frac{\pi}{4}(1 + \ln\frac{h}{h_e}) + \sqrt{\frac{R}{h_x}}\left(\tan^{-1}\sqrt{\frac{R}{h_x}}\theta - \tan^{-1}\sqrt{\frac{R}{h_x}}\varphi\right) \tag{2}$$

where; h_e is the thickness of the strip at the entry of roll bite; h_x is the thickness of the strip at the exit of roll bite; h is the thickness of the strip at any section where the calculation is made. In these equations, ϕ is the angle between the calculation section and the exit section, R is the roll radius, θ is the angle of bite and k is the resistance to plane strain deformation. k = $1.115\sigma_f$, σ_f being unidirectional flow stress of steel. Equation 1 is valid for the zone between the neutral section and exit section. Equation 2 is valid for the zone between the entry section and the neutral section and. Using Sims' theory, roll force from is calculated by trapezoidal rule of numerical integration from the equation:

$$P = Rb\int_0^\theta s\,d\varphi \tag{3}$$

where; b is the strip width.

Tselikov's theory derives the following equation for mean roll bite pressure.

$$S_{av} = \frac{2k}{\Delta h}\left(\frac{h_e}{\delta - 2}\left(\left(\frac{h_e}{h_n}\right)^{\delta-2} - 1\right) + \frac{h_x}{\delta + 2}\left(\left(\frac{h_n}{h_x}\right)^{\delta+2} - 1\right)\right) \tag{4}$$

where; $\delta = \mu\dfrac{2\sqrt{R\Delta h}}{\Delta h}$

In this equation, Δh is the draft, b is the strip width, is the coefficient of friction and h_n is the thickness at the neutral section. Roll force using the above pressure equation can be written as,

$$P = Rbs_{av} \tag{5}$$

Figure 12.1 shows the conceptual diagram of the mathematical-ANN hybrid model. The inverse activation function (AF) values of mathematical models are taken as the first two inputs of the ANN model. The basic structure of the feed-forward network of ANN with BPA of training is used in the hybrid model, but the training methodology has been modified. In conventional ANN models, weights, and bias are initialized with random numbers. But in the hybrid model, weights, and biases have been initialized with particular fixed values. The initial weight from the first input to the first hidden layer node is taken as 1. Similarly, the initial weight from the second input node to the second hidden node is taken as 1. The initial weights from hidden nodes to the output node are taken as 0.5 each. Initial values of all other weights and biases are taken as zero. The selection of initial values of weights and bias has been carried out in such a way that when the first sample is given to the untrained ANN model, it gives an output which is the average of roll force values predicted by Sim's and Tselikov's theories. A hybrid thermal model and hybrid roll gap model were also developed using the similar concept of the hybrid roll force model.

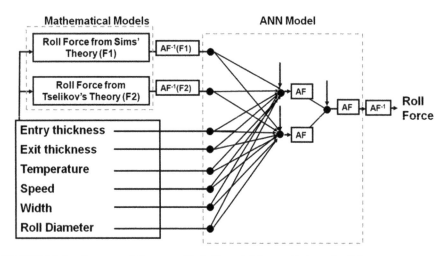

FIGURE 12.1   Conceptual diagram of hybrid model for prediction of roll force.

Figure 12.2 shows the flow chart for the determination of the reduction schedule during hot rolling by using the hybrid models of roll force, temperature, and roll gap. Constrained multivariable optimization algorithm optimizes the reduction schedule with the objective function of either minimization of energy or maximization of productivity under mill constraints of allowable force, torque, and power.

The context diagram of the data flow diagram (DFD) is shown in Figure 12.3. It shows the receipt of data from different PLCs and other systems. The data from PLCs are received by the OPC communication system, whereas the data from VAX and ERP are obtained by file transfer protocol (FTP) communication. Similarly, the calculated data from the model moves from the model system to PLCs through OPC communication.

Figure 12.4 shows a partial screenshot of the ASP. Net based intranet website. This screen shows the model output to mill operators and operation managers. There are special web pages for model developers for fine-tuning of the model from remote locations.

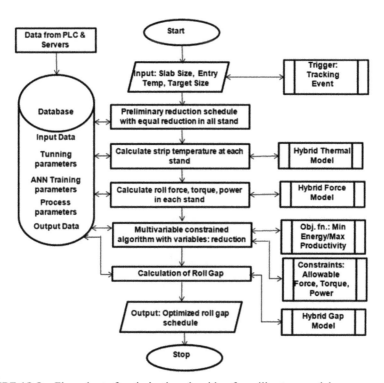

FIGURE 12.2   Flow chart of optimization algorithm for mill set up model.

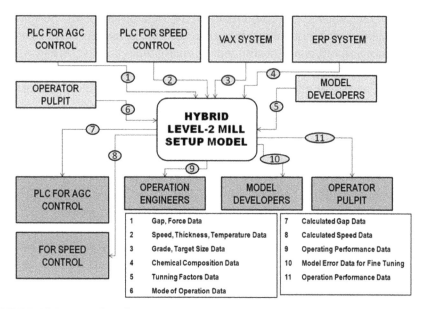

FIGURE 12.3   Data flow diagram (DFD) of mill setup model.

OPERATOR CONTROL STATION (OCS)			Speed			AGC				
Coil at R1	Grade	Width	Coil Thick	Coil Box	R2Temp (Stat)	Op Thick	Op Width	[C,%]	[Si,%]	[SiEq.%]
H19023	WTCRCC	936	1.9	0	1134	270	1040	0.03	0.021	-0.26

Coil at R2	Grade	Width	Coil Thick	Coil Box	R2 Temp	R2 Time	
H19018	WTCRCC	936	2.3	0	1133.637	7/14/2015 3:03:56 PM	

MODEL SETTING: R1	F6	F5	F4	F3	F2	F1
Roll Gap	218	307	474	575	694	1156
Speed	820	663	492	358	236	136

◉ L2-Manual   ○ L2-SemiAuto   ○ L2-FullAuto   Send Model Setting to PLC   0   Recalculate

LAST COIL SETUP	F6	F5	F4	F3	F2	F1
Roll Gap	230	315	490	590	705	1175
Speed	800	660	492	362	241	139

FIGURE 12.4   Screenshot of intranet website of mill setup model.

12.2.2   RESULTS AND DISCUSSIONS ON CASE STUDY-I

The measurable parameters for which there are sensors in the mill are roll force of different stands, temperature before and after finishing mill and final strip thickness. The hybrid model predictions were validated with mill data of different grades of steel processed in the mill. Some typical validation results are given in this chapter. Figure 12.5 shows the validation result 2409 no of coils of 50C700 grade of steel. The model error is found to be 5.2% with root mean square error (RMSE) of 1.25 MN. Similarly, the validation result of the final strip thickness of these coils is shown in Figure 12.6. The r-square value is found to be 0.9131. Both figures show that the model is accurate enough for industrial applications.

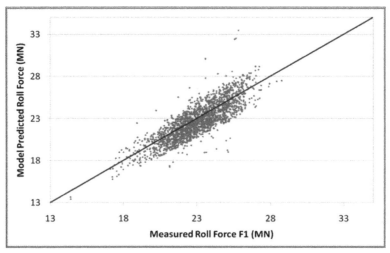

FIGURE 12.5 Validation of roll force.

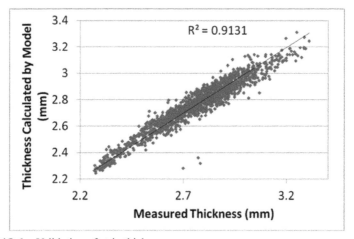

FIGURE 12.6 Validation of strip thickness.

The model was tried at different campaigns in the mill. The difficulties faced in a campaign were analyzed, and the model was fine-tuned to avoid such problems in the future. The model has successfully rolled 668 hot rolled coils with the optimized reduction schedule.

12.2.3   ANALYSIS OF A CASE OF MODEL FAILURE

As discussed in the previous section, the hybrid mill setup model success-fully rolled 668 coils. However, there was a failure of the model during the rolling of one particular coil which led to cobble in the mill. Failure analysis indicates that the speed set-up signal transferred from the model server to PLC was giving a value of "zero" at a particular time interval. The mill motors got the signal to stop at that time. In the next moment, the motors were given the signal to run at the desired speed. The mill control system started to fluctuate abnormally due to this wide variation of set-up speed leading to the cobble in the mill. The mill operation was discontinued for about 50 minutes leading to loss of time besides the loss of material. It was found that there was a communication failure between the model (Level-2) and PLC (Level-1) systems thereby setting mill speed to zero. Later the Level-1 program was modified to avoid this problem. The system retains the last set-point value and uses it in case of no communication is received from the Level-2 system.

12.3   CASE STUDY-II: MACHINE LEARNING FOR PREDICTION OF MECHANICAL PROPERTIES

ML tools are of great use for the prediction of material properties of hot rolled products. In this case study, the methodology of the development of a hybrid model for prediction of mechanical properties like yield strength (YS), UTS, and percentage elongation (%EL) of material just after rolling is described.

12.3.1   METHODOLOGY OF HYBRID MODEL DEVELOPMENT

Semi-empirical equations were selected from the literature for prediction of grain size of the material of the strip during rolling in a hot rolling mill. Different symbols used in the equations are [C] for C in steel composition

(%), [Mn] for Mn in steel composition (%), [P] for P in steel composition (%), [S] for S in steel composition (%), [Si] for Si in steel composition (%), [Al] for Al in steel composition (%), [Nf] for free N in steel composition (%), etc. In these equations, ε is used for strain during rolling, ε· for strain rate (sec^{-1}), ε_r for accumulated strain below the recrystallization temperature, R for universal gas constant (8.31451 J/K/mol), T for the absolute temperature of the material, t for the time in second, Q for activation energy, C_r for Cooling rate (°C/sec) and d_γ for austenite grain size prior to transformation into ferrite (micron). The following equations are compiled by Ginzburg [43].

The grain growth equation during reheating is given by:

$$D_o = A.t^m . \exp\left(-\frac{Q}{RT}\right) \tag{6}$$

Where constitutive material constants for C-Mn grade of steel are A = 2.93 × 10^5, m=0.194 and Q = 94,000 J/mole. Special grades of steel have different material constants which are determined from experiments.

During deformation in the rolling process, static recrystallization (SRX), dynamic recrystallization (DRX), meta dynamic recrystallization (MDRX) and grain growth take place. Empirical equations for C-Mn grades of steel for these processes are given below:

$$\text{Peak strain, } \varepsilon_p = 4.90 \, x10^{-4} \dot{\varepsilon}^{0.15} d_o^{0.5} \exp\left(\frac{5629}{T}\right) \tag{7}$$

$$\text{Critical strain, } \varepsilon_c = 3.68 \, x10^{-4} \dot{\varepsilon}^{0.19} d_o^{0.44} \exp\left(\frac{7130}{T}\right) \tag{8}$$

$$\text{DRX grain size, } d_{drx} = 1.60 \, x10^4 \dot{\varepsilon}^{-0.23} \exp\left(\frac{-8299}{T}\right) \tag{9}$$

$$\text{MDRX grain size, } d_{mdrx} = 2.60 \, x10^4 \dot{\varepsilon}^{-0.23} \exp\left(\frac{-8299}{T}\right) \tag{10}$$

Time required for 50% of static recrystallization is given by:

$$t_{0.5x} = 1.14 \, x10^{-13} \varepsilon^{-3.8} \dot{\varepsilon}^{-0.41} \exp\left(\frac{-30310}{T}\right) \tag{11}$$

Volume fraction of SRX, $X = 1 - \exp\left(-0.639\dfrac{t}{t_{0.5x}}\right)^{2.0}$ (12)

SRX grain size, $d_{srx} = 343\varepsilon^{-0.5}d_o^{0.4}\exp\left(\dfrac{-5412}{T}\right)$ (13)

SRX grain growth is calculated from the following equation:

$$d_{gg}^7 = d_{srx}^7 + 1.5 \times 10^{27}(t - 4.32t_{0.5x})\exp\left(\dfrac{-48110}{T}\right) \qquad (14)$$

Ferrite grain size after cooling is given by,

$$d_\alpha = (1-0.45\varepsilon_r^{0.5})[1.4+5.0\ C_r^{-0.5}+22(1-\exp(-0.015d_\gamma))\ ] \qquad (15)$$

The structure-property correlation equations were also given as follows: Pickering equation for yield stress [43] is given by:

$$\sigma_y = 53.9 + 32.3[Mn] + 83.2[Si] + 354[N_f]^{0.5} + 17.4d_\alpha^{-0.5} \qquad (16)$$

Hodgson and Gibbs [43] have proposed the following equation for yield stress:

$$\sigma_y = 62.6 + 26.1[Mn] + 60.2[Si] + 759[P] + 212.9[Cu] + 3286[N_f] + 19.7d_\alpha^{-0.5} \qquad (17)$$

Pickering equation for ultimate tensile strength (UTS),

$$\sigma_t = 29.4 + 27.7[Mn] + 83.2[Si] + 3.8[\%\,pearlite] + 7.7d_\alpha^{-0.5} \qquad (18)$$

Hodgson and Gibbs have proposed the following equation for UTS:

$$\sigma_t = 164.9 + 634.7[C] + 53.6[Mn] + 99.7[Si] + 651.9[P] + 472.6[Ni] + 3339.4[N_f] + 11d_\alpha^{-0.5} \qquad (19)$$

Total strain at fracture is proposed by Pickering as

$$\varepsilon_T = 1.4 - 2.9[C] + 0.20[Mn] + 0.16[Si] - 3.9[P] - 2.2[S] + 0.25\ [Sn] + 0.017d_\alpha^{-0.5} \qquad (20)$$

The constitutive material constants were collected from the literature. Different researchers have proposed different equations for the three properties. The approach adopted in this present work was not to evaluate the equations proposed by individual researchers. All the equations were selected as components of the hybrid model.

The mechanical properties predicted by the empirical models are not highly accurate as the empirical equations have been formulated with some simplified assumptions and laboratory data which is not fully suitable for industrial applications. Therefore, an ANN program has been used along with the empirical models as shown in Figure 12.7.

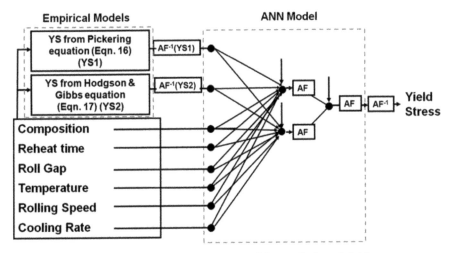

FIGURE 12.7   Conceptual diagram of hybrid model for prediction of yield stress.

The conceptual diagram of the hybrid model is shown in Figure 12.7. The ANN model consists of one input layer of 8 input nodes, one output layer with 1 node and one hidden layer with two nodes. The ANN network is a feed-forward network in which the node value of each hidden node is calculated by multiplying weight factors to input parameters and adding bias value to it. An AF is used for normalization of the hidden layer value and also to take care of non-linearity in the relation. In this case, the AF is chosen as a sigmoid function so that all the calculated values are normalized between 0 and 1. The hybrid model is coded in ASP.NET using VB.NET programming language. The front end of the program is a series of "aspx" files with a cascading style sheet (CSS). The back end of the program is equipped with Microsoft SQL Server RDBMS which is connected to the ASP.NET program using Microsoft. Net framework object SQLClient. Similar hybrid models were also developed for prediction of UTS and percentage elongation.

12.3.2   RESULTS AND DISCUSSIONS ON CASE STUDY-II

The model was validated with data obtained from an industrial plate mill. A validation plot for 37 plates is shown in Figure 12.8. This plot shows that there is a close match between predicted and measured values YS.

Figure 12.9 shows the histogram of Model Error. The Model error is slightly skewed towards the right. This figure also shows that the model predicts the exact value as the measured value for 20% plates indicating the accuracy of the hybrid model is fairly acceptable for the industrial condition.

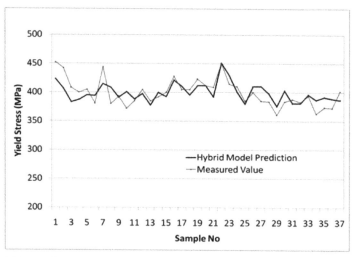

FIGURE 12.8   Validation of YS.

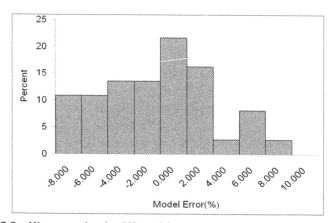

FIGURE 12.9   Histogram showing YS model error.

12.4 CASE STUDY-III: SVM BASED COBBLE PREDICTION SYSTEM

Cobble generation is an abnormality of a hot strip mill operation. During rolling, coils are stuck in mill stands leading to loss of material and production time. The objective of the work was to predict the possibility of cobble generation in a hot strip mill using signal analysis. Two methods have been used in this model for the prediction of cobble. The first method is a statistical method. The principle of the statistical method is shown in Figure 12.10.

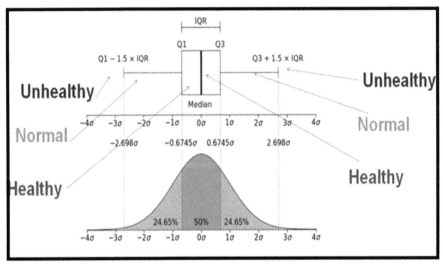

FIGURE 12.10 Principle of statistical classification of cobble generation in hot strip mill.

First quartile (Q1), third quartile (Q3) and interquartile range (IQR) are calculated from the previously recorded signals of the mill. When the real time signal is less than Q1–1.5xIQR or more than Q3+1.5xIQR, it indicates the unhealthy condition of the mill which may result in a cobble.

The second method is the SVM based method. In this method, the SVM is first trained with signals of cobble and no-cobble data. The trained two-class classifier is used to predict the possibility of cobble generation in the mill. SVM was selected due to its simplicity, robustness to the outliers, and efficiency in binary classification. The kernel function and associated parameters are calibrated empirically to obtain the best training and testing performances. The available datasets were randomly divided into two sets-training and testing: 70% of datasets for training and the remaining 30% of datasets for testing before training and testing. A total number of 255 features are generated from the raw dataset for the training of SVM. However, all these 255 features may not be relevant for the classification of the existence of cobble into two classes-Cobble and No-Cobble. Therefore, 113 features out of the available 255 features were selected based on mutual information. A threshold for mutual selection is selected empirically, the features carrying higher mutual information with respect to the class labels are selected for this purpose. After training of the SVM classifier, it was used to predict cobble generation using online real-time signals. Both the statistical and SVM classifiers were superimposed to predict cobble with high reliability. A partial screenshot of the software screen is shown in Figure 12.11.

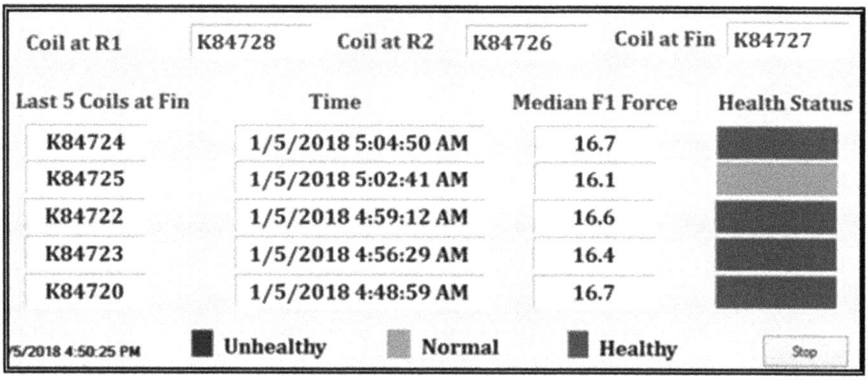

Coil at R1	K84728	Coil at R2	K84726	Coil at Fin	K84727

Last 5 Coils at Fin	Time	Median F1 Force	Health Status
K84724	1/5/2018 5:04:50 AM	16.7	
K84725	1/5/2018 5:02:41 AM	16.1	
K84722	1/5/2018 4:59:12 AM	16.6	
K84723	1/5/2018 4:56:29 AM	16.4	
K84720	1/5/2018 4:48:59 AM	16.7	

1/5/2018 4:50:25 PM	■ Unhealthy	Normal	■ Healthy	Stop

FIGURE 12.11   Screenshot of the real-time cobble prediction software for hot strip mill.

12.5   SUMMARY

- Applications of ML in different units of the steel industry, including coke oven, sinter plant, BF, steel melting shop, rolling mills have been discussed in the chapter. The application of ML for the product development process is also discussed.
- Three case studies of the use of ML applications in the steel industry are discussed in the chapter.
- The first case discusses the methodology of the development of a mathematical-ANN auto-adaptive Level-2 mill set-up model of a hot strip mill. Industrial trials carried out using the model.
- Failure of the model in a particular case, due to communication failure, had led to cobble in the mill resulting in loss of material and rolling time.

- The second case study describes is the methodology of the development of a hybrid model for the prediction of mechanical properties. The prediction data were validated with measured data.
- The third case study describes the methodology development of a cobble prediction system in a hot strip mill using a combined statistical method and SVM technique.

ACKNOWLEDGMENT

The author is thankful to the engineers of Hot Strip Mill and C&IT Department, Rourkela Steel Plant and engineers of Hot Strip Mill and C&A Department, Bokaro Steel Plant for their support. The author is also grateful to Prof. Aurobinda Routray, Department of Electrical Engg., IIT, Kharagpur, and his team for developing algorithms for SVM classifier for cobble. The author is grateful to the management of the R&D Center for Iron and Steel (RDCIS), SAIL for supporting the work.

KEYWORDS

- **artificial intelligent**
- **artificial neural network**
- **genetic algorithm**
- **industrial internet of things**
- **machine learning**

REFERENCES

1. Carayannis, G., (1993). Artificial intelligence and expert systems in the steel industry. *JOM*, 43–51.
2. Zhao, J., Liu, Q., Wang, W., Pedrycz, W., & Cong, L., (2012). Hybrid neural prediction and optimized adjustment for coke oven gas system in steel industry. *IEEE Transactions on Neural Networks and Learning Systems, 23*, 439–450.
3. North, L., Blackmore, K., Nesbitt, K., Hockings, K., & Mahoney, M., (2017). A novel approach to coke strength prediction using self organizing maps. *Int'l Conf. Data Mining (DMIN'17)*, 17–23.
4. Khandelwal, H., Shrivastava, S., Ganguly, A., & Roy, A., (2020). Prediction and control of coke plant wastewater quality using machine learning techniques. *Coke Chem., 63*, 47–56.
5. Beşkardeş, A., & Çevik, S., (2016). Coke optimization with machine learning method in sinter plant. In: *2016 National Conference on Electrical, Electronics, and Biomedical Engineering (ELECO)* (pp. 170–173). Bursa.

6. Zhou, P., Yuan, M., Wang, H., & Chai, T., (2015). Data-driven dynamic modeling for prediction of molten iron silicon content using ELM with self-feedback. *Mathematical Problems in Engineering, 11.* 326160.

7. Zhang, H., Zhang, S., Yin, Y., & Chen, X., (2018). Prediction of the hot metal silicon content in blast furnace based on extreme learning machine. *Int. J. Mach. Learn. & Cyber., 9,* 1697–1706.

8. Kim, K., Seo, B., Rhee, S., Lee, S., & Woo, S. S., (2019). Deep learning for blast furnaces: Skip-dense layers deep learning model to predict the remaining time to close tap-holes for blast furnaces. *Proceedings of the 28th ACM International Conference on Information and Knowledge Management,* 2733–2741.

9. Laha, D., Ren, Y., & Suganthan, P. N., (2015). Modeling of steelmaking process with effective machine learning techniques. *Expert Systems with Application, 42,* 4687–4696.

10. Laha, D., (2013). ANN modeling of a steelmaking process. *International Conference on Swarm, Evolutionary, and Memetic Computing,* 308–318.

11. Das, A., Maiti, J., & Banerjee, R. N., (2010). Process control strategies for a steel making furnace using ANN with Bayesian regularization and ANFIS. *Expert Systems with Applications, 37,* 1075–1085.

12. Rajesh, N., Khare, M. R., & Pabi, S. K., (2010). Feedforward neural network for prediction of end blow oxygen in LD converter steelmaking. *Materials Research, 13*(1), 15–19.

13. Pican, N., Fridbric, A., & Patrick, B., (1996). Artificial neural networks for presetting of a steel temper mill. *IEEE Expert,* 22–27.

14. Cho, S., Jang, M., Yoon, S., Chot, Y., & Cho, H., (1997). A hybrid neural network/mathematical prediction model for tandem cold mill. *J. Computers & Industrial Engineering, 33,* 453–456.

15. Schlang, M., Feldkeller, B., Lang, B., Poppe, T., & Runkler, T., (1999). Neural computation in steel industry. *Proc. European Control Conference,* 2922–2927. Karlsruhe.

16. Kusiak, J., Lenard, J. G., & Dudek, K., (1999). Artificial intelligence approach to the modeling of rolling loads in technology design for cold rolling processes. *Proceedings of the Second International Conference on Intelligent Processing and Manufacturing of Materials (IPMM '99),* 543–548. Honolulu.

17. Kim, Y., Yum, B., & Kim, M., (2001). Robust design of artificial neural network for roll force prediction in hot strip mill. *Proc. Int. Joint Conference on Neural Networks (IJCNN'01)* (Vol. 4, pp. 2800–2804). Washington DC.

18. Lee, D., & Lee, Y., (2002). Application of Neural-network for improving accuracy of roll force model in hot rolling mill. *J. Control Engineering Practice, 10,* 473–478.

19. Yang, Y., Linkens, D. A., Silva, J. T., & Howard, L., (2003). Roll force and torque prediction using neural network and finite element modeling. *ISIJ International, 43,* 1957–1977.

20. Lee, D. M., & Choi, S. G., (2004). Application of on-line adaptable neural network for the rolling force set-up of a plate mill. *Engg. Applications of Artificial Intelligence, 17,* 557–567.

21. Son, J., Lee, D., Kim, L., & Choi, S., (2005). A study on on-line learning neural network for prediction for rolling force in hot-rolling mill. *J. Material Processing Technology, 165,* 1612–1617.

22. Yang, J., Che, H., Xu, Y., & Dou, F., (2006). Application of adaptable neural networks for rolling force set up in optimization of rolling schedules. *Advances in Neural Networks* (pp. 864–869). Springer Berlin.

23. Rath, S., Singh, A. P., Sengupta, P. P., Bhaskar, U., & Krishna, B., (2007). *Determination of Flow Stress Coefficient for Nb-Micro Alloyed Steel Using Parameter Estimation Techniques, 29,* 100–104. Steel India.

24. Rath, S., Singh, A. P., Bhaskar, U., Krishna, B., Santra, B. K., Rai, D., & Neogi, N., (2010). Artificial neural network modeling for prediction of roll force during plate rolling process. *International Journal of Materials and Manufacturing Processes, 25,* 149–153.

25. Ding, J., Hu, X., Jiao, J., She, G., & Liu, X., (2008). Application of adaptive threading technique to hot strip mill. *Journal of Iron and Steel Research International, 15,* 29–31.

26. Cao, G., Cheng-Gang, L., Guo-Ping, Z., Zhen-Yu, L., Di, W., Guo-Dong, W., & Xiang-Hua, L., (2010). Rolling force prediction for strip casting using theoretical model and artificial intelligence. *J. Cent. South Univ. Technol., 17,* 795–800.

27. Chen, J., (2011). The application of the mathematical model of hot rolling process control. *Proc. 2nd International Conference on Artificial Intelligence, Management Science and Electronic Commerce (AIMSEC),* 7327–7331.

28. Rath, S., Sengupta, P. P., Singh, A. P., Marik, A. K., & Talukdar, P., (2013). Mathematical-artificial neural network hybrid model to predict roll force during hot rolling of steel. *Int. J. Computational Materials Science and Engineering, 2,* 16. 1350004.

29. Vannucci, M., Colla, V., & Dimatteo, A., (2013). Improving the estimation of mean flow stress within hot rolling of steel by means of different artificial intelligence technique. *Proc. 7th IFAC Conference on Manufacturing Modeling, Management, and Control, International Federation of Automatic Control,* 945–950.

30. Jose, C. L., Casteleiro-Roca, J. L., Quintián, H., & Meizoso-Lopez, M., (2013). A hybrid intelligent system for PID controller using in a steel rolling process. *Expert Systems with Applications, 40,* 5188–5196.

31. Lechwar, S., Rauch, Ł., & Pietrzyk, M., (2015). Use of artificial intelligence in classification of mill scale defects. *Steel Research Int., 86,* 266–277.

32. Krajewski, S., & Nowacki, J., (2016). Artificial intelligence in the AHSS steel mechanical properties and microstructure analysis. *Przegląd Elektrotechniczny, 92,* 102–105.

33. Rath, S., Talukdar, P., & Singh, A. P., (2017). Application of artificial neural network for flow stress modelling of steel. *American Journal of Neural Networks and Applications, 3,* 36–39.

34. Tian, S., & Xu, K., (2017). An algorithm for surface defect identification of steel plates based on genetic algorithm and extreme learning machine. *Metals, 7*(311), 1–11.

35. Bhadeshia, H. K. D. H., (1999). Neural networks in materials science. *ISIJ International, 39,* 966–979.

36. Dumortier, C., & Lehert, P., (1999). Statistical modeling of mechanical tensile properties of steels by using neural networks and multivariate data analysis. *ISIJ International, 39,* 980–985.

37. Datta, S., Sil, J., & Banerjee, M. K., (1999). Petri neural network model for the effect of controlled thermomechanical process parameters on the mechanical properties of HSLA steels. *ISIJ International, 39,* 986–990.

38. Warde, J., & Kimowles, D. M., (1999). Application of neural networks to mechanical property determination of ni-base superalloys. *ISIJ International, 39,* 1006–1014.

39. Femminella, O. P., Starink, M. J., Brown, M., Sinclair, I., Harris, C. J., & Reed, P. A. S., (1999). Data pre-processing/model initialization in neurofuzzy modeling of structure-property relationships in Al-Zn-Mg-Cu alloys. *ISIJ International*, *39*, 1027–1037.

40. Wang, J., Wolk, P. J. V., & Zwaag, S. V., (1999). Effects of carbon concentration and cooling rate on continuous cooling transformations predicted by artificial neural network. *ISIJ International*, *39*, 1038–1046.

41. Lenard, J. G., Pietrzyk, M., & Cser, L., (1999). *Mathematical and Physical Simulation of the Properties of Hot Rolled Products* (pp. 172–177). Elsevier, UK.

42. Doll, R., Sorgel, G., Daum, M., & Zouhar, C., (1999). *Control of Mechanical Properties*, 200–202. Asia Steel.

43. Ginzburg, V. B., (2005). *Metallurgical Design of Flat Rolled Steels*. Marcel Dekker.

CHAPTER 13

Experiments Synergizing Machine Learning Approaches with Geospatial Big Data for Improved Urban Information Retrieval

KAVACH MISHRA,[1] ASFA SIDDIQUI,[2] and VINAY KUMAR[3]

[1]*Geomatics Engineering Group, Civil Engineering Department, Indian Institute of Technology Roorkee, Roorkee, Uttarakhand, India, E-mail: kmishra@ce.iitr.ac.in*

[2]*Urban and Regional Studies Department, Indian Institute of Remote Sensing, Indian Space Research Organization, Dehradun, Uttarakhand, India*

[3]*Photogrammetry and Remote Sensing Department, Indian Institute of Remote Sensing, Indian Space Research Organization, Dehradun, Uttarakhand, India*

ABSTRACT

Geospatial big data produced by airborne or ground-based hyperspectral sensors have high spectral resolution and therefore account for the heterogeneity of urban areas. Machine learning approaches like support vector machine (SVM) successfully handle noise and variability in such datasets. SVM performs intermediate of spectral angle mapper (SAM) and object-based image analysis (OBIA) in retrieving buildings and natural features from the 2 m airborne hyperspectral data over Reno. However, such data acquisition is not economically viable for large scale detailed urban information extraction. Sensor optics design also forbids the exchanging of descriptive spectral and spatial content. Super-resolution (SR) reconstruction offers a solution. Using iterative back projection (IBP) and bicubic interpolation over the Washington DC scene shows that IBP creates a higher spatial resolution image at the same scaling ratio without retaining spectral characteristics. Algorithms sparse regression and natural prior (SRP), and anchored neighborhood regression (ANR) ensure input spectral information preservation while reconstructing the scene for Ahmedabad by learning the relationship between the spectral response and the feature patches. Visual examination and quality metric evaluation show that SRP outperforms ANR. SAM, SVM, and OBIA classify the best and worst super-resolved products to prepare urban material and land cover maps. A comparative assessment evinces that radial kernel-based SVM classifies the SRP generated output most favorably. These real data experiments thus establish SR as a tool for synthesizing spatially and spectrally rich datasets and highlight the flexibility of machine learning for geospatial big data tasks.

13.1   INTRODUCTION

Global urban coverage is projected to increase from 0.7-0.9 million km2 in 2010 to 1.2-3.1 million km^2 in 2050 [2]. Cities are thus experiencing a continuous change in land cover with urban core densification and infrastructure up-gradation comprising new or altering constructions. Although concentrated within a smaller portion of the Earth, the built-up area constituents, whether natural or human-made, undergo modification in biophysical properties, which hugely impacts the biogeochemical cycles and climate as well as the economy and the community. Monitoring urban expansion and its effects thus necessitate a standardized quantification of its constituents and their detection and mapping consistently [50].

Traditional ground surveying consists of instruments such as chains, tapes, ranging rods, theodolites, and dumpy levels. More recently, automatic levels, total stations, global positioning systems (GPS) serve this purpose, along with the interpretation of aerial photographs. However, they are tedious, require a highly-skilled workforce, have small aerial coverage, and costly. Remote sensing systems, whether active or passive, help to monitor urban areas by addressing these difficulties [25]. Active or radar sensors record the backscatter received from the target illuminated by the radar beam. They provide data independent of weather conditions at both day and night to study object texture and structure [58].

On the other hand, passive or optical sensors detect the sunlight reflected from the object of interest and give information about the Earth's surface only in cloud-free circumstances. They can be multispectral or hyperspectral, depending upon the slicing of the electromagnetic spectrum. The former measures the reflected sunlight in a few spectral bands with broad bandwidths, while the latter has more than 200 spectral channels with a narrow bandwidth. However, only a few imaging spectrometers are available with a 20 m to 30 m resolution against the numerous multispectral sensors in space, which have ground observing capability from less than 0.5 m to 1 km. Consequently, the probability of the occurrence of mixed pixels increases, thereby limiting the possibility of obtaining explicit spectral content of urban areas from the hyperspectral image. Therefore, very high spatial and spectral resolutions will ideally allow detailed differentiation of the surface materials occurring in the built-up areas [20] and its continuous monitoring but are not currently present.

In the three-dimensional data cube representation of a hyperspectral image, the X-Y plane shows the location of each image pixel, and the Z-axis shows the spectral response of the feature(s) dotting that pixel across the electromagnetic spectrum sliced into bands. The variations in the reflectance spectrum can be intra-image as well as inter-image owing to the surrounding environment [22], illumination [69], sun sensor geometry [19], sensor, and diversification within the same material class [11]. Such datasets are received at the data processing centers in large volumes in near real-time, and thus are an essential source of geospatial big data. As a result, new algorithms such as fast line of sight atmospheric analysis of hypercubes (FLAASH) for atmospheric correction, linear spectral unmixing and spectral matching techniques such as SAM came into existence in the first commercial image visualization environment: environment for visualization of images (ENVI) in 1994 [8].

Many processing routines, like the removal of redundant data and noise and classification, employ machine learning (ML) techniques. For instance, the minimum noise fraction (MNF) [34] transform removes the noise in the image before applying principal component analysis (PCA) [27], a class of latent linear models, to reduce the dimensionality of the imagery. Gaussian maximum likelihood (ML) classifier is a popular hyperspectral land cover classification algorithm wherein a multi-variable Gaussian function describes class-wise data distribution through estimated mean vectors and covariance matrices [12]. SVM provides efficient and accurate discrimination among classes based on less training pixels. Being supervised and non-parametric, it handles the multi-class issue prevalent in hyperspectral data [44]. It selects the hyperplane with the most significant margin to separate the data points of classes and thus categorize unclassified data points. SVMs obtain good results from complex and noisy data [78].

OBIA improves urban feature extraction by considering regular geometric shape, size, and arrangement [79]. An object representative of a particular land cover is a group of pixels adjacent to each other, having an identical tone, color, and texture [37]. They reduce the complexity of a high-resolution scene by avoiding the noise between ground features and integrating properties of the spectral domain [36]. Segmentation approaches divide the entire image into objects. For example, multiresolution segmentation commences with a pixel and assumes the local homogeneity criteria for deciding the merger of neighboring image objects [35].

For investigating urban processes, impervious, and built-up surfaces need to be characterized in a detailed manner using high spatial and high spectral resolution datasets. SR algorithms retain the spatial and spectral properties of the low resolution (LR) input in the high resolution (HR) output [74] and thus overcome the challenges posed by other spatial scale improvement methods like fusion, interpolation, and restoration. SR can be of multi-frame or single-frame type based on the number of input images. In multi-frame SR, the misalignment information between numerous LR images of the same area under observation reconstructs the HR picture or sequence [18]. A single LR image serves the purpose of HR scene recovery in single-frame SR. Several papers discuss multi-frame SR [45, 72, 74]. Single-frame SR review works are low in number and at most general [77]. According to [16], single-frame SR methods are divided into reconstruction, learning and hybrid types. For reconstruction algorithms, the input image resolution is increased to the target resolution using interpolation, following which physical characteristics are extracted and added with the interpolated output to obtain the super-resolved output. Determining the relation between HR and LR regions using an independent image database or the input LR image itself forms the essence in learning algorithms. Hybrid methods exploit the characteristic of the occurrence of repetitive structures in natural high-resolution images [5].

The super-resolved outputs undergo quality checks before their utilization for any application. Indices such as bias, correlation coefficient (CC), difference in variance (DIV), and root mean square error (RMSE) test the spatial quality of the products [65]. Entropy (E) looks after the amount of information present in the image by promulgating histogram analysis. Erreur relative globale adimensionnelle de synthese (ERGAS), universal image quality index (Q), and relative average spectral error (RASE) are responsible for spectral quality [57].

In Bias, the mean values of processed and reference images are divided. With the ideal result being zero, a substantial similarity implies between original and processed image by a small positive or negative value. A similar inference draws from DIV, which depends on the variance values of processed and reference pictures. CC ranges from −1 to 1. The processed image is precisely the opposite of reference data when the CC value is −1. 1 indicates the exact similarity between the two. 0 reflects that there is no correlation between the two images. The interpretation of Q is similar to CC. Q measures the processed image quality and ranges between −1 and 1 [68]. ERGAS depends on the scaling factor, and its increased value denotes distortion from the reference. RASE utilizes the mean value of radiance of all bands, unlike ERGAS, which uses only the mean radiance value of each band. RASE figures have a similar connotation as that of ERGAS. The higher the value of E, the more is the information in the processed output. RMSE is affected by outlying values and lower its value, better the agreeability of the processed image with the reference.

13.2 PREVIOUS WORK DONE

Hyperspectral data is most suitable for region-wise urban material mapping due to their capability to record detailed target spectra. Very few such studies are present. Subudhi and Mishra [60] study urban spectral reflectance characteristics in Kanpur city and find that the most suitable bandwidth for mapping of urban areas is blue and near-infrared regions. Hepner et al. [23] use AVIRIS to extract signatures of several urban land cover classes and explains their separability for delineating urban land cover. Clark et al. [10] analyze spectral signatures using the continuum removal approach and generates a map of dust or debris collections in and around the world trade center to aid the 9/11 terrorist attack investigation. Ben-Dor et al. [6] and Herold et al. [24] discuss the essentialities for mapping urban surfaces with imaging spectroscopy data.

A spatial-spectral expanding technique in [53] differentiates the surface materials, automatically examining endmember spectral dissimilarities. Manual or automatic endmember extraction techniques permit one (e.g., N-FINDR, [70]; Iterative error analysis, [48]) or more than one end member (e.g., Multiple endmember spectral mixture analysis (MESMA) [52]) per class to be retrieved from the data thereby avoiding time-consuming and costly fieldwork. Rashed et al. [49], and Wu and Murray [71] analyze intimate spectral mixtures to map urban rooftop and pavement materials. However, there exist linear and non-linear spectral unmixing techniques, when fed with the field-collected pure spectral signatures as end members, distinguish uncertainties occurring due to inter and intra-class variations of surface materials [46, 54]. Such methods map urban land cover descriptively and accurately.

Herold et al. [25] successfully categorize the materials by applying Bhattacharya distance on the spectral signatures compiled in a spectral library developed using field samples and 4 m AVIRIS imagery. Benediktsson et al. [7], Gamba et al. [21], and Van Der Linden et al. [66] propose different methodologies for categorizing cities and their surroundings, such as morphological profiles, object boundaries, and ML techniques, respectively. Enkhbaatar et al. [15] use SAM and SVM to classify the compact airborne spectrographic imager (CASI) [3] high-resolution image into eight different classes. SAM shows more accuracy than the SVM classifier, which is 69% and 62.5%, respectively. SVM reports higher overall accuracy and kappa coefficient than ML in mapping land cover in Qazvin [62]. Attarzadeh and Momeni [4] perform object-based classification for building feature extraction in Isfahan city using Quickbird data and succeed in extracting them with over 80% accuracy. Shrivastava and Rai [55] also extract building automatically using OBIA on high-resolution fused products of Cartosat-1 with IRS-1C and Cartosat-1 with LISS-4.

Efficacy of newly proposed SR methods, whether single or multi-frame, has been evaluated only on test images, and very few SR based resolution enhancement experiments on real data exist [61]. Yang et al. [73] perform SR using single-frame IBP [14]. They interpolate the input LR image by a 5×5 Gaussian kernel that deviates by 0.6. The maximum iterations for back projections are 100. Timofte et al. [64] present three approaches for neighborhood representation of LR patches. The first approach considers a global neighborhood representation for every dictionary atom, whereas each atom adopts a linear representation without any regularization in the other approach. The third approach confines the least-squares solution to only positive values. The earliest work on the sparse coding approach for single-frame SR uses different approaches for dictionary training in the case of LR and HR images [73]. Each hybrid method assumes a distinct set of rules to define the imaging model [26, 39]. Martens et al. [38] use a convolution neural network (CNN) to investigate multi-frame SR on an extensive set of both HR and LR PROBA-V monthly data. The super-resolved output sequence records a more significant signal to noise ratio

(SNR) for a large number of scenes in comparison to the bicubic interpolation of LR dataset.

Recently, Kotthaus et al. [31] derive a London specific spectral library containing the spectral signatures of urban materials in the visible to the thermal infrared region of the electromagnetic spectrum. Okujeni et al. [47] conclude that the incorporation of material-specific pure spectral signatures gathered from multiple sites to train the support vector regression (SVR) model is an efficient methodology to map the cities where field data regarding urban rooftop and pavement materials is not available. The study of Krishna et al. [32] performed on the city of Delhi finds that the Hyperion dataset is capable of extracting land use land cover (LULC) end members and random forest (RF) classifier outperforms SAM and SVM classifiers. Zahiri et al. [75] explore the application of shortwave infrared (SWIR) spectrometry in the classification of concrete samples according to water-to-cement (w/c) ratio and prediction of their density using a partial least square discriminant analysis (PLS-DA) model. Deshpande et al. [13] develop an algorithm for detecting the wavelength range in which the local Indian materials are the most distinguishable. The algorithm uses the Leodoit-Wolf covariance estimator. In Koirala et al. [30], either of Gaussian processes, kernel ridge regression (KRR) [28], or feedforward neural networks relates a real-time hyperspectral data to equivalent linear spectra and calculates abundances by unmixing. Siddiqui et al. [56] focus on mapping 11 features in Ahmedabad city using mixture tuned matched filtering (MTMF) on airborne visible/near-infrared imaging spectrometer-next generation (AVIRIS-NG) sensor data. Checking accuracy at randomly selected spots reveals variations in overall accuracy from 82.3% to 87.7%.

13.3 STUDY AREA AND MATERIALS USED

The sensor ProspecTIR captures the airborne hyperspectral scene with a high spatial resolution on September 13, 2009, at 12:48 pm (Central Time) over a part of the city of Reno, Nevada, in the United States of America. Highway no. 668 and Truckee River are the north and south limits of the study area. As shown in Figure 13.1, commercial, and manufacturing spaces on portions of Greg Street and S. Rock Boulevard dot the study area [40]. The sensor manufactured by SpecTIR LLC, United States of America, has a spectral range of 400 nm–970 nm in the visible near-infrared (VNIR) region and 970 nm–2450 nm in the SWIR region. In the VNIR region, the spectral resolution is 2.9 nm and the radiometric resolution is 12 bit whereas in the SWIR region, the spectral resolution is 8.5 nm and the radiometric resolution is 14 bit [59]. In a typical operation, the sensor scans the target in 360 channels which can extend to a maximum of 500 channels at a field of view (FOV) of 24°.

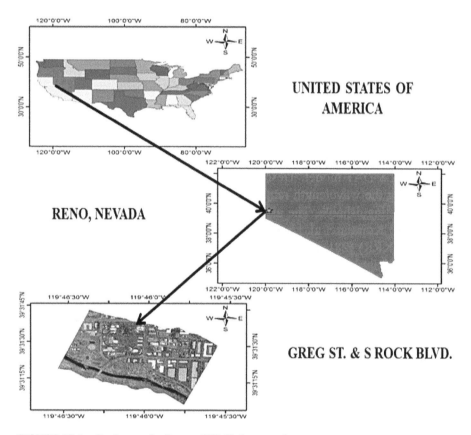

FIGURE 13.1   Study area for ProspecTIR flight campaign.
Source: Reprinted from: Ref. [40]. © Authors.

The National Mall of Washington DC, United States of America, forms the backdrop of the scene acquired by hyperspectral digital imagery collection experiment (HYDICE) in August 1995. Figure 13.2 clearly shows that the area of interest falls between the Lincoln Memorial and the United States Capitol Grounds with the Washington Monument in the middle.

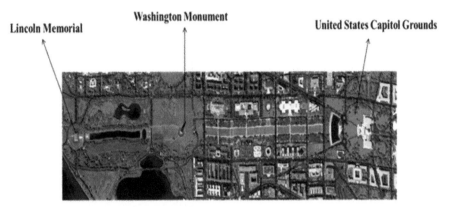

FIGURE 13.2   Study area for HYDICE flight campaign.
Source: Photo by Authors.

The radiometrically corrected dataset has 191 bands over 0.4 to 2.5 µm wavelength range. Around 1208 scan lines with 307 pixels per scan line make up the dataset in a 16-bit unsigned integer format. According to Mitchell [43], HYDICE sensor has a varying spectral resolution of 7.6–16 nm as a function of wavelength; a radiometric resolution of 12 bits; a swath width of 0.9 km and a swath FOV of 8.94°.

The study area chosen for urban information extraction from the Airborne Visible InfraRed Imaging Spectrometer - Next Generation (AVIRIS-NG) dataset is a portion of eastern Ahmedabad city about 4.85 sq. km in size with Kankaria Lake serving as the focal point. Figure 13.3 illustrates the region. Falling within the jurisdiction of the Ahmedabad Municipal Corporation (AMC), parts of five wards under three zones form the study area. The wards and zones are Khadia ward (part; Central Zone), Kankaria ward (full; South Zone), Maninagar ward (part; South Zone), Rajpur ward (part; East Zone) and Gomtipur (part; East Zone).

The date and time of dataset acquisition are February 11, 2016, and 08:01:29 coordinated universal time (UTC), respectively. The scene extends from 22° 59'16.57" N, 72° 25'19.94" E to 23° 3'21.04" N, 72° 45'6.68" E. The reflectance file contains 425 bands distributed over 0.376 µm to 2.5 µm. The spectral sampling is 5 nm, and spatial resolution is 8.1 m. SVC HR-1024 of Spectra Vista Corporation collects spectral signatures of various natural features and urban materials in the study area of Ahmedabad. Trimble Juno SD Handheld GPS records positional information of the sites of collection of spectral signatures.

Building spectral libraries and processing hyperspectral images occur in ENVI 5.0. SR algorithm routines run by modifying the open-source MATLAB codes while stacking and georeferencing of the outputs utilize an R programming language script. The software for map composition is ArcMap 10.5, and spectral signature analyzes are in MS Office Excel 2013.

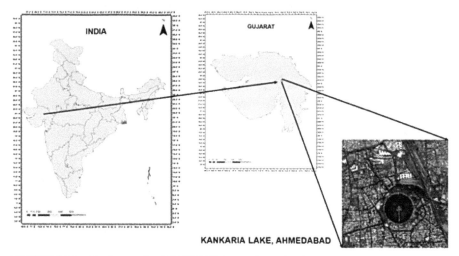

FIGURE 13.3   Study area for AVIRIS-NG dataset investigations.
Source: Photo by Authors.

13.4   METHODOLOGY

The experiments with the three airborne hyperspectral datasets share some significant steps like sensor error corrections, SR implementation, comparison of super-resolved outputs, classification, and accuracy assessment. Flowcharts showing the procedure for each study are in Figures 13.4–13.6, respectively.

13.4.1   DATA PRE-PROCESSING

The dataset provided by ProspecTIR is atmospherically corrected. The input geometry (IGM) file corrects for erroneous terrain. A visual examination of each of the 356 bands for salt and pepper effect leads to the removal of bands 1, 348–352, and 354–356, thereby leaving only 348 bands.

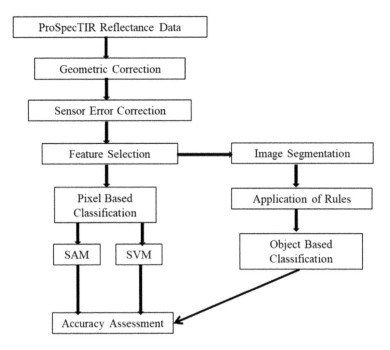

FIGURE 13.4 Methodology for experiments with ProspecTIR data.
Source: Reprinted from: Ref. [40]. © Authors.

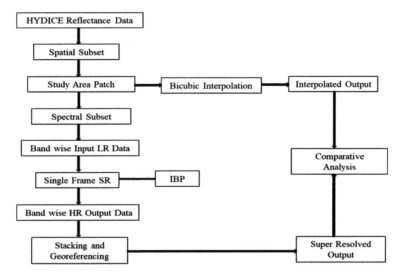

FIGURE 13.5 Overall methodology for experiments with HYDICE data.
Source: Photo by Authors.

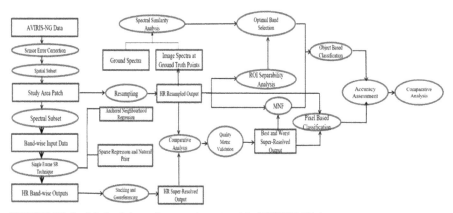

FIGURE 13.6   Methodology for experiments with AVIRIS-NG data.
Source: Photo by Authors.

The AVIRIS-NG dataset is also a Level 2 surface reflectance file containing 425 bands. Only 353 bands remain in the dataset upon removal of noisy bands after the visual examination. Bands removed are 1–12, 196–210, 213, 217, 284–319, 325–328, and 422–424. The defined study area is a region consisting of 272 scan lines and 272 samples. It undergoes subsetting into individual bands to serve as input for the SR routine to assess the computing proficiency of the method.

The HYDICE dataset undergoes corrections for sensor errors, errors due to atmospheric attenuations as well as terrain errors. A patch containing 288 lines and 288 samples forms the study area in such a manner that several art galleries, museums, and cultural institutions dot the landscape along with vegetation. Single bands generated from the patch produce HR outputs using the SR approach.

13.4.2   SINGLE-FRAME SR

Band-wise HYDICE data serves as input for IBP. Iterative refinement of an initial estimate of super-resolved imagery takes place in IBP, followed by a reduction of the error between the band-wise input and LR variety of the super-resolved output. The process stops upon arriving at the most significant number of iterations or a limit in the error value. The patch undergoes bicubic interpolation with the same scaling ratio for comparison with the super-resolved output. Here, the maximum number of iterations is 500, sigma is 0.9, and the scaling ratio is 2 [42]. Both the SR and interpolation routines run in MATLAB with the system configuration: RAM = 4 GB; Processing Speed = 1.6 GHz; and CPU = Intel Pentium Quad-core N3710.

According to literature, SRP [29] and ANR produce results with superior visual standards, are computationally efficient, and can mimic identical properties of real-time LR data. This study, therefore, tests the execution of these two algorithms for enhancement of the visualization of the band-wise input LR AVIRIS-NG data by a factor of 2. Again, the SR routines run in MATLAB by making changes in the source codes provided by the developers of each method and the following system configuration: RAM = 16 GB; Processing Speed = 3.4 GHz; and CPU = Intel Core i7–6700.

ANR combines the neighborhood embedding approach with the sparse coding methodology [76] for performing SR The bicubic interpolation of the input achieves the target spatial resolution. Then first and second-order gradients create unique representation for every identified distinct input patch feature. The trained LR dictionary identifies a nearest neighbor atom corresponding to each representation. Correlation between atoms determines k nearest neighbors, which group together to form the LR neighborhood. With the help of the corresponding HR neighborhood, the LR neighborhood estimates the projection matrix for each identified atom. The product of the input feature patch and the projection matrix gives the HR patch. Such resultant patches upon addition to the interpolated output and averaging the overlapped patches yield the final super-resolved output. The dictionary size is 2048 atoms, and the maximum neighborhood size for each atom is 256 atoms.

Both LR and HR dictionaries utilize the image set used by Zeyde et al. [76] during their separate training processes. Resampling this set according to the scaling factor, generates the LR image set. The difference image of the two sets gives an HR image set without any low frequencies. Similarly, the LR image set retains only high-frequency details upon the application of a high pass filter. Then, different feature patches extracted at location k in both the image concatenate into patch vectors. Execution of PCA on LR patch vectors facilitates easy application of k-singular value decomposition (k-SVD; [1]) algorithm to train dictionary and decrease computational complexity therein. Applying a direct approach using pseudo-inverse [64] on the HR patch vectors obtains the trained HR dictionary.

In SRP, cubic spline interpolation brings the input LR data to the target resolution. A Laplacian function extracts the band frequency components. Considering SR as a regression problem, a sparse matrix offers a solution. For solution initialization, kernel matching pursuit (KMP) [67] selects the basis points. Gradient descent then optimizes the matrix containing n basis points. Evaluating only the candidate points and not the entire training set for choosing the basis point reduces the computational time. For each pixel location, optimizing the basis point and the corresponding nth row of the solution matrix containing the candidate points at the rth step of KMP also recedes the process run time. The criterion for the selection of candidate points is the maximum distance between regressor cost functional minimizer and localized KRR. Nearest neighbors (NN) of each input pixel train the entire KRR for obtaining its localized version. A convex combination of the candidate points determines the pixel value for image location (x, y) of the super-resolved estimate, which sums up to the interpolated result for obtaining the final output. A prior [63] removes the ringing artifacts in the final output around those edge pixels whose Laplacian norm and the sizeable gap between pixel figures of the local region are more than the minimum and maximum limits.

For KRR training and testing, 7×7 and 5×5 are the input and output patch sizes, respectively. 0.05 and 0.5×10exp(–7) are the respective weight and kernel values. The number of basis points and the number of training points are 300 and 200,000 respectively. For combination, 7×7 and 0.04 are the input patch size and the weight value, respectively. The minimum threshold is 0.95, and the maximum threshold is 2.2. The stacking and georeferencing of HR band outputs produce the final super-resolved output.

13.4.3   COMPARATIVE ASSESSMENT OF SUPER-RESOLVED OUTPUTS

The comparison between IBP and interpolated outputs is on spatial resolution, computational efficiency, and visual interpretation. Figure 13.7 shows the location of the three patches taken for visual examination on the false-color composite (FCC) of the interpolated and super-resolved images.

As regards AVIRIS-NG dataset, patches chosen for visual comparison correspond to Nagina Wadi, vegetation, and road junction. As the NN resampling approach preserves the spectral attributes of input LR data [33], the scaled-up study area patch using NN resampling serves as the reference data. Examination of the spectral profiles of the central pixel of each patch assesses the retention of spectral information from the input LR data. A red color cross-hair highlights the central pixel in super-resolved outputs and reference data in Figure 13.11. The coordinates of the three central pixels are Point 1 (293, 341), Point 2 (68, 308), and Point 3 (168, 336). Averaging the process run time recorded for each of 353 executions of the algorithm obtains a mean process run time for comparison purposes. Implementation of quality evaluation in MATLAB using eight indices affirms the efficacy of the SR process. Bias, CC, DIV, Entropy, and RMSE represent spatial quality, whereas ERGAS, RASE, and Q test the spectral nature of the data.

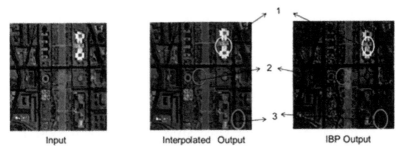

Input   Interpolated Output   IBP Output

FIGURE 13.7   Location of patches for visual examination.
Source: Reprinted from: Ref. [42]. © Authors.

13.4.4   FIELD DATA COLLECTION FOR EXPERIMENTS WITH AVIRIS-NG IMAGERY

The spectroradiometer sensor, when kept perpendicular to the surface at a distance of exactly one meter above the target at the designated point, records the spectral signature in the 0.348 μm to 2.5026 μm range of the electromagnetic spectrum. Acquisition of positional information of 281 points and their photographs occurred in three days. The acquired spectra group into a spectral library. The features include water, concrete, tin, GI sheet, grass vegetation, asphalt, vegetation, tarpaulin, soil, and China mosaic. Figure 13.8 illustrates the constructed spectral library.

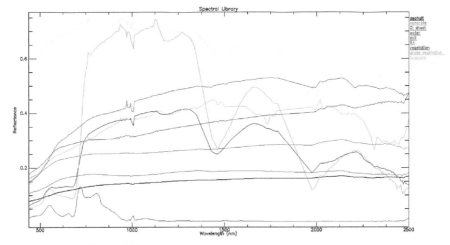

FIGURE 13.8   Spectral library.
Source: Photo by Authors.

13.4.5   CLASSIFICATION

In the absence of ground truth, the detection of LULC classes occurs from the processed ProspecTIR image for classification purposes. The features are tiled roof structure, polymeric composite roof structure, type I metal roof structure, composite roof structure, road, parking, bare ground, vegetation, and water. Regions of interest (ROIs) taken for the identified features function as training samples for supervised SAM and supervised SVM. Figure 13.9 shows the plotted spectral signatures of the ROIs. SAM distinguishes maximum features optimally by keeping 0.5 radians as the threshold, whereas default parameters accompanying radial kernel type yield the best results in case of SVM classification. The parameters are gamma = 0.01; penalty = 100; pyramid levels = 0.0; and classification probability threshold = 0.0.

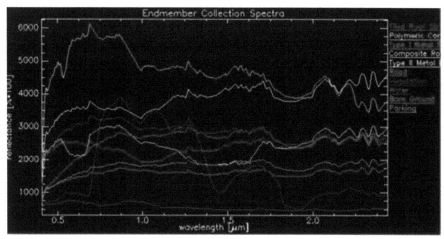

FIGURE 13.9   Characteristic spectra of LULC classes.
Source: Reprinted from Ref. [40]. © Authors.

Multiresolution segmentation segregates the image into image objects. Scale, shape, and compactness are 130, 0.40, and 1.0, respectively. The NN algorithm classifies the objects into each of the 10 classes by taking the mean and standard deviation of each layer into consideration as rules. The chosen parameters mean only for the region under observation and change from dataset to dataset.

In the case of AVIRIS-NG data, supervised SAM, supervised SVM and OBIA classify the reference (Resample_NN), best (Output_SRP) and worst (Output_ANR) super-resolved products obtained as a result of the comparative assessment and quality metric evaluation. Samples of 10 urban material and natural feature classes train SAM and SVM. SAM classifies optimally by adopting different spectral angle threshold for each class. The limits are 0.16, 0.36, 0.30, 0.66, 0.40, 0.136, 0.25, 0.121, 0.11, and 0.10 for soil, vegetation, grass vegetation, water, asphalt, China mosaic, concrete, tin, GI sheet and tarpaulin respectively. In case of SVM, parameters such as kernel type = radial; gamma = 0.03; penalty = 100; pyramid level = 0; and classification probability threshold = 0 yield the optimum outputs.

Before object-based classification implementation, forward MNF transform operates on the three datasets. After arranging the uncorrelated bands from highest to lowest, components considered for classification are 13, 15, and 16 from reference, best, and worst super-resolved outputs. Then, a similarity analysis runs between image spectra at ground truth points and field spectra to detect the presence of the natural feature or urban material. The metrics SAM, spectral feature fitting (SFF) and binary encoding (BE) have an equal weightage of 0.33. Upon identification of the wavelength regions where both the spectra overlap or are very close to each other, ROI separability computations identify the bands which can differentiate the features to be classified distinctly. Pairs of ROIs for the 10 target classes selected on the reference data undergo calculation of transformed divergence (TD) and Jeffries Matusita (JM) distance. Scores more than 1.9 indicate good separability while scores less than 1.0 indicate high similarity between the ROIs.

Multiresolution segmentation divides each dataset consisting of the MNF components stacked together with the optimal bands into objects of the 10 target classes. Table 13.1 shows the segmentation parameters.

TABLE 13.1 Segmentation Parameters

Dataset	Scale	Shape	Compactness
Resample_NN	5	0.2	0.7
Output_SRP	6	0.3	0.9
Output_ANR	7	0.4	0.8

Source: Table by Authors.

Then the NN algorithm classifies the objects, during which standard NN slope sets to 0.2 and the membership function is 0.5. Object attributes considered as rule set are: mean, standard deviation, and the ratio of pixels for each layer; brightness value and maximum difference values of optimal band layers; object connectivity; normalized difference vegetation index (NDVI); and normalized difference water index (NDWI). Here, Band 101 in the NIR region and band 53 in the red region having the central wavelength of 937.41 nm and 696.99 nm respectively help in obtaining NDVI. Band 24 in the green region and Band 58 in the NIR region produce NDWI. They have the respective central wavelength of 551.74 nm and 722.04 nm. The considered parameters are dataset and study area dependent.

13.4.6   ACCURACY ASSESSMENT

Assessing accuracy using an error matrix validates the classification results. The error matrix is an array with the columns denoting detected classes on the classified image, and the rows give the information present on the reference. The last column mentions the total number of actual points per class used for calculating accuracy [9]. Similarly, the sum in the last cell of each column represents the total points per class in the classified image. The bottom of the right-hand side shows the addition output of the diagonal elements used for determining overall accuracy (OA) whereas non-diagonal elements define the errors of omission and commission. Pearson's Kappa coefficient [17], a multi-variable statistical method, also assesses accuracy.

13.5   RESULTS AND DISCUSSION

13.5.1   SR PRODUCTS

IBP takes about 32.42 seconds for one round of its execution while interpolation clocks only about 0.012 seconds. Upon zooming in, the interpolated product appears blurred while the IBP output has finer details than the interpolated product. Visually examining the selected patches reveals that IBP defines and preserves the building edges (figure 13.10, 1) while interpolation retains the natural features (figure 13.10, 2). Nevertheless, IBP output does not preserve the spectral content, especially when different features have similar spectral signatures or experience tonal resemblance (figure 13.10, 3).

1

2

3

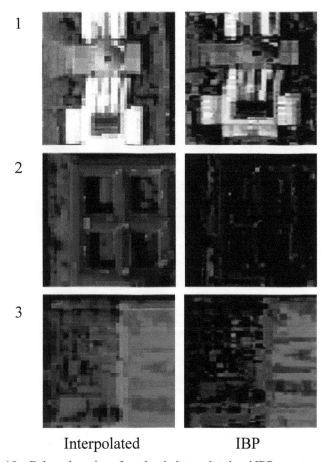

Interpolated   IBP

FIGURE 13.10 Enlarged version of patches in interpolated and IBP outputs.
Source: Photo by Authors.

The super-resolved outputs generated from the LR AVIRIS-NG data have 4.05 m as their spatial resolution. SRP takes only 0.17 seconds to complete once while ANR clocks about 1.32 seconds to produce the final band wise output. Figure 3.11 shows the enlarged version of the selected patches in reference and super-resolved products. The water around Nagina Wadi possesses evenness throughout and has a uniform tone in every super-resolved product (figure 13.11, 1). Grass and tree cover distinguish easily in the vegetation patch with well-defined edges in each super-resolved output (figure 13.11, 2). Edge sharpness is absent in all super-resolved outputs (figure 13.11, 3). Features such as open area, road width, built-up, and vegetation are also clearly visible (figure 13.11, 3).

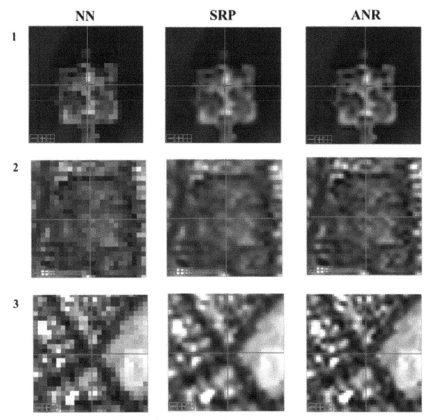

FIGURE 13.11　Magnified version of patches in reference and super-resolved outputs.
Source: Adapted from: Refs. [57] and [41]. https://creativecommons.org/licenses/by/4.0/

From the spectral profiles shown in Figure 13.12, it is evident that each super-resolved output retains the shape of the spectral curve throughout the electromagnetic spectrum. It indicates the preservation of input spectral content to varying degrees in the super-resolved outputs. There is an increase in reflectance value of each band in case of point 1, point 2 and point 3 for each super-resolved output. Except point 1, SRP output reports the closest reflectance values to the reference giving rise to the possibility that it retains maximum spectral content. ANR spectral profiles show significant deviations from the reference indicating partial preservation of spectral content. They also overlap at numerous bands, thereby revealing a stronger resemblance between the two outputs and departure from the input LR data both spatially and spectrally.

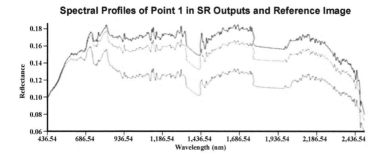

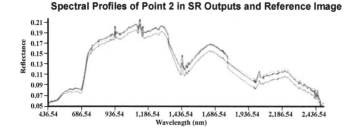

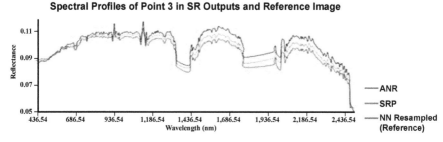

FIGURE 13.12   Spectral profiles of central pixel in selected patches of super-resolved outputs and reference data.
Source: Photo by Authors.

Table 13.2 shows the quality index results wherein the figures highlighted in red indicate the best result of the respective quality index. Q and CC values are above 0.9 for each super-resolved output, indicating the preservation of feature and spectral information at a higher spatial resolution. SRP output reports Q and CC values higher than that of ANR output, implying that SRP has a more considerable resemblance to the input LR data and ANR shows significant deviations. Lowest values of ERGAS and RASE are of SRP, leading to the conclusion that SRP ensures maximum retention of spectral information at a larger spatial scale. SRP output also records values of bias and RMSE lower than ANR product reiterating that SRP output is identical to the input LR data and must be the best performing SR technique. Again, a minimal positive value of DIV in case of output generated by SRP indicates a strong resemblance with the reference data. Entropy values suggest the addition of information to ANR output, whereas SRP output experiences information loss. It is contrary to the results of other index analyzes. Hence, it infers that SRP shows the most promising results and ANR performs poorly on all the parameters under consideration.

TABLE 13.2   Quality Metric Evaluation

Dataset	Quality Metric							
	Bias	DIV	CC	Entropy	ERGAS	Q	RASE	RMSE
Output_SRP	−0.0001	0.0677	0.9763	12.5896	4.0756	0.9757	8.1511	0.0124
Output_ANR	0.0155	−0.1854	0.9082	13.6352	8.5287	0.9048	17.0574	0.026

Source: Table by Authors.

13.5.2   OPTIMAL BANDS SELECTION FOR OBIA

Spectral similarity analysis tests 10 random points corresponding to 10 distinct features found in the study area. This subsection shows the results only for two points. Figure 13.13 shows the location of these points.

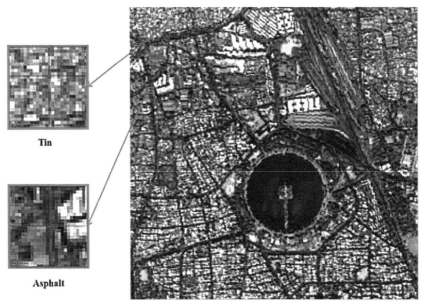

FIGURE 13.13   Location of points selected for spectral similarity analysis.
Source: Photo by Authors.

The entire electromagnetic spectrum was split into three wavelength regions to understand the similarity of the image and ground spectra at the designated point. They are 436.54 nm to 1102.7 nm; 1102.7 nm to 1703.74 nm; and 1703.74 nm to 2500.12 nm. Figure 13.14 shows the spectral similarity analysis results for (85, 19) and (39, 155) in the reference, best, and worst super-resolved outputs.

NN

Similarity Scores X:85, Y:19 — Unknown: X:85 Y:19

Library Spectrum	Score	SAM	SFF	BE
tin	[0.742]	{0.893}	{0.597}	{0.759}
tarpaulin	[0.732]	{0.832}	{0.506}	{0.881}
concrete	[0.693]	{0.659}	{0.680}	{0.561}
china mosaic	[0.684]	{0.830}	{0.548}	{0.694}
soil	[0.664]	{0.785}	{0.531}	{0.697}
vegetation	[0.655]	{0.653}	{0.527}	{0.805}
asphalt	[0.652]	{0.827}	{0.516}	{0.635}
GI sheet	[0.608]	{0.759}	{0.552}	{0.530}
grass vegetation	[0.559]	{0.394}	{0.525}	{0.776}
water	[0.305]	{0.000}	{0.652}	{0.272}

SRP — Unknown: X:85 Y:19

Library Spectrum	Score	SAM	SFF	BE
tin	[0.750]	{0.894}	{0.613}	{0.765}
tarpaulin	[0.741]	{0.840}	{0.512}	{0.892}
concrete	[0.698]	{0.659}	{0.689}	{0.567}
china mosaic	[0.680]	{0.828}	{0.586}	{0.649}
soil	[0.672]	{0.791}	{0.544}	{0.703}
asphalt	[0.658]	{0.829}	{0.525}	{0.640}
vegetation	[0.656]	{0.660}	{0.630}	{0.799}
GI sheet	[0.613]	{0.760}	{0.563}	{0.535}
grass vegetation	[0.561]	{0.399}	{0.529}	{0.771}
water	[0.306]	{0.000}	{0.660}	{0.266}

ANR — Unknown: X:85 Y:19

Library Spectrum	Score	SAM	SFF	BE
tin	[0.736]	{0.894}	{0.585}	{0.751}
tarpaulin	[0.720]	{0.827}	{0.495}	{0.861}
china mosaic	[0.687]	{0.838}	{0.569}	{0.674}
concrete	[0.679]	{0.858}	{0.660}	{0.541}
vegetation	[0.654]	{0.650}	{0.509}	{0.824}
soil	[0.650]	{0.780}	{0.512}	{0.677}
asphalt	[0.642]	{0.824}	{0.507}	{0.615}
GI sheet	[0.598]	{0.757}	{0.545}	{0.510}
grass vegetation	[0.560]	{0.393}	{0.509}	{0.796}
water	[0.310]	{0.000}	{0.646}	{0.292}

Similarity Scores X:85, Y:19

Unknown: X:39 Y:155 — Library Spectrum	Score	SAM	SFF	BE
asphalt	[0.749]	{0.902}	{0.511}	{0.856}
tarpaulin	[0.742]	{0.866}	{0.535}	{0.847}
tin	[0.734]	{0.898}	{0.595}	{0.731}
soil	[0.730]	{0.832}	{0.554}	{0.927}
concrete	[0.729]	{0.839}	{0.617}	{0.754}
china mosaic	[0.710]	{0.808}	{0.560}	{0.782}
GI sheet	[0.681]	{0.805}	{0.577}	{0.683}
vegetation	[0.502]	{0.369}	{0.523}	{0.629}
water	[0.270]	{0.000}	{0.669}	{0.224}

Unknown: X:39 Y:155 — Library Spectrum	Score	SAM	SFF	BE
asphalt	[0.756]	{0.906}	{0.533}	{0.853}
tarpaulin	[0.748]	{0.864}	{0.552}	{0.850}
tin	[0.742]	{0.903}	{0.614}	{0.734}
soil	[0.738]	{0.830}	{0.582}	{0.824}
concrete	[0.732]	{0.836}	{0.630}	{0.751}
china mosaic	[0.716]	{0.809}	{0.582}	{0.779}
GI sheet	[0.686]	{0.804}	{0.595}	{0.680}
vegetation	[0.514]	{0.370}	{0.555}	{0.632}
water	[0.273]	{0.000}	{0.683}	{0.144}

Unknown: X:39 Y:155 — Library Spectrum	Score	SAM	SFF	BE
asphalt	[0.749]	{0.904}	{0.520}	{0.844}
tarpaulin	[0.745]	{0.861}	{0.537}	{0.858}
tin	[0.739]	{0.902}	{0.596}	{0.742}
soil	[0.726]	{0.827}	{0.559}	{0.816}
concrete	[0.718]	{0.834}	{0.606}	{0.737}
china mosaic	[0.712]	{0.807}	{0.579}	{0.771}
GI sheet	[0.677]	{0.801}	{0.586}	{0.666}
vegetation	[0.514]	{0.371}	{0.540}	{0.646}
water	[0.274]	{0.000}	{0.683}	{0.147}

FIGURE 13.14   Spectral similarity analysis results for (85, 19) and (39, 155).
Source: Photo by Authors.

Highlighted values in red reveal the best overall and individual similarity score, thereby indicating the occurrence of that material at the chosen point. The similarity scores are on the higher side of the range 0 to 1, i.e., primarily above 0.5. For the feature 'water' only, the scores are lower than 0.5 in each dataset. The super-resolved outputs obtain similarity scores higher than the reference data. For most features, the image and the field spectral signatures are very close to each other or overlap in the VNIR region up to a wavelength of nearly 1100 nm and then again in the SWIR region from 2000 nm onwards. Hence, these are the regions of the electromagnetic spectrum for carrying out ROI separability computations. The 'average' class separability comprises scores above 1.9 reflecting maximum differentiation among the classes while the 'minimum' class separability has the ones below 1.0 signifying the least possible difference among the features. Therefore, the most suitable set of wavelengths identified in the VNIR region are 516.68 nm, 551.74 nm, 591.81 nm, 596.82 nm, 696.99 nm, 722.04 nm, 937.41 nm, and 1072.65 nm. Similarly, the central wavelengths of the optimal set of bands in the SWIR region are 1127.74 nm, 1623.60 nm, 1643.63 nm, 1653.65 nm, 1668.68 nm, and 1678.69 nm.

13.5.3   URBAN INFORMATION EXTRACTION

Figure 13.15 shows the LULC maps extracted from ProspecTIR data by SAM, SVM, and OBIA. Table 13.3 shows OA and kappa coefficient wherein the figures highlighted in red indicate the best outcome. Figures 13.16(a–c) highlight the class-wise PA and UA for SAM, SVM, and OBIA classifications, respectively.

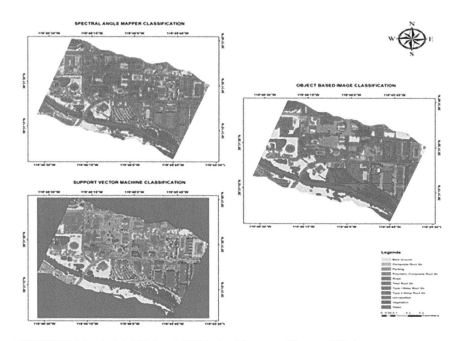

FIGURE 13.15   SAM, SVM, and OBIA classification of ProspecTIR data.
Source: Reprinted from: Ref. [40]. © Authors.

TABLE 13.3   OA and Kappa Coefficient Results for Classification from ProspecTIR Data

Accuracy Assessment			
Classification	**SAM**	**SVM**	**OBIA**
OA (%)	67.99	68.62	86.76
Kappa coefficient	0.6447	0.6455	0.852

Source: Reprinted from: Ref. [40]. © Authors.

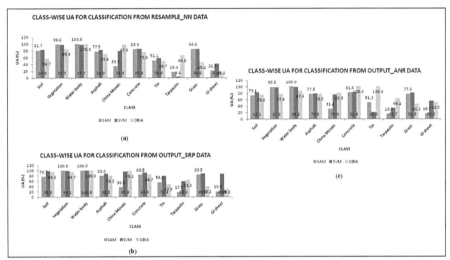

FIGURE 3.16 (a) Class-wise PA and UA results for SAM classification from ProspecTIR data; (b) class-wise PA and UA results for SVM classification from ProspecTIR data; (c) class-wise PA and UA results for OBIA classification from ProspecTIR data.
Source: Photo by Authors.

In SVM output, water pixels merge with background pixels and shadow pixels, causing their classification as water. SAM classifies roads, parking areas, and natural features effectively while SVM identifies structures efficiently. On the whole, object-based classification distinguishes clearly the different types of structures. None of the three classifiers maps motor vehicles and containers as their spectra overlap with that of different structures in the data having a high spatial resolution. As is evident from accuracy assessment results, OBIA outperforms both SAM and SVM in retrieving urban LULC information from ProspecTIR data.

Figure 13.17 presents the urban material and natural feature maps prepared by classifying Resample_NN, Output_SRP, and Output_ANR datasets using SAM, SVM, and OBIA approach. Figure 3.18(a) shows the position of the patch selected for visual investigation of the classified results while Figure 3.18(b) shows its magnified version on each thematic map as well as its Google Earth scene.

The classifiers identify the urban materials and the natural features efficiently in the three datasets. There is no misclassification in the rooftop classes of concrete, China mosaic and tin with the retention of the structural features of the input LR image at the higher spatial resolution. Roads are also visible with well-defined limits in the classified outputs. However, asphalt mixes with other rooftop classes wherever such classes occur together with shadow leading to their designation as asphalt instead. There is also mixing between asphalt and water in SVM outcomes with the former classified as the latter at few spots.

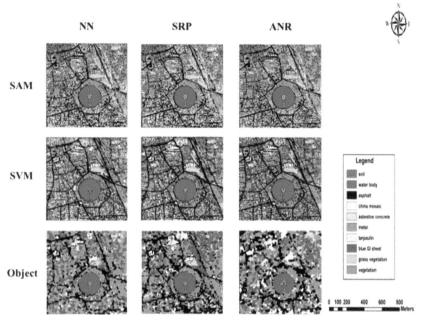

FIGURE 13.17   SAM, SVM, and OBIA classification results of Resample_NN, Output_ SRP, and Output_ANR datasets.
Source: Photo by Authors.

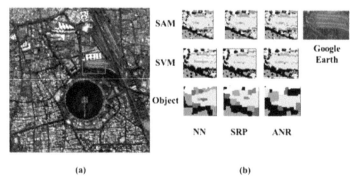

FIGURE 13.18   (a) Location of patch for visual inspection (*Source:* Reprinted from: Ref. [41]; (b) Enlarged version of patch in SAM, SVM, and OBIA classification results of resample_ NN, Output_SRP, and Output_ANR along with google earth image of patch.
Source: Photo by Authors.

Cross-validation with ground samples reveals high accuracy for all the classes. Table 13.4 shows the OA and Kappa Coefficient outcomes. The values highlighted in red are the best possible results.

TABLE 13.4 OA and Kappa Coefficient Results for Classification from Reference and Super-Resolved Outputs

Classification Technique	SAM			SVM			OBIA		
Dataset	NN	SRP	ANR	NN	SRP	ANR	NN	SRP	ANR
OA	70.30	70.52	68.66	82.67	92.73	80.64	74.91	81.95	79.66
Kappa coefficient	0.6581	0.6613	0.6397	0.7973	0.9119	0.7737	0.7083	0.7903	0.7626

Source: Adapted from: Ref. [41].

SVM reports the best accuracy assessment result for SRP generated super-resolved output. Among the datasets, SRP generated output has the highest OA and kappa coefficient across all classifiers, thereby making the process of urban mapping using super-resolved products a success. Compared to the other two classification approaches, SVM performs better as it possesses high learning capacity and better generalization ability producing excellent results from data with high dimensionality and heavy noise.

Figures 13.19(a–c) show the PA of each class for the three datasets. Figures 13.20(a–c) show the UA of each class for the three datasets.

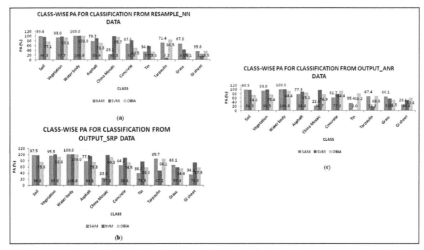

FIGURE 13.19 (a) Class-wise PA result for classification from resample_ NN dataset; (b) class-wise PA result for classification from Output_ SRP dataset; (c) class-wise PA result for classification from Output_ ANR dataset.
Source: Photo by Authors.

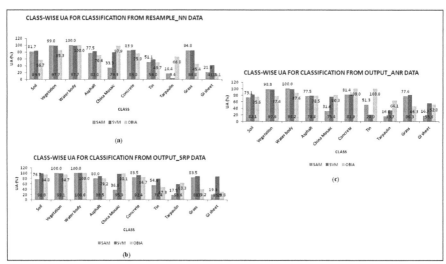

FIGURE 13.20 (a) Class-wise UA Result for Classification from Resample_NN dataset (b) Class-wise UA Result for Classification from Output_ SRP dataset (c) Class-wise UA Result for Classification from Output_ ANR dataset.
Source: Photo by Authors.

Grass, vegetation, water body and soil classes record very high accuracies across all classifiers. SVM shows the most significant PA and UA for asphalt, China mosaic, concrete, and tin classes. Accuracies for GI sheet and tarpaulin classes are moderate and the lowest, respectively. They occur as small proportions in each pixel of the imagery and hard classifiers allocate them to alternative labels. The recorded accuracies being as per convention, thus emphasize the preservation of spectral and spatial content in the SR derived products with magnifications visible in the imagery.

13.6 CONCLUSION

The chapter introduces the concept of hyperspectral data cubes as a form of geospatial big data. The three case studies explore the applicability of ML algorithms for various hyperspectral data processing tasks such as dimensionality reduction, feature selection and classification as well as SR based resolution enhancement of real data in an urban setting.

OBIA delineates urban land use classes in the most promising manner compared to SAM and SVM from high resolution airborne hyperspectral image, thereby establishing its potential to execute extensive mapping from such datasets. Comparative assessment of IBP with bicubic interpolation shows that IBP improves the spatial resolution at the same scaling ratio. However, it is slower and fails to retain the spectral data of the input, thus indicating the need to develop and apply such SR methods that retain spectral information along with improved spatial output.

Single-frame SR methods: SRP and ANR clearly distinguish pavements, rails, and structures which remain undetected in the input LR AVIRIS-NG data. SRP performs better than ANR based on the visual and spectral examinations, the process run times, and quality metric evaluations.

Around 14 bands focused in the visible and SWIR regions of the electromagnetic spectrum are the optimal set of bands that can differentiate all the features present in the imagery and yield classification results by OBIA approach intermediate of that by SAM and SVM. From the OAs and kappa statistics, it is evident that the super-resolved output obtained by SRP gives the best results for the three classifiers. SVM efficiently classifies asphalt, China mosaic, concrete, GI sheet and tin irrespective of the dataset, as seen from the PAs and UAs. The bounding lines of the structures are visible in every thematic map obtained by SVM. Water is the natural feature to be classified most appropriately reporting nearly 100% PAs and UAs across all classifiers and datasets. The three classifiers clearly distinguish all the natural features with the best outputs in SAM.

13.7 RECOMMENDATIONS

Future work can include execution of the SR process for a scale factor of 4 and above and testing for its spatial and spectral fidelity. Training dictionaries from patches of input LR data itself will yield a better super-resolved product. Development of sensor independent tool for both multi and single-frame SR is also the need of the hour. Usage of emittance spectroscopy in tandem with reflectance spectroscopy can aid in the efficient characterization of urban impervious surfaces. Adoption of unmixing strategies for pure pixel extraction and multi-layer object-based image analysis that uses decision trees or neural networks at its base will also help in this objective.

ACKNOWLEDGMENTS

The authors would like to thank SpecTIR LLC, Reno, Nevada, United States of America and Larry L. Biehl (Systems Manager, Purdue Terrestrial

Observatory, West Lafayette, Indiana, United States of America) for providing access to the processed sample datasets acquired by ProSpecTIR and HYDICE sensors respectively. We would also like to thank ISRO-NASA AVIRIS-NG mission team at the Space Applications Centre, the National Remote Sensing Centre and the Indian Institute of Remote Sensing for providing the AVIRIS-NG data. This work would not have been possible without access to the source codes of various SR methods by the respective authors. Lastly, it was also not possible to improve this research work without the constructive comments and suggestions of the editors and anonymous reviewers.

KEYWORDS

- **hyperspectral remote sensing**
- **SVM**
- **OBIA**
- **SR**
- **urban mapping**

REFERENCES

1. Aharon, M., Elad, M., & Bruckstein, A., (2006). K-SVD: An algorithm for designing overcomplete dictionaries for sparse representation. *IEEE Transactions on Signal Processing, 54*(11), 4311–4322.
2. Angel, S., Parent, J., Civco, D. L., Blei, A., & Potere, D., (2011). The dimensions of global urban expansion: Estimates and projections of all countries, 2000–2050. *Progress in Planning, 75*, 53–107. doi: 10.1016/j.progress.2011.04.001.
3. Anger, C. D., Babey, S. K., & Adamson, R. J., (1990). A new approach to imaging spectroscopy. *Proc. SPIE Conference on Imaging Spectrometry of Terrestrial Environment* (Vol. 1298, pp. 72–86). Orlando, Florida.
4. Attarzadeh, R., & Momeni, M., (2012). Object-based building extraction from high resolution satellite imagery. *International Archives of the Photogrammetry, Remote Sensing and Spatial Information Sciences, 39*, B4.
5. Baker, S., & Kanade, T., (2002). Limits on super-resolution and how to break them. *IEEE Transactions on Pattern Analysis and Machine Intelligence, 24*(9), 1167–1183. doi: 10.1109/TPAMI.2002.1033210.
6. Ben-Dor, E., Levin, N., & Saaroni, H., (2001). A spectral based recognition of the urban environment using the visible and near-infrared spectral region (0.4–1.1 m). A case study over Tel-Aviv. *International Journal of Remote Sensing, 22*(11), 2193–2218.

7. Benediktsson, J. A., Palmason, J. A., & Sveinsson, J. R., (2005). Classification of hyperspectral data from urban areas based on extended morphological profiles. *IEEE Transactions on Geoscience and Remote Sensing, 43*(3), 480–491.

8. Boardman, J. W., Biehl, L. L., Clark, N. N., Kruse, F. A., Mazer, A. S., Torson, J., & Staenz, K., (2006). Development and implementation of software systems for imaging spectroscopy. *Proc. Int. Geosci. Remote Sens. Symp. (IGARSS'06)* (pp. 1969–1973). Denver, Colorado.

9. Chandra, A. M., & Ghosh, S. K., (2006). *Remote Sensing and Geographical Information System*. Alpha Science Int'l Ltd.

10. Clark, R. N., Green, R. O., Swayze, G. A., Meeker, G., Sutley, S., Hoefen, T. M., Livo, K. E., et al., (2001). Environmental Studies of the World Trade Center area after the September 11, 2001 attack. U. S. Geological Survey, Open-File Report OFR-01-0429, http://speclab.cr.usgs.gov/wtc/ (accessed on 11 November 2021).

11. Cochrane, M. A., (2000). Using vegetation reflectance variability for species-level classification of hyperspectral data. *International Journal of Remote Sensing, 21*(10), 2075–2087.

12. Dalponte, M., Ørka, H. O., Gobakken, T., Gianelle, D., & Næsset, E., (2012). Tree species classification in boreal forests with hyperspectral data. *IEEE Transactions on Geoscience and Remote Sensing, 51*(5), 2632–2645.

13. Deshpande, S. S., Inamdar, A. B., & Vin, H. M., (2019). Spectral library and discrimination analysis of Indian urban materials. *Journal of the Indian Society of Remote Sensing, 47*(5), 867–877.

14. Elad, M., & Feuer, A., (1996). Super-resolution reconstruction of an image. In: *Electrical and Electronics Engineers in Israel, 1996, 19th Convention* (pp. 391–394). IEEE.

15. Enkhbaatar, L., Jayakumar, S., & Heol, J., (2009). Support vector machine and spectral angle mapper classifications of high resolution hyperspectral aerial image. *Korean Journal of Remote Sensing, 25*(3).

16. Fernandez-Beltran, R., Latorre-Carmona, P., & Pla, F., (2017). Single-frame super-resolution in remote sensing: A practical overview. *International Journal of Remote Sensing.* https://doi.org/10.1080/01431161.2016.1264027.

17. Foody, G. M., (2002). Status of land cover classification accuracy assessment. *Remote Sensing of Environment, 80,* 185–201.

18. Gaidhani, P., (2011). *Super-Resolution.* From Education Information UK, CV online.

19. Galvao, L. S., Ponzoni, F. J., Epiphanio, J. C. N., Rudorff, B. F. T., & Formaggio, A. R., (2004). Sun and view angle effects on NDVI determination of land cover types in the Brazilian Amazon region with hyperspectral data. *International Journal of Remote Sensing, 25*(10), 1861–1879.

20. Gamba, P., & Dell'Acqua, F., (2006). Spectral resolution in the context of very high resolution urban remote sensing. In: Weng, Q., & Quattrochi, D., (eds.), *Urban Remote Sensing* (pp. 377–391). Boca Raton: CRC Press.

21. Gamba, P., Dell'Acqua, F., & Trianni, G., (2007). Rapid damage detection in the bam area using multitemporal SAR and exploiting ancillary data. *IEEE Transactions on Geoscience and Remote Sensing, 45*(6), 1582–1589.

22. Gao, X., Huete, A. R., Ni, W., & Miura, T., (2000). Optical-biophysical relationships of vegetation spectra without background contamination. *Remote sensing of environment, 74*(3), 609–620.

23. Hepner, G. F., Houshmand, B., Kulikov, I., & Bryant, N., (1998). Investigation of the integration of AVIRIS and IFSAR for urban analysis. *Photogrammetric Engineering and Remote Sensing, 64*(8), 813–820.

24. Herold, M., Gardner, M. E., & Roberts, D. A., (2003). Spectral resolution requirements for mapping urban areas. *IEEE Transactions on Geoscience and Remote Sensing, 41*(9), 19071919.

25. Herold, M., Roberts, D. A., Gardner, M. E., & Dennison, P. E., (2004). Spectrometry for urban area remote sensing—development and analysis of a spectral library from 350 to 2400 nm. *Remote Sensing of Environment, 91*(3, 4), 304–319.

26. Huang, J. B., Singh, A., & Ahuja, N., (2015). Single image super-resolution from transformed self-exemplars. In: *IEEE Conference on Computer Vision and Pattern Recognition* (pp. 5197–5206). New Jersey, USA: IEEE.

27. Jolliffe, I., (2014). *Eigenvalues and Eigenvectors in Statistics*. Wiley StatsRef: Statistics Reference Online.

28. Kim, K. I., & Kwon, Y., (2008). Example-based learning for single-image super-resolution. In: *Joint Pattern Recognition Symposium* (pp. 456–465). Springer, Berlin, Heidelberg.

29. Kim, K. I., & Kwon, Y., (2010). Single-image super-resolution using sparse regression and natural image prior. *IEEE Transactions Pattern Analysis Mach Intelligent, 32*(6), 1127–1133. doi: 10.1109/TPAMI.2010.25.

30. Koirala, B., Zahiri, Z., & Scheunders, P., (2020). A machine learning framework for estimating leaf biochemical parameters from its spectral reflectance and transmission measurements. *IEEE Transactions on Geoscience and Remote Sensing, 58*(10), 7393–7405

31. Kotthaus, S., Smith, T. E., Wooster, M. J., & Grimmond, C. S. B., (2014). Derivation of an urban materials spectral library through emittance and reflectance spectroscopy. *ISPRS Journal of Photogrammetry and Remote Sensing, 94*, 194–212.

32. Krishna, G., Sahoo, R. N., Pradhan, S., Ahmad, T., & Sahoo, P. M., (2018). Hyperspectral satellite data analysis for pure pixels extraction and evaluation of advanced classifier algorithms for LULC classification. *Earth Science Informatics, 11*(2), 159–170.

33. Kwan, C., Choi, J. H., Chan, S., Zhou, J., & Budavari, B., (2017). Resolution Enhancement For Hyperspectral Images: A Super-resolution And Fusion Approach Signal Processing, Inc., Rockville, MD 20850 USA Purdue University, West Lafayette, IN 47907 USA, 6180–6184.

34. Lee, J. B., Woodyatt, A. S., & Berman, M., (1990). Enhancement of high spectral resolution remote-sensing data by a noise-adjusted principal components transform. *IEEE Transactions on Geoscience and Remote Sensing, 28*(3), 295–304.

35. Li, H., Gu, H., Han, Y., & Yang, J., (2009). SRMMHR (statistical Region merging and minimum heterogeneity rule) segmentation method for high-resolution remote sensing imagery. *IEEE Journal of Selected Topics in Applied Earth Observations and Remote Sensing, 2*(2), 67–73.

36. Li, X., & Shao, G., (2014). Object-based land-cover mapping with high resolution aerial photography at a county scale in midwestern USA. *Remote Sensing, 6*(11), 11372–11390. https://doi.org/10.3390/rs61111372.

37. MacLean, M. G., & Congalton, R. G., (2012). Map accuracy assessment issues when using an object-oriented approach. In: *Proceedings of the American Society*

for Photogrammetry and Remote Sensing 2012 Annual Conference (pp. 19–23). Sacramento, CA, USA.

38. Märtens, M., Izzo, D., Krzic, A., & Cox, D., (2019). Super-resolution of PROBA-V images using convolutional neural networks. *Astrodynamics, 3*(4), 387–402.

39. Michaeli, T., & Irani, M., (2013). Non-parametric blind super-resolution. In: International Conference on Computer Vision (ICCV) (pp. 945–952). New Jersey, USA: IEEE.

40. Mishra, K., Kumar, V., & Siddiqui, A., (2017). Land use-land cover information extraction from high resolution airborne hyperspectral data. In: *Proc. 38th Asian Conf. Remote Sens. (ACRS)* (Vol. 4, pp. 2721–2728).

41. Mishra, K., Siddiqui, A., & Kumar, V., (2018). A comparative assessment of efficacy of super-resolved airborne hyperspectral outputs in urban material and land cover information extraction. *Int. Arch. Photogram. Remote Sens. Spatial Inf. Sci., XLII-5*, 653–658, https://doi.org/10.5194/isprs-archives-XLII-5-653-2018.

42. Mishra, K., Siddiqui, A., Kumar, V., & Garg, R. D., (2019). Enhancing resolution of hyperspectral data: A comparative study in urban area. In: *ISG-ISRS National Symposium on Innovations in Geospatial Technology for Sustainable Development with Special Emphasis on NER.* North Eastern Space Applications Center (NESAC), Shillong, India.

43. Mitchell, P. A., (1995). Hyperspectral digital imagery collection experiment (HYDICE). In: *Geographic Information Systems, Photogrammetry, and Geological/Geophysical Remote Sensing* (Vol. 2587, pp. 70–95). International Society for Optics and Photonics.

44. Moughal, T. A., (2013). Hyperspectral image classification using support vector machine. *Journal of Physics: Conference Series, 439*, 012042. https://doi.org/10.1088/1742-6596/439/1/012042.

45. Nasrollahi, K., & Moeslund, T. B., (2014). Super-resolution: A comprehensive survey. *Machine Vision and Applications.* https://doi.org/10.1007/s00138-014-0623-4.

46. Neville, R. A., Sun, L., & Staenz, K., (2008). Spectral calibration of imaging spectrometers by atmospheric absorption feature matching. *Canadian Journal of Remote Sensing, 34*(Supplement 1), S29–S42.

47. Okujeni, A., Canters, F., Cooper, S. D., Degerickx, J., Heiden, U., Hostert, P., & Van, D. L. S., (2018). Generalizing machine learning regression models using multi-site spectral libraries for mapping vegetation-impervious-soil fractions across multiple cities. *Remote Sensing of Environment, 216*, 482–496.

48. Plaza, A., Martínez, P., Pérez, R., & Plaza, J., (2004). A quantitative and comparative analysis of endmember extraction algorithms from hyperspectral data. *IEEE Transactions on Geoscience and Remote Sensing, 42*(3), 650–663.

49. Rashed, T., Weeks, J. R., Gadalla, M. S., & Hill, A., (2001). Revealing the anatomy of cities through spectral mixture analysis of multispectral imagery: A case study of the greater Cairo region, Egypt. *Geocarto International, 16*(4), 5–16.

50. Ridd, M. K., (1995). Exploring a V-I-S (vegetation-impervious surface-soil) model for urban ecosystem analysis through remote sensing: Comparative anatomy for cities. *International Journal of Remote Sensing, 16*(12), 2165–2185.

51. Roberts, D. A., & Herold, M., (2004). Imaging spectrometry of urban materials. In: King, P., Ramsey, M. S., & Swayze, G., (eds.), *Infrared Spectroscopy in Geochemistry, Exploration, and Remote Sensing* (pp. 155–181). Mineral Association of Canada: Ottawa, ON, Canada.

52. Roberts, D. A., Gardner, M., Church, R., Ustin, S., Scheer, G., & Green, R. O., (1998). Mapping chaparral in the Santa Monica Mountains using multiple endmember spectral mixture models. *Remote Sensing of Environment, 65*, 267–279.

53. Roessner, S., Segl, K., Heiden, U., & Kaufmann, H., (2001). Automated differentiation of urban surfaces based on airborne hyperspectral imagery. *IEEE Transactions on Geoscience and Remote Sensing, 39*(7), 1525–1532.

54. Roth, K. L., Dennison, P. E., & Roberts, D. A., (2012). Comparing endmember selection techniques for accurate mapping of plant species and land cover using imaging spectrometer data. *Remote Sens. Environ., 127*, 139–152.

55. Shrivastava, N., & Rai, P. K., (2015). An object based building extraction method and classification using high resolution remote sensing data/O metoda de extragere a cladirilor orientata obiect si clasificare folosind date de înalta rezolutie furnizate de teledetectie. In: *Forum Geografic* (Vol. 14, No. 1, p. 14). University of Craiova, Department of Geography.

56. Siddiqui, A., Chauhan, P., Kumar, V., Jain, G., Deshmukh, A., & Kumar, P. (2022). Characterization of urban materials in AVIRIS-NG data using a mixture tuned matched filtering (MTMF) approach. *Geocarto International, 37*(1), 332–347.

57. Singh, S. K., Jain, G., Siddiqui, A., Naik, S., Rathore, B. P., Garg, V., & Thakur, P. K., (2019). Characterization and retrieval of snow and urban land cover parameters using hyperspectral imaging. *Current Science, 116*(7), 1182.

58. Soergel, U., (2010). Radar Remote Sensing of Urban Areas. *Remote Sensing and Digital Image Processing, 15.* Springer Science + Business Media, Dordrecht, the Netherlands.

59. SpecTIR Inc., (2011). *ProSpecTIR TM VS VNIR-SWIR Hyperspectral Instrument* (pp. 1–2).

60. Subudhi, A. P., & Mishra, D., (1989). Study of spectral reflectance characteristics of an urban environment—case study of Kanpur city. *Journal of the Indian Society of Remote Sensing, 17*(3), 127–132.

61. Suganya, P., Mohanapriya, N., & Vanitha, A., (2013). Survey on image resolution techniques for satellite images. *International Journal of Computer Science and Information Technologies, 4*(6), 835–838.

62. Taati, A., Sarmadian, F., Mousavi, A., Pour, C. T. H., & Shahir, A. H. E., (2015). Land use classification using support vector machine and maximum likelihood algorithms by Landsat 5 TM images. *Walailak Journal of Science and Technology (WJST), 12*(8), 681–687.

63. Tappen, M. F., and Freeman, W. T. (2003). Comparison of graph cuts with belief propagation for stereo, using identical MRF parameters. *In: IEEE*, p. 900.

64. Timofte, R., De Smet, V., & Van, G. L., (2013). Anchored neighborhood regression for fast example-based super-resolution. In: *IEEE International Conference on Computer Vision, 1920–1927.* New Jersey, USA: IEEE.

65. Vaiopoulos, A. D., (2011). Developing MATLAB scripts for image analysis and quality assessment. In: *Earth Resources and Environmental Remote Sensing/GIS Applications II* (Vol. 8181, p. 81810B). International Society for Optics and Photonics.

66. Van, D. L. S., Janz, A., Waske, B., Eiden, M., & Hostert, P., (2007). Classifying segmented hyperspectral data from a heterogeneous urban environment using support vector machines. *Journal of Applied Remote Sensing, 1*(1), 013543.

67. Vincent, P., & Bengio, Y., (2002). Kernel matching pursuit. *Machine learning, 48*(1–3), 165–187.

68. Wang, Z., & Bovik, A. C., (2002). A universal image quality index. *IEEE Signal Processing Letters, 9*(3), 81–84.

69. Wendel, A., & Underwood, J., (2017). Illumination compensation in ground-based hyperspectral imaging. *ISPRS Journal of Photogrammetry and Remote Sensing, 129,* 162–178.

70. Winter, M. E., (1999). N-FINDR: An algorithm for fast autonomous spectral end-member determination in hyperspectral data. In: *Imaging Spectrometry V* (Vol. 3753, pp. 266–275). International Society for Optics and Photonics.

71. Wu, C., & Murray, A. T., (2003). Estimating impervious surface distribution by spectral mixture analysis. *Remote Sensing of Environment, 84,* 493–505.

72. Yang, C. H., Ma, C., & Yang, M. H., (2014). Single-image super-resolution: A benchmark. In: *European Conference on Computer Vision* (Vol. 8692, pp. 372–386). Berlin, Heidelberg: Springer.

73. Yang, J., Wright, J., Ma, Y., & Huang, T., (2008). Image super-resolution as sparse representation of raw image patches. *IEEE Computer Vision and Pattern Recognition, 1,* 1–8.

74. Yue, L., Shen, H., Li, J., Yuan, Q., Zhang, H., & Zhang, L., (2016). Image super-resolution: The techniques, applications, and future. *Signal Processing, 128,* 389–408. https://doi.org/10.1016/j.sigpro.2016.05.002.

75. Zahiri, Z., Laefer, D. F., & Gowen, A., (2018). The feasibility of short-wave infrared spectrometry in assessing water-to-cement ratio and density of hardened concrete. *Construction and Building Materials, 185,* 661–669.

76. Zeyde, R., Elad, M., & Protter, M., (2010). On single image scale-up using sparse-representations. In: *International Conference on Curves and Surfaces* (pp. 711–730). Berlin, Heidelberg: Springer.

77. Zhang, H., Yang, Z., Zhang, L., & Shen, H., (2014). Super-resolution reconstruction for multi-angle remote sensing images considering resolution differences. *Remote Sensing, 6,* 637–657. doi: 10.3390/rs6010637.

78. Zhuo, W., & Lili, C., (2010). The algorithm of text classification based on rough set and support vector machine. In: *2010 2nd International Conference on Future Computer and Communication* (Vol. 1, pp. V1–365). IEEE.

79. Zou, X., Zhao, G., Li, J., Yang, Y., & Fang, Y., (2016). Object-based image analysis combining high spatial resolution imagery and laser point clouds for urban land cover. *The International Archives of Photogrammetry, Remote Sensing and Spatial Information Sciences, 41,* 733.

CHAPTER 14

Garbage Detection Using SURF Algorithm Based on Merchandise Marker

LALIT GUPTA, SAMARTH JAIN, DHRUV BANSAL, and
PRINCY RANDHAWA

*School of Automobile, Mechanical, and Mechatronics Engineering;
Department of Mechatronics Engineering, Manipal University Jaipur,
Jaipur, Rajasthan, India, E-mails: guptalalit1997@gmail.com (L. Gupta),
samarthjain.119@gmail.com (S. Jain), deebnsl65@gmail.com
(D. Bansal), princyrandhawa23@gmail.com (P. Randhawa)*

ABSTRACT

- **Purpose:** In garbage detection-based on merchandise marker, from the previous studies, we found that those studies used different and old algorithms like SIFT and FAST which were slow and also were less accurate. The aim of this study is to detect different types of garbage and based on a new algorithm which is a hybrid of the algorithms used in previous studies called SURF algorithm.
- **Design/Methodology/Approach:** Three types, namely paper, plastic, and glass of garbage data (images) was collected by us equal number of images for all three types were collected. By extracting feature points and descriptors from the data given and using that on the new upcoming images for identification for which type of garbage it is. The performance was compared to accuracy and time taken by other algorithms.
- **Findings:** The accuracy of this method was checked by four experiments. The results show that this algorithm is more efficient and accurate with an average accuracy of 93.58% which is way better than that of older algorithms.

- **Practical Implications**: This research can be used in recycling factories and also in reducing the number of people that get in touch with garbage by using this research in automatic separation of garbage.
- **Originality/Value**: Rather than using a pure algorithm, a hybrid algorithm was used. The results showed that by using this algorithm, the accuracy and efficiency was way better. Comparing differences in performance, it was concluded that the SURF algorithm was more suitable algorithm.

14.1 INTRODUCTION

All living beings are affected by garbage and is now a global problem. In India alone, 377 million people living in urban India generate 100,000 metric tons of solid waste every day, of which 45 million are left untreated, causing unnatural health problems and environmental degradation. The main problem is the dumping of non-degradable garbage into the environment as it will remain in the environment for a very long period and hence damages both the living organisms and the environment. The main purpose of segregating garbage is so that the degradable garbage can be dumped in landfills and oceans and Non-degradable garbage can be sent back for reusing and recycling and preventing from getting mixed with degradable waste. The general method of disposal of waste is unplanned and is not discarded by the non-disposal of waste disposal sites. The purpose of this chapter is to create a system for household waste disposal for domestic purposes, which can also be used in public places such as schools, colleges, railway stations and air services. Most of the non-degradable waste consists of some markers, labels, tags or stickers about the merchandise from the manufacturers. Whereas mostly degradable objects are those which comes directly from nature and doesn't have any markers, labels, tags or stickers.

By using same as the feature points for the identification of non-degradable waste, so that the intelligent system can differentiate between both types of garbage and act accordingly as manually separating such mammoth amount of garbage is not practically possible anymore. Speed up robust feature (SURF) is an algorithm which can be used for image registration and classification along with object recognition inspired partially by the scale-invariant feature transform (SIFT). This algorithm is not affected changes take place due to image rotation, measurement, and angle of 3D viewing. Therefore, this method of using images can be used in our chapter to identify and classify the type of waste.

14.2   RELATED WORK

Much research has been done on garbage detection automation over the past few years, although it was slow, but the search to fully automate garbage is ongoing work. In this section, we will discuss how much research has been done and which algorithms were used [8]. Also addresses the drawbacks of the algorithms used, and their contrast with each other. In previous chapters, algorithms such as YOLO, SIFT, etc. [5] were being used, some of which achieved great precision but had some disadvantages. Figure 14.1 shows the comparison of the accuracies obtained with the different algorithms. The algorithms shown in the figure are mostly used by the previous researchers for the segregation of garbage, including SIFT, Wave, ORB, Many-to-many matching and yolo (CNN) [11, 18, 19]. Few studies have been taken place in the past, and artificial intelligence (AI) and deep neural network have shown great results in image processing, which can be used for solving the above problem. automatically detecting urban decoration waste based on video images in the past literature. The proposed fast R-CNN and super-fast R-CNN, respectively [8, 13] improved the detection speed and frame-speed while improving the accuracy of the system. The frame's will hit 5. The difference is that the starting module is not used, but rather a 1×1 layer + 3 $\times$ 3 convolutionary layer to replace, the video can be identified at speed (45 frames) simply by replacing. So YOLO improved its detection speed and saved its precision rate, it offered a new way to incorporate the classification and positioning for the future. Some of these algorithms have generated great results but are followed by some drawbacks and limitations.

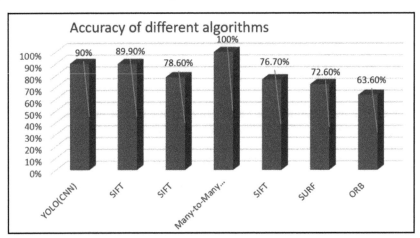

FIGURE 14.1   Various algorithms for garbage detection.

The limitations which came with high accuracies are listed below:

- Time required for training the model was dependent highly on the GPU used. On a GTX 850M, it took 9 h to achieve good detection [10].
- Also, it had to be looked after to prevent over fitting of the model and detecting performance as it can be affected if the model was trained for too long.
- Also, the accuracy is dependent on the parameters used in the model. Therefore, it would require fine-tuning to bring out the best from a model. Maybe the parameters used in Ref. [10] may not be totally appropriate and with fine-tuning may come up with much better results.

Some of the reasons for the difference in results are the following: scale-space sampling, the various definitions of DoG scale space (parameter) lead for the most part to identical detections up to a normalized scale [26]. The results may be different. In addition, the choice of original parameters in the SIFT scheme is not enough to provide an invariance (including translation) theoretical and functional scale, a key argument of the SIFT method [16, 24]. The SIFT algorithm is mainly related to its speed, i.e., SURF is three times faster than that of SIFT and even SURF results in terms of rotational matching, blurring images, different hues, different warp transformations and noise images were better than those achieved by SIFT.

Coming to the algorithm with 100% accuracy, which is a multiple functional algorithm. While this accuracy depends on the edge weights selected for the nodes. The EMD step does not converge on a satisfactory solution when selected or poorly described [14]. The selection of these weights is a hectic task, as weight algorithms have to be run to see weight production, i.e., waiting for the results before the weights selected can't be adjusted.

While ORB use pyramid for scale invariance and strength centroid for rotational invariance, SURF is even more robust than ORB, not only is the problem less precise but also SURF more robust.

Figure 14.2 shows some articles are published in certain years on the same subject as ours, i.e., "Separation of garbage." It can clearly show that the increase in the amount of waste generated also makes it necessary to find new ways to automatically rather than manually separate types of waste. Most papers are released in 2019 and subsequently in 2018 as the need to distinguish various forms of garbage has increased automatically. In the future, more work will be performed at a faster pace.

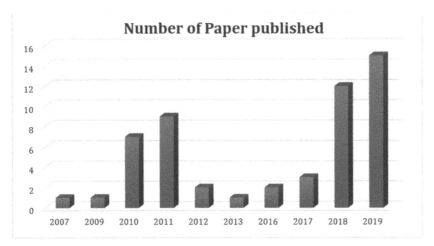

FIGURE 14.2   Various work done on garbage detection.

14.3   BACKGROUND

14.3.1   DIGITAL IMAGE

A digital image is nothing but a collection of real or complex numbers which are signified by bits in a 2-D matrix. A physical image which is captured is first digitalized and store it as an array of binary in the memory of computer [1]. The image data is random in form. Thus, it is necessary to use different kind of techniques like statistical ones to properly process and analyze the image. Image data is quite huge. It needs to be stored in a particular format so that it can be retrieved with ease [2]. In digital imaging, the pixel is the minutest addressable element. Each pixel is a sample of the primary image. Therefore, many pixels usually provide a more accurate representation of the primary. Each pixel value is a variable. In color imaging systems, one color is usually represented by three: red, green, and blue, and in grayscale images, black gives a value of 0, white gives a value of 1. To define an image mathematically it is represented as a 2-D function (x, y) where x and y are the coordinates in spatial coordinate system, and the gray level or intensity of the image at any coordinate pair (x, y) is denoted by the amplitude which is represented by f.

When both the spatial coordinates x and y along with intensity values of f has values within the finite range, i.e., they are a discrete quantity, then the image can be called a digital image [4]. A digital image with gray level A, width P and height Q is defined as:

The major difference between a normal picture and an integral image is explained in Figure 14.3 wherein image each block or pixel consist of a particular value according to the color intensity, the block or pixel in that of an integral image consist of the addition of all the values on the left and top of that particular block.

$$f(x, y) = i(x, y) \cdot i(x, y)$$
$$0 \leq x \leq P$$
$$(x, y) = \{0 \leq y \leq Q$$
$$0 \leq f \leq A$$

Digital image with size P × Q is generally expressed in terms of a 2-D matrix-having P columns and Q row.

$$(0, 0) \dots (0, P - 1)$$
$$f(x, y) = [\vdots \quad \ddots \quad \vdots]$$
$$(Q - 1, 0) \dots f(Q - 1, P - 1)$$

Image

1	2	5	7	2	8	0	6	4	6
9	8	0	4	9	5	10	7	10	3
7	6	10	2	0	10	4	9	10	8
3	8	1	5	4	8	0	9	5	8
9	5	0	1	3	4	1	9	6	1
1	2	5	6	9	9	0	2	4	0
1	2	4	1	6	6	10	4	2	5
5	6	2	10	5	3	9	10	10	2

Integral image

1	3	8	15	17	25	25	31	35	41
10	20	25	36	47	60	70	83	97	106
17	33	48	61	72	95	109	131	155	172
20	44	60	78	93	124	138	169	198	223
29	58	74	93	111	146	161	201	236	262
30	61	82	107	134	178	193	235	274	300
31	64	89	115	148	198	223	269	310	341
36	75	102	138	176	229	263	319	370	403

FIGURE 14.3   Integral image generation.

14.3.2   SPEED UP ROBUST FEATURES (SURF)

The detector used is based on Hessian which is a square matrix of 2 order partial derivations and still uses a very basic calculation. In order to reduce the computation time, it relies on integral images and is thus called a 'fast-Hessian' detector. While the descriptor describes the dispersion of Haar-wavelet reactions near points of interest. Only 64 dimensions have been used to reduce computation time for feature recognition and detection. Hence increasing speed, efficiency, accuracy, and robustness.

14.3.3   INTEGRAL IMAGE GENERATION

Integral images concept is used for the quick operation of box type complicated filters. The entry of an integral image Σx at a location $x = (x, y)$ represents the sum of all pixels in the input image I of a rectangular region formed by the point x and the origin,

$$\Sigma (x) = \overset{i<x\,j<i}{\underset{i=0\;j=0}{\sum (i) \sum I(j)}}$$

With ΣI calculated, rather than summing up the pixels in the image, the total value of the intensities in the requisite region can be computed with only four pixels, without depending on the size of the region.

14.3.4   DETECTING KEY POINTS

The detector is based on the Hessian matrix because of its efficiency in computation time and accuracy. However, it depends on Hessian's decision-maker to choose both the position and the scale. Given a point $x = (x, y)$. In an image I. The Hessian matrix $H(x, \sigma)$ in x at scale s is defined as follows:

$$H(x, \sigma) = [Lxx(x, \sigma)\ Lxy(x, \sigma)]$$

$$Lxy(x, \sigma)\ Lyy(x, \sigma)$$

where; $Lx(x, \sigma)$ is the convolution of the Gaussian second-order derivative with the image I in point x, and similarly for $L(x, \sigma)$, and $Lyy(x, \sigma)$. Scale-space analysis is done using box filters. These can be approximated by second-order Gaussian derivatives and can be estimated very rapidly using the independent shape integral images. Figure 14.4 is the diagram which explains the working of scale-space in SURF algorithm.

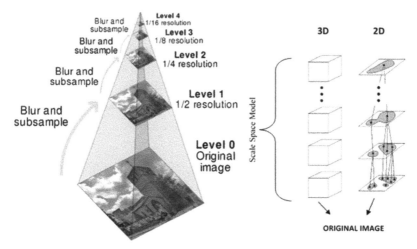

FIGURE 14.4 Scale-space model.

Source: Graphic by Cmglee. https://creativecommons.org/licenses/by-sa/3.0/deed.en

Using integrated images and box filters, it is not necessary to repeatedly insert a single filter for the output of the first filtered layer, but instead of any size, such a filter can be replaced at the same speed directly over the original image. Rather than reducing the size repeatedly, analyzing of scale space is done by scaling the filter size.

14.3.5 SURF DESCRIPTOR

In the first step, on the basis of information from the circular region the reproduction trend is determined. Then, a circular region is created which is connected to the orientation from which the SURF descriptor is extracted. Descriptors are the points around the key points that offers robustness by describing the intensity of distribution around the key point. Descriptors unlike key points change when image is altered; for example, rotating, changing the contrast or brightness of image. Descriptors not only gives robustness but also increases accuracy as it gives algorithms more points to match, decreasing the chances of errors. The key points, descriptors, and their vectors which are formed are shown in Figure 14.5. The point inside the circles is the key point and the area around it inside the circle contain descriptors. In the third image, the black lines shows the vectors formed using key points, these vectors formed are used in calculations and matching input data (images of the garbage) from the sample image [7].

FIGURE 14.5   Example of the detected key points and their descriptors in an image: (a) original image; (b) scaled image; and (c) vectors form.

14.3.6   ORIENTATION ASSIGNMENT

Horizontal and vertical Haar wavelet responses are used by the descriptor orientation assignment. Firstly, the image is converted into grayscale, and then the area around interest points is selected which is known as descriptor of that key point. The descriptor area is further sub-divided into smaller blocks and are assigned with numbers in between 0–1 on the basis of contrast, assigning it 0 for complete black, 1 for complete white and rest of the shades lying between 0 and 1. The average of the values is calculated and then compared as it remains similar even after changing orientation [5].

14.3.7   MATCHING

In the generated image, the features are extracted from the image with the help of key points and descriptors using a fast-Hessian detector. These features are then matched with the input image. If the number of features of sample image matching the number of features of input image surpasses the predefined threshold value, then the image is recognized as non-degradable otherwise considered as degradable. The threshold value was calibrated after in numerous trials choosing the one with the best outcomes.

14.4   RESEARCH METHODOLOGY

The research work was performed in multiple stages as explained below in the specific order.

14.4.1   RESEARCH DATA

Firstly, the data was collected on which the trials of our experiment were performed. The data used for the experiment are the images captured of degradable and non-degradable substances.

The images used for the experiment are of the joint photographic experts group (jpg/jpeg) format with varying size and pixel density. The examples of the images used as research data in the experiment are shown in Figure 14.6 and the table mentioning the number of images (data) that have been used for the experiment are shown in Table 14.1.

FIGURE 14.6   (a) Non-degradable; and (b) degradable.

TABLE 14.1   Number of Images Used Per Category for Testing

Sl. No.	Description	Amount
1.	Degradable substance	15
2.	Non-degradable substance (based on positions)	53
3.	Non-degradable substance (based on rotation)	51
4.	Non-degradable substance (based of scaling)	48
Total		167

14.4.2 TUNING THE RESEARCH DATA

The images used as the research data were tuned before processing. The images were sized according to the limitations and requirements of the software and system. The images were also scaled, rotated, and put at different positions according to the experiment performed to get the end results according to the real-world scenario as practically the orientation and position of the substance will never be same or upright.

14.4.3 DIVIDING THE DATA

To execute the algorithm properly and to process it quickly and efficiently, the data is divided into two subparts viz, the sample data and the testing data. The sample data has the image of the markers, tags, labels, and stickers of the merchandise and the testing data consists of the image of both degradable and non-degradable substances.

14.4.4 TESTING MODEL

The SURF algorithm comprises of four main parts (Figure 14.7):
- Integral image generation;
- Fast-Hessian detector (interest point detection);
- Descriptor orientation assignment; and
- Descriptor generation [6].

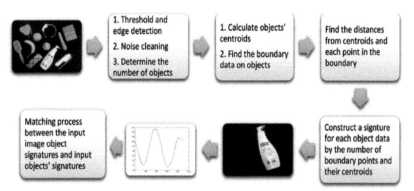

FIGURE 14.7   Steps for testing a model.

Source: Reprinted with permission from [28]. © 2015. Taylor & Francis.

- The integral image is used instead of normal image to increase both the robustness and the speed of the system as it drastically reduces the computation time of the process.
- Fast-Hessian detector is used as it uses the determinant of the Hessian matrix instead of measuring the selecting location and the scale using Hessian-Laplace detector (Figure 14.8).

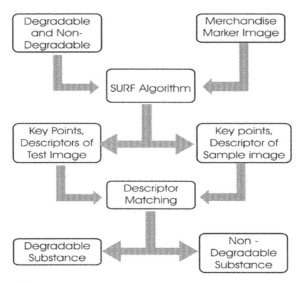

FIGURE 14.8   Working process.

14.5   RESULT AND DISCUSSION

Segregating degradable and non-degradable waste is nothing but differentiating the input image by comparing its features with that of the sample image which is a merchandise marker, tag, label or sticker. When the number of features matched is more than the defined threshold value, than the substance of that image is considered as non-degradable otherwise the substance is considered as degradable.

14.5.1   TYPES OF PARAMETER

We have used four different kinds of images in trials for this experiment to make the results close to the real-world scenario, and those four types are:

(a) degradable substance; (b) non-degradable (scaled); (c) non-degradable (rotated); and (d) non-degradable (positioned) (Figure 14.9).

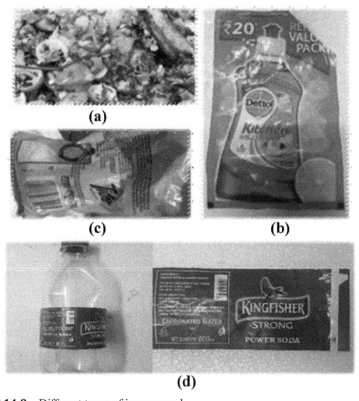

FIGURE 14.9   Different types of images used.

14.5.2 *TRIAL RESULT*

We performed the trials on four different types of images viz., (a) degradable (b) non-degradable (based on scaling); (c) non-degradable (based on rotation); and (d) non-degradable (based on positions); out of which, the degradable image comes with 100%; which means that no degradable image is considered as a non-degradable even once in any condition even if the image is altered on the basis of position, rotation, and scaling. The non-degradable substance images based on the positions and scaling gave exceptional results with the accuracy of 94.30% and 93.75% de-testing almost all the non-degradable substances. The images after rotation gave good results too with the accuracy of 86.27%. The reduction in the accuracy of the rotated images than that of the other images is because the feature changed in the former as hence reducing the number of matching features below the defined threshold value. All the data of the trails have been mentioned in Table 14.2.

TABLE 14.2   Recognition Result

SL. No.	Description	Amount	Degradable	Non-Degradable	Accuracy
1.	Degradable	15	15	–	100%
2.	Non-degradable (based on positions)	53	3	50	94.30%
3.	Non-degradable (based on rotation)	51	7	44	86.27%
4.	Non-degradable (based of scaling)	48	3	45	93.75%
Average					93.58%

14.5.3   GRAPHICAL REPRESENTATION OF THE TRIAL RESULT

In Figure 14.10, we graphically represent the data for accuracy from Table 14.2 by histogram to relate the efficiency of the algorithm between the various types of images used for the trials of the research.

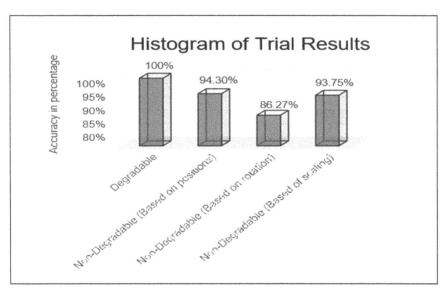

FIGURE 14.10   Graphical representation of trials data.

14.6 CONCLUSION

From this experiment, we can conclude that this method is enormously effective for segregating garbage. The merchandise marker is an important attribute for differentiating between degradable and non-degradable garbage, as the non-degradable garbage mainly consists of man-made material having these, whereas the degradable garbage comprises of natural occurring substances. Along with its effectiveness, this method is faster than other methods [4]. Thus, making it immensely robust. The technique SURF is reliable for use as object identification algorithm.

KEYWORDS

- **digital image**
- **integral image generation**
- **research methodology**
- **scale-invariant feature transform**
- **speed up robust feature**

REFERENCES

1. Jain, A., (1989). *Fundamentals of Digital Image Processing, 1*, 1–569.
2. Madhuri, A. J., (2006). *Digital Image Processing: An Algorithmic Approach, 1*, 1–344.
3. Setiawan, W., Wahyudin, A., & Widianto, G. R., (2018). The use of scale-invariant feature transform (SIFT) algorithms to identification garbage images based on product label. *Proceeding-2017 3rd International Conference on Science in Information Technology: Theory and Application of IT for Education, Industry, and Society in Big Data Era, ICSITech, 2017*, 336–341.
4. Bay, H., Tuytelaars, T., & Van, G. L., (2006). SURF: Speeded up robust features. *Lecture Notes in Computer Science (Including Subseries Lecture Notes in Artificial Intelligence and Lecture Notes in Bioinformatics), 3951 LNCS*, 404–417.
5. Karami, E., Prasad, S., & Shehata, M., (2015). *Image Matching Using SIFT, SURF, BRIEF, and ORB: Performance Comparison for Distorted Images, 1*, 1–5.
6. Swapnali, B. B., & Vijay, K. S., (2014). Feature extraction using surf algorithm for object recognition. *International Journal of Technical Research and Applications, 2*(4), 197–199.
7. Lindeberg, T., (2015). Image matching using generalized scale-space interest points. *Journal of Mathematical Imaging and Vision, 52*(1). https://doi.org/10.1007/s10851-014-0541.

8. Kannan, S., Kumar, S., & Balakrishnan, R. R., (2016). Automatic garbage separation robot using image processing technique. *International Journal of Scientific and Research Publications, 6*(4), 326–328. www.ijsrp.org (accessed on 11 November 2021).

9. Aravindan, B., (2019). Automated domestic waste segregator using image processing. *International Research Journal of Engineering and Technology (IRJET),* 357–360.

10. Valente, M., Silva, H., Caldeira, J., Soares, V., & Gaspar, P., (2019). Detection of waste containers using computer vision. *Appl. Syst. Innov., 2*(1), 11.

11. Bay, H., Tuytelaars, T., & Gool, L. V., (2006). LNCS 3951-SURF: Speeded up robust features. *Computer Vision-ECCV 2006,* 404–417. http://link.springer.com/chapter/10.1007/11744023_32 (accessed on 11 November 2021).

12. Bommert, A., Rahnenführer, J., & Lang, M., (2017). A multicriteria approach to find predictive and sparse models with stable feature selection for high-dimensional data. *Computational and Mathematical Methods in Medicine, 2017.* https://doi.org/10.1155/2017/7907163.

13. Jain, A. K., (1989). *Fundamentals of Digital Image Processing* (p. 569). In: Vision.

14. Demirci, M. F., Shokoufandeh, A., Keselman, Y., Bretzner, L., & Dickinson, S., (2006). Object recognition as many-to-many feature matching. *Int. J. Comput. Vis. 69*(2), 203–222.

15. Lindeberg, T., (1998). Feature detection with automatic scale selection. *International Journal of Computer Vision, 30*(2), 79–116. https://doi.org/10.1023/A:1008045108935.

16. Chomat, O., De Verdiere, V., Hall, D., & Crowley, J., (2000). Local-scale selection for Gaussian based description techniques. In: *Proceedings European Conference on Computer Vision (ECCV 2000), Lecture Notes in Computer Science* (Vol. 1842, pp. I:117–133). Springer-Verlag, Dublin, Ireland.

17. Madhuri, A. J., (2006). *Digital Image Processing (Eastern Ec)*. PHI Learning.

18. Marr, D., (1976). Analyzing natural images: A computational theory of texture vision. In: *Cold Spring Harbor Symposia on Quantitative Biology* (Vol. 40, pp. 647–662). https://doi.org/10.1101/SQB.1976.040.01.060.

19. Marr, D., & Hildreth, E., (1980). Theory of edge detection. *Proceedings of the Royal Society of London-Biological Sciences, 207*(1167), 187–217. https://doi.org/10.1098/rspb.1980.0020.

20. Setiawan, W., Wahyudin, A., & Widianto, G. R., (2017). The use of scale-invariant feature transform (SIFT) algorithms to identification garbage images based on product label. *Proceeding-2017 3ʳᵈ International Conference on Science in Information Technology: Theory and Application of IT for Education, Industry, and Society in Big Data Era, ICSITech, 2017,* 336–341. https://doi.org/10.1109/ICSITech.2017.8257135.

21. Swapnali, B. B., & Vijay, K. S., (2014). Feature extraction using surf algorithm for object recognition. *International Journal of Technical Research and Applications, 2*(4), 2320–8163.

22. Lindeberg, T., (1994). *Scale-Space Theory in Computer Vision*. Springer, Berlin.

23. Harris, C., & Stephens, M., (1988) A combined corner and edge detector. In: *Alvey Vision Conference* (pp. 17–152)

24. Bretzner, L., & Lindeberg, T., (1998). Feature tracking with automatic selection of spatial scales. *Comput. Vis. Image Underst. 71*(3), 385–392.

25. Lowe, D., (1999). Object recognition from local scale-invariant features. In: *Proceedings of International Conference on Computer Vision (ICCV'99)* (pp. 1150–1157). Corfu, Greece.

26. Linde, O., & Lindeberg, T., (2004). Object recognition using composed receptive field histograms of higher dimensionality. In: *International Conference on Pattern Recognition* (Vol. 2, pp. 1–6). Cambridge.
27. Bretzner, L., & Lindeberg, T., (1998). Feature tracking with automatic selection of spatial scales. *Comput. Vis. Image Underst. 71*(3), 385–392.
28. Elsalamony, H.A.M. (2015) Comparing Proposed Signature with SURF in Object Detection Process, IETE Journal of Research, 61:5, 466-474, DOI: 10.1080/03772063.2015.1023371

CHAPTER 15

Evolution of Long Short-Term Memory (LSTM) in Air Pollution Forecasting

SATHEESH ABIMANNAN,[1] DEEPAK KOCHHAR,[2] YUE-SHAN CHANG,[3] and K. THIRUNAVUKKARASU[1]

[1]School of Computer Science and Engineering, Galgotias University, Uttar Pradesh, India, E-mail: satheesha23@gmail.com (S. Abimannan)

[2]School of Computer Science and Engineering, VIT, Vellore, Tamil Nādu, India

[3]Department of Computer Science and Information Engineering, National Taipei University, Taiwan

ABSTRACT

Long short-term memory (LSTM) networks are a tweaked version of the recurrent neural networks (RNN) that enable information persistence and fall under the deep learning domain. It's widely used in various applications, such as air pollution forecasting, flood forecasting, handwriting generation, language modeling, image captioning, question answering, video to text conversion, machine translation, etc. LSTM networks are used to process sequential data that involves the temporal correlation between a given data segment and its previous segment. The chapter starts with a discussion of the LSTM architecture, its variants, and its applications across various domains. The chapter also provides a comprehensive discussion of various types of LSTMs being used to solve the problem of air pollution forecasting, along with discussing a general pipeline used for the same.

15.1 RECURRENT NEURAL NETWORK

The recurrent neural networks (RNNs) are based on the work of David Rumelhart in 1986 [1]. RNN is a neural network branch, and a ML subset

(Figure 15.1). It remembers every piece of information through time. In time series prediction it is only useful to remember previous inputs also because of the feature. This is called long term short memory. RNNs are also used to expand the efficient neighborhood of pixels with convolutional layers.

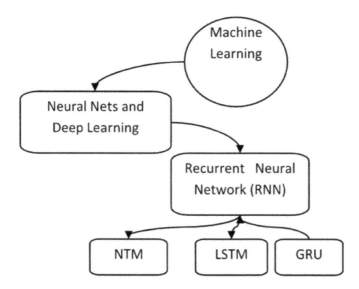

FIGURE 15.1   History of RNN.

RNNs are state-of-the-art sequential data algorithms used by Apple's Siri and Google voice search. RNNs were the first algorithm to retrieve its input from internal memory, making it an ideal fit for problems that involved sequential data. It is one of the algorithms behind the scenes of the incredible accomplishments seen in the last few years of deep learning (DL) (https://builtin.com/data-science/recurrent-neural-networks-and-lstm).

The applications of the RNN are machine translation, time-series analysis, speech recognition and synthesis, music generation, etc. Time forecasting is the most important application of RNN. The study of the time series includes methods of processing time-series data to derive useful statistics and other data characteristics. Time series forecasting is the use of a model to predict future values based on the values previously observed.

Neural Turing machine (NTM), Long short-term memory (LSTM), and Gated recurrent units (GRU) are a few types of RNN models. LSTM has three gates such as input, output, and forget gate. GRU has two gates such as reset and update gate and couples forget as well as input gates. GRU has fewer training parameters and thus consumes less memory, runs faster, and trains faster than LSTM, whereas LSTM is more reliable on the dataset using longer sequences.

More details on the LSTM functions, types, and application of Time Series Forecasting are discussed in further sections.

15.2   LONG SHORT-TERM MEMORY

LSTM [2] is a special kind of RNN that overcomes the vanishing gradient problem and enables information persistence through retaining relevant information for longer periods using its unique arrangement of *gates.* Unlike a normal neuron, an LSTM neuron unit comprises three gates, namely the input gate, the output gate, and the forget gate. These gates are responsible for controlling the flow of data entering and exiting the cell along with deciding parts of information to be retained across time-steps. The forget gate is responsible for deciding which information will be eliminated and which will be retained from the cell. The function of the forget gate is shown in (1) [3].

$$f_t = \sigma\left(W_f \cdot \left[h_{t-1}, x_t\right] + b_f\right) \tag{1}$$

where; W_f is the weight matrices; h_{t-1} is the hidden layer vector of the previous timestep (t–1); b_f is the bias vector parameters; and x_t is the input vector which is added into *Sigmoid* function S(t) to output a value between 0 and 1. The value 0 signifies that the information will be completely forgotten and thus won't be passed to the next stage, while the value 1 signifies that the entire information will be completely retained. The *Sigmoid* function S(t) is shown in (2),

$$S(t) = \frac{1}{1+e^{-t}} \tag{2}$$

Further, the input gate determines the new information to be retained in the given cell state along with the memorized information passed on from the forget gate. The function to determine how much of the new information the cell state needs to retain is shown in (3),

$$i_t = \sigma\left(W_i \cdot \left[h_{t-1}, x_t\right] + b_i\right) \tag{3}$$

Then, the value of i_t is between 0 and 1. It multiplies by i_t and election message $C\sim_t$ is represented in (4) to obtain the information which is to be added into the cell state C_t as shown in (5).

$$C\sim_t = tanh\left(W_C \cdot \left[h_{t-1}, x_t\right] + b_C\right) \tag{4}$$

$$C_t = f_t \times C_{t-1} + i_t \times C\sim_t \tag{5}$$

15.3 TYPES OF LSTM

Vanilla LSTM, stacked LSTM, CNN LSTM, encoder-decoder LSTM, bidirectional LSTM, and generative LSTM are the most important types of LSTMs. The vanilla LSTM consists of a single hidden LSTM layer followed by an activation function and a standard feedforward output layer. It consists of three gates called the input gate, the forget gate, and the output gate. The output of the LSTM block is connected in a recurrent fashion to the inputs of other blocks as well as the gates to control the flow of information. [4]

Gers et al. [5] introduced an adaptive forget gate in the vanilla LSTM that enabled the LSTM cells to reset themselves, thus eliminating the problem of processing continual input streams without explicitly marked sequence ends. Gers et al. [6] further proposed the augmentation of LSTM networks with the introduction of the *peephole connection.* The peephole connections made from internal cells to multiplicative gates allowed the gate layers to observe the internal cell states. This augmentation enabled the LSTMs to efficiently learn precise and stable timing algorithms despite the very uninformative target signals which change very rarely. These two modifications made the original LSTM that we use today. All the other LSTM types are the variants of this development and we mention them briefly below.

A Stacked LSTM variant has multiple hidden LSTM layers where each layer can contain multiple memory cells. The stacked LSTM approach is undertaken to build deep RNNs that are capable of learning complex non-linear sequential data patterns. In a stacked LSTM [7], the output from a lower layer of memory cells is connected to the upper layer of memory cells.

A CNN LSTM is an LSTM variant in which the CNN layers, namely convolutional and pooling layers are used for feature extraction from the data, these layers are followed by the LSTM model, which performs time series analysis of the features extracted by CNN layers. The CNN LSTM architecture enables the learning of spatial features through the CNN channel and the learning of temporal features through the LSTM channel.

The Encoder-Decoder LSTM is based on the RNN Encoder-Decoder system developed by Cho et al. for learning phrase representations [8]. The Encoder-Decoder LSTM variant consists of two LSTM networks namely the encoder and the decoder. The encoder LSTM is used to generate a summary of the input sequential data stream into the final cell state vector [9]. This encoded summary is a vector representation of a fixed length. This vector representation is fed into the decoder LSTM to initialize its cell state for output sequence generation. In the decoder LSTM, the outputs from the previous update are fed as input to the current update. The encoder and decoder LSTMs are jointly trained to model the conditional probability of the target data sequence given the input data sequence. Loss functions are used to maximize the conditional probability.

Schuster et al. introduced the bidirectional LSTMs or BiLSTMs in 1997. The Bidirectional LSTM variant is trained using all available input information in the past and future of a specific time frame [10]. The bidirectional LSTMs overcame the limitations of regular LSTMs of being able to utilize sequential data up to a specified time frame. The cell states in bidirectional LSTMs are split into the forward and backward states so as to enable training using all the available sequential data at once.

Generative LSTMs are not a new variant in terms of LSTM architecture. The name signifies LSTM's application as generative models that are used to learn sequential data patterns from a large data repository and generate new sequences that are representative of the original data. The generative model learns the probabilistic relationships between data points and then generalizes these patterns to generate new data sequences of its own. The generative LSTMs are widely used in language modeling, handwriting generation, music generation, speech generation.

15.4   APPLICATION OF LSTM

Recent developments in LSTMs and its variants have made it the state-of-the-art ubiquitous choice for a variety of applications. The ability of LSTMs to learn relations among data sequences have evolved them not only into efficient forecasting models but also generative models. LSTM networks can manage learning when and what to remember and when and what to forget. We will briefly discuss some of the interesting applications of LSTMs below.

15.4.1   *HANDWRITING RECOGNITION*

Handwriting recognition is one of the hardest problems to accomplish as it highly depends on contextual information and lexicon matching. We, humans, can recognize and differentiate handwritings comparatively easily because we can effectively map the context knitted within it. We can differentiate similar-looking characters as well. Although, there's a standard way to write each and every character, handwritings highly depend on individuals. Every individual's handwriting differs on various parameters such as stroke, curves, etc. (Figure 15.2). Sometimes, we can also guess words even if the writing is not clearly understood. We now understand how hard it becomes to even translate the necessary information for handwriting recognition into recognizable data patterns. The variety available is overwhelming. Over the years, multiple approaches have been developed to solve this problem, and LSTMs perform far better than any other algorithm. Multiple researchers have confirmed the accuracy of LSTMs in handwriting recognition. This is due to the fact that handwriting can also be represented as sequential data patterns. LSTMs learn relations between adjacent characters, curves, etc., by converting various handwriting parameters into multidimensional data. Recently, Carbune et al. [11] have developed an advanced handwriting recognition system at Google that leverages LSTM to support 102 languages. The researchers convert handwriting data to a 5-dimensional point including x-coordinate, y-coordinate, touchpoint timestamp, pen-up or pen-down, and stroke. Apart from this, they used Bézier Curves to present trajectories in space. Handwriting recognition finds useful applications in signature verification, document verification, etc.

FIGURE 15.2   Google handwriting recognition in Gboard.
Source: Reprint from: Ref. [26]; https://ai.google/.

15.4.2   HANDWRITING GENERATION

Handwriting generation is an inverted application of handwriting recognition using LSTMs. As we have discussed in previous sections, LSTMs can be used as generative models to generate sequences of data based on their learning of the probabilistic relationships between data points and then generalizing these patterns to further generate sequences. In Ref. [12] Alex Graves demonstrates how LSTM RNNs can be used to generate complex sequences with long-range structure, simply by predicting one data point at a time. The system developed by the researchers was able to generate highly realistic cursive handwriting in a wide variety of styles. The readers are suggested to get a hands-on real-time demo to experience this application of LSTMs here at-University of Toronto Handwriting Generation demo (https://www.cs.toronto.edu/~graves/handwriting.html). Figure 15.3 illustrates a sample of LSTM generated handwriting.

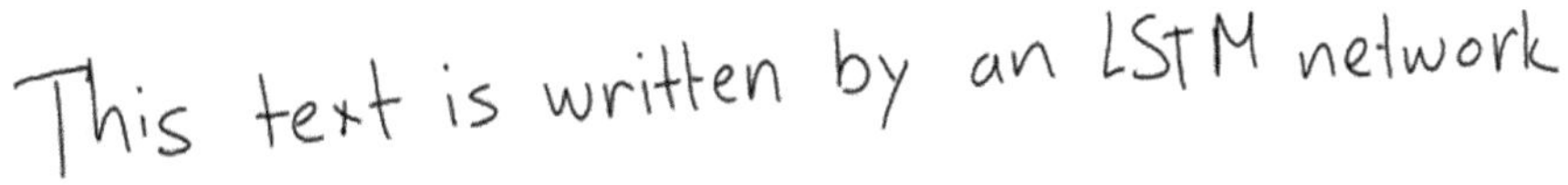

FIGURE 15.3   LSTM generated handwriting.

15.4.3   MUSIC GENERATION

Music generation is one of the most exciting applications of a generative LSTM model. This application was possible because music, just like text, can be represented as a sequence of notes. Due to the inherent ability to learn temporal data patterns, LSTMs can learn note-by-note transition probabilities which enables them to model music structure. Douglas Eck and Jurgen Schmidhuber [13] presented the first look at music composition using LSTM RNNs in 2002. The researchers present experimental results of LSTM learning a form of music and composing novel melodies of the same style. The readers are suggested to take a look at LSTM generated melodies here at-LSTM generated music (http://www.hexahedria.com/files/nnet_music_2.mp3).

15.4.4 TEXT GENERATION

Text generation is another exciting application of generative LSTMs. It can learn the sequences of a text corpus and then generate entirely new data sequences. The language model is the core element of natural text generation. A statistical language model is a probability distribution over sequences of words. It assigns a probability for the likelihood of a given word/sequence of words to follow a sequence of words. Given the input text sequence, with LSTMs we can build a generative model that generates natural language text. After performing tokenization on the input text sequence, we generate a sequence of tokens with uniform lengths (padding applied) to be fed into the LSTM model. With this, the model learns to relate adjacent words/phrases and develops a probability score of next word occurrence based on the input received till that point. Recently, many researchers and developers across the globe have implemented this application using a variety of text corpora including Shakespeare's literature, famous novels, songs, scripts, etc., and found that the generative LSTMs can learn the associated language model very effectively and reproduce plausible results in a fashion strikingly similar to with which it was trained.

While we are in this section, we would like to share some information about *Benjamin*. Benjamin is a self-improving LSTM RNN machine intelligence, trained on the human screenplay which authored a 2016 experimental science fiction short film called sunspring. The script is again a sequence of characters and LSTMs are now a pioneer in learning and absorbing that sequence. With enough quality data, we are now capable of generating sensible movie scripts with LSTM. Our readers are encouraged to experience this amazing application by watching the movie authored by LSTM here at Sunspring (https://youtu.be/LY7x2Ihqjmc).

15.4.5 IMAGE AND VIDEO CAPTIONING

Automated image and video captioning is an amazing example of CNN LSTMs in which the CNN module learns the spatial features which are coupled with temporal feature learning by generative LSTMs to produce relevant captions for images and videos (Figure 15.4). LSTMs consists of a memory cell that maintains the information for a longer period of time which is critical when associating visuals from the image/video to relevant captions. The CNN module in this architecture is also termed as an Encoder because it encodes large image content to a small prominent feature vector. This feature is then fed to the Decoder or LSTM module which decodes this feature vector and associates it to a sequence of words or captions. The normal process of building such a model involves image inputs with each image containing several captions. The CNN LSTM model learns to associate various image points along with relevant captions. Automated image and video captioning is a very exciting application that comes in handy for a variety of applications including but not limited to closed captioning or subtitle generation, real-time scene description for assistive devices for visually impaired people, etc.

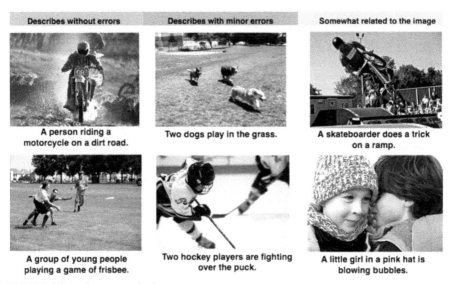

FIGURE 15.4   Image captioning.
Source: Reprint from: Ref. [25]; https://www.oreilly.com/library/view/deep-learning-for/9781788295628/assets/f5c8ceb8–5a77–4f81–8578-ff1458b4268c.png.

15.4.6   LANGUAGE TRANSLATION

Language translation can be achieved through LSTM's sequence to sequence model. The data consists of data tuples of the original and translated language (Figure 15.5). These are then cleaned and tokenized to calculate the word embeddings. The word embeddings are fed to the encoder LSTM. The encoder passes the last state of its recurrent layer to the decoder LSTM. The decoder initializes its first layer with the inputs fed from the encoder's last layer. The decoder LSTM outputs the sequence of translated words that we want. The entire pipeline is optimized through error rate reduction over multiple epochs.

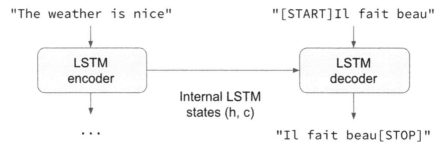

FIGURE 15.5   Language translation using LSTM.
Source: Reprint from: https://blog.keras.io/img/seq2seq/seq2seq-teacher-forcing.png.

15.4.7   *FLOOD FORECASTING*

Floods cause a significant loss of life and property and can cause huge social and economic losses. It strongly affects the locations around the river downstream. Flood mitigation and accurate forecasting become the need of the hour. The traditional methods involve simulation of the hydrodynamic process of the water's flow through mathematical models. These models fail to gain decent accuracy due to data limitation and longer computational times. Daily discharge and rainfall measures can be used to perform a time series analysis for flood forecasting using LSTMs. The LSTM data-driven model can very efficiently learn linear and non-linear patterns of the data and thus offer a promising alternative to the existing mathematical models for the hydrological forecast of streamflow. In [14] Xuan-Hien Le et al. used LSTM to forecast one-day, two-day, and three-day flood flow at the Hoa Binh Station on the Da River, Vietnam. The LSTM model was not dependent on data such as land-use and topography for rainfall-runoff simulation which strengthens its ubiquitous applications. The LSTM model only used data collected at the target station and the upstream meteorological and hydrological stations to forecast the flowrate at the target station. The LSTM model efficiently learned long-term relationships between the sequential series of data and strongly demonstrated reliable outputs and results.

While we have discussed some amazing applications of LSTM in the section above and we can now quite easily realize their power and proficiency to solve complex problems, there are numerous other applications that establish the supremacy of LSTMs. Discussing various LSTM based approaches and analyzing their performance to forecast air pollution is our main focus of this work which we will continue to discuss in detail in the upcoming sections.

15.5 CASE STUDY: AIR POLLUTION FORECASTING

In this section, we begin with a discussion on air pollution forecasting and related terminology and concepts. Followed by this is a section which presents a discussion on general steps involved in a forecasting problem. In the next section, we discuss the data analysis pipeline before moving on to the next section presenting a comprehensive discussion on various LSTM based methods, their architectures, and their implementation methodology for air pollution forecasting.

15.5.1 AIR POLLUTION FORECASTING

The rapid advancements of modern technologies and innovations have no doubt made the world a better place today, but it has also introduced several life-threatening factors as well. Adverse ecological effects such as air contamination are one of them. As we progressed the development of our society socially and technically, advancements in the fields such as transportation, industry, etc., soon coupled with the emission of harmful particulate matter in high concentrations into the atmosphere thereby causing severe health hazards to life on the planet. PM 2.5 is the particulate matter in the atmosphere that is two and one-half microns in size. These fine particles pose the greatest health risk as they can penetrate into the lungs and bloodstream and also have a strong correlation with the effects of cardiovascular disease (CVD). Growing cases of ailments and deaths due to air pollution worldwide proves how deadly these are. Thus, it becomes the need of the hour to develop highly efficient systems that can forecast air pollution with high accuracy and reliability.

In the last few years, severe air pollution and environmental issues have gained global concern due to their adverse effect on the health and well-being of people [15]. As a result, air pollution forecasting has garnered the interest of the research community globally. It is a well-established fact that forecasting air quality and pollution levels for a monitoring station is a problem hard to crack as it is influenced by multiple factors. Air quality is determined by a variety of influences, such as vehicular exhausts, chemical, and industrial pollution, coal combustion, dust, and smoke, urban pollution, community transport, environmental factors, etc. [16]. These factors vary in terms of spatial distributions and temporal patterns and are thus time-dependent on each other, values of a given factor can influence other factors over time or can be influenced by other factors over time. It becomes very difficult to model these data sequences with traditional data models. The accuracy of these traditional data models suffers a lot due to the inability to accommodate the factors varying in time and space. With advanced developments in the DL domain over the years, air quality forecasting with DL has become an active field of research. LSTMs networks have emerged as state-of-the-art RNNs for air pollution forecasting as they are capable of learning time-varying data patterns and thus are highly effective in providing accurate forecasts.

Reliable, accurate, and timely air pollution forecasting plays a crucial role in the air quality management system. We can make use of that in creating *health alerts* for the people so that they can take precautionary measures and have their activities planned accordingly. We can supplement the existing emission control programs to control the emissions across various activities to avoid worsening the situation. Likewise, we can achieve operational planning of a lot of activities that directly or indirectly depends on the air quality, such as sports events, travel, and tourism arrangements, etc.

15.5.2   STEPS FOR FORECASTING

While the various implementations differ with the algorithm being used for air pollution forecasting, the standard pipeline and steps remain the same. Various stages of building a forecasting model generally consist of data acquisition pipeline, data pre-processing or ETL pipeline, feature engineering pipeline, the ML or DL module, the model performance module, and the deployment module. We discuss each of these in subsections.

15.5.2.1   DATA ACQUISITION

The data acquisition or the data collection pipeline is responsible for pooling data from multiple sources and creating a data lake. Some possible data sources for air pollution-related datasets can be local station data, neighboring station data, international station data, emission data including household, industrial, and transport, etc. The data ownership can be either government or private, but the data should ideally be updated with high frequency such as hourly or bi-hourly updates. The acquired data can consist of multiple attributes such as $PM_{2.5}$, PM_{10}, SO_2, O_3, NO_x, CO, rainfall, humidity, date-day-time, month, season, temperature, wind speed and direction [16] for air pollution. The data sources are preferred to be multiple so as to build a comprehensive data repository of high quality that can contain a wide variety of scenarios as this data will directly affect the performance of our model.

15.5.2.2   DATA PRE-PROCESSING

The acquired data comes from different sources and thus might not be in a single standard format. The data might also suffer from missing values or bias due to reasons such as instrumental error, manual entries, and invalid values, etc., along with varying orders of magnitude among attributes of the same data source. Thus, the acquired data is usually not in a direct consumable format and requires various preprocessing and cleaning functions to achieve standard data points.

The missing data values are imputed using various standard techniques such as mean imputation, regression imputation, clustered imputation, etc. The non-numeric attributes are brought to numeric using encoding techniques such as label encoders or one hot encoder. Once the entire data is numeric, we check for the bias and order of magnitudes in various data attributes. We then perform data normalization and data standardization to bring data to the same level. Data normalization and data standardization are essential because otherwise, the attribute with a higher order of magnitude will get more importance by the forecasting model, and the attributes with a lower order of magnitude will get suppressed in the model even if they are very important indicators. This also eliminates different measuring units and makes data a pure dimensionless quantity. The data is also to be transformed into a time series format for LSTM implementations. This is the general pipeline that makes data fit for downstream computations.

15.5.2.3   FEATURE ENGINEERING

Feature engineering is an applied ML methodology of using domain knowledge to identify prominent features from the feature pool. It is pretty obvious that few attributes might have a greater influence on the outcomes than other attributes. These prominent features should be given higher weightage in building the forecasting model. Feature engineering is performed to identify such features using data mining and pattern recognition techniques. Correlation analysis of feature and target vectors is also performed to get a sense of correlation, for example, various studies reveal that ozone, PM10, and PM2.5 share a strong correlation value. Apart from this, some features can be derived from the existing features to better the forecasting model performance. The engineered features are then fed to the downstream pipeline of ML or deep learning modules.

15.5.2.4   MODEL IMPLEMENTATION

As discussed, LSTMs are state-of-the-art models for time series forecasting. Air pollution forecasting comes under the same domain and thus LSTMs and its variants have pioneered this work as evident from various implementations that are discussed in detail in the upcoming sections. The data is first divided into the independent and target feature set and then split into training, testing, and validation sets. The clean and engineered numeric air pollution data in time series format is fed to the LSTM model which is trained with various hyperparameters with constant accuracy check. The hyperparameters are tuned with every cycle to further enhance accuracy. Various methods such as dropout regularization (developed by *Google*) are used for reducing overfitting in the forecasting model. The dropout method drops units out of the neural network to prevent complex co-adaptations on the training data. Apart from the dropout regularization, other regularization techniques such as Lasso (L1) and Ridge (L2) regularization are also used, these are decided based on the use case. The best performing model is saved and used for predicting final values. The predicted values are mapped and tested against the original values to benchmark model performance based on parameters such as accuracy, precision, recall, *f1*-score, root mean square error (RMSE), mean absolute error (MAE), mean absolute percentage error (MAPE), etc.

15.5.2.5   MODEL DEPLOYMENT

After achieving a considerable accuracy and performing necessary testing of the forecasting model, it can be deployed to the air quality monitoring weather stations and used to predict target values such as PM2.5 values for the real-time data input. The model can also be further trained on the newly acquired data points to perform learning on the fly. The model can be deployed to forecast values for a duration such as 1 to 8 hours. The real-time performance of the deployed models can be achieved by doing a quantitative and qualitative analysis of the model predicted values and the actual values.

15.6 METHODS

In this section, we will discuss in detail various variants of LSTM, their architecture, and their implementation for air pollution forecasting.

15.6.1 VANILLA LSTM

The Vanilla LSTM contains a single hidden LSTM layer accompanied by an activation function (AF) and a standard feedforward output layer. It consists of three gates called the input gate, the output gate, and the forget gate. The output of the LSTM block is connected in a recurrent fashion to the inputs of other blocks as well as the gates to control the flow of information [4]. The vanilla LSTMs eliminate the vanishing gradient, exploding gradient, and long-term dependency problem of the RNN by the introduction of the memory blocks. The memory unit comprises the memory cell, multiplicative gates as its input and output, and a constant error carousel value that remains active across the time step. Multiplicative gates control all the operations of the memory unit whereas the input gate checks the cell activation to control the flow of input into the memory unit. The flow of the output into other units is managed by the output gate.

15.6.1.1 VANILLA LSTM ARCHITECTURE

As discussed, the vanilla LSTM consists of three gates, namely the input gate, the forget gate, and the output gate. We present a brief discussion on each of them below:

1. **The Forget Gate:** It receives the outputs of the previous cell state, $h(t-1)$. The forget gate takes the decision of eliminating the irrelevant information from $h(t-1)$ and forward only the relevant information. The forget gate includes a sigmoid AF which generates an output

between 0 and 1 for any given input. This sigmoid value decides the amount of information to be retained from the previous state. The forget gate is multiplied with the previous cell state using the sigmoid output to forget the information chunk that becomes irrelevant. It is represented as (Figure 15.6).

$$f_t = \sigma(W_f.[h_{t-1}, x_t] + b_f \tag{6}$$

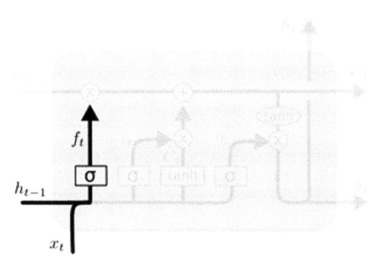

FIGURE 15.6   Vanilla LSTM-forget gate.
Source: Reprint from: https://colah.github.io/posts/2015–08-Understanding-LSTMs/img/LSTM3-focus-f.png.

2. **The Input Gate:** It is used to manage the addition of new information (input) from the present input to the present cell state. It includes the *sigmoid* layer and *tanh* layer; the sigmoid layer decides which values to be updated and the *tanh* layer creates a vector for new candidates to add to the present cell state (Figure 15.7).

$$i_t = \sigma(W_i.[h_{t-1}, x_t] + b_i \tag{7}$$

$$C_t = \tanh(W_C.[h_{t-1}, x_t] + b_C \tag{8}$$

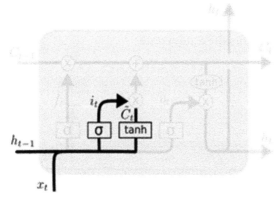

FIGURE 15.7   Vanilla LSTM-Input gate (*Source*: Reprint from https://colah.github.io/posts/2015–08-Understanding-LSTMs/img/LSTM3-focus-i.png).

3. **The Output Gate:** It is used to decide what to present as output from the cell state. It is again controlled by a sigmoid function. The input is multiplied with the *tanh* activation to bring the values between (–1,1) which is then multiplied with the sigmoid output to create the relevant final output (Figure 15.8).

$$O_t = \sigma(W_o[h_{t-1}, x_t] + b_o \tag{9}$$

$$h_t = o_t \times \tanh(C_t) \tag{10}$$

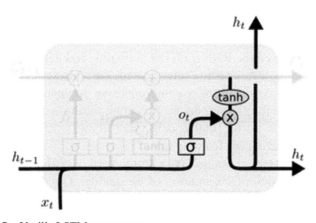

FIGURE 15.8   Vanilla LSTM-output gate.
Source: Reprint from: https://colah.github.io/posts/2015–08-Understanding-LSTMs/img/LSTM3-focus-o.png.

These three gates make up the LSTM architecture. Figure 15.9 shows a single LSTM unit. The f_t represents the forget gate, i_t represents the input gate and the o_t represents the output gate.

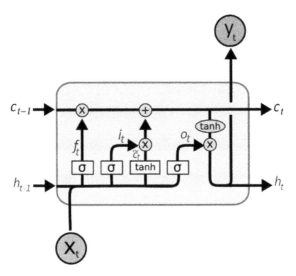

FIGURE 15.9   LSTM cell.

Source: Reprint from: https://www.researchgate.net/profile/   Antoine_Tixier/ publication/327303180/figure/fig8/AS:665167033561091@1535599587965/The-LSTM-unit-Adapted-from-Chris-Colahs-blog.png.

15.6.1.2   *AIR POLLUTION FORECASTING USING VANILLA LSTM*

In DeepAirNet: Applying recurrent networks for air quality prediction [16], Athira et al. have used the RNNs, LSTM networks, and gated recurrent unit (GRU) for building a forecasting model using the time series AirNet data. The researchers also performed a comprehensive comparative analysis to identify the best performing model by executing multiple experiments. The experiments ran for up to 1000 epochs each along with hyperparameter tuning such as adjusting the learning rate.

The AirNet dataset contained data from April 1, 2015, to September 1, 2017, and consisted of six indexes of air quality. The data consisted of 10,593,856 samples and pollutants such as PM_{10}, $PM_{2.5}$, NO_2, CO, O_3, SO_2, AQI. The data was acquired from 1498 facilities of the China national environmental monitoring center (CNEMC). Along with this, the meteorological data were obtained from the global forecasting system (GFS) which was released every 6 hours. The data was preprocessed and normalized before being fed to the LSTM model. RMSprop optimizer coupled with the mean square error (MSE) loss function was used with the target feature for prediction as PM_{10}. The hyperparameters such as the learning rate, epochs, and the batch size were fine-tuned to get maximum accuracy. Performance metrics used for benchmarking model performance were root mean square error (RMSE) and MAPE. Models with small RMSE indicate better performance.

   In the study, the authors analyzed three kinds of models namely RNNs, LSTMs, and GRUs for air pollution forecasting. RMSE and MAPE metrics were computed for all three models and the values achieved were found to be analogous. RNN gave RMSE = 0.40 and MAPE = 0.57, LSTM gave RMSE = 0.40 and MAPE = 0.52 and the GRU gave RMSE = 0.40 and MAPE = 0.45. The GRU model performed slightly better than the LSTM model but the performance of all the models was very well. In Section 15.7, we discuss the performance metrics such as RMSE and MAPE in detail.

15.7   STACKED LSTM

A Stacked LSTM is a vanilla LSTM variant with several hidden LSTM layers where multiple memory cells can be contained in each layer. The stacked LSTM approach is undertaken to build deep RNNs that are capable of learning complex non-linear sequential data patterns. In a stacked LSTM [7], the output from a lower layer of memory cells is connected to the upper layer of memory cells. The stacking of the LSTM hidden layers introduces depth in the model which brings representational optimization and thus enhances the model accuracy. The multiple hidden layers reconstitute the trained representation from previous layers and construct new representations at high abstraction levels [17].

15.7.1   STACKED LSTM ARCHITECTURE

The Stacked LSTM architecture consists of a chain of LSTMs that are stacked on top of each other with the layer getting input which is the output of the previous layer. The upper-level activations in the stacked LSTMs can be accessed to construct the outputs, and hence they should contain all the relevant short term information for the current prediction. As we know that LSTMs model the sequential data and thus addition of multiple layers adds levels of abstraction of input observations over time thereby denoting the problem at different time scales. This method empowers the hidden LSTM states at each level to function at different timescales. The Stacked LSTM architecture is discussed below. The architecture of the basic LSTM cell remains the same as we have discussed in the previous section (Figure 15.10).

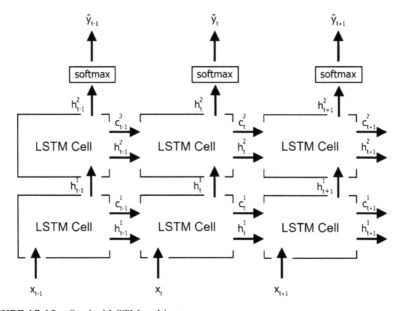

FIGURE 15.10   Stacked LSTM architecture.
Source: Reprint from: Ref. [26]. ©2018, IOS Press.

15.7.2   *AIR POLLUTION FORECASTING USING STACKED LSTM*

In the study, time series based LSTM model to predict air pollutant's concentration for Prominent cities in India [18] researchers at the Samsung Research Institute India have used a stacked LSTM model for predicting pollutant concentration. They model the task of predicting pollutant concentration as a time series problem in which the pollutant levels at the current time step depends on the pollutant levels, meteorological, traffic data, festivals, and national holidays data of the previous time step. The authors identify a set of distinguishing features to predict AQI along with pollutant levels for the next *n* hours and further perform a series of experiments to validate their solution.

The suggested stacked LSTM system demonstrated high performance with the mean RMSE score of pollutant level fewer than 15 for the next

12-hour forecast, an RMSE score of fewer than 8 for the next six-hour forecast, and RMSE score of fewer than five for the next one-hour forecast. This framework was tested against the data acquired in real-time from the Central Pollution Control Board, India. The data used to build the forecasting model was obtained from Delhi and Agra stations for a duration of approximately three months. The authors have used the RMSE performance metric for model evaluation which gave the difference between the actual and the predicted values by the model. The optimizers used in the study are Adam optimizer and the SGD gradient descent optimization algorithm.

Based on multiple experiments conducted, the authors hypothesize that the meteorological factors and pollutant concentration are directly correlated and the meteorological factors greatly influence the pollutant concentration. The levels of CO showed a strong inverse correlation with temperature and a direct correlation with wind speed. Traffic conditions also showed a correlation with the Co and NO_2 concentrations. Festivals involving crackers and colors also influenced the pollution level by exhibiting elevated levels at the time. The PM 2.5 and PM10 concentration levels were found to be less on weekends. The data was duly cleaned and arranged into a time-series format. The categorical variables were encoded into numerical values, and the data was further scaled using *MinMaxScaler*. Random forest (RF) was used to identify the feature importance in predicting a given pollutant level. This data was then fed to the stacked LSTM model for predicting the concentration of pollutants and forecasting the air quality index (AQI).

The results obtained for the stacked LSTM framework demonstrated high accuracy. The predicted AQI values were found to be almost exact to the actual values. Table 15.1 shows the results obtained from this study. As it is evident from the table that the accuracy of prediction for the next one hour is better than the next 6th and 12th hour.

TABLE 15.1 RMSE Values for Both the Experimental Locations

Station	Forecast Hour	NO_2	SO_2	$PM_{2.5}$	PM_{10}	O_3	CO
S. P, Agra	Next 1 hr.	0.6	1	2.513	NA	0.43	1.7
	Next 6 hr.	0.86	1.8	6.82	NA	0.86	11.3
	Next 12 hr.	2.4	3.79	11.4	NA	1.67	15.4
ITO, Delhi	Next 1 hr.	2.0	NA	3.183	4.29	NA	NA
	Next 6 hr.	4.06	NA	12.37	5.8	NA	NA
	Next 12 hr.	10.8	NA	17.58	7.19	NA	NA

Source: Reprinted from: Ref. [18].

15.7.3   CNN LSTM

A CNN-LSTM is an LSTM variant originally called the long-term recurrent convolutional network in which the convolutional neural network (CNN) layers namely convolutional and pooling layers are used for feature extraction from the data, these layers are followed by the LSTM network which performs time series analysis of the features extracted by CNN layers. The CNN LSTM architecture enables the learning of spatial features through the CNN channel and the learning of temporal features through the LSTM channel. The CNNs are excellent at minimizing frequency variations and LSTMs are excellent at temporal modeling [19], and thus their unified architecture provides results better than the individual models.

15.7.3.1   CNN LSTM ARCHITECTURE

The CNN channel of the CNN-LSTM method consists of convolutional and pooling layers arranged into a stack. The convolutional layers perceive spatial information from the input data, this interpretation will be further consolidated or abstracted by the pooling layer. The convolution and pooling stack eventually generates a vector representation of the input sequence using a fully connected layer. LSTM channel is fed with this vector representation as a time-step input to build its internal cell state and weights for temporal learnings. The CNN used can or cannot be a pre-trained model. In the case of a pre-trained model, CNN needs not to be trained otherwise, we need to train CNN by the back-propagating error from LSTM. The high-level architecture of a CNN-LSTM method is shown in Figure 15.11. A thorough discussion on CNNs is beyond the scope of this work, but readers are encouraged to go through the paper ImageNet Classification with Deep Convolutional Neural Networks (DCNN) by Krizhevsky, Sutskever, and Hinton [20] to get a deeper understanding of CNNs. Further, readers can explore ConvNet Playground (https://convnetplayground.fastforwardlabs.com/#/models) for building intuition on how CNNs work.

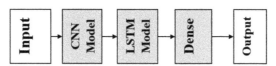

FIGURE 15.11   CNN LSTM high-level architecture.
Source: Reprint from: https://machinelearningmastery.com/cnn-long-short-term-memory-networks/.

15.7.3.2 AIR POLLUTION FORECASTING USING CNN LSTM

The existing research methodologies haven't been successful in extracting the spatiotemporal attributes of pollutants concentration data, thereby failing to achieve high precision and accuracy. In *a novel spatiotemporal convolutional long short-term neural network for air pollution prediction* [21]. Wen et al. have used a convolutional LSTM neural network extended (C-LSTME) model for forecasting the air quality. The researchers used historical air pollutant concentration of the current facility along with the data from adaptive k-nearest neighboring (KNN) stations to build the forecasting model. The model performance was enhanced by making use of the aerosol and meteorological data. The $PM_{2.5}$ concentration values were acquired hourly from 1200+ monitoring stations for air quality from the Ministry of Environmental Protection of China during a time span of 1st January 2016 to 31st December 2017. In order to establish the $PM_{2.5}$ concentration spatiality attribute, the researchers calculated the Pearson correlation coefficient (CC) and Euclidean distance between neighboring stations. It was found that the correlation scores obtained were more than 0.56 which ascertains the fact that pollutant concentration at a given station is correlated with the values at the neighboring stations. Thus, neighboring stations should also be used to increase the accuracy of the existing station's forecasts. Due to the difference in the number of relevant neighboring stations, the researchers used adaptive k-nearest neighboring stations to study spatiotemporal correlation. 3D CNN-stateful LSTM model was used to obtain spatiotemporal attributes of the data from the spatiotemporal matrix obtained after the adaptive KNN operation. These spatiotemporal features thus obtained were represented by an N*1 feature vector. The spatiotemporal eigenvectors were combined with the auxiliary data using a connected layer. The performance metrics used in the study are root mean square error (RMSE), mean absolute error (MAE), and MAPE (MAPE). The R^2 value achieved was found to be 92% and the overall air quality rank prediction accuracy was found to be 87.6%. Tables 15.2 and 15.3 show a comparison of different methods using the above-mentioned performance metrics. From the table, we observe that the CNN-LSTM (C-LSTME) model outperformed all other state-of-the-art models.

TABLE 15.2 Comparison of the Mean Absolute Error of Different Models

MAE($\mu g/m^3$)	1st Hour	2nd Hour	3rd Hour	4th Hour	5th Hour	6th Hour
C-LSTME	5.77	8.85	10.31	11.60	12.25	14.00
LSTME	7.01	9.37	10.44	12.65	15.94	17.96
ST-DNN	7.36	10.83	11.15	14.17	15.35	16.43
LSTM	7.86	10.05	11.59	14.49	15.82	16.22
Zheng	12.73	14.67	18.27	22.94	26.25	28.37
ARMA	18.54	19.47	21.85	23.64	25.81	28.51
SVR	26.79	30.77	33.69	35.74	37.37	38.21
LR	34.27	35.59	37.15	38.41	39.68	40.25

Source: Reprint with permission from Ref. [21]. © 2018 Elsevier.

TABLE 15.3 Comparison of the Performance Using: RMSE, MAE, and MAPE

Method	RSME ($\mu g/m^3$)	MAE ($\mu g/m^3$)	MAPE (%)
C-LSTME	12.08	5.82	17.09
LSTME	17.76	8.02	21.93
ST-DNN	18.25	8.48	22.82
LSTM	21.17	10.57	25.38
Zheng	22.22	11.09	29.93
ARMA	25.95	12.48	30.89
SVR	34.40	28.05	37.54
LR	39.92	29.98	37.23

Source: Reprint with permission from Ref. [21]. © 2018 Elsevier.

15.7.4 ENCODER-DECODER LSTM

The encoder-decoder LSTM is built on RNN Encoder-Decoder developed by Cho et al. for learning phrase representations [8]. The encoder-decoder LSTM variant consists of two LSTM networks namely the encoder and the decoder. The encoder LSTM is used to generate a summary of the input sequential data stream into the final cell state vector [9]. This encoded summary is a vector representation of a fixed length. This vector representation is fed into the decoder LSTM to initialize its cell state for output sequence generation. In the decoder LSTM, the outputs of the last update are passed as input to the current update. The encoder and the decoder LSTMs collectively undergo training to model the conditional probability of the target data sequence given the input data. Loss functions are used to maximize the conditional probability.

15.7.4.1   ENCODER-DECODER LSTM ARCHITECTURE

The encoder-decoder LSTM [22] consists of two LSTM models namely the *encoder* and the *decoder*. The encoder encodes the input data sequence into a fixed-length vector whereas the decoder decodes this fixed-length vector and outputs a predicted sequence, hence the name encoder-decoder LSTM model (Figure 15.12). These models are specifically designed for seq2seq problems. For a given data sequence vector $d = (d_1, ..., d_T)$, the encoder LSTM reads this input and creates a context vector c_i using some nonlinear functions. The decoder consumes this context vector c_i along with all the previously predicted values to predict the value y.' A typical decoder defines a probability over the prediction y by decomposing the joint probability into the conditional order using a nonlinear multi-layered function.

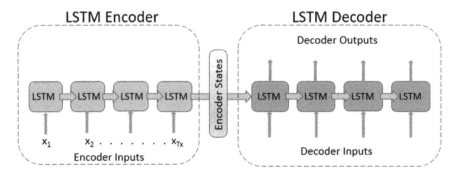

FIGURE 15.12   Encoder-decoder LSTM architecture.
Source: Reprint from: Ref. [28]; https://towardsdatascience.com/time-series-forecasting-with-deep-stacked-unidirectional-and-bidirectional-lstms-de7c099bd918.

15.7.4.2   AIR POLLUTION FORECASTING USING ENCODER-DECODER LSTM

In "*A DL Approach for Forecasting Air Pollution in South Korea Using LSTM*" [23], Tien-Cuong et al. performed research to study the performance of Encoder-Decoder LSTM networks for building $PM_{2.5}$ air quality index (AQI) forecasting models based on time series data. Adam algorithm was used as an optimizer in their study as it outperforms the stochastic gradient descent (SGD) in terms of faster convergence and lower error ratios. The dataset used in the study was pooled from multiple sources for a duration of July 2008 to April 2018. The sources included World Weather Online (https://www.worldweatheronline.com/) and Air Korea, Seoul Clean Air, Chinese PM2.5 report, and Daegu Environment Government private APIs. The data was brought into a consumable format by performing ETL operations and transforming context features into vectors where each vector signified a 1-hour timestamp. The Daegu dataset was split into two classes due to missing data, the first consisted of data from January 2015 to June 2017 and the second one consisted of June 2017 to March 2018. The first model was trained on the first class of data using Encoder-Decoder LSTM and the learned weights were used as a transfer learning component to train the model on the second data class. This prevented training the second model from scratch and thus saved a lot of computational and time resources. The model was tested on the data from the period of February to March 10th, 2018. On the other hand, the Seoul dataset contained complete information from January 2008 to April 2018, with more than 2 million records corresponding to hourly records of 25 districts. Data from 2008 to 2016 from the Seoul dataset was used to train the model, which was further tested on the data from January 2017 to April 2018. It was revealed from the $PM_{2.5}$ AQI Seoul data that the pollutant level peaked in January while substantially on the rise from October to March of a given year. The researchers also found that the $PM_{2.5}$ AQI values varied slightly for a shorter time-span ($<= 5$ hours) and hence the idea is to forecast pollution levels for longer terms. Tables 15.4 and 15.5 obtained from the original work of the authors that demonstrate the performance of Encoder-Decoder LSTMs for air pollution forecasting.

TABLE 15.4   RMSE Values of Different Settings

Model Settings	8 h	12 h	16 h	20 h	24 h
TF + RNN + MAE	**12.41**	13.48	14.48	14.42	17.30
TF + RNN$_s$ + MAE	13.47	**13.19**	**12.85**	**12.79**	**13.54**
Joint + RNN + MAE	13.84	13.18	13.19	13.16	13.79
Joint + RNN$_s$ + MAE	15.17	14.82	14.71	14.85	15.12
TF + RNN + MSE	13.96	13.51	13.47	13.43	14.02
Joint + RNN + MSE	13.73	13.24	13.10	13.30	14.47
TF + RNN$_s$ + MSE	14.26	14.34	14.02	13.89	15.20
Joint + RNN$_s$ + MSE	15.99	15.18	14.76	14.58	14.85

Source: Reprint from: Ref. [23].

Table 15.4 reveals that using MAE in the training model is more effective than MSE, and the transfer method is appropriate for the Daegu dataset. The combination of multiple RNN layers model, MAE loss function, and transfer methods provide outstanding prediction results [23].

TABLE 15.5   Test RMSE for 2017–2018 with Different Settings

Model Settings	8 h	12 h	16 h	20 h	24 h
Joint dataset + RNN$_s$	26.27	27.08	28.61	29.97	31.29
Joint dataset + RNN	25.93	27.61	29.05	30.21	31.52
Seoul dataset + RNN$_s$	27.51	28.49	29.66	30.6	31.8

Source: Reprinted from: Ref. [23]. https://creativecommons.org/licenses/by/4.0/

Table 15.5 presents that a single RNN model performs efficiently only on forecasting 8 hours. In conclusion, utilizing a robust model and joining complete China-related features to training vectors provide the highest accuracies [23].

15.7.5   BIDIRECTIONAL LSTM

Schuster et al. introduced the bidirectional LSTMs or BiLSTMs in 1997. The Bidirectional LSTM variant uses the input in the past and future of a specific time-step for training [10]. The bidirectional LSTMs overcame the limitations of regular LSTMs of being able to utilize sequential data up to a specified time frame. The cell states in bidirectional LSTMs are split into the forward and backward states so as to enable training using all the available sequential data at once.

15.7.5.1   BIDIRECTIONAL LSTM ARCHITECTURE

The bidirectional LSTM architecture (Figure 15.13) basically consists of two independent LSTMs (RNNs) put together so as to allow the model to have both forward and backward data sequence at every time step. Such an arrangement makes it possible to process inputs in two manners; past → future and future → past. The uniqueness of the bidirectional method is the backward run of the LSTM that preserves learnings from the future, and making use of the two hidden states together, we are able to preserve information from both past and future at any point in time. The additional backward run provides extra context to the LSTM to learn the data sequences.

The stacked BiLSTM layers help in capturing the hierarchical attributes in the temporal domain better, thereby enabling utilization of both the past and the future impact on the final forecast.

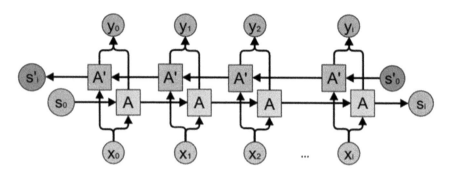

FIGURE 15.13   Bidirectional LSTM.
Source: Reprint from: https://medium.com/@raghavaggarwal0089/bi-lstm-bc3d68da8bd0.

15.7.5.2   *AIR POLLUTION FORECASTING USING BIDIRECTIONAL LSTM*

In "*Air pollutant severity prediction using Bi-directional LSTM Network*" [24], a team of researchers at TCS research, India has forecasted the pollutant severity level using a bi-directional LSTM model. The researchers built a $PM_{2.5}$ severity level ensemble forecasting model. The ensemble model is comprised of three bi-LSTMs to model the long-term, short-term, and immediate effects. The novelty of their approach was to predict severity level or category rather than actual values. This approach to predict discretized values is sufficient for pollution-related planning and significantly improves the prediction accuracy as well. The data consisted of $PM_{2.5}$, PM_{10}, NO_x, etc., along with meteorological data such as rainfall, temperature, etc. The meteorological factors have an indirect influence on the AQI as they might increase or decrease the pollutant concentration. As we are aware of the missingness and abnormality in the data that can happen due to instrumental errors or external factors, the data used by the researchers was also subjected to such issues, and hence before being fed to the prediction pipeline, the data was duly pre-processed. The air pollutant data usually demonstrates long and short-term dependencies. The researchers used a fully connected time-distributed layer between two stacked BiLSTM layers which helped in weighting every time step output before passing it to the next BiLSTM layer and noise decoupling. The dropout method was used to avoid overfitting and Scaled Exponential Linear Unit (*selu*) activation in the fully connected layers. Softmax activation was used in the last layer which acted as a classifier. Further, Adam optimizer with a decay rate of 0.00001 was used. Hourly data was passed into the BiLSTM layer and at every time step, the layer calculated the output based on the current and previous output. This output was passed into a fully connected single-layer neural network-based time distributed layer. This dense representation was then passed into the successive BiLSTM layer and the output resulted in a consolidated representation. This representation was merged with the daily parameter inputs, and eventually, this combined representation was passed to the fully connected layers which acted as a classifier and gave a severity level as output.

15.8   CONCLUSION

This chapter discussed the strong foundational understanding of LSTM and its variants and further provide discussions on their real-world implementations to solve the air pollution forecasting problem. As discussed, LSTMs have become a state-of-the-art ubiquitous choice for time series analysis and holds promising potential for the development of technologies under several domains. LSTMs demonstrated high accuracy for air pollution forecasting and using LSTMs for the same will enable the preemptive planning to mitigate air pollution-related problems thereby saving lives by controlling health hazards.

KEYWORDS

- **long short-term memory**
- **recurrent neural networks**
- **neural Turing machine**
- **gated recurrent units**
- **root mean square error**

REFERENCES

1. Rumelhart, D., Hinton, G., & Williams, R., (1986). Learning representations by back-propagating errors. *Nature, 323*, 533–536. https://doi.org/10.1038/323533a0.

2. Hochreiter, S., & Schmidhuber, J., (1997). Long short-term memory. *Neural Computation, 9*(8), 1735–1780. https://doi.org/10.1162/neco.1997.9.8.1735.

3. Abimannan, S., Chang, Y. S., & Lin, C. Y., (2020). Air pollution forecasting using LSTM-multivariate regression model. In: Hsu, C. H., Kallel, S., Lan, K. C., & Zheng, Z., (eds.), *Internet of Vehicles. Technologies and Services Toward Smart Cities: IOV 2019: Lecture Notes in Computer Science* (Vol. 11894). Springer, Cham. https://doi.org/10.1007/978-3-030-38651-1_25.

4. Greff, K., Srivastava, R. K., Koutník, J., Steunebrink, B. R., & Schmidhuber, J., (2016). LSTM: A search space odyssey. *IEEE Transactions on Neural Networks and Learning Systems, 28*(10), 2222–2232.

5. Gers, F. A., Schmidhuber, J., & Cummins, F., (1999). Learning to forget: Continual prediction with LSTM. In: *1999 Ninth International Conference on Artificial Neural Networks ICANN 99. (Conf. Publ. No. 470)* (Vol. 2, pp. 850–855). Edinburgh, UK. doi: 10.1049/cp:19991218.

6. Gers, F. A., & Jürgen, S., (2000). Recurrent nets that time and count. *Proceedings of the IEEE-INNS-ENNS International Joint Conference on Neural Networks: IJCNN 2000: Neural Computing: New Challenges and Perspectives for the New Millennium, 3*, 189–194.

7. Yao, K., Cohn, T., Vylomova, K., Duh, K., & Dyer, C., (2015). *Depth-Gated LSTM.* arXiv preprint arXiv:1508.03790.

8. Cho, K., Van, M. B., Gulcehre, C., Bahdanau, D., Bougares, F., Schwenk, H., & Bengio, Y., (2014). *Learning Phrase Representations using RNN Encoder-Decoder for Statistical Machine Translation.* arXiv preprint arXiv:1406.1078.

9. Park, S. H., Kim, B., Kang, C. M., Chung, C. C., & Choi, J. W., (2018). sequence-to-sequence prediction of vehicle trajectory via LSTM encoder-decoder architecture. In: *2018 IEEE Intelligent Vehicles Symposium (IV)* (pp. 1672–1678). IEEE.

10. Schuster, M., & Paliwal, K. K., (1997). Bidirectional recurrent neural networks. *IEEE transactions on Signal Processing, 45*(11), 2673–2681.

11. Carbune, V., Gonnet, P., Deselaers, T., Rowley, H. A., Daryin, A., Calvo, M., & Gervais, P., (2020). Fast multi-language LSTM-based online handwriting recognition. *International Journal on Document Analysis and Recognition (IJDAR),* 1–14.

12. Graves, A., (2013). *Generating Sequences with Recurrent Neural Networks.* arXiv preprint arXiv:1308.0850.

13. Eck, D., & Schmidhuber, J., (2002). *A First Look at Music Composition Using LSTM Recurrent Neural Networks* (Vol. 103, p. 48). Istituto Dalle Molle Di Studi Sull Intelligenza Artificiale.

14. Le, X. H., Ho, H. V., Lee, G., & Jung, S., (2019). Application of long short-term memory (LSTM) neural network for flood forecasting. *Water, 11*(7), 1387.

15. Yue-Shan, C., Hsin-Ta, C., Satheesh, A., Yo-Ping, H., Yi_Ting, T., & Kuan-Ming, L., (2020). An LSTM-based aggregated air pollution forecasting model. *Atmospheric Pollution Research, 11*(8), 1451–1463.

16. Athira, V., Geetha, P., Vinayakumar, R., & Soman, K. P., (2018). Deep AirNet: Applying recurrent networks for air quality prediction. *Procedia Computer Science, 132*, 1394–1403.

17. https://machinelearningmastery.com/stacked-long-short-term-memory-networks/ (accessed on 11 November 2021).

18. Sharma, N., Dev, J., Mangla, M., Wadhwa, V. M., Mohanty, S. N., & Kakkar, D., (2021). A heterogeneous ensemble forecasting model for disease prediction. *New Generation Computing*, 1–15.

19. Sainath, T. N., Vinyals, O., Senior, A., & Sak, H., (2015). Convolutional, long short-term memory, fully connected deep neural networks. In: *2015 IEEE International Conference on Acoustics, Speech, and Signal Processing (ICASSP)* (pp. 4580–4584). IEEE.

20. Krizhevsky, A., Sutskever, I., & Hinton, G. E., (2012). ImageNet classification with deep convolutional neural networks. In: *Advances in Neural Information Processing Systems* (pp. 1097–1105).

21. Wen, C., Liu, S., Yao, X., Peng, L., Li, X., Hu, Y., & Chi, T., (2019). A novel spatiotemporal convolutional long short-term neural network for air pollution prediction. *Science of the Total Environment, 654*, 1091–1099.

22. https://machinelearningmastery.com/encoder-decoder-long-short-term-memory-networks/ (accessed on 11 November 2021).

23. Bui, T. C., Le, V. D., & Cha, S. K., (2018). *A Deep Learning Approach for Forecasting Air Pollution in South Korea Using LSTM.* arXiv preprint arXiv:1804.07891.

24. Verma, I., Ahuja, R., Meisheri, H., & Dey, L., (2018). Air pollutant severity prediction using Bi-directional LSTM Network. In: *2018 IEEE/WIC/ACM International Conference on Web Intelligence (WI)* (pp. 651–654). IEEE.

25. https://www.oreilly.com/library/view/deep-learning-for/9781788295628/assets/f5c8ceb8-5a77-4f81-8578-ff1458b4268c.png (accessed on 11 November 2021).

26. Lee, N., Shih, Y. O., Ying, H. P., Seong, O. H., & Syh-Yuan, T., (2018). Study of long short-term memory in flow-based network intrusion detection system, *Journal of Intelligent & Fuzzy Systems, 35*(6), 5947–5957.

27. https://ai.google/ (accessed on 11 November 2021).

28. Manohar, B., (2019). *Time Series Forecasting with Deep Stacked Unidirectional and Bidirectional LSTMs.* https://towardsdatascience.com/time-series-forecasting-with-deep-stacked-unidirectional-and-bidirectional-lstms-de7c099bd918 (accessed on 11 November 2021).

CHAPTER 16

Application of Machine Learning in Stock Market Prediction

P. S. SHEEBA[1] and SUBHASH K. SHINDE[2]

[1]Department of Computer Science & Engineering (IoT & Cyber Security including Blockchain Technology), Navi Mumbai, Maharashtra, India, E-mail: sheebaps@gmail.com

[2]Department of Computer Engineering, Lokmanya Tilak College of Engineering, Navi Mumbai, Maharashtra, India

ABSTRACT

Machine learning is a branch of artificial intelligence (AI), which allows the computer to learn things from the past data and use it to automate the actions in future. It enables the computer to learn by itself using algorithms without explicitly programming. With emerging trends in technology in vast areas of everyday life, machine learning is widely been used in several fields including agriculture, robot locomotion, search engines, forecasting, speech recognition, optimization, data analysis, computer networks, finance sectors, information retrieval, etc. Apart from this, there are wide applications of machine learning in stock markets. Several new dimensions have been added to the applications of machine learning in trading due to the advancements in technology. In this chapter, we explore the application of machine learning in stock market prediction. Prediction of stock market determines the future value of a stock traded in a stock exchange. With accurate prediction of future stock value of a company, an investor can maximize his gains. To increase the efficiency and user-friendliness, stock market trading is getting adopted to new technologies. It is been estimated that 85% of the customer interaction in financial sectors will be without directly interacting with another human. Apart from this, machine learning and AI are used to protect security threats and data breaches. This chapter gives an overview of various algorithms in the application of machine learning in stock market prediction. Proper use of machine learning in stock market can lead to better predictability which in turn reduces the risk involved in the business.

16.1   INTRODUCTION

In today's world, machine learning (ML) plays a very important role in the sustenance of different industries, especially financial sectors. Due to the high computing power and availability of huge data, most of the financial organizations are incorporating ML system for their business operations to improve their efficiency and reduce the production costs. One of the emerging applications of ML is its power to predict stock market value. For traders, accurate prediction of stock value is very important for making their trading decision. It is very difficult to predict the future value of the market just by analyzing the historic data. It requires external factors also to predict the value accurately. As ML is achieved by training the system with an enormous amount of data, it is easier to get more accurate results.

A considerable amount of research is happening in the area of applications of ML for stock market prediction. Extracting meaningful data from the data source, identifying, and analyzing the patterns are very important for prediction. In Ref. [1], the regression analysis method is explored to predict the stock market value in Nigerian Stock Exchange using real time data of three banks. A data mining tool was used to extract patterns for prediction using time series and moving average (MA) method.

Different DL methods has been explored in Ref. [2], in which the prediction was done based on the historical data available. The authors have used the methods like multilayer perceptron, long short-term memory (LSTM), recurrent neural networks (RNNs) and convolution neural network (CNN) for prediction. It was found that the convolution neural network prediction was more accurate than the other methods and even neural network model was outperforming the ARIMA model.

DL for forecasting in financial sectors is discussed in Ref. [3]. The use of neural networks in DL models gave rise to the deep neural networks (DNN). How prediction can be done by the use of multi-stage fuzzy interface systems and wavelet transform is explained in Ref. [4]. The authors also explain the short-term features that is present in the stock trends.

Stock market prediction using particle swarm optimization (PSO) method integrated with least square support vector machine (LS-SVM) is proposed in Ref. [5]. PSO algorithm tries to avoid the local minima by selecting the best parameters using LS-SVM. The model was compared with artificial neural network model and found that the prediction accuracy was improved with the proposed model.

In another chapter [6], authors have used fusion of three ML technologies for prediction of stock market index by means of two stages. In the first stage, statistical parameters were predicted to be used for the later stage. It was found that the prediction error was reduced by means of the fusion model.

Basically, stock market data is nonlinear in nature. Based on the stock market value, people invest in stocks. The method used for stock market should give accurate predictions. In Ref. [7], authors examine a survey on the most popular method for prediction, the regression analysis.

Stock prediction by using two data sources concurrently is discussed in Ref. [8]. Authors explain signal mining platform which uses extreme learning machine (ELM) by means of its design and architecture. They have also done comprehensive experimental comparisons of various algorithms.

Taiwan stock exchange data is used to analyze a statistical learning algorithm which uses self-organizing polynomial neural networks in Ref. [9]. The chapter surveys various individual and hybrid computational intelligence (CI) approaches and found that the hybrid CI approach is a good technique for stock price forecasting.

A predicting model based on PSO and a support vector machine is constructed in Ref. [10] to forecast the behavior of the stock market. The model was analyzed with the Shanghai stock market and Dow Jones index and found that prediction accuracy is much better than the other forecast models.

Various ML algorithms were used to predict the Karachi Stock Exchange and Saudi Stock Exchange in Ref. [11]. Comparison of the various algorithms were done to analyze the performance and accuracy.

In Ref. [12], a linear regression model is used to predict the stock market trading volume. The authors claim that the stakeholders can invest based on the proposed prediction model.

A novel architecture for stock market prediction is proposed in Ref. [13]. The authors have used a combination of Generative adversarial network along with multi-layer perceptron and LSTM for predicting the stock closing price. The generative adversarial network architecture was found to be more accurate in predicting the closing price compared to other ML models and deep learning (DL).

A prediction model for S&P 500 stock index build using artificial neural networks (ANN) and support vector machines (SVMs) is discussed in Ref. [14]. The proposed SVM model performed better than the artificial neural network and regression models.

In Ref. [15], a forecasting model is developed by combining artificial neural networks and decision tree (DT) model. The combination of these two models gave an accuracy of 77% which was better than the prediction accuracy of these models were used separately.

Investing risk can be reduced significantly by accurate forecasting. In Ref. [16], the authors consider both the losses and the gains. They have developed an experimental framework to determine whether the stock prices decrease or increases based on the earlier prices. Random forests (RFs) and gradient boosted DTs were used for the frame work.

The use of sentimental analysis to predict stock market price is discussed in Ref. [17]. It is been observed that the sentiments, opinion, emotions, attitude, etc., of a user can be used to predict the price using the stock market indicators like Sensex and Nifty.

SVM is widely used to predict the stock prices [18]. Macro-economic factors and company specific factors are considered to predict the stock market price. It is been observed that the use of SVM in predicting the stock market price is more powerful compared to other models. A support vector regression (SVR) model is considered in Ref. [19] to predict capitalizations in various markets considering up to the date and time prices. It is observed that during low volatility periods the precision of prediction improved. This chapter gives an overview of the various ML tools which are commonly used for the prediction of stocks.

16.2 MACHINE LEARNING

ML is a process to teach computer to predict things accurately when a data is fed into the system. Data can be of any form, for example, it can be a word, an image or numbers or anything else. Most of the applications which we use on a day to day basis use ML for giving the output. For example, Google, YouTube, Social media applications, voice assistants, etc., use ML algorithms to process the data. ML makes computers to behave like humans without explicitly programming it. It uses a huge amount of data for learning. For example, to identify a particular animal or a fruit, various images of a particular fruit or animal will be fed to the system to teach the system that the image fed is that of a fruit or an animal. So huge amount of data is required for ML. ML and artificial intelligence (AI) are inter-related. With artificial intelligence machines can perform task like humans. Through ML AI can be achieved in a much easier way as writing complicated codes is not required [20, 21].

16.3   TYPES OF MACHINE LEARNING

Machine learning can be of the following types.

16.3.1   SUPERVISED LEARNING

This type of learning uses labeled data. A large amount of labeled data will be fed to the system to train them to identify a particular data as shown in Figure 16.1(a).

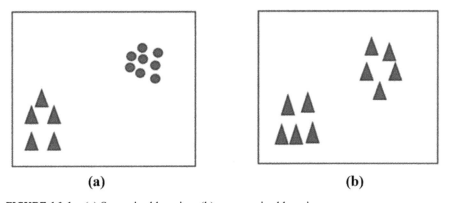

(a)   **(b)**

FIGURE 16.1   (a) Supervised learning; (b) unsupervised learning.

So, in future when we fed an image to the system it can easily recognize it. Even we can train the computer to predict the market prices by training it with a historical data of market. The data required for this type of training is very huge, and usually, labeling is done by means of crowd working services which is a laborious task.

16.3.2   UNSUPERVISED LEARNING

In this type of learning, labeled data is not used. Here computer tries to find similarities in the pattern of data and try to categorize it as given in Figure 16.1(b). This type of learning helps computers visualize and cluster the data based on similarities. It can also help in generating more data. In this type learning is done by finding natural groups and patterns from the input data.

16.3.3   SEMI-SUPERVISED LEARNING

This type of learning is a mix of supervised and unsupervised learning. If a limited set of labeled data is available and a large amount of unlabeled data is available, then the limited labeled data can be used to find similarities in the unlabeled data to train the system to label it. This is called pseudo-labeling. This pseudo labeled data and the labeled data will be used for training the machine. With this type of learning machines can generate new data which can be used for training.

With this type of learning, computational power of machine will be more important than the amount of labeled data used for ML.

16.3.4   REINFORCEMENT LEARNING

This type of learning is basically a trial and error approach in which a certain objective has to be met. If the algorithm it uses helps to get the desired objective then it is rewarded and otherwise penalized. So in every step the performance will get better. The best example of this type of learning is Google deep mind's deep Q network which has been used in several video games.

16.4   MACHINE LEARNING AND FINANCE

Due to the advancements in technology, more ML tools are easily accessible by finance sectors, e.g., TensorFlow by Google. ML is been adopted in most of the financial organizations due to its high computational power and accessible tools. ML has several applications in finance sectors. It can give a new dimension to the business related to customer service, risk management, etc. Let us look into some of the applications which will benefit the finance sectors.

16.4.1 CUSTOMER SERVICE

For the sustainment of every business customer service plays a major role. For financial services it plays a crucial role in retaining the customers. ML helps financial services to study the previous data of customers and take appropriate action for optimizing their business. It also helps them to contact customers in an efficient manner.

One of the most popular AI-based application, Chatbots are becoming more common nowadays in financial organizations to assist the customers. It understands what a customer is asking by natural language processing (NLP) and gives an appropriate response. Chatbots try to learn new things from each customer interaction and use this learning for future interactions. ML also allows chatbots to understand a customer's behavior and respond accordingly.

In the future apart from financial sectors, it will be adopted by various industries by making it as specialized chatbots and will be used by millions of people.

16.4.2 ALGORITHMIC TRADING

Algorithmic trading is otherwise called Automated Trading Systems can make trading decisions extremely faster by making use of complex AI systems. In a day it can make millions of trades. Most of the financial organizations are making use of AI for trading purpose.

To place a trade, a set of predefined instructions are executed by computers in algorithmic trading. Instructions usually consists of the market conditions like quantity, pricing, timing, etc. This helps traders in a competitive advantage.

Trading opportunities can be increased by algorithmic trading as it allows multiple markets operation. These algorithms can learn real-time changes and can easily adapt to it. Since it is an algorithm which is involved in the trading process, decisions can be made without human emotions or sentiments.

The best application of algorithmic trading is that stock trade decisions can be made without human intervention. The system learns from the past data and predicts the future market with high accuracy and trades by its own.

16.4.3   PERSONAL FINANCE

ML can help customers in managing their personal budgets by means of various apps. These apps give guidance and advice to the customers and they can track their daily expenditures on a daily basis through their mobile phones. These data will be used by ML to identify their financial patterns and help them to save in the future. Financial organizations can also track the customer spending patterns and guide them in managing their finance.

Another commonly used application is Robo-advisors which can manage a portfolio of clients and give automated advice and guidance by means of ML.

Smart chatbots and voice assistants help to address customer's query and give financial advice and guidance by reducing the work load of call center executives. The intelligent tools help customers to keep track of payments, to check account balance, expenses, and other activities and help them to optimize their finance plans.

16.4.4   FRAUD AND RISK MANAGEMENT

It has been estimated that insufficient or poor-quality data costs business very much, about more than 3 trillion dollars annually in the US. By making use of ML techniques, financial services can lower their risks as they can analyze large amounts of data before arriving at a financial decision like mortgage or approving loans.

Due to the vast use of the internet and huge amount of online data stored by companies, there involves a huge security risk in maintaining the data. Financial sectors handle large amount of personal and transaction data which are prone to hacking and data theft. Hence organizations are implementing new tools to prevent fraud and manage risks.

Companies have to rely on ML algorithms to detect frauds and prevent security threats. Risk management engines of PayPal can detect the risk level of a customer within milliseconds by means of machine learning. So, it is necessary for companies to have machine learning systems in the future for security purposes, which may require some additional features like voice recognition, face recognition, biometrics, etc., instead of the current user name and password system.

Machine learning algorithms can easily detect an unusual activity by processing large amount of data. Top companies like Google, Microsoft,

Amazon, etc., have already implemented machine learning algorithms in to their cloud services.

16.4.5 PROCESS AUTOMATION

Time consuming tasks can be automated by making use of robotic processes, thereby increasing the production and decreasing the cost of production. Human errors can be eliminated by robotic process automation for repetitive tasks, and financial organizations can optimize the tasks which require human involvement. Some of the tasks in finance organizations which can use machine learning for automation are documentation automation, call center automation, employee training, chatbots, etc. It is been estimated that 50–70% cost reduction can be achieved by making use of process automation.

16.4.6 TRADE SETTLEMENTS

Once the stocks are traded, money should be transferred to the seller's account and securities to be transferred to a buyer's account, this is called trade settlement. Most of the trades are now done automatically so settlement of trades also needs proper attention.

Most of the trade settlements are through automated process but few of them may need manual settlement due to failure in settlement. ML algorithms can identify the reason for failure, and it can predict the future failures and provide solutions. ML can fix a failed trade in a fraction of a second, whereas humans take nearly 5 to 10 minutes to rectify it.

16.4.7 MONEY LAUNDERING

It is been estimated that globally 800 billion dollars to 2 trillion dollars of money is laundered. So, major banks are incorporating ML technology to fight money laundering. Machine learning systems collects transaction data from client's network to detect money laundering. The applications of machine learning is not limited to a few domains, it can be applied to any field of interest.

16.5   MACHINE LEARNING IN STOCK MARKET PREDICTION

Due to the immense growth of the trading process, investing decisions in the stock market is a complicated task today. ML makes the decision process simpler for traders as it has the capability to analyze large data and identify market patterns and predicts stock market value. Due to the unpredictable nature of finance markets, we often encounter with chaotic data structure. It is difficult to extract patterns from this data; hence the information fed to the algorithm should be unbiased.

ML should be able to find hidden laws in the chaotic data while modeling such systems to predict the future. DL is the efficient method to achieve this as it can deal with complex structures and analyze it to make accurate predictions.

The first step in using ML for stock trading is to collect data set for a particular system. This data set is divided into a training set and a test set. Algorithm needs to be trained for the purpose it is used for by means of the training set. Once it is tuned with the training set, it will be tested using the test data set. The result generated by the algorithm will be compared with the real-time data of that stock.

16.5.1   MODELS FOR PREDICTION

To predict the future values of the stock market, we need to use certain algorithmic tools. Some of the commonly used algorithms are discussed.

16.5.1.1   MEAN VALUE

This is the simplest rule everyone follows to predict the future values, which is done by taking the average of all the values for a stipulated time. The accuracy of the predicted value can be checked by taking the mean square error (MSE). The prediction should be accurate otherwise it may result in loss of money in the business. Mean value prediction is shown in Figure 16.2.

To find the error, we need to calculate the difference between a predicted value and the actual value. This error has to be squared and then divided by the total number of data points to get the mean square error value. For example, if there are n data points and errors are given by e_1, e_2, ..., e_n. Then mean squared error is given by,

$$(e_1^2 + e_2^2 + ... + e_n^2)/n \tag{1}$$

Lower the error higher will be the accuracy. These errors can be reduced by considering a MA method which considers the recent data sets for predicting a future value. It includes the previous predicted values and removes the oldest data set for finding the mean value for predicting the future values.

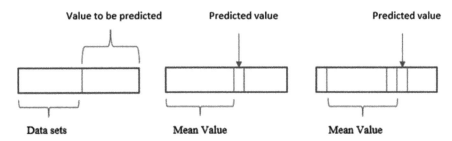

FIGURE 16.2   Mean value prediction.

If the outcome of a market value depends upon various features, then using mean value method for prediction of future values may not give the desired result. For such cases linear regression plays a major role.

16.5.1.2   LINEAR REGRESSION

This is a very commonly used technique for modeling prediction using statistical methods. This method uses a linear equation which consist of independent variables (features) and dependent variables (target). The equation is given by:

$$Y = \alpha_1 x_1 + \alpha_2 x_2 + ... + \alpha_n x_n \tag{2}$$

where; Y is the dependent variable; x_i's are independent variables, and α_i's are weighing coefficients whose values or weights depends on the importance of the parameters under consideration. For representation purpose let us consider only one independent variable.

In Figure 16.3, we observe that many lines can be drawn for various values but only one line will be the best fit for the values. The best fit line means it should give minimum error between the observed value and the predicted value. The best fit line would be the one which is formed by the predicted values that are having minimum error or residuals.

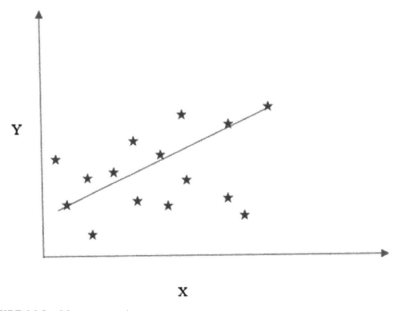

FIGURE 16.3   Linear regression.

Residuals are found by drawing vertical lines between the predicted value and the actual value. Linear regression methods are best suited for predicting sales.

16.5.1.3   LOGISTICAL REGRESSION

This ML algorithm is similar to linear regression. Classification tasks are commonly done by using this algorithm

This algorithm uses a Logistic function which is nothing but a sigmoid function given by the formula:

$$S(x) = \frac{1}{1+e^{-x}}$$ (3)

The sigmoid function is as shown in Figure 16.4.

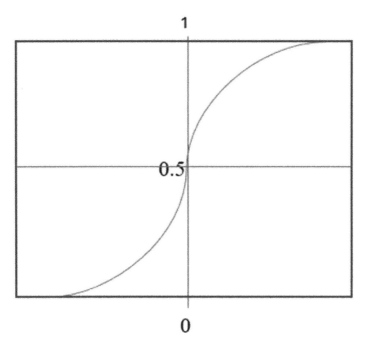

FIGURE 16.4   Sigmoid function.

Artificial neurons use Sigmoid function as activation function (AF). Output is predicted by combining the inputs linearly by means of weights. The output value is binary, either 0 or 1. The output becomes 1 if the curve goes to positive infinity and output becomes zero if the curve goes to negative infinity. More than two output values are modeled by means of multinomial logistic regression (LR). If the dependent variables are ordered then it can be modeled by ordinal logical regression. Bernoulli distribution is followed in Logical regression instead of Gaussian distribution and maximum likelihood is used for estimation. This model is used to predict the probability of outcomes.

16.5.1.4   K-NEAREST NEIGHBORS (KNN)

This is a powerful ML algorithm. This is commonly used in classification problems. The important aspects that need to be considered for selecting any algorithm are: the simplicity in predicting outputs, the time required for calculation, and the power with which it predicts the future values. K-Nearest Neighbor algorithm satisfies all these aspects.

Let us consider an example to illustrate this algorithm. In Figure 16.5, there are different classes stars and diamonds.

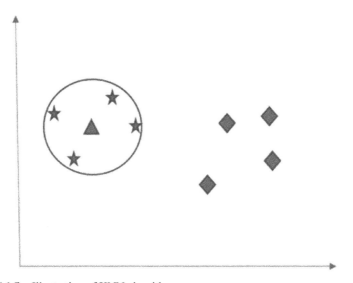

FIGURE 16.5   Illustration of KNN algorithm.

We need to identify in which class triangle belongs to by means of the KNN algorithm. It can belong to either stars or diamonds. This algorithm tries to find the Kth nearest neighbor to the triangle. For this first, we have to decide on the value of K. Let us assume K=4, so a circle is drawn with the triangle position as a center to enclose only four data points. In this case, the result is obvious as all four data points belong to the class stars and hence triangle belongs to the class stars.

With each value of K, boundaries for a particular class can be made. With increasing value of K, the boundary becomes smoother. For accessing different values of K, we need to consider the training error rate and valida-tion error rate. For K=1, the error will always be zero because the closest point is itself. Initially, for lower values of K error rate will be decreasing and reaches a minima and it then increases afterwards. The optimum value of K can be found from the validation error curve and this value of K will be used for future predictions.

This is a simple algorithm which can give highly challenging results for classification problems. This can also be used for regression problems by taking the average of nearest neighbors (NN).

16.5.1.5 *AUTO ARIMA*

Forecasting the price of a product or market values is one of the top skills required for a data scientist. For forecasting one requires the historical data. This requires a time series forecasting algorithm. Auto ARIMA is a time series forecasting method. Time series means data sets are collected and recorded at regular intervals of time, and each data point in this series depends on the previous data point.

Auto ARIMA is a statistical time-series method for forecasting. There are various methods which are used for time series forecasting, namely, Naïve approach, simple average, MA, weighted MA, Simple exponential smoothing, Holt's linear trend model, Holt Winter's method and ARIMA.

Auto-regressive integrated moving averages (ARIMA) is one of the most popular time series forecasting statistical method. This method makes the assumption that the mean and variance of the data set should not vary with time or in other words, the data set is stationary, and the input data must be univariate series as the prediction of future values depends on past values.

In ARIMA, Auto-regressive means for predicting the future value past values are used. MA refers to the past errors occurred in the forecast while predicting future values. Integrated is termed as order of differencing which refers to the total number of times difference operation is done to make the series stationary.

16.5.1.6 *PROPHET*

For stock market prediction, there are various time series techniques which can be implemented in fitting a model, but most of these methods requires a huge amount of data pre-processing. Prophet is an open-source time series forecasting library designed by Facebook which requires no data pre-processing. Implementation of Prophet is also very simple. The parameters used by prophet are intuitive, and it is easy to tune those parameters which does not require expertise in predicting the future values.

16.5.1.7 LONG SHORT-TERM MEMORY (LSTM)

This method is extremely effective in solving sequence prediction problems which are very difficult to solve. The advantage of this method is its ability to store only the important past information for a longer duration and forget the remaining information. This algorithm can be used to predict the sales, identify stock market patterns, predicting the next word in mobile's keyboard, etc. This algorithm is found to be better than the ANNs and RNNs.

For predicting the stock at a given time, RNNs consider the predictions done previously and that information will be used to learn and predict the future values whereas LSTM can remember or forget data selectively. It consists of various memory blocks called cells. Cell state and hidden state are the two states which will be transferred to the next cell. For remembering, memory blocks are used. It works by making use of three gates: (i) the input gate, which adds information to the cell, (ii) the forget gate, which forgets the information that is not required, (iii) the output gate, which selects the information that has to be shown as output.

For stock market prediction, the factors that depends are:

- Previous days trends whether it is upward or downward trends;
- Stock price of previous day as traders check previous day's price before buying a stock;
- Factors which can affect today's price maybe due to the change in business strategies.

All these factors have to be taken in to consideration while predicting the stock value. In LSTM we can model this as:
- Previous state of the cell data;
- Previous cell output or previous hidden state; and
- Current input or the information fed at the current time step.

LSTM can be effectively used for time series and scheduling problems, but the drawback is the complexity in training it.

16.5.1.8 MULTILAYER PERCEPTRON

ML can be done by means of perception. Perceptron can take weighted inputs based on its importance and generates an output of 0 or 1. If so many perceptrons are combined together in multiple layers so as to solve complex problems, then it becomes a multi-layer perceptron. The structure of a perceptron is shown in Figure 16.6.

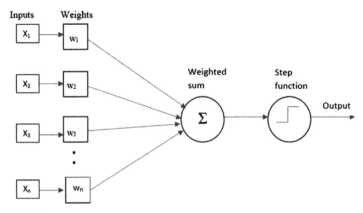

FIGURE 16.6 Perceptron structure.

The perceptrons take real value inputs and multiplied by the weights associated with it based on its importance, and it is summed up to generate the output which can be either 0 or 1 by an AF. In multilayer, this perceptron will be in multiple layers. A three-layer perceptron is shown in Figure 16.7.

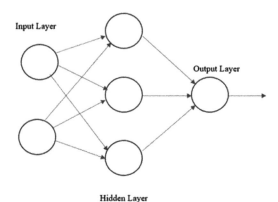

FIGURE 16.7 Multilayer perceptron with three layers.

Each layer has multiple perceptrons and each perceptron is connected to all the perceptrons in the second layer and so on. As the number of layers increases, this network becomes more complex.

The multilayer perceptron are commonly called neural networks. Three-layer perceptron is called shallow neural network or non-deep neural network. Perceptron with four and more layers are called DNN. For the normal perceptron the output is either 0 or 1 but in the case of neural network, the AF can be different from step function which means it can give output values in the range 0 to 1 or –1 to 1. Hence probability based predictions are possible with neural networks. The AF may be linear or non-linear. Most commonly used nonlinear AFs are Sigmoid, TanH, ReLU, etc.

Usually backpropagation algorithm (BPA) is used to tune the weights associated with the inputs so as to reduce the loss. It performs iterative process backwards hence in each step it tries to optimize the weight and hence it can give more accurate predictions.

Most of the neural network uses more complex advanced structures like RNNs and convolution neural networks (CNN). In RNN, two neural network runs in parallel and in CNN a three-dimensional multilayer perceptron is used.

16.5.1.9   BAYESIAN NETWORK

Bayesian network consists of a set of variables and its conditional dependence by means of a statistical graphical model. Bayesian network can be used to predict the events based on the past occurrence. When a sequence of variables is modeled using this network, it is called dynamic Bayesian networks (DBN). Let E1 and E2 be two events that influence the outcome O in Figure 16.8. Each event has two possibilities True (T) and False (F).

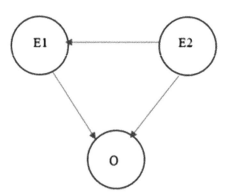

FIGURE 16.8   Bayesian network example.

Function for Joint Probability is given by:

$$P (O, E1, E2) = P (O|E1, E2) P(E1|E2) P(E2) \tag{4}$$

This model can give the probability of E2 (cause), given O (effect) by the conditional probability formula:

$$P(E2{=}T|O{=}T) = \frac{P(O=T,E2=T)}{P(O=T)} = \frac{\sum_{E_1 \epsilon (T,F)} P(O=T,E1,E2=T)}{\sum_{E_1,E2 \epsilon (T,F)} P(O=T,E1,E2)} \tag{5}$$

To determine the structure of the underlying graphs many algorithms has been developed. Various optimization methods have been deployed for the learning of Bayesian networks. Using the Bayesian networks for ML, the learned data can be used to predict the probability of the subsequent events.

One of the simplest Bayes network classifiers is Naïve-Bayes classifier. These classifiers can be trained effectively by supervised learning. The advantage of this classifier is that it requires less amount of data for estimating the parameters for classification. It uses Bayes probability theorem to predict the values of parameters. This classifier algorithm assumes that in a class, the presence of a particular feature is independent of the presence of other features. Performance of Naïve-Bayes classifier algorithm is better compared to some of the other methods like LR.

Some of the other common Naïve-Bayes classifier algorithms are Multinomial Naïve-Bayes, Bernoulli Naïve-Bayes, Gaussian Naïve-Bayes (GNB). For this classifier algorithm the predictors should be independent but in real life scenario most of the predictors are dependent hence it may affect the classifier performance.

Naïve-Bayes algorithm is faster as training data is less and it can be used for multiple class and real time predictions. This can be used for sentimental analysis of customers which is a very important factor in prediction of stock market price.

16.5.1.10   SUPPORT VECTOR MACHINES

SVMs is a supervised ML algorithm used for classification and regression analysis. Data points are classified with decision boundaries called hyperplanes.

In SVM, data points are considered to be n-dimensional vectors, and it has to be classified by means of (n–1)-dimensional hyperplane. The best hyperplane would be the one which separate the data point of different classes with maximum distance. Such hyperplanes with the maximum margin are called maximum margin hyperplane and the classifier is the perceptron of optimal stability. In Figure 16.9, there are two different classes of data and three hyperplanes P_1, P_2, and P_3.

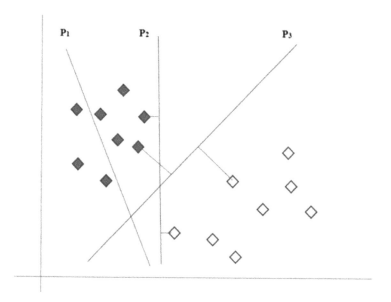

FIGURE 16.9   Hyperplane classification.

We can observe that P_1 is a hyperplane which is not separating the classes. P_2 separates the classes but the margin of separation is very less. P3 separates the classes as well as the margin is maximal.

In this example, P_3 is the best hyperplane which classifies the data. Generalization error of the classifier will be lower if the margin is higher. The data points closer to the hyperplanes are called support vector points and these points only determines the outcome of the algorithm. The distance between these vectors and hyperplanes is called margin.

If the data sets which needs to be classified are not linearly separable, then the finite dimension space has to be mapped to a higher dimension space where the separation becomes much easier. The mapping is done in such a way that the dot product of the data vectors may be computed by defining the original space variables by means of a Kernel function *k (x, y)*. The vectors may be chosen as the linear combination of parameter α_1 of feature vectors

x_i image in database. For example, a point x is mapped from feature space to hyperplane by means of the relation $\sum_i ai\ k(xi,x) =$ constant. Each term in the summation measures the closeness of the base point x_i with the test point x as y moves away from x and if $k\ (x, y)$ is reduced.

The generalization error is increased in higher dimensional feature space. Some of the commonly used kernels are Polynomial (homogenous), Polynomial (Inhomogeneous), Gaussian radial basis function (RBF) and Hyperbolic tangent. Selection of the kernels and its parameters determines the effectiveness of SVM.

For stock market prediction, various parameters like volatility of price, volatility of sector, momentum of sector, momentum of price, macro-economic data, company-specific data, etc., can be taken into account. The feature vectors along with their outcomes has to be fed as the training data to the SVM model for prediction.

This algorithm is faster compared to some algorithms like neural networks. Performance is also better with lesser number of samples.

16.5.1.11   RANDOM FOREST

This is a supervised ML algorithm by constructing DTs at training time for regression and classification. The ensemble of DTs forms the forest and as the DTs increases it will result in a dense and robust forest. DTs are created from data samples and this algorithm make use of voting to select the best solution and averages it thereby reducing the over-fitting.

From the given data samples, the algorithm first selects the random samples and construct DTs for all the samples. From the DTs, it will find the predicted result and voting will be performed on this result and the prediction with the maximum vote will be selected as the final predicted result.

This algorithm works best with large data and it is very flexible and the accuracy is high even without scaling of the data. Even with incomplete data, it gives good accuracy, but it is a very complex algorithm and time consuming.

These are some of the most popular ML algorithms used for stock market prediction. Many researches are going on in developing new algorithms for ML. The modification of these algorithms can give rise to new models of prediction which may give better prediction accuracy and performance.

16.6　CONCLUSION

With the advancement in technology, the use of ML is increasing in every sector, out of which the stock market prediction is considered to be the most widely used one. Decision capability of the humans have limitations when the data is very large. For stock market prediction, the data to be analyzed is very large, which make it a complicated task for humans; hence they have to depend on machines for automated decision making. The machines have to be trained with the available data using various algorithms for predicting the stock market price.

In this chapter, we have discussed about the various algorithms that can be used to train the machine. The accuracy of the prediction depends upon the data used and the algorithm used for training and prediction. Various research is ongoing in this area and the algorithms developed are shown to give accurate predictions. With more and more research happening in this area, we can expect more reliable and accurate algorithms in the future.

KEYWORDS

- **artificial intelligence**
- **computational intelligence**
- **K-nearest neighbors**
- **least square support vector machine**
- **particle swarm optimization**

REFERENCES

1. Abdulsalam, S. S., Adewole, K. S., & Jimoh, R. G., (2011). Stock trend prediction using regression analysis: A data mining approach. *ARPN Journal of Systems and Software, 1*, 154–157.
2. Hiransha, M., Gopalakrishnan, E. A., Vijay, K. M., & Soman, K. P., (2018). NSE stock market prediction using deep-learning models. *Procedia Computer Science, 132*, 1351–1362.
3. Heaton, J. B., Polson, N. G., & Witte, J. H., (2017). Deep learning for finance: Deep portfolios. *Applied Stochastic Models in Business and Industry, 33*, 3–12.
4. Kishikawa, Y., & Tokinaga, S., (2000). Prediction of stock trends by using the wavelet transform and the multi-stage fuzzy inference system optimized by the GA. *IEICE*

Transactions on Fundamentals of Electronics, Communications, and Computer Sciences, 83, 357–366.

5. Osman, H., & Omar, S. S., & Mustafa, A. S., (2013). A machine learning model for stock market prediction. *International Journal of Computer Science and Telecommunications, 14,* 17–23.

6. Jigar, P., Sahil, S., Priyank, T., & Kotecha, K., (2015). Predicting stock market index using fusion of machine learning techniques. *Expert Systems with Applications, 42,* 2162–2172.

7. Ashish, S., Dinesh, B., & Upendra, S., (2017). Survey of stock market prediction using machine learning approach. *International Conference of Electronics, Communication, and Aerospace Technology,* 20–22.

8. Xiadong, L., Haoran, X., Ran, W., Yi, C., Jingjing, C., Feng, W., Huaging, M., & Xiactie, D., (2016). Empirical analysis: Stock market prediction via extreme learning machine. *Neural Computing and Applications, 27,* 67–78.

9. Jui-Yu, W., & Chi-Jie-Lu, (2013). Computational intelligence approaches for stock price forecasting. *Proceedings of the 2012 International Symposium on Computer, Consumer, and Control,* 52–55.

10. Guo, Z., Wang, H., & Liu, Q., (2013). Financial time series forecasting using LPP and SVM optimized by PSO. *Methodologies and Applications, 17,* 805–818.

11. Mustansar, A. G., Saad, A. A., Yasmeen, F. A., Anam, M., Muazzam, M., & Muhammad, A. A., (2017). Machine learning classifiers to predict stock exchange index. *International Journal of Machine Learning and Computing, 7,* 24–29.

12. Farhad, S. G., Tahmineh, H. B., & Seyyed, R. K., (2013). Linear regression approach to prediction of stock market trading volume: A case study. *International Journal of Managing Value and Supply Chains, 4,* 25–31.

13. Kang, Z., Guoqiang, Z., Junyu, D., Shengke, W., & Yong, W., (2019). Stock market prediction based on generative adversarial network. *Procedia Computer Science, 147,* 400–406.

14. Alaa, F. S., Sara, E. M. A., & Hossam, F., (2015). A comparison between regression, artificial neural networks and support vector machines for predicting stock market index. *International Journal of Advanced Research in Artificial Intelligence, 4,* 55–63.

15. Tsai, C. F., & Wang, S. P., (2009). Stock price forecasting by hybrid machine learning techniques. *Proceedings of the International Multi Conference of Engineers and Computer Scientists, 1,* 18–20.

16. Suryoday, B., Saibal, K., Snehanshu, S., Luckyson, K., & Sudeepa, R. D., (2019). Predicting the direction of stock market prices using tree-based Classifiers. *The North American Journal of Economics and Finance, 47,* 552–567.

17. Aditya, B., Yogendra, N., Vanraj, P., & Maitreyee, D., (2015). Sentiment analysis for Indian stock market prediction using Sensex and nifty. *Procedia Computer Science, 70,* 85–91.

18. Zhen, H., Jie, Z., & Ken, T., (2013). Stocks market prediction using support vector machine. *International Conference on Information Management, Innovation Management and Industrial Engineering,* 23, 24.

19. Bruno, M. H., Vinicius, A. S., & Herber, K., (2018). Stock prediction using support vector regression on daily and up to the minute prices. *The Journal of Finance and Data Science, 4,* 183–201.

20. John, D. K., Brian, M. N., & Aoife, D., (2015). *Fundamentals of Machine Learning for Predictive Data Analytics-Algorithms, Worked Examples, and Case Studies*. The MIT Press.

21. Max, K., & Kjell, J., (2018). *Applied Predictive Modeling* (2nd edn.). Springer.

CHAPTER 17

Deep Learning Model for Stochastic Analysis and Time-Series Forecasting of Indian Stock Market

SOURABH YADAV

University of North Texas (UNT), Denton, Texas, USA,
E-mail: sourabhy1797@gmail.com

ABSTRACT

In this period of modernization, the stock costs act as the narrator of all the financial and economic activities of the nation. But high fluctuations in the cost of a stock, the stock market turns into the spot of high hazard and vulnerability. But still, it is drawing great attention due to its exceptional yielding esteem. The stock market gives a clear image of the current economic state, financial stability, and also the growth rate of any country. Therefore, it has become the greatest speculation place for the overall population. This manuscript targets to perform Univariate analysis on a historical dataset of Bombay stock exchange (BSE) SENSEX open value and compares the results of the ARIMA model, deep learning model, FBProhet model to predict the value of BSE SENSEX Open value, i.e., opening cost of stocks, with high exactness and accuracy. The performed analysis validates that FbProphet model developed by Facebook, gives the best possible predicted values of BSE SENSEX, provided that the dataset used contains the historical values of BSE SENSEX on a daily basis.

17.1 INTRODUCTION

The stock market insinuates the collection of business parts and exchanges where standard activities of buying, selling, and issuance of bits of straightforwardly held associations happen. Such monetary related activities are coordinated through systematized conventional exchanges or over-the-counter (OTC) business focuses, which work under a portrayed set of protocols. Every nation has different stock exchanging scenarios or a territory which grants trades in stocks and various sorts of securities. Financial exchange and Stock trade sounds very comparable yet are used then again, the primary term is normally a superset of the past. In case one says that he/she trades the stocks, it suggests that she buys and sells stocks/shares of stock exchange, which are a bit of the general protections trade.

Stock market performance of any nation is very unusual. However, the reality is financial development of any nation exceptionally relies on the securities exchange costs or stock market performance. So on the off chance that one can foresee the stock costs, it will end up being a useful resource, for the individuals who put resources into the stock market. Gross domestic product (GDP) of any nation is directly correlated to the stock cost, so from that point of view also, this prediction model may become a great deal of interest. Moreover, it will give a brief idea to the stock traders as the stock cost anticipation can assist them by recognizing the current pattern of ups and downs of the market. Therefore, they can easily judge the investment amount. The main stock trades in India incorporate the BSE SENSEX, National stock exchange (NSE) Nifty, and the BSE Bankex. These are the prominent national indices, with few others indices maintained in our nation, builds up the core structure for stock market of India. BSE SENSEX is a list/benchmark used to quantify the exhibition of top 30 well-established and monetarily solid organizations recorded in the Bombay stock exchange (BSE). On the off chance that the Sensex goes up, it implies that the costs of the supplies of a large portion of the significant organizations on the BSE have gone up. On the off chance that the Sensex goes down it implies costs have gone down.

Stock Market pattern and Trend faces high fluctuations in daily routine; therefore, it becomes the most troublesome assignment in light and proves to be a great deal in the estimations of the stock costs. Therefore, stock price prediction model must be solid and effective. There are several methods for implementing predication model. Yet, stochastic methodology is viewed as extraordinary compared to other methodology. In addition, stochastic methodology of time-arrangement will generate the most suitable outcomes. Time series of a dataset is the presence of information over a constant time span. Time series determining is a significant territory of AI that is regularly dismissed. It is significant in light of the fact that there are such a significant number of prediction issues that include a period segment. These issues are dismissed on the grounds that it is this time part that makes time-series issues progressively hard to deal with. Basically, time series is normally demonstrated through a stochastic procedure Y(t), i.e., a grouping of arbitrary factors. In a gauging setting forecaster winds up at time t and he is keen on assessing Y(t+h), utilizing just data accessible at time t.

This manuscript centers around the present reality issue in the stock market. The occasional pattern and stream is the feature of the stock market. In the long run, investors, and the stockbroking organization will likewise watch and catch the varieties, consistent development of the record. This will help new investors just as existing individuals will settle on a key choice. It very well may be accomplished by understanding and the steady perceptions by the investors. Moreover, this manuscript explicitly focuses on anticipating the BSE SENSEX relying on the authentic values of recent years [1], utilizing different estimating models and afterward investigating the best model contingent on the mean mistake of different prediction model outcomes. A blend of distinctive forecasting models when applied upon dataset simultaneously and took a gander at all provides best possible yield [2]. Moreover, mistake network is set up for effective gauging of models performance and their blunders. The time series of the information utilized for this manuscript is from January 2001 to April 2020.

17.2 LITERATURE REVIEW

Time-series evaluation had been a prominent area of research from long time. ARIMA model is considered as the base of time-series forecasting. Moreover, many author has tried to modify the ARIMA model and successfully got some great results. In light of the essential ideas of the ARIMA model and Tanaka fuzzy relapse, the Fang-Mei Tsenga has proposed another technique (fuzzy ARIMA) and applied it to estimate the remote swapping scale of NTD to USD for indicating the propriety and adequacy of the proposed technique. The proposed technique not exclusively can make great gauges yet in addition gives the best and most noticeably awful potential circumstances. The author has concluded that fuzzy ARIMA proves to be an effective model as compared to Watada's fuzzy time series and Chen's fuzzy time series [3]. Also, Nochai, and Nochai has employed ARIMA model for forecasting of commodities prices. Basically, they have created a model for three kinds of oil palm cost, were seen as ARIMA(2,1,0) at the homestead cost model, ARIMA(1,0,1) at a discount cost, and ARIMA(3,0,0) at the unadulterated oil cost, in which author concluded with very less MAPE for each model [4]. Additionally, a blend of ARIMA and a fuzzy relapse model is utilized to estimate two occasional time-series information of the total creation estimation of the Taiwan hardware industry and the soda time-series. The expectation of this chapter was, to give a business that is influenced by enhanced administration with another strategy to lead momentarily determining [5]. ARIMA model is considered as the most unmistakable and well-known model for time-series determining. Also, the Artificial Neural Network (ANN) additionally ends up being a successful non-linear model. The half breed of these two models likewise gives an extraordinary outcome in examination with their singular execution [6]. Najeeb Iqbal and Khuda Bakhsh has employed ARIMA model for forecasting the production of wheat in Pakistan for the period of 2002–2020 [7]. Not just the commodities cost like wheat, palm, and so on, are estimated utilizing the base of anticipating, i.e., ARIMA yet additionally costs of power or electricity have been estimated utilizing these models. The chronicled and typically poorly carried on value arrangement is disintegrated utilizing the wavelet change in a lot of better-acted constitutive series. At that point, the future estimations of these constitutive series figures are utilized appropriately and fitted to ARIMA models. Thus, the ARIMA estimates permit, through the converse wavelet change, remaking the future conduct of the value arrangement and in this way to figure costs [8]. Since ARIMA is considered as the base of time-series forecasting, in the present era, many other forecasting models have been introduced like upgraded version of ARIMA, i.e., Seasonal ARIMA (SARIMA), FbProphet, LSTM network of recurrent neural network (RNN). The blend of SARIMA and FbProphet is utilized for the estimation of Traffic of Short-Term. The research depends on transient traffic expectation utilizing SARIMA and the Facebook PROPHET bundle. A PROPHET model and SARIMA model were created to break down transient traffic expectation utilizing the volume check of seven-day on the hourly basis of the National Highway 744. PROPHET model is utilized to get the estimated pattern with all the possible range of the determined date [9]. In addition, the FbProphet model is utilized for understanding the patterns and the examples of the sharp edge's disappointment in turbines. The information accommodated for this research approximated 79 million lines of sensor readings; and for that feature extraction and testing, techniques were employed. In this examination, the FbProphet model is utilized for inconsistency detection and failure forecasting [10]. Additionally, there are researches in which the fundamental target is to give a structure that will permit venture administrators, entrepreneurs, and designers a viable method to figure the pattern in programming deserts inside a product venture in real-time utilizing the blend of ARIMA and FbProphet model [11]. And above all, the recent spread of Covid 19 has affected the world economy very badly. Many researches and analysis is been performed, targeting to build forecasting model, to study the covid outbreak and forecast its spread in world. Basically, researchers are using FbProphet model as it gives flexibility of data frame management for daily, weekly, and yearly perspectives [12]. Additionally, numerous researchers have proposed a half breed model of the long short term memory (LSTM) model for the determining of the instability of the stock costs. Basically, they have coordinated profound deep learning (DL) methods with current estimating models, to set up the Hybrid LSTM model [13]. These days, photovoltaic (PV) power is considered as the most conspicuous wellspring of the sustainable wellspring of energy. Numerous analysts have utilized the recurrent neural network (RNN) LSTM model for foreseeing the yield intensity of PV frameworks [14].

17.3   PROPOSED METHODOLOGY

Figure 17.1 portrays the system utilized in our examination work to make a conjecture model.

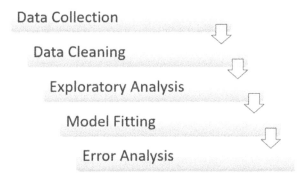

Data Collection

Data Cleaning

Exploratory Analysis

Model Fitting

Error Analysis

FIGURE 17.1   Proposed methodology.

> **Stage 1: Data Collection:** Information Collection is the path toward gathering information from material sources in an intentional way that enables one to react to the huge requests and survey results [15].
>   Information Collection is an effective strategy of gathering and inspecting express information to proffer answers for noteworthy

requests and evaluate the results. It fixates around finding everything on a particular point. Information is accumulated to be furthermore presented to hypothesis testing which hopes to explain a miracle. For authorities of information, there is a scope of results for which the data is gathered. In any case, the key reason for which data is gathered is to place an analyst in a vantage position to make expectations about future probabilities and patterns. The core structure from where data can be gathered must be essential and auxiliary information. While the former is gathered by an analyst through direct sources, the latter is gathered by an individual other than the client. There are a lot of basic purposes behind gathering data, particularly for an analyst. A key explanation behind gathering data, be it through quantitative or subjective strategies is to guarantee that the uprightness of the exploration question is to be sure kept up. The right utilization of proper information assortment of techniques lessens the probability of mistakes reliable with the outcomes. Moreover, to limit the danger of blunders in dynamic, it is significant that precise data is gathered with the goal that the specialist doesn't settle on ignorant choices. Data assortment spares the specialist time and assets that would some way or another be wasted without more profound comprehension of the theme or topic. Also, to demonstrate the requirement for an adjustment in the standard or the presentation of new data that will be broadly acknowledged, it is imperative to gather data as proof to help these cases (Figure 17.2).

FIGURE 17.2   Importance of data collection.

➤ **Stage 2: Data Cleansing:** 'Cleansing' alludes to the way toward expelling invalid information that focuses on a dataset [17]. Much Statistical investigation attempt to discover an example in an informal arrangement, in light of a theory or suspicion about the idea of the information. Cleaning is the way toward expelling the information focuses which are detached with the impact and in addition, a presumption which are should have been secluded. In this procedure, these specific information focuses are overlooked, and investigation has been led on the rest of the information.

Basically, Data cleansing is the most prominent pieces of AI. It has a considerable impact in building a model. It, without a doubt, isn't the most decorated bit of AI, and simultaneously, there is no any sign of covered tricks or puzzles to uncover. Nonetheless, legitimate information cleaning can speak to the choosing snapshot of endeavor. Capable data scientists generally spend an outstandingly gigantic portion of their time on this movement. Clearly, different sorts of data will require different sorts of cleaning. In any case, this efficient methodology can generally fill in as a decent beginning stage (Figure 17.3).

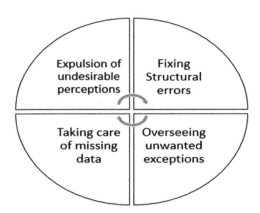

FIGURE 17.3   Methodology for data cleaning.

1   **Expulsion of Undesirable Perceptions:** This incorporates erasing copy/excess or immaterial qualities from your dataset. Copy perceptions most as often as possible emerge during information assortment and irrelevant perceptions may be defined as the particulars that are unable to fit defined issue that is being attempted to be tackled.

2   **Fixing Structural Errors:** The errors that emerge during estimation, the move of information, or other comparable circumstances
are called auxiliary mistakes. Basic blunders remember grammatical
mistakes for the name of highlights, a similar characteristic with an
alternate name, mislabeled classes, for example, separate classes that
should be the equivalent or conflicting capitalization.

3   **Overseeing Unwanted Exceptions:** Anomalies can cause issues
with specific kinds of models. For instance, straight relapse models
are less powerful to anomalies than choice tree models. By and large,
user ought not to expel anomalies until user have an authentic moti-
vation to evacuate them. Now and again, expelling them improves
execution, once in a while not. Along these lines, one must have
a valid justification to expel the anomaly, for example, dubious
estimations that are probably not going to be the piece of genuine
information.

4   **Taking care of Missing Data:** Missing data is a misleadingly precar-
ious issue in AI. One can't simply disregard or expel the missing
perception. They should be taken care of cautiously as they can be
a sign of something significant. Dropping perceptions with missing
qualities and imputing the missing qualities from past perceptions
are the two most regular approaches to manage missing data.

The tool used for data cleansing for our research is MS Excel.
Priority in data cleaning process has been to ensure that there is no
empty field, i.e., no missing cells, and attribute names are defined
fittingly. Once these cleansing procedures are executed successfully
data becomes ready for the further stage, i.e., Exploratory analysis
(Figure 17.4).

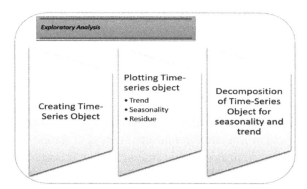

FIGURE 17.4   Exploratory analysis.

➢ **Stage 3: Exploratory Analysis:** This incorporates the exploratory analysis upon the cleaned dataset: Right off the bat in this procedure, the prepared dataset is stacked in a space for performing assorted quantifiable limits on the dataset. Prior to advance procedures, for this research, the dataset has been partitioned till May 2019. Information from May 2019 to March 2020 has been saved for check forms. Information is then changed over as time-series; this implies information exists over a persistent time stretch with equivalent dispersing between every two successive estimations. Changing over the dataset into time series consistently ends up being effective and efficient technique for the examination of any dataset, particularly in the financial analysis [18]. At that point, the output of the time-series performance can be gauged by utilizing time-series object. Time-series plot preparation acts as the next stage of the analysis. Time-series plot gives the basic visuals of dataset performance and presents the actual dynamics of the dataset, due to which it proves to be a very crucial stage in exploratory analysis. Moreover, it assists with examining the crucial components of time-series object data, for example, pattern, irregularity, heteroskedasticity, and stationarity. Therefore, the next stage involves examination of components, i.e., decomposing the dataset. This includes extracting the features like seasonality, residue, trend, etc., from the time-series data [19].

➢ **Stage 4: Model Training:** At that point Stage 4 includes the model training, i.e., deducing the particular model performs exceptionally well upon our dataset relying on our factual outcomes. Distinctive models acquired for this research areas in subsection (Figure 17.5).

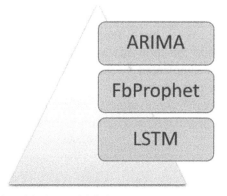

FIGURE 17.5   List of models for model fitting.

17.3.1 *AUTO-REGRESSIVE INTEGRATED MOVING AVERAGE (ARIMA)*

ARIMA is a base model for forecasting that 'clarifies' employed time-series arrangement depending upon its own historical qualities, i.e., its own slacks and the slacked gauge mistakes, so the condition can be utilized to conjecture future qualities. ARIMA is characterized as a measuring method that expands the predicted values of a time-series totally subject to its inertness. Its key application is in the region of transient foreseeing requiring at any rate of 40 chronicled data centers. It works more appropriately when the data shows a consistent or unsurprising model after a few minutes or hours with a base proportion of special cases. It is the supported choice considering its straightforwardness and wide suitability. It acts as the base for working and performing time-series analysis [20]. And this is the reason why it is considered as widely suitable and to the point result presenter model.

ARIMA models give another way to deal with time series anticipating. Exponential smoothing and ARIMA models are the two most generally utilized ways to deal with time arrangement determining and give corresponding ways to deal with the issue. While exponential smoothing models depend on a depiction of the pattern and irregularity in the information, ARIMA models expect to portray the autocorrelations in the information. An ARIMA model is a type of relapse examination that measures the quality of one ward variable comparative with other evolving factors. The model will probably anticipate future protections or money related market moves by inspecting the contrasts between values in the arrangement rather than through genuine qualities.

- Autoregression (AR) alludes to a model that shows a changing variable that relapses all alone slacked, or earlier, values.
- Integrated (I) speaks to the differencing of crude perceptions to take into consideration the time arrangement to get fixed, i.e., information esteems are supplanted by the contrast between the information esteems and the past qualities.
- Moving Average (MA) consolidates the reliance between a perception and a lingering mistake from a moving normal model applied to slack perceptions.

Algorithm for ARIMA
1. #Import   Import the dataset using read_csv()
2. #Plot   Using matplotlib library, plot the dataset
3. #Time-series_object   Define the time series object for the above imported dataset

4. #Plot_Time-Series
    Plotting of time series is done in two phases:
    • With usual differencing;
    • With seasonal differencing.

5. #Model_fitting   Using auto_arima() method and keeping the attributes of auto_arima() depending upon time-series plot, build the Arima model for above imported dataset
6. #forecast   Now, using predict() function perform forecasting for required number of periods.

17.3.2   FBPROPHET

The FbProphet model is an algorithm used for evaluating the time-series object and determining the curvy patterns for the differently differenced dataset, i.e., differenced on a yearly basis, monthly basis, or day to day inconsistency, notwithstanding event impacts. It shows great results for the time-series that have strong infrequent effects and a couple of times of irrefutable data. The prophet is considered a solid model for missing data points extremely curvy patterns and is most frequently used for handling the inconsistency. Prophet is utilized in numerous applications across Facebook for delivering dependable gauges for arranging and objective setting. Facebook researchers has discovered it to perform superior to some other methodology in most of the cases. Researchers fit models in Stan with the goal that you get figures in only a couple of moments. The prophet method incorporates numerous opportunities for clients to change and alter gauges. You can utilize human-interpretable parameters to improve your conjecture by including your space information. Facebook built up a publicly releasing prophet, a gauging instrument accessible in both python and R. It gives instinctive parameters that are anything but difficult to tune. Indeed, even somebody who needs profound mastery in time-arrangement anticipating models can utilize this to create significant forecasts for an assortment of issues in business situations. Prophet normally evaluates check execution and flags give that warrant manual intervention. The most direct evaluation procedure is to define a standard protocol with some fundamental envisioning methodologies (for instance, periodic sincerity, the model mean, glide, etc.). It is useful to differentiate misrepresented and moved to envision methods with choosing if additional execution can be acquired by using a continuously confusing model. An additional substance regression model where indirect trends are perfectly mixed up with yearly, monthly, and daily abnormality, notwithstanding event impacts. A piecewise immediate or vital improvement twists design. Prophet thusly distinguishes changes in designs by picking change points from the data. A yearly periodic part showed using the Fourier course of action. Seven days periodic part using trick factors and uses a customer gave a once-over of huge occasions.

Algorithm for FbProphet
1. #Import Import the dataset using read_csv()
2. #Plot Using matplotlib library, plot the dataset
3. #datastamp FbProphet model only accepts dataframe which contains ds (datestamp) and y (value we want to forecast) column.
4. #instance Prophet class instance is generated and fitted to the data frame.
5. #future_dataframe A new data frame is generated which contains the future dates using make_future_dataframe(). Also state the periods parameter which states the number of forecasts to be made.
6. #prediction predict() function is employed for making prediction and save it in a new data frame. Using this dataframe lower and upper bounds of the uncertain range can be evaluated.

17.3.3   LONG SHORT TERM MEMORY (LSTM) OF RECURRENT NEURAL NETWORK

The long short term memory systems-typically just called "LSTMs" -are an extraordinary sort of RNN, equipped for learning long haul conditions. The LSTM framework, or LSTM compose, is a dreary neural framework that is prepared to use Backpropagation using Time-series and beats the vanishing edge issue. Taking everything into account, in general, it will be used to make huge discontinuous frameworks that in this manner can be used to address irksome progression issues in AI and achieve top tier results. As opposed to neurons, LSTM frameworks incorporate memory blocks which are interfaced using different layers. A block contains portions that strengthen it to become more splendid than an outdated neuron and storage for the last moment entries. A block comprises of gates that manage the block's current state and output. A block implements an information progression and each gate of block utilizes the sigmoid incitation units which control their actuated position or states, revealing the state improvement and extension of information traveling from the block unforeseen. Long short term memory is a kind of repetitive neural system. In RNN yield from the last advance is taken care of as a contribution to the present advance. LSTM was designed by Hochreiter and Schmidhuber. It handled the issue of long haul conditions of RNN in which the RNN can't anticipate the word put away in the drawn-out memory however can give increasingly exact expectations from the ongoing data. As the whole length builds RNN doesn't give productive execution. LSTM can as a matter of course hold the data for a significant stretch of time. It is utilized for preparing, foreseeing, and classifying based on time-series information. The essential work-stream of a long short term memory network is like the work-stream of a recurrent neural network (RNN) with the main distinction being that the internal cell state is additionally passed forward alongside the Hidden State. A long short term memory network comprises of four distinct gates for various purposes as portrayed underneath:

1. **Forget Gate(f):** It basically states the degree of carried data from the past information.
2. **Input Modulation Gate(g):** Its main and basic function is to make data Zero-mean. It takes data from information gates without any specific check of the data. It utilizes chunks of data that internal cells will utilize by making data non-linear, which ends up in making data with zero mean. This step is basically performed for establishing zero-mean data as it is quicker to union this sort of data. And this is the only reason LSTM performance is considered as quicker efficient.
3. **Input Gate(i):** It states the amount of data to be forwarded to the state of Internal Cell.
4. **Yield Gate(o):** It figures out what output (next hidden state) to create from the current internal cell state.

Algorithm for LSTM

1. #Import
   Import the dataset using read_csv()

2. #normalize_dataset
   normalize the dataset using MinMaxScaler() and fit_transform()

3. #spliting_of_dataset
   Split the dataset into training and testing

4. #converting _array_of_values_into _dataset_matrix
   Reshaping of array values to dataset matrix.

5. #model_fitting

   LSTM() method is utilized for Model fitting in LSTM network

6. #make_prediction

   predict() function is employed for making prediction and save it in a new data frame.
   Using this dataframe lower and upper bounds of the uncertain range can be evaluated.

Stage 5 Error Analysis: This deals with error analysis of the above prepared models. Essentially in this progression, examination is made among aftereffects of above expressed models. Officially, error Analysis alludes to the way toward looking at dev set models that your calculation misclassified, with the goal that one can comprehend the hidden reasons for the blunders. This can assist with organizing which issue merits consideration and how much. It provides guidance for taking care of mistakes. Error investigation isn't only a last rescuing activity. It ought to be a piece of standard turn of events. Regularly, it begins with a small model that will undoubtedly have low precision (high mistake). It would then be able to begin assessing this model and examine the errors. As when these mistakes are examined and fixed, one can develop with the model (Figure 17.6).

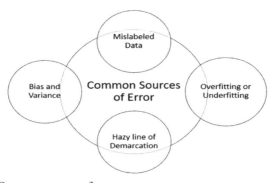

FIGURE 17.6 Common sources of errors.

There are a few wellsprings of errors. Each model would have its own exceptional errors and every one of them should be taken a gander at them independently. In any case, the run of the mill causes are:

1. **Mislabeled Data:** The greater part of the data marking is followed back to people. Data is extricated from the net or reviews or different sources. The fundamental data sources originated from people. Furthermore, people are error inclined. In this way, the reality to recognize is all train/dev/test information has some mislabeled records. In the event that the model is all around assembled and prepared appropriately, at that point it ought to have the option to defeat such blunders.

2. **Dim Line of Demarcation:** Grouping calculations function admirably when the positive and negative are unmistakably isolated. For instance, if the order is made between the pictures of an insect and a human; the division is quite acceptable and that should help accelerate the preparation procedure.

3. **Overfitting or Underfitting:** At the point when the multifaceted nature of the model is unreasonably less for it to gain proficiency with the input data, the model is stated as Underfit. In very simple words, the model neglects to learn properly because of insufficient data points or data values. As a result, the model is unable to learn the basic flow and pattern of the dataset. Underfitting is seen for the model which have very high biasness and low variance

   At the point when the unpredictability of the model is excessively high when contrasted with the information that it is attempting to gain from, the model is recognized as Overfit. In simple words, with expanding model multifaceted nature, Noise present in the data will be also get fitted to the model (e.g., Anomalies). The data learning of model happens excessively well and henceforth neglects to Generalize. Model with low Biasness and high variance results in overfitting

4. **Variance and Bias:** The variance and bias give us a decent understanding of this. In basic words, if the error is high in the preparation set just as dev set, that implies high variance. While if the preparation set is acceptable yet the dev set is terrible, that implies high bias. Variance basically infers that the yield is terrible for all information. Difference infers that the yield is beneficial for certain information and terrible for the rest.

The best fit model is the model which shows least blunders or gives high for the specific dataset. In addition, mistake investigation proposes future scope and improvements need to be made with respect to model fitting and dataset adoption. When error matrix is prepared, various errors are presented for finding the best suited model for forecasting, and some of them are listed below:

i. **Mean Square Error (MSE):** The mean squared error uncovers to you how close line backslide is to a ton of core interests. It is implemented by taking the way from the concentrations to backslide line (these partitions are the "blunders") and making sense of them. The squaring is imperative to oust any negative signs. It also gives more weight to greater differences. It's referred to as the mean squared error as the ordinary of a ton of goofs is being surveyed.

$$MSE = \frac{1}{n}\sum_{i=1}^{n}\left(Y_i - \overline{Y_i}\right)^2$$

ii. **Root Mean Square Error (RMSE):** RMSE quantifies what amount is the blunder between two informational collections. At the end of the day, it looks at an anticipated worth and a watched or known worth. Anyway, it isn't considered as solid for investigation [16].

$$RMSE = \sqrt{\frac{\sum_{t=1}^{T}\left(x_{1,t} - x_{2,t}\right)^2}{T}}$$

iii. **Mean Absolute Percentage Error (MAPE):** MAPE, otherwise called mean absolute percentage deviation (MAPD), is a proportion of expectation exactness of a determining strategy in measurements, for instance in pattern estimation.

$$MAPE = \frac{100\%}{n}\sum_{t=1}^{n}\left|\frac{A_t - F_t}{A_t}\right|$$

iv. **Results and Discussion:** The tool which is utilized for forecasting is python.

Stage 1 of above stated proposed methodology is data collection. For our manuscript, the data contains the nuances of the past 20 years, i.e., from January 2001 to April 2020, on a monthly basis and daily basis, revolves around the most important attribute of the Indian Stock exchange names as Sensex. Sensex likewise called the S&P BSE Sensex record, is the prominent document of the Bombay Stock exchange (BSE). The BSE SENSEX is India's most-followed bellwether file. It is intended to gauge the presentation of the 30 biggest, generally fluid, and monetarily stable organizations across key parts of the Indian economy that are recorded at BSE Ltd. The dataset obtained is in the form. csv format. Two types of datasets are employed for a specific reason, which will be explained afterwards. But for now basic implementation will be done upon yearly differenced dataset. The dataset basically contains two attributes, i.e., Date, and Opening value of stocks for that day (Figure 17.7).

	A	B	C
1	Date	Opening Value of Stocks	
2	01-Jan-01	3990.65	
3	02-Jan-01	3953.22	
4	03-Jan-01	3977.58	
5	04-Jan-01	4180.97	
6	05-Jan-01	4116.34	
7	08-Jan-01	4164.76	
8	09-Jan-01	4114.74	
9	10-Jan-01	4151.58	
10	11-Jan-01	4066.13	
11	12-Jan-01	4059.41	
12	15-Jan-01	4074.32	

FIGURE 17.7   Dataset for analysis.

Stage 2 of proposed methodology comprises of data cleaning. For this research, Dataset is cleaned manually using Microsoft Excel. Basically, the dataset contains many missing points, i.e., there are many instances when the stock market is closed, so for that days past perceptions are taken into consideration. For this research, it is hypothetically considered that when the stock market is closed, the values of stock prices remains the same as of the previous days, that's why past perception is considered for completing missing values (Figure 17.8).

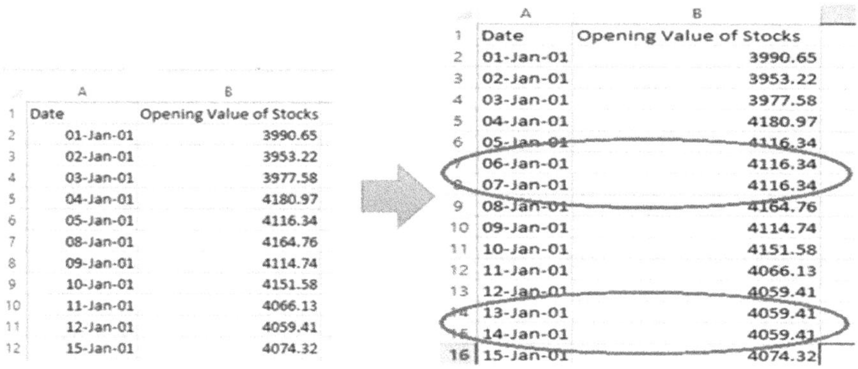

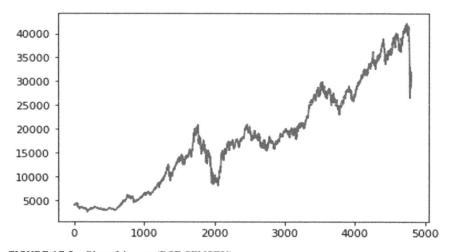

FIGURE 17.8   Dataset before and after data cleaning.

Different Packages identified with the different functionalities portrayed in the proposed methodology, are incorporated as, Pandas package, Matplotlib package, Keras package, Math package, and Sklearn package. Utilizing the previously mentioned tools exploratory analysis is performed to the dataset of the opening value of stocks of BSE SENSEX, and acquired outcomes are discussed underneath in detail (Figure 17.9).

FIGURE 17.9   Plot of dataset (BSE SENSEX).

Further Stage 3 comprises of exploratory analysis. This stage further bifurcated into three more parts, i.e.:

1. **Creation of Time-Series Object:** In the wake of data cleaning, which was the initial step after data collection, the time series object is prepared for the attributes of the dataset. Essentially, in time-series object dataset is set up in a manner on which analysis can be performed contingent on every day, week after week, or yearly premise. Here, the time-series object fundamentally contains two traits, i.e., Dates as datestamp and opening estimation of stocks as another characteristic. Essentially time-series object sets the datestamp as an index for the dataset.

2. **Plotting Time-Series Object:** Once the time-series object is generated, it can easily be plotted using different python libraries like matplotlib. Time-series plot will give the visual of the basic flow of our dataset. For our dataset, dates will be plotted along the x-axis and opening values of stock prices are plotted along the y-axis. The plot of the time series is cited beneath (Figure 17.10):

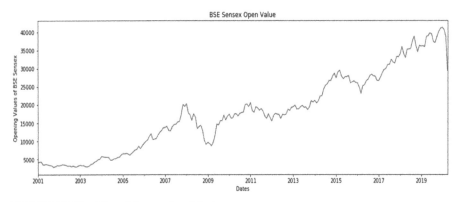

FIGURE 17.10   Plot of time-series object.

3. **Decomposition of Time-Series:** From the above plot, dataset representation is extremely simple. The above plot gives the essential progression of the dataset. After the time series object is plotted, it proposes working upon various segments like trend and seasonality. For more precise view upon various segments like trend and seasonality, time-series object is decomposed using decompose() function. Decomposed function basically decomposes the dataset into various

individual segments like trend, seasonality, and residue. The plot of the decomposed time-series object is cited beneath (Figure 17.11):

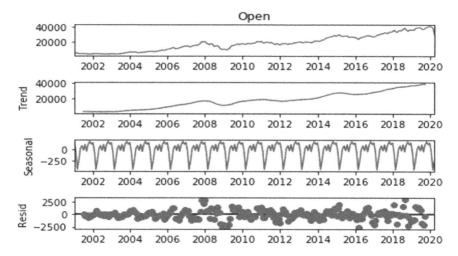

FIGURE 17.11   Decomposed time-series object.

From the above plot, dataset perception is simple. The above plot gives the essential pattern and irregularity example of the dataset. The basic trend and seasonality pattern of the dataset can be deduced very easily. Once the dataset is decomposed, it will be very simple to figure out which model adequately accommodates our dataset.

Stage 4 of proposed methodology implements the model fitting. When the exploratory investigation is finished, distinctive model capacities are applied to the time-series and depending upon their error, the best fit model is chosen. For this step, the dataset is divided into two parts Training and Testing [21, 22]. For this research, basically three different models are applied to the dataset and their results are compared in accuracy matrix. Different models are acquired on the dataset as follow:

1. **ARIMA:** The first and foremost step is to fit an ARIMA model to the whole BSE SENSEX dataset and audit the remaining blunders. Initially, the ARIMA (5,1,0) model is fitted to the dataset. This sets the lag incentive to 5 for autoregression (AR), utilizes a difference order of 1 to make the time series fixed, and utilizes a MA model of 0. While model fitting, a great deal of debug data is given about the fitting of the regression model. This debug data can be killed by

setting the disp contention to 0. The code snippet for model fitting of the ARIMA model is cited in Figure 17.12.

```
series = read_csv('csv_month.csv', header=0, parse_dates=[0], index_col=0, squeeze=True, date_parser=parser)
# fit model
model = ARIMA(series, order=(5,1,0))
model_fit = model.fit(disp=0)
print(model_fit.summary())
# plot
pyplot.plot(test)
pyplot.plot(predictions, color='orange')
pyplot.show()
```

FIGURE 17.12   Code snippet for ARIMA model fitting.

Using the above-cited code predicted values are plotted on the graph with testing data. The resulting graph is cited Figure 17.13.

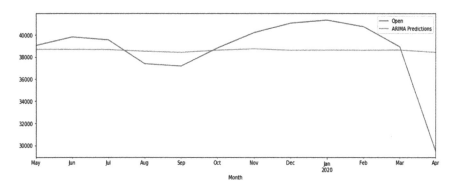

FIGURE 17.13   Plot of testing dataset and ARIMA prediction vs Datestamp.

In the above-cited graph, testing data of dataset is represented by blue line and predicted values are represented by orange line. Clearly visible from the graph that the ARIMA model is not the best fit for the dataset, as it is not even following the trend of the testing data. More conclusive results, i.e., its accuracy matrix will be discussed once all models are implemented.

2. **FbProphet:** After model fitting of ARIMA model, FbProphet is next model in queue. Basically FbProphet model is employed and fitted to the available dataset. Before final model fitting of FbProphet model, few basic changes are made to the dataset depending upon the basic implementation functions of FbProphet library. The code for model fitting of FbProphet model is cited Figure 17.14:

```
dataset= pd.read_csv(r"csv_month.csv")
train_dataset= pd.DataFrame()
train_dataset['ds'] = pd.to_datetime(X["Date"])
train_dataset['y']=y
prophet_basic = Prophet()
prophet_basic.fit(train_dataset)
future= prophet_basic.make_future_dataframe(periods=300)
forecast=prophet_basic.predict(future)
fig1 =prophet_basic.plot(forecast)
```

FIGURE 17.14   Code snippet for FbProphet model fitting.

Once the model fitting is completed, the graph for visualizing the prediction from the model is prepared. The prediction graph is cited Figure 17.15:

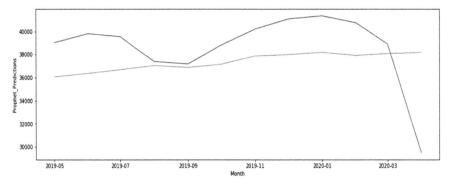

FIGURE 17.15   Plot of testing dataset and prophet prediction vs Datestamp.

It's quite visible from the graph that at least it is showing some trend depending upon the testing dataset. Therefore, if the monthly dataset is replaced by daily dataset, there is high probability of results improvement because daily basis dataset provides more data points to the model for more efficient training of the model. So once the FbProphet model is employed upon daily basis dataset of BSE SENSEX, graph of performance is obtained. The graph for FbProphet model on daily basis dataset is cited Figure 17.16:

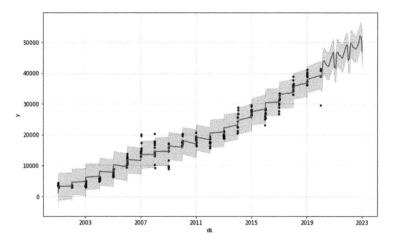

FIGURE 17.16   Plot of prophet prediction vs datestamp ds (dataset of day to day stock prices).

Clearly, it is showing great trends and value pattern for the datasets. So it is clearly evident that FbProphet model is performing exceptionally well for the dataset of daily stock price values.

3. **LSTM:** After FbProphet model fitting, further LSTM model is implemented upon dataset of monthly stock price values. For LSTM model fitting dataset is imported as Pandas Dataframe. LSTMs are touchy to the size of the input data, explicitly when the tanh or sigmoid (default) functions are utilized. It tends to be a decent practice to rescale the information to the scope of 0-to-1, likewise called normalizing. Normalization of dataset can be done by using MinMaxScaler() function from sklearn library. With time-series information, the grouping of qualities is significant. A basic technique that is utilized to split the arranged dataset into train and test datasets. The code beneath computes the file of the split point and isolates the information into the preparation datasets with 67% of the perceptions that can be utilized to train the model, and the remaining 33% of data is used for testing the model. Now the dataset is ready for model fitting and is employed using sequential() and LSTM network function. When the model is fit, the exhibition of the model on the train and test datasets can be evaluated without any problem (Figure 17.17).

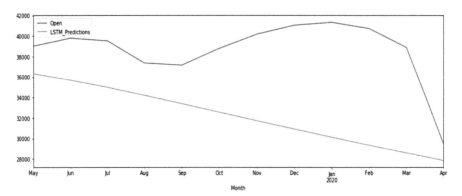

FIGURE 17.17   Plot of testing dataset and LSTM prediction vs. Datestamp.

It is clearly visible that the LSTM model is not following any pattern or trend of the testing dataset. So, for further testing dataset of daily stock price values is taken into consideration. Same algorithm is followed and implied on the new dataset. When arranged, the data is plotted, indicating the main dataset in blue, the forecasts for the preparation dataset in green, and the expectations on the concealed test dataset in red. The graph of prediction and model fitting of dataset containing daily stock price values is cited beneath (Figure 17.18).

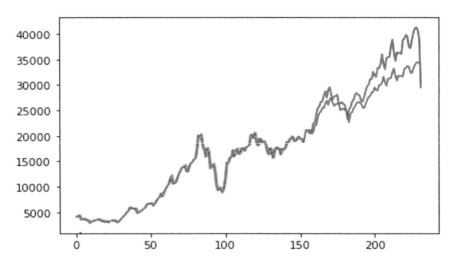

FIGURE 17.18   Plot of actual dataset (red), LSTM training (green), and LSTM prediction (blue).

It's quite evident results are improved drastically. But still there are some ups and downs in predicted values when compared actual testing dataset.

Finally, Stage 5 deals with error analysis of all the above-quoted models [23, 24]. Basically, in this research model fitting is done on two types of dataset, i.e., dataset containing stock prices on monthly basis, and dataset containing stock prices on daily basis. When the above-quoted three models are applied upon dataset containing stock prices on a monthly basis, depending upon their results error matrix is prepared which is as in Table 17.1.

TABLE 17.1 Error Matrix of Different Model Fitting Results for Dataset Containing Monthly Stock Prices

Errors\Models	ARIMA	LSTM	FbProphet
MSE	9355584.551	53818781.04	11719414.3
RMSE	3058.69	7336.128478	3423.36301
MAPE	5.85	16.34	7.41

Moreover, FbProphet, and LSTM models are also applied upon dataset containing day to day stock prices values and their error matrix is as in Table 17.2.

TABLE 17.2 Error Matrix of Different Model Fitting Results for Dataset Containing Day to Day Stock Prices

Errors\Models	FbProphet	LSTM
MSE	9355584.551	53818781.04
RMSE	3279.57	3588.53
MAPE	7.79	8.36

From above-cited Table 17.1 and Figures 17.13, 17.15, and 17.17, it can deduced that ARIMA model shows least error but not following the trends and seasonality in the graph, whereas FbProphet errors are not only quite comparable with ARIMA but also FbProphet graph follows the trend and pattern of testing dataset. Also Table 17.2; Figures 17.16 and 17.18, proves that Fbprophet is best fitted model, when dataset containing day to day stock prices is taken into consideration.

17.5 CONCLUSION

In this manuscript, proposes a data analysis upon univariate time-series dataset. Dataset employed for analysis is BSE SENSEX, which contains datestamp and opening price of stocks as an attribute. The time-series of dataset employed is from January 2001 to April 2020. After employing distinctive forecasting models and fitting the time series upon them, results in diverse determining results and can be broken down based on their forecast plots and error grid. In the wake of analysis, the plots and error lattice for various models is prepared, and it has been inferred that FbProphet execution is feasible, as it follows the fundamental pattern and design and in error framework, it gives the reliably less error, with a little special case, i.e., an error of FbProphet model is comparatively high contrasted with ARIMA model when dataset containing month to month estimations of stock costs is considered.

KEYWORDS

- **artificial neural network**
- **gross domestic product**
- **mean square error**
- **national stock exchange**
- **recurrent neural network**

REFERENCES

1. Sharma, N., & Akanksha, J., (2017). Combining of random forest estimates using LSboost for stock market index prediction. In: *2017 2nd International Conference for Convergence in Technology (I2CT)*. IEEE.
2. Armstrong, J. S., (2001). Combining forecasts. *Principles of Forecasting, 417–439.* Springer, Boston, MA.
3. Tseng, Fang-Mei, T., et al., (2001). Fuzzy ARIMA model for forecasting the foreign exchange market. *Fuzzy Sets and Systems, 118*(1), 9–19.
4. Nochai, R., & Titida, N., (2006). ARIMA model for forecasting oil palm price. *Proceedings of the 2nd IMT-GT Regional Conference on Mathematics, Statistics, and Applications.*
5. Fang-Mei, T., & Gwo-Hshiung, T., (2002). A fuzzy seasonal ARIMA model for forecasting. *Fuzzy Sets and Systems, 126*(3), 367–376.

6. Zhang, G. P., (2003). Time series forecasting using a hybrid ARIMA and neural network model. *Neurocomputing, 50*, 159–175.

7. Iqbal, N., et al., (2005). Use of the ARIMA model for forecasting wheat area and production in Pakistan. *Journal of Agriculture and Social Sciences, 1*(2), 120–122.

8. Conejo, A. J., et al., (2005). Day-ahead electricity price forecasting using the wavelet transform and ARIMA models. *IEEE Transactions on Power Systems, 20*(2), 1035–1042.

9. Chikkakrishna, N. K., et al., (2019). Short-term traffic prediction using sarima and FbPROPHEt. In: *2019 IEEE 16th India Council International Conference (INDICON)*. IEEE.

10. McArdle, J., (2020). *Utilizing Multivariate Time-series Data to Detect Damaged Wind Turbine Blades*. Diss. Utica College.

11. Shrove, M. T., & Jovanov, E., (2020). Software defect trend forecasting in open source projects using a univariate ARIMA model and FBProphet. *Int. J. Softw. Eng., 8*(1), 1–15.

12. Mengistie, T. T., (2020). COVID-19 outbreak data analysis and prediction modeling using data mining technique. *International Journal of Computer (IJC), 38*(1), 37–60.

13. Kim, H. Y., & Chang, H. W., (2018). Forecasting the volatility of stock price index: A hybrid model integrating LSTM with multiple GARCH-type models. *Expert Systems with Applications, 103*, 25–37.

14. Abdel-Nasser, M., & Karar, M., (2019). Accurate photovoltaic power forecasting models using deep LSTM-RNN. *Neural Computing and Applications, 31*(7), 2727–2740.

15. Devers, K. J., & Richard, M. F., (2000). Study design in qualitative research-2: Sampling and data collection strategies. *Education for Health, 13*(2), 263.

16. Historical Values of BSE Sensex, (2020). Indices: S&P BSE SENSEX. Retrieved from https://www.bseindia.com/indices/IndexArchiveData.html (accessed on 11 November 2021).

17. Rahm, E., & Hong, H. D., (2000). Data cleaning: Problems and current approaches. *IEEE Data Eng. Bull., 23*(4), 3–13.

18. Angadi, M. C., & Amogh, P. K., (2015). Time Series data analysis for stock market prediction using data mining techniques with R. *International Journal of Advanced Research in Computer Science, 6*(6).

19. Cleveland, W. P., & George, C. T., (1976). Decomposition of seasonal time series: A model for the census X-11 program. *Journal of the American Statistical Association, 71*(355), 581–587.

20. Mondal, P., Labani, S., & Saptarsi, G., (2014). Study of effectiveness of time series modeling (ARIMA) in forecasting stock prices. *International Journal of Computer Science, Engineering, and Applications, 4*(2), 13.

21. Sharma, N., & Juneja, A., (2019). Extreme gradient boosting with squared logistic loss function. In: *Machine Intelligence and Signal Analysis* (pp. 313–322). Springer, Singapore.

22. Sharma, N., (2018). *XGBoost. The Extreme Gradient Boosting for Mining Applications*. GRIN Verlag.

23. Yadav, S., & Nonita, S., (2018). Homogenous ensemble of time-series models for Indian stock market. *International Conference on Big Data Analytics*. Springer, Cham.

24. Yadav, S., & Nonita, S., (2019). Forecasting of Indian stock market using time-series models. *Computing and Network Sustainability* (pp. 405–412). Springer, Singapore.

CHAPTER 18

Enhanced Fish Detection in Underwater Video Using Wavelet-Based Color Correction and Machine Learning

JITENDRA P. SONAWANE,[1] MUKESH D. PATIL,[1] and GAJANAN K. BIRAJDAR[2]

[1]*Department of Electronics and Telecommunication Engineering, Ramrao Adik Institute of Technology, Nerul, Navi Mumbai – 400706, Maharashtra, India*

[2]*Department of Electronics Engineering, Ramrao Adik Institute of Technology, Nerul, Navi Mumbai – 400706, Maharashtra, India, E-mail: gajanan.birajdar@rait.ac.in*

ABSTRACT

In oceanography, it has become imperative to explore, develop, and protect marine resources. Due to the physical properties of the underwater medium, data considered/obtained in a raw form is often degraded; this result is a combination of low contrast, haziness, blurring details, color deviations, non-uniform illuminations, etc. Thus, enhancement of the scene in an underwater environment has become necessary to raise applications in a practical scenario. As a requisite step in the processing of the underwater scene, enhancement methods vary depending upon the application. The usefulness of the machine learning algorithm has also played a vital role in classification. Machine learning is a technique, which uses a computational method for analyzing data that builds an analytical model. It is a subgroup of artificial intelligence, based on the notion that systems can learn from acquired data, then identify objects/patterns, and make a finding based on the model with minimum human intervention. The proposed approach not only enhances the color content of the underwater video but also can maintain the structure of the original input videos, the delivery of its RGB components should be consistent, but the problem arises in the underwater scene where the wavelength of few colors gets consumed with an increase in depth of water. Therefore, to avoid the effect of this color loss from the underwater videos, pre-processing to be initiated by wavelet-based color correction techniques with different evaluation parameters followed by feature extraction to reduce the amount of redundant data for a given analysis. Besides, fish classification is done using a machine learning approach.

18.1 INTRODUCTION

Imaging in an underwater environment is generally affected by poor visibility, low contrast, and color degradation because of light attenuation in water. The attenuation of light is caused by absorption and scattering. In water, attenuation of light impacts the general execution of the framework for the underwater environment. As the light entering in medium gets collided with molecules/particles present in the water, the incident light gets reflected, refracted, or scattered depending on the wavelength of the incident wave. Forward scattering results in blurring of signal, whereas backward scattering limits the contrast of the images, which then consolidates the impacts on the quality of video received at the processing end [1].

Due to absorption, light strength gets reduced, and the scattering effect reduces both image quality and light strength. The visibility range of the underwater environment can be increased with the use of artificial lighting sources. Underwater images are not only suffered from the problems of light attenuation but also with non-uniform illumination. Filters used in underwater while filming at depth in ambient light are not able to correct the color.

Figure 18.1 shows two frames extracted from two distinct underwater videos from the fish4knowledge database. All the data is collected from fish4knowledge project repositories. As part of the project, the repository has developed a public web-accessible database of the videos and their associated computed descriptors. The objective of the project is to enable, extract useful scientific information from the enormous amount of data provided by the video cameras. By visual analysis of the frames, it is observed that the quality of both frames is poor.

Light enters the water medium causes absorption and scattering. Water molecules and even floating particles in water give rise to the problem of absorption, which is the loss of energy from the signal. As the light travels in the medium may change the direction depending on the refractive index of the medium. As mentioned earlier, scattering is a deflection from a direct propagation path. Scattering of light can occur due to suspended particles and size of which is comparable to that of the wavelength of light [1], which is also known as the diffraction of light, or if the refractive index of the matter is different from the refractive index of water, then refraction will occur.

FIGURE 18.1 Sample frames extracted from underwater videos web-based database 'fish4knowledge' [20]. Photos courtesy of Fish4Knowledge. https://groups.inf.ed.ac.uk/f4k/index.html

Images or videos in the underwater environment are captured using either by installed cameras or by the remotely operated vehicles (ROV), which are used for various applications underwater like monitoring activity, etc. An artificial light source can be used for illumination. Figure 18.2 elaborates on the imaging geometry. The total light intensity that enters the lens of the camera and creates the image is the summation of three components, P1, P2, and P3. P1 is the reflected component of the light from the picture can have useful content. Path P2 is a segment of light which gets scattered before reaching the camera lens. The effect of image blurring is obtained from forward scattered light. P3 is the scattered light while entering the lens, gets collided with particles between the scene and the camera. Additional brightness is added by the P3 component, which causes contrast loss. Scattered light with angle θ is relative to the direction of propagation.

Light entering the medium is not only disrupted by water molecules present but also with the other elements like dissolved organic matter or floating matters, which causes loss in light. Floating particles named as marine snow raises the chances of absorption and scattering. Increasing depth in water causes decay of different colors as per their wavelengths.

Blue color light (430 nm) has least absorption coefficient (0.0144 m^{-1}), green color light (550 nm) has the absorption coefficient of 0.0638 m^{-1}, and for red color light (700 nm) the absorption coefficient is 0.650 m^{-1} with increase in wavelength, absorption coefficient increases.

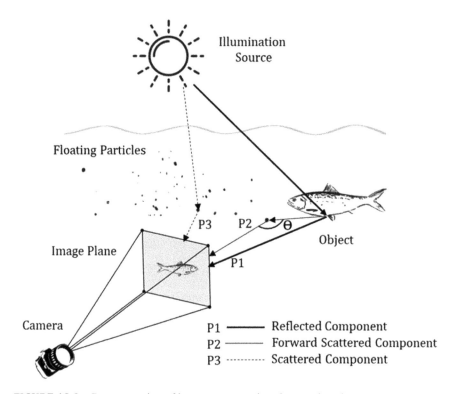

FIGURE 18.2   Representation of image geometry in submerged environment.

Water is marginally blue as an overtone and blends vibrational assimilation of bands, yet far less exceptional, see above reach out through the red piece of the noticeable range with a little top at 739 nm and shoulder at 836 nm, in addition to a littler fourth overtone at 606 nm, and extremely little fifth suggestion (at 514 nm) and consolidated hint (at 660 nm) groups [4]. This spectrum (red light assimilates multiple times more than blue light), along with prominent dissipating of blue light over red light, adds to the blue shade of different sources of water.

At a depth of 5 m, the red color almost vanishes. After 10 m, the orange color is gone. Most of the yellow color is lost by reaching a depth of

20 m. After 30 m depth, the only blue color remains and travels further. Blue, followed by the green color wavelength, travels the larger distance in the water as the wavelength is short. Underwater imaging has various challenges perceived as poor visibility, non-uniform lighting, low contrast, noise, improper color, etc. Image contrast enhancement of a scene can be used so that such images can be processed in computer vision applications. However, selecting a useful algorithm for contrast enhancement is not an easy as different parametric measures are used in defining the image quality expected at the output. As the depth in water increases, the light is reaching the bottom decreases. Even the wavelength penetrating the water will be different for each color. Table 18.1 shows a representation of how the light is absorbed in water.

TABLE 18.1   Light Absorption at Various Depth in Water

Color		Approximate Depth
Red		~ 5 meters
Orange		~ 10 meters (50%)
Yellow		~ 20 meters (25%)
Green		~ 30 meters (12.5%)
Blue		~ 60 meters (06.25%)

At regular depth intervals, sunlight illumination will drop almost by half. Red light is dropped almost by half from the surface, but blue is having shorter wavelengths as it can reach larger depth, as to this reason, most of the scenes are impacted by green and blue color [23].

Therefore, the fact that several factors limit the identification of fish in an underwater environment. Thus, the need arises to enhance underwater videos. We have utilized the wavelet-based color correction technique, which is proposed by Singh et al. in 2015 [8]. Wavelet-based color correction, as presented in [8], is employed to enhance fish classification accuracy. The method possesses the better results even with our data, after application of wavelet, as the approximation coefficient is processed to enhance the colors and detailed coefficient which holds the important structural information are later combined with the results from approximation coefficients. It is observed with different evaluation parameters that technique holds better in comparison with existing techniques. In the following segment of the detection of fish species, the presented machine learning (ML) algorithm using

SVM as a classifier yields a better outcome. The principal motive behind keeping this two-stage approach was to observe whether the enhancement of the videos would present any importance in classification or not, and results indicate the positive impact of the same.

This chapter is organized as follows: In the first section, the brief introduction to the underwater environment and associated concepts are presented. The second section presents a summary of previous research on the enhancement and the fish classification. The third section of the book chapter explains the proposed method comprehensively. In the fourth section, the enhancement technique, along with the evaluation parameters, explained. Machine learning and related methods used for classification and performance evaluation are explained in the fifth section. The sixth section elaborates results collected from both stages of work, and a detailed analysis is presented. The chapter ends with a conclusion and scope of future work.

18.2 LITERATURE REVIEW

In 2010, Raimondo Schettini et al. [1] pointed in the analysis that, to support underwater imaging, an appropriate database of images for various imaging conditions, along with standard models for subjective and objective evaluation of the outcomes is yet expected.

In 2012, Ancuti et al. [2] proposed the underwater image and video enhancement by fusion; the chapter introduces an approach capable of enhancing underwater images and video. The technique is developed on fusion principle, which has marked importance in various applications where reconstruction of image and data reduction is expected. In 2012, Isaak Kavasidis et al. [3] proposed six algorithms; those resulted in better results while the recordings were observed in clear-water and with uniform foundations. At the point, when temporary disturbance like typhoons and tropical storms, were present, the presentation of the considerable number of calculations, in distinguishing objects, degraded, and become impractical.

In 2014, Miao Yang et al. [4] offered the image quality evaluation metric for underwater video; the proposed metric had the option to foresee the relative sharpness/haziness of underwater images effectively and to recognize pictures taken in various scenes. Metric outperforms. The proposed measurement is a reference for image enhancement, classification, and restoration in an underwater environment. Wang et al. in 2014 [5] proposed a contrast enhancement technique in the low light video. The proposed method is based on a segment-wise stretching of the brightness component. The quality of an image is obtained by splitting the brightness component into the darker and brighter part. As per illumination conditions, model parameters were estimated accordingly.

In 2014, Pugh et al. [6] presented a method for the classification of seabed substrates in underwater video. The system proposed, preliminary resulted in various feature realization using Gabor wavelets, histograms also classification part is executed using SVC, K-NN both on full-frame and patched based analysis, resulting in 93% accuracy.

Later in 2015, N. Sathish Kumar et al. [7] offered a frame extraction algorithm having applications in underwater medium, also presented an approach for moving object detection in frames using artificial neural network (ANN). In 2015, Singh et al. [8] presented a wavelet-based approach for the enhancement of underwater imagery with the color correction method. The colors were improvised using DWT to split approximation coefficients of the input scene and then combined later with a detailed coefficient to retain the original structure.

In the same year (in 2015), Ashour et al. [9] presented how to enhance the videos using the median filter, Wiener filter, and Gaussian filter. The technique presented makes use of a database containing the head of a stonefish as a set of images. The features of the fish head are observed by comparing the features of fish-head images with video, by using a Speeded Up Robust Features (SURF) method. The features in video and image datasets are compared with the histogram and k-nearest neighbor (KNN). In 2015, Zhao et al. [10] focused on extracting optical properties from background color, which resulted in the radiation of natural illumination. Therefore, the use of artificial illumination is required.

Qing et al. [11] in 2016, presented a multidimensional underwater video dehazing method for enhancement and restoration of underwater video. The proposed method uses a single image with a dark channel prior. Then, the correlation is calculated between the adjacent video frames transmission and filter background light, as stated by spatial-temporal information fusion; however, movement of objects, camera, and water, etc., the transmission values changes. To mitigate the problem, Qing et al. used the fast-tracking and the least-squares method by adding offset to transmission.

Papp et al. [12] in 2016, proposed the method which can detect, classify, and track individual object recognition, this method utilized the Kalman filter to track the object and Hungarian technique to match pair of an object in consecutive frames, and then classified object using C-SVM technique with the use of RBF kernel. In the year 2016, Jonas Jagar et al. [13] presented work that uses object proposal classification for fish detection; they have used binary SVM for classification of fish and background. Then using multiclass SVM fish recognition is performed. For both, the SVMs used CNN features extracted from AlexNet for prediction.

In the same year, Quevedo et al. [14] offered underwater video enhancement using multi-camera super-resolution, which enhances the objective quality. It is also mentioned that in a complex environment, fusion super-resolution techniques represent good results. The computation time required for the execution of the algorithm is more, which needs to be improvised to cater to the need for real-time implementation.

In 2017, Sun et al. [15] proposed a deep CNN model along with data augmentation for underwater object recognition. Though the training set was insufficient, the transfer approach performed well. To improvise the object detection from video, a weighted probabilities decision mechanism was used.

Honnutagi [16], in the latter year, introduced underwater image enhancement using fusion principal, it also employed weight map techniques, in which it was used to resolve low contrast problem present in underwater is resolved. Also, parameters like MSE, PSNR, entropy used for result representation.

In 2019, Liu et al. [17] proposed an underwater imaging system and constructed the benchmark RUIE. This benchmark targets at the tasks for enhancement like poor visibility, color cast, and higher-level classification. Liu also benchmarked some of the crucial challenges of the underwater image enhancement.

In the year 2019, Anwar et al. [18] proposed a new underwater image synthesis method to offer a robust and data-driven solution. Also incorporated a deep convolutional neural network, which has resulted in higher accuracy, robustness, and flexibility for marine imaging applications.

Jamadandi et al. [19], in 2019, used a deep learning (DL) framework to enhance underwater images. The technique proposed is augmenting network with wavelet corrected transformations, which resulted in recovering highly degraded images. The said algorithm also resulted in low noise and overall better global contrast while preserving the edges, which are blurred by the backscattering of light, and results were characterized by the PSNR and SSIM values. In the same year, Tang et al. [20] put forward a method to enhance the underwater scene based on Retinex. The method composes of the pre-correction of color to achieve uniformity in degraded underwater images and reduce the dominant color preset in the scene depending on the depth of water. The improved multiscale Retinex is associated with the intensity channel to estimate the source component and the reflection component. In the last part, the image is restored. Even as the need arises, the color in the original image can be preserved. BV Deep et al. [25] in 2019 proposed the hybrid CNN approach with SVM and k-NN with DL techniques, and they have tested the framework on the fish4knowledge dataset, which are observed to get a better result using DeepCNN-kNN approach.

18.3   PROPOSED ALGORITHM

We have divided the complete work into two segments as enhancement of the underwater video and classification of the species present in the video based on the dataset. In the first part of enhancement, acquired underwater video is converted to frames, and then the wavelet-based color correction algorithm is used to achieve the enhancement of the video using the wavelet-based method. In the second stage, classification of different types of species from video, calculating the accuracy of prediction on original video and enhanced video as well as observed the impact of the enhancement on the result is obtained.

In this section, we have described the first segment of the proposed approach. There must be a uniform distribution of RGB component to achieve a good quality of image and video quality, but in an underwater environment, this is slightly difficult due to many reasons as colors of particular wavelengths gets eliminated as the depth of water increase. Therefore, to recover from color loss, these images or frames need to be pre-processed by an adequate enhancement algorithm.   The existing image enhancement methods are suitable in the natural air environment only and may not be applicable for underwater image/video, which is affected by insufficient colors, poor visibility, and low contrast.

The enhancement approach presented here not only enhances the color content of underwater images but is also able to maintain the structure of the original input image/videos. Figure 18.3 explains the detailed structure of the enhancement process followed to achieve better results. The frames are extracted from the videos, and discrete wavelet transform is applied on frames. We get two components out of the transform as detailed coefficient and approximated coefficient. Out of these two components, we have preserved the detailed coefficient for further use and apply the contrast correction so that we can reduce the impact of the green-blue color, which impacts the most in an underwater environment.

In the next step, as the imbalance of the color is observed due to contrast correction, the color correction technique is applied. Figure 18.3 explains in detail how the color correction is achieved. In color correction, a maximum and average value of the RGB component are evaluated, then according to the YCbCr color model, the average and maximum luminance are calculated. The color casting factor is also calculated for red, green, blue color according to their maximum, and average white scale factors are evaluated after luminance calculation.

As per the gain factor calculation, the image is color corrected. In the final stage of enhancement, the saturation component is stretched, and then, the inverse discrete wavelet transform is applied to observe the enhancement in frames.

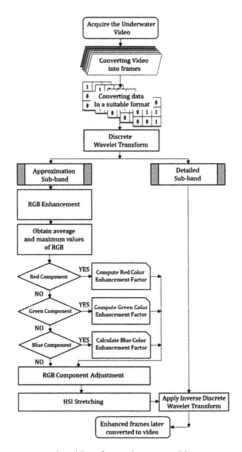

FIGURE 18.3   Enhancement algorithm for underwater video.

The second phase of the proposed system is fish classification. Fish classification is a process of detection and identification of fish species, as per similarities matches with the database and also the features of the fish. Fish classification is often considered as a useful task in fishing and evaluating population density of the different species, also to preserve the rare species. Physical fish classification is a repetitive errand for individuals who are not experts.

Classification of fish is usually done by their characteristics using ML can save time, save effort. Similarly, fish classification automated by ML approach can speed up the process with improvement in the identification of fish species. Several algorithms are presented in various literature for fish species detection, classification/identification. Figure 18.4 explains the approach for fish classification using ML.

FIGURE 18.4 Machine learning approach for classification of fish species.

18.4   VIDEO ENHANCEMENT IN UNDERWATER ENVIRONMENT

18.4.1   *WAVELET TRANSFORM IN TWO DIMENSIONS*

In image processing, 2-D DWT is used, in 2-D DWT, one 2-D scaling function $\varnothing(x,y)$ and three 2-dimensional wavelet functions, $\varphi^H(x,y)$, $\varphi^V(x,y)$, and $\varphi^D(x,y)$ are required. These are the products of 1-D scaling function and corresponding one-dimensional wavelet function, which are given as follows [26]:

$$\varnothing(x,y) = \varnothing(x)*\varnothing(y) \tag{1}$$

$$\varphi^H(x,y) = \varphi(x)*\varnothing(y) \tag{2}$$

$$\varphi^V(x,y) = \varnothing(x)*\varphi(y) \tag{3}$$

$$\varphi^D(x,y) = \varphi(x)*\varphi(y) \tag{4}$$

Where scaling function gives the approximation coefficients ($\varnothing(x,y)$) and wavelet function gives the detailed coefficients those are given as horizontal coefficient ($\varphi^H(x,y)$) vertical coefficients ($\varphi^V(x,y)$), and diagonal coefficients ($\varphi^D(x,y)$).

These, scaled, and translated basis functions are as follows:

$$\varnothing_{j,m,n}(x,y) = 2^{j/2}\varnothing\left(2^j x - m, 2^j y - n\right) \tag{5}$$

$$\varphi^i_{j,m,n}(x,y) = 2^{j/2}\varphi^i\left(2^j x - m, 2^j y - n\right), i = \{H,V,D\} \tag{6}$$

Index i assumes the value H (horizontal), V (vertical), D (diagonal). The discrete wavelet transform of image $f(x,y)$ of size M×N is then

$$W_\varnothing(j_0, m, n) = \frac{1}{\sqrt{MN}}\sum_{x=0}^{M-1}\sum_{y=0}^{N-1} f(x,y)\varnothing_{j_0,m,n}(x,y) \tag{7}$$

$$W^i_\varphi(j, m, n) = \frac{1}{\sqrt{MN}}\sum_{x=0}^{M-1}\sum_{y=0}^{N-1} f(x,y)\varphi^i_{j,m,n}(x,y), i = \{H,V,D\} \tag{8}$$

$f(x,y)$ is obtained via the inverse wavelet transform

$$f(x,y) = \frac{1}{\sqrt{MN}}\sum_m\sum_n W_\varnothing(j_0,m,n)\varnothing_{j_0,m,n}(x,y)$$

$$+\frac{1}{\sqrt{MN}}\sum_{i=H,V,D}\sum_{j=j_0}^{\infty}\sum_m\sum_n W^i_\varphi(j,m,n)\varphi^i_{j,m,n}(x,y) \tag{9}$$

Figure 18.5 shows the diagrammatic approach to explain the process. Analysis filter banks are uses for taking discrete wavelet transform, whereas the synthesis filter banks are used for taking inverse wavelet transform. In the middle of two resulting decompositions are shown.

18.4.2   IMAGE QUALITY ASSESSMENT PARAMETERS

The quality of the images or videos is often determined by the histogram comparison, the peak signal to noise ratio (PSNR), and the structure similarity measure (SSIM) [27]. The following section will take a brief review of the evaluation parameters used in this particular proposed method.

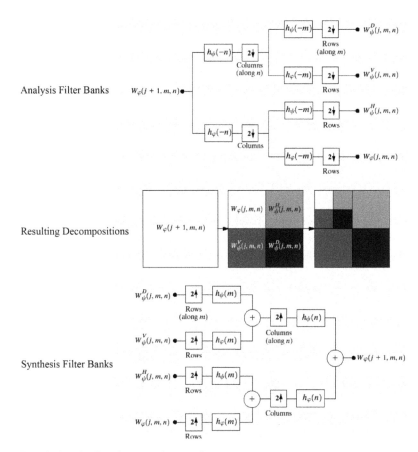

FIGURE 18.5   The 2-D fast wavelet transform.

18.4.2.1   *PEAK SIGNAL TO NOISE RATIO (PSNR)*

PSNR is defined as the ratio of the maximum possible energy of a signal to the energy of noise that is affecting the accuracy. Since numerous signals have an exceptionally wide dynamic range, PSNR is typically represented as the logarithmic decibel scale. The PSNR is most regularly utilized as a proportion of reconstruction quality of lossy compression codecs similar to that of image compression. The signal for this situation is the first information, and the loss is the error presented by compression. While comparing compression codes which is an approximation of capability of a human being for quality of reconstruction; in some exceptional cases, reconstruction of a signal may give off an impression that signal reconstructed is very much similar to that of the original signal even though the PSNR value is low, but as a general case the higher PSNR value represents the better reconstruction. It is just convincingly substantial when it is utilized to look at observations from the equivalent codec and the same content.

$$MSE = \frac{1}{MN}\sum_{i=1}^{M}\sum_{j=1}^{N}\left[I(i,j)-K(i,j)\right]^2 \tag{10}$$

$$PSNR = 20\,log_{10}\left(\frac{MAX_I}{\sqrt{MISE}}\right) \tag{11}$$

where; MAX_I is the maximum value of the image pixel; the value is 255 for images that represent an 8-bit per sample. If the images are represented by B bits per sample, then the value of MAX_I is 2^B-1.

18.4.2.2 STRUCTURE SIMILARITY MEASURE (SSIM)

Expecting that the human visual system is profoundly adjusted to remove basic structural information from the visual perspective, it is recommended that the proportion of auxiliary data or a slight change in the structural information can provide an approximation to the observed image distortion. This procedure can be comprehended by error sensitivity in three distinct manners. To begin with, the error sensitivity approach gauges apparent degradation of the image, changes in structural data may degrade the image. The error sensitivity is an approach, representing the capacity of a significant early-stage component of HVS.

The new top-down approach of representing usefulness is the general functionality of HVS. Finally, the issues of usual picture complexity and decorrelation are additionally kept away from somewhat because the new way of thinking does not endeavor to foresee picture quality by aggregating the errors.

The following section explains the universal image quality index [28]:

$$l(x,y) = \frac{2\mu_x\mu_y}{\mu_x^2 + \mu_y^2} \tag{12}$$

$$c(x,y) = \frac{2\sigma_x\sigma_y}{\sigma_x^2 + \sigma_y^2} \tag{13}$$

$$s(x,y) = \frac{2\sigma_{xy}}{\sigma_x + \sigma_y} \tag{14}$$

By using the above equations, a UIQI is given as:

$$UIQI = l(x,y)c(x,y)s(x,y) = \frac{4\mu_x\mu_y\sigma_x\sigma_y}{\left(\mu_x^2 + \mu_y^2\right)\left(\sigma_x^2 + \sigma_y^2\right)} \tag{15}$$

SSIM technique utilizes three components as luminance, contrast, and structural comparisons for the difference between original and distorted image, as presented in Eqs. (12)–(14) is reflected in Eqn. (15).

$$SSIM = f\left(l(x,y), c(x,y), s(x,y)\right) \tag{16}$$

Here $l(x,y)$ gives the luminance, contrast, and structural components are follows as:

$$l(x,y) = \frac{2\mu_x\mu_y + C_1}{\mu_x^2 + \mu_y^2 + C_1} \tag{17}$$

$$c(x,y) = \frac{2\sigma_x\sigma_y + C_2}{\sigma_x^2 + \sigma_y^2 + C_2} \tag{18}$$

$$s(x,y) = \frac{2\sigma_{xy} + C_3}{\sigma_x + \sigma_y + C_3} \tag{19}$$

where; μ_x, μ_y gives the mean values of original and distorted images. Whereas, σ_x, σ_y denote the standard deviation of original and distorted image respectively, and σ_{xy} gives the covariance of both images. C_1, C_2, and C_3 are small constant to avoid instability, while the denominator is almost zero. Based on the above Eqs. (17)–(19) SSIM is given as:

$$SSIM(x,y) = \left[l(x,y)\right]^\alpha . \left[c(x,y)\right]^\beta . \left[s(x,y)\right]^\gamma \tag{20}$$

where; $\alpha > 0$, $\beta > 0$, and $\gamma > 0$ are parameters used to adjust the relative importance of three components. using $\alpha = \beta = \gamma = 1$ and $C_3 = C_2/2$ the SSIM is given as:

$$SSIM(x,y) = \frac{\left(2\mu_x\mu_y + C_1\right)\left(2\sigma_{xy} + C_2\right)}{\left(\mu_x^2 + \mu_y^2 + C_1\right)\left(\sigma_x^2 + \sigma_y^2 + C_2\right)} \tag{21}$$

for further simplification $C_1 = C_2 = 0$ gives

$$SSIM(x,y) = \frac{4\mu_x \mu_y \sigma_{xy}}{\left(\mu_x^2 + \mu_y^2\right)\left(\sigma_x^2 + \sigma_y^2\right)} \tag{22}$$

18.4.2.3   ENTROPY

The entropy or average information of a signal or an image can be calculated by obtaining information from a histogram. The histogram shows the different gray level probabilities in the image. If we consider entropy as a measure of error, then, as the level of error increases, the entropy also increases, and events become less predictable.

18.5   MACHINE LEARNING

Machine learning (ML) can be elaborated as computerizing and improving the learning procedure of computers, depending on their encounters without being programmed with no human intervention or minimal human intervention. The procedure begins with taking care of good quality information and afterward preparing our machines (computers) by building ML models for utilizing the information and various algorithms. The selection of an algorithm relies upon what sort of information do we have and what sort of assignment we are attempting to automate.

In the ML approach, the information or data on which the execution needs to be done is gathered in suitable for processing, in which, there may be a broad set of N (no. of elements). Better the quality of data better than the modeling. Sometimes, the information fetched needs to be processed as many of the times the information is in a raw form. Thus, incomplete information or an imbalance in data may present less accuracy. Pre-processing is one of the essential steps which can be performed in order to achieve the speedup. After pre-processing, the data is made consistent and relevant; after that, converted to a suitable format which machine can understand. Such a process aims to find useful features from the information which are computationally fast and still, and they preserve the discriminating features.

18.5.1   SUPPORT VECTOR MACHINES (SVMS)

SVMs were introduced in 1992; from there, it was considered to be the beginning of the era of the learning from example. SVMs quickly gained the attention of different communities like pattern recognition due to multiple theoretical and computational advantages. SVM represents the breakthrough in the theory of learning systems. Statistical Learning which is considered as the backbone of SVM, provides the framework for modeling learning algorithms, merges the field of ML and statistics, and inspires new algorithms that overcome most of the difficulties faced by the conventional learning algorithm such as noisy data, high dimensionality, and associated sparseness and non-gaussian distribution of data.

SVM is a powerful supervised ML algorithm. Unlike many other algorithms, like neural network which requires much complex operation in order to achieve a better result, SVM provides better results. When we need to work with a multidimensional approach in SVM, we can use hyperplane. Hence, the hyperplane can be defined as follows:

Consider the two-dimensional case, in which the two dimensional linearly separable data can be divided by a line. The function of line is $y = bx + c$, we rename x with $x1$ and y with $x2$, and we get:

$$bx1 - x2 + c = 0 \tag{1}$$

If we define $x = (x1, x2)$ and $w = (a, -1)$, then:

$$w.x + b = 0 \tag{2}$$

This equation is derived from 2-D vectors but can work with any dimension, and this is a hyperplane. Once we obtain a hyperplane, predictions can be made.

Several selections of kernel functions are available; depending upon the applicability, the choices can be made. We have used the radial basis function (RBF) in order to achieve the maximum possible accuracy of classification of the fish species.

RBF kernel function is defined as:

$$K(xi, xj) = exp\left(-\gamma \|xi - xj\|2\right) \tag{3}$$

18.5.2   K-MEANS CLUSTERING

K-means used to solve the clustering problem. The procedure is to partition a given dataset through a certain number of non-overlapping subgroups, also known as a cluster. Assume the number of these clusters to be k. The purpose is to define k centers, one for each cluster. These centers should be placed in such a manner that by keeping longer distance, different location between clusters produces different results.

In the next step, pick each point representing a given dataset and associate it to the nearest center. When no data point is left, an early clustering is completed. Then evaluate k new centroids as the barycenter of the clusters resulting from the previous step. This is the iterative process, which then results in such that the k centers change their location iteratively until there is no variation. Thus, the error goes on reducing as iteration continues. K-means clustering algorithm proposes an objective function given by:

$$J = \sum_{j=1}^{k} \sum_{i=1}^{n} \left\| x_i^{(j)} - c_j \right\|^2 \tag{4}$$

where; J is an objective function; k is no. of clusters; n is the number of cases; $x_i^{(j)}$ is case i; c_j Centroid for cluster j; $\left\| x_i^{(j)} - c_j \right\|$ is distance function.

18.5.3   FEATURE EXTRACTION

In order to detect the object and to determine the shape in the scene, we have utilized the k-means clustering. We can divide the scene into different parts, known as segments. The idea of processing the entire image is not practical as the complete image may have regions that do not contain the relevant information. By splitting the image into a segment, we can only process the relevant information, thus increase in computational efficiency. An image is a collection of pixels. We can assimilate the pixels that have similar attributes using image segmentation.

In order to obtain features, different image processing techniques are applied like resizing, thresholding, normalization, etc. Features are a vital part of image processing. After that, feature extraction techniques are applied to get features that will be useful in classifying and recognition of images. Feature extraction is a translation of raw data into the inputs that valuable information for a ML model. Some of the intrinsic features can be derived from the raw data. Figure 18.6 shows how the image was extracted and masked for further utilization. We need these intrinsic features so that only relevant information is fed to the model, as with a crucial feature-poor model that can work better over the good model fed with unnecessary features.

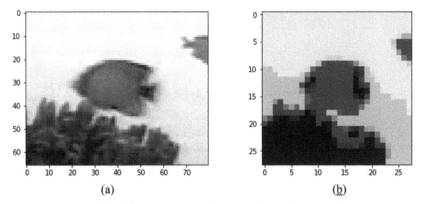

(a)   (b)

FIGURE 18.6   (a) Original image extracted from the video; (b) masked image.

Objects have various visual characteristics, such as shape, texture. The shape of the object represents its profile and structural information. Shape-based features are generally used for the measurement and recognition of an object. The shape-based features can be obtained by two methods; based on boundary and region. With the use of shape features, the target objects can be identified, the accuracy of the shape-based feature depends on the segmentation results. Whereas in texture-based feature extraction, as the texture is a repetitive pattern of information. Texture-based extraction partitions an image into a disjoint set of regions based on certain homogeneous texture characteristics.

18.5.4   EVALUATION PARAMETER FOR MACHINE LEARNING MODEL

In ML, various different parameters play a vital role in representing results. Parameters like confusion matrix, accuracy, precision, recall, specificity, F1-score, precision-recall curve ROC curve, etc., are used to determine the efficiency of the ML model performance.

Accuracy is the most commonly used metric to identify or to present whether a model is working correctly or not and is not a clear indicator of the performance. The results degrade when classes are imbalanced. Precision is a parameter that represents how accurate the model predicts true positives. False positives are the results in which the cases are considered incorrectly as positive, but in actuality, they are negative. While recall represents the ability to find all useful occurrences in a dataset, precision expresses the segment of the data in the model says was relevant and is relevant.

$$Accuracy = \frac{no.\,of\ correct\ predictions}{Total\ no.\,of\ predictions} \tag{5}$$

$$Precision = \frac{no.\,of\ correct\ positives}{.\,of\ correct\ positives + no.\,of\ false\ positives} \tag{6}$$

$$Recall = \frac{no.\,of\ correct\ positives}{total\ no.\,of\ positives} \tag{7}$$

F1 Score is the weighted average, i.e., overall accuracy measure of the model considering Precision and Recall. This score counts both false positives (FP) and false negatives (FN). F1-score is more useful than accuracy, primarily when the dataset represents an uneven class distribution.

$$F1Score = \frac{2*(Recall*Precision)}{(Recall + Precision)} \tag{8}$$

Support is the accuracy of the classifier is in classifying data points in a particular class with a comparison of other classes. The support can be reviewed as, how many numbers of data points lie in the class who are true positives.

18.6   EXPERIMENTAL RESULTS AND DISCUSSION

18.6.1   DATASET: FISH4KNOWLEDGE

The Fish4Knowledge is a funded project, which provides the video and fish analysis dataset. Three sites are having a different number of cameras installed from where the data is available. Dataset provides the 27,370 verified fish images that are divided into 23 clusters, and each cluster is a representation of a particular species. Figure 18.7 shows the types of species, no. of detections, and trajectories from the dataset [20]:

FIGURE 18.7 Each small image represents the species along with ID, Name, no. of detections and value in brackets shows trajectory [20]. Photos courtesy of Fish4Knowledge. https://groups.inf.ed.ac.uk/f4k/index.html

18.6.2 RESULTS OF VIDEO ENHANCEMENT

While performing the video enhancement part, we have compared our results with the existing technique of contrast limited adaptive histogram equalization (CLAHE), which is an alternative to adaptive histogram equalization; the results were also compared with color balance technique [23, 24].

It is observed from the perspective of quantitative and qualitative quality of the video enhancement, the satisfactory results were obtained and which can be observed in Table 18.2 and Figure 18.8, respectively. In Table 18.2, the results are represented for five different videos collected from different sites, time, and camera, provided by web-based database fish4knowledge. On these videos, various methods were implemented and the proposed method is observed to be performing consistently better.

TABLE 18.2   Quantitative Results for Video Enhancement.

Video Name	Technique	Evaluation Parameters		
		PSNR	SSIM	Entropy
Video 1	Proposed method	**20.9243**	**0.9802**	**7.7487**
	CLAHE	20.0983	0.7998	7.6684
	Color balance	10.3713	0.7938	5.2724
Video 2	Proposed method	**50.3815**	**0.9851**	7.1539
	CLAHE	0.7403	0.7787	**7.3506**
	Color balance	11.4756	0.6977	5.6125
Video 3	Proposed method	**27.5167**	**0.9847**	7.8613
	CLAHE	0.6283	0.7996	**7.8996**
	Color balance	9.9516	0.4974	5.8247
Video 4	Proposed method	**27.3100**	**0.9379**	**7.9247**
	CLAHE	0.9430	0.7289	7.8496
	Color balance	13.2930	0.8699	7.3469
Video 5	Proposed method	**37.4801**	**0.9906**	7.8117
	CLAHE	0.6602	0.6602	**7.8879**
	Color balance	17.4606	0.9007	7.7505

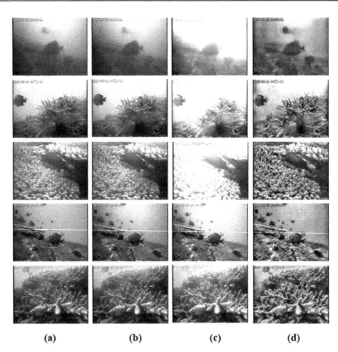

(a)   (b)   (c)   (d)

FIGURE 18.8   Results obtained on various videos; some frames have been extracted to present the results (a) is original frame; (b) result on proposed method; (c) results on color balance technique; (d) CLAHE method for enhancement.

18.6.3 RESULTS ON CLASSIFICATION OF FISH

In the second segment of the proposed technique of fish classification, we have selected one video for representing results of the classification, while dealing with the original video to obtain the results of classification, it is observed that the accuracy of classification is less, for the similar video the results obtained were quite comparable to that of the original video by enhancement technique that we have previously mentioned.

From Table 18.3, it is observed that the accuracy of the enhanced video is improvised along with an increase in precision, recall, and F1-score. As from the value of precision, we can comment that model has classified 68% of samples correctly out of predicted positive samples. The use of the RBF kernel in SVM has presented better results. From macro average value, we can signify that the dataset was imbalanced.

TABLE 18.3 Observations of Fish Classification Using SVM on Original Video and Enhanced Video

Original Video					Enhanced Video				
Accuracy Score: 0.6813573255389113					Accuracy Score: 0.8806174643770551				
Species	Precision	Recall	F1-Score	Support	Species	Precision	Recall	F1-Score	Support
1	0.67	0.92	0.78	9661	1	0.87	0.95	0.91	9661
2	0.60	0.33	0.43	2121	2	0.79	0.82	0.80	2121
3	0.68	0.50	0.57	2918	3	0.84	0.85	0.84	2918
4	0.78	0.67	0.72	3227	4	0.95	0.93	0.94	3227
5	0.66	0.60	0.63	2032	5	0.97	0.96	0.97	2032
6	0.00	0.00	0.00	150	6	0.86	0.48	0.62	150
7	0.54	0.39	0.45	358	7	0.88	0.85	0.87	358
8	1.00	0.01	0.01	183	8	0.88	0.08	0.15	183
9	0.50	0.31	0.38	201	9	0.74	0.33	0.46	201
10	0.85	0.94	0.89	241	10	0.98	0.99	0.98	241
11	0.00	0.00	0.00	79	11	0.50	0.06	0.11	79
12	1.00	0.05	0.10	119	12	0.94	0.41	0.57	19
13	0.00	0.00	0.00	149	13	0.87	0.17	0.29	149
14	0.00	0.00	0.00	73	14	0.00	0.00	0.00	73
15	1.00	0.07	0.12	30	15	0.00	0.00	0.00	30

TABLE 18.3   *(Continued)*

Original Video					Enhanced Video				
Accuracy Score: 0.6813573255389113					Accuracy Score: 0.8806174643770551				
Species	Precision	Recall	F1-Score	Support	Species	Precision	Recall	F1-Score	Support
16	0.68	0.34	0.46	166	16	0.96	0.97	0.96	166
17	0.00	0.00	0.00	40	17	0.83	0.12	0.22	40
18	0.00	0.00	0.00	46	18	0.88	0.48	0.62	46
19	1.00	0.05	0.09	21	19	0.00	0.00	0.00	21
20	0.75	0.19	0.30	16	20	1.00	0.12	0.22	16
21	0.00	0.00	0.00	12	21	1.00	0.08	0.15	12
22	0.00	0.00	0.00	34	22	0.00	0.00	0.00	34
23	0.00	0.00	0.00	19	23	0.00	0.00	0.00	19
Accuracy	–	–	0.68	21896	Accuracy	–	–	0.88	21896
Macro Avg.	0.47	0.23	0.26	21896	Macro Avg.	0.68	0.42	0.46	21896
Weighted Avg.	0.67	0.68	0.65	21896	Weighted Avg.	0.87	0.88	0.87	21896

Papp et al. [21] represented results using C-SVM classifier for whale recognition using which resulted in average precision as 25%, Jonas Jagar et al. [22] have used the seaCLEF database which is derived from fish4knowledge. For species recognition, they have utilized CNN features along with multiclass SVM and obtained a precision of 66%. BV Deep et al. [25] has employed various method for improvizing accuracy the main focus was using a hybrid approach of DL align with CNN and kNN, in result tested on fish4knowledge with SVM result experienced in terms of accuracy were 78.78% whereas in our case after enhancement we have obtained better results.

18.7   CONCLUSIONS

This work presents the enhancement technique for underwater video and classification of fish based on the ML algorithm along with SVM. In the enhancement approach, structural information available in the scene was preserved with the recovery of original colors, the same is being projected by the various parameters PSNR, SSIM, and entropy. In the fish classification part of this work, we have done pre-processing to eliminate the noise and preserve the edges, then k-means clustering is applied for object detection. Finally, SVMs with RBF as a kernel, and with a degree of polynomial equal to three, cross-validation is used for achieving the right metrics. With the enhancement, the results were obtained with an accuracy of nearly about 88%, whereas for the unenhanced version of video observed the accuracy of approximately 68%. In the future, this approach may be extended using some advanced algorithm in order to achieve the greater efficiency in all respect as our model has experienced the higher accuracy but the lower values of precision and recall, which can be improved further, as it was an impact of an imbalanced dataset. Techniques like DL can also be adopted for improvised speed and accuracy [21, 25, 30].

KEYWORDS

- **machine learning**
- **peak signal to noise ratio**
- **remotely operated vehicles**
- **speeded up robust features**
- **structure similarity measure**

REFERENCES

1. Schettini, R., & Corchs, S., (2010). Underwater image processing: State of the art of restoration and image enhancement methods. *EURASIP Journal on Advances in Signal Processing, 2010*, 1–14.
2. Ancuti, C., Ancuti, C. O., Haber, T., & Bekaert, P., (2012). Enhancing underwater images and videos by fusion. In: *2012 IEEE Conference on Computer Vision and Pattern Recognition* (pp. 81–88). IEEE.
3. Kavasidis, I., & Palazzo, S., (2012). Quantitative performance analysis of object detection algorithms on underwater video footage. In: *Proceedings of the 1st ACM International Workshop on Multimedia Analysis for Ecological Data* (pp. 57–60).
4. Yang, M., & Sowmya, A., (2014). New image quality evaluation metric for underwater video. *IEEE Signal Processing Letters, 21*(10), 1215–1219.
5. Wang, D., Niu, X., & Dou, Y., (2014). A piecewise-based contrast enhancement framework for low lighting video. In: *Proceedings 2014 IEEE International Conference on Security, Pattern Analysis, and Cybernetics (SPAC)* (pp. 235–240). IEEE.

6. Pugh, M., Tiddeman, B., Dee, H., & Hughes, P., (2014). Towards automated classification of seabed substrates in underwater video. In: *2014 ICPR Workshop on Computer Vision for Analysis of Underwater Imagery* (pp. 9–16). IEEE.

7. Kumar, N. S., Shobha, G., & Balaji, S., (2015). Keyframe extraction algorithm for video abstraction applications in underwater videos. In: *2015 IEEE Underwater Technology (UT)* (pp. 1–5). IEEE.

8. Singh, G., Jaggi, N., Vasamsetti, S., Sardana, H. K., Kumar, S., & Mittal, N., (2015). Underwater image/video enhancement using wavelet based color correction (WBCC) method. In: *2015 IEEE Underwater Technology (UT)* (pp. 1–5). IEEE.

9. Ashour, H., & Sasi, S., (2015). Recognition of stonefish from underwater video. In: *2015 International Conference on Advances in Computing, Communications, and Informatics (ICACCI)* (pp. 1031–1036). IEEE.

10. Zhao, X., Jin, T., & Qu, S., (2015). Deriving inherent optical properties from background color and underwater image enhancement. *Ocean Engineering, 94*, 163–172.

11. Qing, C., Yu, F., Xu, X., Huang, W., & Jin, J., (2016). Underwater video dehazing based on spatial-temporal information fusion. *Multidimensional Systems and Signal Processing, 27*(4), 909–924.

12. Papp, D., Lovas, D., & Szücs, G., (2016). Object detection, classification, tracking, and individual recognition for sea images and videos. In: *CLEF (Working Notes)* (pp. 525–533).

13. Jäger, J., Rodner, E., Denzler, J., Wolff, V., & Fricke-Neuderth, K., (2016). SeaCLEF 2016: Object proposal classification for fish detection in underwater videos. In: *CLEF (Working Notes)* (pp. 481–489).

14. Quevedo, E., Delory, E., Callicó, G. M., Tobajas, F., & Sarmiento, R., (2017). Underwater video enhancement using multi-camera super-resolution. *Optics Communications, 404*, 94–102.

15. Sun, X., Shi, J., Liu, L., Dong, J., Plant, C., Wang, X., & Zhou, H., (2018). Transferring deep knowledge for object recognition in Low-quality underwater videos. *Neurocomputing, 275*, 897–908.

16. Honnutagi, P., Mytri, V. D., & Lalitha, Y. S., (2019). Fusion-based underwater image enhancement by weight map techniques. In: *Recent Developments in Machine Learning and Data Analytics* (pp. 327–339). Springer, Singapore.

17. Liu, R., Hou, M., Fan, X., & Luo, Z., (2019). *Real-World Underwater Enhancement: Challenging, Benchmark, and Efficient Solutions*. arXiv preprint arXiv:1901.05320.

18. Jamadandi, A., & Mudenagudi, U., (2019). Exemplar-based underwater image enhancement augmented by wavelet corrected transforms. In: *Proceedings of the IEEE Conference on Computer Vision and Pattern Recognition Workshops* (pp. 11–17).

19. Tang, C., Von, L. U. F., Vahl, M., Wang, S., Wang, Y., & Tan, M., (2019). Efficient underwater image and video enhancement based on Retinex. *Signal, Image, and Video Processing, 13*(5), 1011–1018.

20. Bastiaan, J. B., Jiyin, H., Simone, P., Phoenix, X. H., Hsiu-Mei, C., Fang-Pang, L., Concetto, S., & Robert, B. F., (2014). A research tool for long-term and continuous analysis of fish assemblage in coral reefs using underwater camera footage. *Ecological Informatics*. doi: dx.doi.org/10.1016/j.ecoinf.2013.10.006.

21. Jin, L., & Liang, H., (2017). Deep learning for underwater image recognition in small sample size situations. In: *OCEANS 2017-Aberdeen* (pp. 1–4). IEEE.

22. Ocean Networks Canada Data Archive, http://www.oceannetworks.ca, Oceans Networks Canada, University of Victoria, Canada (accessed on 11 November 2021).

23. Yussof, W. N. J. H. W., Hitam, M. S., Awalludin, E. A., & Bachok, Z., (2013). Performing contrast limited adaptive histogram equalization technique on combined color models for underwater image enhancement. *International Journal of Interactive Digital Media, 1*(1), 1–6.

24. Byong, S. M., Dong, K. L., Seung, J. K., & Joo, H. L., (2013). A novel method of determining parameters of CLAHE based on image entropy. in *International Journal of Software Engineering and its Applications* (Vol. 7, No.5, pp. 113–120).

25. Deep, B. V., & Dash, R., (2019). Underwater fish species recognition using deep learning techniques. In: *2019 6th International Conference on Signal Processing and Integrated Networks (SPIN)* (pp. 665–669). IEEE.

26. Gonzalez & Woods, (2002). *Digital Image Processing* (2nd edn.). Prentice-Hall.

27. Zhou, W., Bovik, A. C., Sheikh, H. R., & Simoncelli, E. P., (2004). Image quality assessment: From error visibility to structural similarity. In *Image Processing, IEEE Transactions* (Vol. 13, pp. 600–612).

28. Zhou, W., & Alan, C. B., (2002). A universal image quality index. In: *IEEE Signal Processing Letters* (Vol. 9, No. 3).

29. Fouad, M. M. M., Zawbaa, H. M., El-Bendary, N., & Hassanien, A. E., (2013). Automatic Nile tilapia fish classification approach using machine learning techniques. In: *13th International Conference on Hybrid Intelligent Systems (HIS 2013)* (pp. 173–178). IEEE.

30. Masuda, H., Jukei, T., & Hasegawa, T., (2020). Fish species identification using a CNN-based multimodal learning method. In: *Proceedings of the 2020 2nd International Conference on Image, Video, and Signal Processing* (pp. 15–19).

CHAPTER 19

Fake News Predictor Model-Based on Machine Learning and Natural Language Processing

PRIYANKA BHARTIYA,[1] SOURABH YADAV,[2] VAISHALI WADHWA,[3] and POONAM MITTAL[4]

[1]Gautam Buddha University, Greater Noida, Uttar Pradesh, India, E-mail: bhartiyapriyanka123@gmail.com (P. Bhartiya)

[2]University of North Texas (UNT), Denton, Texas, USA

[3]Panipat Institute of Engineering and Technology, Panipat, Haryana, India

[4]JC Bose University of Science and Technology YMCA, Faridabad, Haryana, India

ABSTRACT

These days, spreading of fake news has become a wide problematic scenario. Fake news is a fabricated disinformation spread via social media or any other broadcast media by malicious people of our society. This news spread has massively increased in recent time by malicious actors, to give harm to one of the other members of the societal environment. Therefore, there is a high requirement of fake news detector, to safeguard the environment from hoaxes and malicious actors. Fake news detection project comes up with many unique challenges which questions our existing technology for the solution. In this manuscript, fake news detection model is proposed to efficiently check and predict the authenticity of the news with accuracy and precision. The latest machine learning algorithm with the perfect blend of natural language processing (NLP) techniques are employed for building this application. This model successfully gives considerable outcomes by filtering out the real news from fake news. Moreover, model proposes the probability of truth, which makes this model different from others.

19.1   INTRODUCTION

Counterfeit news comprises of news which has misinterpreted distortion. Nowadays, fake news is spreading at a raised speed. As the right data stays in numerous structures similarly manufactured news or data abides in numerous structures. Some of them are fraudulent data on the political plan, counterfeit news that produces dread, counterfeit news that makes legends so on. Manufactured news spreads by means of online web-based social networking or wrong individual or conventional news media. Counterfeit news created by an unseemly individual because of numerous elements, for example, to hurt business challengers, to get revenge, to sell items, envious, and so on.

In the present period, significant wellsprings of news are the web. Since its turn of events and wide use, the Internet has immediately become a huge hotspot for news. In today's periods, the maximum amount of time is spent on social media platform. Even peoples are found more interactive towards news on the web than the traditional media. For example, in USA about 49% of common citizen uses social media for day to day news in 2012, whereas this number has drastically changed and increased by more than 12% by the end of 2016. Fabricated information raised at higher speed on social media because of low cost, easily access and rapid raised of information. Various other news goals identify with the radio, paper, and telecom organizations, yet some news affiliations, which generally revolve around political news, simply appear to be on the web. Web-based life stages like Twitter, Facebook, and LinkedIn grant almost anyone to disperse their contemplations or offer stories to the world. The trouble is, numerous individuals don't check the wellspring of the material that they see online before they share it, which can incite fake news spreading quickly or regardless, "turning out to be celebrated online." Counterfeit news makes uproar in our social requests, as people put fake news to create against others. Various people are losing their trust in media as from time to time news channels spread this news to grow their Ratings. In 2019, India was viewed as a selective year for erred distortion. Moreover, society can face very adverse impact due to counterfeit information. It affects our youth decision and believing them in something which is not true. People found harder to distinguish fact from fiction.

Bogus data can affect our day-by-day life that may influence our well-being, faith in bigot thoughts, viciousness against guiltless individuals, and so on. In artificial knowledge, there are numerous devices can be utilized to identify garbage news by developing calculation. These locator exhibitions are phenomenal and have numerous escape clauses. One of them is the composing standard identification that the features are in proficient standard arrangement or not. Second escape clauses manage alter of elegantly composed depictions. Man-made brainpower assumes a significant job in the recognition rules. Identification of phony news will be performed utilizing the python programming language. Utilizing this language you will effortlessly have any kind of effect in genuine or counterfeit news. Natural language processing (NLP) models are utilized to identify counterfeit. Initially, idea of AI was to perform computations and some basic anticipation depending upon the input data, to result in satisfactory range.

19.2 LITERATURE REVIEW

Naïve-Bayes classifier, also known as base of classifiers, is considered an effective algorithm for classification problem which helps in building the quick artificial intelligence (AI) models that can be used to make fast forecasting. Naïve-Bayes classification algorithm aims to be a baseline solution for sentiment analysis tasks. Mykhailo Granik proposed a straightforward methodology for counterfeit news identification utilizing the Naïve-Bayes classifier. This methodology was actualized as a product framework and tried against an informational collection of Facebook news posts. Achieve accuracy around 74% on the test dataset which is a better than average outcome thinking about the overall straightforwardness of the model [1]. Kai Shu and Deepak Mahudeswaran proposed FakeNewsNet dataset, which contains multidimensional dynamic data and social media spreads, latest news items, etc., are some of the key attributes. This dataset was presented to strengthen the data collection of social media spread [2]. NLP models are utilized to distinguish counterfeit news by analyzing the applications, that is deluding reports that are originating from non-trustworthy sources by utilizing the dataset that is obtained from signal media then applying TF-IDF of bi-grams, PCFG then testing of datasets on different classification algorithm [3]. Moreover, in many researches, TF-IDF is considered as an effective feature extraction technique. Moreover, linear support vector machine (SVM) is stated as a leading algorithm for feature extraction. Combination of these two techniques and six different classifier techniques are employed to detect Counterfeit news [4]. Moreover, there are many researches in which author has discussed the variety of deceptive news, each as opposed to certifiable genuine announcing, and gauges their upsides and downsides as a corpus for content examination and prescient displaying, reviewing, shifting, checking on the web data [5]. The main feature is to investigate the phony news or unverified news for that author presented another arrangement of highlights and measure expectation execution of current methodologies and highlights for the programmed location of phony news. The researchers/author talks about how phony news filtering approaches can be utilized in the work on, featuring difficulties and opportunities using supervised learning [6]. Initially in this chapter author propose a novel ML counterfeit news recognition strategy which, by solid news proofs and highlighting social exposure, beats existing technique in the writing, expanding their effectively high precision by up to 4.8%, after which they have implemented their strategy upon chatbot developed by Facebook and approving it as an implementable application, resulting very high precision, i.e., 81.7% [7]. Using a supervised learning approach, a trained classifier is proposed that classifies the dataset on Twitter that the tweets are fake or not fake. Using a supervised learning approach large amount of data is collected, which is very noisy and contains thousands of tweets [8]. Neural Network, SVM, Naïve-Bayes algorithms are adopted by many other researchers as a distinctive techniques for analysis and classification purposes [9]. Moreover, some researchers have utilized Countvectorizer, Tf-idfvectorizer, Naïve-Bayes algorithm, with the blend of NLP algorithms to detect unverified information [10]. Today's era is facing serious problem of Spread of counterfeit information through media and communication. There are many researches that presents the problem and solution for counterfeit news and presented an initial solution to fake image detection [11]. News and reviews both are closely connected phenomena, and both can be fake. Therefore, a model introduced N-gram which is based on six AI techniques with the blend of two distinctive techniques of feature extraction that is specifically used to detect deceptive news and deceptive reviews [12]. Earlier the work proposed for deceptive news detection was in English but Korean has too many problems with this model. Therefore, convolutional network is employed for solving this problem [13]. Researchers has proposed a multilayer supervised learning method for the prediction of deceptive news based on dataset relabeling and iterative learning [14]. Counterfeit news problem is solved by machine learning (ML) algorithm and NLP. Data analysis is performed upon three distinctive datasets which contains the bundle of feature that were extracted from headline and description. Comparison between the seven algorithms and F1 scores gradient boosting performs best with accuracy 88% and the F1 score 0.9 [15]. Raw data generally contains some missing values that can generate some problems in detecting deceptive news. A preprocessing method is used for missing values and categorical feature. Missing values are replaced with the earlier one and in numerical feature, mean value of the column. Multi-layer perceptron (MLP) classifier was proposed with in-built pre-processing technique which beats baselines and improves the expectation precision by over 15%. [16]. Moreover, Supervised ML techniques used to detect deceptive news. The author has divided the dataset into train and test set using python module Scikit-learn and extracted feature using Tf-idf. Using this model probabilistic and linear classification approaches are tested [17]. Moreover, in general machine learning is being prominent techniques for classification, Analysis, and forecasting [18, 19].

19.3   PROPOSED METHODOLOGY

Figure 19.1 gives a deliberation of the whole system. The cited design in Figure 19.1 can be actualized in three stages.

FIGURE 19.1   System architecture.

19.3.1   DATA ACCOMMODATION

Data accommodation first and foremost step to be implemented. In this step, data is prepared for model training. Dataset in its raw form contains many irrelevant information, sometimes it may contain false values. Moreover, data if not collected from trustworthy location, performance of the model can get affected very badly.

Data is categorized into two categories:

1. **Qualitative Data:** It is the data of numbers, values, and quantity. Measurable terms are used to describe the data.
2. **Quantitative Data:** It is the data with values which are descriptive rather than numeric. It cannot be measured easily moreover it is less concrete.

Basically, this step is further bifurcated into two parts:

1. **Data Collection:** It is an effective technique of gathering and inspecting unequivocal information to proffer answers for noteworthy requests and survey the results [20]. It fixates around finding everything on a particular subject. Data is assembled to be also presented to hypothesis testing which hopes to explain a marvel. For specialists of data, there is an extent of results for which the information is assembled. Regardless, the key purpose behind which information is assembled is to put an investigator in a vantage position to make assumptions regarding future probabilities and examples. The center structure from where data can be accumulated must be basic and assistant data. While the previous is assembled by an examiner through direct sources, the last is accumulated by an individual other than the customer. There are a great deal of fundamental purposes behind gathering information, especially for an investigator. A key clarification behind gathering information, be it through quantitative or abstract systems is to ensure that the uprightness of the investigation question is to be certainly kept up. The correct usage of legitimate data grouping of strategies decreases the likelihood of mix-ups dependable with the results. Also, to restrain the risk of goofs in powerful, it is critical that exact information is accumulated with the objective that the specialist doesn't choose oblivious decisions. Data combination saves the expert time and resources that would somehow be squandered without an increasingly significant appreciation of the topic or point. Likewise, to show the prerequisite for a change in the norm or the introduction of new data that will be comprehensively recognized is basic to assemble information as evidence to support these cases. Data collection is the way toward gathering and estimating data from endless various sources. So as to utilize the data gathered for creating functional artificial intelligence and AI solutions, it must be gathered and put away such that bodes well for the business issue closely. Gathering data permits to catch a record of past occasions with the goal that it tends to be utilized for information examination to discover repeating designs. From those examples, prescient models can be fabricated utilizing AI calculations that search for patterns and anticipate future changes. Prescient models are just on a par with the information from which they are constructed, so acceptable information assortment rehearses are urgent to growing high-performing models. The information should

be without errors (trash in, trash out) and contain significant data for the job that needs to be done (Figure 19.2).

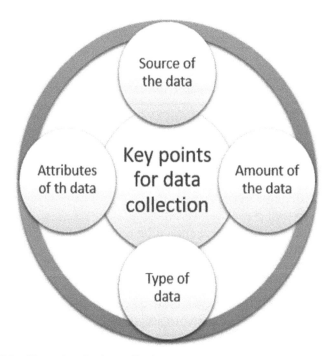

FIGURE 19.2   Key points for data collection.

2. **Data Cleaning:** 'Cleaning' alludes to the way toward expelling invalid information that focuses on a dataset [21–23]. Data cleaning is the way toward fixing or expelling erroneous, adulterated, inaccurately organized, copy, or inadequate information inside a dataset. When joining different information sources, there are numerous open doors for data to be copied or mislabeled. On the off chance that data is wrong, results, and calculations are problematic, despite the fact that they may look right. There is no supreme approach to endorse the specific strides in the data cleaning process. It will fluctuate from dataset to dataset. So it is very important to prepare some comprehensive procedures for the data cleaning process so that data cleansing things can be done in the correct way unfailingly (Figure 19.3).

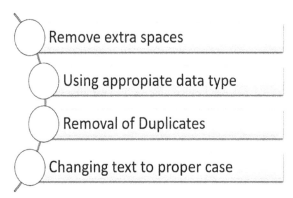

FIGURE 19.3 Different technique for data cleaning.

There are different ways of data cleaning:

- Extra spaces in the dataset should be removed at the early stages as it may cause inconsistency in the dataset which will lead to inappropriate model training.
- Dataset contains many different types of attributes such as dates, integers, etc. Their data type must be selected appropriately so that model can identify the datatypes accordingly for its evaluation.
- Repeated values must be deleted so that there is no inconsistency in the trained model.
- Appropriate cases must be used so that when dataset is taken to the integrated development environment, there is no mismatch for calling the required attributes.

19.3.2 MODEL TRAINING

Once dataset is collected and cleaned, it becomes ready for analysis. For analysis perspective, first, and foremost thing done to the dataset is data split. Basically, training, and testing datasets are prepared in data split by differentiating dataset into two distinctive parts depending upon the differentiating ratio:

1. **Training Dataset:** The dataset used for preparing the model (loads and predispositions on account of Neural Network) is considered as Training Dataset. The model sees and gains from this data.

2. **Testing Dataset:** The test dataset is basically employed for maintaining quality level which further can be used to evaluate the model. It is simply used once a model is completely prepared. The test dataset is once utilized in whole analysis to assess contending models.

Once the data split is performed successfully, datasets are ready for the model fitting. One more important step is performed before moving to model fitting, i.e., extraction of classifying feature from the dataset. Once the classifying feature is extracted, it is passed to the classifiers. Different classifiers are employed for performing analysis upon the extracted features. There are diverse classifiers for performing analysis and few of these models are listed below.

Figure 19.4 portrays different classifiers, which can be employed for performing analysis upon extracted feature from training dataset.

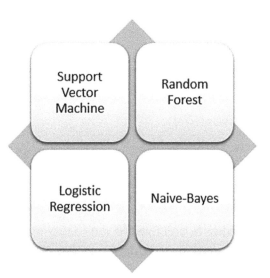

FIGURE 19.4   Different classifiers.

1. **Support Vector Machine (SVM):** These have a special method of usage compared to other available AI calculations procedures. Due to their capacity of dealing with different unstoppable factors, they have got immense appreciation. An SVM model is basically a representation of distinctive classes of hyperplane in a space with multi-dimensions. SVM prepares the hyperplane in an iterative way whose main goal is to limit the mistakes. The key task of SVM is to

differentiate the datasets into distinctive classes so that maximum marginal hyperplane (MMH) can be located (Figure 19.5).

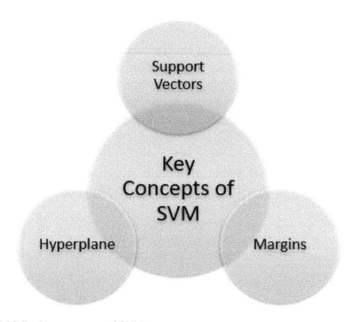

FIGURE 19.5   Key concepts of SVM.

  i.   **Support Vector:** Support vectors are defined as the data points with the least difference from the hyperplane. The assistance of information focus is employed for characterizing the isolating line.
 ii.   **Hyperplane:** It is defined as a deciding plane or space which is differentiated among a large number of articles containing a number of distinctive classes.
iii.   **Margins:** It is generally defined as the distance or difference among multiple linear developed upon the nearest information purposes of two distinct classes. It can also be determined as a perpendicular distance among support vector line. Decent Margine are also known as Enormous margin whereas terrible margins as also known as little margin.

Algorithm for implementing SVM classifier:

➢   **Step 1:** #Import_packages

import Pandas package.
- ➢ **Step 2:** #import_dataset

Dataset imported using read.csv() command.

- ➢ **Step 3:** #spliting_dataset
  Differentiating dataset into training and testing using sklearn.
- ➢ **Step 4:** #import_SVM_classifier
  Import SVM classifier from predefined library sklearn.
- ➢ **Step 5:** #model_fitting
  Fit SVM model by utilizing svc() function.
- ➢ **Step 6:** #predict

Call predict() using SVM algorithm.

2. **Random Forest:** This model is stated as directed learning calculation procedure that is being utilized to perform two group-ings similar to relapse. As it is clearly understood that woods is contained trees and more trees infer continuously ground-breaking forest areas. Thus, initially, RF prepares decision trees (DTs) using provided datasets and secondly, it generates the expecta-tion from every tree produced, and then lastly extracts the effec-tive arrangement using casting ballot method. It is known as an ensemble methodology that is proved to be better than solitary DT as it basically lessens ups the over-fitting of the model by defining the mean of the outcomes. Moreover, it is clearly stated by many researchers, RF calculation beats the issue of overfitting by averaging or consolidating the consequences of various choice trees. It functions admirably for a huge scope of data items than a solitary DT does. It has less fluctuation than a solitary DT. RFs are truly adaptable and have high precision. Scaling of data isn't required for RF calculation. It keeps up great exactness consider-ably in the wake of giving data without scaling. RF calculations keep up great precision even if the enormous extent of the data is absent. It likewise gives a quite decent pointer of the component significance. Scikit-learn gives an extra factor of the model, which results in the relative essentialness or responsibility of every part in the figure. It naturally registers the significance score of each component in the preparation stage. At that point, it downsizes the significance with the goal that the aggregate of all scores is 1. This score will assist you with picking the most significant highlights and drop the least significant ones for model structure. RF utilizes

Gini significance or means a diminishing in error values to figure the significance of each element. This is how much the model fit or exactness diminishes when variable is dropped. The bigger the abatement, the more critical the variable is. Here, the mean lessening is a noteworthy parameter for variable determination. The Gini list can portray the general logical intensity of the factors. RF is viewed as a particularly precise and solid procedure taking into account the quantity of DTs considering intrigue at the same time. It doesn't encounter the worst impacts of the overfitting. The main reason is considered as it recognizes the normal of the considerable number of expectations, which counterbalances the predispositions. RF can deal with the null values. There are two methods for dealing: using center points to supplant ceaseless factors, and registering the vicinity weighted normal of missing qualities. You can get the relative element significance, which helps in choosing the most contributing highlights for the classifier (Figure 19.6).

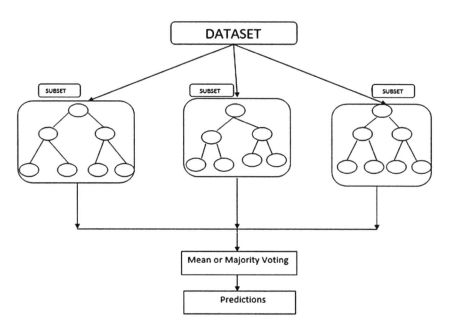

FIGURE 19.6   Random forest classifier.

Algorithm for random forest classifier:

➢ **Step 1:** import packages.

> **Step 2:** Read dataset using read.csv() command.
> **Step 3:** #preprocessing
> Preprocessing of data.
>> **Step 4:** Split the dataset into train dataset for model fitting and test dataset for testing.
>> **Step 5:** #model_fitting

Build the Random Forest Classifier Model.

>> **Step 6:** Prediction using model.
>> **Step 7:** Accuracy check

3. **Logistic Regression:** In ML, LR is one of the most widely used supervised classification algorithm. It is a technique to analyze the dataset in which dependent variables and one or more independent variables are present to predict the outcomes. Independent variables are also called predictors and dependent variables are called target. It predicts the outcome in categorical value, i.e., in binary form 0 or 1. Output(Y) can predict only discrete values for a given set of inputs(x). LR is usually used for binary classification and can also modify the logistic regression (LR) for multiple classifications. Predicts the probability of the event using the log function. Prediction greater than 0.5 is considered to be 1 and lesser than 0.5 are to be 0. Much the same as linear regression accept that the information follows a linear function, LR models the information utilizing the sigmoid function. Sigmoid is scientific capacity having a trademark that can take any genuine worth and guide it to between 0 to 1 formed like the letter "S." The sigmoid capacity additionally called a calculated capacity.

The purpose of LR is to gauge the probabilities of occasions, including deciding a connection among highlights and the probabilities of specific results. LR is the best algorithm when you are dealing with binary data. This also can be used as a performance baseline. It is quite easy and simple to implement and efficient to train. It doesn't require too many computational (arithmetic, numerical) techniques. Input features don't require to be scaled. LR can also be used in building neural networks in the deep learning (DL) model (Figure 19.7).

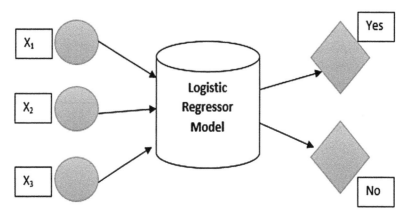

FIGURE 19.7   Logistic regressor model.

Algorithm for LR classifier:
- ➤ **Step 1:** Import module.
- ➤ **Step 2:** Read dataset using read.csv() command.
- ➤ **Step 3:** Train a classifier
- ➤ **Step 4:** Fit model
- ➤ **Step 5:** Make a prediction using such classifier

4. **Naïve-Bayes:** In ML, Naïve-Bayes Classifier is defined as a directed learning algorithm which is dependent on the implementation of Bayes theorem and probabilistic procedures employed for solving the classification problem. Moreover, it is a family of algorithms and involves the idea that the predictor variable in a model is autonomous from each other. In actual-world problems, predictor variables are not always independent of each other there may be some correlations between them but In Naïve-Bayes each predictor variables are considered to be independent of other variables Predictor variables are categorical in nature that means it will store values either true or false, i.e., binary value. Using Gaussian distribution, Multinomial distribution, and Bernoulli distribution Naïve-Bayes algorithm is created. A portion of the utilization is a content arrangement, spam sifting, recommendation system, real-time forecasts, and so forth. Favorable circumstances that Naive Bayes has over other order calculations is its capacity to deal with a very huge number of highlights. Python library, Scikit learn is the most valuable library that causes us to assemble a Naïve Bayes model in Python.

One of the most important obstacles of Naïve Bayes grouping is its strong component opportunity in light of the fact that, in reality, it is essentially hard to have a ton of features that are self-sufficient of each other. Another issue with Naïve Bayes request is it's zero repeats' which suggests that if a straight out factor has a grouping anyway not being seen in the planning data record, by then, Naïve Bayes model will consign a zero probability to it and it will be not ready to make an expectation.

Algorithm for Naïve-Bayes classifier:

> **Step 1:** Import module.
> **Step 2:** Read dataset using read.csv() command.
> **Step 3:** Convert the dataset in the frequency table.
> **Step 4:** Make a table by calculating the probability of each(Likelihood table).
> **Step 5:** Now calculates posterior probability using naïve Bayes.

19.3.3   USER INTERACTION

Basically this module of the proposed methodology implements the user interface of the proposed model. This user interaction acts as a user interface and above stated modules works on the backend of the predictor model. User interface comprises of three subclasses, i.e., User Input, Validation of user input using classifier, and lastly resulting the output of classifier as the probability of truthness (Figure 19.8).

1. **User Inputs:** This is basically defined as the input for the classifier model. Depending upon these inputs performance of classifier model is gauged. So it's very important to pass accurate and precise input to the model. These inputs must be grammatically correct and properly arranged.
2. **Validation Using Classifier Model:** Basically, a system with multiple classifier models, one of the classifier is selected at the end, which acts as the main model for the forecasting or prediction. User input is passed to that model, depending upon its model training and learning, it results as the probability of truthfulness. Classifier model acts as the processing unit for the predictor model, similar to the CPU of the computer system.

3. Truth Probability: It is basically the output of the classifier model. It gives the results of evaluation performed by classifier. For predictor model, it tells about the probability of truthfulness. It will result as Yes or No with the probability of matching.

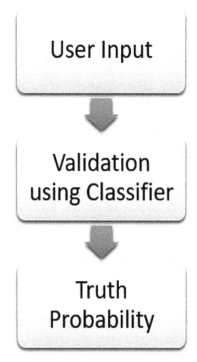

FIGURE 19.8   User interaction module.

19.4   SYSTEM IMPLEMENTATION

This research targets to build a predictor model, in which model will take user input of news headlines or description of headlines, to gauge whether that headline is real or fake. For the evaluation purpose, dataset employed is generated manually and stored in a csv format.

Figure 19.7 portrays the basic implementation of the predictor model. Tool used for implementing the predictor model in Python. Figure 19.9 portrays the basic flow of the model.

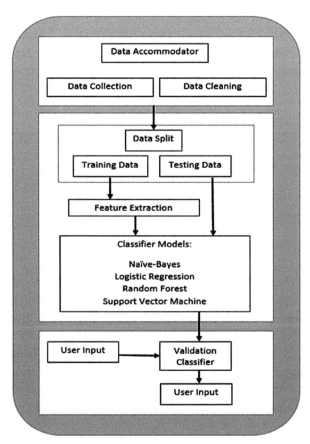

FIGURE 19.9 System implementation.

Stage 1 of system comprises of Data Accommodator. In data accommodator basically dataset is prepared. Basically, dataset carries two attributes that are Statements and Label. Statements attribute contains the headlines and the description of the news. These statements are collected from various trustworthy resources. Label attribute contains the labels that whether this statement is true or false. This label attribute acts as the key for deducing that whether the input headline is true or false. There is no any null value in either of the attributes, and if in any case, it existed, it was removed in the data cleaning process. Moreover, Data cleaning procedure are followed to improve the quality of the dataset and make dataset in easily understandable form for the classifiers.

It is quite visible from Figure 19.10 there are two attributes, statement attribute carries the news information and label attribute carries book value, i.e., whether the news information is true or not. Once the data accommodator step is finished, the dataset will be ready for further analysis.

	A	B
1	Statement	Label
2	We have less Americans working now than in the 70s.	FALSE
3	When Obama was sworn into office, he DID NOT use the Holy Bible, but instead the Kuran (Their equivalency to our Bible, but very different beliefs).	FALSE
4	Says Having organizations parading as being social welfare organizations and then being involved in the political combat harkens back to why the statute a hundr	FALSE
5	Says nearly half of Oregons children are poor.	TRUE
6	On attacks by Republicans that various programs in the economic stimulus plan are not stimulative, "If you add all that stuff up, it accounts for less than 1 percen	TRUE
7	Says when armed civilians stop mass shootings with guns, an average of 2.5 people die; otherwise, an average of 18 people die.	FALSE
8	Says Tennessee is providing millions of dollars to virtual school company for results at the bottom of the bottom.	TRUE
9	The health care reform plan would set limits similar to the socialized system in Britain, where people are allowed to die if their treatment would cost more than	FALSE
10	Says Donald Trump started his career back in 1973 being sued by the Justice Department for racial discrimination because he would not rent apartments in one o	TRUE
11	Bill White has a long history of trying to limit or even disenfranchise military voters.	TRUE
12	John McCains chief economic adviser during the 08 race estimated that Trumps promises would cause America to lose 3.5 million jobs.	TRUE
13	Says 21,000 Wisconsin residents got jobs in 2011, but 18,000 of them were in other states.	FALSE
14	State revenue projections have missed the mark month after month.	TRUE

FIGURE 19.10   Dataset for model implementation.

Stage 2 comprises of passing the dataset for model training. Before passing the data to the classifier, the dataset need to be splitted. For that purpose data splitter module of the model is employed. Basically data splitter will differentiate the acquired dataset into two, one for training the model and one for testing the model. It is basically a python code which will convert the main dataset into two csv files, i.e., train.csv and test.csv. This python code constitutes different user defined functions which will basically create the distribution of dataset, check the quality of the dataset, i.e., check whether there is any null value or not, etc. Figure 19.11 portrays the function in data splitting code.

```
#process the data
def process_data(data,exclude_stopword=True,stem=True):
    tokens = [w.lower() for w in data]
    tokens_stemmed = tokens
    tokens_stemmed = stem_tokens(tokens, eng_stemmer)
    tokens_stemmed = [w for w in tokens_stemmed if w not in stopwords ]
    return tokens_stemmed

#Stemming
def stem_tokens(tokens, stemmer):
    stemmed = []
    for token in tokens:
        stemmed.append(stemmer.stem(token))
    return stemmed

#data integrity check (missing label values)
#none of the datasets contains missing values therefore no cleaning required
def data_qualityCheck():

    print("Checking data qualitites...")
    train_news.isnull().sum()
    train_news.info()

    print("check finished.")

    #below datasets were used to
    test_news.isnull().sum()
    test_news.info()
```

FIGURE 19.11   Data splitter module.

Once the dataset is bifurcated in training and testing parts, dataset are ready to be passed to the feature extraction module. Before training the model for predictor system, some special feature from the dataset must be extracted. Special feature extraction means reducing the weight of the unstructured elements of the dataset into the uniform set of attributes. For our research bag of words (word count) is considered for feature extraction. For feature extraction dataset passed is training dataset. Feature extraction is done by importing the sklearn library of python. Figure 19.12 portrays the basic function for extracting features from the dataset.

```python
def features(sentence, index):
    """ sentence: [w1, w2, ...], index: the index of the word """
    return {
        'word': sentence[index],
        'is_first': index == 0,
        'is_last': index == len(sentence) - 1,
        'is_capitalized': sentence[index][0].upper() == sentence[index][0],
        'is_all_caps': sentence[index].upper() == sentence[index],
        'is_all_lower': sentence[index].lower() == sentence[index],
        'prefix-1': sentence[index][0],
        'prefix-2': sentence[index][:2],
        'prefix-3': sentence[index][:3],
        'suffix-1': sentence[index][-1],
        'suffix-2': sentence[index][-2:],
        'suffix-3': sentence[index][-3:],
        'prev_word': '' if index == 0 else sentence[index - 1],
        'next_word': '' if index == len(sentence) - 1 else sentence[index + 1],
        'has_hyphen': '-' in sentence[index],
        'is_numeric': sentence[index].isdigit(),
        'capitals_inside': sentence[index][1:].lower() != sentence[index][1:]
    }
```

FIGURE 19.12   Feature extraction module.

After feature extraction, extracted dataset is passed to the different classifiers. Distinctive classifiers are employed for our research, such as RF classifier, Naiver-Bayes classifier, LR classifier, and SVM classifiers. Extracted features are passed to these classifiers and model fitting is performed. After model fitting of all the classifiers, confusion matrix is compared for all the classifiers and two best performing models are identified. Then GridSearchCV method is employed for effective parameter tuning of best performing models. In our research, LR, and RF classifiers have performed extremely well. Figure 19.13 portrays there performance graphs.

Once the GridSearchCV method successfully implemented on these two classifiers, best performing classifier among these two will be deduced. In our research, LR classifier is chosen as a final classifier model. Once the final classifier is recognized, the model will only be left final user interaction phase. Till then backend processes of deducing best performing model are successfully implemented.

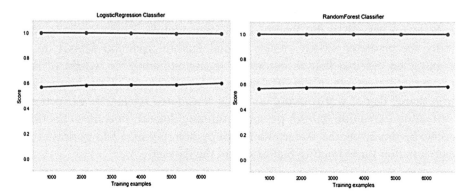

FIGURE 19.13   Performance graph of two best performing classifiers.

Finally, stage 3, comprises of User interaction part. Basically, here user will give the statement or headline which he/she wants to validate. That statement will act as the input for the classifier model. Classifier model will perform the analysis and check that input into the dataset. The final results of the classifier model contain the probability of truthness and classification output. Figure 19.14 portrays the final output of the model.

```
Please enter the news text you want to verify: OBAMA IS A PRESIDENT
You entered: OBAMA IS A PRESIDENT

UserWarning: Trying to unpickle estimator Pipeline fr(
r own risk.
The given statement is  False
The truth probability score is  0.24184794293219997
>>>

Please enter the news text you want to verify: Building a wall on the U.S.-Mexico border will take literally years
You entered: Building a wall on the U.S.-Mexico border will take literally years

UserWarning: Trying to unpickle estimator Pipeline from
r own risk.
The given statement is  True
The truth probability score is  0.568017336920146
>>> |
```

FIGURE 19.14   Final outputs of the model.

19.5   CONCLUSION

In this manuscript, ML approach are preferred to detect the deceptive news. For analysis and prediction purpose manuscript demonstrates a predictive model that will detect the accuracy of information or news. For this research, various natural processing technique and ML algorithms are employed to detect fake news using sci-kit module. The proposed manuscript gives the error free, accurate, and precise predictor model for validating the news spread. The software prefer for model development is Python. For development of predictor model, system architecture contains three basic modules, i.e., data accommodator, model fitting, and user interaction. Each module has its own significance. Data accommodator comprises of collection and cleaning of dataset. Model fitting comprises dataset splitting, feature extraction, and model training. Lastly, User Interaction module takes the statement or headline, which user wants to validate, passes it to the best performing classifier, and results as the probability of truthiness. In model fitting, basically four different classifiers of ML are employed and dataset is fitted upon them. Depending upon there confusion matrix best fit model is selected. In our research, LR classifier fits best to our dataset. Moreover, this manuscript also contains the code snippets of different modules, which show different pre-defined libraries are employed for implementation of this predictor model.

KEYWORDS

- **artificial intelligence**
- **maximum marginal hyperplane**
- **multi-layer perceptron**
- **natural language processing**
- **support vector machine**

REFERENCES

1. Granik, M., & Mesyura, V., (2017). Fake news detection using naive Bayes classifier. In: *2017 IEEE First Ukraine Conference on Electrical and Computer Engineering (UKRCON)* (pp. 900–903). IEEE.
2. Shu, K., Mahudeswaran, D., Wang, S., Lee, D., & Liu, H., (2018). *Fake Newsnet: A Data Repository with News Content, Social Context and Dynamic Information for Studying Fake News on Social Media.* arXiv preprint arXiv:1809.01286.
3. Gilda, S., (2017). Evaluating machine learning algorithms for fake news detection. In: 2017 *IEEE 15*[th] *Student Conference on Research and Development (SCOReD)* (pp. 110–115). IEEE.

4. Ahmed, H., Traore, I., & Saad, S., (2017). Detection of online fake news using N-gram analysis and machine learning techniques. In: *International Conference on Intelligent, Secure, and Dependable Systems in Distributed and Cloud Environments* (pp. 127–138). Springer, Cham.

5. Rubin, V. L., Chen, Y., & Conroy, N. J., (2015). Deception detection for news: Three types of fakes. *Proceedings of the Association for Information Science and Technology, 52*(1), 1–4.

6. Reis, J. C., Correia, A., Murai, F., Veloso, A., Benevenuto, F., & Cambria, E., (2019). Supervised learning for fake news detection. *IEEE Intelligent Systems, 34*(2), 76–81.

7. Della, V. M. L., Tacchini, E., Moret, S., Ballarin, G., DiPierro, M., & De Alfaro, L., (2018). Automatic online fake news detection combining content and social signals. In: *2018 22nd Conference of Open Innovations Association (FRUCT)* (pp. 272–279). IEEE.

8. Helmstetter, S., & Paulheim, H., (2018). Weakly supervised learning for fake news detection on twitter. In: *2018 IEEE/ACM International Conference on Advances in Social Networks Analysis and Mining (ASONAM)* (pp. 274–277). IEEE.

9. Aphiwongsophon, S., & Chongstitvatana, P., (2018). Detecting fake news with machine learning method. In: *2018 15th International Conference on Electrical Engineering/ Electronics, Computer, Telecommunications, and Information Technology (ECTI-CON)* (pp. 528–531). IEEE.

10. Agudelo, G. E. R., Parra, O. J. S., & Velandia, J. B., (2018). Raising a model for fake news detection using machine learning in python. In: *Conference on e-Business, e-Services, and e-Society* (pp. 596–604). Springer, Cham.

11. Choraś, M., Giełczyk, A., Demestichas, K., Puchalski, D., & Kozik, R., (2018). Pattern recognition solutions for fake news detection. In*: IFIP International Conference on Computer Information Systems and Industrial Management* (pp. 130–139). Springer, Cham.

12. Ahmed, H., Traore, I., & Saad, S., (2018). Detecting opinion spam and fake news using text classification. *Security and Privacy, 1*(1), e9.

13. Lee, D. H., Kim, Y. R., Kim, H. J., Park, S. M., & Yang, Y. J., (2019). Fake news detection using deep learning. *Journal of Information Processing Systems, 15*(5).

14. Rasool, T., Butt, W. H., Shaukat, A., & Akram, M. U., (2019). Multi-label fake news detection using multi-layered supervised learning. In: *Proceedings of the 2019 11th International Conference on Computer and Automation Engineering* (pp. 73–77).

15. Bali, A. P. S., Fernandes, M., Choubey, S., & Goel, M., (2019). Comparative performance of machine learning algorithms for fake news detection. In: *International Conference on Advances in Computing and Data Sciences* (pp. 420–430). Springer, Singapore.

16. Kotteti, C. M. M., Dong, X., Li, N., & Qian, L., (2018). Fake news detection enhancement with data imputation. In: *2018 IEEE 16th Intl. Conf. on Dependable, Autonomic, and Secure Computing, 16th Intl. Conf. on Pervasive Intelligence and Computing, 4th Intl. Conf. on Big Data Intelligence and Computing and Cyber Science and Technology Congress (DASC/PiCom/DataCom/CyberSciTech)* (pp. 187–192). IEEE.

17. Al Asaad, B., & Erascu, M., (2018). A tool for fake news detection. In: *2018 20th International Symposium on Symbolic and Numeric Algorithms for Scientific Computing (SYNASC)* (pp. 379–386). IEEE.

18. Sharma, N., & Juneja, A., (2019). Extreme gradient boosting with squared logistic loss function. In: *Machine Intelligence and Signal Analysis* (pp. 313–322). Springer, Singapore.

19. Sharma, N., (2018). *XGBoost. The Extreme Gradient Boosting for Mining Applications.* GRIN Verlag.

20. Devers, K. J., & Richard, M. F., (2000). Study design in qualitative research-2: Sampling and data collection strategies. *Education for Health, 13*(2), 263.

21. Rahm, E., & Hong, H. D., (2000). Data cleaning: Problems and current approaches. *IEEE Data Eng. Bull., 23*(4), 3–13.

22. Yadav, S., & Nonita, S., (2018). Homogenous ensemble of time-series models for Indian stock market. *International Conference on Big Data Analytics.* Springer, Cham.

23. Yadav, S., & Nonita, S., (2019). Forecasting of Indian stock market using time-series models. *Computing and Network Sustainability* (pp. 405–412). Springer, Singapore.

CHAPTER 20

Machine Learning on Simulation Tools for Underwater Sensor Network

MAMTA NAIN and NITIN GOYAL

Chitkara University Institute of Engineering and Technology, Chitkara University, Punjab, India

ABSTRACT

As we know, 71% part of the earth is covered by water. So, underwater sensor networks (USN/UWSN) is getting plenty of attention from the research community and becoming a prominent area of research. The characteristics of UWSN are thoroughly different from other networks like terrestrial network in terms of medium. As acoustic signal is preferred in comparison of radiofrequency signal in UWSN because RF signal cannot propagate through a long distance. To analyze the dynamic behavior of sensor network the machine learning (ML) techniques can be used. ML helps in the requirement of redesigning the routing process based on its models. Researchers are observing an increasing interest in UWSN because it offers help in many application areas like pollution monitoring, disaster prevention, etc., while its architecture is susceptible to many challenges like sensor node deployment, node localization, limited battery power, and many others. Due to complex network topology and tools, underwater sensor networks study is very inflated. But simulation environment and tools help to study the real underwater conditions. Numerous underwater network simulation tools are accessible nowadays, so the selection of a suitable tool is a significant task. This chapter gives an in-depth examination of numerous underwater simulation tools with key features and coding parameters. Also, a researcher will be able to identify the correct tool based on needs and availability.

20.1   INTRODUCTION

In the modern world, wireless sensor network (WSN) is becoming a dominant technology. The applications of WSN creating a huge impact on society
by providing valuable information after development as well as research in
this domain [23, 38]. WSN models can be trained using machine learning
(ML) models. ML is derived from artificial intelligence (AI) in 1950, which
is nowadays used successfully in various fields like computer science,
mathematics, neuroscience, and statistics [21]. Whether it may be WSN or
underwater sensor network (USN) ML techniques help to address the issues
like fault detection, anomaly detection, event detection, routing, localization, congestion control, coverage, and connectivity, data aggregation, target
tracking, clock synchronization, energy harvesting, mobile sink deployment
and quality of service (QoS). ML works on the authentic data and this data
is obtained by monitoring of any area or zone. In UWSN it becomes fruitful
when it is done in real-time and with accurate results. The experiment and
results validation are an extortionate process in UWSN. Every time to
conduct the experiment is not that easy because it necessitates a portion of
costly equipment and time also [19]. Therefore, simulation-based testing
facilitates the researcher to understand whether time and cost investment is
valuable or not for the proposed method. Simulation is considered as the best
approach to test new protocols for USN [6, 26, 34]. Novel characteristics of
USN are the biggest hurdle to simulate wired and WSNs without alteration
in the simulator. Results of simulation are not so perfect as of real-world
environment. Because of worldwide interest of researchers in UWSN, many
simulation tools proposed but maximum out of these are configuration
specific or application-specific. So, the choice of suitable simulation tool
according to study is pivotal. Simulators are generally application-specific
or configuration dependent [9, 12]. Simulation is also classified into three
different categories as Monte Carlo, Discrete event and Trace event simulation. Monte Carlo simulation is used for simulating engineering difficulties
because of its mathematical simulation techniques. Simulators which drive
discrete event functions are mainly engaged in WSNs owing to their highest
efficiency against a wide range of specific applications based on sensor
nodes. Such simulators have a gamut of starting, input, and output and trace
routine as well as help subscribers, especially in dynamic memory administration. Trace driven simulation facilitates with different services and
commonly used in real systems [33]. UWSN is also used to observe environmental conditions, so a network should be engineered in such a way that it

becomes successful in exploring underwater resources, discrete prevention, geographical monitoring, etc. UWSN contains sensor nodes, anchor nodes and through the communication of these nodes, data is communicated, and at the end, data is transferred to the surface station [13, 14]. The working architecture of UWSN can be classified into four different categories as shown in Figure 20.1.

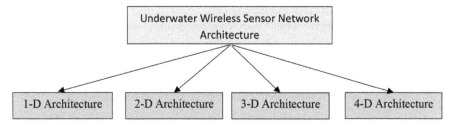

FIGURE 20.1   UWSN architecture classifications.

1. **1-D Architecture:** In 1-D Architecture, every sensor node acts as a system itself. Each sensor node gathers the data and passes this data to remote stations. In this node can be conveyed for a specific period and afterwards float towards the surface to transmit the sensor data to remote stations. It can be an autonomous underwater vehicle (AUV) that drives inside water, detect or gather the submerged data and transmit to the specific data receiver. 1-D design is used for UWSN where single-hop transmission occurs between sensor node and remote station [25].

2. **2-D Architecture:** Cluster of sensors nodes are used in 2-D architecture and sensor nodes are associated with underwater sink or anchor nodes. This node receives the data from other deployed nodes in that clusters that is passed to cluster head. Further, after processing information, it is transferred to the surface station. In 2-D architecture, two types of communication are used as vertical and cluster communication. Anchor nodes uses vertical communication to pass confirmation or communication with surface stations while the cluster communication occurs with horizontal. Anchor nodes and other nodes uses horizontal communication to communicate with each other [5].

3. **3-D Architecture:** In 3-D architecture, collection of sensor nodes forms a group and float at various levels of depth. Due to excessive distance between sensor nodes deployed at variable height require

communication which goes above 2-D. Three types of communication occur in this are as follows:

  i. **Intra Cluster Communication:** i.e., the communication between the anchor node and cluster node.

  ii. **Inter-Cluster Communication:** Cluster nodes communicate with each other through gateway node.

  iii. **Anchor-Buoyant Communication:** Nodes that are involved are anchored or surface nodes.

 4. **4-D Architecture:** This UWSN architecture is a combination of 3-D UWSN with mobility. Mobile submerged sensors systems are made up of remotely employable submerged vehicles (ROVs). It gathers data from anchor nodes and passes this gathered data to the base station. Every sensor node can be free in transmitting the data legitimately to ROVs. As information is passed straightforwardly to ROV, sensors having little information to transmit or far from ROV can utilize acoustic connection whereas the nodes having huge information and near to ROVs can utilize radio connections. Thus, the kind of correspondence among ROVs and stay nodes relies on the two variables: separation among nodes and amount of information to be sent [3, 18, 20].

  Many researchers provide a thorough analysis of simulation tools in their study that can be used for UWSN [15–17, 22]. Simulation tools can also be divided into two categories as commercial and open source. This chapter helps researchers to select the appropriate simulation tool based on the specific research requirements as well as to apply ML models on them.

20.2 SIMULATION MODELS WITH ML FOR UWSN

Simulation results are utilized by ML approaches. Simulation helps in the verification and validation of different algorithms and protocols in a network approximate to real world deployment. ML models contain algorithmic code and tools to offer more flexibility to the researchers. In this section numerous simulator tools used for simulating and applying ML approaches are discussed:

 1. **NS-2 Simulator:** Network simulator (NS) is an open-source and discrete event handler NS. In 1996 it was designed by National Science Foundation and Defense Agency DARPA. It helps to understand the

dynamic nature of the communication network that could be wired and wireless. In-house mechanism of simulation objects is defined by C++ in backend and front end is explained by object tool command language (OTcL) with suitable scripting adaptability in Linux. Installation of NS-2 is itself a time consuming and complex task. Also, some of the inbuilt protocol packages are available with NS-2.30 only. Users should be aware of modeling techniques, queuing theory and scripting language as it lacks Graphical user interface (GUI). Visualizer in NS-2 is Network animator (NAM). Nam is the animation tool that graphically represent the network with packet traces as well. Network outline is created with the help of scripting in TcL, and as a result of the simulation, trace files are produced that keeps a record of events that are occurring in the network. To analyze the performance, trace file plays a vital role. Open-source trace file analyzer software is used for the wireless, wired, and mobile network to analyze the trace files of NS-2 [7]. The basic workflow of NS-2 is also shown in Figure 20.2.

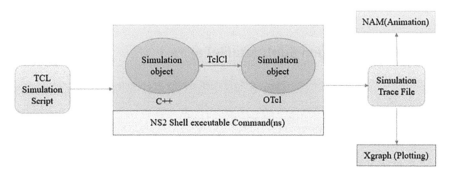

FIGURE 20.2   NS-2 simulator working model [7].

> **Merits:** Cost is less, expressive range of protocols in various layers are supported by NS-2. As it is free to open source so users can change and modify online documents and can modify the code to develop their code.
> **Demerits:** NS-2 is complex and tough to write and learn tool command language (Tcl). The development of protocol is time-consuming and as it is command based so less support to GUI.

The basic example of NS-2 depicting coding is shown in two parts below as a screenshot in Figures 20.3(a) and 20.3(b).

```
set topo_ [new Topography]

$topo load_cubicgrid $opt(x) $opt(y) $opt(z)


#$ns_ use-newtrace

set tracefd       [open $opt(tr) w]

$ns_ trace-all $tracefd

set nf [open $opt(nam) w]

$ns_ namtrace-all-wireless $nf $opt(x) $opt(y)


set data [open $opt(datafile) a]


set total_number_ [expr $opt(nn)-1]

set god_ [create-god_ $opt(nn)]


$ns_ at 0.0 "$god__set_filename $opt(datafile)"


set chan_1_ [new $opt(chan)]
```

FIGURE 20.3(a)   Example of NS-2 part 1.

```
$ns_ node-config -adhocRouting $opt(adhocRouting) \

                    -llType $opt(ll) \

                    -macType $opt(mac) \

                    -ifqType $opt(ifq) \

                    -ifqLen $opt(ifqlen) \

                    -antType $opt(ant) \

                    -propType $opt(prop) \

                    -phyType $opt(netif) \

                    #-channelType $opt(chan) \

                    -agentTrace ON \

              -routerTrace ON \

              -macTrace ON\

              -topoInstance $topo\

              -energyModel $opt(energy)\

              -txPower $opt(txpower)\

              -rxPower $opt(rxpower)\

              -initialEnergy $opt(initialenergy)\

              -idlePower $opt(idlepower)\

              -channel $chan_1_
```

FIGURE 20.3(b)   Example of NS-2 part 2.

The sample output obtained after running the NS2 code will be in the text format as shown in Table 20.1 with some of the possible fields of sending node number (num_send), receiving node number (num_received).

TABLE 20.1   Sample Output of NS2 Results

num_send	num_received	Comm_delay	Energy Consumption
1	46	4.858645	271.63
2	48	6.818	404.118
0	49	8.77	596.178
1	47	10.73	788.237

Here ML can be applied for predicting the average energy consumed in-network, the model can be trained by using communication delay (comm_delay) w.r.t. the num_send, and num_received as inputs. After training, energy consumption can be predicted to locate the sensors perfectly. Here, simple regression algorithms can be used.

2. **AQUA Sim:** This is also an NS-2 based open-source simulator that can effortlessly combine to the present code of NS-2. For the study of underwater WSN, UWSN lab at University of Connecticut develops Aqua-Sim [31]. Aqua-sim helps in 3-D deployment. Any alteration in the wireless package does not affect the Aqua-Sim. Aqua-Sim can be planned with extensible and adaptable choices. Aqua-Sim can be proficiently simulated for acoustic signal attenuation and data collision in UWSN. This also makes use of object-oriented design. Entities, interface, and functions are three basic classes available in Aqua-Sim. Network entities are described by network entity classes, common interfaces are represented by pure interface class, and these act as the base class for others. Functions of other classes that are very common, are served by common function classes and can be coordinated with Aqua-Sim classes. Both CMU wireless communication package and Aqua-Sim are parallel and independent. Aqua-Sim is independent of other packages, so don't interfere with other packages in NS-2 [37]. The basic architecture of AQUA-Sim is shown in Figure 20.4.

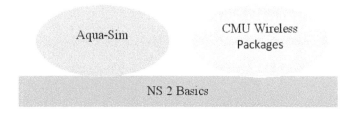

FIGURE 20.4   AQUA-sim simulator working model [37].

The application range of aqua-sim is separated into four fundamental organizers:

1. **UW-Common:** Underwater sensor nodes and traffic related content is stored in this folder.
2. **UW-MAC:** MAC protocols and acoustic channels are stored here.
3. **UW-Routing:** This folder comprises of routing protocol.
4. **UW-TcL:** For the validation of Aqua-Sim, OTcL scripts are stored in this folder.

➢ **Merits:** Aqua-Sim is a discrete event-driven simulator that helps in the 3-D deployment of network and also simulate mobile network. With high fidelity, underwater acoustic channels are simulated. Designed with extensible and flexible options so new protocols can easily import.
➢ **Demerits:** Low signal strength.

The sample output obtained after execution of sample code of Aqua-Sim will be with information as shown in Table 20.2 with some of the possible fields of sending no. of nodes, packets sent, and packets received with packet delivery fraction (PDF).

TABLE 20.2   Sample Output of Using Aqua-Sim Results

Tool Used	Number of Nodes	Packets Sent	Packet Received	PDF
Aqua-Sim	10	2023	548	0.27
	50	4022	1432	0.35
	100	12011	3463	0.28

A lot of results/data can be generated based on the no. of nodes. Further, it can be used for implementation using ML for predicting PDF based on packet sent and packet received as input to the predictor.

3. **NS-3:** Network simulator version 3 (NS-3) is also used for discrete event networks simulator like NS-2. NS-3 was invented from scratch and was not an enhancement of NS-2. NS-3 is implemented in C++, and for scripting as well as for visualization, Python is used. This is also a command-line based GNU. GPL v2-licensed project that was developed for enhancing the pragmatism of models. NS-3 was designed to make the model implementation closer to actual software implementation and increasing the practicality of the model. The model set in NS-3 presents, how the web and system work however

it is not restricted to a web framework only. Work on NS-3 began in 2006 as a freeware project originally funded with financial backing from three NFS grants and from French Government, University of Washington, Sophia Antipolis, INRIA, and Georgia Tech University (Atlanta). Different releases of NS-3 are NS-3.20, 3.21, 3.22, 3.23, etc., and all the versions supports visualization. NetAnim is another visualization package incorporated within NS-3, in addition to the default visualizer. NetAnim is an animated version that shows how network will appear in real and how data will be shifted from one node to other. Trace files are used to follow the route of nodes those helps us in keeping track of how considerable data is transferred. To analyze the trace files trace metrices software was developed. To get all details about the packets files like pcap are generated, these files can be seen using Wireshark packet analyzer software [24]. The basic work model of NS3 simulator is shown in Figure 20.5.

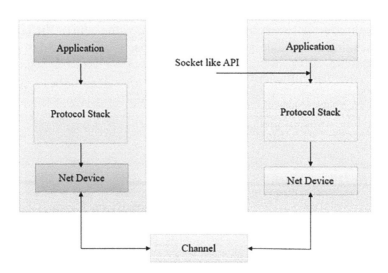

FIGURE 20.5   NS3 simulator working model [1].

> **Merits:** User can run genuine execution code in the simulator in NS-3 as compare to NS-2. The whole system is modularized, and permission for the modular libraries is provided to the node to use external routing. Individual modules contain directory structure.
> **Demerits:** Lack of credibility and maximum modules and components are based on NS-2. NS-3 requires a lot of maintenance as well.

The basic example of NS-3 depicting coding is shown as a screenshot in Figure 20.6.

```
class UdpHeader : public Header
{
public:
    void SetDestination (uint16_t port);
    ...
    void Serialize (Buffer::Iterator start) const;
    uint32_t Deserialize (Buffer::Iterator start);
private:
    uint16_t m_sourcePort;
    uint16_t m_destinationPort;
    uint16_t m_payloadSize;
    uint16_t m_initialChecksum;
void
UdpHeader::Serialize (Buffer::Iterator start) const
{
    Buffer::Iterator i = start;
    i.WriteHtonU16 (m_sourcePort);
    i.WriteHtonU16 (m_destinationPort);
    i.WriteHtonU16 (m_payloadSize + GetSerializedSize ());
    i.WriteU16 (0);
    if (m_calcChecksum)
      {
        uint16_t checksum = Ipv4ChecksumCalculate (...);
        i.WriteU16 (checksum);
      }
}
```

FIGURE 20.6 Example of NS-3.

The sample output obtained after execution of sample code of NS3 will be with information as shown in Table 20.3 with some of the possible fields like cluster size of nodes, packet delivery rate and delay with throughput.

TABLE 20.3 Sample Output for NS-3 Results

Cluster Size	Packet Delivery Rate	Delay	Throughput
80	84.75	3.44	243.92
80	70.67	4.89	445.02
40	90.7	0.8	119.2
40	89.52	1.4	229.3

Here, if the accuracy of throughput obtained is to be examined, then the model can be trained by taking cluster size, packet delivery rate and delay as inputs to the model. Also, in the same way cluster size estimation can also be approximated by using simple regression algorithms.

4.   **OPNET:** A 20 years old student Alain Cohen developed optimized network tools (OPNET) in 1986. First, this was developed as MIL in 1986, but later in 2000 MIL-3 name changed to OPNET. It has been diversified to provide a range of solutions for research purpose and network design/analysis. It is an event-based simulator. This simulator functions at packet level that is the information-carrying entity that circulates among system components. Packets can be formatted or unformatted in three tired OPNET hierarchy. Three domains for this are node, network, and process domain:

   i.   **Node Domain:** It is that internal architecture of node, i.e., defined as functional elements with data flow also.

   ii.   **Network Domain:** It is comprised of nodes, links, and subnets where a subnet may consist of nodes in different network devices. Network domain may be a group of devices like consists of routers, servers, etc. Here link is a point to point connection that can be wired or wireless.

   iii. **Process Domain:** OPNET process model is made up of blocks of C-codes, state transition diagram, kernel procedure, state variable and temporary variables.

In OPNET, debugging, and analysis are GUI based. The basic building block of OPNET Architecture is shown in Figure 20.7.

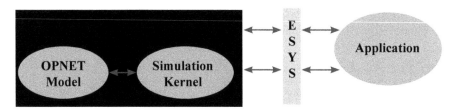

FIGURE 20.7   OPNET architecture [32].

GUI based analysis and debugging is possible in OPNET. C and C++ programming languages are used for OPNET.

➢ **Merits:** Good support, portable model and a good combination of the graphical and programmable interface. On a different platform, the model can be shared.

➢ **Demerits:** Expensive, consume lots of memory. Hard to modify readymade models and GUI operations are complex.

5. **GloMoSim:** It is global mobile simulator having satellite network simulation for huge wireless as well as a wired network. It was established in UCLA's Parallel computing laboratories as a public domain simulator. The simulation of networks can be done which contain thousands or a large number of nodes and asymmetric and heterogeneous links, through GloMoSim. This is a discrete event simulation using OSI Network model and using this numerous network systems are developed having a layered approach using API. Distinct people at different layers develop a discrete model and then they are integrated. GloMoSim is a library-based simulator and that library is developed using PARSEC that is a C-based parallel simulation tool. This is also open-source. To learn this simulator, C programming and basic knowledge of PARSEC is essential. Windows and Linux both operating systems can be used for this [4, 8, 28]. The basic building block of GloMoSim is shown in Figure 20.8.

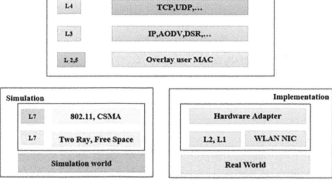

FIGURE 20.8   GloMoSim architecture [27].

➢ **Merits:** It supports ad-hoc network protocols. With thousands of asymmetric nodes, network can be scaled up. For research and academic purpose, it's free and open source.

➤ **Demerits:** GloMoSim provides poor documentation. Because of the commercial version of QualNet, team is having less interest in updating of GloMoSim commercial version. GloMoSim supports only wireless networks. Simulation of large sensor network is hard.

6. **QualNet:** This is also a popular simulation tool provided by scalable network technologies (SNT). QualNet is a testing, planning, and training tool that simulates the activities near to actual communicating network. This provides a good and complete designing environment because of the graphical user interface (GUI) with many options to design a network. This is a commercial product based on GloMoSim. Real-time speed can be maintained in Qualnet. This Qualnet is based on C++, mainly modeled as a finite state machine and this act as network evaluation software. It considers or support both Cartesian coordinate and geographic coordinate system so it helps in studies related to localization problems. Both wired, as well as wireless radio networks, can be simulated through Qualnet. All channel properties and domain characteristics should be modeled so that simulation of UWSN through Qualnet becomes possible [10, 11]. Some features available in Qualnet are:

● Editing tool in Qualnet is Qualnet file editor;
● Command-line access is provided by the command-line interface;
● Graphical packet trace analyzer is Qualnet packet tracer;
● Qualnet architect is a visualization tool.

The basic working model of Qualnet is shown in Figure 20.9 to analyze the network performance by statistical tools that are available in Qualnet Analyzer.

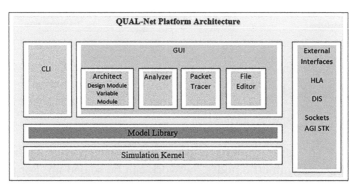

FIGURE 20.9   QUALNet architecture [2].

> ➤ **Merits:** Its GUI is user friendly and facilitate sophisticated animation. It is able to implement on the cluster, multi-core, and multi-processor systems with high speed.
> ➤ **Demerits:** Installation of Qualnet on Linux is tough. Simulation software through Qualnet on java-based user interface is slow.

7. **OMNET++** Andras Varga from the Tech University of Budapest has invented this discrete event simulator. OMNet++ (Objective Modular Network in C++) is a free-ware simulator used to simulate both mobile and wireless networks. Powerful GUI support and simulation model can be embedded into the application programming model. OMNeT++ provides an architecture that is component-based, hierarchical, modular, and extensible. C++ is used to program modules or components for random number generation and kernel, topology discovery, statistics collection, etc., helps in developing new modules. The module is a basic entity and they can be atomic. Modules connect through sending and receiving packets. It can be executed on most of the operating systems because of its convenient nature to use. For the academic purpose, it is free, but one must have to obtain a license or have to pay for commercial use. It also offers an Eclipse-based IDE [36]. The overall processing of OMNet++ is shown in Figure 20.10.

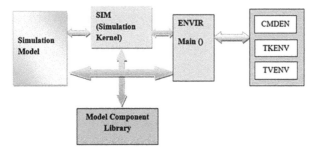

FIGURE 20.10   OMNet++ internal architecture [39].

> ➤ **Merits:** Simulation is easy and powerful GUI. As compared to other simulators tracing and debugging is easy.
> ➤ **Demerits:** Available protocols are not enough. High probability report bugs.

The basic example of OMNET++ depicting coding is shown in Figure 20.11.

```
#include <string.h>
#include <omnetpp.h>

using namespace omnetpp;

/**
 * Derive the Txc1 class from c Simple Module. In the Tictoc1 network,
 * Both the `tic' and `toc' modules are Txc1 objects, created by OMNeT++
 * At the beginning of the simulation.
 */
class Txc1: public cSimpleModule
{
  protected:
    // The following redefined virtual function holds the algorithm.
    virtual void initialize () override;
    virtual void handleMessage (cMessage *msg) override;
};

// The module class needs to be registered with OMNeT++
Define_Module (Txc1);

void Txc1::initialize()
{
    // Initialize is called at the beginning of the simulation.
    // To bootstrap the tic-toc-tic-toc process, one of the modules needs
    // to send the first message. Let this be `tic'.

    // Am I Tic or Toc?
    if (strcmp ("tic", getName ()) == 0) {
        // create and send first message on gate "out". "tictocMsg" is an
        // arbitrary string which will be the name of the message object.
        cMessage *msg = new cMessage("tictocMsg");
        send (msg, "out");
    }
}
```

FIGURE 20.11   Example of OMNET++.

20.3   CONCLUSION

The maximum area on this planet is enclosed with water and a lot of activities are going on beneath the sea level. These activities result in Tsunami, Earthquake, and affect water animal lives also. These activities cater the application areas like underwater monitoring, assisted navigation, underwater sports, disaster management, military applications, etc. So, USNs are getting plenty of attention from the research community and becoming a prominent area of research. ML helps to manage the UWSN dynamic behavior by implementing different models and approximating the accuracy of results obtained. This area replaced the manual monitoring task. But still, due to the complex network, its real-time study is very hard. So, it's better to first test the environment with the help of simulators. Nowadays, several underwater simulation tools are available, but the selection of a suitable tool is a significant task. In this chapter, the author's presented an analysis of various underwater simulation tools with key features and coding parameters. This chapter also gives us a brief idea of using ML techniques for forecasting the behavior of our system. So, now research community can select the best model as per the requirement and availabilities.

KEYWORDS

- artificial intelligence
- machine learning
- quality of service
- underwater sensor network
- wireless sensor network

REFERENCES

1. Amewuda, A. B., Katsriku, F. A., & Abdulai, J. D., (2018). Implementation and evaluation of WLAN 802.11 ac for residential networks in NS-3. *Journal of Computer Networks and Communications, 2018.*
2. Arvind, T., (2016). A comparative study of various network simulation tools. *International Journal of Computer Science & Engineering Technology, 7*(8), 374–378.
3. Awan, K. M., Shah, P. A., Iqbal, K., Gillani, S., Ahmad, W., & Nam, Y., (2019). *Underwater Wireless Sensor, 2019*, p. 20, Article ID: 6470359. https://doi.org/10.1155/2019/6470359.
4. Bajaj, L., Takai, M., Ahuja, R., Tang, K., Bagrodia, R., & Gerla, M., (1999). Glomosim: A scalable network simulation environment. *UCLA Computer Science Department Technical Report, 990027*(1999), 213.
5. Bhambri, H., & Swaroop, A., (2014). Underwater sensor network: Architectures, challenges, and applications. In: *2014 International Conference on Computing for Sustainable Global Development (INDIACom)* (pp. 915–920). IEEE.
6. Bilalb, S. M., & Othmana, M., (2013). *A Performance Comparison of Network Simulators for Wireless Networks*. arXiv preprint arXiv:1307.4129.
7. Das, A. P., & Thampi, S. M., (2016). Simulation tools for underwater sensor networks: A survey. *Network protocols and Algorithms, 8*(4).
8. Dhurandher, S. K., Obaidat, M. S., & Gupta, M., (2012). An acoustic communication based AQUA-GLOMO simulator for underwater networks. *Human-centric Computing and Information Sciences, 2*(1), 3.
9. Dhviya, V. P., & Arthi, R., (2014). Analysis of simulation tools for underwater wireless sensor networks. *International Journal of Computer Science & Engineering Technology (IJCSET)*.
10. Dinesh, S., & Sonal, G., (2014). QualNet simulator. *International Journal of Information & Computation Technology.* ISSN, 0974-2239.

11. Doerffel, T., (2009). *Simulation of Wireless Ad-Hoc Sensor Networks with QualNet.* Documentation.

12. Goyal, N., Dave, M., & Verma, A. K., (2014). Fuzzy based clustering and aggregation technique for underwater wireless sensor networks. In: *2014 International Conference on Electronics and Communication Systems (ICECS)* (pp. 1–5). IEEE.

13. Goyal, N., Dave, M., & Verma, A. K., (2016a). Energy-efficient architecture for intra and inter cluster communication for underwater wireless sensor networks. *Wireless Personal Communications, 89*(2), 687–707.

14. Goyal, N., Dave, M., & Verma, A. K., (2016b). Congestion control and load balancing for cluster based underwater wireless sensor networks. In: *2016 Fourth International Conference on Parallel, Distributed, and Grid Computing (PDGC)* (pp. 462–467). IEEE.

15. Goyal, N., Dave, M., & Verma, A. K., (2017a). Improved data aggregation for cluster based underwater wireless sensor networks. *Proceedings of the National Academy of Sciences, India Section A: Physical Sciences, 87*(2), 235–245.

16. Goyal, N., Dave, M., & Verma, A. K., (2017b). Trust model for cluster head validation in underwater wireless sensor networks. *Underwater Technology, 34*(3), 106–113.

17. Goyal, N., Dave, M., & Verma, A. K., (2018). Adaptive error control technique for cluster-based underwater wireless sensor networks. In: *International Conference on Wireless Intelligent and Distributed Environment for Communication* (pp. 269–280). Springer, Cham.

18. Goyal, N., Dave, M., & Verma, A. K., (2019a). Protocol stack of underwater wireless sensor network: Classical approaches and new trends. *Wireless Personal Communications, 104*(3), 995–1022.

19. Goyal, N., Dave, M., & Verma, A. K., (2020). SAPDA: Secure authentication with protected data aggregation scheme for improving QoS in scalable and survivable UWSNs. *Wireless Personal Communications, 113*(1), 1–15.

20. Goyal, N., Sandhu, J. K., & Verma, L., (2019b). Machine learning based data agglomeration in underwater wireless sensor networks. *International Journal of Management, Technology, and Engineering, 9*(6), 240–245.

21. Gupta, O., Goyal, N., Anand, D., Kadry, S., Nam, Y., & Singh, A., (2020). Underwater networked wireless sensor data collection for computational intelligence techniques: Issues, challenges, and approaches. *IEEE Access, 8*, 122959–122974.

22. Kabir, M. H., Islam, S., Hossain, M. J., & Hossain, S., (2014). Detail comparison of network simulators. *International Journal of Scientific & Engineering Research, 5*(10), 203–218.

23. Kamboj, P., & Goyal, N., (2015). Survey of various keys management techniques in MANET. *International Journal of Emerging Research in Management & Technology, 4*(6).

24. Katkar, P. S., & Ghorpade, D. V. R., (2016). Comparative study of network simulator: NS2 and NS3. *International Journal of Advanced Research in Computer Science and Software Engineering, 6*(3).

25. Khajuria, V., & Kaur, M., (2018). Underwater wireless sensor network: Architecture, applications, and challenges. In: *2018 2nd International Conference on Trends in Electronics and Informatics (ICOEI)* (pp. 939–944). IEEE.

26. Kumar, M., & Goyal, N., (2014). Reviewing underwater acoustic wireless sensing networks. *International Journal of Computer Science and Technology, 5*(2), 95–98.

27. Lee, J., Lee, J., Yi, Y., Chong, S., Proutière, A., & Chiang, M., (2009). Implementing utility-optimal CSMA. In: *2009 47ᵗʰ Annual Allerton Conference on Communication, Control, and Computing (Allerton)* (pp. 102–111). IEEE.

28. Martin, J., (2001). *GloMoSim. Global Mobile Information Systems Simulation Library.* UCLA Parallel Computing Laboratory.

29. Nayyar, A., & Balas, V. E., (2019). Analysis of simulation tools for underwater sensor networks (UWSNs). In: *International Conference on Innovative Computing and Communications* (pp. 165–180). Springer, Singapore.

30. NS-3, (2020). Retrieved from https://www.nsnam.org/ (accessed on 11 November 2021).

31. Obinet.engr.uconn.edu. (2020). *AQUA Lab-Professionals in Water Treatment.* Retrieved from: https://www.aqua-lab.eu/en/index-en.html (accessed on 11 November 2021).

32. Opnet-tutorials.blogspot.com. (2020). *OPNET.* [online] Available at: http://opnet-tutorials.blogspot.com/ (accessed on 11 November 2021).

33. Ovaliadis, K., & Savage, N., (2013). Underwater sensor network simulation tool (USNeT). *International Journal of Computer Applications, 71*(22).

34. Siraj, S., Gupta, A., & Badgujar, R., (2012). Network simulation tools survey. *International Journal of Advanced Research in Computer and Communication Engineering, 1*(4), 199–206.

35. Team, O., (2020). *Getting Started-OMNeT++ Tutorials.* Docs.omnetpp.org. Retrieved from https://docs.omnetpp.org/tutorials/tictoc/part1/ (accessed on 11 November 2021).

36. Varga, A., & Hornig, R., (2008). An overview of the OMNeT++ simulation environment. In: *Proceedings of the 1ˢᵗ International Conference on Simulation Tools and Techniques for Communications, Networks, and Systems & Workshops* (p. 60). ICST (Institute for Computer Sciences, Social-Informatics, and Telecommunications Engineering).

37. Xie, P., Zhou, Z., Peng, Z., Yan, H., Hu, T., Cui, J. H., & Zhou, S., (2009). Aqua-Sim: An NS-2 based simulator for underwater sensor networks. In: *OCEANS 2009* (pp. 1–7). IEEE.

38. Yu, F., & Jain, R., (2011). *A Survey of Wireless Sensor Network Simulation Tools.* Washington University in St. Louis, Department of Science and Engineering.

39. Zarrad, A., & Alsmadi, I., (2017). Evaluating network test scenarios for network simulators systems. *International Journal of Distributed Sensor Networks, 13*(10), 1550147717738216.

CHAPTER 21

Prediction and Analysis of Heritage Monuments Images Using Machine Learning Techniques

GOPAL SAKARKAR,[1] NILESH SHELKE,[2] AYON MOITRA,[1] MANOJ SHANTI,[1] and PRAVIN GHATODE[1]

[1]G. H. Raisoni College of Engineering, Nagpur, Maharashtra, India, E-mails: gopal.sakarkar@raisoni.net (G. Sakarkar), moitra_ayon.ghrcecs@raisoni.net (A. Moitra), pravin.ghatode@raisoni.net (P. Ghatode)

[2]Priyadarshini Indira Gandhi College of Engineering, Nagpur, Maharashtra, India, E-mail: nileshshelke08@gmail.com

ABSTRACT

Landmark acknowledgment could be a challenging issue within the space of picture classification due to gigantic varieties within the design of diverse landmarks. The diverse introduction of the frame plays a crucial role in recognizing the landmarks in their pictures. This chapter suggests an approach to classifying numerous popular monuments as per the characteristics of the monument images. The latest machine learning algorithm is used to extract representations. This demonstration is prepared on representations of distinctive Indian as well as outside landmarks, gotten from pictures, which show geographic and social differences. Tests have been carried out on the physically pro-cured dataset that's composed of pictures of distinctive landmarks where each landmark has pictures from diverse precise sees with its ancient and modern pictures. The tests appear the execution of the demonstration when it is prepared on representations of edited pictures of the different landmarks.

21.1 INTRODUCTION

The foreseeing an age and its past authentic data of the pictures taken amidst the estimation of a building resource is a basic errand inside the computerized documentation of social legacy. A huge number of pictures are more often than not dealt with, so their classification may be a repetitive errand (and thus inclined to mistakes) and routinely devours a part of the time. The accessibility of programmed strategies to encourage these sorting assignments would progress a critical portion of the advanced documentation preparation. All of this has been connected to classifying components of intrigued in pictures of buildings with building legacy esteem.

As the genuine estate's estimating of any building depends on one of the foremost vital parameters, i.e., age of building. Creators proposed that building's age can be extricated by analyzing pictures appearing the outside see of houses [1].

Laser checking and photogrammetry are getting to be progressively broad within the recording of social legacy destinations. [2]

The authors propose a computer-aided calculation of the include extraction in combination with an SVM classifier in Ref. [3] to classify the surfaces. The calculation uses whichever group of planar networks and returns the categorize items.

Aradhya Saini [6] used deep convolutional neural networks (DCNN), a method to classify various Indian monuments found on the characteristics of the monument images. As a result, when it was trained, it represents crop images of various monuments and that have geographic and cultural diversity. Computer vision methods are progressively utilized to encourage and make strides the documentation, conservation, and reclamation prepare of engineering legacy. The most objective looked for is the application of computer vision methods based on profound learning for the classification of pictures of building legacy, notwithstanding of the innovation utilized to get them; and the particular utilize of convolutional neural systems for these assignments.

21.2 IMAGE PROCESSING AND MACHINE LEARNING

Generally, signal processing is often referred to as image processing during which the inputs are images, and therefore the output of the image processing is often either a picture or a series of properties or parameters associated with the image [7]. All image processing functioning are often divided into a variety of techniques: image enhancement, image analysis, image preprocessing image restoration, image display, image data compression, image reconstruction [8, 9].

As per Muthuselvi and Prabhu [10], image processing is an analysis and manipulation of a digitalized image, especially in order to improve the quality of image processing.

Now we can understand various basic techniques used in image processing. In image representation, descriptions are generated from the visual content of an image. In this way, pictures are written and saved in the computer. The image display approaches are separated into four categories:

- Block-based;
- Pixel-based;
- Hierarchical-based; and
- Region-based [11].

21.2.1 PIXEL-BASED REPRESENTATION

The pixel depiction is that the straightforward depiction for outlining a picture. In digital imaging, a pel, a pixel, or image details are a corporeal point during a rectangular image or the tiny admissible feature during a display device admissible to all or any points. Each pixel holds the foremost convincing local records for every element. The variability of elements within the illustration is usually large and is employed to represent the image. There are programs for scientific imaging in which each pixel has been given its own personal significance [12].

21.2.2 BLOCK-BASED REPRESENTATIONS

In which, an image is separated into a fixed two-dimensional array size. The numeral of things is hardly but with based on pixel completely, but few resident facts are saved that correspond to those of based on pixel depictions. When it is based on block the full depictions might be accomplished for somewhat grayscale as well as for any binary image. The depiction is used for compressing, segmenting, extracting various photo functions, etc. [13].

21.2.3 REGION-BASED REPRESENTATIONS

Similarly referred to a super-pixel depiction. Here the areas are not rectangular and are broadly shaped by grouping comparable and related pixels. The adjacency records among areas are generally presented as a Region Adjacency Graph or combinatorial map. Furthermore, an image is put forward for object recognition and breakdown, but exclusive associations on several regions must be taken into account [13].

21.2.4 HIERARCHICAL REPRESENTATIONS

The representation uses a maximum in all probability associations of regions of regional representations. The photo display can be carried out in exclusive scales. Examples are minimum and maximum tree, α tree, quadtree, bin tree, etc. Applications consist of photo segmentation, video segmentation, object recognition, photo segmentation and filtering, image simplification and many more [14].

21.2.5 MACHINE LEARNING

Simon [16] defines that machine learning (ML) is an field in computer science that has industrialized with enough of research of pattern detection also with the help of thesis of computer-assisted learning in artificial intelligence (AI).

One other very famous definition given by Tom is that ML is a mainframe block of codes to understand from past experience, i.e., Ex regarding few task Ta in addition few presentation measure Pe. If it's presentation on Ta, as unrushed via Pe, advances with experience Ex.

Basically, ML is divided into two type of task:

- First is supervised and second one is unsupervised ML: In supervised machine algorithms, the block of code is trained on a preprocessed set of "trained data," which at that moment enable its capability to attain a correct result when given new data.
- On the other hand, in unsupervised machine algorithms, in this performance, agreed a group of data and need to discover shapes and associations within.

New upcoming trained found in AI is reinforcement learning (RL), in which system is educated to process precise conclusions. The whole thing like this: the system is uncovered to a milieu in which it trained itself frequently the usage of reward and punishment. This gadget absorbs from past enjoy and attempts to acquire the high-quality feasible know-how to make correct business decisions.

Some of the very basic ML techniques are as follows:

- Logistic regression;
- Linear regression;
- Random forest;
- SVM;
- Decision tree;
- K-means; and
- Bayesian networks.

21.2.6 LINEAR REGRESSION MACHINE LEARNING ALGORITHM

It is made to predict real life values (price of clubs, prediction of weight and height, sum of business, etc.), based on nonstop variables. Here, we create relationship among dependent and independent objects by best-fitting a line. This best-fit of the line is called line of regression also denoted with a linear equation, i.e., $Y = (a \times X) + b$.

There are two primary sorts of linear regression: Simple linear regression as well as multiple linear regression. Simple linear regression is categorized by one independent variable. And, multiple linear regression is categorized by more than 1 independent variable.

21.2.7 LOGISTIC REGRESSION MACHINE LEARNING ALGORITHM

Basically, it's a cataloging technique not like regression technique. It is also used to predict distinct results, e.g., bool results similar to 0 or 1, on or off, yes or no, true or false as per on assumed group of independent objects. In meek words, it envisages the likelihood of an event occurring by fitting the best data to a Logit Function. Therefore, it is similarly called logit regression. In the meantime, it envisages possibility, its output solutions are expected to be among 0 and 1.

21.2.8   DECISION TREE MACHINE LEARNING

A decision tree (DT) creates a tree-like assembly to find possible solutions to a problem that is primarily based on certain constraints. It is so named that it starts with an unmarried simple decision or root, which when divides into several branches until a choice or prediction is made and forms a tree [17].

They are preferred because of their ability to formalize the problematic process, which in turn helps identify potential solutions faster and more appropriately than others. Examples: Decision stump, iterative dichotomiser 3 (ID3), classification, and regression tree (CART), M5, C4.5 and C5.0, chi-squared automatic interaction detection (CHAID), conditional DTs, etc.:

1. **SVM-Support Vector Machine Learning Algorithm:** SVM can be a separate collection. It makes use of a setting apart hyperplane or a choice plane to demarcate decision limitations among a fixed of information points classified with distinctive labels. It is a precisely supervised classification set of rules. In other words, the set of rules defines a most accurate hyperplane utilizing input records or training information and this choice aircraft in turns categories new set of examples. Based on the kernel in use, SVM can execute both linear and nonlinear classification.

2. **K-Means Clustering Machine Learning Algorithm:** Grouping or clustering is a form of unsupervised learning method which once recruits, makes companies on its own. The objects that have similar properties are placed in the similar collection. This technique or algorithm is known as k-means since it makes ok unique clusters. The recommendation of the results in a specific collection is the center of that collection which is also known as cluster [18].

21.2.7   BAYESIAN NETWORKS MACHINE LEARNING ALGORITHM

It is a graphical model that is made to demonstrate relationships among thoughts and activities to conclude chances and doubts related to those thoughts or events. Predictions, facts, and patterns retrieval, as per restricted input and reputation software is some primary packages of BN [19].

In this algorithm namely Bayesian Networks assembly S is known as directed acyclic graph also referred as DAG with the other nodes in S are in one to one communication with the few topographies X. There are arcs that signify unintentional influences between the topographies during the nonappearance of possible arcs in S which further encodes provisional independencies. Furthermore, a feature generally termed as node is provisional independent from its non-offspring given its parents that means Xi is conditionally independent from Xii.

21.3   AGENT

An agent by way of mentioning to a module of application or hardware which is enough proficient of short-term firmly so as to complete responsibilities on behalf of the user [20]. Agents could also be classified by their agility, which means by their capability to ploy around few networks. This produces the classes of static and mobile agents.

Nevertheless, there can be a multitude of meanings of the terminology agent, which comprise a properties that is not unusual for all sellers: the agent behaves on behalf of its users as well as a multitude of supplementary properties: the agent connects with one another marketers in a multiple agent structure, behaves separately, is intelligent, understands from previous experience; act both proactively and reactively, is modeled or coded using human-like traits namely are beliefs, intentions, goals, actions, etc., is mobile and many more [21].

21.4   PROJECTED WORK

The primary objective of the anticipated task is to calculate the age from verifiable pictures and landmarks using image processing and to supply detailed data of landmarks with the assistance of ML strategies. This work proposed procedures based on ML for the classification of pictures of structural legacy, particularly through the utilization of the straightforward straight iterative clustering (SLIC) calculation for picture saliency [5], OpenCV calculations, etc.

21.5   DATASET

Numerous pictures to prepare ML calculation talked about over are required, utilizing fine-tuning, it is conceivable to utilize little dataset. Despite the fact that there are numerous non-exclusive picture banks with numerous labeled pictures. As the work in this regard has not started, it is very hard to discover a particular dataset of building legacy pictures prepared to be utilized. In this work, we utilized a dataset created by Basura Fernando [4]. This dataset comprises of ancient and modern pictures of the same area. This dataset comprises more than 3700 pictures of distinctive verifiable places in the world counting the Taj Mahal, Eiffel Tower, Galle Face Hotel, Notredame, Temple Tooth, and numerous more.

21.6   PROPOSED ARCHITECTURE

From Figure 21.1, to begin with of all, a picture has been captured by program, at that point utilizing SLIC (Simple Linear Iterative Clustering) calculation that's utilized to discover out around decide where the protest of intrigued was. Once a correct section of landmarks or building extricated frame picture, another task is to discover out the relevance of picture, within the following organize preparing information set is utilized to discover out correct title of building/ landmarks. This data is allotted to a specialist, a specialist at that point discover more data either from online Wikipedia (on the off chance that accessible) or it take subtle elements from put away database and at long last detail data of landmark will make available.

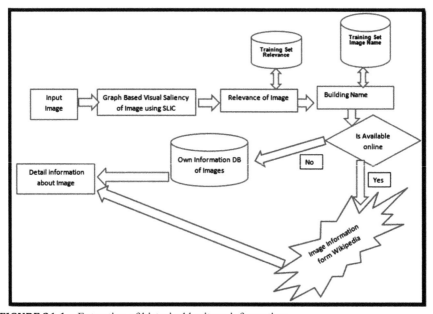

FIGURE 21.1   Extraction of historical heritage information.

21.7   RESULT AND ANALYSIS OF WORK

In this work, we had utilized Microsoft sky blue AI stage for picture classification and predication. We consider five places for result investigation that
incorporate Taj Mahal, Paris Gare de Lyon, Noter-Dame, Eiffel Tower, Sacre
Coeur for preparing and testing purposed. Each chronicled place having its
ancient and unused images (Figure 21.2).

FIGURE 21.2   Dashboard of Microsoft azure platform [*].

In this training, we are used 15 images of each place for training purpose
(Figure 21.3).

Author has received an AI for Earth Microsoft Azure Compute Grant.

FIGURE 21.3   Performance prediction.

In this step, we train the images and as a result we received precision, recall, and average precision (Figure 21.4).

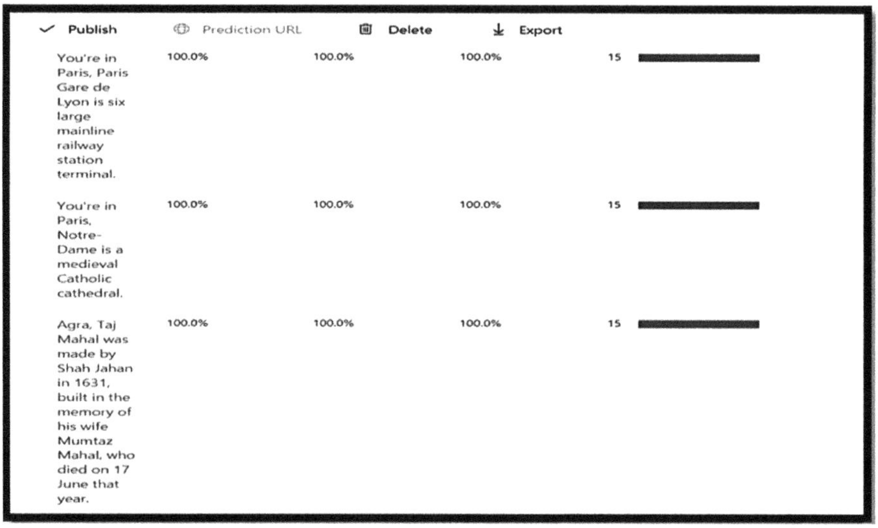

Publish
Prediction URL
Delete
Export
You're in Paris, Paris Gare de Lyon is six large mainline railway station terminal.
100.0%
100.0%
100.0%
15
You're in Paris, Notre-Dame is a medieval Catholic cathedral.
100.0%
100.0%
100.0%
15
Agra, Taj Mahal was made by Shah Jahan in 1631, built in the memory of his wife Mumtaz Mahal, who died on 17 June that year.
100.0%
100.0%
100.0%
15

FIGURE 21.4 Tagging of images.

After effective execution, another step is to tag the pictures with legitimate data. In this, each picture gets appropriately tag with its verifiable information (Figures 21.5 and 21.6).

Predictions
Tag
Probability
Agra, Taj Mahal was made ... 99.9%
You're in Paris, Sacre Coeur ..0%
You're in Paris, Paris Gare d...0%
You're in Paris, Notre-Dam... 0%
You're in Paris, the Eiffel To...0%

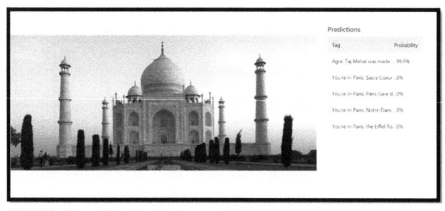

FIGURE 21.5 Predication about Taj Mahal image.

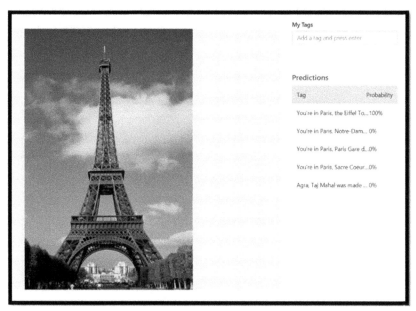

FIGURE 21.6   Predication about Eiffel tower.

21.8   ACCURACY OF ALGORITHMS

1. Loss per epoch:
    i.   **Epoch:** One epoch means one iteration of training;
    ii. **Loss:** It is a measure of evaluating how well a model has learned to predict for a given set of dataset samples (Figure 21.7).

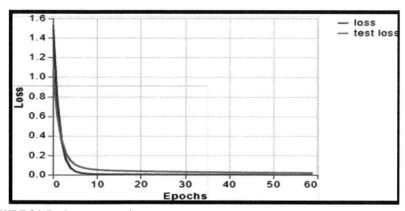

FIGURE 21.7   Loss per epoch.

2. Accuracy per epoch:
   i. **Accuracy:** It is the percentage of classification that a model can get during training. For example, 8 samples got right from 10, and accuracy would be 80%=0.8 (Figure 21.8).

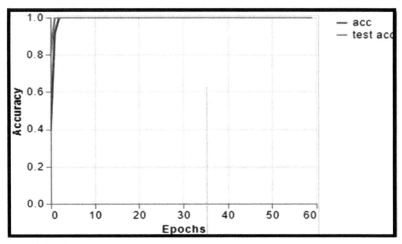

FIGURE 21.8 Accuracy per epoch.

Confusion matric is a combination of true positives, false positives (FP), true negatives, and FN. From Figure 21.9, there were 14.96 true positives, monuments that were correctly classified with respect to the dataset. These

Confusion Matrix

		ACTUAL	
		HAS CLASSIFIED	HAS NOT CLASSIFIED
PREDICTED	HAS CLASSIFIED	14.96	0.04
	HAS NOT CLASSIFIED	0.03	11.97

FIGURE 21.9 Confusion matrix.

are monuments that were correctly identified by the algorithm. There were 11.97 true negatives, monuments that were not classified as per the dataset. These are predictions taken on the monuments other than the training dataset. There were 0.03 FN, monuments that were misclassified with respect to the target prediction, these are the monuments that were misclassified by the algorithm, and there were 0.04 FP, buildings that were misclassified with respect to the target prediction, these are the buildings that were misclassified by the algorithm as if it is a monument.

21.9 CONCLUSION

The primary goal of this project is to create the use of ML and AI to classify authentic images and landmarks. It arranges to confirm the genuine value of some of these networks to assist within the assignments of computerized documentation we are proposing to create an unused dataset. Architectural heritage components information is set to perform all of these tests. In outline, the ultimate objective of the inquire about displayed is to get a valuable apparatus for researchers and history specialists to encourage the programmed classification of pictures of structural legacy and help within the computerized documentation process.

KEYWORDS

- **chi-squared automatic interaction detection**
- **classification and regression tree**
- **deep convolutional neural networks**
- **machine learning**
- **straightforward straight iterative clustering**

REFERENCES

1. Matthias, Z., Miroslav, D., Muntaha, S., David, K., & Mario, D., (2018) *Automatic Prediction of Building Age from Photographs.* ICMR '18. Yokohama, Japan.
2. Boehler, W., & Marbs, A., (2004). 3D scanning and photogrammetry for heritage recording: A comparison. *Proc. 12th International Conference on Geo-informatics* (pp. 7–9). University of Gavle, Sweden.
3. Bassier, M., Vergauwen, M., & Van, G. B., (2017). Automated classification of heritage buildings for as-built BIM using machine learning techniques. *ISPRS Annals of the Photogrammetry, Remote Sensing and Spatial Information Sciences, IV-2/W2.*

4. Basura, F., Tatiana, T., & Tinne, T., (2015). Location recognition over large time lags. *Computer Vision and Image Understanding, 139,* 21–28.

5. https://towardsdatascience.com/saliency-based-image-segmentation-473b4cb31774 (accessed on 11 November 2021).

6. Saini, A., Gupta, T., Kumar, R., Gupta, A. K., Panwar, M., & Mittal, A., (2017). Image based Indian monument recognition using convoluted neural networks. In: *2017 International Conference on Big Data, IoT, and Data Science (BID)* (pp. 138–142). Pune.

7. Deepika, C., Anjali, L., & Sandeep, Y., (2014). Overview of image processing. *International Journal for Research in Applied Science & Engineering Technology (IJRASET), 2*(X).

8. Ravi, P., & Ashokkumar, A., (2017). Analysis of various image processing techniques. *International Journal of Advanced Networking & Applications (IJANA), 8*(5), 86–89.

9. Jayme, G. A. B., (2013). Digital image processing techniques for detecting, quantifying, and classifying plant diseases. *SpringerPlus, 2,* 660.

10. Muthuselvi, S., & Prabhu, P., (2016). *Digital Image Processing Techniques: A Survey* (Vol. 5, No. 11). Golden Research Thoughts, ISSN: 2231-5063 Impact Factor: 3.4052(UIF).

11. Bineeth, K., & Preena, K. P., (2015). A review on 2D image representation methods. *International Journal of Engineering Research & Technology (IJERT).* ISSN: 2278–0181 IJERTV4IS041201.

12. Rafael, C. G., & Richard, E. W., (2009). *Digital Image Processing.* Pearson Education India.

13. Jayaraman, S., Veerakumar, T., & Esakkirajan, S., (2009). *Digital Image Processing.* Tata McGraw-Hill Education.

14. Kuan-Ting, Y., Shih-Huan, T., & Li-Chen, F., (2012). Learning hierarchical representation with sparsity for RGB-D object recognition. *Intelligent Robots and Systems (IROS), 2012 IEEE/RSJ, International Conference.* IEEE.

15. Ayodele, T. O., (2010). Types of machine learning algorithms. *New Advances in Machine Learning, 3,* 19–48.

16. Annina, S., Mahima, S. D., Venkatesan, S., & Ramesh, B. D. R., (2015). An overview of machine learning and its applications. *International Journal of Electrical Sciences & Engineering (IJESE), 1*(1), 22–24.

17. Kajaree, D., & Rabi, N. B., (2017). A survey on machine learning: Concept, algorithms, and applications. *International Journal of Innovative Research in Computer and Communication Engineering, 5*(2).

18. Ayon, D., (2016). Machine learning algorithms: A review. *International Journal of Computer Science and Information Technologies, 7*(3), 1174–1179.

19. Iqbal, M., & Zhu, Y., (2015). Supervised machine learning approaches: A survey. *ICTACT Journal on Soft Computing, 5*(3).

20. Hyacinth, S. N., (1996). Software agents: An overview. *Knowledge Engineering Review, 11*(3), 205–244. Cambridge University Press.

21. Costin, B., Zoran, B., Hans-Dieter, B., & Mirjana, I., (2011). Software agents: Languages, tools, platforms. *ComSIS, 8*(2).

Index